Dealing With Diversity

The Anthology

J.Q. Adams

Pearlie Strother-Adams

Western Illinois University

KENDALL/HUNT PUBLISHING COMPANY

4050 Westmark Drive   Dubuque, Iowa 52002

Book Team

President and Chief Executive Officer   Mark C. Falb
Vice President, Director of National Book Program   Alfred C. Grisanti
Editorial Development Supervisor   Georgia Botsford
Developmental Editor   Liz Recker
Vice President, Production Editorial   Ruth A. Burlage
Production Manager   Jo Wiegand
Production Editor   Carrie Maro
Permissions Editor   Colleen Zelinsky
Design Manager   Jodi Splinter
Cover Designer   Deb Howes

Contents

Preface   vii
About the Authors   ix

Class 1
Course Overview:
Who In The World Is In Here?   1

Chapter 1
A Different Mirror   *Ronald Takaki*   3

Chapter 2
What Is Culture?   *Eugene Garcia*   13

Class 2
Social Interaction Model   23

Chapter 3
Understanding Social Interaction in Culturally
Diverse Settings   *J.Q. Adams*   25

Class 3
Negotiating Cross Cultural
Communication   31

Chapter 4
Intercultural Communication:
A Current Perspective   *Milton Bennett*   33

Class 4
The Changing Face of America and
the World   53

Chapter 5
Diversity and Multiculturalism on the Campus:
How are Students Affected?   *Alexander Astin*   55

Chapter 6
Campus Resegregation and Its Alternatives
Gary Orfield   63

Class 5
Immigration, Social Policy, and
Employment   73

Chapter 7
Building A Nation Through Immigration
L. Edward Purcell   75

Chapter 8
The Business Case for Diversity   *Samuel Betances
and laura M. Torres Souder*   85

Class 6
Race Our Most Dangerous Myth   89

Chapter 9
Racial Identity and the State: The Dilemmas of
Classification   *Michael Omi*   91

Chapter 10
Motivations That Drive Prejudice and
Discrimination: Is the Scientific Community
Really Objective?   *Duane Jackson*   103

Class 7
Social Class Issues In the USA   111

Chapter 11
Where Do Students of Color Earn Doctorates
in Education?: The "Top 25" Colleges and
Schools of Education   *Stafford Hood and
Donald Freeman*   113

Chapter 12
Discrimination   *Richard T. Schaefer*   127

Class 8
Gender Issues In the USA   145

Chapter 13
Interactive Phases of Curricular Revision: A
Feminist Perspective   *Peggy McIntosh*   147

CLASS 9
Native Americans In the USA (Part I)   161

Chapter 14
Civic Literacy, Sovereignty, and Violence: Ojibwe Treaty Rights and Racial Backlash in the North Country   *Guy Senese*   163

CLASS 10
Native Americans In the USA (Part II)   173

Chapter 15
Native Nations and American Indians, Culture, Curriculum, and Social Justice *James V. Fenelon*   175

CLASS 11
Hispanic/Latino Americans (Part I)   183

Chapter 16
Immigrant Latino Parents' Values and Beliefs About Their Children's Education: Continuities and Discontinuities Across Cultures and Generations   *Ronald Gallimore and Claude Goldenberg*   185

CLASS 12
Hispanic/Latino Americans (Part II)   217

Chapter 17
The Cultural Patterning of Achievement Motivation: A Comparison of Mexican, Mexican Immigrant, Mexican American, and Non-Latino White American Students   *Marcelo Suarez-Orozco and Carola E. Suarez-Orozco*   219

CLASS 13
African Americans (Part I)   237

Chapter 18
What Ever Happened to Integration?
Tamar Jacoby   239

Chapter 19
U.S. News Media: A Content Analysis and Media Case Study   *Pearlie Strother-Adams*   247

CLASS 14
African Americans (Part II)   257

Chapter 20
The Essentials of Kwanzaa: A Summary
Maulana Karenga   259

Chapter 21
Afrocentricity and Multicultural Education: Concept, Challenge and Contributions
Maulana Karenga   265

Chapter 22
The Silenced Dialogue: Power and Pedagogy in Educating Other People's Children
Lisa Delpit   279

Chapter 23
Reframing the Affirmative Action Debate
Lani Guiner   293

CLASS 15
Asian Americans   307

Chapter 24
Understanding Asian Americans: Background for Curriculum Development
Shin Kim   309

Chapter 25
Educating Asian-Americans Students: Past, Present, and Future   *Ming-Gon John Lian*   317

CLASS 16
Middle Eastern Americans   327

Chapter 26
Image and Identity: Screen Arabs and Muslims
Jack Shaheen   329

CLASS 17
Emergence of New European Americans   343

Chapter 27
Beyond Vasco Da Gama: Unlearning Eurocentric Phallacies in the Classroom   *Nada Elia*   345

CLASS 18
Creole and Mixed Ethnic Americans   351

Chapter 28
The Americanization of Black New Orleans, 1850-1900   *Arnold Hirsch and Joseph Logsdon*   353

CLASS 19
Ethnocentric Groups In America   389

Chapter 29
The Evolution of Race   *David Duke*   391

CLASS 20
Sexual Orientation Issues   403

Chapter 30
Opening Classroom Closets: Teaching About Lesbians, Gay Men, and Bisexuals in a Multicultural Context   *Jovita Baber and Brett Beemyn*   405

CLASS 21
Physical/Mental Ability Issues   417

Chapter 31
The Microculture of Disability   *Jacqueline Rickman*   419

CLASS 22
Age Issues: From Young to Old   427

Chapter 32
Breaking Down the Myths of Aging   *John Rowe and Robert Kahn*   429

CLASS 23
A New South Africa?: Lessons for the USA   441

Chapter 33
Now That The TRC Is Over: Looking Back, Reaching Forward   *Charles Villa-Vicencio*   443

Chapter 34
African Mysteries   *Patti Waldmeir*   453

CLASS 24
Diversity Issues and Answers   461

Chapter 35
Surprisingly Singing and Women's Day Song   *Barry Feinberg*   463

PREFACE

As the 21st century opens the United States and other nations around the world will continue to struggle on a planet that has been reduced to a global village. The challenges are both inter-cultural and intra-cultural. Continued immigration from around the world brings new ethnic/racial and cultural challenges to an already diverse society. Demographic projections indicate that by the year 2050, one half of the U.S. population will be made up of people of African, Asian, and Latino/Latina backgrounds. This shift in demographics will also reflect in the increase in other definable groups, such as the disabled, the aged, gays, lesbians and a variety of other special interest groups.

Dealing With Diversity: The Anthology, though conceived as an accompanying text/reader for the *Dealing With Diversity II* teleclass, which originated out of Governor's State University, can be used as a text/reader independent of the teleclass. Any courses that have as their objective the expansion of students' knowledge and experience in relationship to the multicultural world and society in which they live, would benefit from this text/reader. I would like to recommend this text/reader for use in university diversity and multicultural courses that are concerned with race, class, and gender issues. Such courses could include courses in ethnic studies, American studies, and social problems. In reading *Dealing With Diversity: The Anthology*, your students can experience, first hand, how people living in the same world can be presented with a different set of challenges.

The articles and chapters selected for this issue of *Dealing With Diversity: The Anthology* are largely the results of interviews I conducted as part of the updating of the **Dealing With Diversity (DWD)** teleclass. The first DWD Teleclass was created in 1991 and has enjoyed critical success having been adopted by more than 125 colleges and universities since its beginning ten years ago. The initial series relied on a number of writings that dealt with social problems addressing most of the topics in the teleclass. In 1999, I began the process of updating the DWD teleclass by interviewing additional experts in the field as well as selecting new in-studio guests in preparation for teaching a revised DWD teleclass during the spring of 2000. During this process it occurred to me that the students who take DWDII would benefit by having even greater access to the views and ideas of our new video and in-studio guests. Therefore, when possible I requested that our "experts" provide a selection that could be included in an anthology that might help students further understand the subject matter discussed in the teleclass.

The *Dealing With Diversity Anthology* is composed of 35 selections, chronologically organized to follow the twenty-four class segments in the DWDII teleclass and the *Dealing With Diversity Study Guide*. There are several selections included in the anthology from authors who do not appear as either video or in-studio guests. They represent a certain expertise (Takaki, for example) that adds richness intellectually and in many cases culturally.

It is, however, important to emphasize that some of the ideas and views expressed in this anthology (David Duke, for example) are not shared by the editors and/or any one else associated with the development of this project. It is our sincere hope this anthology as well as the study guide and the teleclass serve as a vehicle for both helping our audience to gain knowledge and to seek respect and tolerance for the diversity of the many groups and their ideas that make up our uniquely diverse society and world.

Dealing With Diversity: The Teleclass Study Guide, ISBN 0-7872-8144-1, is available through Kendall/Hunt Publishing. This study guide is designed to assist you throughout the telecourse. It provides the key concepts, reading assignments, and discussion questions for each class. To order contact Customer Service at 1-(800) 228-0810.

J.Q. Adams
Pearlie Strother-Adams

ABOUT THE AUTHORS

A Professor in the Department of Educational and Interdisciplinary Studies at Western Illinois University, Macomb, Illinois, J.Q. Adams is an award winning teacher who has worked extensively in the area of multicultural education as a consultant, presenter, and curriculum development specialist. Known for the SIMS Model, an interaction model, he is a published author and has recently developed a second Dealing With Diversity teleclass which incorporates a variety of interviews he conducted with scholars, politicians, writers, and students around the country and in South Africa as well. His first Dealing With Diversity teleclass is distributed nationally by PBS.

An Associate Professor in the Department of English and Journalism at Western Illinois University, Macomb, where she teaches courses in the area of journalism and mass communication, Pearlie Strother-Adams has focused her research on media depictions of traditionally marginalized groups in the United States, with special emphasis on the representations of African American males in popular culture and in news media. She is currently working on a book chronicling the lives of women who worked in the civil rights struggle in the 1960s but did not receive recognition in history for their efforts.

CLASS 1

Course Overview:
Who In the World Is In Here?

CHAPTER 1
A Different Mirror

Ronald Takaki

This introduction to Takaki's award winning book sets the tone for an insightful alternative view on the actions, attitudes, beliefs and values that shaped the development of the U.S.A.

CHAPTER 2
What Is Culture?

Eugene Garcia

Eugene Garcia gives us a comprehensive definition of culture. He details the many different components of this multifaceted concept and how its meaning shifts from context to contact.

CHAPTER 1

A Different Mirror

Ronald Takaki

One of the foremost nationally recognized scholars of multicultural studies, Ronald Takaki is the grandson of Japanese migrant plantation laborers in Hawaii, he holds a Ph.D. in American history from the University of California, Berkeley, where he has been a professor of Ethnic Studies for over two decades. Takaki is the author of the critically acclaimed *Iron Cages* and the prize-winning *Strangers from a Different Shore.*

I had flown from San Francisco to Norfolk and was riding in a taxi to my hotel to attend a conference on multiculturalism. Hundreds of educators from across the country were meeting to discuss the need for greater cultural diversity in the curriculum. My driver and I chatted about the weather and the tourists. The sky was cloudy, and Virginia Beach was twenty minutes away. The rearview mirror reflected a white man in his forties. "How long have you been in this country?" he asked. "All my life," I replied, wincing. "I was born in the United States." With a strong southern drawl, he remarked: "I was wondering because your English is excellent!" Then, as I had many times before, I explained: "My grandfather came here from Japan in the 1880s. My family has been here, in America, for over a hundred years." He glanced at me in the mirror. Somehow I did not look "American" to him; my eyes and complexion looked foreign.

Suddenly, we both became uncomfortably conscious of a racial divide separating us. An awkward silence turned my gaze from the mirror to the passing landscape, the shore where the English and the Powhatan Indians first encountered each other. Our highway was on land that Sir Walter Raleigh had renamed "Virginia" in honor of Elizabeth I, the Virgin Queen. In the English cultural appropriation of America, the indigenous peoples themselves would become outsiders in their native land. Here, at the eastern edge of the continent, I mused, was the site of the beginning of multicultural America. Jamestown, the English settlement founded in 1607, was nearby: the first twenty Africans were brought here a year before the Pilgrims arrived at Plymouth Rock. Several hundred miles offshore was Bermuda, the "Bermoothes" where William Shakespeare's Prospero had landed and met the native Caliban in *The Tempest.* Earlier, another voyager had made an Atlantic crossing and unexpectedly bumped into some islands to the south. Thinking he had reached Asia, Christopher Columbus mistakenly identified one of the islands as "Cipango" (Japan). In the wake of the admiral, many peoples would come to America from different shores, not only from Europe but also Africa and Asia. One of them would be my grandfather. My mental wandering across terrain and time ended abruptly as we arrived at my destination. I said good-bye to my driver and went into the hotel, carrying a vivid reminder of why I was attending this conference.

QUESTIONS like the one my taxi driver asked me are always jarring, but I can understand why he could not see me as American. He had a narrow but widely shared sense of the past—a history that has viewed American as European in ancestry. "Race," Toni Morrison explained, has functioned

From *A Different Mirror: A History of Multicultural America*, 1993, Little Brown & Company, New York. Reprinted by permission of the Balkin Agency.

as a "metaphor" necessary to the "construction of Americanness": in the creation of our national identity, "American" has been defined as "white."

But America has been racially diverse since our very beginning on the Virginia shore, and this reality is increasingly becoming visible and ubiquitous. Currently, one-third of the American people do not trace their origins to Europe; in California, minorities are fast becoming a majority. They already predominate in major cities across the country—New York, Chicago, Atlanta, Detroit, Philadelphia, San Francisco, and Los Angeles.

This emerging demographic diversity has raised fundamental questions about America's identity and culture. In 1990, *Time* published a cover story on "America's Changing Colors." "Someday soon," the magazine announced, "white Americans will become a minority group." How soon? By 2056, most Americans will trace their descent to "Africa, Asia, the Hispanic world, the Pacific Islands, Arabia—almost anywhere but white Europe." This dramatic change in our nation's ethnic composition is altering the way we think about ourselves. "The deeper significance of America's becoming a majority nonwhite society is what it means to the national psyche, to individuals' sense of themselves and their nation— their idea of what it is to be American."

Indeed, more than ever before, as we approach the time when whites become a minority, many of us are perplexed about our national identity and our future as one people. This uncertainty has provoked Allan Bloom to reaffirm the preeminence of Western civilization. Author of *The Closing of the American Mind*, he has emerged as a leader of an intellectual backlash against cultural diversity. In his view, students entering the university are "uncivilized," and the university has the responsibility to "civilize" them. Bloom claims he knows what their "hungers" are and "what they can digest." Eating is one of his favorite metaphors. Noting the "large black presence" in major universities, he laments the "one failure" in race relations—black students have proven to be "indigestible." They do not "melt as have *all* other groups." The problem, he contends, is that "blacks have become blacks": they have become "ethnic." This separatism has been reinforced by an academic permissiveness that has befouled the curriculum with "Black Studies" along with "Learn Another Culture." The only solution, Bloom insists, is "the good old Great Books approach."

Similarly, E. D. Hirsch worries that America is becoming a "tower of Babel," and that this multiplicity of cultures is threatening to rend our social fabric. He, too, longs for a more cohesive culture and a more homogeneous America: "If we *had* to make a choice between the *one* and the *many*, most Americans would choose the principle of unity, since we cannot function as a nation without it." The way to correct this fragmentization, Hirsch argues, is to acculturate "disadvantaged children." What do they need to know? "Only by accumulating shared symbols, and the shared information that symbols represent," Hirsch answers, "can we learn to communicate effectively with one another in our national community." Though he concedes the value of multicultural education, he quickly dismisses it by insisting that it "should not be allowed to supplant or interfere with our schools' responsibility to ensure our children's mastery of American literate culture." In *Cultural Literacy: What Every American Needs to Know,* Hirsch offers a long list of terms that excludes much of the history of minority groups.

While Bloom and Hirsch are reacting defensively to what they regard as a vexatious balkanization of America, many other educators are responding to our diversity as an opportunity to open American minds. In 1990, the Task Force on Minorities for New York emphasized the importance of a culturally diverse education. "Essentially," the *New York Times* commented, "the issue is how to deal with both dimensions of the nation's motto: 'E pluribus unum'—'Out of many, one.'" Universities from New Hampshire to Berkeley have established American cultural diversity graduation requirements. "Every student needs to know," explained University of Wisconsin's chancellor Donna Shalala, "much more about the origins and history of the particular cultures which, as Americans, we will encounter during our lives." Even the University of Minnesota, located in a state that is 98 percent white, requires its students to take ethnic studies courses. Asked why multiculturalism is so important, Dean Fred Lukermann answered: As a national university, Minnesota has to offer a national curriculum—one that includes all of the peoples of America. He added that after graduation many students move to cities like Chicago and Los Angeles and thus need to know about racial diversity. Moreover, many educators stress, multiculturalism has an intellectual purpose. By allowing us to see events from the viewpoints of different groups, a multicultural curriculum enables us to reach toward a more comprehensive understanding of American history.

What is fueling this debate over our national identity and the content of our curriculum is America's intensifying racial crisis. The alarming signs and symptoms seem to be everywhere—the killing of Vincent Chin in Detroit, the black boycott of a Korean grocery store in Flatbush, the hysteria in Boston over the Carol Stuart murder, the battle between white sportsmen and Indians over tribal fishing rights in Wisconsin, the Jewish-black clashes in Brooklyn's Crown Heights, the black-Hispanic competition for jobs and educational resources in Dallas, which *Newsweek* described as "a conflict of the have-nots," and the Willie Horton campaign commercials, which widened the divide between the suburbs and the inner cities.

This reality of racial tension rudely woke America like a fire bell in the night on April 29, 1992. Immediately after four Los Angeles police officers were found not guilty of brutality against Rodney King, rage exploded in Los Angeles. Race relations reached a new nadir. During the nightmarish rampage, scores of people were killed, over two thousand injured, twelve thousand arrested, and almost a billion dollars' worth of property destroyed. The live televised images mesmerized America. The rioting and the murderous melee on the streets resembled the fighting in Beirut and the West Bank. The thousands of fires burning out of control and the dark smoke filling the skies brought back images of the burning oil fields of Kuwait during Desert Storm. Entire sections of Los Angeles looked like a bombed city. "Is this America?" many shocked viewers asked. "Please, can we get along here," pleaded Rodney King, calling for calm. "We all can get along. I mean, we're all stuck here for a while. Let's try to work it out."

But how should "we" be defined? Who are the people "stuck here" in America? One of the lessons of the Los Angeles explosion is the recognition of the fact that we are a multiracial society and that race can no longer be defined in the binary terms of white and black. "We" will have to include Hispanics and Asians. While blacks currently constitute 13 percent of the Los Angeles population, Hispanics represent 40 percent. The 1990 census revealed that South Central Los Angeles, which was predominantly black in 1965 when the Watts rebellion occurred, is now 45 percent Hispanic. A majority of the first 5,438 people arrested were Hispanic, while 37 percent were black. Of the fifty-eight people who died in the riot, more than a third were Hispanic, and about 40 percent of the businesses destroyed were Hispanic-owned. Most of the other shops and stores were Korean-owned. The dreams of many Korean immigrants went up in smoke during the riot: two thousand Korean-owned businesses were damaged or demolished, totaling about $400 million in losses. There is evidence indicating they were targeted. "After all," explained a black gang member, "we didn't burn our community, just *their* stores."

"I don't feel like I'm in America anymore," said Denisse Bustamente as she watched the police protecting the firefighters. "I feel like I am far away." Indeed, Americans have been witnessing ethnic strife erupting around the world—the rise of neo-Nazism and the murder of Turks in Germany, the ugly "ethnic cleansing" in Bosnia, the terrible and bloody clashes between Muslims and Hindus in India. Is the situation here different, we have been nervously wondering, or do ethnic conflicts elsewhere represent a prologue for America? What is the nature of malevolence? Is there a deep, perhaps primordial, need for group identity rooted in hatred for the other? Is ethnic pluralism possible for America? But answers have been limited. Television reports have been little more than thirty-second sound bites. Newspaper articles have been mostly superficial descriptions of racial antagonisms and the current urban malaise. What is lacking is historical context; consequently, we are left feeling bewildered.

How did we get to this point, Americans everywhere are anxiously asking. What does our diversity mean, and where is it leading us? *How* do we work it out in the post-Rodney King era?

Certainly one crucial way is for our society's various ethnic groups to develop a greater understanding of each other. For example, how can African Americans and Korean Americans work it out unless they learn about each other's cultures, histories, and also economic situations? This need to share knowledge about our ethnic diversity has acquired new importance and has given new urgency to the pursuit for a more accurate history.

More than ever before, there is a growing realization that the established scholarship has tended to define America too narrowly. For example, in his prize-winning study *The Uprooted*, Harvard historian Oscar Handlin presented—to use the book's subtitle—"the Epic Story of the Great Migrations That Made the American People." But Handlin's "epic story" excluded the "uprooted" from Africa, Asia, and Latin America—the other "Great Migrations" that also helped to make "the American People." Similarly, in *The Age of Jackson*, Arthur M. Schlesinger, Jr., left out blacks and Indians. There is not even a mention of two marker events—the Nat Turner insurrection and Indian removal, which Andrew Jackson himself would have been surprised to find omitted from a history of his era.

Still, Schlesinger and Handlin offered us a refreshing revisionism, paving the way for the study of common people rather than princes and presidents. They inspired the next generation of historians to examine groups such as the artisan laborers of Philadelphia and the Irish immigrants of Boston. "Once I thought to write a history of the immigrants in America," Handlin confided in his introduction to *The Uprooted*. "I discovered that the immigrants *were* American history." This door, once opened, led to the flowering of a more inclusive scholarship as we began to recognize that ethnic history was American history. Suddenly, there was a proliferation of seminal works such as Irving Howe's *World of Our Fathers: The Journey of the East European Jews to America*, Dee Brown's *Bury My Heart at Wounded Knee: An Indian History of the American West*, Albert Camarillo's *Chicanos in a Changing Society*, Lawrence Levine's *Black Culture and Black Consciousness*, Yuji Ichioka's *The Issei: The World of the First Generation Japanese Immigrants*, and Kerby Miller's *Emigrants and Exiles: Ireland and the Irish Exodus to North America*.

But even this new scholarship, while it has given us a more expanded understanding of the mosaic called America, does not address our needs in the post-Rodney King era. These books and others like them fragment American society, studying each group separately, in isolation from the other groups and the whole. While scrutinizing our specific pieces, we have to step back in order to see the rich and complex portrait they compose. What is needed is a fresh angle, a study of the American past from a comparative perspective.

While all of America's many groups cannot be covered in one book, the English immigrants and their descendants require attention, for they pos-

sessed inordinate power to define American culture and make public policy. What men like John Winthrop, Thomas Jefferson, and Andrew Jackson thought as well as did mattered greatly to all of us and was consequential for everyone. A broad range of groups has been selected: African Americans, Asian Americans, Chicanos, Irish, Jews, and Indians. While together they help to explain general patterns in our society, each has contributed to the making of the United States.

African Americans have been the central minority throughout our country's history. They were initially brought here on a slave ship in 1619. Actually, these first twenty Africans might not have been slaves; rather, like most of the white laborers, they were probably indentured servants. The transformation of Africans into slaves is the story of the "hidden" origins of slavery. How and when was it decided to institute a system of bonded black labor? What happened, while freighted with racial significance, was actually conditioned by class conflicts within white society. Once established, the "peculiar institution" would have consequences for centuries to come. During the nineteenth century, the political storm over slavery almost destroyed the nation. Since the Civil War and emancipation, race has continued to be largely defined in relation to African Americans—segregation, civil rights, the underclass, and affirmative action. Constituting the largest minority group in our society, they have been at the cutting edge of the Civil Rights Movement. Indeed, their struggle has been a constant reminder of America's moral vision as a country committed to the principle of liberty. Martin Luther King clearly understood this truth when he wrote from a jail cell: "We will reach the goal of freedom in Birmingham and all over the nation, because the goal of America is freedom. Abused and scorned though we may be, our destiny is tied up with America's destiny."

Asian Americans have been here for over one hundred and fifty years, before many European immigrant groups. But as "strangers" coming from a "different shore," they have been stereotyped as "heathen," exotic, and unassimilable. Seeking "Gold Mountain," the Chinese arrived first, and what happened to them influenced the reception of the Japanese, Koreans, Filipinos, and Asian Indians as well as the Southeast Asian refugees like the Vietnamese and the Hmong. The 1882 Chinese Exclusion Act was the first law that prohibited the entry of immigrants on the basis of nationality. The Chinese condemned this restriction as racist and tyrannical. "They call us 'Chink,'" complained a Chinese immigrant, cursing the "white demons." "They think we no good! America cuts us off. No more come now, too bad!" This precedent later provided a basis for the restriction of European immigrant groups such as Italians, Russians, Poles, and Greeks. The Japanese painfully discovered that their accomplishments in America did not lead to acceptance, for during World War II, unlike Italian Americans and German Americans, they were placed in internment camps. Two-thirds of them were citizens by birth. "How could I as a 6-month-old child born in this country," asked Congressman Robert Matsui years later, "be declared by my own Government to be an enemy alien?" Today, Asian Americans represent the fastest-growing ethnic group. They have also become the focus of much mass media attention as "the Model Minority" not only for blacks and Chicanos, but also for whites on welfare and even middle-class whites experiencing economic difficulties.

Chicanos represent the largest group among the Hispanic population, which is projected to outnumber African Americans. They have been in the United States for a long time, initially incorporated by the war against Mexico. The treaty had moved the border between the two countries, and the people of "occupied" Mexico suddenly found themselves "foreigners" in their "native land." As historian Albert Camarillo pointed out, the Chicano past is an integral part of America's westward expansion, also known as "manifest destiny." But while the early Chicanos were a colonized people, most of them today have immigrant roots. Many began the trek to El Norte in the early twentieth century. "As I had heard a lot about the United States," Jesus Garza recalled, "it was my dream to come here." "We came to know families from Chihuahua, Sonora, Jalisco, and Durango," stated Ernesto Galarza. "Like ourselves, our Mexican neighbors had come this far moving step by step, working and waiting, as if they were feeling their way up a ladder." Nevertheless, the Chicano experience has been unique, for most of them have lived close to their homeland—a proximity that has helped reinforce their language, identity, and culture. This migration to El Norte has continued to the present. Los Angeles has more people of Mexican origin than any other city in the world, except Mexico City. A mostly mestizo people of Indian as well as African and Spanish ancestries, Chicanos currently represent the largest minority group in the Southwest, where they have been visibly transforming culture and society.

The Irish came here in greater numbers than most immigrant groups. Their history has been tied to America's past from the very beginning. Ireland represented the earliest English frontier: the conquest of Ireland occurred before the colonization of America, and the Irish were the first group that the English called "savages." In this context, the Irish past foreshadowed the Indian future. During the nineteenth century, the Irish, like the Chinese, were victims of British colonialism. While the Chinese fled from the ravages of the Opium Wars, the Irish were pushed from their homeland by "English tyranny." Here they became construction workers and factory operatives as well as the "maids" of America. Representing a Catholic group seeking to settle in a fiercely Protestant society, the Irish immigrants were targets of American nativist hostility. They were also what historian Lawrence J. McCaffrey called "the pioneers of the American urban ghetto," "previewing" experiences that would later be shared by the Italians, Poles, and other groups from southern and eastern Europe. Furthermore, they offer contrast to the immigrants from Asia. The Irish came about the same time as the Chinese, but they had a distinct advantage: the Naturalization Law of 1790 had reserved citizenship for "whites" only. Their compatible complexion allowed them to assimilate by blending into American society. In making their journey successfully into the mainstream, however, these immigrants from Erin pursued an Irish "ethnic" strategy: they promoted "Irish" solidarity in order to gain political power and also to dominate the skilled blue-collar occupations, often at the expense of the Chinese and blacks.

Fleeing pogroms and religious persecution in Russia, the Jews were driven from what John Cuddihy described as the "Middle Ages into the Anglo-American world of the *goyim* 'beyond the pale.' " To them, America represented the Promised Land. This vision led Jews to struggle not only for themselves but also for other oppressed groups, especially blacks. After the 1917 East St. Louis race riot, the Yiddish *Forward* of New York compared this anti-black violence to a 1903 pogrom in Russia: "Kishinev and St. Louis—the same soil, the same people." Jews cheered when Jackie Robinson broke into the Brooklyn Dodgers in 1947. "He was adopted as the surrogate hero by many of us growing up at the time," recalled Jack Greenberg of the NAACP Legal Defense Fund. "He was the way we saw ourselves triumphing against the forces of bigotry and ignorance." Jews stood shoulder to shoulder with blacks in the Civil Rights Movement: two-thirds of the white volunteers who went south during the 1964 Freedom Summer were Jewish. Today Jews are considered a highly successful "ethnic" group. How did they make such great socioeconomic strides? This question is often reframed by neoconservative intellectuals like Irving Kristol and Nathan Glazer to read: if Jewish immigrants were able to lift themselves from poverty into the mainstream through self-help and education without welfare and affirmative action, why can't blacks? But what this thinking overlooks is the unique history of Jewish immigrants, especially the initial advantages of many of them as literate and skilled. Moreover, it minimizes the virulence of racial prejudice rooted in American slavery.

Indians represent a critical contrast, for theirs was not an immigrant experience. The Wampanoags were on the shore as the first English strangers arrived in what would be called "New England." The encounters between Indians and whites not only shaped the course of race relations, but also influenced the very culture and identity of the general society. The architect of Indian removal, President Andrew Jackson told Congress: "Our conduct toward these people is deeply interesting to the national character." Frederick Jackson Turner understood the meaning of this observation when he identified the frontier as our transforming crucible. At first, the European newcomers had to wear Indian moccasins and shout the war cry. "Little by little," as they subdued the wilderness, the pioneers became "a new product" that was "American." But Indians have had a different view of this entire process. "The white man," Luther Standing Bear of the Sioux explained, "does not understand the Indian for the reason that he does not understand America." Continuing to be "troubled with primitive fears," he has "in his consciousness the perils of this frontier continent. . . . The man from

Europe is still a foreigner and an alien. And he still hates the man who questioned his path across the continent." Indians questioned what Jackson and Turner trumpeted as "progress." For them, the frontier had a different "significance": their history was how the West was lost. But their story has also been one of resistance. As Vine Deloria declared, "Custer died for your sins."

By looking at these groups from a multicultural perspective, we can comparatively analyze their experiences in order to develop an understanding of their differences and similarities. Race, we will see, has been a social construction that has historically set apart racial minorities from European immigrant groups. Contrary to the notions of scholars like Nathan Glazer and Thomas Sowell, race in America has not been the same as ethnicity. A broad comparative focus also allows us to see how the varied experiences of different racial and ethnic groups occurred within shared contexts.

During the nineteenth century, for example, the Market Revolution employed Irish immigrant laborers in New England factories as it expanded cotton fields worked by enslaved blacks across Indian lands toward Mexico. Like blacks, the Irish newcomers were stereotyped as "savages," ruled by passions rather than "civilized" virtues such as self-control and hard work. The Irish saw themselves as the "slaves" of British oppressors, and during a visit to Ireland in the 1840s, Frederick Douglass found that the "wailing notes" of the Irish ballads reminded him of the "wild notes" of slave songs. The United States annexation of California, while incorporating Mexicans, led to trade with Asia and the migration of "strangers" from Pacific shores. In 1870, Chinese immigrant laborers were transported to Massachusetts as scabs to break an Irish immigrant strike; in response, the Irish recognized the need for interethnic working-class solidarity and tried to organize a Chinese lodge of the Knights of St. Crispin. After the Civil War, Mississippi planters recruited Chinese immigrants to discipline the newly freed blacks. During the debate over an immigration exclusion bill in 1882, a senator asked: If Indians could be located on reservations, why not the Chinese?

Other instances of our connectedness abound. In 1903, Mexican and Japanese farm laborers went on strike together in California: their union officers had names like Yamaguchi and Lizarras, and strike meetings were conducted in Japanese and Spanish. The Mexican strikers declared that they were standing in solidarity with their "Japanese brothers" because the two groups had toiled together in the fields and were now fighting together for a fair wage. Speaking in impassioned Yiddish during the 1909 "uprising of twenty thousand" strikers in New York, the charismatic Clara Lemlich compared the abuse of Jewish female garment workers to the experience of blacks: "[The bosses] yell at the girls and 'call them down' even worse than I imagine the Negro slaves were in the South." During the 1920s, elite universities like Harvard worried about the increasing numbers of Jewish students, and new admissions criteria were instituted to curb their enrollment. Jewish students were scorned for their studiousness and criticized for their "clannishness." Recently, Asian-American students have been the targets of similar complaints: they have been called "nerds" and told there are "too many" of them on campus.

Indians were already here, while blacks were forcibly transported to America, and Mexicans were initially enclosed by America's expanding border. The other groups came here as immigrants: for them, America represented liminality—a new world where they could pursue extravagant urges and do things they had thought beyond their capabilities. Like the land itself, they found themselves "betwixt and between all fixed points of classification." No longer fastened as fiercely to their old countries, they felt a stirring to become new people in a society still being defined and formed.

These immigrants made bold and dangerous crossings, pushed by political events and economic hardships in their homelands and pulled by America's demand for labor as well as by their own dreams for a better life. "By all means let me go to America," a young man in Japan begged his parents. He had calculated that in one year as a laborer here he could save almost a thousand yen—an amount equal to the income of a governor in Japan. "My dear Father," wrote an immigrant Irish girl living in New York, "Any man or woman without a family are fools that would not venture and come to this plentyful Country where no man or woman ever hungered." In the shtetls of Russia, the cry "To America!" roared like "wild-fire." "America was in everybody's mouth," a Jewish immigrant recalled. "Businessmen talked [about]

it over their accounts; the market women made up their quarrels that they might discuss it from stall to stall; people who had relatives in the famous land went around reading their letters." Similarly, for Mexican immigrants crossing the border in the early twentieth century, El Norte became the stuff of overblown hopes. "If only you could see how nice the United States is," they said, "that is why the Mexicans are crazy about it."

The signs of America's ethnic diversity can be discerned across the continent—Ellis Island, Angel Island, Chinatown, Harlem, South Boston, the Lower East Side, places with Spanish names like Los Angeles and San Antonio or Indian names like Massachusetts and Iowa. Much of what is familiar in America's cultural landscape actually has ethnic origins. The Bing cherry was developed by an early Chinese immigrant named Ah Bing. American Indians were cultivating corn, tomatoes, and tobacco long before the arrival of Columbus. The term *okay* was derived from the Choctaw word *oke,* meaning "it is so." There is evidence indicating that the name *Yankee* came from Indian terms for the English—from *eankke* in Cherokee and *Yankwis* in Delaware. Jazz and blues as well as rock and roll have African-American origins. The "Forty-Niners" of the Gold Rush learned mining techniques from the Mexicans; American cowboys acquired herding skills from Mexican *vaqueros* and adopted their range terms—such as *lariat* from *la reata, lasso* from *lazo,* and *stampede* from *estampida.* Songs like "God Bless America," "Easter Parade," and "White Christmas" were written by a Russian-Jewish immigrant named Israel Baline, more popularly known as Irving Berlin.

Furthermore, many diverse ethnic groups have contributed to the building of the American economy, forming what Walt Whitman saluted as "a vast, surging, hopeful army of workers." They worked in the South's cotton fields, New England's textile mills, Hawaii's canefields, New York's garment factories, California's orchards, Washington's salmon canneries, and Arizona's copper mines. They built the railroad, the great symbol of America's industrial triumph. Laying railroad ties, black laborers sang:

Down the railroad, um-huh
Well, raise the iron, um-huh
Raise the iron, um-huh.

Irish railroad workers shouted as they stretched an iron ribbon across the continent:

Then drill, my Paddies, drill—
Drill, my heroes, drill,
Drill all day, no sugar in your tay
Workin' on the U.P. railway.

Japanese laborers in the Northwest chorused as their bodies fought the fickle weather:

A railroad worker—
That's me!
I am great.
Yes, I am a railroad worker.
Complaining:
"It is too hot!"
"It is too cold!"
"It rains too often!"
"It snows too much!"
They all ran off.
I alone remained.
I am a railroad worker!

Chicano workers in the Southwest joined in as they swore at the punishing work:

Some unloaded rails
Others unloaded ties,
And others of my companions
Threw out thousands of curses.

Moreover, our diversity was tied to America's most serious crisis: the Civil War was fought over a racial issue—slavery. In his "First Inaugural Address," presented on March 4, 1861, President Abraham Lincoln declared: "One section of our country believes slavery is *right* and ought to be extended, while the other believes it is *wrong* and ought not to be extended." Southern secession, he argued, would be anarchy. Lincoln sternly warned the South that he had a solemn oath to defend and preserve the Union. Americans were one people, he explained, bound together by "the mystic chords of memory, stretching from every battlefield and patriot grave to every living heart and hearthstone all over this broad land." The struggle and sacrifices of the War for Independence had enabled Americans to create a new nation out of thirteen separate colonies. But Lincoln's appeal for unity fell on deaf ears in the South. And the war came. Two and a half years later, at Gettysburg, President Lincoln declared that "brave men" had fought and "consecrated" the ground of this battlefield in order to preserve the Union. Among the brave were black men. Shortly after this bloody battle, Lincoln acknowledged the military contributions of blacks. "There will be some black men," he wrote in a letter to an old friend, James C. Conkling, "who can remember that with silent tongue, and clenched teeth, and steady eye, and well-poised bayonet, they have helped mankind on to this great consummation. . . ." Indeed, 186,000 blacks served in the Union Army, and one-third of them were listed as missing or dead. Black men in blue, Frederick Douglass pointed out, were "on the battlefield mingling their blood with that of white men in one common effort to save the country." Now the mystic chords of memory stretched across the new battlefields of the Civil War, and black soldiers were buried in "patriot graves." They, too, had given their lives to ensure that the "government of the people, by the people, for the people shall not perish from the earth."

Like these black soldiers, the people in our study have been actors in history, not merely victims of discrimination and exploitation. They are entitled to be viewed as subjects—as men and women with minds, wills, and voices.

In the telling and retelling of their stories,
They create communities of memory.

They also re-vision history. "It is very natural that the history written by the victim," said a Mexican in 1874, "does not altogether chime with the story of the victor." Sometimes they are hesitant to speak, thinking they are only "little people." "I don't know why anybody wants to hear my history," an Irish maid said apologetically in 1900. "Nothing ever happened to me worth the tellin'."

But their stories are worthy. Through their stories, the people who have lived America's history can help all of us, including my taxi driver, understand that Americans originated from many shores, and that all of us are entitled to dignity. "I hope this survey do a lot of good for Chinese people," an immigrant told an interviewer from Stanford University in the 1920s. "Make American people realize that Chinese people are humans. I think very few American people really know anything about Chinese." But the remembering is also for the sake of the children. "This story is dedicated to the descendants of Lazar and Goldie Glauberman," Jewish immigrant Minnie Miller wrote in her autobiography. "My history is bound up in their history and the generations that follow should know where they came from to know better who they are." Similarly, Tomo Shoji, an elderly Nisei woman, urged Asian Americans to learn more about their roots: "We got such good, fantastic stories to tell. All our stories are different." Seeking to know how they fit into America, many young people have become listeners; they are eager to learn about the hardships and humiliations experienced by their parents and grandparents. They want to hear their stories, unwilling to remain ignorant or ashamed of their identity and past.

The telling of stories liberates. By writing about the people on Mango Street, Sandra Cisneros explained, "the ghost does not ache so much." The place no longer holds her with "both arms. She sets me free." Indeed, stories may not be as innocent or simple as they seem to be. Native-American novelist Leslie Marmon Silko cautioned:

I will tell you something about stories . . .
They aren't just entertainment.
Don't be fooled.

Indeed, the accounts given by the people in this study vibrantly re-create moments, capturing the complexities of human emotions and thoughts. They also provide the authenticity of experience. After she escaped from slavery, Harriet Jacobs wrote in her autobiography: "[My purpose] is not to tell you what I have heard but what I have seen—and what I have suffered." In their sharing of memory, the people in this study offer us an opportunity to see ourselves reflected in a mirror called history.

In his recent study of Spain and the New World, *The Buried Mirror,* Carlos Fuentes points out that mirrors have been found in the tombs of ancient Mexico, placed there to guide the dead through the underworld. He also tells us about the legend of Quetzalcoatl, the Plumed Serpent: when this god was given a mirror by the Toltec deity Tezcatlipoca, he saw a man's face in the mirror and realized his own humanity. For us, the "mirror" of history can guide the living and also help us recognize who we have been and hence are. In

A Distant Mirror, Barbara W. Tuchman finds "phenomenal parallels" between the "calamitous 14th century" of European society and our own era. We can, she observes, have "greater fellow-feeling for a distraught age" as we painfully recognize the "similar disarray," "collapsing assumptions," and "unusual discomfort."

But what is needed in our own perplexing times is not so much a "distant" mirror, as one that is "different." While the study of the past can provide collective self-knowledge, it often reflects the scholar's particular perspective or view of the world. What happens when historians leave out many of America's peoples? What happens, to borrow the words of Adrienne Rich, "when someone with the authority of a teacher" describes our society, and "you are not in it"? Such an experience can be disorienting—"a moment of psychic disequilibrium, as if you looked into a mirror and saw nothing."

Through their narratives about their lives and circumstances, the people of America's diverse groups are able to see themselves and each other in our common past. They celebrate what Ishmael Reed has described as a society "unique" in the world because "the world is here"—a place "where the cultures of the world crisscross." Much of America's past, they point out, has been riddled with racism. At the same time, these people offer hope, affirming the struggle for equality as a central theme in our country's history. At its conception, our nation was dedicated to the proposition of equality. What has given concreteness to this powerful national principle has been our coming together in the creation of a new society. "Stuck here" together, workers of different backgrounds have attempted to get along with each other.

People harvesting
Work together unaware
Of racial problems,

wrote a Japanese immigrant describing a lesson learned by Mexican and Asian farm laborers in California.

Finally, how do we see our prospects for "working out" America's racial crisis? Do we see it as through a glass darkly? Do the televised images of racial hatred and violence that riveted us in 1992 during the days of rage in Los Angeles frame a future of divisive race relations—what

Arthur Schlesinger, Jr., has fearfully denounced as the "disuniting of America"? Or will Americans of diverse races and ethnicities be able to connect themselves to a larger narrative? Whatever happens, we can be certain that much of our society's future will be influenced by which "mirror" we choose to see ourselves. America does not belong to one race or one group, the people in this study remind us, and Americans have been constantly redefining their national identity from the moment of first contact on the Virginia shore. By sharing their stories, they invite us to see ourselves in a different mirror.

CHAPTER 2

What Is Culture?

Eugene García

Professor of Education and Psychology at the University of California, Santa Cruz, Eugene Garcia was director of the Office of Bilingual Education and Minority Language Affairs in the Department of Education during the Clinton Administration. He is widely recognized as a leading researcher and is the author of numerous publications.

When we speak of the **culture** to which an individual belongs, we generally refer to the system of understanding characteristic of that individual's society, or of some subgroup within that society. This system of understanding includes values, beliefs, notions about acceptable and unacceptable behavior, and other socially constructed ideas that members of the culture are taught are "true." This is the common definition of culture employed by many anthropologists, who analyze the behavioral patterns and customs of groups of people. The word *culture*, however, can have a variety of different connotations in general usage.

Recently I taught a class in which I asked a group of university juniors and seniors preparing for careers in education to break into small groups and identify, very specifically, attributes of their individual cultures. It was no surprise to me that one student responded, "I'm White. I have no culture." Such responses occur all too frequently. "Of course you have a culture," I answered as the other students scrutinized our interaction. "Everyone has culture." They all went off, some a bit reluctantly, to complete the assignment.

At the end of the exercise, each group reported their findings and analysis. Yes, they all had culture, but with a diverse set of students it was not easy to discuss individual cultural characteristics. These students, like most of us, usually do not sit down and expose their culture. They live it.

They can recognize it when they see it. And they can determine when they are not in it, and that usually distresses them. These students also seemed distressed in speaking openly about culture to one another, as if exposing their culture would leave them vulnerable to criticism and negative feelings of attribution regarding who they were or what they might represent.

My students all survived their initial distress and discovered in a few minutes the basic tenets of the science of anthropology. To define a culture by its attributes might be a start, but this in itself is not particularly useful. The students did identify cultural attributes. They indicated that their cultures were made up of many distinguishable attributes: familial, linguistic, religious and spiritual, aesthetic, socioeconomic, educational, diet, gender roles, and so on. The list was quite long. But what seemed quite evident was that they all came to the conclusion that this thing—culture—was not easy to define because it meant (1) defining these attributes in relation to specific individuals who live in distinct physical and social contexts and (2) taking into consideration the previous histories of those individuals and those social contexts. In short, they determined culture to be not only complex but dynamic, yet for individuals living their cultures, quite recognizable.

Having begun with the ideas of novice educators and their conceptualizations of culture, it seems appropriate to turn now to the "experts." I must warn you that even professional anthropologists struggle with the same questions as bedeviled my students. Their thinking is more systematic, though, and that will help us.

THE GROUP-ORIENTED CONCEPT OF CULTURE

The **culture concept,** with its technical anthropological meaning, was first defined by Edward Tylor in 1871 as "that complex whole which includes knowledge, belief, art, law, morals, custom, and other capabilities and habits acquired by man as a member of society" (Kroeber and Kluckhohn, 1963, p. 81). Since Tylor's time, many other definitions of culture have been advanced by anthropologists. These definitions, like Tylor's, commonly attempt to encompass the totality (or some subset of the totality) of humanity's achievements, dispositions, and capabilities. Virtually every anthropologist considers culture to be something that is learned and transmitted from generation to generation.

Most definitions of culture include another dimension, the notion that culture is something that members of a group share in common. A recently published textbook on anthropology states, for example, that behaviors and ideas may be considered cultural only insofar as they are shared among members of a social group (Nanda, 1990). This formulation is useful for anthropological comparisons between societies or subgroups within societies. Its basic assumption, however, is that of uniformity in the cultural attributes of individual members of societies and subgroupings of societies. In this formulation, the primary focus of culture is some kind of group.

Anthropologists do acknowledge that members of all societies display individual differences in their behaviors and ways of thinking. That is to say, societies are characterized to some extent by intercultural heterogeneity. But these differences are not significant for anthropologists and usually are noted only insofar as they determine the "looseness" or "tightness" of a society's cultural system. When researchers in anthropology proceed to write their ethnographies, their deep descriptions and analyses of any group, they tend to ignore individual variations and to abstract what they apparently consider "an essential homogeneity from the background noise of insignificant diversity" (Schwartz, 1978, p. 419).

Along these lines, anthropologist Ralph Linton defined culture as "the sum total of ideas, conditioned emotional responses and patterns of habitual behavior which the members of a society have acquired through instruction or imitation and which they share to a greater or less degree" (quoted in Kroeber and Kluckhohn, 1963, p. 82). Although ideas or learned behavioral habits need not be totally shared by everyone in a group, it is nevertheless this property of sharing, the commonality of attributes, that defines the domain of culture.

Educational Considerations

Some emphasis on shared traits is basic to any conceptual understanding of the role of culture in education. However, such an emphasis leaves little if any room for the recognition of each student's individuality within the framework of the culture concept. Individuality becomes the domain of psychology, relevant only to discussions of personality, while "culture" is used to refer to ideas and behaviors that prevail in the individual's group. Using the culture concept as a basis for theories of education might be appropriate if the goal is to educate (or reeducate) a group, as in modernization programs applied by developing countries to their peasant populations. But the focus of most education, as all who have taught for any time know, is the education of the individual student, not the education of his or her ethnic group.

The relevance of this problem lies in the possible consequences of the group-oriented concept of culture for the perceptions and expectations of teachers in their interactions with culturally diverse children. A group-oriented concept may serve to distract the teacher's attention from the student's particular experience of culture-generating processes, in and outside of school. The culture concept adopted by the teacher greatly affects teacher-student interaction. The assumptions a teacher makes about the student's "culture," whether right or wrong, may stereotype the student and thus preclude the flexible, realistic, and open-minded quality of teacher-student interaction needed for effective instruction. The effect of this stereotyping on students is significant, since the educational process is fundamentally a process of social interaction, with socialization as a primary goal.

Let's consider an example of how the group culture concept might operate in a teacher-student interaction. Picture a situation where the teacher is perplexed by some action or response by a student of minority status. A teacher who has studied some anthropological descriptions of the student's ethnic culture may leap to an interpretation of the student's behavior based on idealized characteristics anthropologists have attributed to that culture. The teacher may mean well, but to construe an individual's behavior solely on the basis of generalization about group traits is to stereotype the individual, no matter how valid the generalizations or how well meaning one's intentions.

It would be better for the teacher to encounter the student in the way anthropologists most often come to understand the people they study. Though they write about cultures in collective terms, anthropologists build their understandings through observations of individuals. The teacher's efforts to understand the individual student could (and should) be supplemented by knowledge of cultural attributes widely held in the student's ethnic community. But this fund of knowledge should be viewed only as background information. The question of its applicability to the particular student should be treated as inherently problematical. Many studies (for example, Rodriguez, 1989; Tharp and Gallimore, 1989) also caution educational personnel against hasty "ethnographic/cultural" generalizations on the grounds that all linguistic-cultural groups are continuously undergoing significant cultural changes.

The student-teacher interaction is a powerful phenomenon. Thomas Carter's research (1968) into the effects of teacher's expectations on student learning and classroom behavior are particularly pertinent. Carter showed that Chicano students may sometimes actualize in their behavior the negative expectations held for them by teachers. It may be expected, of course, that a pattern of negative expectation would be less likely among teachers who have elected to teach in bilingual and bicultural settings in which both Spanish and English are used for instruction. We have to remember, though, that many teachers teach in bilingual and bicultural settings that have not been so formally designated and for which these teachers received little preparation.

Even teachers of the same minority status as their students may be considered in some ways culturally different from the children of their own ethnic group. This observation is not recent.

Guerra (1979) points to linguistic and other cultural variations both within (student-student) and between (student-teacher) generations of bilingual populations. Cuellar (1980, p. 198) argues that one's understanding of the meaning and value of culture and language must take into account the fact that "a community's characteristics reflect the composition of the different generational cohorts in the different age strata." What this adds up to is individual variation within cultures, of particular importance to educators.

THE INDIVIDUAL-ORIENTED CONCEPT OF CULTURE

The group culture concept is not the only instrument available for understanding individuals and groups. Fortunately, anthropological theory contains an individual-oriented concept of culture developed and used by a number of anthropologists with interests in psychology. As Ted Schwartz notes, these theorists criticized the group culture concept for the way it can "lead one to imagine culture as floating somehow disembodied in the noösphere or, at best, carried by human beings as a conductor might carry an electric current containing information" (Schwartz, 1978, p. 434). Rather than work with an abstract idea of culture, these theorists were interested more in how culture was manifested in the lives of individual human beings.

An early expression of the individual-oriented concept of culture is seen in the work of anthropologist J. O. Dorsey. U.S. anthropologist Edward Sapir (quoted in Pelto and Pelto, 1975, p. 1) wrote the following of Dorsey's orientation:

> Living as long as he did in close touch with the Omaha Indians, [Dorsey] knew that he was dealing, not with a society nor with a specimen of primitive man but with a finite, though indefinite, number of human beings who gave themselves the privilege of differing from each other not only in matters generally considered as "One's own business" but even on questions which clearly transcended the private individual's concerns.

Advocates of the individual-oriented concept of culture frequently describe a society's culture as a "pool" of constructs (rules, beliefs, values, etc.) by which the society's members conceptually order the objects and events of their lives. The participation of individuals in this pool is seen as variable. Spiro (1951), for example, distinguished between the cultural "heritage" of all members of a society (that which has been made available to them by their predecessors) and each individual's particular cultural "inheritance" (that portion of the group's heritage that the individual has effectively received, or "internalized," from the past). Ted Schwartz adds that the individual also manipulates, recombines, and otherwise transforms these inherited constructs. This process of transformation, together with the outright creation of new constructs, is a major source of culture change (Schwartz, 1978). The individual's own portion of a society's culture is termed by Goodenough as a "propriocept" (1981), by Wallace as a "mazeway" (1970), and by Schwartz as an "idioverse" (1978). All of these specialized terms are variations on a core nature of culture: each individual assembles his or her own version of the larger culture.

For some of the anthropologists who employ an individual-oriented concept of culture, "the private system of ideas of individuals is culture" (Pelto and Pelto, 1975, pp. 12–13). Other anthropologists of like mind reject the implication in such a notion of individual cultures. As they see it, the contents of one subjective system alone cannot be considered a culture. Like Schwartz, these theorists consider a cultural system to consist of all the constructs available to a society's members. Nevertheless, the society is itself not the locus of culture; its individual members are. The culture thus is a **distributive** phenomenon in that its elements are widely distributed among the individual members of a society. A major implication of this **distributive model of culture** is a rejection of the traditional assumption of cultural homogeneity—that is, the idea that all members of a culture share all that culture's attributes. The distributive model instead implies that each individual's portion of the culture differs in some ways from that of any other.

According to Schwartz, Wallace's antidote to the homogeneous view of culture is an overdose, leading to the opposite malady of ignoring the degree of cultural sharing that does occur between individuals. Schwartz's own model of culture takes into account both the sharing and nonsharing of cultural constructs between members of a society, and he argues that both are fundamentally essential to a society's viability. Diversity, he argues, increases a society's cultural inventory, whereas what any individual could contain within his or her head would make up a very small culture pool. Commonality then permits communication and coordination in social life. In Schwartz's own words, "It makes as little sense to depict the distribution of a culture among the members of a society as totally heterogeneous and unique in each individual as it did to argue for complete homogeneity. We must dispense with the *a priori* assumption of homogeneity, but, similarly, we are not served by an *a priori* assumption of heterogeneity" (Schwartz, 1978, p. 438).

Educational Considerations

I view Schwartz's formulation of the distributive model of culture as the most appropriate for addressing issues of cultural diversity in the schools. This formulation permits, within the framework of culture, simultaneous recognition of a student's "ethnic" culture and those characteristics that define the student as a unique individual. Students share with their ethnic peers constructs they do not share with others, but all individuals are in some ways different from their ethnic peers. The distributive model also permits recognition of traits that members of subgroups share with members of the larger culture, such as those acquired through acculturation.

Schooling is a major variable in **acculturation,** which is the process by which the members of a society are taught the elements of the society's culture. The acculturation process is a crucial consideration in the analysis of ethnic minorities in plural societies. Variety in acculturation also contributes significantly to the heterogeneity of ethnic cultures. Writing about the U.S. cultural subgroup labeled "Hispanic," Bell, Kasschau, and Zellman (1976) note that among Chicanos, "many have ancestors who came to North America several centuries ago, but others are themselves recent immigrants. Hence, a simple cultural characterization of [this] ethnic group should be avoided" (p. 7). These authors also caution against a simplistic view of the process of acculturation, noting that it "may not be linear, in the sense that one simply loses certain Mexican attributes and replaces them with Anglo attributes" (1976, pp. 31–32). Acculturation may be characterized by more complex patterns of combination and by ongoing recombination than by simple substitution. Thus, language minority children who hear some English spoken at home experience a different process of acculturation than children who hear only the home language. These children may all belong to the same ethnic subgroup, but their different acculturation makes them each unique.

Some people are likely to respond to the individual-oriented concept of culture with the question "What about customs?" Chicanos, for example, might point out that all the members of their group are alike in that they recognize certain *costumbres* that distinguish them from the larger society. Customs occupy a realm of culture that is highly shared and is more likely to belong to the public sphere than to form a specific part of an individual's subjective orientation. Referring to the "layered" nature of culture, anthropologist Benjamin Paul (1965, p. 200) has observed:

> What we call customs rest on top and are most apparent. Deepest and least apparent are the cultural values that give meaning and direction to life. Values influence people's perceptions of needs and their choice between perceived alternative courses of action.

I purposely emphasize the problematic nature of cultural variability and sharing. The variable nature of acculturation and the individual uniqueness that it engenders are, I believe, no less important for the education of culturally diverse students than are the "real" cultural differences between ethnic groups. Education must deal with both the individual and the culture.

I hasten to add that teachers who work with children from linguistically or culturally diverse populations must be not only keenly aware of the instructional objectives of education but also knowledgeable about and sensitive to the impact that culture and language have on the student.

The Culture of School

The classroom has many, if not all, of the characteristics that anthropologists and sociologists tell us belong to culture. There are tacit rules, patterns, formal structures of organization, and an ecological component. Most important are the tacit dimensions. We tend to think that school is all about learning "the Three R's." Parents and children, and sometimes teachers themselves, do not recognize that the school makes cultural demands

on students in addition to the intellectual ones.

As in our earlier discussion of culture, we need to distinguish between competing concepts of the nature and purpose of school. Recent research acknowledges that schools are social situations which are constructed through the interactions between individuals (Feldman, 1986; Gardner, 1983). More traditional views represent schools as institutions with stable traits generally impervious to individual influence. It is important for educators to understand how our society views the concept of school. This concept underlies how we approach the teaching of students in schools. If we see teaching and learning as embedded within a cultural context, we are more likely to recognize that performance will vary as a function of that context.

STUDENT RESPONSE TO SCHOOL CULTURE

Some examples from research into the cultural demands of school will demonstrate this point. Philips (1982, 1984) examined the classroom performance of Native American students. Observed in the schools, Native American students appeared to conform exactly to the stereotype of "the silent Indian child." Philips was puzzled, however, since her observations also indicated that outside the classroom these children were certainly not silent. She identified what is now considered an important aspect of school culture: **participant-structured demand,** or the demands of instruction that are imposed by the organization of the learning environment itself. She was able to make this discovery only because she observed the children across a number of situations—in community settings, in their homes, and in the school.

Philips found that classroom lessons imposed varying demands on the children. The classrooms were organized in an individualistic, competitive way. Children were expected to stand up alone in front of the classroom and to respond competitively to the teacher's questions. The Native American children were not doing well in this arrangement. Philips contrasted the demands of the school with the demands of the home. There were definite demands in each culture. In the homes of the Native American children, she found a culture in which children were working cooperatively in groups, not competitively. For an individual to stand out, to act on his or her own, independent of the group, was to violate the norm of the home. Conversely, it was to violate the norm of the classroom not to stand out. The children were caught in a bind between the competing demands of home and school.

Other studies have compared home and school cultures. Shirley Brice Heath's work, conducted in a number of different areas, contributes a good deal to our knowledge base. Heath (1982) noted in her study of low-income black and white Appalachian children that their teachers, who came from different economic and cultural backgrounds, talked to children differently than did the children's parents. Heath described a difference in language used between home and school. The school placed a great demand on children to display their knowledge. Children would often be asked a question for which the teacher already had the answer. If, for example, a child correctly answered the question "What time is it?" the teacher would not respond "Thank you" but "Very good," indicating that the child's knowledge had been tested. The teacher did not need the information. At home, however, when a child was asked "What time is it?" the underlying assumption was that the child had information needed by another member of the family. Interestingly, middle-income parents often use a questioning strategy similar to the teacher's. They play games such as peek-a-boo that also have a dimension of information. But Heath found that in low-income families, there was little imitation of the conversational demands of school. These children were not gaining practice at home with a linguistic device essential to their school performance.

THE SCHOOLS' RESPONSE TO CHILDREN

Both Heath's work and Philips's study portray ways in which a school culture may deviate from a student's home culture. This and other research demonstrate quite clearly that a school culture truly does exist and can directly or indirectly influence children's performance and teacher perceptions. Since we cannot ask children to leave their cultures at the door, we must ask, how can schools allow for a better balance of these disparate demands?

One recommendation is to allow cultural elements that are relevant to the children to enter the classroom freely. Some refer to this practice as **scaffolding.** The school provides a set of supports that utilize the child's home language, discourse style, participation orientation, and so on, enabling the child to move through relevant experiences from the home toward the demands of the school as representative of the society. It is not a subtraction of culture, and it is not an attempt to reproduce home environments in the context of the school. The idea is to encourage the child to respect the demands of the school culture while preserving the integrity of the home culture.

Primarily, we must first comprehend the fact that children—all children—come to school motivated to enlarge their culture. But we must start with their culture. We need not regard them, certainly not initially, as organisms to be molded and regulated. We look first to determine how they seek to know themselves and others and how their expertise and experience can be used as the fuel to fire their interests, knowledge, and skills. We do not look first at their deficits: what they do not know but need to know. Far from having deficits, they are rich in assets. As teachers, we enter their world in order to aid them and to build bridges between two cultures (Sarason, 1990).

Teaching in a Cultural Context

If by understanding culture and cultural diversity and respecting individuality, educators can better serve culturally diverse students, have they fulfilled their obligations as teachers? I believe they have not. Our culturally diverse populations continue to be highly vulnerable in today's society and in our schools. They will carry us all to either a bright or a beleaguered future.

Recognizing the present circumstances and the magnitude of this challenge, what is called for? What must we do? Sensitivity toward "culture," while necessary, will not be sufficient. Earlier we saw how even well-meaning teachers may stereotype students when trying to allow for cultural differences. There are three additional ingredients for effective teaching in a context of student cultural diversity:

- Personal commitment
- Knowledge of what makes a difference
- Educational leadership

Let's look more closely at these elements and take an inventory of them in our schools today.

PERSONAL COMMITMENT

We need not be fooled by liberal or conservative rhetoric. We have not achieved educational equality for our culturally diverse populations, and substantive progress requires further resolve. It is often trumpeted that Head Start, school choice, restructuring, site-based management, cooperative learning, the whole language approach, educational technology (computer-assisted instruction), and so forth have already or will soon reverse the pattern of underachievement among linguistically and culturally diverse populations. Doubtlessly these contributions are important, but our own part in the U.S. educational system suggests that we as teachers should resist the notion of a miracle cure. No new methodologies, reorganizations, or curricula will satisfactorily address the problem of underachievement unless the individuals who implement these initiatives are deeply committed to the enterprise. The change that is necessary must be fueled by the type of social energy that our nation has tapped in the past. As in the eras of Kennedy's "New Frontier" or Johnson's "War on Poverty," we must grasp the spiritual importance of this new educational challenge.

More than a decade after Jimmy Carter warned of a crisis of spirit in America—a warning that proved politically disastrous for him and a boon to rival Ronald Reagan—a broad spectrum of the nation's social and intellectual leadership is concluding that Carter was right. In fact, they say, the crisis has deepened. It was heresy when Carter declared, "we've always had a faith that the days of our children would be better than our own." We are losing that faith, and it is no longer possible to conceal it from ourselves.

A consensus has emerged that a lack of confidence among Americans, in the future and in one another, lies at the heart of the nation's ills. A nation that passed much of the 1970s, in the aftermath of Vietnam, in search of its soul and self spent the 1980s in what many see as a self-consuming materialism. We now enter the 1990s in a cynical, dispirited mood. "There is disturbing evidence to suggest that most forms of responsibility toward others have eroded in recent decades," asserts Derek Bok, former president of Harvard University, in his 1990 book, *Universities and the Future of America.* The percentage of people who feel that most individuals in power try to take advantage of others has doubled over the last two decades and now exceeds 60 percent.

One source of information about prevailing attitudes in the United States is the book *The Cynical Americans* (1989), by Donald L. Kanter and Philip H. Mirvis. Based on a national survey of attitudes, Kanter concludes that "the tendency to behave cynically is being reinforced to an unprecedented degree by a social environment that seems to have abandoned idealism and increasingly celebrates the virtue of being 'realistic' in an impersonal, acquisitive, tough-guy world. In citizen and country alike, there seems to be a loss of faith in people and in the very concept of community. A recent national survey found that 43 percent of Americans—and more than half of those under age 24—believe selfishness and fakery are at the core of human nature." Large majorities of those sampled say they feel most people lie if they can gain by it, sacrifice ethical standards when money is at stake, and pretend to care about others more than they really do.

It is difficult to believe that the picture is truly bleak. Most of us know people who are generous and creative in their interactions with others—even heroic in small ways, considering the multiple stresses and strains of modern life. They work hard, tend to their families, and contribute to their communities. There are many people who care deeply about individual and collective welfare in the United States. It is possible that our current cynicism is simply a measure of disappointed idealism, of surprise and dismay that our work as a nation is not done and may never be "done," and that we must continue to call upon the inspiration, resolve, commitment, and passion of everyone.

Some have argued that we have lost the ability to inspire our children. Others say we have lost the ability to inspire ourselves. But inspiration is the spark that leads to resolve and commitment, and we cannot afford to be without it. Borrowing from Jaime Escalante, the noted California educator characterized in the popular 1988 film *Stand*

and Deliver, we will need *ganas*—the desire that fires the will to overcome great challenges.

KNOWLEDGE OF WHAT MAKES A DIFFERENCE

We will also need a new knowledge base. Recent research has pinpointed the problem of educational vulnerability. It has destroyed stereotypes and myths about the educational needs of culturally diverse students and laid a foundation upon which to reconceptualize present educational practices and to launch new initiatives. As we saw earlier in this chapter, the basis for change is a new understanding of individual uniqueness within a cultural context. No one set of descriptions or prescriptions will suffice for all students of a given cultural background.

We should pay attention to what seems to work. Recent research summarized by García (1992) has documented educationally effective practices with linguistically and culturally diverse students in selected sites throughout the United States. These descriptive studies identified specific schools and classrooms that serve students of minority status and that were particularly successful academically. The case study approach adopted by these studies included examination of preschool, elementary, and high school classrooms. The researchers interviewed teachers, principals, parents, and students and conducted specific classroom observations that assessed the "dynamics" of the instructional process.

The results of these studies for elementary schools provide important insights into general instructional organization, literacy development, and academic achievement in such content areas as math and science. The results also yield enlightening information on the perspectives of students, teachers, administrators, and parents. The interviews showed that these classroom teachers were highly committed to the educational success of their students. They perceived themselves as instructional innovators utilizing "new" learning theories and instructional philosophies to guide their practice. Most of these teachers were involved in professional development activities such as participating in small-group support networks with other educators. They had a strong, demonstrated belief in the importance of communication between the school and the home (several teachers were interacting weekly with parents)

and felt they had the autonomy to create or change the instruction and curriculum in their classrooms, even if it did not exactly meet district guidelines. They had high academic expectations for all their students ("Everyone will learn to read in my classroom") and served as advocates for their students. They rejected any conclusion that their students were intellectually or academically disadvantaged.

This and other research shows that curriculum, instructional strategies, and teaching staffs that are effective are rooted in sharing "expertise" and experiences through multiple processes of communication. Abundant and diverse opportunities for speaking, listening, reading, and writing, along with home-to-school bridges that help guide students through the learning process, constitute an effective curriculum. Effective schools also encourage culturally diverse students to take risks, construct meaning, and reinterpret the knowledge they acquire as it applies to their lives. Within this curriculum, skills are taught as tools for acquiring further knowledge. Research into such effective programs should continue. The more we know about what makes them effective, the more equipped we will be to educate diverse student groups.

EDUCATIONAL LEADERSHIP

The leadership necessary to mobilize this growing commitment and knowledge will recognize four interlocking domains that pertain especially to teachers.

Knowledge Dissemination

We will need to disseminate knowledge about effective practices to those who can utilize it. This requires training, retraining, and more retraining. Individually and institutionally, new knowledge must be appropriated by people working in the field of education. It is of no use to students if researchers share their knowledge only among themselves. New avenues for knowledge dissemination and appropriation are required. Leadership in this domain is required.

Professional Development

New knowledge alone does not automatically lead to a new set of pedagogical or curricular skills ready for use by practitioners. Knowledge must be transferred to teachers and adapted for use in specific instructional contexts. Time and energy must be devoted to the collaboration required between teachers and researchers to develop new skills. Moreover, these new pedagogical and curricular skills must be evaluated "in the field"—they must prove themselves effective for students. We will need to hold ourselves and others "automatically" accountable. This requires leadership in both knowledge dissemination and professional skill development.

Disposition for Leadership

Many are called, but few will self-select. We need a generation of educational leaders who are willing to sacrifice, work very hard and very long, take risks, learn from failure, rise above frustration, rethink existing paradigms, and support and collaborate with their colleagues. Those who do not possess this set of dispositions must step aside, minimize obstruction, and otherwise admit that if they cannot be part of the solution, they will not be part of the problem.

Affective Engagement

We will need leadership that welcomes, adopts, nurtures, celebrates, and challenges our culturally diverse students. "They" must become "we." Anything short of raw advocacy every minute of every day will not suffice. Too many of these students have given up hope in themselves. We must not give up hope.

Mostly, educators need to act. Presidents and governors "proclaim" and set national education-al goals. Educators need to move beyond such proclamations. The task at hand is not only to see the future but to enable it. With commitment, knowledge, and leadership, educators can enable the future for our culturally diverse society.

Conclusion

In this chapter, I have tried to set the context for a more thorough discussion of the educational challenges facing this country's educators. The challenge stands for all students and specifically for those who are culturally diverse. This country's educational future will be much different from our educational past. We will have to be capable of responding to transformations in social structures and institutions, in global organization, and in values. Historically, our schools' efforts to merge diverse groups into a homogenized "American" culture have not resulted in academic success for culturally diverse students. However, new insights into educational concepts, new research, and new educational practices suggest that we can meet this challenge successfully.

We must continue to build a knowledge base regarding children, families, communities, and schools. Research studies that add dimension to what we already know about culturally diverse students will be valuable pieces of the puzzle. However, as the discussion in the preceding pages has indicated, merely building this knowledge base is not enough.

CLASS 2

Social Interaction in Diverse Settings: The SIM's Model

CHAPTER 3
Understanding Social Interaction in Culturally Diverse Settings
J. Q. Adams

J. Q. Adams has developed a model that can be used as an analytical tool for understanding human interaction in any setting. The article provides a step by step introduction to each component of the model and the requisite language necessary to use the model effectively. A variety of examples are given to help readers understand how the model can be applied.

Understanding Social Interaction in Culturally Diverse Settings

J.Q. Adams

My primary teaching responsibilities at Western Illinois University involve instructing graduate teaching majors in the area of educational psychology, multicultural education, and alternatives to traditional educational practices. Given the dramatic demographic changes within the state of Illinois and across the nation, it is incumbent upon Colleges of Education, as well as other disciplines, to prepare students who can successfully understand and participate in the culturally diverse settings. In order to teach these skills, I have developed a social interaction model (SIM) and theory that breaks down the primary components of individual and group social interaction characteristics in a variety of cultural settings or scenes.

The SIM and theory have four major components: the ego, the cultural scene, decision making, and event familiarity. Each of these components helps students to understand the complexities of social interaction in society and in the classroom. The model also helps the students to understand their own interaction styles and cultural backgrounds and provides practical strategies to enhance their ability to become more effective participants in culturally diverse settings.

The Individual or Ego

Each ego or individual has developed his or her own unique propriospect or personal culture which is the result of enculturation. Goodenough (1971) states that propriospect embraces an individual's cognitive and affective ordering of his experiences which include:

> The various standards for perceiving, evaluating, believing, and doing what he attributes to other persons as a result of his experiences of their actions and admonitions. By attributing standards to others, he makes sense of their behavior and is able to predict it to a significant degree. By using what he believes to be their standards for him as a guide for his own behavior, he makes himself intelligible to them and can thereby influence their behavior well enough, at least to permit him to accomplish many of his purposes through them. (p. 36)

The problem that certain ethnic group(s)/culturally different students(s) (EG/CDS) encounter is that their primary culture is often foreign to the mainstream, operating culture of the anglicized schools in which they must interact and to the anglicized teachers from whom they must learn. By anglicized I am referring to the Euroethnic/WASP cultural dominance of the U.S. educational system in which the vast majority of instructors are Euroethnic. This idea of personal culture may be linked to recent work on cognitive knowledge structures called schemas. In discussing their schema approach, Schank and Abelson (1977) state that, "People know how to act appropriately because they have knowledge about the world they live in." (p. 36) They go on to describe the two classes of knowledge that humans recognize: general knowledge and specific knowledge. General knowledge is that basic information that all humans understand, such as the need for water and food. Specific knowledge, on the other hand, is used to interpret and participate in events we have been through many times. This type of detailed specific knowledge allows the individual to do less processing and wondering about frequently experienced events. Therefore, if we assume that Goodenough's (1965) contentions are accurate, EG/CDS face a daily dilemma of reordering their "recipes" or what Schank and Abelson (1977) call *scripts,* so as to make sense of and perform the new rules of operating behavior competently enough to achieve their goals.

Each ego also processes an individual idiolect, as Goodenough (1965) again reminds us: "No two speakers of what we regard as the 'same' language actually operate with identical systems and articulation of systems." (p. 8)

This, of course, is compounded when a setting is multicultural or multiethnic with several language and dialect possibilities likely to be in operation. Given the demographic changes occurring in this nation, most colleges and universities already fit this culturally diverse description.

Both a person's propriospect and his or her idiolect are reflective of the resources available through his or her (or the parents'/guardians') socioeconomic status (SES). SES, in this instance, is being used as an index that describes such features as residence, occupation, income, and educational level. These SES factors contribute either more positively or negatively to the performance level of competencies an individual possesses for any given event. These competencies or skills are performed in a manner that would fall somewhere on the continuum between novice and expert.

The Cultural Scene

Spradley (1972) suggests that a cultural scene is the information shared by two or more people that defines some aspect of their experience. Cultural scenes are closely linked to recurrent social situations. Complex social organizations, such as colleges and universities, provide numerous settings that qualify as cultural scenes. Within each cultural scene the individual or ego faces a range of potential interactions with the other participants present, depending on their varying roles, status, scripts, plans, and goals, and the physical constraints of the setting.

It is important to elaborate on the definitions of status and role as they will be used in the context of this chapter. Goodenough (1965), drawing on the research of Linton (1936), Merton (1957), and Hoebel (1954), described statuses as a combination of rights and duties in which individuals have social identities that are either ascribed or achieved. Goodenough maintains that statuses contain the following two properties: what legal theorists call rights, duties, privileges, powers, liabilities, and immunities and the ordered ways these are distributed in what will be called identity relationships. Rights and duties form the boundaries within which individuals in any given cultural scene are expected to confine their behavior based on their knowledge of the rules of sociocultural behavior applicable to that given situation. Goodenough (1965) provides this example:

> When I am invited out to dinner, it is my hostess' right that I wear a necktie; to wear one is my duty. It is also her right that its decoration be within the bounds of decency. But she has no right as to how it shall be decorated otherwise; it is my privilege to decide this without reference to her wishes.

Goodenough goes on to state:

> As for powers, they and their liability counterparts stem from privileges, while immunities result from rights and the observance of duties. (p. 3)

Social identity in Goodenough's scheme refers to that aspect of an individual that determines how one's rights and duties distribute to specific others. This identity is to be distinguished from one's personal identity which relates to the way one may express one's privileges. It is also important to note that each individual has a variety of social identities. A student, for example, can also be an older and/or younger sibling, a football player, student government president, a sorority/fraternity member, and belong to a specific church. One's rights and duties vary according to the identities one assumes, as well as the identities assumed by the other participants with whom one interacts in the cultural scene. When an EG/CDS, for example, is in the classroom, it is the instructor's right to insist that the EG/CDS participate in the classroom activities; classroom participation is the EG/CDS' duty. It is also the instructor's right to demand that the EG/CDS' classroom behavior, while participating, is within the institution's acceptable range of behavior. But the teacher has no right to tell the EG/CDS with whom they should interact within the classroom on a personal level. It is the EG/CDS' privilege to decide with whom they will develop social relationships, without regard for the instructor's wishes. Thus, the exercise of the choices of privileges expresses an individual's "sense" of identity.

Since each individual possesses a myriad of identities, we must ask, how is it that an identity is selected? As Linton (1936, p. 115) contends, some identities are ascribed while others are achieved. A person's gender and age identity in most instances are a given. An 18-year-old male has the social responsibility to represent himself as a young adult and a man. But, on the other hand, he has no obligation to reveal that he is a member of the football team or what his religious preference is. Goodenough (1965) stated that there were several considerations that govern the selection of identities. For example: (a) the individual has the qualifications for selecting identities, (b) the interaction has a direct bearing on the choice of identities by the individuals present, (c) the setting of the interaction helps determine the identity, (d) an individual has only a limited number of appropriate matching responsibilities available for any identity assumed, and (e) finally, an individual is likely to have more than one identity-relationship for each cultural scene. The sum of one's selected identities is referred to as the "social persona" in the cultural scenes interaction.

Combining Spradley (1972) and Goodenough's (1965) theoretical approach leads to the proposal that in each possible cultural scene the identity relationships created among individuals have their corresponding specific allocation of rights and duties. The reciprocal agreement of these rights and duties constitutes a status relationship. Status relationships elaborate on the differences in this relationship between minorities and majorities and/or successful/unsuccessful students. In summary, a culturally ordered system of social relationships, then, is composed (among other things) of identity relationships, status relationships, and finally the ways they are mutually distributed. Goodenough describes an individual's role as the aggregate of its composite statuses. In other words, it would be equivalent to all the duty-statuses and right-statuses for a given identity. Each individual identity will differ in some ways, with some having greater privileges and possibilities for gratification than others. Therefore, each individual identity has a different place or function in the social system in which he or she resides. In order to sum up this discussion on status and roles, Cicourel (1974) states:

> Statuses, like general rules or policies, require recognition and interpretation during which interacting participants must elicit and search appearances for relevant information about each other. Role-taking and role-making require that the actor articulate general rules or policies (norms) with an emergent (constructed) action scene in order to find the meaning of one's own behavior or that of some other. (p. 29)

Cicourel's statement is especially apt in the context of this paper since the individuals under scrutiny are EG/CDS who are oftentimes unaware of the full range of nuances involved in recognizing the status and/or the roles of the more anglicized faculty, staff, and students. This, of course, also applies to the anglicized students' ability to recognize and accurately construct the status and roles of EG/CD faculty, staff, and students in their enculturative settings as well as to assess what their status and roles are in the acculturative scenes of the anglicized school.

Each individual or ego reacts to a given setting or cultural scene based on his or her own individual enculturative experiences, among other things. For most situations, "schemata," or "scripts," have already been established for what is to be expected and how the individual should act based on the constraints and cues present in any given situation. Recipes can be thought of as cognitive routines established over time through repetition to meet the needs of a particular situation. Schank and Abelson describe scripts as a way of economizing familiar episodes into a generalized standard episode. In other words, scripts handle typical everyday situations.

There are numerous cultural scenes and settings within the college/university ranging from the academic classroom, to the residence hall, to extracurricular activities, and to the University

Union. Each specific cultural scene in the school context has its own unique set of constraints and participants.

The Decision-Making Process

Given the constraints of the various cultural scenes EG/CDS encounter within the college/university, the EG/CDS are constantly faced with such decisions as to where, when, and with whom they should interact. While some cultural scenes within the college/university, such as the classroom, have pre-selected or tracked populations and perhaps fixed seating requirements, other settings such as the residence halls, dining rooms, or the hallways outside classrooms, are more open and feature a wider range of peers with whom one can interact. Since these cultural scenes are reoccurring situations or events, the participants have developed recipes or scripts to govern their behavior in them. Events according to Nelson (1986) are more of a macro order; they involved people in purposeful activities acting on objects and interacting with each other to achieve some result.

Let us take, for example, a script we will call the CLASSROOM. According to Schank and Abelson (1977), all participants in the classroom would bring with them specific knowledge and detail about the standard events that occur in the anglicized classroom, including information about the various roles (instructor, students, graduate assistant), props (instructor's desk, student's desk, books, homework, chalkboards), and event tracks (lecture, laboratory, exam). Since much of what takes place in the classroom frequently occurs in a specific "expectable" order, we can assume that the participants are familiar with the corresponding repertoire of behaviors necessary for a high level of social competence in that setting. However, assuming that in some cases the EG/CDS' original script of the classroom will possess some cultural differences as a result of their different enculturative experiences, modifications will have to be made in their CLASSROOM script in order to accommodate the specific knowledge necessary to perform in the mainstream anglicized classroom. Some students will bring more deficit scripts into the classroom than other students whose high school, community college, or other experiences may be more transferable. Thus, one might propose that initially, at least, the EG/CDS utilize the general knowledge from their EG/CD CLASSROOM script as a foundation for the development of their new anglicized CLASSROOM script.

Within this larger body of knowledge we call the CLASSROOM script are specific tracks such as the lecture hall, the laboratory, the practicum, and the various academic classes (math, science, English), each with its own unique set of events that separates it from the other tracks that make up the CLASSROOM script. Schank and Abelson also point out that there are ways more than one script can be active at once. Take for example a situation where "student Alpha," an anglicized student, asks "student Beta," an EG/CDS, if he is going to the soccer match after classes. The question asked by Alpha departs from the situational CLASSROOM script and activates the personal FRIENDSHIP script of both participants. This type of script shifting is not unusual; however, for the novice EG/CDS, the cross-cultural differences in the anglicized FRIENDSHIP script may create some cognitive dissonance, especially for the newly arrived international student or the more ethnically traditional EG/CDS. On the other hand, their more acculturated peers, who have been in anglicized situations longer, have had more time to acquire the nuances of the anglicized FRIENDSHIP script. This greater knowledge of anglicized culture will enable them to demonstrate a higher level of expertise in this event. Thus, Beta understands that Alpha's statement is really an invitation, which is a specific track of the FRIENDSHIP script, and responds appropriately, "Yes, I am planning to go to the game. Would you like to sit together?" Another problem with this form of script-shifting is that the teacher may interpret this brief communication between Alpha and Beta as a breach in the classroom rules and exact some form of discipline and/or penalty if it continues. Script-shifting is sometimes employed as a strategy by the student to gain attention from one's peers or as an expression of not understanding what is going on in the classroom script. A discussion of event familiarity and degrees of expertise will be presented in the next section.

EG/CDS who come from less anglicized cultural settings than the predominantly anglicized college/universities face the obstacles of developing new schema to support the recipes or scripts necessary for appropriate behavior in any given event. Underlying the need for expertise in script interaction is the need for understanding. Schank and Abelson state:

> Understanding then is a process by which people match what they see and hear to pre-stored groupings of actions that they have already experienced. New information is understood in terms of old information. By this view, man is seen as a processor that only understands what it has previously understood. (p. 67)

Understanding allows an individual to not only be predictive in nature but also have the ability to adapt to events with which he or she does not have previous experience. This point is critical. Effective teaching in our culturally diverse classrooms requires that we should take the time to make sure our students understand and can operate the necessary scripts to give them the best opportunity for success.

Event Familiarity—From Novice to Expert

Given that EG/CDS bring into the anglicized school scripts that were based on the social-cultural knowledge of their own enculturative experience in their primary culture, and given that the cultural scenes they face in anglicized settings are often very different from the cultural scenes in their culture of origin, each EG/CDS can be expected to respond to each new cultural scene with differing degrees of experience or expertise. Fivush and Slackman (1986) state:

> We believe that even the simplest action routine is imbued with social meaning. The social meaning defines not only what this particular event is about, but also how it fits into the larger cultural context. (p. 72)

We can assume, therefore, that even though EG/CDS will have scripts from which to access general knowledge about the classroom and academic success, they may lack the specific knowledge necessary for accurate prediction and appropriate behavior.

Slackman, Hudson, and Fivush (1986) discuss this phenomenon as "event familiarity." Borrowing from the research of Taylor and Winkler (1980), they describe four phases of expertise in adults which I believe would also apply to college-age students: (a) the rudimentary (or episodic) phase where knowledge of an example is used to make inferences about other apparently similar instances. An example of this would be EG/CDS making assumptions about what happens in anglicized schools based on a single experience of registering for classes; (b) the stereotypic phase where only the most representative attributes are featured. In the school example prototypical actions such as reading, writing, and studying are characteristic of most schools anywhere; (c) the relative expert phase where greater emphasis is placed on inconsistencies; and finally, (d) the automatic, or "mindless" phase. Thus, when EG/CDS go to predominantly anglicized colleges/universities, they would automatically know what to do in any cultural scene without necessarily being aware of the steps in the process.

Summary

In this chapter I sought to develop a theoretical model of social interaction in culturally diverse settings. This model contains four major components: (a) the individual or ego, (b) the cultural scene, (c) the decision-making process, and (d) the event familiarity range from novice to expert.

Each of these components is based upon the premise that culture is a kind of knowledge individuals acquire through the memory of personal experiences and episodes. Cognitive theorists such as Anderson (1980), Schank and Abelson (1977), and Nelson (1986), have developed a script theory through which to study events. Events involve people who are acting on objects and interacting with each other in purposeful activities to achieve some results. The events are often organized around goals and are usually made up of smaller units or episodes, each with its own schema. Scripts refer to an ordered sequence of actions appropriate to a particular spatial-temporal context and organized around a goal. Scripts specify the actors, actions, and props used to carry out these goals within specified circumstances.

The specific circumstances in this paper are referred to as cultural scenes as defined by Spradley (1972) and include the information shared by two or more people and explain some aspect of their experiences. Cultural scenes are closely linked to recurrent social situations. Thus, the scripts developed for these scenes should allow the actors to predict what the appropriate behavioral and communicative responses are in these settings. Since the social-cultural knowledge of EG/CDS' enculturative experience often differs from that of anglicized students, the scripts that EG/CDS have for the various cultural scenes may be too general in nature to provide them with the specific anglicized knowledge needed to interact appropriately. This would be especially true in the predominant Euro-American classroom.

According to this model, the level of event familiarity that EG/CDS possess influences the kind of decision-making they are likely to exhibit, given the constraints of the situation. EG/CDS who have developed more anglicized classroom scripts are more likely to be academically successful than those who have more traditional cultural scripts and thus are more likely to maintain their more anglicized classroom scripts. The development of anglicized scripts suggests that the individuals possess social interaction skills that have reached either the relative expert or automatic stage, while their more traditional peers possess anglicized social interaction skills at the rudimentary or the stereotypic stage. The implications for these levels of expertise are twofold: (a) those students who have reached the relative expert or automatic phase continue to become more proficient in their social interaction skills each time they use them, and (b) these students have the advantage of utilizing their academic success to assist them in reaching their career and/or social goals.

References

Anderson, J. R. (1980). *Cognitive psychology and its implications*. San Francisco: W. H. Freeman.

Cicourel, A. V. (1974). *Cognitive sociology*. New York: The Free Press.

Fivush, R., & Slackman, E.A. (1986). The acquisition and development of scripts. In K. Nelson (Ed.), *Event knowledge*. (pp. 71–96). Hillsdale, NJ: Lawrence Erlbaum Associates.

Goodenough, W. H. (1965). Rethinking status and role. In M. Banton (Ed.), *The relevance of models for social anthropology* (pp. 1–14). London: Tavistock.

Goodenough, W. H. (1971). *Culture, language, and society*. Reading, MA: Addison-Wesley.

Hoebel, A. E. (1954). *The law of primitive man*. Cambridge, MA: Harvard University Press.

Linton, R. (1936). *The study of man*. New York: Appleton-Century Crofts.

Merton, R. K. (1957). *Social theory and social structure*. (rev. ed.). New York: Free Press.

Nelson, K. (1986). *Event knowledge*. Hillsdale, NJ: Lawrence Erlbaum Associates.

Schank, R. C., & Abelson, R. P. (1977). *Scripts, plans, goals and understanding*. Hillsdale, NJ: Lawrence Erlbaum.

Slackman, S. A., Hudson, J. A., & Fivush, R. (1986). Actions, actors, links, and goals: The structure of children's event representation. In K. Nelson (Ed.), *Event knowledge*. (pp. 47–69). Hillsdale, NJ: Lawrence Erlbaum Associates.

Spradley, J. P. (1972). *Culture and cognition: Rules, maps, and plans*. San Francisco: Chandler.

Taylor, S. E., & Winkler, J. D. (1980). *The development schemas*. Paper presented at the meeting of the American Psychological Association, Montreal, Canada.

CLASS 3

Negotiating Cross Cultural Communication

CHAPTER 4
Intercultural Communication: A Current Perspective
Milton Bennett

Milton Bennett's article is a primer for anyone engaging in inter-cultural contact. It provides fertile background and knowledge to help readers understand their own cultures as well as the cultures of others. Bennett shares many of his own personal experiences traveling and living in other cultures. Readers also get the opportunity to benefit from the research he has studied and analyzed from other well respected inter-cultural scholars in the field.

Intercultural Communication: A Current Perspective

Milton J. Bennett

An international consultant on inter-cultural communication, Milton Bennett is co-founder and co-director of the Intercultural Communication Institute in Portland, Oregon. Bennett served in the Peace Corps in Micronesia and was on the faculty at Portland State University. He has written numerous articles and is the editor of *Basic Concepts of Intercultural Communication: Selected Readings.*

The study of intercultural communication has tried to answer the question, "How do people understand one another when they do not share a common cultural experience?" Just a few decades ago, this question was one faced mainly by diplomats, expatriates, and the occasional international traveler. Today, living in multicultural societies within a global village, we all face the question every day. We now realize that issues of intercultural understanding are embedded in other complex questions: What kind of communication is needed by a pluralistic society to be both culturally diverse and unified in common goals? How does communication contribute to creating a climate of respect, not just tolerance, for diversity? The new vision and innovative competencies we bring to this changing world will determine the answer to another question about the global village posed by Dean Barnlund: "Will its residents be neighbors capable of respecting and utilizing their differences or clusters of strangers living in ghettos and united only in their antipathies for others?"[1]

Dealing with Difference

If we look to our species' primate past and to our more recent history of dealing with cultural difference, there is little reason to be sanguine. Our initial response to difference is usually to avoid it. Imagine, if you will, a group of our primate ancestors gathered around their fire, gnawing on the day's catch. Another group of primates comes into view, heading toward the fire. I wonder how often the first group looked up and said (in effect), "Ah, cultural diversity, how wonderful." More likely it was fight or flight, and things have not changed that much since then. We flee to the suburbs or behind walls to avoid cultural difference, and if we are forced to confront it, there often is a fight.

Historically, if we were unsuccessful in avoiding different people, we tried to convert them. Political, economic, and religious missionaries sought out opportunities to impose their own beliefs on others. The thinking seemed to be, "If only people were more like us, then they would be all right to have around." This assumption can still be seen in the notion of the "melting pot" prevalent this century in the United States. It is difficult for many people to believe that any understanding at all is possible unless people have become similar to one another.

When we could not avoid or convert people who were different from ourselves, we killed them. Examples of genocide are not so very far away from us, either in time or distance, and individual cases of hate crimes are tragically frequent. Of course, one doesn't need to physically terminate the existence of others to effectively eliminate them. When we make their lives miserable in our organizations and neighborhoods, we also "kill" them—they cannot flourish, and often they do not survive.

Given this history of dealing with difference, it is no wonder that the topic of difference—understanding it, appreciating it, respecting it—is central to all practical treatments of intercultural communication. Yet this emphasis on difference departs from the common approaches to communication and relationships based within a single culture.

Monocultural communication is *similarity-based*. Common language, behavior patterns, and values form the base upon which members of the culture exchange meaning with one another in conducting their daily affairs. These similarities generally allow people to predict the responses of others to certain kinds of messages and to take for granted some basic shared assumptions about the nature of reality. In monocultural communication, difference represents the potential for misunderstanding and friction. Thus, social difference of all kinds is discouraged.

Intercultural communication—communication between people of different cultures—cannot allow the easy assumption of similarity. By definition, cultures are different in their languages, behavior patterns, and values. So an attempt to use one's self as a predictor of shared assumptions and responses to messages is unlikely to work.[2] Because cultures embody such variety in patterns of perception and behavior, approaches to communication in cross-cultural situations guard against inappropriate assumptions of similarity and encourage the consideration of difference. In other words, the intercultural communication approach is *difference-based*.[3]

Upper-Case Culture and Lower-Case culture

When people anticipate doing something *cultural* of an evening, their thoughts turn to art, literature, drama, classical music, or dance. In other words, they plan to participate in one of the *institutions* of culture—behavior that has become routinized into a particular form. I refer to this aspect of culture as "Culture writ large," with a capital "C." The more academic term that is used by most writers is *objective culture*.[4] Other examples of objective culture might include social, economic, political, and linguistic systems—the kinds of things that usually are included in area studies or history courses. The study of these institutions constitutes much of the curriculum in both international and multicultural education. For instance, courses in Japanese culture or African American culture are likely to focus on the history, political structure, and arts of the groups. While this is valuable information, it is limited in its utility to the face-to-face concerns of intercultural communication. One can know a lot about the history of a culture and still not be able to communicate with an actual person from that culture. Understanding objective culture may create knowledge, but it doesn't necessarily generate competence.

The less obvious aspect of culture is its *subjective* side—what we can call "culture writ small." Subjective culture refers to the psychological features that define a group of people—their everyday thinking and behavior—rather than to the institutions they have created. A good working definition of subjective culture is *the learned and shared patterns of beliefs, behaviors, and values of groups of interacting people*. Understanding subjective cultures—one's own and others'—is more likely to lead to intercultural competence.

Of course, social reality is constructed of both large and small "c" aspects of culture; people learn how to behave through socialization into the institutions of the culture, which leads them to behave in ways that perpetuate those same institutions.[5] As noted above, traditional international and multicultural education tends to focus only on the objective mode of this process; in contrast, intercultural communication focuses almost exclusively on the subjective mode. For instance, interculturalists are concerned with *language use* in cross-cultural relationships, rather than in linguistic structure. They study how language is modified or supplanted by culturally defined *nonverbal behavior*, how cultural patterns of thinking are expressed in particular *communication styles*, and how reality is defined and judged through cultural *assumptions and values*. In the following pages, examples in each of these areas will illustrate how understanding subjective culture can aid in the development of skills in cultural adaptation and intercultural communication.

Levels of Culture

The definition of subjective culture also provides a base for defining "diversity" in a way that includes both international and domestic cultures at different *levels of abstraction.* National groups such as Japanese, Mexican, and U.S. American and pan-national ethnic groups such as Arab and Zulu are cultures at a high level of abstraction—the qualities that adhere to most (but not all) members of the culture are very general, and the group includes a lot of diversity. At this level of abstraction we can only point to general differences in patterns of thinking and behaving between cultures. For instance, we might observe that U.S. American culture is more characterized by individualism than is Japanese culture, which is more collectivist.

Analysis at a high level of abstraction provides a view of the "unifying force" of culture. The very existence of interaction, even through media, generates a commonality that spans individuals and ethnicities. For instance, despite their significant individual and ethnic differences, Mexicans spend more time interacting with other Mexicans than they do with Japanese. They certainly spend more time reading Mexican newspapers and watching Mexican television than they do consuming Japanese media. This fact generates Mexican "national character"—something that distinguishes Mexicans from Japanese (and from other Latin Americans as well).

U.S. Americans are particularly resistant to recognizing their national culture. Despite the fact that nearly everyone else in the world immediately recognizes them as Americans, many of them still insist on labeling themselves as "just individuals" or "a mixture of cultures." Of course, the very commonality of this tendency is an example of U.S. American national culture; no other people in the world but U.S. Americans are so quick to disavow their cultural affiliation. This is probably a manifestation of the individualism that is generally attributed to U.S. Americans.[6] Whatever the reason, it is perilous for U.S. Americans to fail to see the cultural force that unifies them. It leads them to see ethnic and other cultural differences as more of a threat to national unity than they are.

While cultural difference at a high level of abstraction provides a rich base for analyzing national cultural behavior, there are significant group and individual differences within each national group that are concealed at this level. These differences provide a diversifying force that balances the unifying force of national culture.

At a lower level of abstraction, more specific groups such as ethnicities can be described in cultural terms. In the United States, some of these groups are African American, Asian American, American Indian, Hispanic/Latino American, and European American. People in these groups may share many of the broad national culture patterns while differing significantly in the more specific patterns of their respective ethnicities. It should be noted that in terms of subjective culture, ethnicity is a cultural rather than a genetic heritage; dark skin and other Negroid features may make one "black," but that person has not necessarily experienced African American enculturation. Most black people in the world are *not* American in any sense. Similarly, "whites" are not necessarily European American, although in the United States it is difficult for them to escape being socialized in the patterns that are currently dominant in U.S. American society.

Other categories of subjective cultural diversity usually include gender, regionality, socioeconomic class, physical ability, sexual orientation, religion, organization, and vocation. The concept can embrace other long-term groupings such as single parents or avid sports fans, as long as the groups maintain the clear patterns of behavior and thinking of an "identity group."[7] By definition, individuals do not have different cultures; the term for patterns of individual behavior is "personality."

Stereotypes and Generalizations

Whenever the topic of cultural difference is discussed, the allegation of stereotyping usually is not far behind. For instance, if cultural patterns of men and women are being compared, someone may well offer that she is a woman and doesn't act that way at all.

Stereotypes arise when we act as if all members of a culture or group share the same characteristics. Stereotypes can be attached to any assumed indicator of group membership, such as race, religion, ethnicity, age, or gender, as well as national culture. The characteristics that are assumedly shared by members of the group may be respected by the observer, in which case it is a *positive stereotype*. In the more likely case that the characteristics are disrespected, it is a *negative stereotype*. Stereotypes of both kinds are problematic in intercultural communication for several obvious reasons. One is that they may give us a false sense of understanding our communication partners. Whether the stereotype is positive or negative, it is usually only partially correct. Additionally, stereotypes may become self-fulfilling prophecies, where we observe others in selective ways that confirm our prejudice.

Despite the problems with stereotypes, it is necessary in intercultural communication to make *cultural generalizations*. Without any kind of supposition or hypothesis about the cultural differences we may encounter in an intercultural situation; we may fall prey to naive individualism, where we assume that every person is acting in some completely unique way. Or we may rely inordinately on "common sense" to direct our communication behavior. Common sense is, of course, common only to a particular culture. Its application outside of one's own culture is usually ethnocentric.

Cultural generalizations can be made while avoiding stereotypes by maintaining the idea of *preponderance of belief*.[8] Nearly all possible beliefs are represented in all cultures at all times, but each different culture has a preference for some beliefs over others.[9] The description of this preference, derived from large-group research, is a cultural generalization. Of course, individuals can be found in any culture who hold beliefs similar to people in a different culture. There just aren't so many of them—they don't represent the preponderance of people who hold beliefs closer to the norm or "central tendency" of the group. As a specific example (see Figure 1), we may note that despite the accurate cultural generalization that U.S. Americans are more individualistic and Japanese are more group-oriented, there are U.S. Americans who are every bit as group-oriented as any Japanese, and there are Japanese who are as individualistic as any U.S. American. However, these relatively few people are closer to the fringe of their respective cultures. They are, in the neutral sociological sense of the term, "deviant."

Deductive stereotypes occur when we assume that abstract cultural generalizations apply to every single individual in the culture. While it is

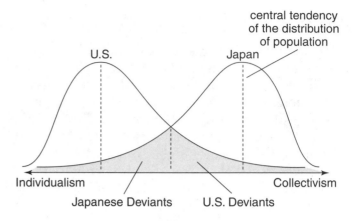

FIGURE 1 GENERALIZATION DISTRIBUTIONS

appropriate to generalize that U.S. Americans as a group are more individualistic than Japanese, it is stereotyping to assume that every American is strongly individualistic; the person with whom you are communicating may be a deviant. Cultural generalizations should be used tentatively as working hypotheses that need to be tested in each case; sometimes they work very well, sometimes they need to be modified, and sometimes they don't apply to the particular case at all. The idea is to derive the benefit of recognizing cultural patterns without experiencing too much "hardening of the categories."

Generalizing from too small a sample may generate an *inductive stereotype*. For example, we may inappropriately assume some general knowledge about Mexican culture based on having met one or a few Mexicans. This assumption is particularly troublesome, since initial cross-cultural contacts may often be conducted by people who are deviant in their own cultures. ("Typical" members of the culture would more likely associate only with their cultural compatriots—that's how they stay typical.) So generalizing cultural patterns from any one person's behavior (including your own) in cross-cultural contact is likely to be both stereotypical and inaccurate.

Another form of inductive stereotype is derived from what Carlos E. Cortés calls the "social curriculum." He notes that school-children report knowing a lot about Gypsies, even though few of the children have ever met even one member of that culture. According to Cortés' research, the knowledge was gained from old horror movies![10] Through media of all kinds we are besieged with images of "cultural" behavior:

African Americans performing hip-hop or bringing warmth to medical practice; Hispanic Americans picking crops or exhibiting savvy in the courtroom; European Americans burning crosses or exercising altruism toward the homeless. When we generalize from any of these images, we are probably creating stereotypes. Media images are chosen not for their typicality, but for their unusualness. So, as with initial cross-cultural contacts, we need to look beyond the immediate image to the cultural patterns that can only be ascertained through research.

Assumptions of an Intercultural Communication Perspective

Beyond its emphasis on cultural difference, intercultural communication is based on some assumptions that both identify it with and distinguish it from other social sciences.

ANALYSIS OF PERSONAL INTERACTION

Like interpersonal communication, intercultural communication focuses on face-to-face (or at least person-to-person) interaction among human beings. For this kind of communication to occur, each participant must perceive him- or herself being perceived by others. That is, all participants must see themselves as potentially engaged in communication and capable of giving and receiving feedback. This assumption allows us to understand why interculturalists are not particularly focused on mass media. Even though the issues of international satellite broadcasting and culture-specific cable productions are fascinating, they are essentially one-way events. However, individual, mediated communication such as faxing, e-mailing, and Internet chat room dialogue does fit the definition of person-to-person communication.

It is surprising to some that intercultural communication does not often generate comprehensive descriptions of culture, or ethnographies. While such descriptions are crucial for any cross-cultural study, they do not in themselves constitute cases of cross-cultural interaction. An intercultural perspective leads researchers to hypothesize, given some difference in the described cultures, how members of the cultures might interact.

Another useful distinction in this context is that between *cultural interaction* and *cultural comparison*. When social science studies deal with culture at all, they frequently compare one aspect of a culture to a similar phenomenon in another. For instance, psychologists might compare how Northern European depth perception differs from that of Amazonian Indians. Or sociolinguists might analyze the differences in ritual greeting between European Americans and African Americans. While interculturalists use these kinds of comparisons for their knowledge base, they focus less on the differences themselves and more on how the differences are likely to affect face-to-face interaction.

This emphasis on interaction does not mean that interculturalists neglect knowledge about specific cultures. On the contrary, it is considered a prerequisite for interculturalists to have expert knowledge of at least their own cultures (an often-neglected skill in other academic fields). Most interculturalists are particularly knowledgeable about one or more cultures in addition to their own.

CULTURE-SPECIFIC AND CULTURE-GENERAL APPROACHES

Interaction analysis and skill development can be undertaken at two levels. At the *culture-specific* level, differences between two particular cultures are assessed for their likely impact on communication between people of those cultures. For instance, the generalization that Hispanic American patterns of cross-status communication differ from the more egalitarian patterns of European Americans[11] could be analyzed for its possible effect on interaction between employees and managers from the two cultures. Training in alternative cross-status communication styles could then help members of both cultures appreciate and deal more effectively with each other in the workplace. This approach, based on specific ethnographies, is an intercultural form of "emic" cultural analysis.[12]

Culture-general approaches to interaction describe general cultural contrasts that are applicable in many cross-cultural situations. For instance, Edward T. Hall's definition of high-context and low-context cultures[13] is a culture-general contrast that suggests a source of miscommunication among many diverse cultures. Similarly, culture-general skills are communication competencies that would be useful in any cross-cultural situation. They usually include cultural self-awareness, nonevaluative perception, cultural adaptation strategies, and cross-cultural empathy. This approach, based on more abstract categories and generalizable skills, is the intercultural equivalent of "etic" cultural analysis.

EMPHASIS ON PROCESS AND THE DEVELOPMENT OF COMPETENCE

The process of communication can be thought of as the mutual creation of meaning—the verbal and nonverbal behavior of communicating and the interpretations that are made of that behavior. The meaning itself, whatever it is, can be called the *content* of the communication. Everyday communication mainly stresses content, while studies of communication tend to emphasize the process and give less attention to the content. This is particularly true for intercultural communication, where apparently familiar or understandable content may mask radically different cultural processes.

Another implication of this assumption is that knowledge of content does not automatically translate into mastery of process. I have already noted that knowledge about objective cultural institutions does not necessarily yield competence in communicating with the people whose behavior maintains those institutions. Even knowledge about subjective cultural contrasts, while more directly applicable to communication, is still not sufficient in itself for intercultural competence. Specific knowledge of subjective culture needs to be framed in culture-general categories and coupled with an understanding of both the general and specific intercultural processes involved. A knowledge of the differences between U.S. American and Japanese decision-making styles is not, in itself, particularly useful. It needs to be framed in more general value contrasts (e.g., individualism and collectivism), linked with an understanding of how individualists and collectivists generally misconstrue each other's behavior, joined by an awareness of how those misunderstandings manifest themselves in dysfunctional communication patterns (e.g., negative spirals), and finally applied to avoiding negative spirals and other miscommunication in an actual joint decision-making effort.

Focus on Humanistic Phenomena

Most approaches to intercultural communication (and communication in general) treat it as a purely human phenomenon, not, for instance, as an expression of a divine plan. Any assumption of transcendental guidance to communication immediately runs afoul of cultural differences in religious beliefs. And if one believes that his or her communication style is dictated by a divine authority, adapting that style to a different cultural context will be difficult at best. Interculturalists generally leave questions of supernatural order to contexts where improving communication is not the goal.

In a similar vein, interculturalists tend to avoid purely ideological analyses of discourse. When communication behavior is labeled as "Marxist," or "imperialist," or "racist," or "sexist," the human aspects of that behavior are overshadowed by the reifications of principle. Polarization usually supplants any hope of inclusivity, and further exploration of communication differences is drowned out by the political commotion.[14]

I do not mean to say here that the abuse of power is inconsequential to communication. On the contrary, no improvement of intercultural relations is likely to occur in a climate of oppression and disrespect, and interculturalists have a role in changing that climate through their explication and facilitation of interaction. I do, however, mean to suggest that the professional work of interculturalists is not primarily ideological (except insofar as any action taken is inherently political, to some degree). Critical social analysis is an important part of political change. But when the question is how to understand and adapt to another culture more successfully, as it is in intercultural communication, purely ideological analyses yield little light and much heat.

Historical analyses of cultural behavior have some of the same disadvantages as ideological approaches. While it might be accurate to note that U.S. American individualism has Calvinistic roots nurtured in a wild frontier and that Japanese collectivism has grown out of Shintoism and close-knit agricultural communities, such an observation tells us little about how the values of individualism and collectivism are likely to affect the behavior of an American person with a Japanese person today. Similarly, understanding the history of immigration into the United States, while important for other reasons, is not particularly useful in analyzing the cross-cultural aspects of interethnic communication. In both cases, the immediate behavior and its cultural context may be occluded by a preoccupation with historical causes.

The avoidance of history as an analytical frame does not mean that interculturalists neglect the subject altogether. People of most cultures feel respected if the person they encounter knows something about the history of their group, and mutual respect is a major goal of intercultural communication. Also, the acknowledgment of history is particularly important if an oppressor/oppressed relationship existed (or continues to exist) between the communication partners. Any disavowal of that history on the part of a dominant culture member is likely to be interpreted as evidence of continuing (albeit possibly unintentional) oppression. For instance, the failure by European Americans to recognize the history of slavery or of American Indian genocide in the United States is often seen as racist. A knowledge of history is also important for interpreting those aspects of people's behavior that mainly are responses to past and present mistreatment. Scottish people, for instance, take particular umbrage at being confused with the English, their historical oppressors. But, while acknowledging historical context, interculturalists usually focus on patterns of behavior in the here and now. Specifically, they analyze the human interaction that is created each time different cultural patterns are brought into contact through face-to-face communication.

Another aspect of humanism is its assumption of personal and cultural relativity. This means that behavior and values must be understood both in terms of the uniqueness of each person and in terms of the culture of that person. Absolute judgments about the goodness or badness of behavior and values are avoided, as far as communication is concerned. Interculturalists generally consider that evaluations of culturally different behavior are likely to be ethnocentric and that in any case they interfere with the communication necessary to become informed about the worldview context in which the behavior must be interpreted. In the simplest terms, cultural relativity is a commitment to understanding all events in cultural context, including how the event is likely to be evaluated in that context.

It is important to note here that cultural relativity is not the same as ethical relativity. The end result of understanding events in cultural context is not "... whatever." Like most other people, interculturalists are both professionally and personally committed to ethical positions. They may be, however, particularly concerned that their ethical commitments are not based on ethnocentric absolutes.[15]

Intercultural Communication Processes

For the rest of this chapter, processes and skills of intercultural communication will be reviewed. In this section, the review will be restricted to communication process. In the following sections, applications of these concepts to culture-general issues of intercultural adaptation and sensitivity will be considered.

LANGUAGE AND THE RELATIVITY OF EXPERIENCE

Many students (and some teachers) view language only as a communication tool—a method humans use to indicate the objects and ideas of their physical and social world. In this view, languages are sets of words tied together by rules, and learning a foreign or second language is the simple (but tedious) process of substituting words and rules to get the same meaning with a different tool.

Language does serve as a tool for communication, but in addition it is a "system of representation" for perception and thinking. This function of language provides us with verbal categories and prototypes that guide our formation of concepts and categorization of objects; it directs how we experience reality.[16] It is this "reality-organizing" aspect of language that engages interculturalists.

A memorable statement of how language organizes and represents cultural experience is now known as the Whorf/Sapir hypothesis:

> We dissect nature along lines laid down by our native languages. The categories and types that we isolate from the world of phenomena we do not find there because they stare every observer in the face; on the contrary, the world is presented in a kaleidoscopic flux of impressions

which has to be organized by our minds—and this means largely by the linguistic systems in our minds.[17]

In this statement, Benjamin Lee Whorf advances what has come to be called the "strong form" of the hypothesis: language largely determines the way in which we understand our reality. In other writings, Whorf takes the position that language, thought, and perception are interrelated, a position called the "weak hypothesis." Interculturalists tend to use the weak form of the hypothesis when they discuss language and culture.

An example of how various languages direct different experiences of reality is found in how objects must be represented grammatically. American English has only one way to count things (one, two, three, etc.), while Japanese and Trukese (a Micronesian language) each have many different counting systems. In part, these systems classify the physical appearance of objects. For instance, one (long) thing is counted with different words from one (flat) thing or one (round) thing in Trukese. We could imagine that the experience of objects in general is much richer in cultures where language gives meaning to subtle differences in shape. Indeed, Japanese aesthetic appreciation of objects seems more developed than that of Americans, whose English language has relatively simple linguistic structures to represent shapes.

In addition, both Japanese and Trukese count people with a set of words different from all others used for objects. We might speculate that research on human beings that quantifies behavior "objectively" (i.e., like objects) would not arise as easily in cultures where people were counted distinctly. And indeed, quantitative research on human beings is much more common in Western cultures, particularly U.S. American.

Another example of the relationship of syntax and experience can be found in the grammatical representation of space. In American English, things can be either "here" or "there," with a colloquial attempt to place them further out "over there." In the Trukese language, references to objects and people must be accompanied by a "location marker" that specifies their position relative to both the speaker and listener. A pen, for instance, must be called this (close to me but away from you) pen, this (midway between us) pen, that (far away from both of us but in sight) pen, or that (out of sight of both of us) pen. We may assume that Trukese people, who live on islands, experience "richer" space than do Americans, whose language does not provide so many spatial boundary markers and for whom space is therefore more abstract.

Language syntax also guides our social experience. Perhaps the simplest and best-known examples are linguistic differences in "status markers." Thai, Japanese, and some other Asian languages have elaborate systems of second-person singular (*you*) words that indicate the status of the speaker relative to the listener. In Thai, there are also variable forms of *I* to indicate relative status. Thus, I (relatively lower in status) may be speaking to you (somewhat higher in status) or to you (much higher in status), using a different form of *I* and *you* in each case. It seems apparent that cultures with languages which demand recognition of relative status in every direct address will encourage more acute experience of status difference than does American culture, where English provides only one form of *you*. European cultures, most of whose languages have two forms of *you*, indicating both status distinctions and familiarity, may represent the middle range of this dimension. Europeans are more overtly attentive to status than are Americans, but Europeans are no match for Asians in this regard.

The preceding examples indicate a relationship between language syntax and the experience of physical and social reality. The relationship between language and experience can also be found in the semantic dimension of language. Languages differ in how semantic categories are distinguished and elaborated. For instance, several stages of coconut growth are described with separate words in the Trukese language, while English has only one word to describe the nut. On the other hand, English has an elaborate vocabulary to describe colors, while Trukese describes only a few colors and does not distinguish between blue and green. It is clear that Americans without the extra vocabulary cannot easily distinguish coconuts in their different stages; that is, they do not have the experience of the coconuts as being different. Similarly, it appears that Trukese people without additional color categories do not experience the difference between blue and green.

Other examples abound of how categories are differentiated to greater or lesser degrees. Wine connoisseurs maintain a highly differentiated set of labels for the experience of wine, as opposed to the two or three categories (red, white, and maybe blush) used by casual drinkers. Skiers distinguish more kinds of snow than do nonskiers, and so forth. Of even greater interest are situations where an entire kind of experience seems to disappear when the vocabulary for it is missing. For instance, while English has many words to describe boredom and ennui, Trukese seems to lack any reference to the entire concept. Although we cannot be sure, linguistic relativity would predict that Trukese people do not experience boredom in the same way as English speakers do until they learn to distinguish a category for it.

In summary, categories are constructed differently in different cultures and languages, and with the different constructions go different experiences of physical and social reality. These particular experiences are not *determined* by language, in the sense that other forms of experience are precluded without concomitant linguistic support. Research on color perception[18] and other phenomena indicate that distinctions can be made without a specific "naming strategy." Rather, linguistic relativity suggests that we are predisposed by our languages to make certain distinctions and not others—our language encourages habitual patterns of perception.

This formulation of linguistic and cultural relativity is central to intercultural communication. Without the assumption of relativity at the very root of our experience of reality, naive practitioners of intercultural relations veer toward itemizing different customs and providing tips for minor adjustments of behavior. More sophisticated interculturalists realize that their study is of nothing less than the clash of differing realities and that cultural adaptation demands the apprehension of essentially alien experience.

PERCEPTUAL RELATIVITY

The Whorf/Sapir hypothesis alerts us to the likelihood that our experience of reality is a function of cultural worldview categories. At the basic level of perception, language and culture guide us in making *figure/ground distinctions.* From the "kaleidoscopic flux" (ground) of undifferentiated phenomena, we create a boundary that distinguishes some object (figure) from the ground.[19] These figures may literally be objects, or they may be concepts or feelings. Collections of figures are "categories." What we think exists—what is real—

depends on whether we have distinguished the phenomenon as figure. And since culture through language guides us in making these distinctions, culture is actually operating directly on perception.

Micronesians, for example, are far more likely than Americans to see wave patterns—interactions of tide and current on the ocean surface that are used for navigation. To a typical American, the ocean is just "ground," and only boats or other objects are figures. But this same American may single out an automobile sound as indicating imminent mechanical failure, while to the Micronesian it is simply part of the background noise. In general, culture provides us with the tendency to perceive phenomena that are relevant to both physical and social survival.

The boundaries of constructed objects are mutable. For instance, as mentioned earlier, speakers of Trukese do not make a blue/green distinction. (One word, *araw*, refers to both colors, and "araw" is the response to either question, "What color is the sea?" or "What color is the grass?") Yet Trukese children are routinely taught to perceive the difference in color as part of their training in English as a second language. The mutability of perceptual boundaries supports the idea that perceivers actively organize stimuli into categories. And evidence from physiological studies of vision indicate that people do indeed see different objects when looking in the same direction.[20] The human eye and brain respond selectively to stimuli, depending on whether the visual system is tuned to the stimulus as figure or as ground.

The observation that perceptual figure/ground distinctions are learned and lead to different experiences of reality contradicts the traditional view of the perceiver who confronts a specific, objective reality. Instead, the perceiver is assumed to respond to culturally influenced categorizations of stimuli. Like the assumption of linguistic relativity, this assumption of perceptual relativity lies at the heart of intercultural communication. If we fail to assume that people of different cultures may sincerely perceive the world differently, then our efforts toward understanding are subverted by a desire to "correct" the one who has it wrong.

NONVERBAL BEHAVIOR

There is an entire universe of behavior that is unexplored, unexamined, and very much taken for granted. It functions outside conscious awareness and *in juxtaposition to words*.[21]

Verbal language is *digital,* in the sense that words symbolize categories of phenomena in the same arbitrary way that on/off codes symbolize numbers and operations in a computer. Nonverbal behavior, by contrast, is *analogic.* It represents phenomena by creating contexts which can be experienced directly. For instance, it is digital to say "I love you." It is analogic to represent that feeling with a look or a touch. Digital symbolizations are more capable of expressing complexity ("I love you twice as much now as I did last week"), but analogic representations are more credible because they are generally less easily manipulated.[22]

Some languages put more emphasis on the digital quality than others. English, for instance, is strongly digital in the way that it divides continua of human feeling and thought into discrete, abstract categories, providing speakers with many words to name particular affective and cognitive states. In contrast, Japanese is a more analogic language. It demands that its speakers imply and infer meaning from the context of relatively vague statements—the way it's said, by whom, to whom, where, at what time, and just before or after what other statement.[23]

Cultures such as Japanese that stress analogic communication are referred to as "high context."[24] Hall, who coined that term, defines it as a communication "in which *most* of the information is already in the person, while very little is in the coded, explicit, transmitted part of the message."[25] Cultures such as U.S. American that emphasize digital forms of communication are called "low context," defined as communication "where the mass of information is vested in the explicit code."[26]

In both high- and low-context cultures, all verbal messages in face-to-face interpersonal communication are accompanied by nonverbal behavior which provides an analogic background for the digital words.[27] Voice, gestures, eye contact, spacing, and touching all provide direct analogic expressions of emotion that modify (in low context) or supplant (in high context) the verbal message. Even in low-context cultures, only a small percentage of the meaning created in a social communication exchange is based on verbal language,[28] so understanding the more important nonverbal aspects of communication is vital to an overall comprehension of intercultural events.

In low-context cultures such as U.S. American, nonverbal behavior is unconsciously perceived more as a commentary on the verbal message than as a part of the message itself. This tendency is particularly noticeable in the use of voice tone, such as that used in the communication of sarcasm. Words such as "My, what a nice tie" can be modified by a tone of voice that indicates to the listener, "Don't take these words seriously." In other words, the nonverbal cue (tone of voice, in this case) establishes the sarcastic relationship in which the words should be interpreted.

Paralanguage, which also includes the pitch, stress, volume, and speed with which language is spoken, lends itself readily to misinterpretation cross-culturally. The potential for misunderstanding begins with perception. Is the communication stimulus even discriminated as figure from the ground of other behavior? U.S. Americans are likely to miss shadings of tone which in higher-context cultures would scream with meaning. Within the United States, European American males are less likely than some African American males to perceive the use of movement to signal a shift from talking to fighting. And conversely, black males may fail to discriminate the fighting cue of "intensity" in the tone of white male talk.[29]

In cross-cultural situations we may also perceive the appearance of a cue when none was intended. An example of this occurs around the American English use of a pitch drop at the end of sentences. The pitch of our voices goes up on the next to the last syllable and then down on the last syllable in a spoken statement. How quickly the pitch is dropped makes a difference. In even a short utterance such as "Come in," a medium pitch drop signifies normal interaction, while an abrupt drop may signify anger, frustration, anxiety, or impatience. Conversely, an elongated pitch drop usually indicates friendliness and relaxation, but an elongated pitch *increase* at the end of a statement can imply a manipulative or misleading intent. These implications are instantly recognized and reacted to by native speakers.

Nonnative English speakers may not respond to or generate voice tones in the same way. For instance, for native speakers of Cantonese, pitch changes are important within words but are not used to modulate sentences. So a Cantonese speaker of English as a second language may not generate an ending pitch drop. Additionally, Cantonese may sound rather staccato and a little loud to American ears. The combination of these factors leads some native English speakers to evaluate Chinese people as brusque or rude. If a native speaker generated loud, staccato, flat pitch statements, it might indeed indicate rudeness. But when the native Cantonese speaker talks that way in English, it probably means that he or she is using the English language with Cantonese paralanguage. The failure to observe intended cues or the discrimination of nonexistent cues based solely on one's own culture can be termed *ethnocentric perception.*

Finally, we may correctly perceive that a nonverbal cue has been generated but misinterpret its meaning. This is most likely to occur when we assume (perhaps unconsciously) that particular behavior carries the same meaning in every culture. For example, the clipped speech of some British is noticed both by other British and by U.S. Americans. For the British, however, the paralanguage cues are likely to indicate social status, home region, or place of education. For the Americans, the cues may be interpreted simply as haughtiness. This tendency to assign meaning to events solely in the context of one's own culture can be called *ethnocentric interpretation.* Both ethnocentric perception and interpretation are consistent with the idea of cultural relativity—that our experience of reality differs culturally as well as individually.

The form of nonverbal interaction analysis used in the paralanguage examples above is also generally applied to the area of kinesics, or "body language." To illustrate this, we can imagine different degrees of gesturing placed on a continuum extending from the nearly motionless presentation of some Asians and Native Americans to the dramatic sweeps of Greeks and Italians. When they come into contact, people at contrasting positions on the continuum may fall prey to ethnocentric perception and interpretation. For instance, those in the middle of the continuum, such as European Americans, may interpret Native American reserve as "lacking ambition and self-esteem." Native Americans, on the other hand, may interpret European American gesturing as "intrusive and aggressive." African Americans, whose gesturing is a bit further along the continu-

um, may be interpreted by some Asians (Koreans, for example) as being "violent and unpredictable." The greater reserve of the Koreans might fit into an African American interpretation of "unfriendly (perhaps because of racism)." As should be obvious from these examples, "simple" misinterpretations of nonverbal behavior may contribute to tragic failures in our educational system and terrible social strife.

Another practical consequence of nonverbal ethnocentrism occurs around turn taking in conversation, particularly in group discussion. The European American pattern involves eye contact to cue turns. The speaker ends with his or her eyes in contact with the conversational heir-apparent. If the speaker lowers her eyes at the end of an utterance, a confused babble of fits and starts may ensue. In contrast to this pattern, some Asian cultures routinely require averted eyes and a period of silence between speakers. In groups including more eye-intensive cultures, unacculturated Asians may never get a turn. And on the other end of this continuum, some forms of African American, Middle Eastern, and Mediterranean cultures tend to prefer more of a "relay-race" pattern of turn taking. Whoever wants the turn next just begins talking, and eventually the conversational baton may be passed on to her. Both Asian and European Americans may interpret this last pattern as interrupting. The simple task of facilitating a group discussion increases dramatically in complexity when even this one intercultural dimension is introduced.

COMMUNICATION STYLE

Habitual patterns of thought are manifested in communication behavior. Since our habits of thought are largely determined by culture, in cross-cultural situations we should see contrasts in these styles of communication. One of the most striking differences is in how a point is discussed, whether in writing[30] or verbally, as illustrated in the following example.

European Americans, particularly males, tend to use a *linear* style that marches through point *a*, point *b*, and point *c*, establishes links from point to point, and finally states an explicit conclusion. When someone veers off this line, he or she is likely to hear a statement such as "I'm not quite following you," or "Could we cut to the chase," or

"What's the bottom line?" In many school systems, this style has been established as the only one indicative of clear critical thinking. It is, however, a culturally rare form of discourse.

An example of a contrasting style occurred in a group of international and U.S. American students. I had asked a question about early dating practices, and the Americans all answered with fairly concise statements that made some explicit connection to the question. When a Nigerian in the group replied, however, he began by describing the path through his village, the tree at the end of the path, the storyteller that performed under the tree, and the beginning of a story the storyteller once told. When, in response to the obvious discomfort of the Americans in the group, I asked the Nigerian what he was doing, he said, "I'm answering the question." The American students protested at that, so I asked, "How are you answering the question?" He replied, "I'm telling you everything you need to know to understand the point." "Good," said one of the Americans. "Then if we're just patient, you will eventually tell us the point." "Oh no," replied the Nigerian. "Once I tell you everything you need to know to understand the point, you will just know what the point is!"

What this student was describing is a circular, or *contextual*, discussion style. It is favored not only by many Africans but also typically by people of Latin, Arab, and Asian cultures. And in the United States, the more circular style is commonly used by African Americans, Asian Americans, Native Americans, Hispanic Americans, and others. Even among European Americans, a contextual approach is more typical of women than of men. The only natural cultural base for the linear style is Northern European and European American males. That doesn't make the style bad, of course, but it does mean that other, more prevalent styles need to be considered as viable alternatives. To some extent, this issue has been addressed in the context of gender differences,[31] and it is getting increasing attention in the context of multicultural classrooms.[32]

When people who favor a contextual approach generate an ethnocentric interpretation of the linear style, they may see it as simple or arrogant: simple because it lacks the richness of detail necessary to establish context, and arrogant because the speaker is deciding what particular points you should hear and then what point you should draw from them! On the other hand, proponents of a linear style are likely to interpret the circular style as vague, evasive, and illogical. Interculturalists sometimes approach this kind of mutual negative evaluation with the idea of *strengths and limits.* In this case, the strength of a linear style may be in efficient, short-term task completion, while its limit is in developing inclusive relationship. Conversely, the strength of a contextual style is its facilitation of team building and consensual creativity, while its limit is that it is slow. The goal of education and training in this area, in addition to developing awareness and respect for alternative styles, may be to develop "bistylistic" competency.

Another area where differences in communication style are particularly obvious is around confrontation. European and African Americans tend to be rather direct in their style of confrontation, compared with the indirectness of many Asians and Hispanics. Adherents of the direct style favor face-to-face discussion of problems, relatively open expression of feeling, and a willingness to say yes or no in answer to questions. People socialized in the more indirect style tend to seek third-person intermediaries for conducting difficult discussions, suggest rather than state feelings, and protect their own and others' "face" by providing the appearance of ambiguity in response to questions.[33]

I was once involved in an incident involving indirect style in Malaysia. The guide had provided our group with a wonderful day of sights and cultural insight, and we were anticipating a trip to the jungle the next day with him. Upon leaving us off at the hotel, he stated somewhat offhandedly, "It will rain tomorrow." I joked back, "Oh, that's all right, we're used to getting wet." But he repeated the statement, this time adding, "It will rain really hard." More seriously this time, I said, "Our schedule is set, so we'll have to make this trip, rain or shine." He said okay and left. The next (sunny) morning, we arrived at our departure point to find a substitute guide who spoke no English. When someone in our party asked me why the original guide hadn't just said he couldn't make it the next day, I found myself ruefully explaining about indirectness and loss of face. Knowledge does not equal intercultural competence.

An elaboration of this basic contrast between direct and indirect styles can be applied to understanding a difficulty in communication between

Northern Europeans and U.S. Americans. Northern Europeans (particularly Germans) tend to be direct about intellectual topics but relatively indirect about relational matters. For instance, Northern Europeans are more likely than most U.S. Americans to say, "That idea is the stupidest thing I've ever heard." But those same Northern Europeans are less likely than Americans to discuss their feelings about casual relationships with the people involved. In contrast, U.S. Americans are more likely to be indirect on intellectual topics, making comments such as "Perhaps there is another way to think about that" or simply "Hmmm, interesting." But those same Americans may be quick to state to his or her face how much they like a new acquaintance. So Americans often think that Northern Europeans are relationally haughty, while Northern Europeans may think that Americans are intellectually shallow. Ethnocentric perception leads U.S. Americans to fail to recognize indirectness in relational commentary, while Northern Europeans similarly fail to detect indirectness in intellectual discourse. Additionally, ethnocentric interpretation leads Americans to mistake normal Northern European argument for the intellectual arrogance it would represent in most U.S. contexts, and Northern Europeans to mistake normal American relational openness for the boorishness it would represent in many European contexts.

VALUES AND ASSUMPTIONS

Cultural values are the patterns of goodness and badness people assign to ways of being in the world. For instance, Japanese people typically assign goodness to being interdependent in groups (even if they often act individually), while U.S. Americans typically assign goodness to being independently self-reliant (even if they often act interdependently). To shorten this, we would state the generalization that, relative to the other culture, Japanese value collectivism and U.S. Americans value individualism. Conversely, Japanese tend to disvalue many manifestations of individualism as unnecessarily selfish, while U.S. Americans disvalue many forms of collectivism as unduly conformist.

Cultural assumptions are interrelated with values but refer to the existence of phenomena rather than the assignment of value to them. So, in terms of the above example contrasting Japanese and U.S. Americans, most Americans assume the existence of an individual identity, which is necessary for the self-reliance of individualism to exist. Most Japanese, on the other hand, assume the existence of a kind of collective consciousness ("we Japanese"), which is necessary for interrelationships of collectivism to occur. In most intercultural analyses of situations, it is necessary to ascertain both what cultural assumptions are being made in the situation and what values are being placed on those assumptions.

The system that has been used traditionally by interculturalists for analyzing cultural values is the one developed by Florence R. Kluckhohn and Fred L. Strodtbeck.[34] Based on research with several cultures, the system defines five dimensions of cultural assumptions: peoples' relationship to the environment, to each other, to activity, to time, and to the basic nature of human beings. Constituting each of these dimensions is a continuum of possible relationships that people might assume with the subject. For instance, people may assume that they can control the environment, that they can live in harmony with it, or that they are subjugated by the environment. Kluckhohn and Strodtbeck state that all positions on the continuum will be represented to some degree in all cultures, but that one position will be *preferred*. It is this general preference that constitutes a cultural value. For example, most U.S. Americans prefer to think that nature is controllable—witness their damming of rivers, their programs to conquer space, and so forth. We could say that, in general, U.S. Americans value being in control of their environment. Other assumptions about an appropriate relationship to nature are present in U.S. society, of course. But with some exceptions, those assumptions are not as yet preferred and so are not now considered general cultural values.

Many modifications of the Kluckhohn and Strodtbeck approach have proved useful for intercultural value analysis. John C. Condon[35] has expanded the original five dimensions into a list that can be applied to a broader range of more specific cultural phenomena, as has L. Robert Kohls.[36] Edward C. Stewart has done the most to develop the theoretical potential of the approach by defining the contrast-American approach to value analysis[37] and by redefining the original dimensions in particularly useful ways.[38]

Another approach to value analysis has been developed by Geert Hofstede.[39] As opposed to the deductive approach of Kluckhohn and Strodtbeck, Hofstede used the inductive technique of surveying a large number of people from various national cultures about their values and preferences in life. Using the statistical technique of factor analysis, he then isolated four dimensions (and later a fifth) that accounted for a large amount of the variation in answers. He named the four dimensions *Power-Distance,* referring to the assumption of status difference; *Masculinity,* referring to (among other things) the assumption of gender difference; *Individualism,* referring to the assumption of self-reliance; and *Uncertainty Avoidance,* referring to the assumption of intolerance of ambiguity. In later studies, he added the dimension of *Confucian Dynamism* or *Long-Term Orientation,* referring to focus on future rewards.[40] Returning to the data from each national culture, he was then able to rank-order the cultures in terms of each dimension. For instance, Japanese ranked 7th out of fifty countries on Uncertainty Avoidance, while the United States ranked 46th; on Individualism the United States scored 1st and Japan 22nd. By statistically combining factors, Hofstede was able to map clusters of cultures in several dimensions. Many contemporary studies of cultural values now use, at least in part, the Hofstede categories.

Cultural Adaptation

In many ways, the crux of intercultural communication is in how people adapt to other cultures. Yet the intercultural concept of adaptation is frequently misunderstood. To clarify the idea, it is useful to distinguish *adaptation* from *assimilation.* Assimilation is the process of resocialization that seeks to replace one's original worldview with that of the host culture. Assimilation is "substitutive." Adaptation, on the other hand, is the process whereby one's worldview is expanded to include behavior and values appropriate to the host culture. It is "additive," not substitutive. The assumed end result of assimilation is becoming a "new person," as Israel Zangwill wrote in his play *The Melting Pot.*[41] The assumed end result of adaptation is becoming a bicultural or multicultural person. Such a person has new aspects, but not at the cost of his or her original socialization. The identity issues around adaptation are quite complex, and understanding them is one of the new frontiers of intercultural communication.

DEVELOPMENTAL APPROACHES TO CULTURAL ADAPTATION

Cultural adaptation is not an on/off phenomenon. Like many other human abilities, it appears that cultural adaptation develops through stages, in much the same way as does cognition as described by Jean Piaget[42] or ethicality as described by William G. Perry Jr.[43] With descriptions of the stages of development, interculturalists who are responsible for facilitating cross-cultural encounters are able to diagnose learners' levels of development and thus design their interventions more effectively.

A straightforward form of developmental thinking can be illustrated with one of the best-known of all intercultural concepts: *culture shock.* The evolution of this concept began with a relatively simple statement of how disorientation can occur in a different cultural context, along with the implication that culture shock was something like a disease that could be prevented, or caught and cured.[44] From this distinctly nondevelopmental beginning, the concept gained complexity as it was described in terms of *U* or *W* curves extending through time.[45] Then Peter S. Adler[46] suggested that culture shock was a process that went through five stages: the euphoria of Contact, when cultural difference is first encountered; the confusion of Disintegration, when loss of self-esteem intrudes; the anger of Reintegration, when the new culture is rejected and the old self reasserted; the relaxed self-assuredness of Autonomy, when cross-cultural situations can be handled with relative ease; and the creativity of Independence, when choice and responsibility accompany a deep respect for one's own and others' cultures. These ideas were placed in an even broader developmental context by Janet M. Bennett,[47] who defined culture shock as a special case of the typical human response to any transition, loss, or change.

So when even a relatively simple aspect of cultural adaptation—culture shock—is cast in developmental terms, it attains a level of complexity that makes it a richer and more useful descriptor of peoples' experiences. When the broader topic of cultural adaptation in general is described in

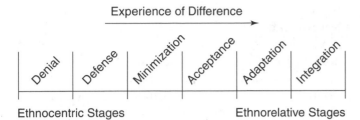

Experience of Difference →

Denial | Defense | Minimization | Acceptance | Adaptation | Integration

Ethnocentric Stages   Ethnorelative Stages

FIGURE 2 DEVELOPMENT OF
INTERCULTURAL SENSITIVITY

developmental terms, the result is even more descriptive of complex experience. One example of this attempt is the Developmental Model of Intercultural Sensitivity (DMIS).[48] Based on "meaning-making" models of cognitive psychology and radical constructivism,[49] the DMIS links changes in cognitive structure to an evolution in attitudes and behavior toward cultural difference in general. The DMIS is divided into *Ethnocentric Stages* and *Ethnorelative Stages*.

Ethnocentric is defined as using one's own set of standards and customs to judge all people, often unconsciously. *Ethnorelative* means the opposite; it refers to being comfortable with many standards and customs and to having an ability to adapt behavior and judgments to a variety of interpersonal settings. Following are short descriptions of each of six stages of development.

Denial. People at the denial stage are unable to construe cultural differences in complex ways. They probably live in relative isolation from other cultures, either by happenstance or by choice. Either they do not perceive cultural differences at all, or they can conceive only of broad categories such as "foreigner," "people of color," or "Africans." People at this stage may use stereotypes in their description of others that are not meant to denigrate but are based on knowing only one or two things about the other people. For instance, many U.S. Americans seem to think that all Africans live near jungles and have encounters with wild animals; or many Asians seem to think that all Americans from the Pacific Northwest live on ranches and ride horses.

In contrast to the complexity of our own worldview, the simplicity of these stereotypes makes "their" seemingly sparse experience seem less real than "our" demonstrably rich experience. Consequently, when actually confronted by cultural diversity, people in denial unconsciously attribute less than human status to the outsiders. They may then use power for purposes of exploiting the others, and in extreme cases of threat, they may further dehumanize the outsiders to enable genocide.

Defense. People at the defense stage have more ability to construe cultural difference, but they attach negative evaluations to it. They combat the threat of change to their stable worldview by denigrating others with negative stereotypes and by attaching positive stereotypes to themselves. Consequently, they view their own culture as the acme of "development" and tend to evaluate different cultures as "underdeveloped." A few people may enter a reversed form of defense, wherein they vilify their own culture and become zealous proponents of an adopted culture. For example, some U.S. Americans spurn their European roots while idealizing Native Indian cultures, and some U.S. Americans, when traveling, label most of their compatriots as "the ugly Americans." In all cases, however, defense is characterized by the polarization of a denigrated "them" with a superior "us."

People in defense consider themselves under siege. Members of socially dominant cultures may attempt to protect privilege and deny opportunities to outsiders, while nondominant culture members may aggressively protect their ethnic identity from suppression by the majority. Ironically, while personally directed violence may be more common in defense than in denial, the threat of systematic genocide is reduced by the greater humanity accorded one's enemy.

Minimization. People at the minimization stage try to bury cultural differences within already-familiar categories of physical and philosophical similarity. They recognize and accept superficial cultural differences such as eating customs and other social norms, but they assume that deep down all people are essentially the same—just human. As a consequence of this assumption, certain cultural values may be mistaken for universal desires; for instance, U.S. Americans may believe that people everywhere desire individual freedom, openness, and competition. Religious people may hold that everyone is a child of God, is subject to Allah's will, or acquires karma "whether they know it or not." Political and economic minimizers may suppose that we are all victims of historical Marxist forces or that we are all motivated by the private enterprise of capitalism. While people at the minimization stage are considerably more knowledgeable than those in denial and a lot nicer than those in defense, they are still ethnocentric in their adherence to these culture-bound universalistic assumptions.

In domestic intercultural relations in the United States, minimization is the classic "white liberal" position. It is usually accompanied by strong support for the "melting pot" idea, a distrust of ethnic and other labels for cultural diversity, and an abiding belief in the existence of equal opportunity. While eschewing power exercised through exploitation and denial of opportunity, people in minimization unquestioningly accept the dominant culture privileges built into institutions. People who do not enjoy these privileges—people of color and others who experience oppression in U.S. society—tend not to dwell at this somewhat self-congratulatory stage.

Acceptance. People at the acceptance stage enjoy recognizing and exploring cultural differences. They are aware that they themselves are cultural beings. They are fairly tolerant of ambiguity and are comfortable knowing there is no one right answer (although there are better answers for particular contexts). "Acceptance" does not mean that a person has to agree with or take on a cultural perspective other than his or her own. Rather, people accept the *viability* of different cultural ways of thinking and behaving, even though they might not like them. This is the first stage in which people begin to think about the notion of cultural relativity—that their own behavior and values are not the only good way to be in the world.

People in acceptance tend to avoid the exercise of power in any form. As a consequence, they may at times become paralyzed by the dilemmas posed by conflicting cultural norms. At this stage, people have moved beyond ethnocentric rules for behavior and may not yet have developed ethnorelative principles for taking action.

Adaptation. People at the adaptation stage use knowledge about their own and others' cultures to intentionally shift into a different cultural frame of reference. That is, they can empathize or take another person's perspective in order to understand and be understood across cultural boundaries. Based on their ability to use alternative cultural interpretations, people in this stage can mod-

ify their behavior in ways that make it more appropriate to cultures other than their own. Another way to think about this is that people in adaptation have increased their repertoire of behavior—they have maintained the skills of operating in their own cultures while adding the ability to operate effectively in one or more other cultures. This intercultural competence may include the ability to recognize how power is being exercised within a cultural context, and some people may themselves be able to exercise power in ways that are appropriate to the other culture. Advanced forms of adaptation are "bicultural" or "multicultural," wherein people have internalized one or more cultural frames in addition to that in which they were originally socialized. Bicultural people can completely shift their cultural frame of reference without much conscious effort.

Most people at the adaptation stage are generally interculturally sensitive; with varying degrees of sophistication, they can apply skills of empathy and adaptation of behavior to any cultural context. However, in some cases people have become "accidently bicultural," wherein they received primary socialization in two or more cultural frames of reference. (Children of bicultural marriages and of long-term expatriates may fall into this category.) Sometimes these people are very good at shifting between the two cultures they have internalized, but they cannot apply the same adaptation skills to other cultures. In addition, some people in adaptation do not exhibit intercultural sensitivity toward groups that they do not consider cultures. For instance, some people who are otherwise interculturally skilled retain negative stereotypes of gay, lesbian, and bisexual people. When these groups are defined in cultural terms, people in adaptation are more likely to be able to relate to them in interculturally competent ways.

Integration. People at the integration stage of development are attempting to reconcile the sometimes conflicting cultural frames that they have internalized. In the transition to this stage, some people become overwhelmed by the cultures they know and are disturbed that they can no longer identify with any one of them. But as they move into integration, people achieve an identity which allows them to see themselves as "interculturalists" or "multiculturalists" in addition to their national and ethnic backgrounds.[50]

They recognize that worldviews are collective constructs and that identity is itself a construction of consciousness. As a consequence, they may seek out roles that allow them to be intercultural mediators and exhibit other qualities of "constructive marginality."[51] They also tend to associate with other cultural marginals rather than people from any one of the cultures they know.

People in integration are inclined to interpret and evaluate behavior from a variety of cultural frames of reference, so that there is never a single right or wrong answer. But, unlike the resulting paralysis of action that may occur in earlier stages, people in integration are capable of engaging in "contextual evaluation." The goodness or ethicality of actions is not given by absolute (and ethnocentric) principles but is constructed by human beings who thereby take responsibility for the realities they are creating. Thus, people in integration face the unending task of guiding their own behavior along the ethical lines that they themselves have created.

Ethnorelative Ethics

Much of the controversy surrounding the development of intercultural sensitivity is about ethics. Some people seem to think that being interculturally sensitive means giving up any set of ethical principles or moral guidelines. They think cultural relativity is the same thing as moral relativism or situational ethics. To understand that criticism, we can turn to yet another developmental model, the Perry Scheme of Cognitive and Ethical Development.[52]

Perry outlines a process whereby people develop ethical thinking and behavior as they learn more about the world. The model describes movement from "dualism" (one simple either/or way of thinking) to "multiplicity" (many ambiguous and equally good ways of thinking), and then on to "contextual relativism" (different actions are judged according to appropriate context) and "commitment in relativism" (people choose the context in which they will act, even though other actions are viable in different contexts).

People who are most critical of multiculturalism seem to be at Perry's stage of dualism. They think of ethics and morality as absolute, universal rules. In this dualistic view, the acceptance of dif-

ferent cultures leads only to multiplicity, where all options are equal and ethical chaos reigns. Therefore, goes the dualistic argument, either you choose the absolutist ethical path that rejects cultural relativism, or you accept cultural relativism and the only alternative it offers to absolutism, moral relativity and situational ethics.

Interculturalists by and large reject this dualistic view in favor of a third alternative, one where ethnorelativism and strong ethical principles coexist. The reconciliation of culture and ethics occurs in parallel to the latter two stages of Perry's model. In contextual relativism, actions must be judged within context. Thus, at this stage, ethical actions must be judged within a cultural context. There is no universal ethical behavior. For instance, it is not universally ethical to be openly honest in dealing with others. That such is the case, however, does not imply that one should be dishonest whenever it is convenient or situationally normative (e.g., "Everyone else is lying to get those payments, so why shouldn't I?"). On the contrary, Perry's last stage suggests that we commit to acting within the context we wish to maintain. If we want a reality in which open honesty is normative, then it is ethical to act in ways that support the viability of that behavior. Perhaps this doesn't mean that someone with such an ethical commitment is openly honest in every situation. But it probably does mean that actions that contradict or undermine a context in which "honesty is the best policy" would be avoided.

Some antagonists of intercultural and multicultural thinking[53] have suggested that interculturalists are the same as any other ethical absolutist in their adherence to the "goodness" of contextual relativity. In so doing, these critics neglect that important aspect of language called "logical type."[54] The statement "It is good to have three wives" is different in logical type from the statement "It is good to know that forms of marriage are evaluated differently in different cultures." The latter statement is actually a "metastatement," a statement about other statements. Interculturalists would certainly think it was good to make that metastatement, but this thought is significantly different in type from thinking that it is good or bad to have one or three wives. Another such metastatement is "absolutists and relativists differ in their belief in the importance of contextual evaluation." It is good to be able to make this distinction, but doing so says nothing about the goodness of either absolutists or relativists. Absolutists might be judged as "bad" in the context of intercultural communication not for any particular beliefs they hold but because they reject seeing their own behavior in cultural context.

Personal Endnote

As you can see, I think an intercultural perspective offers more than an effective way to analyze interaction and facilitate adaptation. In my opinion, intercultural communication envisions a reality which will support the simultaneous existence of unity and diversity, of cooperation and competition in the global village, and of consensus and creative conflict in multicultural societies. In this vision, our different voices can be heard both in their uniqueness and in synergistic harmony. While there are many paths which can converge into this future, the focus brought by interculturalists rests on individuals and relationships. We strive to bring culture into individual consciousness and in so doing bring consciousness to bear on the creation of intercultural relationships.

1. Dean Barnlund, "Communication in a Global Village," this volume.

2. Milton J. Bennett, "Overcoming the Golden Rule," this volume.

3. LaRay M. Barna, "Stumbling Blocks in Intercultural Communication," this volume.

4. For example, see Peter L. Berger and Thomas Luckmann, in *The Analysis of Subjective Culture*, edited by Harry C. Triandis (New York: John Wiley, 1972).

5. Peter L. Berger and Thomas Luckmann, *The Social Construction of Reality: A Treatise in the Sociology of Knowledge* (New York: Doubleday, 1966).

6. Edward C. Stewart and Milton J. Bennett, *American Cultural Patterns: A Cross-Cultural Perspective*, rev. ed. (Yarmouth, ME: Intercultural Press, 1991).

7. Marshall R. Singer, "Culture: A Perceptual Approach," this volume.

8. David S. Hoopes, "Intercultural Communication Concepts and the Psychology of Intercultural Experience," in *Multicultural Education: A Cross Cultural Training Approach*, edited by Margaret D. Pusch (LaGrange Park, IL: Intercultural Press, 1980).

9. Florence R. Kluckhohn and Fred L. Strodtbeck, *Variations in Value Orientations* (1961; reprint, Westport, CT: Greenwood Press, 1973); Stewart and Bennett, *American Cultural Patterns*.

10. Carlos E. Cortés, "Pride, Prejudice and Power: The Mass Media as Societal Educator on Diversity," in *Prejudice, Polemic or Progress?*, edited by James Lynch, Celia Modgil, and Sohan Modgil (London: Falmer Press, 1992), 367–81.

11. Stewart and Bennett, *American Cultural Patterns*; Eva S. Kras, *Management in Two Cultures: Bridging the Gap between U.S. and Mexican Managers*, rev. ed. (Yarmouth, ME: Intercultural Press, 1995); John C. Condon, *Good Neighbors: Communicating with the Mexicans*, 2d ed. (Yarmouth, ME: Intercultural Press, 1997).

12. Judith N. Martin and Thomas K. Nakayama, *Intercultural Communication in Contexts* (Mountain View, CA: Mayfield Publishing, 1997).

13. Edward T. Hall, *Beyond Culture* (1976; reprint, New York: Anchor/Doubleday, 1981).

14. Deborah Tannen, *Gender and Discourse* (New York: Oxford University Press, 1994).

15. William G. Perry Jr., *Forms of Intellectual and Ethical Development in the College Years: A Scheme* (Fort Worth, TX: Harcourt Brace, 1970).

16. Stewart and Bennett, *American Cultural Patterns*.

17. Benjamin Lee Whorf, "Science and Linguistics," this volume.

18. Brent Berlin and Paul Kay, *Basic Color Terms: Their Universality and Evolution* (Berkeley: University of California Press, 1969); Stewart and Bennett, *American Cultural Patterns*.

19. G. Spencer Brown, *Laws of Form* (Toronto: Bantam Books, 1972); Heinz von Foerster, "On Constructing a Reality," in *The Invented Reality*, edited by Paul Watzlawick (New York: W. W. Norton, 1984): 41–62.

20. von Foerster, "On Constructing a Reality."

21. Edward T. Hall, *The Silent Language* (1959; reprint, New York: Anchor/Doubleday, 1981).

22. Paul Watzlawick, Janet H. Beavin, and Don D. Jackson, *Pragmatics of Human Communication* (New York: Norton, 1967).

23. Kichiro Hayashi, *Intercultural Insights into Japanese Business Methods*, Senior Executive Seminar, Pacific University, Forest Grove, Oregon, Nov. 1990.

24. Hall, *Beyond Culture*.

25. Edward T. Hall, "The Power of Hidden Differences," this volume.

26. Ibid.

27. Watzlawick, Beavin, and Jackson, *Pragmatics,* 53.

28. Lawrence B. Rosenfeld and Jean Civikly, *With Words Unspoken: The Nonverbal Experience* (New York: Holt, Rinehart & Winston, 1976), 5; James A. Banks and Cherry A. McGee Banks, eds., *Handbook of Research on Multicultural Education* (New York: Simon and Schuster, 1995); Christine I. Bennett, *Comprehensive Multicultural Education: Theory and Practice,* 2d ed. (Boston: Allyn and Bacon, 1990).

29. Thomas Kochman, *Black and White Styles in Conflict* (Chicago: University of Chicago Press, 1981), 47.

30. Robert B. Kaplan, "Cultural Thought Patterns" in *Toward Multiculturalism,* edited by Jaime S. Wurzel (Yarmouth, ME: Intercultural Press, 1988), 207–21.

31. Mary Field Belenky et al., *Women's Ways of Knowing: The Development of Self, Voice, and Mind* (New York: HarperCollins, 1997); Nancy Goldberger et al., *Knowledge, Difference, and Power: Essays Inspired by Women's ways of Knowing* (New York: HarperCollins, 1996).

32. Jaime S. Wurzel and Nancy Fishman, producers, *A Different Place* and *Creating Community: The Intercultural Classroom* (Boston: Intercultural Resource Corporation, 1993), video.

33. Sheila J. Ramsey, "Interactions between North Americans and Japanese: Considerations of Communication Style," this volume; William B. Gudykunst, Stella Ting-Toomey, and Elizabeth Chua, *Culture and Interpersonal Communication,* vol. 8 (Newbury Park, CA: Sage, 1988).

34. Kluckhohn and Strodtbeck, *Variations in Value Orientations.*

35. John C. Condon and Fathi Yousef, *An Introduction to Intercultural Communication* (New York: Macmillan, 1975).

36. L. Robert Kohls, *Values Americans Live By* (Duncanville, TX: Adult Learning Systems, 1988).

37. Edward C. Stewart, Jack Danielian, and Robert J. Foster, "Cultural Assumptions and Values," this volume.

38. Stewart and Bennett, *American Cultural Patterns.*

39. Geert Hofstede, *Culture's Consequences: International Differences in Work-Related Values,* abridged ed., vol. 5, Cross-Cultural Research and Methodology Series (Beverly Hills, CA: Sage, 1984).

40. Geert Hofstede, *Cultures and Organizations: Software of the Mind* (London: McGraw-Hill, 1991).

41. Israel Zangwill, *The Melting Pot: Drama in Four Acts* (New York: Macmillan, 1921).

42. Jean Piaget, *Construction of Reality in the Child* (New York: Ballantine Books, 1954).

43. Perry, *Forms of Intellectual and Ethical Development.*

44. Kalvero Oberg, "Cultural Shock: Adjustment to New Cultural Environments," *Practical Anthropology* 7 (1960): 177.

45. John Gullahorn and Jeanne Gullahorn, "An Extension of the U-Curve Hypothesis," *Journal of Social Issues* 19, no. 3 (1963).

46. Peter S. Adler, "Culture Shock and the Cross-cultural Learning Experience," in *Readings in Intercultural Communication,* vol. 2, edited by David S. Hoopes (Pittsburgh, PA: Regional Council for International Education, June 1972).

47. Janet M. Bennett, "Transition Shock: Putting Culture Shock in Perspective," this volume.

48. Milton J. Bennett, "Towards Ethnorelativism: A Developmental Model of Intercultural Sensitivity," in *Cross-Cultural Orientation: New Conceptualizations and Applications,* edited by R. Michael Paige (New York: University Press of America, 1986).

49. Paul Watzlawick, ed., *The Invented Reality* (New York: W. W. Norton, 1984).

50. Peter S. Adler, "Beyond Cultural Identity: Reflections on Multiculturalism," this volume.

51. Janet M. Bennett, "Cultural Marginality: Identity Issues in Intercultural Training," in *Education for the Intercultural Experience,* 2d ed., edited by R. Michael Paige (Yarmouth, ME: Intercultural Press, 1993).

52. Perry, *Forms of Intellectual and Ethical Development.*

53. Dinesh D'Souza, *The End Of Racism: Principles for a Multiracial Society* (New York: Free Press, 1995); Arthur M. Schlesinger Jr., *The Disuniting of America: Reflections on a Multicultural Society* (1991; reprint, New York: W. W. Norton, 1998); Dinesh D'Souza, *Illiberal Education: The Politics of Race and Sex on Campus* (New York: Random House, 1998).

54. Bertrand Russell, *Human Knowledge, Its Scope and Limits* (New York: Simon and Schuster, 1948).

CLASS 4

The Changing Face of America and the World

CHAPTER 5
Diversity and Multiculturalism on the Campus: How are Students Affected?
Alexander Astin
Alexander Astin's study reports the results of a survey of over 25,000 students attending 217 colleges and universities in the U.S.A. The students were surveyed during their freshmen year and again four years later. The findings suggest that multi-cultural classes and activities have a positive impact on students' cognitive and affective development.

CHAPTER 6
Campus Resegregation and Its Alternatives
Gary Orfield
Gary Orfield's research reveals the alarming trend of racial and ethnic segregation that exists on our nation's campuses. He seeks to provide strategies that will help college and university campuses become integrated learning and social communities.

CHAPTER 5

Diversity and Multiculturalism on the Campus: How are Students Affected?

Alexander W. Astin

Professor of Higher Education and Director of the Higher Education Research Institute at the University of California, Los Angeles, Alexander Astin is a highly respected researcher and scholar in several areas of higher education. Among his publications are *Assessments for Excellence: The Philosophy and Practice of Assessment* and *Evaluation in Higher Education; What Matters in College: Four Critical Years Revisited;* and "What Matters in General Education: Provocative Findings from a National Study of Student Outcomes."

Amidst debates over multiculturalism, diversity, and political correctness by academics and the news media, claims and counterclaims about the dangers and benefits of multiculturalism have abounded, but so far little hard evidence has been produced to support any of these claims. Most of the "evidence" injected into the debate thus far is of a purely anecdotal nature, with the veracity of the ancedotes cited by critics on one side of the argument usually disputed by critics on the other side.

As a political animal, I might have certain strong views about multiculturalism—whether it is a good or a bad idea—but as an educator and a researcher, my most important question about multiculturalism and diversity is how students are affected by campus policies and practices. I recently had the opportunity to examine this question empirically in a major national study of undergraduates attending 217 four-year colleges and universities. Published this year [1993], the study involved 82 outcome measures on 25,000 students who entered college as freshmen in the fall of 1985 and were followed up four years later in 1989. It also included data that enabled us to determine how much each institution emphasized diversity and multiculturalism, and measures of each individual student's direct experience with diversity and multiculturalism.

The following analysis of this study addresses several pertinent questions: How are students' values and beliefs about other races and cultures affected by their institutions' policies on diversity and multiculturalism? What difference does it make in students' attitudes and behavior when their professors emphasize diversity issues in the classroom or in their research? How are students' academic progress and values affected by direct involvement in "diversity" experiences?

Method

The basic purpose of this research project was to determine how various student outcomes are affected by environments. The larger study of student development, which provides the data for the findings reported here, included 82 different student outcome measures covering a wide range of cognitive and affective development: attitudes, values, beliefs, aspirations, and career plans, as well as measures of undergraduate achievement and degree completion and scores on nationally standardized tests such as the GRE, MCAT, and LSAT. Since many of these outcomes were pre-tested when the students entered college as freshmen and post-tested four years later, we can determine how students actually changed during the four years. The study also incorporated more than 190 measures of the students' environmental experiences, including characteristics of the curriculum, faculty, and student peer group (for details, see Astin, 1993). Of particular relevance to this article are seven environmental measures reflecting a) the institution's and its faculty's policies on diversity issues and b) the student's direct experience with diversity and multiculturalism at the institution. Given the centrality of these seven environmental measures to the issue of diversity on campus, more detailed discussion of each is in order.

Measures of Diversity/Multiculturalism

The study incorporated three types of environmental measures relating to issues of diversity or multiculturalism: Institutional Diversity Emphasis, Faculty Diversity Emphasis, and Student Diversity Experiences (five measures).

The first two measures are based on the responses of the faculty at each of the 217 institutions to an extensive questionnaire administered during the 1989–90 academic year. The mean faculty responses to a large number of questionnaire items were computed and then factor analyzed in order to identify clusters of items that "go together" as determined by the patterns of faculty responses. Environmental measures for any institution were then obtained by averaging the responses of its faculty separately for each cluster of questions. Institutional Diversity Emphasis, for example, reflects the extent to which faculty believe that their institution is committed to each of the following five goals:

1. to increase the number of minority faculty;

2. to increase the number of minority students;

3. to create a diverse multicultural environment;

4. to increase the number of women faculty;

5. to develop an appreciation for multiculturalism.

By looking at the faculty's perception of the degree of institutional emphasis on diversity and multiculturalism, as one might guess, a considerable variation emerges among the 217 institutions in their degree of emphasis on diversity.

Faculty Diversity Emphasis is defined in terms of four other questionnaire items, which also were shown by the factor analyses to produce similar response patterns:

1. instructional technique that incorporates readings on women and gender issues;

2. instructional technique that incorporates readings on racial and ethnic issues;

3. research or writing focused on women or gender;

4. research or writing focused on racial or ethnic minorities.

Note that Faculty Diversity Emphasis is based on the faculty's own scholarly and pedagogical practices, while Institutional Diversity Emphasis reflects the faculty's perceptions of the overall institutional climate. The latter measure presumably reflects not only faculty values and behavior, but also the policies of the administration and possibly even the trustees. As would be expected, these two environmental measures are substantially correlated ($r = .55$), which means simply that faculty who emphasize diversity issues in their teaching and research are likely to be found in institutions that also emphasize diversity and multiculturalism in their admissions and hiring policies. However, the fact that the correlation is far from perfect indicates that there are some institutions where the institutional emphasis on diversity is strong but where the faculty do not emphasize diversity issues in their teaching or research and, conversely, some institutions where the reverse pattern occurs. The two measures, in other words, are not completely interchangeable.

Student Diversity Experiences were measured in terms of five items from the follow-up questionnaire completed by the 25,000 students during the 1989–90 academic year. Each of these items is treated separately in the analysis:

1. took ethnic studies courses;

2. took women's studies courses;

3. attended racial/cultural awareness workshops;

4. discussed racial or ethnic issues;

5. socialized with someone from another racial/ethnic group.

Analysis of Environmental Effects

The method used for analyzing the effects of these seven environmental variables on the 82 student outcomes has been described in detail in earlier works (Astin, 1991, 1993). Pre-tests and other entering student characteristics assessed in 1985 are controlled first by means of stepwise regression analyses, after which the possible effects of environmental variables are examined. Basically, the analyses are designed to "match" students statistically in terms of their entering characteristics before evaluating the effects of environmental variables on the outcome measures obtained four years later. In effect, this method attempts to determine whether students change differently under differing environmental circumstances.

Before discussing the specific findings from these analyses, it should be mentioned that 26 of the 82 outcome measures were specifically identified as directly relevant to the goals of general education as spelled out in the considerable literature on this subject (Astin, 1992). These 26 goals include a variety of cognitive and academic outcomes, as well as completion of the baccalaureate degree, interest in and enrollment in graduate study, and several value and attitudinal measures. In reporting the findings, I pay special attention to these 26 measures because one of the critical policy questions is whether or not the overall goals of general education are facilitated by emphasizing diversity and multiculturalism.

Institutional Diversity Emphasis

The effects of Institutional Diversity Emphasis are of some practical as well as theoretical interest, since the factors that make up this environment measure are presumably under the direct control of the institution. Its strongest positive effects are on two outcomes: cultural awareness and commitment to promoting racial understanding. Cultural awareness is one of the developmental outcomes that was identified as particularly relevant to the goals of most general education pro-

grams. It is based on the students' estimate of how much their undergraduate experience has enhanced their understanding and appreciation of other races and cultures. The fact that a strong emphasis on diversity enhances the students' commitment to promoting racial understanding is of special interest, given that some critics have alleged that emphasizing issues of race and multiculturalism tends to exacerbate racial tensions on the campus. Quite the opposite seems to be the case.

Emphasizing diversity also has positive effects on several measures of student satisfaction with the college experience: overall satisfaction, as well as satisfaction with student life, opportunities to take interdisciplinary courses, facilities, and the quality of instruction. Institutional Diversity Emphasis also has positive effects on political liberalism, libertarianism, and participation in student protests.

Consistent with its positive effect on the students' personal commitment to promoting racial understanding, Institutional Diversity Emphasis has a negative effect on the belief that racial discrimination is no longer a problem in America. It also has negative effects on the students' chances of joining a social fraternity or sorority, or getting married while in college, and on the belief that the chief benefit of college is to increase earning power. This last measure is another outcome judged as relevant to the goals of most general education programs, since such programs would hopefully weaken the students' tendency to see liberal learning in strictly instrumental or monetary terms.

What, then, are the consequences for students who are associated with a strong institutional emphasis on issues of diversity and multiculturalism? If one were to attach values to the outcomes just discussed, emphasizing diversity appears to have uniformly positive effects, not only on those outcomes that are relevant to the goals of general education—heightened cultural awareness and satisfaction and reduced materialism—but also on the students' commitment to promoting racial understanding. The positive effect on political liberalism could be judged as either a plus or minus, given one's own political preferences. The same goes for participation in campus protests, which might be considered by some as a negative outcome. However, to render such a judgment, it is first necessary to determine what effects protest participation itself has on the students' subsequent development. This issue will be addressed shortly.

Faculty Diversity Emphasis

Faculty Diversity Emphasis produces a pattern of effects that is very similar to the pattern associated with Institutional Diversity Emphasis. The strongest positive effects are on cultural awareness and overall satisfaction with the college experience. Faculty Diversity Emphasis also had a positive effect on the students' chances of voting in the 1988 presidential election. This item was included as a measure of "citizenship," another of the 26 outcomes that were included among the goals of general education.

That Faculty Diversity Emphasis and Institutional Diversity Emphasis produce very similar patterns of effects does not mean that these two measures are entirely redundant. Both measures, for example, produced independent effects on cultural awareness, overall satisfaction, and participation in campus protests. By "independent," we mean that the faculty's focus on diversity issues contributes to these outcomes over and above the contribution of the overall institutional emphasis.

Direct Student Experience with Diversity

Let us now consider the effects of individual Student Diversity Experiences. Even though these "effects" were obtained only after all student input and faculty environmental measures were controlled for, the fact that the student experiences occurred after the student actually enrolled in college requires that we interpret these effects with caution. Even so, the pattern and results are very interesting.

Critics of political correctness have focused much of their attack on efforts to diversify the curriculum. Our data base included two items bearing on this issue: the number of ethnic studies courses and the number of women's studies courses taken by the students during their undergraduate years. These two measures produced almost identical patterns of effects on student outcomes. The strongest positive effects were on cul-

tural awareness and commitment to promoting racial understanding, as well as a commitment to helping clean up the environment. There were also weaker, but still significant, positive effects on participation in campus protests, political liberalism, listening ability, foreign language skills, and attendance at recitals and concerts. Only one outcome was negatively associated with taking ethnic or women's studies courses: the belief that racial discrimination is no longer a problem in America. Once again, taking ethnic studies or women's studies courses is associated with a wide range of generally positive outcomes rather than alienating students of different races from each other.

Another controversial issue concerns whether the campus administration should sponsor "cultural awareness" workshops designed to enhance racial/cultural understanding among students from different backgrounds. A large number of outcomes are significantly associated with attending such workshops: commitment to promoting racial understanding, participating in campus demonstrations, cultural awareness, and social activism. Of particular interest is that participation in such workshops is positively associated with undergraduate retention (completion of the bachelor's degree) as well as with six different measures of satisfaction with various aspects of the undergraduate experience and six different measures of academic development (critical thinking, general knowledge, public speaking ability, listening ability, writing ability, and preparation for graduate school). Participation in racial/cultural awareness workshops has negative effects on materialistic values and on two beliefs: that racial discrimination is no longer a problem and that the individual can do little to change society. This last item was included among our 82 outcomes as a measure of "empowerment," the student's sense that he or she can actually make a difference through individual effort and dedication. In effect, participating in such workshops appears to strengthen a student's sense of personal empowerment to effect societal change.

Another item from the list of individual Student Diversity Experiences was the frequency with which the student socialized with persons from different racial/ethnic groups. While this experience has its strongest positive effects on cultural awareness and commitment to promoting racial understanding, it also has significant positive associations with commitment to helping clean up the environment, attending recitals and concerts, and—most importantly—with practically all measures of the student's academic development and satisfaction with college. It has negative associations with the beliefs that racial discrimination is no longer a problem in America and that the individual can do little to change society. It is of some interest to note that socializing with persons from different racial/ethnic groups, in contrast to most of the other diversity experiences discussed so far, does not have positive effects either on political liberalism or on participation in campus protests.

Interestingly enough, the largest number of positive effects was associated with the frequency with which students discussed racial/ethnic issues during their undergraduate years. As would be expected, the strongest effects are on commitment to promoting racial understanding and cultural awareness. This item showed other positive and negative effects that closely follow the pattern associated with the other diversity variables. However, one of the strongest effects not found for most of these other diversity variables is the positive impact on the student's commitment to developing a meaningful philosophy of life. This value, which was also included among the 26 goals of general or liberal education, is what we call our "existential" value question. It was the most popular value question on surveys that we conducted in the early 1970s, but its importance to students has since dropped precipitously. That frequent discussions of racial/ethnic issues should appear to strengthen students' commitment to developing a philosophy of life is interesting and provocative. Could it be that issues of race, culture, and ethnicity represent promising curricular subject matter for confronting some of the existential dilemmas that many contemporary students seem to be avoiding?

Effects of Campus Activism

Since emphasizing diversity on the campus seems to enhance the likelihood that students will engage in some kind of protest activity during their undergraduate years, it is important to ask how activism itself affects the student's development. The strongest positive associations are with political liberalism, cultural awareness, and com-

mitment to promoting racial understanding. In other words, individual participation in campus protest activities does not, as some critics would have us believe, serve to alienate students from each other. On the contrary, it seems to strengthen students' sense of cultural awareness and appreciation and to reinforce their commitment to promoting greater understanding between the races. Campus protest participation is also associated with strengthened commitment to helping clean up the environment and developing a meaningful philosophy of life, growth in artistic interests and leadership abilities, aspirations for advanced degrees, and increased chances of voting in a presidential election. Participating in campus protests is negatively associated with materialistic values and the beliefs that racial discrimination is no longer a problem and that the individual can do little to change society. About the only outcome associated with protest participation that might be considered negative is a positive effect on the student's degree of hedonism (defined in this study as drinking beer, smoking cigarettes, and staying up all night). Hedonism, it should be stressed, was not affected one way or the other by any of the environmental diversity measures or individual Student Diversity Experiences.

In short, participation in campus protest activities is associated with a pattern of outcomes that is quite similar to the pattern associated with diversity activities, with the exception of its positive effects on hedonism, voting in a presidential election, artistic inclination, leadership, and aspiration for advanced degrees.

Reflections

Through these analyses I have attempted to shed some new light on the heated debate over political correctness and multiculturalism on college campuses by seeking some empirical answers to the following questions: Does emphasizing or not emphasizing diversity issues have any real consequences for students? How are students actually affected by some of the policies and practices that conservative critics find so objectionable? The findings present a clear-cut pattern: emphasizing diversity either as a matter of institutional policy or in faculty research and teaching, as well as providing students with curricular and extracurricular opportunities to confront racial and multicultural issues, are all associated with widespread beneficial effects on a student's cognitive and affective development. In particular, such policies and experiences are associated with greater self-reported gains in cognitive and affective development (especially increased cultural awareness), with increased satisfaction in most areas of the college experience, and with increased commitment to promoting racial understanding. Emphasizing diversity and multiculturalism is also associated with increased commitment to environmental issues and with several other positive outcomes: leadership, participation in cultural activities, citizenship, commitment to developing a meaningful philosophy of life, and reduced materialistic values. If we confine our analyses just to outcomes that are relevant to the goals of most general education programs, the effects of emphasizing multiculturalism and diversity appear to be uniformly positive.

Perhaps the only outcome consistently associated with diversity variables that might be considered "negative" is the positive effect on participation in student protests. While protest activities are often seen by some faculty, and especially by campus administrators, as a nuisance or possibly even as detrimental to campus order and tranquility, engaging in such protests seems to be associated with generally positive outcomes for the individual student participating. It is also true that an emphasis on multiculturalism is associated with increases in the student's political liberalism, but how one chooses to value such an effect would depend on one's political orientation.

While these findings provide strong evidence supporting campus attempts to emphasize issues of diversity and multiculturalism, there are other aspects of the PC debate which we have not directly addressed in this study. One particularly touchy issue is speech codes. Perhaps the most bizarre and ironic aspect of the PC debate is that, when it comes to speech codes, people at the extremes of the political spectrum seem to have switched sides. Those on the left who have supported codes that outlaw racist and other forms of hateful speech and conduct on the campus come from the same political camp that has always championed first amendment rights and supported the dismantling of *in loco parentis*. At the same time, those on the political right who have, with the help of the news media, promoted the PC issue, come from a political perspective that has

regularly advocated censorship in speech, writing, and the arts and that has endorsed restrictive codes of student conduct on the campus.

Ironically, the PC debate has once again underscored the critical importance of academic freedom and tenure in academia. Tenure, lest we forget, was established primarily to protect academic freedom. I am a living example of the necessity for tenure, since some of what I have to say in my writing and speechmaking does not fall on receptive ears in my own university. While I like to think of myself as a free thinker, there is a serious question in my mind as to whether I might be much more circumspect in what I say and do if there were no academic freedom and tenure. I might even be in a different line of research.

That emphasizing multiculturalism and diversity reinforces political liberalism on the campus, should come as no surprise. Nor should academics necessarily feel defensive or apologetic about such effects. The very values and traditions of academia naturally attract people of a liberal persuasion. An environment that places a high value on teaching, learning, discovery, artistic expression, independence of thought, critical thinking and freedom of speech and expression naturally tends to attract such people, since these are values that have traditionally been very important to people from the left. In the same way, the corporate and military worlds have tended to attract people from the right because business and the military have traditionally placed a high value on power, control, hierarchy, authority, capitalism, free enterprise, and making money.

Academics should more openly acknowledge that the PC critics are right when they claim that the expression of right-wing viewpoints is not warmly received in a liberal campus climate. What the PC critics themselves fail to do, however, is to make any distinction between the right to express a particular point of view and the right to have others agree with it. There is no such thing as a "right" to expect agreement. As a matter of fact, liberal academics don't even agree with each other on matters like speech codes and curricular reform. If the PC critics want people to agree with them, then they should look, instead, into conservative politics, corporate business, fundamentalist religion, or the military.

Despite the liberal leanings of most faculties, I would submit that in academia there is still far more tolerance shown for the expression of deviant viewpoints than in any other social institution. In other words, an employee in business, government, or the military has much less freedom of expression—especially when it comes to expressing deviant political viewpoints—than does an employee in academia. And this is as it should be. This is our tradition, our strength.

One thing that we tend to forget about academic freedom is that it is not merely an end in itself but that it has a larger purpose: the pursuit of truth. The link between academic freedom and the pursuit of knowledge is often overlooked in the PC debate, but the underlying logic is really very simple: the quickest and surest way to the truth is to encourage the expression of diverse points of view and to promote active discussion and debate of these different views. This is really what academic freedom is all about.

Related Readings

Astin, A. W. (1991). *Assessment for excellence: The philosophy and practice of assessment and evaluation in higher education.* Phoenix: Oryx.

Astin, A. W. (1992, Fall). What matters in general education: Provocative finding from a national study of student outcomes. *Perspectives,* 22(1), 23–46.

Astin, A. W. (1993). *What matters in college? Four critical years revisited.* San Francisco: Jossey-Bass.

CHAPTER 6

Campus Resegregation and Its Alternatives

Gary Orfield

Professor of Education and Social Policy at the Graduate School of Education and the John F. Kennedy School of Government, Harvard University, Gary Orfield is Co-director of the Civil Rights Project. He has also chaired a National Institute of Education study group on school desegregation and served as a court appointed expert in school desegregation cases in Los Angeles, St. Louis, and San Francisco. Orfield's Publications include Dismantling Desegregation: The Quiet Reversal of Brown v. Board of Education, and The Closing Door: Conservative Policy and Black Opportunity. He received his Ph.D. in political science from the University of Chicago.

After a generation of serious efforts by U.S. colleges and universities to reverse their historic exclusion of African Americans, Latinos, and American Indians, these institutions are suddenly facing a frontal attack on the programs, policies, and commitments born of those efforts. Threatened by court decisions, referenda, political attacks, and lawsuits, colleges are struggling to foresee the consequences of abandoning affirmative action and to devise viable alternatives for promoting and preserving campus diversity. This volume documents and examines that struggle.

As the communities around them become more and more diverse, many campuses that have been forced to end affirmative admissions are now rapidly turning whiter. There are fewer minority applicants, and those who are admitted often choose to go elsewhere rather than face severe isolation. These changes can create a vicious circle of resegregation. Denying the benefits of a college education to groups that are destined to become the majority in many cities and states raises explosive issues. The first troubling examples are already evident. At the leading public law schools in Texas and California, states where the majority of students are now Latino or black, the enrollment of blacks and Latinos has dropped dramatically:

the University of Texas (UT) Law School's entering class in fall 1997 was less than 1 percent black; in California black enrollment dropped by 63 percent while Latino enrollment was down by 34 percent.

The U.S. Supreme Court's 1978 decision in *Regents of the University of California v. Bakke* permitted colleges to consider race as one of a variety of factors in admissions, but forbade the use of racial quotas. The key opinion, by Justice Lewis Powell, cited Harvard University's multidimensional admissions process, which seeks to promote diversity of many kinds.

The rate of access to college for black high school graduates relative to whites had reached its peak just before *Bakke*, because of a variety of trends in the 1960s and early 1970s. These included a vast expansion of federal aid for low-income college students; the rapid growth of low-cost four-year state colleges; and programs from the War on Poverty, such as Upward Bound, designed to identify promising low-income students and give them both training in key pre-collegiate skills and support in preparing for and applying to college. *Bakke* enabled colleges wanting to maintain a significant minority presence to do so even as these anti-poverty programs were dismantled in the 1980s, and in spite of continuing large gaps in the preparation of minority students.

Under *Bakke,* colleges were allowed to work out something short of a quota that would boost minority access. There were few legal or political challenges to these affirmative admissions programs for a generation, while public debate focused on more visible issues such as school busing, racially defined voting districts, and affirmative action in employment. The conflicts over race on campus were about curriculum, harassment, racially defined housing and educational programs, and faculty recruitment. The few researchers who concentrated on these issues gave most attention to the problems of minority students on predominantly white campuses.

Everything changed suddenly in 1996, when federal courts of appeals in Texas and California, the two largest states, outlawed race-conscious college admissions policies. Several other states were affected by a third appeals court decision in Maryland that prohibited racially targeted financial aid. The U.S. Supreme Court, which had already limited race-conscious remedies in minority contracting, voting rights, and school desegregation, refused to hear any of these three key cases, thus effectively limiting the *Bakke* principle in large parts of the country.

As this book is published, legislative and legal challenges to affirmative admissions have been launched in several other states. Lawyers are advising some institutions to cut back on their existing admissions policies, and minority scholarships are being terminated in a number of states. In response, civil rights groups are attacking the use of standardized tests and seeking other basic changes in college admissions policies.

Higher education is fundamentally different from other civil rights arenas. Civil rights policies are usually challenged by institutions that are being forced to pursue racial goals they oppose. Most affirmative admissions and aid policies, on the other hand, are purely voluntary efforts to achieve goals the colleges themselves support. Outside the South, colleges have not faced court orders or federal sanctions to force them to admit minority students; even in the South, there has been little such enforcement. The great majority of colleges want to maintain their civil rights policies. But white students and right-wing legal action groups trying to impose a change on these institutions are asking federal courts to prohibit these voluntary efforts and prescribe different admissions policies.

In the states most affected thus far, minority communities are reacting with shock and anger. Some campuses have erupted in protests of the sort not seen since the Vietnam War. A college education has become a central part of the American dream; slamming shut the gates of college and professional school clearly threatens the future of the communities affected. But high-pitched demands for action can lead legislatures and academic administrators to consider any alternative that sounds plausible.

Education leaders and policymakers face a difficult challenge. The courts are increasingly responsive to white claims of racial discrimination while dismissing minority concerns over the continuing effects of historic discrimination. Many campuses are therefore trying to figure out how to maintain diversity without any explicit consideration of race in admissions. It would be simple if race were simply a proxy for other conditions, but, as the research in this volume shows, it is not. Race overlaps with class, educational, and job inequality, and with geographic isolation, giving rise to the hope that one or more of those factors might be an easy substitute. But race in truth is unique in its significance and impact, both historic and contemporary.

It is also true that any overt effort to specify a set of multiple factors that are obviously intended to duplicate the effect of racial selection would be seen as defiance of the court orders, because institutions may not do by subterfuge what they are prohibited from doing directly. In this complex situation, policymakers are likely to adopt new strategies that sound as if they might work with little or no serious analysis of their viability or educational consequences. Such decisions often have unanticipated consequences. If a policy turns out to be based on unworkable premises, it could discredit the goal.

For example, if a new admissions policy succeeds in admitting many minority students with far weaker preparation than those admitted under the old policy, universities would temporarily maintain minority enrollment levels but would find themselves flunking out a growing percentage of minority students unless they mounted a massive remediation effort. Because highly selective schools have few instructors skilled in remedial work and give no rewards for such work, major problems would be likely.

Moreover, Stanford Professor Elizabeth Cohen and others have shown that race relations are improved when there is equal status interaction—that is, when racial differences are not reinforced by class differences and very large achievement differences. Admitting only very poor black or Latino students from very weak schools would tend to reinforce racial stereotypes and diminish the probability of positive interracial contacts. It would be better for developing positive race relations and reducing stereotypes to find a way to admit those minority students most ready for college work.

When race-conscious admissions policies are outlawed, the easiest alternative for colleges seeking to admit significant numbers of minorities is to target high-poverty, low-achieving schools, because very few whites attend such schools. But the students from these schools will also be the least likely to succeed in college. It is extremely difficult to identify, using only nonracial criteria, those African-American and Latino applicants most likely to succeed in a selective college, because they are often middle-class students attending more competitive, less impoverished schools. (These students, of course, still face a variety of obstacles related to historic and current forms of discrimination—obstacles that opponents of affirmative action simply deny.)

The problem is complex: any purely voluntary affirmative admissions program must produce good enough results to maintain the support, or at least the acceptance, of the faculty and administration. If the policy does not work it may be terminated at any point, leaving no policy at all and fostering a belief that there is no feasible solution. It is very important, in other words, that new policies be likely to work.

Many university leaders have strongly reaffirmed their belief that maintaining campus diversity is crucial. But belief is not enough. These leaders must be prepared both for the coming legal challenges and for the possibility that they will find their accustomed authority in these matters suddenly limited. What they will need, first of all, is much better information on the likely consequences of policy alternatives. One goal of this book is to provide that information.

The Rise and Fall of Affirmative Admissions

U.S. college campuses historically reflected the dominant groups in American society, choosing students with no interference from federal courts or agencies. There were, of course, pressures from trustees, alumni, sports teams, fundraisers, and contributors to admit certain students. Most students were white Protestant males from more affluent and educated families. Nineteen states maintained racially separate public campuses for black and white students, and seventeen (where the large majority of blacks lived) had mandatory segregation laws until 1954. Even after the Supreme Court outlawed public school segregation, very little changed until the late 1960s.

Selective colleges historically tended to reflect the biases of the larger society, including anti-Semitism and racism. Even at the few northern colleges that admitted significant numbers of black graduate students before the civil rights era, discrimination was often overt. The University of Chicago, for example, segregated its student housing and participated in a campaign to keep its neighborhood all-white through restrictive real-estate covenants.

Things began to change after World War II, when the G.I. Bill brought hundreds of thousands of less affluent students to campus. Soon the United States began a huge expansion of higher education. During the 1960s and 1970s, state and federal governments tried to make some kind of college education possible for anyone who could benefit from it. Financial aid programs were created; the War on Poverty encouraged the poor to attend college; and civil rights laws directly challenged the tradition of racial exclusion. This revolution began to open the door to white colleges for blacks.

Affirmative policies for student recruitment, admissions, and aid were important elements of this effort. Given the unequal educational backgrounds of minority students, the history of unconstitutional segregation, the continued existence of segregated and unequal public schools, the huge gaps in test scores, and the failure of limited efforts in the preceding decade to significantly integrate elite colleges and universities, many institutions devised much more focused race-conscious policies in the late 1960s and early 1970s. The basic lesson of the first decade of civil rights policymaking was that the problems were systemic: they would tend to be self-perpetuating even when overt racial barriers fell. Real change, therefore, would mean prying open the doors through a conscious plan to overturn long-standing traditions.

Those policies were often attacked as government-imposed quotas, but they were actually voluntary goals. The government could have used its authority under the 1964 Civil Rights Act to force change, but it did not. That law forbade discrimination in institutions receiving federal aid and gave the Department of Education authority to regulate institutions on issues of nondiscrimination. Even after the Office for Civil Rights was ordered by federal courts to require equity and desegregation plans in the states that had intentionally segregated students, it never used its power to cut off funds against those falling far short of their goals for minority access. In the rest of the nation, there were no regulations and no required plans for racial equity. The one major enforcement case developed in the 1970s, against the University of North Carolina, was quickly dropped when President Reagan took office.

Ironically, probably the most aggressive investigation of admissions issues was by the Reagan administration on behalf of Asian-American students who complained that an increased emphasis on verbal skills at the University of California (UC) at Berkeley would result in the admission of fewer Asians. Under threat, the university backed down. No similar threat regarding admissions or tests that have the effect of reducing enrollment has ever been made on behalf of black, Latino, or American Indian students. Many states, in fact, have recently adopted higher admissions requirements with disproportionate negative impact on these minorities.

Most colleges and universities devised their own policies for their own reasons. The urban upheavals of the 1960s and the assassination of Martin Luther King, Jr., lent urgency to these efforts, and fostered the belief that colleges should try to develop interracial leadership for the future good of society. Colleges exercised their traditional discretion in admissions, and their authority under *Bakke*, to devise policies and practices that would identify, admit, and assist larger numbers of minority students.

Even at its peak, this effort at equity fell far short of reflecting the nation's overall population or its population of high school graduates. It came closest to equalizing rates of college entrance among white and black high school graduates in the late 1970s, just before *Bakke* and the rapid

tuition increases and aid cuts of the 1980s. But there was always a large gap in graduation rates. By the early 1980s, there was a serious drop in the percentage of minority students entering college compared to whites, a racial gap that grew during the decade.

Access to college for minority families was threatened on a number of fronts. Cutbacks in state and federal funding and huge rises in tuition compounded the impact of sharp cuts in the buying power of the largest aid program, the Pell grants. The Reagan administration loosened civil rights requirements and called for the raising of entrance requirements. It also mounted an all-out attack on race-conscious civil rights remedies, announcing that states need not achieve the racial goals set for their higher education systems—even those states that had never desegregated their institutions. The administration asked the courts to permit race-based remedies only where clear discrimination was proved and, even then, only for a few years. Where there was no overt historic discrimination, it argued, no affirmative policies should be allowed because they would amount to discrimination against whites. Presidents Reagan and Bush went on to appoint the majority of all sitting federal judges; the courts increasingly leaned toward their limited vision.

By the late 1990s, this view had reshaped the law of affirmative action in employment, voting rights, minority contracting, and school desegregation. In each case the Supreme Court restrained the lower federal courts, turning authority over to state and local officials. As court-imposed remedies were terminated, the courts became more responsive to claims that even voluntary race-conscious efforts discriminated against whites. The recent appeals courts' decisions in Texas, California, and Maryland clearly reflect this transformation.

When Admissions Are Driven by Tests and Grades

Once affirmative action was stripped away in the two largest states, the consequences of ranking applicants by standardized tests became much more obvious. The studies included in this volume confirm reports from several highly selective campuses and professional schools: under the new rules there have been devastating declines in the admission of underrepresented minority students. And a recent California study suggests that, even without the use of standardized tests, differences in grades alone would produce major drops in the enrollment of black and Latino students.

Dropping racial targeting will have similar effects nationwide—particularly at the 20 percent of U.S. colleges with genuinely selective admissions—given the existing gaps in test scores and grades between whites and underrepresented minorities. Thomas Kane of Harvard's Kennedy School of Government analyzes the probable impact of such a change on the fortunes of white applicants, compared with general public perceptions of affirmative action. Because there are far more whites in the pool of eligible applicants at selective schools, Kane reasons, a drastic reduction in the number of minorities admitted would produce only a small increase in the acceptance rates of whites and Asians. At Harvard College, for instance, even if no blacks or Latinos were admitted at all, a white or Asian applicant's chances of acceptance would rise by only one or two percent. "If more than one or two percent of those who were originally denied admission believe that they would have been admitted but for affirmative action," Kane writes, "then the perceived costs of the policy overstate the true cost."

Kane's analysis illuminates a fallacy in the thinking of many critics of affirmative action, who exaggerate its actual impact and thus play on the resentment of whites who are inclined to blame it for their own disappointments. Reversing affirmative action will cause substantial harm to minority group representation on selective campuses and deepen minority skepticism about the possibility of racial progress, and yet help few whites or Asians.

The end of affirmative action on key selective campuses will reverberate throughout the educational system. Jerome Karabel of Berkeley reports that restricting enrollment of Mexican Americans in the UC and UT systems would gravely affect Latino medical school applications nationwide. Thus the entire country's supply of Latino doctors could be harmed by policy changes at just two large state university systems. From these and other data, Karabel concludes that the demise of affirmative action will mean "a return to a level of racial and ethnic segregation in American higher education not seen in more than a quarter of a century." The American Medical Association

reports that minority applications to medical school fell by 11 percent in 1997.

Ending affirmative action not only limits admission to higher education but also sends a much broader signal to minority groups, who are especially sensitive to symbols. In a racially polarized society, minorities watch closely for signs of hope or of reversal. When they see what seem to be unmistakable signs that doors are being closed, many decide that they will not be allowed in. So even before the new admissions policies took effect in Texas and California, there were sharp drops in the numbers of inquiries and applications from minorities. Susanna Finnell's study of Texas A&M University documents a dramatic decline in applications from Latinos and blacks for its academic scholarships following the news that the court had outlawed affirmative action. At the same time, there was a surge of applications from whites and Asians—perhaps reflecting their overestimate of the impact of affirmative action on their groups.

Texas A&M's academic scholarships are reserved for students with high SAT or ACT scores who are also in the top segment of the graduating class. These scholarships were originally designed in part to recruit talented minority students, who are underrepresented on campus. In the year after the Texas court of appeals decision, applications for the scholarships from Latinos dropped by 36 percent; applications from blacks dropped 71 percent. The number of white applicants went up 103 percent.

Elementary and secondary public school enrollment in Texas is now 53 percent nonwhite. If current trends continue, Latinos will be the majority group in the state's public schools within a few years, but they will be largely excluded from its selective colleges.

Finnell describes Texas A&M's efforts to attract minority students to its historically white campus in recent years, including a highly effective invitational summer program targeted at talented minority youth. With such racially targeted recruitment efforts now illegal in Texas, if the university wants to continue the program it must open it to whites, quintupling its size and defeating its purpose. The result is that no one is invited. An effort to overcome a campus's historic image of racial bias through personal visits is simply abandoned. This outcome only reinforces problems rooted in a history of discrimination.

Will Race-Blind Alternatives Work?

Faced with catastrophic declines in black and Latino enrollment, policy-makers and advocates in Texas and California have begun a hurried search for race-blind alternatives that seem likely to preserve some degree of diversity on campus.

Because the courts have forbidden only the consideration of race, and because affirmative action arises from notions of redressing disadvantage, people naturally think of different definitions of disadvantage that might work. The one most often discussed in affirmative action debates is poverty, because blacks, Latinos, and American Indians are much more likely than whites to be poor. They are also likely to attend segregated, high-poverty schools.

But using poverty as a proxy for race will not preserve diversity, as analyses by Kane and Karabel show. Most poor people in the United States are neither black nor Latino, and many of the minority students admitted to college through race-conscious affirmative action are not poor. A ranking of students below the poverty line by their test scores would result in a pool of favored applicants that was mostly Asian and white—many of them from temporarily poor families who managed to send their children to competitive schools that prepared them for college entrance exams.

Recent immigrants from Asia, for example, often are highly educated people who cannot practice their professions in the United States, at least until they receive a new certification; their children, however, have the immense advantage of the parents' education and often are able to attend suburban schools because they face less housing discrimination than blacks or Latinos. The stereotype that Asian children encounter in these schools is generally positive, not negative. A policy that gives preferential admissions to such students, who enjoy family and school advantages and have experienced little discrimination in the United States, while excluding minorities who face serious discrimination, would have serious unanticipated consequences. (Some Asian refugee groups do not, of course, enjoy these advantages and in fact face problems much more like those confronting Latinos.)

To maintain the current level of black and Latino representation through preferences based on poverty instead of race, selective colleges would have to reserve six times as many places for poor students as they currently reserve for under-represented minorities, according to Kane's analysis. Few, if any, colleges could afford to pursue such a course.

One seemingly easy but race-blind way to insure some minority representation would be to target high-poverty schools. Very few white students attend such schools; schools in which more than 90 percent of the students are black or Latino are 16 times as likely as mostly white schools to have a majority of poor kids. It is not surprising, then, that the Texas legislature, seeking a way to preserve minority access to college, fixed on this solution. It declared that the top 10 percent of students in every high school are eligible for admission to the University of Texas. This approach includes high-poverty schools in the admissions pool, using traditional measures of achievement within the school, not race, to select individual students.

Segregation is widespread but far from absolute in Texas schools, and so there is no guarantee that the top-scoring students even in heavily non-white schools will be African American or Latino. But a serious problem arises from the strikingly unequal preparation of this cohort of students.

College admissions officers have long known that class rank is hardly comparable from one high school to the next. The top students in many high-poverty schools are woefully unprepared for college. Ignoring this fact and admitting these students presents universities with a difficult choice. If nothing else changes, many of the new students will simply flunk out and the policy will be discredited. To avoid this outcome, colleges will have to invest in effective remedial strategies, something selective campuses have been notoriously reluctant to do. Many, in fact, have raised their admissions requirements in recent years and cut back remedial programs. Thus, a seemingly simple solution has the unintended effect of excluding many of the best-prepared minority students and requiring other complex changes in policy.

The assault on affirmative action has brought into much sharper focus the social consequences of relying on standardized tests in the college admissions process. Black, Latino, and American Indian students have always fared poorly on such tests. The reasons for their poor performance are complex and not entirely understood. What is clear, however, is that if colleges are forced into a slavish adherence to cutoff scores in admitting applicants, the numbers of blacks, Latinos, and American Indians on campus will fall precipitously. The enrollment figures in California and Texas law and business schools have already sparked intense scrutiny of the validity and predictive power of admissions tests, and testing policies have become principal targets of civil rights advocates.

Tests are often assumed to be neutral and highly reliable measures of merit, but experts have long known that they have large margins of error in assessing any individual student, and that their overall predictive power accounts for only a modest portion of the variance in achievement among first-year college students. Given the difficulties of choosing among thousands of similar applicants, it is easy to understand why colleges rely on an indicator that helps even a little, provides very simple, easily interpreted data, and shifts the costs to the students. As the power of tests increases, however, advocates are calling for changes in the nature and uses of those tests. A university committee in California has recommended dispensing with standardized testing entirely. Others call for the construction of different kinds of assessment that are more related to actual performance on the job, or that reflect more of the talents and experiences of minority students. Some California campuses tried to do this.

Following the court decisions ending affirmative action in Texas and California, the Texas state legislature responded to large initial losses by trying to preserve minority access by providing automatic access to the university for any student finishing in the top 10 percent of his or her high school class. University of California campuses had to admit at least half of their students purely on the basis of test scores and grades; since many applicants had perfect or near-perfect grades, the test scores alone would be decisive for them. The California campuses tried to come up with a number of other measures and procedures to address other forms of disadvantage. The most selective California campuses, however, experienced drastic declines in African American, Latino, and American Indian students.

The total of African Americans, Latinos, and American Indian undergraduates admitted at Berkeley fell from 23 percent to 10 percent, and from 20 percent to 13 percent at UCLA—this at a time when the state's minority population was rapidly rising. In Texas, in spite of the 10 percent plan, fewer blacks were admitted at Austin, and there was no increase in the number of Latinos. The group that benefited most from the 10 percent plan was Asians, who had not suffered from the end of affirmative action. At the University of Texas at Tyler, less than 15 percent of the students admitted under the 10 percent plan were minorities. The net effect was that there was no recovery from the dramatic declines that occurred following the circuit court ruling in *Hopwood v. Texas*. Schools in both states often mentioned the severe problems they had faced in recruiting those students who were admitted, caused by ending minority scholarships. Eligible black and Latino students had to consider whether or not to accept less financial aid, and whether to attend schools where they would be more isolated due to greatly reduced enrollment of minority students.

These issues will be addressed in detail in a future volume from the Harvard Civil Rights Project. They already figure prominently, however, in the early reaction to post-affirmative action problems in some states. One of the many ironies of the current situation is that those most convinced that tests truly measure "merit" are creating a political climate in which tests may ultimately be downgraded in importance.

Some universities have reacted to the crisis by belatedly deciding to develop admissions policies that comply with the spirit of *Bakke*. As Jorge Chapa and Vincent Lazaro make clear in their essay in this volume, the UT Law School provided a tempting target for white litigants because its admissions procedure clearly violated the Supreme Court's *Bakke* principle—that race could be considered only as one of many variables in a complex admissions process. Too many selective public universities did not create such a process; they simply used the standard test scores and grades and added in race. The UT Law School created a "Texas Index" by combining test scores and grades, and then treated minority and white applicants differently. It was a two-factor analysis—nothing like the *Bakke* model. This meant that applicants were arrayed on a relatively simple continuum and admissions decisions were then adjusted by taking race into account as the decisive factor.

At very selective colleges where many applicants have high grades and the choice hangs on just two variables—tests scores and race—the admissions process is particularly vulnerable to challenge. Because such systems use no other cross-cutting factors, the loss of minority students can be precipitous once race is eliminated as a criterion. Certainly any campus that retains such a flawed process after the appeals court ruling in *Hopwood* is exposing itself to the maximum risk of judicial takeover of its admissions process.

Complying with the *Bakke* model is a logical but costly alternative. A study of changes in the admissions process at UC Irvine by Susan Wilbur and Marguerite Bonous-Hammarth suggests that a multidimensional system of assessing student potential can help produce a more diverse campus. They report that the new system, implemented in the wake of a UC regents' vote ending affirmative action, resulted in significant increases in the admission of black and Latino applicants above the numbers admitted through a simple formula based on tests and grades. Their study suggests that if public universities invest in admissions processes designed to assess a broader array of talents, they may be able to remain diverse. The Irvine system did this, but the campus still had substantial drops in black and Latino admissions in 1998.

Still another important way of thinking about the problem is to reconceptualize the goals of the selection process. Admissions criteria should be seen as a way to fulfill the values of the institution and to create the most effective learning community that embodies those values. Advocates of a one-dimensional "merit"-based system seem to suggest that admission to college is simply a reward for the students who are most "deserving," as measured on the scale of test scores and grades. But universities are not passive receptacles; they are dynamic communities that profoundly affect the development of students on many dimensions that are not readily quantified. The most important intellectual interactions many students ever experience take place in college—often with other students. Universities must foster the creation of knowledge and the training of leadership for the community and its professions. Because of these critical functions of universities, admissions processes reflect considerations important to the fulfillment of community as well

as individual goals. This is precisely what the Supreme Court recognized in the *Bakke* case.

Gregory Tanaka, Marguerite Bonous-Hammarth, and Alexander Astin suggest in this volume that it would be appropriate for universities to make interracial experience a "plus factor" for admissions. They cite evidence that multiracial campuses offer important advantages and that creating such communities should be a fundamental goal of a university in diverse society. Their research suggests that students who bring interracial experience with them to college may be valuable assets for these institutions. Diversity by itself, without people who understand how to make it work, may confer fewer benefits and create more problems than on campuses with many such people. If it is reasonable, Tanaka and colleagues argue, to give admissions preference to student athletes on the grounds that they enhance student life and increase external support for the school, is it not also reasonable to consider experience and skills in multiracial settings an asset? Positive race relations contribute to both the productive sharing of ideas on campus and to good institutional relationships with the outside community.

There may be other legitimate considerations in admissions. Because most colleges look only at English verbal test scores, they often underestimate students who have another first language. Outside the United States, fluency in two or more languages is considered a hallmark of an educated person. In the United States, by contrast, it is rare for students to graduate from college with a working knowledge of a second language, in spite of the importance of such knowledge in a global economy. Demonstrated fluency in a second world language could well be a plus factor in admissions decisions.

Other attributes and skills directly relate to success in careers and professions and could be incorporated into the admissions process. Leadership talent, the ability to work with others, verbal confidence, resilience, perseverance in the face of setbacks, and many other qualities are valued by employers and could be considered by admissions committees. Colleges have every right to take such qualities into account.

Every crisis presents opportunities for progress. In the long run, colleges and universities must take advantage of the affirmative action crisis to sharpen and reaffirm their goals, to develop recruitment and admissions policies that look at the whole person and recognize more of the accomplishments of minority students, and to reflect critically on how better to achieve their goals after the students arrive on campus. In the short run, however, a great deal remains at risk.

Conclusion and Recommendations

The reversal of affirmative admissions in higher education can drastically reduce black, Latino, and American Indian enrollment on highly selective campuses. The increased use of tests and grades as entrance standards will tend to exacerbate the existing inequities in U.S. society. If affirmative action is outlawed nationally, as it has been in Texas, the impact on access to leading public and private universities would be enormous. Many of our most able students would find themselves on campuses overwhelmingly dominated by white and Asian students. The severe isolation characteristic of our more affluent suburbs would become the rule in the institutions that train the leaders of our society and our professions. This threatens critical educational functions of universities and their ability to fully serve their communities.

The research reported in this volume shows that there is no good substitute for affirmative admissions efforts targeted at historically excluded groups. Any substitute criteria will be likely to bypass many of the best-prepared black and Latino students, who may face many forms of racial discrimination but are neither poor nor isolated in the weakest schools. The likely outcome of substituting poverty for race will be the admission of fewer and less-prepared black and Latino students. Therefore, the highest priorities for supporters of minority access to college should be:

- a vigorous defense of race-conscious affirmative action admissions policies that comply with *Bakke*, which rightly called for the creation of a multidimensional admissions process that takes account of a wide variety of applicants' talents;

- documentation of the academic benefits of diversity (the subject of the second volume in this series); and

- strong efforts to counter inaccurate and polarizing claims about minority admissions.

If affirmative action is struck down, universities should undertake a long-overdue examination of the entire admissions process. The same kind of narrow formulaic approach that is most likely to exclude minorities is also likely to exclude other students with talents that are not easily measured by tests and grades and, conversely, to reward students from the most affluent and educated families and communities. If colleges define "merit" as, in effect, being born into a highly educated, suburban white or Asian family and attending a highly competitive white high school, they are serving to maintain a stratified society rather than to truly reward merit and ability. As access to college becomes more and more decisive in shaping life chances, leaders of higher education have a growing responsibility to reach out for talent and make mobility possible. Universities that grafted affirmative action onto a flawed admissions process a quarter century ago now risk losing diversity unless they build a better process. Even if they eventually are successful in defending affirmative action in the Supreme Court, the radical reversals in some regions, the experiments they produce, and the legitimate criticisms of some of the existing systems all argue for change.

The essays in this book show that research can play an important role in the affirmative action debate. But far too few rigorous studies have addressed the important issues raised in the courts and in political debates. Very little previous work addressed the basic issues before the courts today; researchers could, for example, contribute important knowledge on the history of discrimination and its continuing effects, which is the strongest legal basis for race-conscious policies. Documenting the nature of the disadvantages that middle-class blacks and Latinos still face is crucial for their continued access to higher education.

The rollback of affirmative action in higher education requires all members of the university community to consider soberly a profound social change that they have hitherto taken for granted. A generation of multiracial campuses—the only such generation in U.S. history—was the product of both a great social movement and the commitment of university leaders three decades ago. Too little has been done to renew that commitment or to make the resulting levels of diversity work even better.

Now that our campuses are threatened with a return to almost total domination by the most privileged racial and ethnic communities, educational and political leaders must ask how much they value that hard-won diversity and what they are willing to do to keep it. From that debate could emerge a new understanding of common goals—and the energy to build a more democratic system for educating the future leaders of our rapidly changing society.

CLASS 5

Immigration, Social Policy, and Unemployment

CHAPTER 7
Building A Nation Through Immigration
L. Edward Purcell
L. Edward Purcell provides an insightful overview of the history of immigration in the U.S.A. He highlights the changes that came in immigration laws in response to the changing populations entering the country.

CHAPTER 8
The Business Case For Diversity
Samuel Betances and Laura M. Torres Souder
Samuel Betances and Laura M. Torres Souder have isolated a number of diversity initiatives necessary for the success of entities with a diverse workforce. They argue that entities that do not take these steps run the risk of not maximizing the potential of their workforce or marketplace opportunities.

CHAPTER 7

Building a Nation Through Immigration: Immigrate

L. Edward Purcell

L. Edward Purcell is an independent historian, editor, and journalist who has written over a dozen books and numerous articles, many of them on historical topics. He is currently an adjunct lecturer in American history at both Drake University, Des Moines, Iowa and Grand View College, Des Moines, Iowa.

Social Issues in America History (1995)

Factors in both Europe and the United States surfaced immediately after the end of the Napoleonic wars that set off a long, steady period of immigration, which coincided with the development of America as a strong, prosperous nation. The story of modern immigration begins after 1815 and is closely intertwined with the story of how the United States changed from a small nation of colonists clinging to the eastern seaboard into a transcontinental country of immense power and potential.

Modern Immigration Begins

Until 1820, all statistics about the numbers of immigrants and their origins are educated guesses (although they are quite likely to be accurate). In 1820, however, the United States began to keep records of arrivals, so despite many discrepancies and demographic inadequacies, there is reasonably good data from then on. However, it should be noted that the U.S. government has used political, not ethnic, definitions to count immigrants; in other words, the nation of origin has been used to designate immigrants whether or not the persons involved were really part of that nation's language and culture. This was not a major problem in 1820, but became one by the end of the 19th century when the policy obscured a great deal about immigration from European empires. Hundreds of thousands of Poles, for example, were counted as Germans or Russians, because Poland had been divided between the two countries.

During the decade between 1820 and 1830, slightly under 152,000 immigrants arrived in America. During the 1830s, the number was just short of 600,000. Immigration jumped during the 1840s to more than 1.7 million, and during the 10 years just before the Civil War, 2.6 million arrived. In total, well over 5 million new Americans immigrated between 1815 and 1860, adding to a total population of more than 30 million, nearly 10 times the number at the time of the Revolution.

The classic explanation of immigration is called the "push-pull" theory, which says that elements must be in place at both ends for immigration to occur: elements in the old land must push immigrants to uproot themselves and leave home; other elements in the new land must look so attractive that immigrants are pulled to a new place. During the decades from 1815 to 1860, both sorts of incentives were at work.

First of all, Europe entered a prolonged period of peace. The widespread and awesomely destructive wars of the French Revolution and the Napoleonic Era came to an end and were not repeated in such scale until World War I. There were several small wars, such as in the Crimea in the 1850s, and many violent revolutions and civil skirmishes, but none brought the violence that had pinned people in place during the last years of the 18th century and the first of the 19th. For many years, it was possible to move from the interior of Europe to a sea port and then across the Atlantic. Hamburg, Liverpool, and Le Havre became thriving, bustling points of embarkation.

Most of the immigration came from northern and western Europe, including more than two million Irish and more than a million Germans, who lived in places where particular circumstances calculated to stimulate movement. One of the most important circumstances, and least understood by historians and demographers, was the huge explosion of population in much of Europe and the British Isles. There were simply more and more people every year, with the result that any form of political or economic dislocation triggered mass migration. There was also some political immigration after the great political revolutions of 1830 and 1848, and these immigrants tended to have high profiles in their new lands. The actual numbers of political exiles to America were relatively small, but their influence was relatively large.

There was also a major shift in governmental policy in many European nations when the viewpoint became widespread that excess population was a threat to a nation's prosperity. Countries that had previously restricted emigration began to encourage it, hoping to avoid the liabilities of too many people, especially poor ones. Great Britain, most of the German states, Holland, and Sweden all changed policies and in some cases were only too glad to see people leave.

The rapid industrialization of Britain and western Europe also added immeasurably to the factors pushing immigrants to the New World. The growth of the factory system and numerous advances in scientific farming moved tens to hundreds of thousands of small farmers or renters off the land. People who had lived on small parcels of land following essentially the same patterns of agricultural life familiar for centuries were abruptly forced to give up and leave. The only livelihood they could find was in the new industrial cities, so they came to America.

The allure of land in America was nearly irresistible. The idea of nearly an entire continent for the taking was overwhelmingly attractive to many Europeans who wanted to live rural lives but could not find land in their original countries. The fact that land in the United States was relatively expensive-it cost hundreds of dollars in hard cash to buy even the smallest farm-and often came with difficulties and conditions unfamiliar to Europeans meant little in the face of the romantic attraction of what appeared to be limitless acres rolling out toward the Pacific.

Moreover, a great deal of impetus for Europeans considering a move to the United States came from the thousands of previous immigrants who sent glowing accounts in what became known as "American letters." These letters often motivated many from the writer's former home to seek a new life abroad.

There were also several kinds of promoters at work during most of the first part of the 19th century. Many individual American states actively recruited in Europe with advertising, distribution of literature, and promotional offices. Land agents recruited in Europe as did shipping companies and railroads. All had something to gain by encouraging immigration.

Part of the immigration boom was inspired by the fact that transportation grew increasingly simpler and cheaper. During the first decades of the 19th century, travel across the Atlantic was still slow and uncertain, with sailing ships at the mercy of the seas and the weather. But the cost of transport dropped as shippers, headed to America to pick up loads of timber and cotton to bring back to Europe, sought to fill their vessels and avoid deadhead runs to America. Between the end of the Napoleonic Wars and the 1850s, trans-Atlantic fares dropped by as much as 75 percent. Eventually the the steamship made the trip quicker and relatively healthier.

Transportation once the immigrants reached America also improved markedly during the period. Early in the 19th century, water travel was still the cheapest and easiest way to get to the interior. For example, the fare for travel from New York City to Detroit by way of the Hudson River, the Erie Canal, and the Great Lakes was as low as eight dollars. By the 1850s, rail transport was common in the northeastern part of the nation, and immigrants took full advantage of it to reach settlements in the growing states of the upper Midwest.

Until very late in the 1800s, the individual states, not the federal government, had responsibility for processing immigrants. Massachusetts and New York shouldered the largest burdens because of the popularity of Boston and New York City as immigrant landing ports. Massachusetts tried to improve conditions for immigrants in the 1840s by collecting a landing fee that was used to set up a hospital. New York, which came to be the busiest port of entry for immigrants from Europe, established a Board of Emigration in 1847 to regulate the influx and processing of newcomers. There were essentially no restrictions on entering the country, but the Board wanted procedures to register immigrants. The New York Board took over Castle Garden on Manhattan Island in 1855, which became the primary receiving point for immigrants to America until it was superseded by the new Federal facility at Ellis Island in 1892.

New York made some efforts to protect recent arrivals from the exploiters who found the "greenhorns" (as the immigrants were known) easy victims for fraud and deception. Because many of the arriving immigrants were disoriented, could not understand the language, and knew little of the customs, con men sold them phony rail tickets or offered other services that, of course, never materialized after the immigrants paid cash in advance. The worst abuses came from immigrants' fellow countrymen, who put the greenhorns at ease by speaking their language and assuming the role of friendly guide, then left them stranded and penniless. New York's immigrant registration procedure included a brief indoctrination designed to help the greenhorns avoid the most obvious confidence games.

The patterns of distribution of immigrants during the years before the Civil War followed the path of the nation's development. The growing importance of cities was emphasized by the tendency of many immigrants to choose urban life once in America. Many of the most dynamic American cities such as New York, St. Louis, Cincinnati, Chicago, Cleveland, Detroit, and San Francisco were about half populated by foreign-born immigrants by 1860; others had from one-fourth to one-third immigrant populations.

Of course, there were hundreds of thousands of immigrants who turned toward the farming states of the upper Midwest, especially the prairie lands of Illinois, Iowa, Wisconsin, and Minnesota. Some groups such as the Scandinavians, skipped over the cities almost entirely in order to reach the fertile soils of the interior.

The one section that few immigrants chose was the South. In general, the newcomers saw the slave societies and slave economies as unattractive: there was little place in southern agriculture for free immigrant labor, and the only available land was taken by well-established Scotch-Irish and other earlier immigrants. The South had few important cities outside the sea coast ports and not much industry to provide jobs for immigrants. By 1861 and the final breach between North and South, only about 13 percent of the nation's foreign born lived in the southern states, and most of these were concentrated in a few port cities.

The Second German Immigration

Following the defeat of Napoleon and the restoration of peace in Europe, German immigration to America resumed. From 1815 to past the turn of the 20th century, this tide of people was so large that immigrants of German origin outnumbered all others, with only the Irish coming close. The pattern of German immigration was relatively modest during the 1820s, but rose steadily, peaking in the decade surrounding the Civil War and during the 1880s. Between 1820 and 1920 (a period for which moderately reliable figures are available), more than 5.7 million Germans immigrated to the United States.

Basic changes in the structure of the economy and society in the German states had much to do with impelling people to emigrate. The development of larger and larger cities, the growth of industry, and political changes all helped to create an atmosphere in which the old ways of life were more and more difficult to maintain. The widespread (and largely inexplicable) population growth that affected most of Europe hit Germany also. The result of these changes was to motivate small farmers, merchants, and artisans to find new occupations or new places to live.

The majority of German immigrants to America before the late 1840s came from the southwestern states of Wurtemburg, Bavaria, and Baden, which were heavily agricultural regions. The immigrants included many families that had been forced off the land by debt and poor harvests; the same potato blight that struck farms in Ireland ravaged crops in Germany, but with less human toll. The changes and failures in the German agricultural system prompted many to leave before reaching the crisis stages, so the greatest numbers of immigrant German farmers of this period were not destitute, though they were usually far from prosperous.

The flow of German immigration also included a significant number of reasonably wealthy farmers who lacked faith in the future of the German economy and saw a chance to invest in American lands, and substantial artisans and merchants who simply wanted a change.

One of the most colorful groups to emigrate from Germany, and one that for a long time almost monopolized the attention of historians, was the small but important number of political activists in the failed revolutions of 1848, when the German states were swept by a wave of liberalism that captured the imagination of some of the most talented Germans. When the movement collapsed and repressive conservative regimes regained power, most of the revolutionaries were forced to flee, many of them choosing the United States as their refuge.

These "Forty-Eighters," as they were known, included writers, scholars, editors, doctors, lawyers, and others of similar background and experience. Not surprisingly, they tended to move into positions of leadership among the German communities of their new homeland. Several individuals subsequently had major influence in American life, most notably Carl Schurz, a 19-year-old Bonn student radical in 1848 who escaped Germany and after sojourns in France and England immigrated to the United States in 1852. He made his way to the Midwest and by the outbreak of the Civil War was a successful businessman and one of the most powerful leaders of the new Republican Party. He served as a Union general in the war and subsequently as a diplomat, Secretary of the Interior, and editor of Harper's Weekly.

The majority of German immigrants were, of course, less influential than Schurz and other Forty-Eighters, but the tendency of most Germans to preserve their national and ethnic identity gave them a pervasive cultural influence in any of the several German enclaves or German-dominated cities. Unlike the German immigrants of the previous century, who predominately secured farms and populated rural Pennsylvania with "Dutch" settlers, many among the second wave of Germans turned to the growing American cities (although there were significant numbers of 19th-century German immigrant farmers). By the time of the Civil War, places such as Cincinnati, Milwaukee, and St. Louis were heavily German in appearance and style, and New York had a huge German population that lived primarily in a "Little Germany."

Because so many German immigrants came with valuable skills, it is not surprising that they had a major economic impact wherever they went. They set up breweries, packinghouses, saw mills, and machine shops, for example, and usually they prospered. Skilled German workers also found work in businesses owned by native-born Americans and gave a strong boost to the development of industrialism in the United States.

German taverns, beer gardens, Turnvereins (social and athletic clubs), bands, orchestras, literary clubs, newspapers, churches, choral groups, and similar cultural organizations were found in every American city that supported a significant German population. German was the language of instruction in many local schools, and German language and customs were fostered through several generations. However, almost all of this elaborate German culture was destroyed virtually overnight during the anti-German hysteria that gripped the country during World War I.

Although by far the great majority of German immigrants during the 19th century came as families or individuals-mostly from the ports of Le Harve or Hamburg after a sometimes difficult overland journey-there were also notable but unsuccessful efforts at group colonizations. Several groups came to Texas, for example, during the years while it was an independent republic, including the founders of New Braunfels in 1845 who were participants in the settlement scheme of several German noblemen. German immigrant families paid the organizers of the New Braunfels colony a set fee in return for transportation, a log house, and a 160-acre Texas farm. The scheme failed, but many Germans came to Texas, nonetheless. Other German immigrant colonists moved to Minnesota, where they began a colony at New Ulm in 1857 that was a model of social planning. The New Ulm Germans formed a land association and set up "Turner" clubs and halls.

Mixed among the hundreds of thousand of German immigrants were many German Jews, who began to come to America in important numbers during the 1820s as part of the general migration from the German states. These Jews had a significant economic and social impact on the long-established but relatively small communities of Sephardic (Hispanic) Jews that had settled in America previously. By the Civil War, there were as many as 150 Jewish communities in the United States and more than 40,000 Jews in New York City alone. Few of these German-Jewish immigrants opted to take up farming, although some moved to rural areas as peddlars and merchants. The greatest numbers settled into the cities of the eastern sea board and began building urban Jewish communities.

The Irish

The history of Ireland-"that most distressful nation"-is full of drama and tragedy, but nothing rivals the astounding story of what happened to the Irish during the mid-19th century and how millions of Irish came to live in America.

Although the peak of the drama was the years of the devastating potato famine from 1845 to 1848, immigration historians point out that emigration from Ireland was significant before the famine and continued very strong until the turn of the 20th century: in the 100 years between the first recording of immigrants in 1820 and the passage of immigration restrictions in 1924, well over 4.5 million Irish immigrated to the United States.

However, no matter how important the long-range Irish immigration pattern was, the statistics of the famine years are astounding. At the beginning of the decade of the 1840s, when the economy and agricultural production were still adequate, there were roughly 8.2 million people living in Ireland. Ten years later the population has been reduced to 6.6 million-more than a million and a half people had disappeared. A very large percentage had died from starvation or diseases related to malnutrition; the rest fled. It seems certain that at least a million persons emigrated from Ireland to America in the years surrounding the famine. This is, perhaps, the clearest example of "push" factors in all of immigration history.

The prefamine immigration of the Irish had some of the same background factors but without the tragic urgency and scale. Ireland had nearly doubled in population during the first decades of the 1800s, and repeated division of the small land holdings made producing adequate food supplies more and more difficult. Only the high-nutritional value and low-production cost of the potato allowed the Irish to survive. Moreover, Ireland was subject to the political control of the British, who were seen as oppressors. When added to the fact that transportation across the Atlantic was relatively cheap, these conditions motivated about 300, 000 Irish to immigrate to America between 1820 and 1840. Most of the prefamine immigrants were apparently single men who found jobs as laborers in the North and Northeast-jobs on the lowest rungs of the free-market economic ladder but still a step up from their former situations in Ireland.

Another characteristic behavior pattern of the Irish immigrants in the prefamine years was a practice that came to be known as "chain migration." The earliest immigrants found jobs, saved assiduously, and sent passage money (often pre-paid tickets) to relatives in the old country. By very hard work and dedication, immigrants financed the passage of entire families in this way. It was difficult and took remarkable courage and perseverance, but it worked. Many other immigrant groups used the technique as well; in fact it is still common practice at the end of the 20th century. However, the Irish were among the first to use it on an important scale.

When the potato crop failed disastrously in 1845 and for several years thereafter, a large percentage of those Irish who managed to survive sailed for America. When they arrived they formed a high-profile immigrant group that was distinctly different. First of all, almost all the Irish immigrants of this period were Roman Catholic. Despite the early attempt of Lord Baltimore to establish a haven for Catholics in Maryland in the 17th century, America was solidly Protestant and erected a wall of prejudice against Catholics. The circumstances of the arrival of the famine refugees, who had almost no capital and were often in ill health, added to Americans' poor opinion of Catholics, and their very large numbers caused anxiety. The Irish "hordes" were the targets of discrimination for decades: they were perceived by many Americans as poor, dirty, uneducated, and practitioners of an alien religion. It was not, perhaps, until the 1960 election of President John Kennedy, a Roman Catholic descendent of prefamine Irish immigrants, who faced anti-Catholic propaganda throughout his career, that the Irish finally shrugged off the effects of discrimination.

The Irish of the famine years (and the decades following) moved more or less in the same patterns as their prefamine predecessors: they remained in the cities of the North and Northeast, seeking employment as construction workers or, as in the case of many Irish immigrant women, as domestic servants. On the whole, the Irish had no interest in moving back onto the land. Even though land in America was relatively rich and plentiful compared to home, very few had the money to buy farms.

During the decades after the end of the famine immigration, the balance of Irish immigrants changed gradually from mainly men to mainly women, although in all cases the average age of Irish immigrants was very young. The Irish immigrant women tended to stay in domestic service jobs or in mill work, but the men gradually moved up the economic ladder during the late 19th century. As the immigrant and second-generation Irish discovered the power of the vote in the American system and as American cities grew and needed people to operate the expanding governments and public services, the Irish virtually took over such occupations as urban firemen and police.

Nativism before the Civil War

There is nothing unusual about people viewing newcomers as strange and curious; this is a natural human reaction to someone or something new. Americans have always reacted to immigrants in this way, particularly if the immigrants spoke a language other than English and came from a place where the clothing, customs, and experiences were quite different than those of the United States.

However, this sort of healthy curiosity has frequently given way to nativism, a virulent, often violent, paranoid, and irrational hatred and fear of immigrants. At its least destructive, nativism is the motive for relatively mild government regulation, such as prolonging the waiting period for naturalization. At its worst, nativism edges over into bigotry and something resembling racial hatred, although "race" is seldom involved despite some nativists's tendency to use such labels. (Nativists around the turn of the century

confused cultural differences based on national customs and language with true genetic differences between races.)

Until 1924, when nativism finally triumphed in the passage of restrictive laws and regulations, immigration to the United States was open to all (with the exception of the formal exclusion of the Chinese and the informal barring of the Japanese). There were few serious movements to restrict immigration; however, there were several periods in which nativism came to the forefront of American life and politics.

The first important nativist movement was in the 1830s, 1840s, and 1850s, concerned almost entirely with Protestant American fears of Roman Catholicism and the importation of Catholic worship by European immigrants.

The Irish and the German Catholics bore the worst of the nativist outbreak during the period before the Civil War because they were the most prominent Catholic newcomers. There were public protests against Catholics in New York in the early 1830s, with newspapers and Protestant preachers at the forefront. In 1834, a Protestant mob in Boston burned down an Ursuline convent. Ten years later in Philadelphia, a conflict over schools and the use of the Catholic translation of the Bible escalated into full-scale rioting that destroyed blocks of houses in the Irish section of town and resulted in 13 deaths.

By the 1850s, the nation was in a precarious state of unity and balance, with divisions over the issue of slavery producing constant tension and anxiety. Many basic American institutions, such as political parties and religious denominations, seemed in jeopardy and the national consensus that held the nation together began to fail. Against this background, nativists organized on a national scale.

They argued that recent immigrants were wicked slum-dwellers who had imported alien customs and could never adapt to the practices of pure American democracy. These exact arguments have appeared over and over in American history whenever older generations have felt threatened by newcomers. These arguments never seem to lose their power over a certain part of the population who tend to make scapegoats out of newcomers whom they cannot be bothered to understand. One of the most potent recurring arguments has been that immigrants are too uneducated and politically degenerate to ever understand the American system, and therefore they are a threat to the essential American characteristic: democracy.

The nativist political party organized in the 1850s was known as the Know-Nothing Party, because its members were supposedly sworn to secrecy and replied that they "knew nothing" when asked about the organization. It began humbly but grew very rapidly, in part because the other established political parties-the Whigs and the Democrats-were disintegrating over the issue of slavery. The Know Nothings had a single principle, which was to oppose Catholicism and by extension to oppose immigrants.

In 1854, the Know-Nothing Party won astounding victories in Massachusetts, where it captured the entire state government, in Pennsylvania and in Delaware. A year later, the party won in five more states and showed strongly in seven more. Oddly enough, even with electoral success-there were several Know-Nothing members of Congress-the party never was able to actually pass much legislation against Catholics or immigrants. For example, bills to restrict entrance and create a 21-year waiting period for citizenship died before coming to a vote in the House of Representatives.

In Massachusetts, where they had seized full political and governmental power, the Know Nothings did pass a state requirement for a long naturalization waiting period and managed to establish a law restricting state office holders to the native born.

As strong as the Know-Nothing movement seemed in the mid-1850s and as rapidly as it grew, it also dissolved rapidly. The party nominated former President Millard Fillmore as its national candidate in the election of 1856, but he failed to attract support at the polls except in Maryland. The concerns of the nation over sectionalism and slavery came to a head by the end of the decade and the impending crisis of the Civil War left little time or energy for side issues such as immigration. The nativist movement collapsed for the time being.

The Civil War and After

Recent immigrants-most of whom lived in the North and Northeast-played important roles in the great national disaster of the Civil War. The foreign-born flocked to the standard of the Union and joined the northern army in droves. Any questions about their loyalty or commitment to the American ideal were swept away between 1861 and 1865, when immigrant soldiers provided the backbone of many of the regiments in the field. Hundreds of thousands of immigrants, the Germans and Irish most conspicuously, served in the ranks, and there were several all-immigrant units.

After the last gun sounded, America moved into one of the most dynamic periods of growth in its history. During the two decades after the war, the country expanded westward, pulled by the railroads and the Homestead Act, and the great industrial cities of the Northeast and Midwest began the economic developments that eventually made the nation prosperous and powerful.

Immigrants were closely involved in all of these national movements, particularly in the growth of cities and industry. During the late 1860s, total annual immigration climbed back to pre-Civil War levels, and during the early 1870s, twice passed the 400,000 mark, with people coming from more or less the same source countries as before the war. The flows from Germany and Ireland continued, although at a reduced pace from the boom years. A steady stream came from Britain (including the Welsh and the Cornish) and there were smaller but important groups such as the French Canadians and the Dutch.

The Scandinavians

The three Scandinavian nations-Sweden, Denmark, and Norway-sent slightly more than two million immigrants to the United States between the early 1800s and early 1900s. The greatest numbers came in the decades from 1870 to 1910, and the majority skipped over the cities of the East and headed directly for the great farm lands of the upper Midwest, where they created a lasting Scandinavian presence.

The relationships among the three Scandinavian nations have been historically complex, with political dominance shifting several times in the modern era: Denmark held all of Norway and Sweden at one time, then Sweden gained the upper hand, with Norway emerging as a more-or-less sovereign nation only in 1814 (complete separation did not come until 1905). The Norwegian and Danish languages are virtually the same, and Swedish speakers can usually understand the other two.

The immigration history of each nationality had its own characteristics, but there were also strong similarities. The majority of Scandinavians came seeking land and farms, and many of them came with enough capital to make landowning a reality. For most of the period of immigration, Scandinavians came as families and settled whenever possible in communities that often became rural ethnic enclaves. Later in the period, more single immigrants made the journey as conditions changed in the homelands.

The most potent force pushing immigrants from Scandinavia was the widespread and pervasive dislocation of small farmers. During the 19th century, land became extraordinarily hard for the average person to obtain, and the only choice was to change from an agricultural existence or to emigrate. In addition to land hunger and a desire to remain farmers, many Scandinavians were happy to leave behind the overbearing state Lutheran churches of their native lands. While seeking religious freedom was probably not the predominate goal of most Scandinavian immigrants, it was an important reason to emigrate.

Until 1840, the Swedish-Norwegian government officially discouraged emigration with a national law restricting individuals from leaving. However, widespread economic dislocations and a major growth in population forced the withdrawal of these prohibitions. There were simply too many people for the limited supply of land to support, and all controls were dropped by 1860.

Immigration from Sweden before 1840 had consisted of a small scattering of middle-class businessmen and professionals, but shortly before the American Civil War relatively affluent small farmers, usually traveling in groups with families, began to arrive. The pattern continued for 15 years after the war, with the Swedish immigrants moving to the fertile northern prairies of Illinois and Minnesota because of the expansion and promotion of the new western railroads. During the 1880s, more and more Swedish immigrants who had been agricultural workers and probably had never owned land at home arrived. The decade between 1880 and 1890 marked the biggest years of Swedish immigration with nearly 400,000 arriving. By the turn of the 20th century, the character of Swedish arrivals changed again, as rural immigrants gave way to younger single men and women from the Swedish cities.

Not all Swedish immigrants fit the stereotype of midwestern farmers, and there was a significant number of Swedes who settled in industrial cities. Chicago, for example, had a heavily ethnic Swede Town until well into the 1900s.

The smaller numbers of Danish immigrants followed a similar pattern, with the bulk of the first wave coming from the low- to middle-socioeconomic ranks, mostly in family clusters. After the turn of the century, the same shift occurred to younger, unmarried urban immigrants. We know a great deal about the Danish immigrants because the Danish police kept meticulous records of all emigrants from 1869 to 1914, and historians have made a thorough study of the social and economic patterns. Once in America, the Danes were more inclined to disperse than the Swedes or the Norwegians, but about three in 10 Danes ended up in Iowa, Wisconsin, or Minnesota.

The pressure to emigrate created by a lack of land was undoubtedly greatest in Norway, where the 19th-century growth in population dramatically outstripped the small amount of farmland wedged between the coasts, fjords, and mountains: no more than about 4 percent of the land in Norway can be farmed. In addition, the Norwegian Lutheran church seemed particularly oppressive to many lower-class Norwegians-the first boatload of immigrants in 1825 were religious dissenters-and the political domination of Norway by Sweden gave extra motivation to leave.

In all, close to 700,000 Norwegians came to America between 1860 and 1920, which was roughly equivalent to half of the total population of the country in 1845. Most of these immigrants sought the land they had been denied at home, and an absolute majority settled in the midwestern farm states of Wisconsin, Minnesota, and North Dakota, often in rural ethnic clusters.

The Chinese

The most unusual immigrant group of the 19th century, and by far the worst received, were the Chinese who came to America between the

1850s and 1882. They were treated differently from all other nationalities: the Chinese The first Chinese to enter the United States were a handful of students were discriminated against, physically attacked, and finally excluded. Their story is one of the unhappiest in American history. brought to this country in the late 1840s by a missionary. One of them, Yung Wing, graduated from Yale in 1854 and became a naturalized citizen, although his citizenship was later revoked.

Most Chinese, however, immigrated to the United States originally as sojourners-immigrants who intended from the beginning to return to their native lands. They were almost exclusively males who left their families in China and came to improve their economic lot. About 90 percent of the Chinese immigrants to America came from the same region of Canton in South China. Before immigration was cut off in 1882, about 300,000 Chinese found their way to America, most of them to California.

The original attraction was gold in the California mountains, a factor that set off a rush among many immigrants of all nations. Although a large percentage of Chinese became miners, it was a difficult occupation for them because of persecution by other American miners. The white miners took Chinese claims by force, pushing the Chinese miners to less productive diggings, and continually harassed and attacked them. The state of California passed a series of discriminatory laws that reduced the Chinese to second-class status and specifically put them under legal penalties that were borne by no other group.

When the Union Pacific Railroad began construction of the western portion of its line in 1864, thousands of Chinese laborers were hired to build a railroad over the challenging western landscape. They were extremely hard workers, lived in difficult conditions with little or no complaint, and were willing to sacrifice for the sake of wages.

Although often accused by opponents of participating in "coolie" labor systems, which were illegal arrangements used in South America and the Caribbean to import Chinese workers under conditions of near slavery, most Chinese immigrants to California were individuals. There was, however, a thriving system of underground finance that allowed men in China to pledge themselves to pay back transportation loans at high rates. This was a twist on the old indentured servant and redemptioner systems, but in the skewed vision of Chinese opponents, the idea seemed somehow to threaten the American free labor market.

The center of Chinese culture in California was indisputably a small section of San Francisco that was transformed into an all-Chinese enclave known as Chinatown. Other immigrant groups also tended to cluster in city neighborhoods, but none did so with the thoroughness of the Chinese in San Francisco. Virtually all Chinese in the city lived in Chinatown, including both rich and poor, and there was never any significant movement out of the enclave as individual members of the community advanced economically-the racism of the surrounding natives made it impossible. Ironically, the separation of the Chinese was used as a weapon to attack them for exclusiveness.

Part of American suspicion was directed against what was seen as a sinister "invisible government" among the Chinese community. In truth, the Chinese relied on a system of associations known as the Six Companies, based originally on clan and village affiliations. The Six Companies supplied social services to the Chinese community, particularly newcomers, and acted as spokesmen to the outside world. The Six Companies were often confused in the minds of critics with the so-called tongs, which were completely separate criminal organizations that were also tinged by Chinese domestic revolutionary politics.

The Federal Naturalization Act of 1870 was the forerunner of a series of legal and policy decisions against the Chinese. The Act limited naturalization to whites and people of "African descent," which meant that of all the immigrants to America, only the Chinese were barred from citizenship. In effect, the Chinese were put on notice by this law that they would never be allowed to enter the society of the United States on the same footing as all others.

The economic depression of the 1870s led to even more repressive measures. As has commonly been the case, when times turn bad, a certain segment of Americans express their anxieties by turning on immigrants. As jobs dried up, the cry that cheap Chinese labor was pushing aside "good Americans" gained momentum in California. The idea was a fiction, because the Chinese amounted to less than 10 percent of the state's population and probably contributed much more economically than they withdrew.

Facts usually have little effect on such nativist hostility, however.

In 1876, a California state legislative investigation accused the Chinese of failure to satisfactorily assimilate and detailed a long list of supposed moral and intellectual inadequacies that the investigators claimed were Asian racial characteristics. During the same year, out-of-work American laborers, led by an Irish immigrant sailor named Denis Kearney, began regularly to attack Chinese neighborhoods and individual Chinese who were unlucky enough to be on the street. The attacks escalated during the following years and included several full-scale riots and instances of violence in other California towns where Chinese had come to work.

By the late 1870s, the United States government had begun to put diplomatic pressure on China to limit immigration. The efforts continued and intensified until the official treaty between the nations was modified to allow the United States to regulate entry of Chinese immigrants.

The final inequity was carried out in 1882, when the federal Chinese Exclusion Act suspended the immigration of Chinese laborers altogether. Additional laws eventually prohibited all immigration of Chinese workers and put humiliating conditions on the entry of any Chinese national into the United States. These laws marked the first time that the United States had taken action to limit or stop immigration from a foreign land. Until the Chinese Exclusion Act, the very concept of an illegal immigrant was virtually impossible. Afterward, American immigration policy would never quite be the same again, although more than 40 years lapsed before restriction clamped down on European immigrants.

The Exclusion Act also denied naturalization to Chinese in America and refused to allow Chinese to return to America if they left to visit China. The result was a warped sort of Chinese immigrant society in America (the center remained in San Francisco) made up of a large percentage of males who were cut off from their families. This "bachelor" society was characteristic of Chinese immigrant communities for decades.

The Japanese

Although initially fewer in number than the Chinese, Japanese immigrants became the target of similar anti-Asian discrimination and racially based immigration restriction. However, by the time pressure began to build on the West Coast to keep out new Japanese, Japan had become one of the major military powers in the world, after victory over the Russian Empire in 1905. It was dangerous to offend the entire nation by excluding its immigrants.

The earliest Japanese immigrants, about 30,000, had come to Hawaii in the second half of the 1880s as agricultural workers. When Hawaii was annexed by the United States in 1898, the Japanese population shifted to the West Coast mainland. Most of the Japanese of the first generation of immigrants became farmers or agricultural workers, and in some parts of California almost dominated the industry. The influx of new immigrants was mostly male farm workers.

In 1907, the U.S. government was forced to deal with the rising tide of anti-Japanese prejudice in California when the school board of San Francisco tried to segregate Japanese and Japanese American students. The insult to Japanese pride was blatant. President Theodore Roosevelt got the school board to rescind the plan, and in return he negotiated what was known as the Gentleman's Agreement with Japan. In order to avoid further friction, the Japanese imperial government agreed to stop allowing farm workers to emigrate. The agreement halted almost all immigration by Japanese males, but significant numbers of Japanese women immigrated each year until 1924, when new restriction laws barred all Japanese. The 1920 census counted 111,010 Japanese and their descendents in the United States, more than 85 percent of them living in California.

L. Edward Purcell, *CHAPTER: 3: Building a Nation Through Immigration.* Vol. 1, Immigration: Social Issues in American History, 01-16-1995.

CHAPTER 8

The Business Case for Diversity

Dr. Samuel Betances & Dr. Laura M. Torres Souder

Professor Emeritus of Sociology at Northeastern Illinois University where he taught undergraduate and graduate students for twenty years, Samuel Betances is a well known and frequent lecturer on topics of diversity, social change, gender and race relations, demographic changes, and the impact of the global economy on group relations in the U.S.A. He is also Senior Consultant with Souder, Betances, and Associates, Inc. Chicago, Illinois.

Laura Souder is the CEO/President of the very successful consulting firm of Souder, Betances and Associates, Inc. Chicago, Illinois.

Diversity initiatives must respond to multiple and ever-changing challenges in the workplace—globalization, increasing technology, a shrinking workforce, fewer males, downsizing of military installations and the ensuing displaced labor pools, the changing roles of women in the labor market, work and family issues, sexual preference, anti-discrimination legislation, greater ethnic awareness, immigration, religious beliefs, the aging workforce, and the quest for people with mental or physical disabilities to make greater contributions. These and other related factors make diversity initiatives legitimate bottom-line issues.

The interplay between all of these forces in society have a direct impact on what organizations can or cannot do. Constant change equals constant challenges for leadership. The quest to forge team members from diverse backgrounds into becoming respectful and trusting of each other is indeed of growing concern to managers and one that has direct impact on the bottom line. Customs, traditions, and media stereotypes tend to work against that goal. Diversity initiatives seek to eliminate dysfunctional personal and organizational behaviors which might frustrate efforts at developing quality relationships in the workplace. In doing so, diversity initiatives promote a wiser use of resources by strengthening the human factor in modern organizations in view of interest group agendas and demographic trends.

Brainstorming sessions which focus on how these forces are impacting a particular organization may be helpful in challenging mindsets to embrace diversity as a legitimate issue in the organization. Good planning will benefit from team reports based on the feedback from such sessions. Senior managers guiding their organizations towards a more prosperous future are challenged to create a workplace climate in which diverse interest group members feel respected, empowered, and rewarded for providing quality goods and services.

Harnessing the rainbow of the total workforce—it's diverse ways of knowing, world views, insights, passions, and talents—for the bottom line, will in fact add value to the organization and its goals. Diversity initiatives become useful as a business imperative when building quality teams is the goal of organizations. Every ounce of intelligence available to the modern organization must be harnessed. To discriminate is deadly. To be inclusive is just plain good for business. The future is screaming at us with new demographic trends which announce a new world reality in which to do business. The changing face of America requires a positive response. Part of that response is the implementation of diversity initiatives in the workplace.

For real organizational change to occur, several conditions must be met. There must be dissatisfaction with the way things are. There has to be a vision of where the organization wants to go and a process by which to get there. Insightful visionary leaders seeking a more prosperous and profitable future will embrace the challenge of change. They will work at implementing a process to connect their vision with the needs of a changing reality at home and abroad. Diversity initiatives become a useful option for them.

Nonetheless, diversity training is not *the* exclusive answer. It is not a panacea to all that challenges organizations. But in a time when everything below the neck is minimum wage, no answer or course of action which ignores diversity initiatives as a positive force for good, can be realistically pursued. Leadership must harness the rainbow of diversity. Embrace it and make it work for their organizations.

Caution! Focusing on a single issue tends to contribute to faulty assumptions about the role of diversity in the workplace. Also, be wary of putting a racial or gender face on the issue. Race and gender are factors which must be evaluated in the context of momentous changes and the lack of a common history of having white males work at par with non-traditional members at every level of the organization.

A holistic approach is best. In view of the demographic trends and interest group behavior in the larger society, the issues have more to do with how managers might create a hospitable climate which reduces dysfunctional tensions by promoting respect and productive teamwork. This will serve as a powerful incentive for employees to make their organization their employer of choice.

Comparing and contrasting Diversity Initiatives with Compliance Programs, such as Affirmative Action, Equal Opportunity, and Equal Employment Opportunity, is an essential step when making the business case for diversity. To some ideologues, diversity is defined in a negative light as "affirmative action," which when viewed as a buzzword by them, spells disaster for the workplace. Diversity initiatives must never become a twisted game focusing on what Dr. Abdin Noboa has labeled as the perverse act of counting heads rather than making heads count. However, diversity initiatives are likely to be trivialized or vilified as "perversity" by the unin-

formed, the fearful, or by those unwilling to change and who may not want to share in the responsibilities, burdens, or rewards which result from meeting organizational goals. Diversity can only equal perversity when the initiatives are ridiculed and sabotaged by influentials on the basis that such programs are branded as a process by which coercive laws and practices seek the replacement of talented white males in the workplace by a bunch of unqualified minorities.

White male bashing must not be allowed in workforce diversity training. The goal of diversity initiatives is about shaping new systems, not about demeaning groups who have benefited from past imbalances. The reason is simple. There is nothing to be gained by poisoning relationships. The goal is to heal, to build, to shape new non-racist, non-sexist, non-discriminatory systems.

There is a great need for strong persuasive voices of reason in diversity initiatives which applaud the organizations built by members of all groups, but primarily with the visible leadership of white males, while challenging those talented leaders to help build inclusive systems so that the promise of a more prosperous future for all will be realized. Simply put, we need each other. We must build coalitions of interest, not of color. Effective diversity training initiatives invite consultants to guide meaningful discussions on how to best transform systems, which may be exclusive in nature, to become empowering, inclusive, productive systems. Everyone will benefit. White males will also benefit since the good work which lies before those organizations requires the collaboration of all. This is the essential reason why, as all interest group, white males will want to exercise leadership in creating new non-racist, non-sexist, and in other ways inclusive systems in partnership with women and members of emerging majorities, (groups typically labeled as "minorities").

Women constitute the biggest source of brain power in our society today, as they continue to outnumber men, and must therefore be represented at every level of the organization. Sexism must end. Racism must also end. African Americans, together with numerous other interest groups, will reap the rewards of a non-racist system. As an interest group, they have struggled most consistently to eliminate discrimination. Their struggle has proven a blessing to every group seeking to be included, respected, and rewarded for their work. All groups, therefore, must take a strong position against racism, sexism, and all other forms of discrimination.

Effective diversity training will guide senior managers in the process of identifying barriers in the organization which frustrate the quest of achieving a balanced workforce. These barriers, once identified, must be targeted for removal. Some barriers identified by our clients in previous training sessions are immediately recognizable. Consider the feminist complaint that the "good ole boy" networking on the golf course has traditionally excluded women and those who don't have access to country club memberships from participating in a vital forum for decision making in some corporate circles. Or the complaint that there aren't any interested persons of color to fill management positions while exclusively recruiting from Ivy League colleges—how about opening recruitment efforts to include non-traditional institutions of training such as largely black colleges and universities. Then there is the familiar practice of pigeonholing employees into certain types of positions based on ethnic group, gender, or other such "identity" categories. Another example is advertising a vacancy while grooming a preferred candidate, placing that selected person in an acting capacity, and claiming nonetheless that the position is "open." Disappointment turns to deep resentment and lack of trust among hopeful employees who learn that the position was "wired," in the jargon of some organizations. Pre-selection of job candidates sabotages the hopes of employees to have a fair chance of being prepared for promotions.

The study of the cultural behavior of an organization must be embraced with vigor and honesty. Our emphasis is on the cultural behavior of the organization, not the behavior of cultural groups in the organization. Instead of sponsoring workshops which focus on the culture of underrepresented groups in organizations, diversity initiatives require that managers, as members of work teams, study the culture of the organization which keeps certain groups underrepresented. For example, have a workshop on recruitment. Explain how changing recruiting strategies might yield different results in terms of hiring talent from previous underrepresented groups. Examine how informal mentoring strategies might be augmented by formal mentoring so as to enhance the career development of women and members of emerging majorities, alongside white males in the workplace. In other words, the study of hidden rules in organizations and the normal way of doing business in the past may reveal patterns which will not suffice for creating the organizational culture useful in responding to the challenge of change. Action steps to identify and target barriers in the culture must then follow. Targeting the elimination of barriers by clearly denoting resources needed, setting timeframes for implementing new policies and practices, specifying the role of senior management, and how to measure the success of such initiatives will tie these activities to the bottom line.

The most senior executives in an organization must demonstrate their full commitment to diversity initiatives by word and deed to assure success. They must welcome and implement a curriculum which makes the business case for diversity in view of monumentous changes taking place all around us. Diversity Initiatives must not be dismissed on the grounds of a poor presentation in an awareness event of the past. Simply put, leadership cannot ignore the business case for diversity if their organizations are to develop and/or maintain a competitive advantage. Once the bottom line concerns are identified for an organization and a course of action is determined, a high powered motivational session to launch the organization's diversity initiative is in order. Buy-in by the top level decision makers and an unveiling of the plan to all employees, to obtain their commitment as well, is not only desirable but essential.

There are many resources in the marketplace which are helpful to leadership and practitioners who are interested in implementing diversity initiatives. The book by Ann Morrison, *The New Leaders*, has been the most useful in our quest for knowledge on the issues. The book *Implementing Diversity* by Marilyn Loden is also helpful and practical. Leadership should also seek input from informed members of diverse interest groups within their organization. The quest to grow from *awareness*, to *understanding*, and then to the ultimate goal of creating organizational *change* will illustrate to all stakeholders that diversity in the specific context of their particular organization, is not a fad or a response to political pressure, the erosion of sound values, or any other cynical factors. It is a useful tool by which to gain a competitive edge as we face the challenges of a new century.

The most valuable asset of any organization is its people. Diversity initiatives seek to upgrade the capacity of the workplace to recruit, retain, and promote talented people of every interest group who have ideas, ideals, intelligence, and fire in their belly to be serious about success by working with equally minded people to achieve the measurable goals of their teams. For too long in our heterogeneous society we have lived segregated lives. The media has recycled damaging stereotypes. We do not always have a balanced view of each other. Some of us belong to groups defined by their worst elements. Others by their best. Because we tend to worship with, live next to, socialize, recruit from, befriend, and marry those who are most like us, we are either indifferent, or in some cases, afraid or suspicious of those who differ from ourselves. One of the aims of diversity training is to help reduce fears. It also challenges an organization to qualify non-traditional members of the workforce along with white males, so that they can form parts of teams. The literature indicates that the best way to reduce prejudice is to create teams of people, who are equally qualified but from diverse backgrounds. They then become interdependent on each other to achieve the goals of an organization through teamwork. Without a diverse workforce, the talent war will not be won.

CLASS 6

Race: Our Most Dangerous Myth

CHAPTER 9
Racial Identity and the State:
The Dilemmas of Classification
Michael Omi
Michael Omi examines the difficulty people have in identifying themselves
within the socially constructed categories provided by the state and federal
government as well as other social organizations in the country.

CHAPTER 10
Motivations That Drive Prejudice and Discrimination:
Is the Scientific Community Really Objective
Duane Jackson
Duane Jackson's essay traces the origins of scientific racism in the U.S.A. He
draws the links between the development of the Eugenics movement to the
pseudo-science presented in the *Bell Curve*. He closes with an overview of the
challenges yet to be resolved by social scientists as the 21st century begins.

CHAPTER 9

Racial Identity and The State:
The Dilemmas of Classification

Michael Omi

Associate Professor of Asian American Studies and Ethnic Studies, Michael Omi is the author of *Racial Formation in the United States*. He teaches courses on the history of Asians in America, on Asian American politics and racial theory and politics. In 1990, he was the recipient of Berkeley's Distinguished Teaching Award. He received his Doctoral Degree from the University of California, Berkeley.

Introduction

The February 1995 *Chronicle of Higher Education* featured an article on racial classification and the sciences which highlighted an interesting dilemma facing scientists in the United States.[1] On one hand, scientists routinely use racial categories in their research and regularly make comparisons between the races with respect to health, behavior, and intelligence.[2] On the other hand, many scientists feel that racial classifications are meaningless and unscientific.[3] For example, Professor Kenneth Kennedy of Cornell University is quoted in the article as saying, "In the social sense, race is a reality. In the scientific sense, it is not."[4] It is the reality of race "in the social sense" that I want to explore by focusing on the racial categories used by the federal government, the problems associated with these categories, and their deeply political character.

My initial interest in state-defined classifications of race was inspired by a Louisiana case from the early 1980s.[5] In 1977, Susie Guillory Phipps, who was then forty-three years old, found herself in need of her birth certificate to process a passport application.[6] Believing all her life that she was White, she was stunned when a clerk at the New Orleans Division of Vital Records showed her that she was designated as "colored.[7] As Mrs. Phipps told reporters, "It shocked me. I was sick for three days.[8] The only person apparently aware of Mrs. Phipps' racial designation on her birth certificate was the mid-wife who wrote it down.[9] "I was brought up white, I married white twice.[10]

Mrs. Phipps' racial classification was assigned under an old Louisiana state law which allowed anyone with "any traceable amount" of black ancestry to be legally defined as "black."[11] According to the state's genealogical investigation, Mrs. Phipps great-great-great-great grandmother was a black slave named Margarita.[12] Given this information, state stood by the designation of "colored" on Mrs. Phipps' birth certificate.[13]

The logic of Louisiana's racial classification is consistent with what anthropologist Marvin Harris calls the principle of *hypodescent*.[14] This rule provides that any "White" person who is known to have had a black ancestor is classified as black.[15] Therein lies a particular kind of racial logic commonly deployed, that anyone with a black ancestor, however distant, is also black. Ms. Phipps sued the state of Louisiana to change her racial designation from "colored" to "White."[16] She lost.[17] In 1986, the Louisiana Supreme Court denied her motion to appeal.[18] Later that same year, the U.S.

From *Law & Inequity: A Journal of Theory and Practice*, Vol. XV, No.1, pages 7-23. Used with permission of the University of Minnesota.

Supreme Court refused to review the case and thus left standing the lower court's decision.[19]

The *Phipps* case dramatically illustrates the disjuncture between state-imposed definitions of race and how individuals perceive their own racial identity. A thorough analysis of state definitions of race reveals their deeply problematic construction and highlights the difficulty—if not impossibility—of defining and utilizing coherent and consistent categories over time. The discussion which follows examines some of the problems.

State Definitions of Race

HOW THE STATE CLASSIFIES RACE

The designation of racial categories and the determination of racial identity is no simple task. Over the last several centuries, it has provoked numerous debates in this country, including intense disputes over natural and legal rights, who could become a naturalized citizen and who could marry whom.[20]

Racial and ethnic categories in the U.S. historically have been shaped by the political and social agendas of particular times. The first U.S. census in 1790 distinguished holders of the franchise, namely White males, from the general population.[21] The practice of slavery motivated changes in categorization such as grouping blacks into free and slave populations.[22]

The current categories of racial classification were assigned and implemented by the U.S. Office of Management and Budget (OMB) in response to the anti-discriminatory and equal opportunity laws of the 1960s and 1970s.[23] Statistical Directive No. 15 (Directive 15), issued in 1977 by the OMB, fosters the creation of "compatible, nonduplicated, exchangeable racial and ethnic data by Federal agencies.[24] Directive 15 defined the basic racial and ethnic categories to be utilized by the federal government for three reporting purposes: statistical, administrative and civil rights compliance.[25]

THE PROBLEMS IN DIRECTIVE 15 CLASSIFICATIONS

An investigation of Directive 15 classifications reveals significant problems in their construction and meaning. While most of the categories rely on a concept of "original peoples," only one of the definitions is specifically racial, only one is cultural and only one relies on a notion of affiliation or community recognition.[26] There are few comparable criteria deployed across the categories. For example, Directive 15 defines a black person as one having her or his "origins in any of the black racial groups of Africa," but it does not define a White person with reference to the White racial groups of Europe, North Africa, or the Middle East.[27] Indeed "Black" is the only category which is defined with an explicit racial designator[28]—one which is quite problematic. What, we might ask, are the "black racial groups of Africa"?

Hispanics are not considered and classified as a race but as an ethnic group.[29] The Hispanic category is, in fact, the only ethnicity that the state is interested in explicitly identifying and classifying. The category is defined through cultural designators—a person of "Mexican, Puerto Rican, Cuban, Central or South American or other Spanish culture or origin.[30] In this definition, Hispanics can be of any race.[31]

The category of "American Indian or Alaskan Native" reveals another intriguing definitional issue. Individuals who are to be counted in this category not only must have their origins in any of the original peoples of North America, but must also maintain "cultural identification" through "tribal affiliation or community recognition."[32] Directive 15 does not impose that requirement of cultural identification on any of the other groups.[33]

In addition to these facially apparent problems associated with these definitions, there are cracks in this system of classification in that particular groups cannot be situated within its framework. For example, the native peoples of Central and South America do not fall within any category, and Brazilians, although South American, are not of Spanish culture or origin.[34]

CHALLENGING FEDERAL DEFINITIONS

These problems and concerns have led to a serious questioning of the existing federal standards for racial and ethnic classification. The obvious inconsistencies and omissions in the current classifications warrant analysis and may need corrections. In February 1994, I participated in a two-day workshop convened by the National Research Council at the request of the OMB.[35] The purpose of the meeting was to assess the existing racial and ethnic categories as defined in Directive 15, to isolate problems in its use as a research and administrative tool and to consider options for a revision of Directive 15.

During the sessions, we heard directly from and about different groups who were advancing political claims for recognition and change in the existing standards. Some argued for a Hispanic category which would combine race and ethnicity and be mutually exclusive of the other four race categories.[36] Groups of native Hawaiians expressed the desire to move from the category of "Asian and Pacific Islander" to "American Indian or Alaskan Native."[37] They argued that because of history and current sovereignty claims they have much more in common with other indigenous peoples than, for example, East Asians.[38] Some Arab American groups are currently lobbying for a Middle Eastern category.[39] Noting that they are now classified as White, they argue that the data Arab Americans need in order to address issues such as discrimination are not available due to the lack of a specific racial designator.[40]

Perhaps the most controversial proposal was to add a multiracial category to the next census.[41] Much of the momentum for this idea comes from school districts which have seen a dramatic rise in children of mixed race."[42] Their visible presence has led to questions regarding how to classify them for reporting and planning purposes.

Proposed changes to the existing standards, emanating from various political claims, have left some demographers and statisticians unsettled. They would prefer to remove the determination of categories from the realm of politics, and transfer it to the arena of academic research. Such a move, in their view, would allow more precise and scientifically determined categories to be constructed and utilized for administrative reporting and the collection of data.

Any attempt to frame such structured categories, however, immediately confronts a range of contradictory choices and gaps in our understanding about racial classification and identity. The following discussion surveys some of these problems.

The Problems in Racial Classification

THE CONFLICT BETWEEN STATE DEFINITIONS AND INDIVIDUAL/GROUP IDENTITIES

The first significant problem in racial classification is the gap between administrative requirements and popular consciousness. The government's interests in identifying and tracking individuals by race and ethnicity compel limitations that fail to acknowledge the nuances of racial identity in reality.

The federal, state and local agencies involved in compiling and analyzing racial and ethnic data do so with the intent to track socio-economic progress, assess health trends, and determine patterns of discrimination, well-being and life chances. Because tracking such data requires longitudinal analyses, agencies want relatively static categories which can be objectively determined. Ideal racial and ethnic categories for such purposes would be conceptually valid, exclusive and exhaustive, measurable and reliable over time. The Census Bureau and most government agencies currently uses three different questions and concepts to describe and categorize individuals: race,[43] ethnicity[44] and ancestry.[45]

Such categories contrast sharply with conceptions of race and ethnicity which recognize their dynamic nature and their "slippery" subjective indicators such as identity. Partially because of these limitations, administrative definitions may not be meaningful to the very individuals or groups they purport to represent. This is evident in Clara Rodriguez's study of Latinos which reveals a strong group rejection of the dominant mode of conceptualizing racial categories in the United States.[46] For example, the Census Bureau reports that 40% of Hispanic respondents in 1980 and 1990 answered the race and ethnicity questions "wrong." That is they failed to check both a race box and an ethnicity box.[47] In addition, it is estimated that over 97% of persons reporting in the "other race" category were Hispanic.[48]

Part of the problem lies with individual and group differences in conceptualizing race. With respect to new immigrant populations, for example, it is important to examine the shifts in racial self-identity as immigrants move from a society organized around specific concepts of race, to a new society with a different mode of conceptualization.

CHANGING SELF-IDENTIFICATION

The second significant problem in racial classification is the ever-changing character of racial identification, stemming both from changes in state definitions and from shifts in how individuals or groups identify themselves. These constant changes frustrate the needs and intentions of the government institutions that seek to clearly assign racial categories.

A fascinating example of changing self-identification is the dramatic increase in the American Indian population. The number of American Indians increased from 552,000 in 1960 to 1,959,000 in 1990—a 255% increase in thirty years.[49] This rate of increase is virtually impossible demographically, but much of the increase is explained by changes in racial self-identification. These changes are driven by shifts in attitudes toward American Indians,[50] a romanticization of the past and tangible benefits tied to American Indian identification.[51]

Researchers are likely to elicit different responses on racial and ethnic identification in different historical periods. They are also likely to elicit different responses from the same individual at different points in her or his life cycle. Given the contextual nature of racial and ethnic identification, it may be difficult or perhaps impossible to achieve the necessary reliability and consistency in time series data and analysis.

LIFE CYCLE EFFECTS

Another problem surfaces in that race is often identified by third parties whose only basis for the racial assignment is the individual's outward appearance. Since 1989 births have been categorized by the race of the mother.[52] Racial classification at death, by contrast, is designated by a third party, either a physician or funeral director.[53] This has led to a peculiar situation where a person may be born one race, and die another. In fact, studies have suggested that there is an over-assignment of deaths to the white category, a small under-assignment of deaths to the black category and significant underassignment of deaths to American Indian and Asian categories.[54]

This systematic discrepancy has led to significant errors in statistical analysis and record keep-

ing. For example, Robert Hahn, an epidemiologist at the Centers for Disease Control and Prevention, found that established infant-mortality rates for some groups are fraught with error.[55] Linking birth and death certificates, he found that the infant-mortality rates were 46.9% higher than previously reported for American Indians, 48.8% higher for Japanese Americans and 78.7% higher for Filipinos.[56] From birth to death, current systems of racial classification are arbitrary and inconsistent.

In addition to the apparent problems with existing classifications above,[57] there is also the temporal effect of evolving racial and ethnic labels. New labels come into vogue, old groups dissolve through assimilation and new groups emerge as a result of changes in civil status or patterns of immigration. Two particular historical trends have emerged as significant causes of changed racial designations: panethnicity and multiracial consciousness.

PANETHNICITY

The reorganization of old groups and the creation of new groups are features of changing political and social contexts.[58] The rise of panethnic consciousness and organization is a dramatic political development in the post-Civil Rights era.[59] Groups whose previous national or ethnic identities were quite distinct became consolidated into a single racial (or in the case of Latinos, ethnic) category.

Prior to the late 1960s, for example, there were no people who identified as "Asian American."[60] In the wake of the civil rights movement, distinct Asian ethnic groups, primarily Chinese, Japanese, Filipino and Korean Americans, began to frame and assert their "common identity" as Asian Americans.[61] This political label reflected the similarity of treatment that these groups historically encountered at the hands of state institutions and the dominant culture at large.[62] Different Asian ethnic groups had been subject to exclusionary immigration laws,[63] restrictive naturalization laws,[64] labor market segregation[65] and patterns of "ghettoization" by a polity and culture which treated all Asians as alike.

The panethnic organization of Asian Americans involved the muting of profound cultural and linguistic differences and significant historical antagonisms, which existed among the distinct nationalities and ethnic groups of Asian origin. In spite of diversity and difference, Asian American activists found the political label a crucial rallying point for raising political consciousness about the problems in Asian ethnic communities and in asserting demands on political institutions.

Panethnic formations such as this are not stable. Conflicts often occur over the precise definition and boundaries of various panethnic groups as well as their adequate representation in census counts, reapportionment debates and minority aid programs. Panethnic consciousness and organization are, to a large extent, situationally and strategically determined. There are times when it is advantageous to be in a panethnic bloc, and times when it is seen as more desirable to mobilize along particular ethnic lines.

Lumping various groups together may result in a flattening of important distinctions we, as researchers and policy makers, may wish to discern and analyze. Some groups may "all look alike," but they are not homogeneous. How meaningful, for example, is an Asian American category for analysis when both Japanese and Laotian Americans are subsumed under it? Such categorization ignores significant differences between these two groups of people.[66] The conflation of important "differences" is a hazard with the construction and use of particular categories.

MULTIRACIAL IDENTIFICATION

An important emerging issue is the inability of existing state definitions to encompass people of "mixed racial descent." While the number of such individuals is unclear and contingent on self-definition, the 1990 Census counted two million children under the age of eighteen whose parents were of different races.[67]

In response to these demographic changes, there has been a concerted effort from school boards and organizations such as Project RACE (Reclassify All Children Equally) to add a "multiracial" category to the Census.[68] This proposal has been opposed by many civil rights organizations.[69] Some groups fear a reduction in their numbers[70] and worry that such a multiracial category would spur debates regarding the protected status of groups and individuals.[71] According to the Census Bureau, 75% percent of those who currently identify themselves as black could identify themselves as multiracial.[72] Though it is impossible to know whether these qualifying people

would so identify, complex issues of identity would emerge from the institutionalization of a multiracial category.[73]

The debate over a multiracial category reveals an intriguing aspect about how we conceptualize race. The very terms "mixed race" or "multiracial" imply the existence of "pure" and distinct races. Drawing attention to the socially constructed nature of this category and the meanings attached to it reveals the inherent fluidity of our concepts of race.

THE SHIFTING MEANING OF RACIAL/ETHNIC IDENTIFICATION FOR WHITE AMERICANS

The meaning of racial/ethnic identification for specific groups and individuals varies enormously. Recent research on White Americans suggest that they do not experience their ethnicity as a definitive aspect of their social identity.[74] Rather, they perceive it dimly and irregularly, picking and choosing among its varied strands that allows them to exercise—as sociologist Mary Waters suggests in her study—an "ethnic option."[75] Waters found that ethnicity was flexible, symbolic and voluntary for her White respondents in ways that they were not for non-Whites.[76]

Jeffrey Passel's analysis of the open-ended question on ancestry or descent which first appeared in the 1980 Census underscores the fluid nature of white ethnic identification.[77] The question, "What is this person's ancestry?" was followed by an open-ended, write-in box. Below the box a group of more than a dozen options were listed. What is intriguing is that the examples provided below the question had a dramatic influence on responses. For example, in 1980 English was listed as an option but was dropped in 1990.[78] As a result, the English population of the United States declined by 34%.[79] French was listed in 1980 and when dropped in 1990, the French population fell by 20%.[80] By contrast, the Cajun population grew by more than 6,000% between 1980 and 1990 as a result of the group's addition to the 1990 set of examples.[81]

The loose affiliation with specific European ethnicities does not necessarily suggest the demise of any clear group consciousness and identity. The twilight of European ethnicity may in fact signal the growth of a White racial identity. In an increasingly diverse workplace and society Whites are increasingly wondering what it means to be "White." What was previously a transparent and "natural" category has now been rendered problematic as Whites experience a profound racialization.

The racialization process for Whites is very evident on many university campuses as White students encounter a heightened awareness of race which calls their own identity into question. Interviews with White students at the University of California-Berkeley produced responses such as these:[82]

> Many whites don't feel like they have an ethnic identity at all and I pretty much feel that way too. It's not something that bothers me tremendously but I think that maybe I could be missing something that other people have, that I am not experiencing.[83]

> Being white means that you're less likely to get financial aid . . . . It means that there are all sorts of tutoring groups and special programs that you can't get into, because you're not a minority.[84]

> If you want to go with the stereotypes. Asians are the smart people, the Blacks are great athletes, what is white? We're just here. We're the oppressors of the nation.[85]

Here we see many of the themes and dilemmas of White identity in the current period: the absence of a clear culture and identity, the perceived disadvantages of being White with respect to the distribution of resources and the stigma of being perceived as the oppressors of the nation. Such comments underscore the new problematic meanings attached to the category of White. The debates about Whiteness will deepen in the years to come.

Assigning Race: The Debate's Meaning for Social Research and Social Policy

In the midst of all of this uncertainty, however, there is one indisputable conclusion: state definitions of race have inordinately shaped the discourse of race in the United States. Originally conceived solely for the use of federal agencies, Directive 15 has become the de facto standard for state and local agencies, the private and nonprofit sectors, and the research community. Social scientists use the Directive 15 categories because they are the data codings that are available.

Among scholars there is a continuous temptation to think of race as an *essence*, as something fixed, concrete and objective. There is also an opposite temptation: to imagine race as a mere *illusion*, a purely ideological construct which masks some other more fundamental division, such as class.

Much of sociological research, though firmly committed to a social as opposed to biological interpretation of race, nevertheless slips into a kind of objectivism about racial identity and racial meaning. There is a marked tendency to treat race as an independent variable and to downplay its own variability and historically contingent character. Thus, sociologists can correlate race and residential patterns, race and crime, as well as race and intelligence (as *The Bell Curve*[86] controversy[87] dramatically reminds us), without problematizing the concept of race itself.

There is no discussion among scholars about the constantly shifting parameters through which race is considered—how group interests are conceived, status is ascribed, agency is attained and roles performed. Although abstractly acknowledged to be a socio-historical construct, race in practice is often treated as an objective fact: one simply *is* one's race.

Sociologists have debated the validity of race and have questioned whether to eliminate the concept, scale it back in usage to specific and verifiable applications, or leave it alone. David Decker argues that a proper sociological protocol requires that:

> [T]he use of race be defined explicitly when it is used in research so that it is clear whether the term is being used to refer to a mythical but perceived relationship between superficial anatomical characteristics and specific social groups, or pointing to patterns and processes of discrimination, or to the history of the use and abuse of the term in human societies. It should not be used in a haphazard manner to seek correlates between race as a variable and other variables. It should not be used when researchers have not explained how and why the concept has been defined and is being used.[88]

As an example, Decker states that there is little basis for presenting criminal arrest rates by race without explicitly explaining the meaning of race.[89] Is race being used to indicate the inequity of arrest procedures? Or is it being used to show how processes of racial discrimination and its socio-economic consequences have an impact upon the likelihood of criminal involvement? Or is it suggesting that some groups are by genes or culture more predisposed to criminal activity?

A few central questions continue to haunt policy-oriented research: What is it that we are trying achieve in defining racial and ethnic categories? What do we want to know and why? The federal government is currently grappling with these questions.

Some political conservatives have seized upon the difficulty of establishing coherent racial categories as an excuse to call for the abolition of all racial classification and record keeping.[90] Such a move, they argue, would save federal dollars and minimize racial/ethnic distinctiveness, consciousness and divisive politics. Yet accurate racial classification and record keeping is essential to systematically track patterns of discrimination and to gather data useful for evaluating policy with respect to racial inequality.[91]

Other social scientists and statisticians want to retain a system of classification, but are arguing for categories which are conceptually valid, exclusive and exhaustive, measurable and reliable over time. The discussion above, however, illustrates the problems in defining and maintaining such an "objective" system of classification.

Race and ethnicity will continue to defy our best efforts to establish coherent definitions over time. The real world is messy with no clear answers. Nothing demonstrates this convolution better than the social construction of racial and ethnic categories.

Conclusion

The strange and twisted history of the classification of Asian Indians in the United States provides an instructive note in conclusion. During and after the peak years of immigration, Asian Indians were referred to and classified as "Hindu" though the clear majority of them were Sikh. In *United States v. B.S. Thind*,[92] the U.S. Supreme Court held that Thind, as a native of India, was indeed "Caucasian," but he was not "White" and therefore was ineligible to become a naturalized citizen.[93] It may be true," the Court declared, "that the blond Scandinavian and the brown Hindu have a common ancestor in the dim reaches of antiquity, but the average man knows perfectly well that there are unmistakable and profound differences between them today."[94]

Asian Indians' status was revised after World War II when they were allowed to naturalize as a consequence of the favorable postwar environment.[95] The Asian Indians' classification story, however, further demonstrates the problems associated with rigid classification efforts. In the post-Civil Rights era, Asian Indian leaders sought to change their classification in order to seek "minority" group status.[96] The 1980 Census added the category "Asian Indian" to include immigrants from India and their descendants.[97] Currently, young Asian Indian activists prefer the term "South Asian" in order foster panethnic identification with those from Pakistan and Bangladesh among other countries.

The point of this discussion is that racial and ethnic categories are often the effects of political interpretation and struggle and that those categories in turn have political effects. This understanding is crucial for the ongoing debates around the federal standards for racial and ethnic classification.

Endnotes

1. David L. Wheeler, *A Growing Number of Scientists Reject the Concept of Race*, CHRON. HIGHER EDUC., Feb. 17, 1995, at A8.

2. *Id.* at A8.

3. *Id.*

4. *Id.* at A15. Professor Kennedy's view is shared by many scientists who believe that there are no meaningful biological differences between members of different races. In a social context, however, racial differences are often dramatic.

5. Doe v. Department of Health and Human Resources, 479 So. 2d 369 (La. Ct. App. 1985).

6. Calvin Trillin, *American Chronicles: Black or White*, NEW YORKER, Apr. 14, 1986, at 62 (recounting the details of Ms. Phipps' experience).

7. *Id.* at 62.

8. *Id.*

9. *Id.* at 63.

10. *Id.*

11. *Id.* In 1970, the classification was changed to require a person with more than 1/32 black blood to be legally defined as "black." *Id.* The 1970 statute read, in relevant part:

> In signifying race, a person having one thirty-second or less of Negro blood shall not be deemed, described, or designated by any public official in the state of Louisiana as 'colored,' a 'mulatto,' a 'black,' a 'Negro,' a 'griffe,' an 'Afro-American,' a 'quadroon,' a 'mestizo,' a 'colored person,' or a 'person of color.'

Doe v. Department of Health and Human Resources, 479 So. 2d 369 (La. Ct. App. 1985) (quoting LA. REV. STAT. 42:267). This statute was repealed in 1983. Trillin, *supra* note 6, at 63.

12 *Id.* at 71.

13. After complicated calculations, the state investigator was ready to prove Ms. Phipps was actually 5/32 black. *Id.* at 76.

14. MARVIN HARRIS, PATTERNS OF RACE IN THE AMERICAS 56 (1964).

15. *Id.* Brian Bégué, Ms. Phipps' attorney also classifies this type of thinking as an issue of denial of equal protection. "If you're a little bit black, you're black. If you're a little bit white, you're still black." Trillin, *supra* note 6, at 78.

16. Doe v. Department of Health and Human Resources, 479 So. 2d 369 (La. Ct. App. 1985).

17. *Id.* at 371. The Louisiana Court of Appeals affirmed the trial court's decision which held that the defendant state officers had no legal duty to alter the birth certificates unless the appellant could show that white was the correct racial designation. *Id.* at 372. The court stated, "[t]he voluminous record before us contains fascinating evidence of race as a matter of physical appearance, heredity, self-perception, community recognition, and cultural bias . . . . The intriguing . . . issues raised by this evidence belie simple legal questions—the only questions courts of law are authorized, or indeed able, to answer." *Id.* The court acknowledged that the repealed statute which provided the original basis for the racial classification "was based upon wholly irrational and scientifically insupportable foundations." *Id.* at 372. Nonetheless, the court also recognized that the Louisiana Supreme Court had found the statute constitutional. *Id.* at 373 (Armstrong, J., concurring in part, dissenting in part) (citing State *ex rel.* Plaia v. Louisiana Bd. of

Health, 296 So. 2d 809 (La. 1974)). The court concluded, "[w]hile our present opinion should not be interpreted to imply that we are bound today by social and cultural precedent, we are nonetheless bound by legal precedent." *Id.* at 372.

18. Doe v. Department of Health and Human Resources, 485 So. 2d 60 (La. 1986).

19. Doe v. Department of Health and Human Resources, 479 U.S. 1002 (1986) (dismissing appeal for want of a substantial federal question).

20. It was not until 1967 that all state anti-miscegenation laws were ruled unconstitutional. *See* Loving v. Virginia, 388 U.S. 1 (1967).

21. COMMISSION OF BEHAVIOR AND SOC. SCIENCES AND EDUC., COMMITTEE ON NAT'L STATISTICS, SPOTLIGHT ON HETEROGENEITY: THE FEDERAL STANDARDS FOR RACIAL AND ETHNIC CLASSIFICATION 5 (Barry Edmonston et al. eds., 1996) [hereinafter SPOTLIGHT ON HETEROGENEITY]. This first census was largely concerned with political apportionment and taxation. In addition to noting slaves, American Indians were counted separately for taxation purposes. *Id.* The census distinguished U.S. inhabitants by five classes: "[1] Free white Males of sixteen years and upwards, including heads of families; [2] Free white Males under sixteen years; [3] Free white Females including heads of families; [4] All other free persons; [5] Slaves." CENSUS OF 1790, *reprinted in* FIRST CENSUS OF THE U.S., 1790, No. 1 (1990).

22. *See* SPOTLIGHT ON HETEROGENEITY, *supra* note 21, at 5. The editors concluded that racial and ethnic categorizations "have always been closely associated with the politics and the social agendas of the times. . . ." *Id.*

23. As federal and state governments enact anti-discrimination and equal opportunity laws, governmental determination of minority status and the collection of racial and ethnic data becomes essential. *Id.* at 6. An example of these enactments includes the Civil Rights Act of 1964, 42 U.S.C. § 2000d (1964), which provides that no person may, "on ground of race, color, or national origin, be excluded from participation in, or denied the benefits of . . . any program receiving federal financial assistance." *Id.* Additionally, the Equal Opportunity Act, 42 U.S.C.§ 2000e (1964), makes it an unlawful employment practice to discriminate on the basis of "race, color . . . or national origin." *Id.* § 2000e-2(a)(1).

24. OFFICE OF MANAGEMENT AND BUDGET, STATISTICAL DIRECTIVE NO. 15 (May 12, 1977) [hereinafter DIRECTIVE 15]. Directive 15, entitled "Race and

Ethnic Standards for Federal Statistics and Administrative Reporting," provides:

1. Definitions

   The basic racial and ethnic categories for Federal Statistics and program administrative reporting are defined as follows:

   a. *American Indian or Alaskan Native.* A person having origins in any of the original peoples of North America, and who maintains cultural identification through tribal affiliation or community recognition.

   b. *Asian or Pacific Islander.* A person having origins in any of the original peoples of the Far East, Southeast Asia, the Indian subcontinent, or the Pacific Islands. This area includes, for example, China, India, Japan, Korea, the Philippine Islands, and Samoa.

   c. *Black.* A person having origins in any of the black racial groups of Africa.

   d. A person of Mexican, Puerto Rican, Cuban, Central or South American or other Spanish culture or origin, regardless of race.

   e. *White.* A person having origins in any of the original peoples of Europe, North Africa, or the Middle East.

25. *Id.*

26. *Id.*

27. *Id.*

28. *Id.*

29. *Id.*

30. *Id.*

31. Existing data collection efforts tend to assume that persons of Hispanic ethnicity are either black or white, rendering affiliations with other racial categories nonexistent. *See, e.g.,* SPOTLIGHT ON HETEROGENEITY, *supra* note 21, at 28.

32. DIRECTIVE 15, *supra* note 24.

33. *Id.*

34. SPOTLIGHT ON HETEROGENEITY *supra* note 21, at 25.

35. The workshop is summarized in SPOTLIGHT ON HETEROGENEITY, *supra* note 21.

36. *Id.* at 28.

37. *Id.* at 31. This suggestion was met with resistance at the workshop from some groups representing American Indians. While native Hawaiians may have more cultural or social experiences in common with American Indians as native people in land taken by Americans, these groups argued that the legal relationship between the U.S. and American Indians differs significantly from that of the U.S. and Hawaiians. *Id.* The rationale for including native Hawaiians with American Indians could also be extended to members of groups currently classified under "Asian and Pacific Islander." The inclusion of native Hawaiians and possibly other Pacific Islanders in a new "Indigenous People" category is an example of a possible new panethnic formation and demonstrates some of the conflicts related to the concept. *See* discussion *infra* notes 57–66 and accompanying text.

38. *Id.* at 31.

39. *Id.* at 33. A "Middle East" or "Arab American" panethnic identity currently is being encouraged by some groups to aid in the fight against discrimination and to fill other special needs of Arab Americans, totaling over one million at the time of the 1990 Census. *Id.* The issuance of new racial categories in the census, however, is done cautiously, taking size, social, economic and legal factors into consideration. *Id.*

40. *Id.*

41. *Id.* at 38.

42. *Id.* at 13.

43. The 1990 Census asked the respondent to fill in one circle indicating the race that person considered himself or herself to be. BUREAU OF THE CENSUS, OFFICIAL 1990 U.S. CENSUS FORM (1990). There were sixteen racial categories as options: White, Black or Negro, Indian (American), Eskimo, Aleut, one of the identified Asian or Pacific Islander groups (Chinese, Filipino, Hawaiian, Korean, Vietnamese, Japanese, Asian Indian, Samoan, or Guamanian), other Asian or Pacific Islander, or other race. *Id.* at 2. American Indians were also asked to note their enrolled or principal tribe. *Id.*

44. The ethnicity question asked whether the person was of Spanish/Hispanic origin. *Id.* If so, the respondent was asked to note one of three categories: Mexican, Mexican-American, Chicano; Puerto Rican, Cuban; or other Spanish/Hispanic. *Id.*

45. The ancestry question was open-ended with no precoded categories, but listed examples such as German, Italian and Afro-American. BUREAU OF THE CENSUS, 1990 CENSUS OF POPULATION F-7 (1993). In 1980, the question asked, "What is this person's ancestry?" and in 1990 asked, "What is this person's ancestry or ethnic origin?" SPOTLIGHT ON HETEROGENEITY, *supra* note 21, at 22. The ancestry question is given only on "long form" questions,

which are administered to one-sixth of the population. *Id.* at 21.

46. Clara E. Rodriguez, *Race, Culture, and Latino "Otherness" in the 1980 Census*, 73 Soc. Sci. Q. 930, 930 (1992).

47. Spotlight on Heterogeneity, *supra* note 21, at 21. Approximately 9.8 million people reported identified as "Other race." *Id. See* also Rodriguez, *supra* note 46, at 932.

46. "In no state—including Hawaii—did more than 2 percent of the non-Hispanic population indicate that they were of 'other race.'" *Id.*

49. Jeffrey S. Passel, Racial and Ethnic Differentiation in the United States: Comments and Observations, Address at the Workshop on Race and Ethnicity Classification, 17 (Feb. 17–18, 1994) (transcript on file with *Law and Inequality: A Journal of Theory and Practice*). In addition to the rise in self-identified American Indians, the number of Americans claiming American Indian ancestry increased from 6.8 million in 1980 to 8.8 million in 1990. *Id.*

50. *Id.*

51. *Id.*

52. Robert A. Hahn et al., *Inconsistencies in Coding of Race and Ethnicity Between Birth and Death in US Infants*, 267 JAMA 259, 260 (1992). A somewhat complex system was used prior to 1989. In the previous system, newborns were classified according to the race of the parents, if both were the same race; by the race of the non-white parent, if one parent was white and the other was not; and if both parents were non-white, the baby was classified according to the race of the father (except if one parent was Hawaiian, in which case, the baby was classified as Hawaiian). Spotlight on Heterogeneity, *supra* note 21, at 26 n.6 (citing National Ctr. for Health Statistics, U.S. Dep't of Health and Human Serv., Vital and Health Statistics 21 (1995).

53. Hahn, *supra* note 52, at 260. Racial classification at death typically is assigned by the person or official who fills out the death certificate. Often this classification is based on the statements of the next of kin.

54. *Id.* at 261. Whites were over-assigned at death by 2.5%, while blacks were under-assigned by 1.9% and Filipinos were underassigned 44.5%.

55. *Id.* at 262.

56. *Id.* at 261.

57. *See supra* notes 24–42 and accompanying text (discussing OMB's Directive 15 which set guidelines for racial classifications by the federal government).

58. *See generally* David Lopez & Yen Le Espiritu, *Panethnicity in the United States: A Theoretical Framework*, 13 Ethnic & Racial Stud. 198 (1990) (discussing the historical process of panethnic association).

59. *Id.* at 198 ("[P]anethnicity . . . is an essential part of ethnic change.").

60. *See* Yen Le Espiritu, Asian American Panethnicity: Bridging Institutions and Identities 19–20 (1992) ("[I]mmigrants from Asian countries did not think of themselves as Asians.").

61. *Id.*

62. *See id.* at 14.

63. *Id.* at 19.

64. *Id.* at 54.

65. *Id.* at 10.

66. Among Japanese Americans, only 28.4% are foreign born, the median family income is 137% of the national average, the poverty rate is 4.2%, and 55.9% speak English at home exclusively. At the same time, among Laotians, 93.7% are foreign-born, the median family income is 26% of the national average, the poverty rate is 67.2% and 3.4% speak English at home exclusively. Bureau of the Census, U.S. Dep't of Commerce, We, the Asian and Pacific Islander Americans 11–16 (1988).

67. Michael Marriott, *Multiracial Americans Ready to Claim Their Own Identity*, N.Y. Times, July 20, 1996, at Y1.

68. Linda Mathews, *More Than Identity Rides on a New Racial Category*, N.Y. Times, July 6, 1996, at Y1.

69. *See, e.g.,* Raul Yzaguirre, *Multiracial Census Category Would Undercount Hispanics*, (July 10, 1996), press release distributed by the Progressive Media Project, Madison, Wisconsin, (on file with *Law & Inequality: A Journal of Theory & Practice*) Yzaguirre argues that a multiracial category would lead to inaccurate data collection and undermine the data's purpose of profiling the economic and social status of groups of people who have something in common.

70. Mathews, *supra* note 68, at Y1.

71. "Clear and consistent federal data collection on race and ethnic groups has gone a long way in ensuring civil rights, due-process protections and equal allocation of federal resources to minority groups and economically disadvantaged commu-

nities." Yzaguirre, *supra* note 69; *see also* Mathews, *supra* note 68, at Y1.

72. Lawrence Wright, *One Drop of Blood*, NEW YORKER, July 25, 1994, at 46, 48.

73. For a detailed discussion of this debate, see Wright, *supra* note 72.

74. See infra notes 75–85 and accompanying text.

75. *See generally,* MARY C. WATERS, ETHNIC OPTIONS: CHOOSING IDENTITIES IN AMERICA (1990) (analyzing socioeconomic differences based on ethnicity as reported in the 1980 census).

76. *Id.* at 147–50.

77. *See* Passel, *supra* note 49, at 21.

78. *Id.* at 21.

79. *Id.*

80. *Id.*

81. *Id.*

82. INSTITUTE FOR THE STUDY OF SOC. CHANGE, THE DIVERSITY PROJECT: THE FINAL REPORT 37 (1991).

83. *Id.*

84. *Id.*

85. *Id.*

86. RICHARD J. HERRNSTEIN & CHARLES MURRAY, THE BELL CURVE: INTELLIGENCE AND CLASS STRUCTURE IN AMERICAN LIFE (1994). This book created a storm of controversy by arguing that intelligence is largely a genetic trait, and that significant differences in I.Q. scores exist between racial or ethnic groups and between social classes. The policy implications are that most forms of social intervention to raise I.Q. scores are doomed to fail.

87. *See generally* THE BELL CURVE DEBATE: HISTORY, DOCUMENTS, OPINIONS (Russell Jacoby & Naomi Glauberman eds., 1995); THE BELL CURVE WARS: RACE, INTELLIGENCE, AND THE FUTURE OF AMERICA (Steven Fraser ed., 1995). Both works examine the concept of intelligence in detail, repudiate the claim that it is genetically inherited and stress the social context in which racial and class differences in intelligence and economic performance should be considered.

88. David L. Decker, The Use of Race in Social Research 13 (1994) (unpublished paper presented at the 65th Annual Pacific Sociological Association Meeting, San Diego, Cal., April 12–17, 1994) (on file with *Law & Inequality: A Journal of Theory & Practice*).

89. *Id.* at 13–14.

90. *See, e.g.* Clint Bolick, *Discriminating Liberals*, N.Y. TIMES, May 6, 1996, at A15; *Black? White? Asian? Why Not American?* GREENSBORO NEWS & REC., Jul. 10, 1994, at F2.

91. *"Let's Keep Black Folks in the Dark": Proposed Restrictions on Collecting Census Information*, 10 J. BLACKS HIGHER EDUC. 20, 20, (Winter 1995/1996).

92. 261 U.S. 204 (1923).

93. *Id.* at 213.

94. *Id.* at 209.

95. Sucheta Mazumbar, *Race and Racism: South Asians in the United States, in* FRONTIERS OF ASIAN AM. STUD. 26, 30 (1989).

96. *Id.* at 35.

97. BUREAU OF THE CENSUS, OFFICIAL 1980 U.S. CENSUS FORM (1980).

Motivations that Drive Prejudice and Discrimination: Is the Scientific Community Really Objective?

Duane M. Jackson

Chair of the Department of Psychology at Morehouse College, Duane Jackson is a graduate of the University of Illinois' Comparative Psychology and Behavior-Genetics program. His research and publications focus on various aspects of animal behavior, including relationships between learning and memory. He is a member of the Board of Governors for the National Conference on Undergraduate Research. As a teacher and scientist he is interested in incorporating multicultural perspectives into the teaching of science and scientific research.

We are taught that science, unlike religion and philosophy, is based on empirical evidence, that science is a dynamic process and is self-correcting. Existing theories are constantly being modified or abandoned in the face of new evidence. But what truly sets science apart from other disciplines is **objectivity**. As an African American scientist and a student of history, I do not question the objectivity of science as a discipline, but science is done by individuals, and I question the objectivity of scientists and the scientific community. Prejudice (perceptions) and discrimination (actions based on prejudice) have prevented the scientific community from being objective. I will examine the historical roots of this discrimination in science—scientific racism and the eugenics movement, race, intelligence and the IQ controversy, the misuse of heritability, and the inability of the field of psychology to deal with the issue of race.

When we look for motives behind discrimination and prejudice in science, we see three types of individuals emerge: the don't-know, the don't-want-to-know, and the know-and-will-not-accept. The three types are driven by prejudice but the latter two are also driven by discrimination. Individuals who fall into the don't-know category are simply unaware of the accomplishments and contributions that African Americans have made in science. Don't-want-to-know individuals believe African Americans cannot make contributions in science, in part because such accomplishments undermine the don't-want-to-know type's belief in themselves. Individuals who know-but-will-not-accept are the most dangerous of the three, however, since they will attempt to discredit, block, or conceal the truth about the actual scientific contributions African Americans have made.

Three African American Scientists

When I gave a talk, titled "Carver, Just, and Turner: Scientists Against the Odds," at a predominantly European American institution during Black History Month several years ago, I began my paper by asking the audience if they knew who George Washington Carver, Ernest Everett Just, and Charles Turner were. The majority of the audience were aware of Carver, but only a few African Americans knew of Just, and no one in the audience had ever heard of Turner. These three

Reprinted by permission of the author.

men had several things in common. They were all African Americans born in the 19th century who spent part of their careers teaching and doing research in Historically Black Colleges (HBCs).

Just taught at Howard University in Washington D.C., Carver taught at Tuskegee Institute (now Tuskegee University) in Alabama; and Turner taught at Clark University (now Clark-Atlanta University) in Atlanta. Being 19th-century African Americans at HBCs worked against them since HBCs had far fewer resources than their European American counterparts. Further, being educated and intellectual African Americans in the 19th century presented a problem: they were not supposed to exist. That they did challenged the very foundation of the European American belief that African Americans were intellectually and socially inferior.

Just and Turner spent most of their lives in frustration. Both Just and Turner received their doctorates from the University of Chicago. As noted above, Just taught at Howard University; he spent twenty years during the summer doing research at Woods Hole Marine Biology Laboratory in Woods Hole. Massachusetts. Known worldwide, this laboratory has attracted scientists and students to pursue research in the areas of biology, chemistry, physics, and geology. Just's research on cell membrane activity demonstrated that the cell's cytoplasm and ectoplasm are equally important as the nucleus for heredity. Just was prolific: he wrote two books and over sixty articles. Though he was respected and honored in the scientific capitals of Europe, he received little recognition for his accomplishments in the United States. Because of racial prejudice and discrimination in the scientific community in the United States, he spent the last ten years of his life in voluntary exile in Europe.

Charles Turner, the first African American animal behaviorist, published over fifty papers. His first, "Psychological notes upon the gallery spider" (1892a) published in 1892, appears to be the first published paper in psychology written by an African American. It is believed, but difficult to document, that his paper, "A few characteristics of the avian brain," published in Science (1892b) was the first paper by an African American published in that highly respected scientific journal. Some of his work was published by T. C. Schneirla and E. L. Thorndike, two eminent scientists of the time

who initiated detailed laboratory studies in insect (Schneirla) and animal learning (Thorndike).

Convinced that education was the key to overcoming prejudice, Turner developed an argument drawing from comparative psychology and a comparative study of history.

> Among men . . ., dissimilarity of minds is a more potent factor in causing prejudice than unlikeness of physiognomy. . . . [T]he new Southerner is prejudiced against the new Negro because the new Negro is very unlike him. He does not know that a similar education and a like environment have made the new Negro and himself alike in everything except color and features. (1902, pp. 163–164)

He goes further to suggest the problem was that "the white trash and the vagrant Negro form a wedge separating the new Southerner from the new Negro so completely that they cannot know each other" (1902, p. 164). He later suggested that the only way to overcome this was to transform the white trash and the vagrant Negro into new Southerners and new Negroes through education. But we shall see that traditional education is not enough to cover some prejudice and discrimination; in fact, in some ways, traditional education has actually perpetuated these problems.

This is evident when men of "science" such as Jensen (1969). Herrnstein (1973), Rushton, (1988), and Herrnstein and Murray (1994) in their recently published book, The Bell Curve, propose that genetic differences exist among the races and that these differences create inequalities among the races in regard to behaviors from intelligence to criminality. The educational system has either ignored or, in many cases, been inadequate in educating students about the role genes play in behavior and about the interaction between genes and the environment.

Turner's dream of eventually having a position at a major European American research institution never materialized. He spent his last years as a professor of biology and psychology at Sumner High School and Teacher College in St. Louis where his duties included collecting meal tickets at the school cafeteria.

Carver, Just, and Turner all made major contributions in science. Why then is Carver remembered and Just and Turner forgotten? How was Carver able to gain, to some degree, the respect and recognition of the scientific community for his accomplishments? Several factors could account for this. First, Carver was raised by European Americans. He never knew his father, and his mother disappeared when he was an infant. He was adopted by his former slave master. Additionally Carver, unlike Turner and Just, received the majority of his primary and secondary education from European Americans. Also, Carver taught at an HBC that was an industrial and agricultural school, while Turner and Just taught at HBCs that were liberal arts institutions. Teaching African Americans to be farmers and factory workers was more palatable to the European American community than teaching African Americans to be lawyers, doctors, and scientists.

Carver's research was applied, while Just's and Turner's work was for the most part theoretical. Carver's research on the peanut was far easier to grasp than Just's research on the internal workings of cells and Turner's research on the cognitive abilities of insects. It may have been far easier to accept an African American man doing applied rather than theoretical research.

Finally, however, I propose that the most important factor helping Carver gain some acceptance by the European American scientific community was his political activism. Carver had seen and experienced the brutality of racism, but he had been raised and taught by European Americans. This created a dilemma. He attempted to resolve this conflict by working for racial harmony. He was very active on the Commission on Interracial Cooperation and with the YMCA. Despite all of this, however, even Carver never received full recognition for his accomplishments.

The Eugenics Movement and the Roots of Scientific Racism

The eugenics movement attempted to legitimize racism under the guise of science and served as a foundation for scientific racism. Allen Chase defines scientific racism as "the creation and employment of a body of legitimately scientific, or patently pseudoscientific data as rationales for the preservation of poverty, inequality of opportunity for upward mobility and related regressive social arrangements" (1977, p. 72). According to Chase, during its conception, scientific racism was not concerned much with racial or cultural differences. Although it was anti-Semitic, anti-Catholic, and white supremacist, it was primarily concerned with profit. The founding father of scientific racism. Thomas Malthus, laid out the purpose of scientific racism in 1826: to maximize profits and to minimize taxes on those profits. Malthus also stated in *An Essay on the Principle of Population* (1826) that the state is not obligated to support the poor.

The eugenics movement, founded by Francis Galton, guaranteed a future for scientific racism. Galton (1869) coined the word *eugenics* from the Greek word *eugenes*, meaning well born. The primary purpose of the movement was to improve the races by boosting the birthrate of the "well born" and decreasing the birthrate of the less well born. The eugenics movement has a long history of racism and its doctrines have been used to justify racist ideologies. Galton, in 1869, stated that black people were inferior to the lowest of whites and he went further to state, without empirical evidence, ". . . that the average intellectual standard of the negro [sic] race is some two grades below our own" (p. 327).

The eugenics movement had an impact on immigration and sterilization laws in the United States during the early part of this century. President Theodore Roosevelt, who was greatly influenced by the eugenics movement, wrote a letter on January 14, 1913 to the Committee to Study and to Report on the Best Practical Means of Cutting Off the Defective Germ-Plasm in the American Population, a committee started by the American Breeders Association's Eugenics Section. Roosevelt stated:

> It is obvious that if in the future racial qualities are to be improved, the improving must be wrought mainly by favoring the fecundity of the worthy types. . . . At present, we do just the reverse. There is no check to the fecundity of those who are subordinate. . . . (cited in Chase, 1977, p. 15)

The eugenics movement was most fully exploited by Nazi Germany. Its doctrine was perfect for a regime that sought to rule the world by breeding a "master race." The eugenics movement gave scientific justification for breeding programs, the creation of Nazi Eugenics Court, and the extermination of an entire "race." The German

Sterilization Act of 1933, which was enforced by the Nazi Eugenics Court, was based on the Model Eugenical Sterilization Law written by Harry L. Laughlin (1922) at the Eugenics Record Office of Cold Spring Harbor in New York.

Dr. Lothrop Stoddard, an American eugenicist, who was widely read by Hitler's closest advisors, went to Germany, met with Hitler, and sat on the Eugenics Court. Stoddard stated in his book, *Into the darkness: Nazi Germany today:* "... once the jews [sic] and other inferior stocks were annihilated, the Nazi state would be able to concern itself with the improvements within racial stock that are recognized everywhere as constituting the modern science of eugenics, or racial betterment" (1940, p. 189). Eugenics was interwoven into the very fabric of the Nazi creed. Although the Nazi Third Reich fell almost fifty years ago, we have seen in the nineties in Eastern Europe similar atrocities committed in the name of "ethnic cleansing."

The Search for the Genetic Basis of Intelligence
The Race-Intelligence Controversy

The question as to whether African Americans as a group are genetically inferior to European Americans in regard to intelligence is like a vampire. This question keeps rising out of the grave, and no one seems to have the wooden stake to lay this question to an eternal rest. The notion that different ethnic groups were different in regard to intelligence has its roots in Galton's 1869 book, *Hereditary Genius.* As the title implies, Galton believed that intelligence was inherited, although he had no scientific basis for this conclusion: The test that Galton used to measure intelligence lacked reliability as well as validity, and genetics was not a science until the triple rediscovery of Mendel's work in 1990 (Hirsch, 1982, p. 1).

The first intelligence test to demonstrate reliability and validity (validity in regard to academic performance) was developed by Alfred Binet in 1905. The French government commissioned Binet to construct a test to identify students who had low academic aptitudes. Unfortunately, this test, which was designed to help educators identify students with learning disabilities, has over time become synonymous with intelligence testing. The Americanized version, the Stanford-Binet, was published by Lewis Terman (1916) in a book titled *The Measurement of Intelligence.*

Many of the early pioneers in the American testing movement—Lewis Terman, Henry Goddard, and Robert Yerkes—were members of the eugenics movement. These individuals concluded that the Stanford-Binet test measured an "innate intelligence," and this test could be used to identify genetically inferior individuals (Kamin, 1974, pp. 5–6). Terman in *The Measurement of Intelligence* states:

> ... [I]n the near future intelligence tests will bring tens of thousands of these high-grade defectives under the surveillance and protection of society. This will ultimately result in curtailing the reproduction of feeble-mindedness and in the elimination of an enormous amount of crime, pauperism, and industrial inefficiency. (pp. 6–7)
>
> ... [A]mong spanish-indian [sic] and Mexican families of the Southwest and also among negroes [sic] dullness seems to be racial, or at least inherent in the family stocks from which they come.... Children of this group should be segregated in special classes.... They cannot master abstractions, but they can often be made efficient workers.... There is no possibility at present of convincing society that they should not be allowed to reproduce, although from a eugenic point of view they constitute a grave problem because of their unusually prolific breeding. (pp. 91–92)

However, there was also strong resistance in the field of psychology to the notion that genetics had a role in individual differences in behavior. This resistance was led by the behaviorists who felt that all individual differences could be explained by environmental factors. Watson, in his 1930 book, *Behaviorism,* stated:

> Our conclusion, then, is that we have no real evidence of the inheritance of traits. I would feel perfectly confident in the ultimately favorable outcome of careful upbringing of a *healthy, well formed baby* born of a long line of crooks, murderers and thieves, and prostitutes. Who has evidence to the contrary? (p. 103)

He goes on to say:

> I should like to go one step further now and say, "Give me a dozen healthy infants, well-formed, and my own specified world to bring them up in

and I'll guarantee to take any one at random and train him to become any type of specialist I might select—doctor, lawyer, artist, merchant-chief and, yes, even beggar-man and thief, regardless of his talents, penchants, tendencies, abilities, vocations, and race of his ancestors." I am going beyond my facts and I admit it but so have the advocates of the contrary and they have been doing it for thousands of years. (p. 104)

When we look at the race-intelligence controversy, we see that what Watson said over sixty years ago is still correct. Individuals on both sides have gone beyond their facts.

Problems to Resolve Before the Search Begins

I do not question the legitimacy nor the ethics in the search for the genetic basis of intelligence. In a survey of 134 psychology majors at Morehouse College, where I teach, when asked "what is your view of scientific investigators asking questions dealing with **race and intelligence**," the responses were enlightening. Twenty-two percent felt that it was a valid question, twenty-seven percent wanted to know the answer, and forty-six percent felt that the question has racist overtones and implications (Jackson, 1997). William Tucker (1994) in his book *The Science and Politics of Racial Research*, proposed that much of the work in this area has been motivated by the desire to promote some political, economic, or social policy agenda. I feel that looking for genetic correlates to intelligence is a legitimate line of scientific enquiry, but I strongly believe certain problems must be resolved before this can become a worthwhile scientific endeavor. These problems are: 1) the lack of clear definitions of race and intelligence; 2) the limitations of the investigators in the field; and 3) the misconception that the underlying genetic basis for intelligence consists of a few genes or genetic systems.

What does it mean to be intelligent? Some view the use of language and abstract reasoning as the hallmark of intelligence. Others think intelligence is uniquely associated with the mind and thinking, while still others see intelligence as the ability to learn or to adapt to changes in the environment. Unfortunately, no universally accepted operational definition of intelligence exists. One might think it would be far easier to define race, but this has also been a problem.

Yee, Fairchild, Weizmann, and Wyatt (1993), in a paper titled "Addressing Psychology's Problem with Race," deal with the difficulties science has had in clearly defining race. Yee and his co-writers state that not having a scientific definition for race results in investigators conceptualizing and using race in a variety of ways, causing confusion and controversy. Having no clear definitions of intelligence or race limits research design and theory building. It also calls into question "race difference" research: How does one claim a race difference if the researchers have not agreed upon a definition of race that allows them to say the races they are referring to are different races?

The second problem I see is that many investigators involved in searching for the genetic basis of intelligence have limited training. Many psychologists have limited training in genetics, so they go outside their field to geneticists for advice. Most geneticists, however, have little training in psychology.

Finally, there exists an oversimplification of the genetic basis for intelligence and a misuse of the concept of heritability. Heritability is a dynamic population measure that must be recalculated each generation and holds only for the single population investigated at the time it was investigated. Yet we see some investigators using it as a static individual measure.

Evidence tends to support strongly the notion that the genetic basis of intelligence is far from simple. For example, Tryon (1940) demonstrated genetic variation in maze learning in rats when he created a strain of "bright" rats and "dull" rats to run a maze. But in 1949 Pearle ran these selectively bred strains through a variety of mazes and found that on some tasks the bright strain was superior to the dull strain and on some tasks the reverse was true. He concluded

The finding . . . indicates that a "general intelligence" factor, if it exists at all, may be regarded as of little or no importance. . . . [F]rom this together with the intercorrelational evidence that brights and dulls are differently organized it may be assumed that the differences in the maze-learning ability represent differences in patterns of behavior traits rather than in degree of any single psychological capacity. (p. 320)

The importance of this work is that it demonstrates that "intelligence" even in the rat is complex and not governed by one gene. As a graduate student I was able to demonstrate through bidirectional selective breeding for high and low memory and average learning in blowflies in a classical conditioning test that learning and memory in blowflies was governed by **two different** genetic systems (1990). If there are different genetic systems for maze learning in rats, and for learning and memory in blowflies, the number of genes and genetic systems involved in human intelligence, which has still not been clearly defined, must be very large. Yet we see genetic models and the misuse of heritability reducing the genetic basis of intelligence to a simple system.

After we have clear, concise definitions of race and intelligence and individuals who have thorough training in genetics and psychology, then we may be able to deal with the complex search for the genetic correlates of behavior and to tackle the far more complex problem of the genetic X environment interaction. It is also hoped that line of research will be motivated to look for differences among groups rather than the superiority of some groups.

Prejudice and discrimination in science exist because science is done by scientists who are no different from other members of society. In a recent article by Schulman, et al (1999) it was shown in a controlled experiment that medical doctors, when presented with two patients that have identical problems, will prescribe different treatments based on race and sex. However, there is hope in science, for in science, old theories and concepts are modified or abandoned when new evidence is presented. Science can abandon old ideas based on prejudice and discrimination in the face of existing data, and scientists must do the same.

References

Chase, A. (1977). *The legacy of Malthus: The social costs of the new scientific racism.* New York: Alfred A. Knopf.

Galton, F. (1869). *Hereditary genius.* London: Macmillan.

Herrnstein, R. J. (1973). *IQ in the meritocracy.* Boston: Atlantic-Little Brown.

Herrnstein, R. J., & Murray, C. (1994). *The bell curve.* New York: The Free Press.

Hirsch, J. (1982). Introduction. In J. Hirsch & T. McGuire (Eds.), *Behavior-genetic analysis.* Stroudsburg, PA: Hutchinson Ross.

Jackson, D. (1990). *Behavior-genetic analysis of conditioning and retention in Phormia regina (blow flies): A search for relationships between learning and memory.* Unpublished doctoral dissertation, University of Illinois, Champaign-Urbana.

Jackson, D. (1997). Behavior genetic analysis and the African American community: Objective science or voodoo genetics. Paper presented at the European Behavioral and Neural Genetics Society, Orlcans, France.

Jensen, A. (1969). How much can we boost IQ and scholastic achievement? *Harvard Educational Review, 39,* 1–123.

Kamin, L. (1974). *The science and politics of I.Q.* New York: John Wiley & Sons.

Laughlin, H. L. (1922). *Eugenical sterilization in the United States, Chicago: Psychopathic laboratory of the municipal court of Chicago* (rev. ed., 1926). New Haven, CT: American Eugenics Society.

Malthus, T. (1826). *An essay on the principle of population, it affects the future improvement of society* (6th ed.). London: Norton.

Rushton, J. P. (1988). Race differences in behaviour: A review and evolutionary analysis. *Personality and Individual Differences, 9,* 1009–1024.

Schulman, K. et al. (1999). The effect of race and sex on physicians' recommendations for cardiac catheterization. *The New England Journal of Medicine, 340,* 618–626.

Searle, L. V. (1949). The organization of hereditary maze-brightness and maze-dullness. *Psychology Monographs, 39,* 283–325.

Stoddard, L. (1940). *Into the darkness: Nazi Germany today.* New York: Duell, Sloan, & Pearce.

Terman, L. M. (1916). *The measurement of intelligence.* Boston: Houghton Mifflin.

Tryon, R. C. (1940). Genetic differences in maze-learning ability in rats. *Thirty-ninth yearbook of the national society for the study of education.* Bloomington, IL: Public School Publishing.

Tucker, W. (1994). *The science and politics of racial research.* Urbana, IL: University of Illinois Press.

Turner, C. H. (1892a). Psychological notes upon the gallery spider. Illustration of intelligent variations in the construction of the web. *Journal of Comparative Neurology, 2,* 95–110.

Turner, C. H. (1892b). A few characteristics of the avian brain. *Science, 19,* 16–17.

Turner, C. H. (1902). Will the education of the Negro solve the race problem? In D. W. Culp (Ed.). *Twentieth century Negro literature or cyclopedia of thought on the topics relating to the American Negro* (pp. 162–166). Naperville, IL: J. L. Nichols.

Watson, J. B. (1930). *Behaviorism.* Chicago: University of Chicago Press.

Yee, A., Fairchild, H. F., Weizmann, F, & Wyatt, G. (1993). Addressing psychology's problem with race. *American Psychologist, 48,* 1132–1140.

CLASS 7

Social Class Issues in the USA

CHAPTER 11
Where Do Students of Color Earn Doctorates in Education?: The "Top 25" Colleges and Schools of Education
Hood, Stafford and Freeman, Donald

Stafford Hood and Donald Freeman provide insight into both the success and the lack of success among our nation's premier "colleges and schools of education" (CSE's) in recruiting and graduating students of color. The authors identify the top 25 schools that produce the largest share of students of color with doctorates, while also identifying the characteristics that appear to make these institutions successful. Their efforts dispel some of the contemporary notions of what might be viewed as acceptable successful practices.

CHAPTER 12
Discrimination
Richard T. Schaefer

Richard Schaefer provides a comprehensive examination of discrimination in all its many forms in the U.S.A. This work examines the causes as well as some of the strategies to undo this social problem. Issues like the affirmative action debate and the glass ceiling effect are covered.

Where Do Students of Color Earn Doctorates in Education?: The "Top 25" Colleges and Schools of Education

Stafford Hood and Donald Freeman

An Associate Professor of Counseling/Counseling Psychology at Arizona State University, Stafford Hood has published in major journals and anthologies on program evaluation, educational assessment, teacher education, and bias in testing. He is co-editor of *Beyond the Dream: Meaningful Program Evaluation and Assessment to Achieve Equal Opportunity at Predominantly White Universities* and is a consultant in program evaluation and bias in testing for universities, state court systems, and professional licensing agencies.

A Professor of Learning and Instructional Technology in the Division of Psychology in Education at Arizona State University, over the course of his career, Donald Freeman has logged more than 20 years of experience into the designing and conducting of research and programs in the area of evaluation studies. He has published extensively in scholarly journals in the areas of program evaluation, professional development schools, and classroom instruction. He has served as an evaluation consultant in the area of school program evaluation.

Although African Americans and other students of color have sought graduate degrees in education more often than in any other academic field, non-white students are consistently underrepresented in the proportions of doctoral degrees awarded in education (National Research Council, 1976–1988). During academic year 1989–90, for example, only 518 African Americans, 161 Hispanics, 95 Asian Americans/Pacific Islanders, and 38 American Indians/Alaskan Natives earned doctorates in education (National Center for Education Statistics, 1992b). The 812 individuals in this group represented only about 11.7% of all of the doctorates awarded in education during that academic year.

Discussions of efforts to attract more students of color to academic careers are typically cast in terms of supply and demand (Quality Education for Minorities Project, 1990). Early work in this field focused on the recruitment and retention of African American graduate students (Pruitt, 1985;

Thomas, Mingle, & McPartland, 1981), faculty (Epps, 1989; Moore & Wagstaff, 1974), and other delineated conditions that tend to limit the supply of African Americans at both levels. Given the limited supply of doctoral recipients of color in education and other fields (Thomas, 1987, 1992; Trent, 1991), it is not surprising that professors of color are grossly underrepresented on university faculties across all academic disciplines (Blackwell, 1987; Bowen & Schuster, 1986; Jackson, 1991; Moore, 1988; Moore & Wagstaff, 1974). Although the field of education can generally claim to have the highest levels of racial representation, a severe shortage of faculty of color exists in colleges and schools of education throughout the United States (National Center on Postsecondary Education, 1990). This shortage is particularly acute in the nation's elite research universities (Schneider, Brown, Denny, Mathis, & Schmidt, 1984).

Two general areas of concern that are directly related to these racial representation issues

Reprinted by permission of the author.

prompted the present investigation. First, we wanted to know which universities have been the most successful in preparing students of color for leadership positions in education in general. That is, which schools or colleges of education are most likely to have prepared those doctoral recipients of color who have chosen to work in our nation's public schools or in other applied settings? Second, we wanted to know which schools and colleges of education have been most successful in preparing students of color for leadership positions in educational research and development.

In addressing the first question, we adopted an analysis strategy similar to that used by Cooper and Borden (1994) to generate a list of the 100 universities (the "Top 100") that have conferred the highest number of doctoral degrees to racial minorities across all academic disciplines. As an extension of that approach, we narrowed our focus to the field of education and began our analyses by determining which institutions have awarded the highest numbers of doctoral degrees in education to students of color during each of four academic years: 1984–85, 1989–90, 1990–91, and 1991–92. We also determined which colleges and schools of education have been most successful in achieving this goal across the three most recent years for which these data were available: 1989–1992. Our goal was to identify the 25 institutions that headed each of these lists. To circumvent the issue of ties, we varied the actual numbers of colleges and schools of education that were included on this "Top 25" list from one year to another. The number of universities identified ranges from 23 institutions in 1991–92 to 25 institutions in 1984–85 and 1989–90, while 26 universities headed the list for the three most recent years, 1989 to 1992.

Our first set of research questions centered on the "Top 25" lists. They were as follows:

- Do the top 25 universities account for a significant proportion of all of the doctoral degrees in education that were awarded to students of color?

- Was minority doctoral production at these universities stable from one year to the next?

- Do the top 25 lists feature proportional representations of institutions from different regions of the country?

- Do the lists include a reasonable representation of elite research universities?

To determine which institutions have been most successful in preparing students of color for leadership positions in educational research and development, our attention shifted to colleges and schools of education at the nation's major research institutions. As Jackson (1991) and others have noted, students of color are often reluctant to enroll in graduate programs at major research universities because the campus climate and opportunities to develop satisfactory relationships with faculty are viewed as problematic. As a result, many doctoral recipients of color do not have the opportunity to participate in the social networks that typically prevail within and among elite research institutions. These social networks may provide opportunities to participate in externally funded research projects, to co-author research papers and publications with faculty, to establish personal contacts with other prominent researchers nationwide, and to participate in other forms of mentoring in research (Jackson, 1991; Padilla, 1994; Schneider, 1984). Because those who have functioned in social networks such as these have a competitive edge over those who have not, and because graduation from an elite research university is often a prerequisite for employment in other institutions of this type, the pool of candidates of color who can assume leadership positions in educational research and development may be severely restricted (Hood & Hood, 1993).

Thus, our second set of research questions centered on the number of doctorates in education awarded to students of color by the leading educational research institutions. They were:

- Which of the leading educational research universities have been the most successful in awarding doctorates in education to students of color?

- What proportion of those students of color who have earned doctorates in education have graduated from these major research institutions?

- Do the records of success in awarding doctorates in education vary among major research institutions located in different regions of the country?

- How does the proportion of doctoral recipients of color who earned their degrees from prestigious education research universities compare with the corresponding statistic for colleges and schools of education that ranked lower in academic productivity?

Method

DATA SOURCE

The graduation rates reported in this analysis were derived from surveys conducted by the U.S. Department of Education. These surveys asked representatives of the postsecondary institutions that participated in the Integrated Postsecondary Education Data System (IPEDS) to report the number of academic degrees they awarded to various subgroups of students in a given academic year. IPEDS surveys were conducted during each of the four academic years considered for the present investigation: 1984–85, 1989–90, 1990–91, and 1991–92. Although the incidence of missing data for graduates of doctoral programs was relatively rare, it is important to recognize that the frequencies reported throughout this analysis may underestimate the actual numbers of doctorates earned by students of color to at least some degree. This issue was especially problematic in 1990–91, when usable data were not available for four relatively large and prestigious institutions: the University of California-Los Angeles, Harvard University, New York University, and Stanford University.

DATA ANALYSES

The analyses that serve as the focus of this report were derived from printouts of IPEDS data summarized in cross-tabulations depicting the number of students earning doctorates in education in a given academic year by individual institutions, states, gender, race, and ethnicity. Six categories of race/ethnicity were reported: nonresident alien, non-Hispanic White, non-Hispanic Black, Hispanic, Asian/Pacific Islander, and American Indian/Alaskan Native. Because this investigation focused on the preparation of students of color for leadership positions in our nation's public schools and universities, the data for nonresident aliens were not included in any of the analyses that were conducted.

The initial phase of data analysis focused on efforts to identify the institutions that awarded the highest numbers of doctorates in education to students of color during each of the four academic years that were considered. A list of the "Top 25" institutions for 1984–85 is presented in Table 1 as an illustration of the results of these analyses. Comparable tables were also prepared for 1989–90, 1990–91, and 1991–92. Data from the three most recent IPEDS surveys were then combined and a list of the 26 institutions that awarded the most doctorates in education to students of color during the three-year period from 1989 to 1992 was compiled.

The second phase of the data analysis centered on the minority doctoral production rates of the leading research institutions. A precondition for conducting these analyses was the identification of the colleges and schools of education (CSEs) that constitute the leading educational research institutions in the United States. In this case, a choice had to be made between the results of two recent national surveys of colleges and schools of education: one conducted by two professors from the University of Illinois that identified the "most productive" colleges of education (West & Rhee, 1995); and the other a survey published by *U.S. News & World Report,* which identified America's "best graduate schools for education and other disciplines ("America's Best Graduate Schools," 1995).

The choice was relatively straightforward. The West and Rhee survey identified 31 colleges and schools of education that have ranked highest in academic productivity in recent years. These rankings were based on multiple indicators of academic productivity including: (a) the number of articles and documents published by each institution's faculty in the Educational Resources Information Center (ERIC) database from 1983 to mid-1990, (b) the number of citations of faculty publications from 1972 to mid-1990, (c) the number of faculty who served as editors of prestigious professional journals in 1979 and 1989, (d) the level of external funding the school or college received during the 1989–90 academic year, and (e) the number doctoral graduate of these institutions who have joined the other elite research institutions. By contrast, the *U.S. News & World Report* ratings were based on independent rankings of each institution across four different cate-

Table 1. Doctorates in education awarded to students of color in 1984–85: the "Top 25" institutions

	State	AA	AI/AN	A/PI	H	Total Minority	% of all grads
Columbia U.	NY	20	0	5	1	26	18.2%
Temple U.	PA	16	0	4	5	25	16.7%
Nova U.	FL	20	0	0	2	22	16.5%
Clark Atlanta U.	GA	21	0	0	0	21	91.3%
Kansas State U.	KS	14	0	4	1	19	24.1%
U. of Massachusetts—Amherst	MA	11	0	0	7	18	20.2%
Florida State U.	FL	15	0	0	2	17	23.6%
U. of Michigan	MI	12	0	0	3	15	17.9%
Southern Illinois U.—Carbondale	IL	10	0	3	1	14	19.2%
U. of Texas—Austin	TX	1	1	1	11	14	14.1%
George Washington U.	DC	11	0	1	1	13	35.1%
Michigan State U.	MI	8	0	2	3	13	10.9%
U. of Pittsburgh (main campus)	PA	12	0	1	0	13	9.3%
Wayne State U.	MI	11	0	0	1	12	26.1%
Pennsylvania State U. (main campus)	PA	2	1	0	9	12	14.6%
East Texas State U.	TX	6	1	0	4	11	20.0%
Vanderbilt U.	TN	10	0	0	1	11	13.4%
Georgia State U.	GA	11	0	0	0	11	11.7%
Ohio State U. (main campus)	OH	8	1	2	0	11	10.8%
Fordham U.	NY	7	0	0	3	10	17.9%
U. of Alabama	AL	10	0	0	0	10	14.7%
U. of Nebraska	NE	5	0	2	3	10	14.3%
U. of Maryland—College Park	MD	9	0	0	1	10	8.3%
Harvard U.	MA	3	1	2	3	9	14.8%
U. of Wisconsin	WI	4	1	0	4	9	10.3%
Totals for top 25 institutions		257	6	27	66	356	16.5%
Totals for other institutions (n=158)		242	37	46	85	410	10.2%
Combined totals (n=183)		499	43	73	151	766	12.4%

Note: Nonresident aliens were not included in this or any of the other analyses considered in this report. Subgroups: AA=African American; AI/AN=American Indian/Alaskan Native; A/PI=Asian/Pacific Islander; H=Hispanic.

gories: student selectivity, faculty resources, research activity, and institutional reputation among deans, university faculty, and school district superintendents. The indicators of research activity in this latter survey were limited to: (a) the total level of external funding received by each institution in 1994, and (b) that total divided by the number of faculty members engaged in research. The West and Rhee survey considered a wider range of indices of academic productivity than did the *U.S. News & World Report* rankings and was not confounded with other measures that are not directly related to research or academic productivity such as student selectivity and reputations among educators. Thus, the results of West and Rhee's analyses were used in our identification of the leading education research universities. Nevertheless, some of the data from the *U.S. News & World Report* analysis was considered in our presentation of findings.

In the second phase of the data analysis, the number of doctorates awarded to students of color for the three years from 1989 to 1992 was determined for each of the 31 CSEs that ranked highest in academic productivity in West and Rhee's survey. Analyses contrasting the levels of success of these units in recruiting and retaining advanced graduate students of color were also conducted. However, these analyses are limited because data on the actual number of students of color who were recruited, applied, admitted, and subsequently graduated from each of the reported CSEs were not available to the researchers.

Results

HOW MANY DOCTORATES IN EDUCATION WERE AWARDED TO STUDENTS OF COLOR?

The total numbers of doctorates in education earned by students of color during the years in question are summarized in Table 2. As noted earlier, these statistics may represent somewhat conservative estimates of the actual number of doctoral recipients of color in a given year. Nevertheless, they suggest that the total numbers of doctorates in education earned by students of color were fairly stable from one year to the next. The same was true of the proportions of doctorates earned by members of each of the four nonwhite subgroups. From 1989 to 1992, for example, at least 1,442 African Americans, 466 Hispanics,

316 Asian Americans/Pacific Islanders, and 104 American Indians/Alaskan Natives earned doctorates in education. These 2,328 individuals accounted for about 13% of all doctorates in education attained during that three-year period, with the respective groups accounting for 8.1%, 2.6%, 1.8%, and 0.6% of the total number of doctorates in education awarded.

WHICH UNIVERSITIES AWARDED THE MOST DOCTORATES IN EDUCATION TO STUDENTS OF COLOR?

The 25 universities that awarded the most doctorates in education to students of color in 1984–85 are listed in Table 1. The 26 universities that headed the list of minority doctorates in education during the three-year period from 1989 to 1992 are presented in Table 3. Fifteen of the universities that ranked in the "Top 26" list from 1989 to 1992 also ranked on the "Top 25" list in 1984–85.[1] Thus, the records of success in the recruitment and retention of advanced graduate students of color for this subset of 15 universities are shown to have spanned a period of at least eight years. Other universities that were included on at least one of the Top 25 lists for each of the four academic years were the University of Alabama (1984–85), the University of California-Los Angeles (1991–92), East Texas State University

Table 2. Number of doctorates in education awarded to students of color (1984–85, 1989–90, 1990–91, 1991–92)

	Number of institutions reporting	AA	AI/AN	A/PI	H	W	Minority totals	% of all grads
1984–85	183	499	43	73	151	5,431	766	12.4%
		(8.1%)	(0.7%)	(1.2%)	(2.4%)	(87.6%)	766	12.4%
1989–90	170	495	37	95	143	5,010	770	13.3%
1990–91	188	455	35	122	141	5,086	753	12.9%
1991–92	196	492	32	99	182	5,457	805	12.9%
Totals, 1989–92		1,442	104	316	466	20,984	2,328	13.0%
		(8.1%)	(0.6%)	(1.8%)	(2.6%)	(87.0%)		

Note: Nonresident aliens were not included in this or any of the other analyses considered in this report. Subgroups: AA=African American; AI/AN=American Indian/Alaskan Native; A/PI=Asian/Pacific Islander H=Hispanic.

Table 3. Doctorates in education awarded to students of color from 1989 to 1992: the "Top 26" institutions

		Subgroups						Totals by years			
	State	**AA**	**AI/AN**	**A/PI**	**H**	**Totals**	**% all grads**	**89-90**	**90-91**	**91-92**	**84-85**
Nova U.	FL	80	3	31	12	126	19%	42*	47*	37*	22*
Columbia U.[a]	NY	75	2	21	25	123	23%	44*	44*	35*	26*
Clark Atlanta U.	GA	78	0	0	0	78	98%	45*	14*	19*	21*
U. of Massachusetts—Amherst	MA	43	1	3	30	77	22%	27*	23*	27*	18*
U. of Maryland—College Park[a]	MD	44	1	3	4	52	15%	18*	15*	19*	10*
Wayne State U.	MI	31	2	2	9	44	18%	10*	24*	10*	12*
Temple U.	PA	26	0	7	7	40	11%	14*	13*	13*	25*
Fordham U.s	NY	12	0	2	24	38	30%	7	11*	20*	10*
Florida State U.[a]	FL	25	1	2	9	37	17%	10*	12*	15*	17*
Vanderbilt U.[a]	TN	33	1	0	2	36	16%	19*	3	14*	11*
U. of New Mexico	NM	4	1	2	28	35	25%	8	10*	10*	6
U. of Illinois—Urbana[a]	IL	20	2	6	7	35	14%	14*	8	13*	5
Texas Southern U.	TX	34	0	0	0	34	81%	15*	7	12*	8
Ohio State U.[a]	OH	26	0	5	3	34	11%	10*	12*	12*	11*
U. of Texas—Austin[a]	TX	8	1	2	23	34	10%	12*	14*	8	14*
U. of San Francisco	CA	16	0	9	8	33	17%	13*	12*	8	7
Pennsylvania State U.[a]	PA	13	7	2	10	32	15%	14*	12*	6	12*
Harvard U.[a]	MA	10	1	7	10	28	21%	22*	?	6	9*
U. of Pittsburgh[a]	PA	23	0	4	1	28	11%	11*	9*	8	13*
U. of South Carolina	SC	25	1	0	1	27	69%	13*	14*	0	?
U. of Wisconsin[a]	WI	10	3	5	9	27	12%	8	11*	8	9*
Northern Illinois U.	IL	15	0	5	7	27	13%	7	10*	10*	3
Texas A&M	TX	10	1	1	14	26	12%	9*	10*	7	2
Seattle U.	WA	24	0	0	1	25	38%	2	2	21*	1
Loyola U. of Chicago	IL	18	0	4	3	25	17%	10*	10*	5	6
Virginia Polytechnic Institute[a]	VA	23	0	1	1	25	13%	8	12*	5	7
Totals: top 26 institutions		726	28	124	248	1,126	18.5%				
Totals: all institutions		1,442	104	316	466	2,328	13.0%				
% of all minority doctorates from 1989 to 1992		50.3%	26.9%	39.2%	53.2%	48.4%					

*Institutions ranked among the top 25 universities in the number of minority doctorates in education awarded that year
[a]Universities ranked among the top 31 colleges of education in academic productivity by West and Rhee (1955) (see Table IV)
? = missing data

(1984–85), George Washington University (1984–85 and 1991–92), Georgia State University (1984–85), the University of Hawaii-Manoa (1990–91), the University of Houston (1989–90), Iowa State University (1991–92), Kansas State University (1984–85 and 1990–91), the University of Miami (1991–92), the University of Michigan (1984–85), Michigan State University (1984–85), the University of Nebraska (1984–85), New York University (1989–90 and 1991–92; the data for 1990–91 were missing), the University of North Texas (1990–91), Pepperdine University (1991–92), Rutgers University (1989–90), Southern Illinois University (1989–90), and historically Black Tennessee State University (1990–91 and 1991–92).

Proportions of Doctorates Earned. As the data presented in Table 1 indicate, 356 students of color earned doctorates in education from the Top 25 universities in 1984–85. This number represents 46.5% of the 766 doctorates in education earned by racial/ethnic minority students during that academic year. The corresponding percentages for the other three academic years were 54.5% for the Top 25 universities in 1989–90, 50.7% for the Top 24 universities in 1990–91, and 45.1% for the Top 23 universities in 1991–92. In other words, a relatively small subset of from 23 to 25 universities accounted for about one-half of all of the doctorates in education that were awarded to students of color for each year.

The numbers of doctoral recipients of color who completed their graduate studies at one of the Top 26 universities during the three-year period from 1989 to 1992 are also summarized in Table 3. As these data indicate, 1,126 students of color earned doctorates in education during this three-year period at one of the 26 universities cited on this list. This figure represents nearly one-half (48.4%) of the total number of doctorates in education earned by students of color from 1989 to 1992 ($n = 2,328$). This subset of 26 universities also accounts for slightly more than one-half of all doctorates in education awarded to African Americans (50.3%) and Hispanics (53.2%) during those three years.

Consistency Across Years. A total of 46 universities qualified for one or more of the Top 25 lists for the four academic years considered in these analyses. As shown by the asterisks in the column labeled "Totals by Years" in Table 3, 9 universities qualified for all four of the lists, 5 appeared on three of the lists, and 10 qualified for two of the

lists. Thus, 24 universities ranked among the Top 25 institutions in numbers of doctorates in education awarded to students of color for at least two of the four academic years that were considered, while 22 institutions qualified for only one of the four lists.

Regional Contrasts. As a closer review of the data in Table 3 confirms, more than one-third of the 26 institutions that ranked highest in numbers of doctorates in education awarded to students of color during the three-year period from 1989 to 1992 were located in states east of the Mississippi River ($n = 9$). By contrast, only 6 of the 26 universities on this list were located west of the Mississippi, including four universities in Texas. Moreover, although three Pacific Athletic Conference (PAC-10) universities ranked among the top 25 institutions on Cooper and Borden's (1994) list of the 100 universities that conferred the most doctoral degrees to students of color across all academic disciplines in 1990–91, none of the colleges or schools of education in this conference qualified for our Top 26 list of institutions awarding doctorates in education to students of color from 1989 to 1992.

Representation of the Major Research Universities. As shown in Table 3, the Top 26 list for the three-year period from 1989 to 1992 includes elite research universities as well as other four-year institutions that are not generally recognized for their research productivity. The same is true for the Top 25 lists for each of the four academic years. Those universities that were included in both West and Rhee's (1995) list of the 31 most academically productive colleges of education in the United States and on our list of the top 26 U.S. universities that awarded the highest numbers of doctorates in education to students of color from 1989 to 1992 are noted in the first column of Table 3. As the table indicates, a total of 12 universities had the distinction of being included on both lists.

HOW MANY STUDENTS OF COLOR EARNED DOCTORATES FROM THE MOST ACADEMICALLY PRODUCTIVE COLLEGES/SCHOOLS OF EDUCATION?

Variations in Levels of Success in Awarding Doctorates in Education to Students of Color. Data summarized in Table 4 describe the number of doctorates in education awarded to students of color by each of the 31 North American CSEs that ranked highest in academic productivity in West and Rhee's (1995) survey. As these graduation data indicate, considerable variation exists in the total number of doctorates in education earned by students of color during the three years from 1989 to 1992. Only about one-fourth of these 31 CSEs awarded doctorates to more than 25 students of color during this three-year period. One of these institutions, Columbia Teachers College, located in New York City, granted a total of 123 doctorates in education to non-white students and easily outdistanced all of the other leading education research universities in this regard. At the other end of the continuum, five of the institutions on this list awarded fewer than 10 doctorates in education to students of color during the same three-year period. The final column of Table 4 reports the total amount of publicly and privately funded research dollars (in millions) that were administered by each of these institutions in 1994, according to the *U.S. News & World Report* analysis. These data reveal that the median level of research funds distributed to each of these 31 research institutions in 1994 was $5.65 million.

Proportions of Doctorates Earned. The wide variation in the number of graduate students enrolled at each of the leading research institutions suggested the importance of determining the proportions of doctorates awarded to students of color at each university. Here again, considerable variation was found by institutional category. In 6 of the 31 CSEs with distinguished records of academic productivity, more than 15% of all doctorates were awarded to students of color during the three-year period from 1989 to 1992. By contrast, students of color accounted for less than 10% of all doctorates in education awarded by 10 of the 31 elite education research universities during this same period.

Contrasts Between Graduation Rates at Major Research Universities and Other Institutions. During the three years from 1989 to 1992, a total of 745 students of color earned doctorates in education from one of the 31 academically productive CSEs listed in Table 4—an average of about 250 students per year. These individuals represented 12.2% of the 6,127 doctorates in education awarded by this subset of universities during this period of time. During this same period, 1,583 students of color earned doctorates in education from CSEs within the IPEDS system (*n* = approximately 155 institu-

tions each year) that ranked lower in academic productivity. These individuals accounted for 13.5% of the 11,760 doctorates in education awarded by this larger subset of institutions. Therefore, the proportion of doctorates awarded to students of color by the 31 CSEs that ranked highest in academic productivity was lower than that of CSEs with less distinguished records of research productivity (12.2% compared to 13.5%).

Viewed from a different perspective, the 745 students of color who completed their doctorates in education at one of the 31 colleges and schools of education listed in Table 4 represent 32.0% of the 2,328 doctorates in education awarded to students of color nationwide from 1989 to 1992, including 30.9% of all doctorates earned by African Americans, 33.7% of all doctorates awarded to American Indians/Alaskan Natives, 32.6% of all doctorates earned by Asian Americans/ Pacific Islanders, and 34.8% of all doctorates awarded to Hispanics. The consistency of these proportions from one racial/ethnic subgroup to another is striking. Collectively, these statistics suggest that approximately one-third of all students within each of these four subgroups who received doctorates in education from 1989 to 1992 earned their degrees from one of the 31 most academically productive CSEs in the country.

Regional Contrasts. As a closer analysis of the data presented in Table 4 confirms, significant differences exist in minority graduation rates among major research institutions located in different regions of the country. Consider, for example, the contrast between the eight midwestern universities of the Big 10 Conference that were included on West and Rhee's (1995) list and the six PAC-10 universities that were also included on this list. The mean number of doctorates awarded to students of color from 1989 to 1992 by these two subsets of universities are summarized in Table 5.

As the data in Table 5 indicate, the graduation rates for students of color were roughly equal across the eight universities of the Big 10 and the six of the PAC-10 (with means of 3.0 and 2.9 graduates of color per institution, respectively). Given the racial/ethnic differences in demographics across the two regions of the country that these two conferences represent, it is not surprising that the universities in the Big 10 were more successful than their PAC-10 counterparts in recruiting and retaining African Americans graduate students. What is surprising, however, is that the universi-

Table 4. Doctorates in education awarded to students of color from 1989 to 1992 by the 31 colleges and schools of education ranked highest in academic productivity by West and Rhee (1995)

	Rankings AP vs. US[a]	AA	AI/AN	A/PI	H	Totals	% all grads	1994 research funds[b]
U. of Wisconsin—Madison	1–5	10	3	5	9	27	12.0%	$10.9
U. of Illinois (main campus)	2–7.5	20	2	6	7	35	14.2%	$7.3
Ohio State U.	3–9	26	0	5	3	34	11.2%	$15.4
Stanford U.[c]	4–2	5	2	3	4	14	22.2%	$7.4
U. of Minnesota—Twin Cities	5–25.5	10	4	2	7	23	7.8%	$11.0
Indiana U.—Bloomington	6–13	7	0	4	3	14	7.2%	$2.4
Michigan State U.	7–7.5	13	0	1	1	15	6.7%	$13.3
Columbia Teachers College	8–4	75	2	21	25	123	23.1%	$11.5
U. of Georgia	9–15	9	0	2	4	15	4.9%	$14.5
Pennsylvania State U.—University Park	10–25.5	13	7	2	10	32	14.8%	$4.6
U. of Maryland—College Park	11–21	44	1	3	4	52	15.0%	$7.0
U. of Texas—Austin	12–27	8	1	2	23	34	10.0%	$1.2
U. of Michigan—Ann Arbor	13–22	8	1	2	2	13	13.1%	$2.3
Arizona State U. (main campus)	14–47	4	4	5	7	20	13.8%	$3.3
U. of California—Los Angeles	15–10.5	6	0	6	6	18	18.2%	$8.0
U. of Washington	16–18	3	1	4	1	9	9.9%	$5.7
U. of California—Berkeley	17–3	5	3	3	4	15	14.7%	$14.0
U. of Chicago	18–19	7	0	1	1	9	12.2%	$3.3
Harvard U.[c]	19–1	10	1	7	10	28	20.9%	$7.1
U. of Virginia	20–13.5	13	0	2	1	16	8.1%	$4.4
Vanderbilt U. (Peabody College)	21—6	33	1	0	2	36	16.0%	$16.8
U. of North Carolina—Chapel Hill	22–32	15	0	1	2	18	12.4%	$1.4
U. of Florida	23–36	8	1	1	6	16	11.9%	$2.9
Florida State U.	24—30	25	1	2	9	37	17.1%	$6.2
Syracuse U.	25–28	3	0	0	0	3	2.9%	$5.6
U. of Arizona	26.5–35	3	0	2	8	13	12.0%	$4.0
U. of Nebraska—Lincoln	26.5–48	6	0	4	0	10	4.8%	$2.4
Virginia Polytechnic Institute	28–<50	23	0	1	1	25	12.7%	?
State U. of New York—Buffalo	29.5–39	6	0	1	1	8	8.3%	$1.9
U. of Missouri—Columbia	29.5–34	4	0	1	0	5	2.5%	$5.3
U. of Pittsburgh (main campus)	31–44	23	0	4	1	28	10.9%	$3.8
Totals for the 31 AP institutions		445	35	103	162	745	12.2%	
Totals for all institutions		1,442	104	316	466	2,328	13.0%	
% of all doctorates awarded by the 31 AP institutions		30.9%	33.7%	32.6%	34.8%	32.0%		

Notes:
[a]AP = rankings of academic productivity derived from West and Rhee (1995); US = *U.S. News & World Report* rankings of graduate schools of education.
[b]Data in this column were taken from the *U.S. News & World Report* analysis and represent total dollars in research grants awarded to each institution during the 1994–95 academic year (in millions).
[c]Data for 1990–91 were missing for these universities; numbers therefore represent totals for two rather than three years.
? = missing data

Table 5. Mean number of doctorates in education awarded to students of color in Big 10 and PAC-10, 1989–92*

Conference	African Americans	American Indians	Asian Americans	Hispanics	Total
Big 10 (n=8)	13.4	2.1	3.4	5.3	24.2
PAC-10 (n=6)	5.3	1.8	4.6	5.8	17.5

*The means for the PAC-10 schools are adjusted to include interpolations of missing data for the 1990–91 academic year from the University of California-Los Angeles and Stanford University.

ties in the Big 10 were nearly as successful as the PAC-10 institutions in recruiting and retaining American Indian and Hispanic graduate students. Likewise, although the PAC-10 research universities were more successful in recruiting and retaining Asian Americans, the difference in graduation rates among CSEs in the two conferences was not as large as we expected.

Discussion

Interpretations of the results of this investigation are likely to vary from one reader to the next; however, our findings should be meaningful in one way or another to nearly all stakeholders in education. For example, when viewed from one perspective, these results should provide a better understanding of why the number of applicants of color for faculty positions at major educational research institutions is typically meager. As noted earlier, faculty search committees at such universities are likely to view persons who received their doctoral degrees from comparable institutions as the most viable candidates for faculty positions. Moore (1988) takes this line of reasoning one step further by contending that faculty members of search committees function as gatekeepers for the "ruling class" of educational elites at these predominantly white institutions and may pose a significant barrier to the selection and hiring of faculty of color. Given these conditions and the findings of this investigation, which suggest that only about 250 students of color complete their doctorates at the 31 most prestigious educational research institutions each year, it is evident that the national

pool of viable applicants of color for faculty positions at major education research institutions is severely restricted. The size of this pool is further reduced because students of color who complete their doctorates at major research universities may be more likely than their white counterparts to accept non-university positions such as school- or district-level administrative assignments in public schools or positions in state departments of education (Brown, 1988). Given these and other conditions such as the uneven distribution of doctoral recipients of color across specialty areas within education, the national pool of qualified applicants of color in some educational fields—for example, educational measurement and statistics—may be minuscule (Hood & Freeman, 1995).

This self-perpetuating cycle is not likely to be broken until the graduate faculties at most major educational research universities become more aggressive in recruiting and retaining students of color in their doctoral programs. Steps must also be taken to improve the professional lives of untenured faculty of color at the most prestigious research institutions so that these positions will become more appealing to doctoral recipients of color who have earned their degrees from comparable institutions. Moreover, faculty search committees at these institutions must also begin to take more deliberate steps to encourage qualified doctoral recipients of color working in non-university settings to apply for the university-based faculty positions they are trying to fill.

Shifting to a different area of concern, the findings of these analyses might also serve as a springboard for further research related to issues of minority representation in education. These results could provide the logistical foundation for a variety of research investigations in this field. Future studies might address questions such as the following:

- Why have some of the CSEs identified in this study been very successful in recruiting and retaining doctoral students of color while others have not?

- Why have the graduation rates for students of color seeking doctorates in education been considerably higher for universities located in the East and throughout the Midwest than for universities located in the West?

- Why have minority graduation rates been lower at prestigious education research universities than at universities that rank lower in academic productivity?

- Would an in-depth analysis of a university (or universities) that has established a noteworthy record of success in recruiting and retaining doctoral students of color shed additional light on this issue? (A comprehensive study of the recruitment and retention practices of Columbia Teachers College might prove to be especially fruitful in this regard.)

- In what ways, if any, have the career paths of students of color who earned doctorates in education from one of the major education research universities differed from those of their white counterparts and from minority doctoral recipients who earned their degrees from one of the other colleges or schools of education listed in Table 3?

Further, university professors and administrators might use the results of our analyses to compare their institution's success in preparing students of color for leadership positions in education with that of other colleges and schools of education nationwide. Faculties in universities that have enjoyed high levels of success in this regard should welcome the results of this investigation and view them as a recognition of their noteworthy accomplishments. Consider, for example, the record of success Columbia Teachers College (CTC) has established in recruiting and retaining minority doctoral students in education. Bear in mind that CTC ranked eighth in academic productivity among all of the North American CSEs surveyed by West and Rhee (1995), and fourth in

the *U.S. News & World Report* (1995) listing of "America's Best Graduate Schools" of education. Notwithstanding, during the three-year period from 1989 to 1992, a total of 123 students of color earned doctorates in education from this prestigious institution. This number (a) was more than double that of the academically productive university that ranked second in the number of doctoral recipients of color from 1989 to 1992—namely, the University of Maryland-College Park ($n = 52$ doctorates in education); (b) accounted for more than 5% of all of the doctorates in education awarded to students of color nationwide from 1989 to 1992, including 5.2% of all African Americans, 6.6% of all Asian Americans, and 5.4% of all Hispanics; and (c) accounted for a higher percentage of all doctorates in education awarded to students of color from 1989 to 1992 than the six most academically productive institutions in the PAC-10 combined (5.3% compared to 4.5%). Indeed, Columbia Teachers College ranked first among CSEs in the number of its students of color who earned doctorates in education during the 1984–85 academic year, the earliest of the four years considered in these analyses (see Table 1). Simply stated, for at least eight years, this institution's distinguished record of success in recruiting and retaining doctoral candidates of color in education was unchallenged by any other prestigious university in the country.

Other academically productive universities that may have assumed significant roles in the preparation of leaders of color in education during the three-year period from 1989 to 1992 include the University of Maryland-College Park, Florida State University, Vanderbilt University's Peabody College, the University of Illinois at Champaign-Urbana, the University of Texas-Austin, Ohio State University, and Pennsylvania State University-University Park (see Table 4). These and the other institutions listed in the Top 26 list summarized in Table 3 assumed comparable roles in the preparation of educational leaders of color for our nation's public schools and schools and colleges of education.

At the other end of the continuum, the results of this investigation also provide reason to believe that the graduate faculties of most CSEs are content to take a reactive stance rather than a proactive one with respect to minority recruitment and retention at the doctoral level—whereby qualified candidates of color may be admitted if—and only if—they take the initiative to apply. The results of this analysis of doctorates in education awarded to students of color across the 31 most academically productive CSEs are especially problematic in this regard. As our results indicate, the proportion of students of color who earned doctorates in education from these prestigious universities from 1989 to 1992 was lower than the corresponding statistic for less prestigious universities (12.2% compared to 13.5%). This finding seems to support Jackson's (1991) contention that students of color often view the campus climates of major research universities as problematic. Thus, faculties of major research institutions should be challenged to examine the psychological climate of their colleges or schools of education and the forms of personal and academic support their institutions provide for advanced graduate students in education.

The findings of the present study should also challenge the graduate faculties at most of these institutions to explain why their records of success in recruiting and retaining doctoral students in education lag behind the national norm. Our own informal interactions with graduate faculty from a number of different educational research institutions suggest that shortcomings in this area are often attributed to one or more of the following reasons: (a) the lack of sufficient funds directed toward this effort that would enable these institutions to become competitive with other universities that are also trying to recruit qualified students of color, (b) the undesirable geographical locations of the low-minority institutions, (c) the lack of a large enough pool of qualified minority candidates in the state or region in which these institutions are located, and/or (d) the limited presence of faculty of color in their colleges or schools of education. Although these 31 academically productive institutions appear to have ample funds from research grants to make them competitive with other universities in this regard, when Columbia Teachers College is posed as a counter example, most of them are hard pressed to provide convincing evidence that CTC is better positioned on all (or even most) of these variables.

Conclusion

The results of this investigation support those who contend that the differential levels of success in recruiting and retaining doctoral students of color in education are more closely related to the level and consistency of institutional commitment to this goal than to the combined effects of differences in available funds, geographical locations, accessible pools of qualified minority applicants, or numbers of faculty of color. Collectively, our findings seem to indicate that the graduate faculties of most major educational research institutions have adopted a passive rather than an assertive stance when it comes to preparing increasing numbers of students of color for leadership positions in educational research and development. This is true even in the present era, in which the ever-increasing levels of racial and cultural diversity in our nation's public schools and universities have become obvious to just about everyone.

Based on our reading of the data, more than a few of our colleagues at elite CSEs seem to lack a strong and consistent commitment to the production of students of color for faculty positions. Yet, we find it hard to accept that the success of Columbia Teachers College cannot be reasonably duplicated by more of its peer institutions. We urge faculties at these CSEs to take a close, critical look at their recruitment and retention practices relative to students of color. Their goal should be to establish noteworthy rather than questionable records of success in this regard.

Endnotes

1. The 1984–85 graduation rates for each of the Top 26 institutions are starred in the last column of Table 3 (labeled "89–90").

References

America's best graduate schools. (1995, March 20). *US. News & World Report* (Special Supplement).

Blackwell, J. E. (1987). *Mainstreaming outsiders: The production of Black professionals.* Dix Hills, NY: General Hall.

Bowen, H., & Schuster, J. (1986). *American professors: A national resource imperiled.* New York: Oxford University Press.

Brown, S. V. (1988). *Increasing minority faculty: An elusive goal.* Princeton, NJ: Educational Testing Service.

Cooper, A., & Borden, V. (1994, May 19). Top 100 degree producers. *Black Issues in Higher Education, 11(6),* 49–87.

Epps, E. G. (1989). Academic culture and the minority professor. *Academe, 36(5),* 23–26.

Hood, S., & Freeman, D. (1995, April). Breaking the tradition: Increasing the production of doctoral recipients of color in research methodology, educational measurement, and statistics. Paper presented at the annual meeting of the American Educational Research Association, San Francisco.

Hood, S., & Hood, D. W. (1993, April). The production of minority teachers and faculty: Are colleges of education at major research universities pulling their weight? Paper presented at the annual meeting of the American Educational Research Association, Atlanta, GA.

Jackson, K. (1991). Black faculty in academia. In P. C. Altbach & K. Lomotey (Eds.), *The racial crisis in American higher education* (pp. 135–148). Albany, NY: State University of New York.

Moore, W. (1988). Black faculty in White colleges: A dream deferred. *Educational Researcher, 17,* 117–121.

Moore, W., & Wagstaff, L. H. (1974). *Black educators in White colleges.* San Francisco, CA: Jossey-Bass.

National Center for Education Statistics (NCES). (1992a, January). *Characteristics of doctorate recipients: 1979, 1984, and 1989* (NCES Report 91-384). Washington, DC: U.S. Department of Education, Office of Educational Research and Improvement.

National Center for Education Statistics, (1992b, May). *Race/ethnicity trends in degrees conferred by institutions of higher education: 1980–81 through 1989–90* (NCES Report 92-039). Washington, DC: U.S. Department of Education, Office of Educational Research and Improvement.

National Center on Postsecondary Education. (1990). *Faculty in higher education institutions, 1988.* Washington, DC: U.S. Department of Education, Office of Educational Research and Improvement.

National Research Council. (1976–1988). *Doctorate recipients from United States universities.* Washington, DC: National Academy Press.

Padilla, A. M. (1994). Ethnic minority scholars, research, and mentoring: Current and future issues. *Educational Researcher, 23,* 24–27.

Pruitt, A. S. (1985). Discrimination in recruitment, admission, and retention of minority graduate students. *Journal of Negro Education, 54(4),* 526–536.

Quality Education for Minorities Project. (1990). *Education that works: An action plan for the education of minorities.* Cambridge: Massachusetts Institute of Technology, Quality Education for Minorities Project.

Schneider, B. (1984). Graduate programs in schools of education: Facing tomorrow, today. In M. Pelezar & L. Solomon (Eds.), *Keeping graduate programs responsive to national needs* (pp. 57–63). San Francisco: Jossey-Bass.

Schneider, B., Brown, L., Denny, T., Mathis, C., & Schmidt, W. (1984). The deans' perspective: Challenges to perceptions of status of schools of education. *Phi Delta Kappan, 65,* 617–630.

Thomas, G. E. (1987). Black students in U.S. graduate and professional schools in the 1980s: A national and institutional assessment. *Harvard Educational Review, 57(3),* 261–282.

Thomas, G. E. (1992). Participation and degree attainment of African American and Latino students in graduate education relative to other racial and ethnic groups: An update from Office of Civil Rights data. *Harvard Educational Review, 62(1),* 45–65.

Thomas, G. E., Mingle, J. R., & McPartland, J. M. (1981). Recent trends in racial enrollment segregation, and degree attainment in higher education. In G. D. Thomas (Ed.), *Black students in higher education* (pp. 107–125). Westport, CT: Greenwood Press.

Trent, W. T. (1991). Focus on equity: Race and gender differences in degree attainment, 1975–76 to 1980–81. In W. Allen, E. Epps, & N. Haniff (Eds.), *Colleges in Black and White: African American students in predominantly White and historically Black public universities* (pp. 41–60). Albany, NY: State University of New York Press.

West, C. K., & Rhee, Y. (1995). Ranking departments or sites within colleges of education using multiple standards: Departmental and individual productivity. *Contemporary Educational Psychology, 20,* 151–171.

CHAPTER 12

Discrimination

Richard T. Schaeter

Richard T. Schaefer is Chair of the Sociology Department in the College of Liberal Arts & Sciences at DePaul University in Chicago, Illinois. Schaefer has authored two popular text books, *Sociology,* 6th Edition and *Racial & Ethnic Groups,* 7th Edition.

Discrimination can take many forms. As the next two incidents indicate, discrimination can be direct or the result of a complex combination of factors. It can lead to indignities or to death.

Lawrence Otis Graham (1995) had "arrived" by the standards of most people in the United States. He was a graduate of Harvard Law School, married, and had become a well-regarded member of a Manhattan law firm. But he was also Black. Despite his success in securing clients for himself and his firm, Graham had noticed that White attorneys seemed to get a jump on him because of their associations with corporate leaders at private clubs. By tradition, the clubs were exclusively White. Graham decided to take time out from his law firm and learn more about the workings of these private clubs that allowed some Whites to mingle in an informal atmosphere and so contributed to their establishing networks. These networks in turn allowed people to establish contacts that advanced their success in the business world. Rather than present himself as a successful Ivy League college graduate to become a member, he presented himself as a working-class African American seeking a job as a waiter. From the vantage point of a server. Graham figured he could observe the network of these predominantly White country-club members. This was not to be the case. He was not given a job at club after club. Despite all sorts of encouragement when he talked to employers over the phone, he was denied a job when he presented himself, and they saw that this articulate, well-mannered young man was Black. Eventually he obtained a job as a bus boy, clearing tables in a club where the White servers commented that he could do their job better than they could.

Cynthia Wiggins was also African American, but she lived in a different world from Lawrence Otis Graham. She was a seventeen-year-old single mother struggling to make a living. She had sought jobs near her home but had found no employment opportunities. Eventually she found employment as a cashier, but it was far from her home, and she could not afford a car. Still, she was optimistic and looked forward to marrying the man to whom she was engaged. In 1995, she made the fifty-minute bus ride from her predominantly Black neighborhood in Buffalo, New York, to her job at the Galleria, a fancy suburban shopping mall. Every day, charter buses unloaded shoppers from as far away as Canada, but city buses were not allowed on mall property. The bus Wiggins rode was forced to stop across the lot and across a seven-lane highway without sidewalks. On a December day, with the roadway lined with mounds of snow, she tried to cross the highway, only to be struck by a dump truck. She died three weeks later. Later investigation showed that the bus company had been trying to arrange for the bus to stop in the mall parking lot, but the shopping center authorities had blocked the move. Prior to the incident, the mall said they would consider allowing in suburban buses but not public buses from the city. As one mall store owner put it, "You'll never see an inner-city bus on the mall premises" (Barnes 1996:33; Gladwell 1996).

Discrimination has a long history, right up to the present, of taking its toll on people. For some, like Lawrence Otis Graham, discrimination is being reminded that even when you do try to seek employment, you may be treated like a second-class citizen. For others, like Cynthia Williams, discrimination meant suffering for the unjust decisions made in a society that quietly discriminated. Williams lost her life not because anyone actually intended to kill her, but because decisions made it more likely that an inner-city resident would be an accident victim. Despite legislative and court efforts to eliminate discrimination, members of dominant and subordinate groups pay a price for continued intolerance.

Understanding Discrimination

Discrimination is the denial of opportunities and equal rights to individuals and groups because of prejudice or for other arbitrary reasons. Some people in the United States find it difficult to see discrimination as a widespread phenomenon. "After all," it is often said, "these minorities drive cars, hold jobs, own their homes, and even go to college." This does not mean that discrimination is rare. An understanding of discrimination in modern industrialized societies such as the United States must begin by distinguishing between relative and absolute deprivation.

RELATIVE VERSUS ABSOLUTE DEPRIVATION

Conflict theorists have said correctly that it is not absolute, unchanging standards that determine deprivation and oppression. It is crucial that, although minority groups may be viewed as having adequate or even good incomes, housing, health care, and educational opportunities, it is their position relative to some other group that offers evidence of discrimination.

The term **relative deprivation** is defined as the conscious feeling of a negative discrepancy between legitimate expectations and present actualities. After settling in the United States, immigrants often enjoy better material comforts and more political freedom than were possible in their old country. If they compare themselves to most other people in the United States, however, they will feel deprived because, while their standard has improved, the immigrants still perceive relative deprivation.

Absolute deprivation, on the other hand, implies a fixed standard based on a minimum level of subsistence below which families should not be expected to exist. Discrimination does not necessarily mean absolute deprivation. A Japanese American who is promoted to a management position may still be a victim of discrimination, if he or she had been passed over for years because of corporate reluctance to place an Asian American in a highly visible position.

Dissatisfaction is also likely to arise from feelings of relative deprivation. Those members of a society who feel most frustrated and disgruntled by the social and economic conditions of their lives are not necessarily worse off in an objective sense. Social scientists have long recognized that what is most significant is how people perceive their situations. Karl Marx pointed out that, although the misery of the workers was important in reflecting their oppressed state, so, too, was their position relative to the ruling class. In 1847, Marx wrote that

> Although the enjoyment of the workers has risen, the social satisfaction that they have has fallen in comparison with the increased enjoyment of the capitalist. (Marx and Engels 1955:94)

This statement explains why the groups or individuals who are most vocal and best organized against discrimination are not necessarily in the worst economic and social situation. They are likely, however, to be those who most strongly perceive that, relative to others, they are not receiving their fair share. Resistance to perceived discrimination, rather than the actual amount of absolute discrimination, is the key.

TOTAL DISCRIMINATION

Social scientists—and increasingly policy makers—have begun to use the concept of total discrimination. **Total discrimination,** as shown in Figure 3.1, refers to current discrimination operating in the labor market *and* past discrimination. Past discrimination experienced by an individual includes the relatively poorer education and job experience of racial and ethnic minorities compared to that of many White Americans. When considering discrimination, therefore, it is not enough to focus only on what is being done to people now. Sometimes a person may be dealt with fairly but may still be at a disadvantage because he or she suffered from poorer health care, inferior counseling in the school system, less access to books and other educational materials, or a poor job record resulting from absences to take care of brothers and sisters.

We find another variation of this past-in-present discrimination when apparently nondiscriminatory present practices have negative effects because of prior intentionally biased practices. Although unions that purposely discriminated against minority members in the past may no longer do so, some people are still prevented from achieving higher levels of seniority because of those past practices. Personnel records include a cumulative record that is vital in promotion and selection for desirable assignments. Blatantly discriminatory judgments and recommendations in the past, however, remain part of a person's record.

INSTITUTIONAL DISCRIMINATION

Individuals practice discrimination in one-to-one encounters, while institutions practice discrimination through their daily operations. Indeed, a consensus is growing today that this institutional discrimination is more significant than that committed by prejudiced individuals.

Social scientists are particularly concerned with the ways in which patterns of employment, education, criminal justice, housing, health care, and government operations maintain the social significance of race and ethnicity. **Institutional discrimination** refers to the denial of opportunities and equal rights to individuals and groups that results from the normal operations of a society.

Civil rights activist Stokely Carmichael and political scientist Charles Hamilton are credited with introducing the concept of *institutional racism*. Individual discrimination refers to overt acts of individual Whites against individual Blacks; Carmichael and Hamilton reserved the term *institutional racism* for covert acts committed collectively against an entire group. From this perspective, discrimination can take place with-

out an individual's intending to deprive others of privileges and even without the individual's being aware that others are being deprived (Ture and Hamilton 1992).

How can discrimination be widespread and unconscious at the same time? The following represent a few documented examples of institutional discrimination:

1. Standards for assessing credit risks work against African Americans and Hispanics seeking to establish businesses because many lack conventional credit references. Businesses in low-income areas where these groups often reside also have much higher insurance costs.

2. IQ testing favors middle-class children, especially the White middle class, because of the types of questions included.

3. The entire criminal justice system, from the patrol officer to the judge and jury, is dominated by Whites who find it difficult to understand life in poverty areas.

4. Hiring practices often require several years experience at jobs only recently opened to members of subordinate groups

In some cases, even apparently neutral institutional standards can turn out to have discriminatory effects. In 1992, African American students at a Midwestern state university protested a policy under which fraternities and sororities that wished to use campus facilities for a dance were required to post a $150 security deposit to cover possible damage. The Black students complained that this policy had a discriminatory impact on minority student organizations. Campus police countered that the university's policy applied to *all* student groups interested in using these facilities. However, since overwhelmingly White fraternities and sororities at the school had their own houses, which they used for dances, the policy indeed affected only African American and other subordinate groups' organizations.

The U.S. population is becoming more diversified, and examples of institutional discrimination are confronting more different groups. Many Asian peoples have distinctive customs honoring their deceased family members. Among these traditions is the burning of incense at the grave site, placing food on the grave markers, and leaving fake money. These practices stem from ancestor worship but are often followed by Christian Chinese Americans who try to hold on to some of the "old ways." Cemetery proprietors maintain standards of what they regard as proper grave decoration in order to maintain a tidy appearance. Consequently, people of Asian descent find they are unable to bury their loved ones in the cemeteries most convenient to them and must travel to cemeteries that are more open to different ways of memorializing the dead. Cemeteries do not consciously seek to keep people out because they are Asian, but they develop policies, often with little thought, that fail to recognize the pluralistic nature of society (M. Eng 1998).

Institutional discrimination continuously imposes more hindrances on, and awards fewer benefits to, certain racial and ethnic groups than it does to others. This is the underlying and painful context of American intergroup relations.

The Informal Economy

The secondary labor market affecting many members of racial and ethnic minorities has come to be called the informal economy. The **informal economy** refers to transfers of money, goods, or services that are not reported to the government. This label describes much of the work in inner-city neighborhoods and poverty-stricken rural areas, in sharp contrast to the rest of the marketplace. Workers are employed in the informal economy seasonally or infrequently. The work they do may resemble the work of traditional occupations, such as mechanic, cook, or electrician, but these workers lack the formal credentials to enter such employment. Indeed, workers in the informal economy may work sporadically or may moonlight in the regular economy. The informal economy also includes unregulated child-care services, garage sales, and the unreported income of crafts people and street vendors.

The informal economy, sometimes referred to as the **irregular** or **underground economy,** exists worldwide. In 1996, wide publicity was given to the presence of sweatshops throughout the world and in urban America that supplied clothing for major retailers such as Kmart. Most of these employees were immigrants or non-Whites. Conflict sociologists in particular note that a significant level of commerce occurs outside traditional economies. Individually, the transactions are small, but they can be significant when taken together. Within the apparel industry, it has been estimated that perhaps half of all U.S.-produced garments in small shops are made in businesses where two or more of the following laws are routinely violated: child labor, health and safety, minimum wage, and overtime. The informal economy taken in total makes up 10 to 20 percent of all economic activity in the United States (R. Ross 1998: D. Sontag 1993).

According to the **dual labor market model,** minorities have been relegated to the informal economy. While the informal economy may offer employment to the jobless, it provides few safeguards against fraud or malpractice that victimizes the workers. There are also few of the fringe benefits of health insurance and pension that are much more likely to be present in the conventional marketplace. Therefore informal economies are criticized for promoting highly unfair and dangerous working conditions. To be consigned to the informal economy is thus yet another example of social inequality.

Sociologist Edna Bonacich (1972, 1976) outlined the dual or split labor market that divides the economy into two realms of employment, the secondary one being populated primarily by minorities working at mental jobs. Labor, even when not manual, is still rewarded less when performed by minorities. In keeping with the conflict model, this dual-market model emphasizes that minorities fare unfavorably in the competition between dominant and subordinate groups.

The workers in the informal economy are ill prepared to enter the regular economy permanently or to take its better-paying jobs. Frequent changes in employment or lack of a specific supervisor leaves them without the kind of job résumé that employers in the regular economy expect before they hire. Some of the sources of employment in the informal economy are illegal, such as fencing stolen goods, narcotics peddling, pimping, and prostitution. More likely, the work is legal but not transferable to a more traditional job. An example is an "information broker," who receives cash in exchange for such information as where to find good buys or how to receive maximum benefits from public assistance programs (S. Pedder 1991).

Workers in the informal economy have not necessarily experienced direct discrimination.

Because of past discrimination, they are unable to secure traditional employment. Working in the informal economy provides income but does not lead them into the primary labor market. A self-fulfilling cycle continues that allows past discrimination to create a separate work environment.

The Underclass

Many members of the informal economy, along with some employed in traditional jobs, compose what is called the underclass of American society.

The **underclass** consists of the long-term poor who lack training and skills. Conflict theorists, among others, have expressed alarm at the proportion of the nation's society living at this social stratum. Sociologist William Wilson (1987, 1988:15, 1996) drew attention to the growth of this varied grouping of families and individuals who are outside the mainstream of the occupational structure. While estimates vary depending on the definition, in 1990 the underclass included more than 3 million adults of working age, not counting children or the elderly. In the central city, about 49 percent of the underclass in 1990 comprised African Americans; 29 percent, Hispanics (or Latinos); 17 percent, Whites; and 5 percent, other (O'Hare and Curry-White 1992).

The discussion of the underclass has focused attention on society's inability to address the problems facing the truly disadvantaged—many of whom are Black or Hispanic. Some scholars have expressed concern that the portrait of the underclass seems to blame the victim, making the poor responsible. Wilson and others have stressed that it is not bad behavior but structural factors, such as the loss of manufacturing jobs, that have hit ghetto residents so hard. As the labor market has become tighter, the subordinate groups within the underclass are at a significant disadvantage. Associated with this structural problem is isolation from social services. The disadvantaged lack contact or sustained interaction with the individuals or institutions that represent the regular economy. It is the economy, not the poor, that needs reforming (J. DeParle 1991; W. Kornblum 1991; S. Wright 1993).

While the concept of underclass has been useful, its use reflects the division over issues involving race and poverty. Proponents of intervention use the underclass to show the need for a basic restructuring of the economy. Others use the term to describe a lifestyle whose practitioners refuse to try to move out of poverty and conclude that the poor reject responsibility for their plight. There is little evidence to support this pessimistic conclusion. Wilson (1996), in a 1978–1988 survey of African Americans living in poor neighborhoods, found that they believed in the work ethic and felt that plain hard work was important to getting ahead. The underclass, therefore, describes a segment of the population whose job prospects, as well as educational opportunities, are severely limited.

It is a commonly held notion that there are jobs available for the inner-city poor but they just do not seek them out. A study looked at jobs that were advertised in a help-wanted section of *The Washington Post*. The analysis showed that most of the jobs were beyond the reach of the underclass—perhaps 5 percent of all openings could even remotely be considered reasonable job prospects for people without skills or experience. During interviews with the employers, researchers found that an average of 21 people applied for each position, which typically was filled within three days of when the advertisement appeared. The mean hourly wage was $6.12 and 42 percent offered no fringe benefits, and the remaining positions offered "meager" fringe benefits after six months or one year of employment. The researchers concluded that this study, like others before it, counter the folk wisdom that there are plenty of jobs around for the underclass (Pease and Martin 1997).

Poverty is not new, yet the concept of an underclass describes a very chilling development: workers, whether employed in the informal economy or not, are beyond the reach of any safety net provided by existing social programs. Concern in the late 1990s about government spending and federal deficits have led to cutbacks of many public assistance programs and close scrutiny of those remaining. In addition, membership in the underclass is not an intermittent condition but a long-term attribute. The underclass is understandably alienated and engages sporadically in illegal behavior. This alienation and the illegal acts gain the underclass little support from the larger society to address the problem realistically.

The term *underclass* is often invoked to establish the superiority of the dominant group. Even if it is not stated explicitly, there is a notion that society and institutions have not failed the underclass but that somehow they are beyond hope. All too frequently, the underclass is treated as a homogeneous group, the object of scorn, fear, and embarrassment.

Discrimination Today

Dateline NBC in August 1998 sent two young men—one African American and the other White—to shopping malls. They looked at merchandise in Eddie Bauer, Timberland, and other stores. Consistently, the Black shopper was tailed by in-store security. Often the guards, many of whom were themselves Black, left their assigned posts at the front of the store to follow the Black shopper. Confronted with the differential treatment of their customers, store executives indicated they gave no instructions to follow Black customers closely. White viewers were surprised by what they saw, while Black viewers generally saw little new to them in the report. Discrimination may take many forms and surface due to specific procedures or feelings of distrust (NBC News 1998).

Discrimination is widespread in the United States. It sometimes results from prejudices held by individuals. More significantly, it is found in institutional discrimination and the presence of the informal economy. The presence of an underclass is symptomatic of many social forces, and total discrimination—past and present discrimination taken together—is one of them.

Not so subtly, discrimination shows itself even when people are prepared to be customers. A 1990 study had Black and White men and women follow a script to buy new cars in the Chicago area. After 164 visits, the results showed that a White woman could be expected to pay $142 more for a car than a White man, a Black man $421 more, and a Black woman $875 more. African Americans and women were perceived as less knowledgeable, and therefore were the victims of a higher markup in prices. A similar study in housing, nationwide in twenty-five metropolitan areas, showed that African Americans and Hispanics faced discrimination in a majority of their responses to advertisements. Housing agents showed fewer housing units to Blacks and Hispanics, steered them to minority neighborhoods, and gave them far less assistance in finding housing that met their needs. Other recent studies reveal that lenders are 60 percent more likely to turn down a mortgage request from a minority applicant than from an equally qualified White and that lenders give minority applicants far less assistance in filling out their forms (I. Ayres 1991; J. Yinger 1995).

Discrimination also emerges when we look at data for groups other than Blacks and Hispanics. National studies have documented that White ethnics, such as Irish Catholics and Jewish Americans, are less likely to be in certain positions of power than White Protestants, despite equal educational levels (Alba and Moore 1982). The victims of discrimination are not limited to people of color.

MEASURING DISCRIMINATION

How much discrimination is there? As in measuring prejudice, problems arise in quantifying discrimination. Measuring prejudice is hampered by the difficulties in assessing attitudes and by the need to take many factors into account. It is further restrained by the initial challenge of identifying different treatment. A second difficulty of measuring discrimination is assigning a cost to the discrimination.

Some tentative conclusions about discrimination can be made, however. Figure 1 uses income data to show vividly the disparity in income between African Americans and Whites, men and women. The first comparison is of all workers. White men, with a median income of $36,118, earn almost 34 percent more than Black men and 89 percent more than Hispanic women, who earn only $19,676 in wages.

Clearly, White males earn most, followed by Black males. White females, Black females, Hispanic men, and Hispanic females. The sharpest drop is between White and Black males. Even worse, relatively speaking, is the plight of women. **Double jeopardy** refers to subordinate status twice, defined as experienced by women of color. This disparity between Black women and White men has remained unchanged over the more than fifty years during which such data have been tabulated. It illustrates yet another instance of the double jeopardy experienced by minority women. Also, Figure 1 includes only data for full-

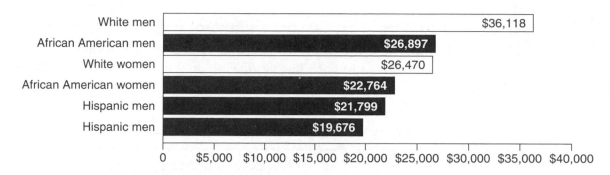

FIGURE 1 MEDIAN INCOME BY RACE, ETHNICITY, AND GENDER, 1997
Even a brief analysis reveals striking differences in earning power between White men in the United States and other groups. Furthermore, the double jeopardy is apparent for African American and Hispanic women.

Note: Median income is from all sources and is limited to year-round, full-time workers over 15 years old.
Source: Bureau of the Census 1998b:28,29.

time, year-round workers, and therefore the figure excludes housewives and the unemployed. Even in this comparison, the deprivation of Blacks, Hispanics, and women is confirmed again.

Are these differences entirely the result of discrimination in employment? No, individuals within the four groups are not equally prepared to compete for high-paying jobs. Past discrimination is a significant factor in a person's present social position. As discussed previously, past discrimination continues to take its toll on modern victims. Taxpayers, predominantly White, were unwilling to subsidize the public education of African Americans and Hispanics at the same levels as White pupils. Even as these actions have changed, today's schools show the continuing results of this uneven spending pattern from the past. Education is clearly an appropriate variable to control.

In Table 3.1, median income is compared, holding education constant, which means that we can compare Blacks and Whites and men and women with approximately the same amount of formal schooling. More education means more money, but the disparity remains. The gap between races does narrow somewhat as education increases. However, both African American and women lag behind their more affluent counterparts. The contrast remains dramatic: women with a degree or graduate work ($29,781) earn less than men who fail to finish college ($30,536).

What do these individual differences look like if we consider them on a national level? Economist Andrew Brimmer (1995), citing numerous government studies, estimates that about 3 or 4 percent of the gross domestic product (GDP, or

the value of goods and services) is lost annually by the failure to use African Americans' existing education. There had been little change in this economic cost from the mid-1960s to the mid-1990s. This estimate would be even higher, of course, if we took into account economic losses due to the underutilization of the academic talents of women and other minorities.

Now that education has been held constant, is the remaining gap caused by discrimination? No, not necessarily. Table 3.1 uses only the amount of schooling, not its quality. Racial minorities are more likely to attend inadequately financed schools. Some efforts have been made to eliminate disparities among school districts in the amount of wealth available to tax for school support, but with little success. In a 1973 case, *San Antonio Independent School District* v. *Rodriguez*, the U.S. Supreme Court ruled that attendance at an underfinanced school in a poor district does not constitute a violation of equal protection. The inequality of educational opportunity may seem less important in explaining sex discrimination. Even though women are usually not segregated from men, educational institutions encourage talented women to enter fields that pay less (nursing or elementary education) than occupations requiring similar amounts of training.

ELIMINATING DISCRIMINATION

Two main agents of social change work to reduce discrimination: voluntary associations organized to solve racial and ethnic problems and the federal government including the courts. The

Table 1. Median Income by Race and Sex, Holding Education Constant
Even at the very highest levels of schooling, the income gap remains between Whites and Blacks. Education also has little apparent effect on the income gap between male and female workers.

	Race, 1996		Ratio	Sex, 1997		Ratio
	White	Black	Black to White	Male Workers	Female Workers	Women to Men
Total	$25,876	$20,262	.78	$28,919	$15,573	.54
High School						
1–3 years	15,135	13,054	.86	16,818	8,861	.53
4 years	21,307	17,285	.81	25,453	13,407	.53
College						
Some college	25,587	22,283	.87	30,356	17,153	.56
Bachelor's degree						
or more	36,941	31,639	.86	47,126	29,781	.63

Sources: Bureau of the Census 1998b: 26,27; 1998c.
Notes: Figures are median income from all sources except capital gain. Included are public assistance payments, dividends, pensions, unemployment compensation, and so on. Incomes are for all workers over twenty-five years of age. Data for Whites are for White non-Hispanics. "Some college" includes Associate Degree-holders for Race, excludes them for Sex data.

two are closely related: most efforts initiated by the government were urged by associations or organizations representing minority groups, following vigorous protests against racism by African Americans. Resistance to social inequality by subordinate groups has been the key to change. Rarely has any government of its own initiative sought to end discrimination based on such criteria as race, ethnicity, and gender.

All racial and ethnic groups of any size are represented by private organizations that are to some degree trying to end discrimination. Some groups originated in the first half of the twentieth century, but most have either been founded since World War II or have become significant forces in bringing about change only since then. These include church organizations, fraternal social groups, minor political parties, and legal defense funds, as well as more militant organizations operating under the scrutiny of law-enforcement agencies. The purposes, membership, successes, and failures of these resistance organizations dedicated to eliminating discrimination are discussed throughout the balance of this book.

Government action toward eliminating discrimination is also relatively recent. Anti-discrimination actions have been taken by each branch of the government: the executive, the judicial, and the legislative.

The first antidiscrimination action at the executive level was President Franklin D. Roosevelt's 1943 creation of the Fair Employment Practices Commission (FEPC), which handled thousands of complaints of discrimination, mostly from African Americans, despite strong opposition by powerful economic and political leaders and many southern Whites. The FEPC had little actual power. It had no authority to compel employers to stop discriminating but could only ask for voluntary compliance. Its jurisdiction was limited to federal government employees, federal contractors, and labor unions. State and local governments and any business without a federal contract were not covered. Furthermore, the FEPC never enjoyed vigorous support from the White House, was denied adequate funds, and was part of larger agencies that were hostile to the commission's existence. This weak antidiscrimination agency was finally dropped in 1946, to be succeeded by an even weaker one in 1948. The judiciary, charged with interpreting laws and the U.S. Constitution, has a much longer history of involvement in the rights of racial, ethnic, and religious minorities. Its early decisions, however, protected the rights of the dominant group, as in the 1857 U.S. Supreme Court's *Dred Scott* decision, which ruled that slaves remained slaves even when living or traveling in states where slavery was illegal. Not until the 1940s did the Supreme Court revise earlier decisions and begin to grant African Americans the same rights as those held by Whites. The 1954 *Brown* v. *Board of Education* decision, which stated that "separate but equal" facilities, including education, was unconstitutional, heralded a new series of rulings, arguing, in effect, that to distinguish among races in order to segregate was inherently unconstitutional.

It was assumed incorrectly by many that *Brown* and other judicial actions would lead quickly to massive change. In fact, little change occurred initially, and resistance to racism continued. The immediate effect of many court rulings was minimal because the Executive branch and the Congress did not wish to violate the principle of **states' rights,** which holds that each state is sovereign in most of its affairs and has the right to order them without interference from the federal government. In other words, supporters of states' rights felt that the federal government had to allow state governments to determine how soon the rights of African Americans would be protected. Gradually, U.S. society became more committed to the rights of individuals. Legislation in the 1960s committed the federal government to protecting civil rights actively, rather than merely leaving action up to state and local officials.

The most important legislative effort to eradicate discrimination was the Civil Rights Act of 1964. This act led to the establishment of the Equal Employment Opportunity Commission (EEOC), which had the power to investigate complaints against employers and to recommend action to the Department of Justice. If the Justice Department sued and discrimination was found, the court could order appropriate compensation. The act covered employment practices of all businesses with more than twenty-five employees, as well as nearly all employment agencies and labor unions. A 1972 amendment broadened the coverage to employers with as few as fifteen employees.

The act also prohibited the application of different voting registration standards to White and Black voting applicants. It prohibited as well discrimination in public accommodations, that is, hotels, motels, restaurants, gasoline stations, and amusement parks. Publicly owned facilities, such as parks, stadiums, and swimming pools, were also prohibited from discriminating. Another important provision forbade discrimination in all federally supported programs and institutions, such as hospitals, colleges, and road construction projects.

The Civil Rights Act of 1964 covered discrimination based on race, color, creed, national origin, and sex. Although the inclusion of gender in employment criteria had been forbidden in the federal civil service since 1949, most laws and most groups pushing for change showed little concern about sex discrimination. There was little precedent for attention to sex discrimination even at the state level. Only Hawaii and Wisconsin had enacted laws against sex discrimination before 1964. As first proposed, the Civil Rights Act did not include mention of gender. One day before the final vote, opponents of the measure offered an amendment on gender bias in an effort to defeat the entire act. The act did pass with prohibition against sex bias included—an event that can only be regarded as a milestone for women seeking equal employment rights with men (Commission on Civil Rights 1975; E. Roth 1993).

The Civil Rights Act of 1964 was not perfect. Since 1964, several acts and amendments to the original act have been added to cover the many areas of discrimination it left untouched, such as criminal justice and housing. Even in those areas singled out for enforcement in the Civil Rights Act of 1964, discrimination still occurs. Federal agencies charged with its enforcement complain that they are underfunded or are denied wholehearted support by the White House. Also, regardless of how much the EEOC may want to act in a case, the individual who alleges discrimination has to pursue the complaint over a long time, marked by long periods of inaction.

Although civil rights laws have often established rights for other minorities, the Supreme Court made them explicit in two 1987 decisions involving groups other than African Americans. In the first of the two cases, an Iraqi American professor asserted that he had been denied tenure because of his Arab origins; in the second, a Jewish congregation brought suit for damages in response to the defacing of its synagogue with derogatory symbols. The Supreme Court ruled unanimously that, in effect, any member of an ethnic minority may sue under federal prohibitions against discrimination. These decisions paved the way for virtually all racial and ethnic groups to invoke the Civil Rights Act of 1964 (S. Taylor 1987a).

A particularly insulting form of discrimination seemed finally to be on its way out in the late 1980s. Many social clubs had limitations forbidding membership to minorities, Jews, and women. For years, exclusive clubs argued that they were merely selecting friends, but in fact, a principal function of these clubs has been providing a forum to transact business. Denial of membership meant more than the inability to attend a luncheon; it also seemed to exclude one from part of the marketplace, as Lawrence Otis Graham observed at the beginning of this chapter. The Supreme Court ruled unanimously in the 1988 case *New York State Clubs Association* v. *City of New York* that states and cities may ban sex discrimination by large private clubs where business lunches and similar activities take place. Although the ruling does not apply to all clubs and leaves the issue of racial and ethnic barriers unresolved, it did serve to chip away at the arbitrary exclusiveness of private groups (S. Taylor 1988).

Memberships and restrictive organizations remain perfectly legal. The rise to national attention in 1996 of the amateur champion and professional golfer Tiger Woods, of mixed Native American, African, and Asian ancestry, brought to public view that there were at least twenty-three golf courses he would be prohibited from playing by virtue of race (J. McCormick and S. Begley 1996; H. Yu 1996).

The inability of the Civil Rights Act, similar legislation, and court decisions to end discrimination is not due entirely to poor financial and political support, although they played a role. The number of federal employees assigned to investigate and prosecute bias cases declined in the 1990s. By 1996, the EEOC was looking at 121,230 unresolved complaints. Thus, even if the EEOC had been given top priority, discrimination would remain. The civil rights legislation attacked the most obvious forms of discrimination. Many discriminatory practices, such as those described as institutional discrimination, are seldom obvious (D. Price 1996).

Environmental Justice

Discrimination takes many forms and is not necessarily apparent even when its impact can be far-reaching. Take the example of Kennedy Heights, a well-kept working-class neighborhood nestled in the southeastern part of Houston. This community faces a real threat, and it is not from crime or drugs. The threat they fear is under their feet, in the form of three oil pits abandoned by Gulf Oil back in 1927. The residents, most of whom are African American, argue that they have suffered high rates of cancer, lupus, and other illnesses because the chemicals from the oil fields poison their water supply. The residents first sued Chevron USA back in 1985, and the case is still making its way through the courtrooms of no less than six states and the federal judiciary.

Lawyers and other representatives for the residents say that the oil company is guilty of *environmental racism* because it knowingly allowed a predominantly Black housing development to be built on the contaminated land. They are able to support this charge based on documents, including a 1954 memorandum from an appraiser who suggested that the oil pits be drained of any toxic substances and the land filled for "low-cost houses for White occupancy." When the land did not sell right away, an oil company official in a 1967 memorandum suggested a tax-free land exchange with a developer who intended to use the land for "Negro residents and commercial development." For this latter intended use by African Americans, there was no mention of environmental cleanup of the land. The oil company counters that it just assumed the developer would do the necessary cleanup of the pits (A. Manning 1997; S. Verhovek 1997).

The conflict perspective sees the case of the Houston suburb as one where pollution harms minority groups disproportionately. **Environmental justice** refers to the efforts to ensure that hazardous substances are controlled so that all communities receive protection regardless of race or socioeconomic circumstance. Following Environmental Protection Agency and other organization reports documenting discrimination in the locating of hazardous waste sites, an Executive Order was issued in 1994 that requires all federal agencies to ensure that low-income and minority communities have access to better information about their environment and have an opportunity to participate in shaping government policies that affect their community's health. Initial efforts to implement the policy have met widespread opposition, including criticism from some proponents of economic development who argue that to conform to guidelines unnecessarily delays or blocks altogether locating new industrial sites. Effort by the EPA to further clarify environmental justice guidelines in 1998 created more problems when the agency proceeded without sufficient consultation with states, cities, and industry (J. Cushman 1998).

Sociologist Robert Bullard (1990) has shown that low-income communities and areas with significant minority populations are more likely to be adjacent to waste sites than are affluent White communities. Similarly, undergraduate student researchers at Occidental College in California found in 1995 that the poor, African Americans, Hispanics, Asian Americans, and Native Americans were especially likely to be living near Los Angeles County's 82 potential environmental hazards (Moffat 1995). Issues of environmental justice are not restricted to metropolitan areas. Another continuing problem is abuse of Native American reservation land. Many American Indian leaders are concerned that tribal lands are too often regarded as "dumping grounds" for toxic waste that go to the highest bidder. We will return to this aspect of environmental justice in Chapter 6.

As with other aspects of discrimination, experts disagree. There is controversy within the scientific community over the potential hazards of some of the problems, and there is even some opposition within the subordinate communities being affected. This complexity of the issues in terms of social class and race is apparent, as some observers question the wisdom of an Executive Order that slows economic development coming to areas in dire need of employment opportunities. On the other hand, some counter that such businesses typically employ few less-skilled workers and only make the environment less livable for those left behind. Despite such varying viewpoints, environmental justice offers an excellent example of resistance and change in the 1990s that could not have been foreseen by the civil rights workers of the 1950s.

Affirmative Action

Affirmative action is the positive effort to recruit subordinate-group members including women for jobs, promotions, and educational opportunities. The phrase *affirmative action* first appeared in an Executive Order issued by President Kennedy in 1961. The order called for contractors to "take affirmative action to ensure that applicants are employed, and that employees are treated during employment, without regard to their race, creed, color, or national origin." However, at this early time no enforcement procedures were specified. Six years later, the order was amended to prohibit discrimination on the basis of sex, but affirmative action was still defined vaguely.

Today *affirmative action* has become a catch-all term for racial-preference programs and goals. It has also become a lightning rod for opposition to any programs that suggest special consideration of women or racial minorities.

AFFIRMATIVE ACTION EXPLAINED

Affirmative action has been viewed as an important tool for reducing institutional discrimination. Whereas previous efforts had been aimed at eliminating individual acts of discrimination, federal measures under the heading of affirmative action have been aimed at procedures that deny equal opportunities even if they are not intended to be overtly discriminatory. This policy has been implemented to deal with both the current discrimination and the past discrimination outlined earlier in this chapter.

The Commission on Civil Rights (1981:9–10) gave some examples of areas where affirmative action had been aimed at institutional discrimination:

- Height and weight requirements that are unnecessarily geared to the physical proportions of White males without regard to the actual requirements needed to perform the job and therefore exclude females and some minorities.

- Seniority rules, when applied to jobs historically held only by White males, that make more recently hired minorities and females more subject to layoff—the "last hired, first fired" employee—and less eligible for advancement.

- Nepotism-based membership policies of some unions that exclude those who are not relatives of members, who, because of past employment practices, are usually White.

- Restrictive employment-leave policies, coupled with prohibitions on part-time work or denials of fringe benefits to part-time workers, which make it difficult for the heads of single-parent families, most of whom are women, to get and keep jobs and also meet the needs of their families.

- Rules requiring that only English be spoken at the workplace, even when not a business necessity, which result in discriminatory employment practices toward individuals whose primary language is not English.

- Standardized academic tests or criteria, geared to the cultural and educational norms of middle-class or White males, when these are not relevant predictors of successful job performance.

- Preferences shown by law and medical schools in the admission of children of wealthy and influential alumni, nearly all of whom are White.

- Credit policies of banks and lending institutions that prevent the granting of mortgages and loans in minority neighborhoods or prevent the granting of credit to married women and others who have previously been denied the opportunity to build good credit histories in their own names.

Employers have also been cautioned against asking leading questions in interviews, such as "Did you know you would be the first Black to supervise all Whites in that factory?" or "Does your husband mind your working on weekends?" Furthermore, the lack of minority-group (Blacks, Asians, Native Americans, and Hispanics) or female employees may in itself represent evidence for a case of unlawful exclusion (Commission on Civil Rights 1981).

THE DEBATE

How far can an employer go in encouraging women and minorities to apply for a job before it becomes unlawful discrimination against White males? Since the late 1970s, a number of bitterly debated cases on this difficult aspect of affirmative action have reached the U.S. Supreme Court. The most significant cases are summarized in Table 3.2. Furthermore, as we will see, the debate has moved into party politics.

In the 1978 *Bakke* case (*Regents of the University of California* v. *Bakke*), by a narrow 5–4 vote, the Court ordered the medical school of the University of California at Davis to admit Allan Bakke, a qualified White engineer who had originally been denied admission solely on the basis of his race. The justices ruled that the school had violated Bakke's constitutional rights by establishing a fixed quota system for minority students. The Court added, however, that it was constitutional for universities to adopt flexible admissions programs that use race as one factor in making decisions.

Colleges and universities responded with new policies designed to meet the *Bakke* ruling while broadening opportunities for traditionally underrepresented minority students. However, in 1996, the Supreme Court allowed a lower court decision to stand that affirmative action programs for African American and Mexican American students at the University of Texas law school were unconstitutional. The ruling effectively prohibited schools in the lower court's jurisdiction of Louisiana, Mississippi, and Texas from taking race into account in admissions. Given this action, further challenges to affirmative action can be expected in higher education (Lederman and Burd 1996).

Even if the public in the United States acknowledges the disparity in earnings between White males and others, growing numbers of people doubt that everything done in the name of affirmative action is desirable. In 1991, national surveys showed that 24 percent of respondents agreed that "affirmative action programs designed to help minorities get better jobs and education go too far these days." Further analysis of the survey data reveals sharp racial division. In 1995, 46 percent of Whites and only 8 percent of African Americans indicated that affirmative action had gone too far (D. Lauter 1995).

Beginning in the 1980s, the Supreme Court, increasingly influenced by conservative justices, has issued many critical rulings concerning affirmative action programs. In a key case in 1989 the Court invalidated, by a 6—3 vote, a Richmond,

Table 2. Key Decisions on Affirmative Action

In a series of split and often very close decisions, the Supreme Court has expressed a variety of reservations in specific situations.

Year	Favorable/ Unfavorable to Policy	Case	Vote	Ruling
1971	+	Griggs v. Duke Power Co.	9–0	Private employers must provide a remedy where minorities were denied opportunities even if unintentional
1978	–	Regents of the University of California v. Bakke	5–4	Prohibited specific number of places for minorities in college admissions
1979	+	United Steelworkers of America v. Weber	5–2	OK for union to favor minorities in special training programs
1984	–	Firefighters Local Union No. 1784 (Memphis, TN) v. Stotts	6–1	Seniority means recently hired minorities may be laid off first in staff reductions
1986	+	International Association of Firefighters v. City of Cleveland	6–3	May promote minorities over more senior Whites
1986	+	New York City v. Sheet Metal	5–4	Approved specific quota of minority workers for union
1987	+	United States v. Paradise	5–4	Endorsed quotas for promotions of state troopers
1987	+	Johnson v. Transportation Agency, Santa Clara, CA	6–3	Approved preference in hiring for minorities and women over better-qualified men and Whites
1989	–	Richmond v. Croson Company	6–3	Ruled a 30 percent set-aside program for minority contractors unconstitutional
1989	–	Martin v. Wilks	5–4	Ruled Whites may bring reverse discrimination claims against court-approved affirmative action plans
1990	+	Metro Broadcasting v. FCC	5–4	Supported federal programs aimed at increasing minority ownership of broadcast licenses
1995	–	Adarand Constructors Inc. v. Peña	5–4	Benefits based on race are constitutional only if narrowly defined to accomplish a compelling interest
1996	–	Texas v. Hopwood	*	Let stand a lower court decision covering Louisiana, Mississippi, and Texas, that race could not be used in college admissions

* 5th U.S. Circuit Court of Appeals decision.

Virginia, law that had guaranteed 30 percent of public works funds to construction companies owned by minorities. In ruling that the Richmond statute violated the constitutional right of White contractors to equal protection under the law, the Court held that affirmative action programs are constitutional only when they serve the "compelling state interest" of redressing "identified discrimination" by the government or private parties. More recently, in 1994, a divided Supreme Court, by a 5—4 vote in *Adarand* v. *Peña*, held that federal programs that award benefits on the basis of race are constitutional only if they are "narrowly tailored" to accomplish a "compelling governmental interest." The Court's ruling was expected to encourage further legal challenges to federal affirmative action programs (Commission on Civil Rights 1995; L. Greenhouse 1989).

Has affirmative action actually helped to alleviate employment inequality on the basis of race and gender? This is a difficult question to answer given the complexity of the labor market and the fact that there are other antidiscrimination measures, but it does appear that affirmative action has had significant impact in the sectors where it has been applied. Sociologist Barbara Reskin (1998) studied available studies looking at workforce composition in terms of race and gender in light of affirmative action policies. She found that gains in minority employment can be attributed to affirmative action policies. This includes both firms mandated to follow affirmative action guidelines and those that took them on voluntarily. There is also evidence that some earnings gains can be attributed to affirmative action. Economists M. V. Lee Badgett and Heidi Hartmann (1995), reviewing twenty-six other research studies, came to similar conclusions: affirmative action and other federal compliance programs have modest impact, but it is difficult to assess, given larger economic changes such as recessions or the massive increase in women in the paid labor force.

Sometimes the impact of affirmative action is clear, such as during the 1970s and 1980s—a period during which courts ordered about 40 percent of the nation's police departments to engage in affirmative action because they had systematically discriminated against minorities and women. Another 42 percent of police departments adopted voluntary plans, leaving over 80 percent of the nation's law enforcement departments working ambitiously to improve representation. The result is dramatic in that minority representation among police officers increased from 7 percent to 22.5 percent, and women's presence rose from 2 percent to 9 percent (Martin 1991).

REVERSE DISCRIMINATION

While researchers debated the merit of affirmative action, the general public— particularly Whites but also some affluent African Americans and Hispanics— questioned the wisdom of the program. Particularly vocal were the charges of **reverse discrimination:** that government actions cause better-qualified White males to be bypassed in favor of women and minority men. Reverse discrimination is an emotional term because it conjures up the notion that somehow women and minorities will subject White males in the United States to the same treatment received by minorities during the last three centuries. Increasingly, critics of affirmative action called for color-blind policies, which would end affirmative action and, they argue, allow all people to be judged fairly. Of major significance, often overlooked in public debates, is that a color-blind policy implies a very limited role for the state in addressing social inequality between racial and ethnic groups (A. Kahng 1978; D. Skrentny 1996; H. Winant 1994).

Is it possible to have color-blind policies in the United States as we move into the twenty-first century? Supporters of affirmative action contend that as long as businesses rely on informal social networks, personal recommendations, and family ties. White men will have a distinct advantage built upon generations of being in positions of power. Furthermore, an end to affirmative action should also mean an end to the many programs that give advantages to certain businesses, homeowners, veterans, farmers, and others. The vast majority of these preference-holders are White (M. Kilson 1995; R. Mack 1996).

Consequently, by the 1990s, affirmative action had emerged as an increasingly important issue in state and national political campaigns. Generally, discussion focused on the use of quotas in hiring practices. Supporters of affirmative action argue that hiring goals establish "floors" for minority inclusion but do not exclude truly qualified candidates from any group. Opponents insist that these "targets" are, in fact, quotas that lead to reverse discrimination. However, according to the U.S. Department of Labor, affirmative action has caused very few claims of reverse discrimination by White people. Fewer than 100 of the more than 3,000 discrimination opinions in federal courts from 1990 to 1994 even raised the issue of reverse discrimination, and reverse discrimination was actually established in only six cases (Joint Center for Political and Economic Studies 1996).

The state of California, in particular, was a battleground over this controversial issue. The California Civil Rights Initiative was placed on the ballot in 1996 as a referendum to amend the state constitution and prohibit any programs that give preference to women and minorities for college admission, employment, promotion, or government contracts. Overall, 54 percent of the voters backed the state proposition, with 61 percent of men in favor compared to only 48 percent of women. Whites, who represented 74 percent of the voters, voted in favor of the measure overwhelmingly, with 63 percent backing Proposition 209. This compares to 26 percent of African Americans, 24 percent of Hispanics, and 39 percent of Asian Americans favoring the end of affirmative action in state-operated institutions. Obviously, those voters—Whites and men—who perceived themselves as least likely to benefit from affirmative action overwhelmingly favored Proposition 209.

Legal challenges continue concerning Proposition 209, which is being implemented unevenly throughout the state. Much of the attention has focused on the impact that reducing racial preference programs will have in law and medical schools, where competition for admission is very high. Initial evidence is that there has been a significant decline at elite institutions, particularly at UCLA and the University of California at Berkeley, but that less impact is being experienced at most institutions. These charges come just as a study in the prestigious *Journal of the American Medical Association* showed that while giving preference to ethnicity yields "powerful effects on the diversity of the student population," there is "no evidence of diluting the quality of the graduates" (Davidson and Lewis 1997:1153).

Ironically, just as supporters of Proposition 209 were cheering its passage, national attention was riveted on a scandal involving alleged discrimination at the highest levels of Texaco—the nation's fourteenth largest corporation. Audio tapes were released that showed senior company executives plotting to destroy documents demanded in a discrimination suit and using racial epithets in discussing Black employees. Texaco, facing a threatened nationwide boycott, agreed to pay $176 million in compensation for outstanding grievances and complaints concerning racial discrimination. The company agreed to give about 11,000 African American employees an 11 percent pay hike, spend millions more on programs designed to wipe out discrimination, and let outsiders come inside to monitor progress (Roberts and White 1998).

The Glass Ceiling

We have been talking primarily about racial and ethnic groups as if they have uniformly failed to keep pace with Whites. While that is accurate, there are tens of thousands of people of color who have matched and even exceeded Whites in terms of income. For example, in 1991 there were more than 133,000 Black households and over 134,000 Hispanic households that earned over $100,000. What can we say about affluent members of subordinate groups in the United States?

Prejudice does not necessarily end with wealth. Black newspaper columnist De Wayne Wickham (1993) wrote of the subtle racism he had experienced. He had witnessed a White clerk in a supermarket ask a White customer if she knew the price of an item the computer would not scan; when the problem occurred while the clerk was ringing up Wickham's groceries, she called for a price check. Affluent subordinate-group members routinely report being blocked as they move toward the first-class section aboard airplanes or seek service in upscale stores. Another journalist, Ellis Cose (1993), has termed these insults the soul-destroying slights to affluent minorities that lead to the "rage of a privileged class."

Discrimination persists for even the educated and qualified from the best family backgrounds. As subordinate-group members are able to compete successfully, they sometimes encounter attitudinal or organizational bias that prevents them from reaching their full potential. They have confronted what has come to be called the **glass ceiling.** This refers to the barrier that blocks the promotion of a qualified worker because of gender or minority membership. Often people entering non-traditional areas of employment become *marginalized* and made to feel uncomfortable, much like the situation of immigrants who feed a part of two cultures, as we discussed in Chapter 1.

The reasons for glass ceilings are as many as the occurrences. It may be that one Black or one woman vice-president is regarded as enough, so the second potential candidate faces a block to movement up through management. Decision makers may be concerned that their clientele will not trust them if they have too many people of color or may worry that a talented woman could become overwhelmed with her duties as a mother and wife and thus perform poorly in the workplace.

Concern about women and minorities climbing a broken ladder led to the formation in 1991 of the Glass Ceiling Commission, with the U.S. Secretary of Labor chairing the twenty-one-member group. Initially, it regarded some of the glass ceiling barriers as:

- Lack of management commitment to establishing systems, policies, and practices for achieving workplace diversity and upward mobility

- Pay inequities for work of equal or comparable value

- Sex-, race-, and ethnic-based stereotyping and harassment

- Unfair recruitment practices

- Lack of family-friendly workplace policies

- "Parent-track" policies

- Limited opportunities for advancement to decision-making positions

The commission report documented that the underrepresentation of women in managerial positions is due in large part to the presence of glass ceilings. As the commission noted, 97 percent of the senior managers of Fortune 1000 industrial and Fortune 500 service companies are White, and about 96 percent are male. A follow-up study in 1996 found little change, with only 2 percent or 50 of the top 2,500 executives women in the Fortune 500 companies (Department of Labor 1993, 1995; S. Silverstein 1996).

While glass ceilings have been widely described and condemned in business during the 1990s, this does not necessarily mean that there has been a dramatic move to remove them. A 1998 survey of Chicago's top 100 companies found only modest representation by women (7.5 percent) and minorities (5.8) among boards of directors. Yet 53 percent of the Chicago-area CEOs declared that they were satisfied with the makeup of their board of directors (Chandler 1998).

Glass ceilings are not the only barrier. Catalyst, a nonprofit research organization, conducted interviews in 1992 with senior and middle managers from larger corporations. The study found that, even before glass ceilings are encountered, women and racial and ethnic minorities face **glass walls** that keep them from moving laterally. Specifically, the study found that women tend to be placed in staff or support positions in areas such as public relations and human resources and are often directed away from jobs in core areas such as marketing, production, and sales. Women are assigned, and therefore trapped, in jobs that reflect their stereotypical helping nature and encounter glass walls that cut off access to jobs that might lead to broader experience and advancement (J. Lopez 1992).

How do members of subordinate groups respond to glass walls and glass ceilings? Some endure them, but others take their potential and begin their own businesses. Susan Crowe Chamberlain, past president of Women in Management, summarized it succinctly by saying that for many women and minority men, the real way to get to the top is to get out. Instead of fighting the ceiling, they form their own companies (R. Richman 1992: sec. 6, 11).

Focusing on the employed and even the relatively affluent should not lead us to ignore the underclass people employed in the informal economy or Native Americans without economic opportunities on isolated reservations. Surveying the past ten years, Urban League President John Jacob said in 1994 that Blacks can do only so much themselves; self-development cannot succeed without an "opportunity environment." He called on President Clinton to endorse a "Marshall Plan for America" that would focus on job creation and job training (*USA Today* 1994). Yet even the affluent subordinate-group person is reminded of her or his second-class status through subtle racism or a glass ceiling.

Conclusion

Discrimination takes its toll, whether a person who is discriminated against is part of the informal economy or not. Even members of minority groups who are not today being overtly discriminated against continue to fall victim to past discrimination. We have also identified the costs of discrimination to members of the privileged group. The attitudes of Whites and even members of minority groups themselves are influenced by the images they have of racial and ethnic groups. These images come from what has been termed statistical discrimination, which causes people to act based on stereotypes they hold and the actions of a few subordinate-group members.

From the conflict perspective, it is not surprising to find the widespread presence of the informal economy proposed by the dual labor-market model and even an underclass. Derrick Bell (1994), an African American law professor, has made the sobering assertion that "racism is permanent." He contends that the attitudes of dominant Whites prevail, and society is willing to advance programs on behalf of subordinate groups only when they coincide with needs as perceived by those Whites. Bell observes that the criticism of the affirmative action program in the 1990s exceeded any concern over corporate downsizing, which led to a loss of 1.6 million manufacturing jobs from 1989 to 1993 alone.

Women are a particularly vulnerable group, for whether the comparisons are within or across racial and ethnic groupings, they face significant social disparities. This inequality will be a recurring theme throughout this book, but we can observe that it is present even in developing fields such as computer science. In 1990, women accounted for 35 percent of computer systems analysts and programmers, but data for 1997 shows the proportion to be down to 29 percent. Is computer science openly discriminating against women? There is little evidence of blatant discrimination, but increasing numbers of women drop out of the field claiming they are not taken seriously, have few role models, and face a family-unfriendly environment. So, is the industry taking steps to address this need? Actually, the major initiative has been for the computer industry to lobby the federal government to increase the number of legal immigrants with the desired computer skills who are allowed to enter the country (Piller 1998).

The surveys presented in Chapter 3 show gradual acceptance of the earliest efforts to eliminate discrimination but that support is failing, especially as it relates to affirmative action. Indeed, concerns about doing something about alleged reverse discrimination are as likely to be voiced as racial or gender discrimination or penetrating glass ceilings and concrete walls.

Institutional discrimination remains a formidable challenge in the United States. Attempts to reduce discrimination by attacking institutional discrimination have met with staunch resistance. Partly as a result of this outcry from some of the public, especially White Americans, the federal government gradually deemphasized its efforts in affirmative action during the 1980s and 1990s. Yet resistance continues. States and the federal government have not been as quick to jump on the anti-affirmative action bandwagon as many had predicted in the wake of the passage of Proposition 209. Indeed, even in California the resistance has been clear (Bobo 1998).

As we turn to examine the various groups that make up the American people, through generations of immigration and religious diversity, look for the types of programs designed to reduce prejudice and discrimination that were discussed here. Most of the material in this chapter has been about racial groups, especially Black and White Americans. It would be easy to see intergroup hostility as a racial phenomenon, but that would be incorrect. Throughout the history of the United States, relations among some White groups have been characterized by resentment and violence. The next two chapters examine the nature and relations of White ethnic groups.

For Further Information

William G. Bowen and Derek Bok. *The Shape of the River: Long-Term Consequences of Considering Race in College and University Admissions.* Princeton, NJ: Princeton University Press, 1998. A thorough statistical analysis of data (grades, SAT scores, and so forth) gathered on 93,000 students of all races at 34 elite colleges and universities. The authors conclude that eliminating affirmative action would not do much to help Whites who are rejected for admission.

Sharon M. Collins-Lowry. *Black Corporate Executives: The Making and Breaking of a Black Middle Class.* Philadelphia, PA: Temple University Press, 1997. Based on extensive interviews with African American executives in Chicago concerning their success and barriers to further advancement.

Barbara F. Reskin. *The Realities of Affirmative Action in Employment.* Washington, DC: American Sociological Association, 1998. Offers a concise (121 pages) but comprehensive look at affirmative action in the labor market.

John Yinger. *Closed Doors, Opportunities Lost. The Continuing Costs of Housing Discrimination.* New York: Russell Sage Foundation, 1995. Economist Yinger provides a history of fair housing and fair lending enforcement and examines the underlying causes of discrimination present.

STATISTICAL SOURCES

Hundreds of federal government publications provide statistical data comparing racial and ethnic groups to each other and women to men. The *Current Population Report Series* P-20 and P-60 and the annual *Statistical Abstract of the United States* are among the best. Increasing numbers of data sets are first available, and sometimes only available, on the Bureau of the Census WEB site at http//www.census.gov.sources.

CLASS 8

Gender Issues in the USA

CHAPTER 13
Interactive Phases of Curricular Revision:
A Feminist Perspective
Peggy McIntosh
Peggy McIntosh discusses five interactive phases of personal and curriculum
change that occur when educators begin the process of incorporating
women's studies materials into the curriculum.

Interactive Phases of Curricular Re-Vision: A Feminist Perspective

Peggy McIntosh

Associate Director of the Wellesley Center for Research on Women, Peggy McIntosh is founder and co-director of the national S.E.E.D. (Seeking Educational Equity and Diversity) Project for Inclusive Curriculum. She travels worldwide as a consultant on the issue of creating gender fair and multicultural curricula. She has written and given invited lectures on the Wittgensteinian notion of "language games" in the U.S. and abroad and has co-authored several articles linking philosophy and pedagogy.

I want to speculate here about a theory of five interactive phases of personal and curriculum change which occur when new perspectives and new materials from Women's Studies are brought into a traditional curriculum or a traditional consciousness. After a number of years of work in curriculum revision involving Women's Studies, I found that my colleagues and I were frequently making judgments without having made the grounds of our judgments explicit. That is, we were seeing some efforts of curriculum revision as better than others, more advanced along a spectrum of curricular possibilities which had not yet been described. My theory is an attempt to describe the spectrum.

Such theories have their dangers. Typologies scare me because abstract schema have so often left out most people, including me. Stage theories in particular are dangerous because they can so easily reinforce present hierarchies of power and value. Nevertheless, I want to speak in terms of curricular phases here, partly because colleagues in Women's Studies on many campuses are making similar analyses, speaking and writing about the process of curriculum change as if we could see in it identifiable varieties and types of change. "Such and such a course still has a long way to go," we say. A long way toward what? This is

what I will try to spell out here. I like the tentativeness with which others interested in stage or phase theories in this field have drawn their pictures. D'Ann Campbell, Gerda Lerner, Catherine Stimpson, Marcia Westkott and the faculty development team of Arch, Tetrault, and Kirschner at Lewis and Clark College have developed theories that do not entail ranking and labeling of a sort which perpetuates oppression and exclusion. I take them as models.

For my own analysis, I have adopted, instead of the word "stages," the phrase suggested by Prof. Joan Gunderson of St. Olaf College: "interactive phases." Initial phases of perception do not disappear, but can be felt continually in the mind or the discipline, as one moves toward or away from a more inclusive body of knowledge, a more active process of learning, and a greater ability to see the dominant modes of thought and behavior which we wish to challenge or change.

I begin also with a sense of indebtedness to many other colleagues, including especially the women and men who have taken part over the last four years in the Mellon Seminars at the Wellesley College Center for Research on Women. These seminars are focused on liberal arts curriculum re-vision in two senses: **re-seeing** and **remaking** of the liberal arts curriculum. Each year,

McIntosh, Peggy. (1990). WABC-TV: New York, August 10, #778, Wellesley College Center for Research on Women, Wellesley, MA 02481-8203. Used by permission of the author.

the Mellon Seminar participants meet together once a month for five hours to consider each of their academic areas or disciplines in turn. The questions we ask in that seminar for each discipline are the same: "What is the present content and scope and methodology of the discipline?" (Or, to use a phrase of Elizabeth Minnich's: "What are the **shaping dimensions** of the discipline at present?") And then. "How would the discipline need to change to reflect the fact that women are half the world's population and have had, in one sense, half the world's experience?"

The phases in curricular revision which I will describe owe their conceptualization in part to the work of the seminar. Sometimes after a presentation, a member of this group will say, "We really can't get any further in my field on this question." Or "I think you can get further ahead in Religion than we can in Philosophy; we can't make most women's experience visible, given the self-definition of the field." There is a sense among the seminar members that degrees of change do exist in the process of curriculum transformation. I will trace here what I think are the types of curriculum corresponding to five phases of perception.

In naming the five phases I will use history as the first example. I call Phase 1 Womanless History; Phase 2 Women in History; Phase 3 Women as a Problem, Anomaly, or Absence in History; Phase 4 Women As History; and Phase 5 History Redefined or Reconstructed to Include us All.

Analogously, we can have Womanless Political Science, then Women in Politics, then Women as an Absence, Anomaly or Problem for Political Science (or in Politics); next, Women As Political, (the study of women's lives in all their political dimensions, or, to use a phrase from Elizabeth Janeway's, *The Powers of the Weak,* the politics of the family, the school, the neighborhood, and the curriculum, the politics of culture, class, race and sex); and finally, Politics Redefined or Reconstructed to include multiple spheres of power, inner and outer.

Or we can have Womanless Biology, followed by (great) Women in Biology. Here, Phase 2 tends to be about a few of the few who had access to lab equipment, a handful of women still remembered for their work. In Phase 3 we have Women as Problems or Absences or Anomalies in Biology, for example as analyzed in the collection of essays called *Women Look at Biology Looking at Women.* In Phase 4 we have women taking the initiative to do

science in a new way, on a differing base of assumptions and finally, we can imagine Biology Reconstructed to Include us All.

The Phase 1 syllabus is very exclusive; Phase 4 and 5 syllabi are very inclusive. Individuals and courses do not, as I have said, exist in fixity in given phases, but will show points of dynamic interaction among several of the phases, if the teacher or researcher is conscious of the magnitude of the problem of women's invisibility, and of the many forms of the problem. I think that superficial curriculum change gets arrested in what I have called Phases 2 and 3.

In proposing these phases of curriculum change. I may seem to be creating yet another ladder of values and arranging things so that Phase 1 is the bottom and Phase 5 is the top. This is not quite so; in one respect it is the reverse of what I intend, and what I see in my mind's eye. For Phase 1 thinking reinforces what we have been taught is the "top" and Phase 4 corresponds to what we have been taught is the "bottom" according to present hierarchies of knowledge, power and validity. Phase 5 puts what we were taught to devalue and to value into a new revolutionary relation to each other.

For me, the varieties of curriculum change in order to be accurately understood need to be set against models of the larger society and should be overlaid on an image of a broken pyramid. This image has come for me to stand for our culture as a whole. In my imagination it represents our institutions and also our individual psyches. I want to spend some time now developing this image of the broken pyramid and setting what I see as phases or types of curriculum development against the background of that image.

The upper part of the broken pyramid consists of peaks and pinnacles, peaks and pinnacles particularly in the public institutional life of nations, of governments, of militia, universities, churches, and corporations. Survival in this world is presented to us as a matter of winning lest you lose. We are taught to see both our institutions and ourselves within this framework: either you are a winner or you are among the losers. The winners are few, and high up on narrow bits of land which are the peaks; the losers are many and are low down, closer to the bottom. Institutions, groups, and individuals are seen as being on their way to the bottom if they are not on their way to the top.

The mountainous and pyramidal form of our society and of our psyches is a social construct invented by us. The shape of the pyramid was not necessarily inherent in the human materials but developed in our minds, and has now become reified, not only in our minds but in our institutions and in our behavior. We are taught that civilization has a clear top and a clear bottom. The liberal arts curriculum has been particularly concerned with passing on to students the image of what the "top" has been.

Both our public institutions and collective as well as innermost psyches have taken on the hierarchical structure of this winning-versus-losing kind of paradigm. Those who climb up get power; we are taught that there is not power for the many but there is power at the top for those few who can reach the peaks and pinnacles. College liberal arts catalogues, which package liberal arts education for sale to incoming students and to parents of students, make the claim that colleges help students to realize themselves, to discover their individual uniquenesses and to develop confidence which will lead to achievement, accomplishment, and success in the world outside the university. Most of this language masks. I think, the actual liberal arts function which is, at present, to train a few students to climb up to pinnacles and to seize them so as to have a position from which power can be felt, enjoyed, exercised and imposed on others. Images of upward mobility for the individual pervade the admissions literature of most of our colleges and universities today. We are taught that the purpose of education is to assist us in climbing up those peaks and pinnacles to enjoy the "fulfillment of our potential," which I take to mean the increased ability to have and use power for our individual selves.

As I have said, we are taught that only a few will be able to wield power from the summits. Behind the talk about scholarly excellence and teaching is hidden a voice that says: "The territory of excellence is very small. Only a few will be allowed to gain the peaks, having had access to excellent teaching and having earned excellent grades." A few will be "winners," perhaps featured in the subject matter of future courses, as winners in the history of the world—those worthy of the limelight. A few will be tenured and promoted in the pyramid of the college or the university or in the pyramids of legal, medical, finan-

cial, and governmental institutions, but the rest in some sense or other are made to be or feel like losers. The words "success," "achievement," and "accomplishment" have been defined in such a way as to leave most people and most types of life out of the picture.

Now, Womanless History is characteristic of thinking which reflects the society's pyramidal winning-vs-losing mentality. Phase 1 curriculum in the United States reflects only the highest levels of the existing pyramids of power and value. Womanless History specializes in telling about those who had most public power and whose lives were involved with laws, wars, acquisition of territory, and management of power. History is usually construed, in other words, to exclude those who didn't possess a good deal of public power. This kind of history perfectly reinforces the dominant political and social systems in that nonwhite males and women, the vast majority of the world's population, are construed as not worth studying in a serious and sustained way, and not worth including in the version of reality passed on to students.

Womanless History, in other words, is about "winning" and has been written by the "winners." Feminist analysts of that version of reality have come to realize that a privileged class of men in western culture have defined what is power and what constitutes knowledge. Excluded from these definitions and hence from consideration in the traditional History curriculum are types of power and versions of knowledge which this privileged class of men does not share. Hence a corrective is called for if the definitions of power and knowledge are to become more complete.

At first glance, the Phase 2 corrective, Women in History, appears to be an improvement over Phase 1, but Phase 2 History is very problematical for me and for many of my colleagues. I have come to think that it is worse than the traditional curriculum, worse than Womanless History in that it pretends to show us "women" but really shows us only a famous few, or makes a place for a newly-declared or a newly-resurrected famous few. It is problematical to argue **against** Phase 2 history at a time when many are concerned that young women have something up there on the pinnacles for them to look at and when many others want to restore to women of the past a historical record which has been taken from them. But Phase 2 is all too often like an affirmative action program which implies that institutions are model places which need only to help a few of the "inferior" Others to have the opportunity to climb onto these pinnacles with their "superiors." Affirmative action programs rarely acknowledge that the dominant group can and should learn from the Other. Phase 2 curricular policies, like most affirmative action programs, assume that our disciplines are basically functioning well, and that all that women or Blacks or Chicanos could need or want is to be put into higher slots on the reading list. In other words, the World Civilization course just needs a little attention to Africa, as a disadvantaged culture, giving Africa the time of day but from a position of "noblesse oblige."

In Phase 2 History the historians' spotlight is simply trained a little lower than usual on the pinnacles, so that we see people like Susan B. Anthony trying to scramble up the rocks. Anthony is featured as a hero in that she tried to make it into men's territory and succeeded. And she gets on the silver dollar. But there were all the other women on behalf of whom she was speaking whose lives remain completely invisible to us. That's the trouble with Phase 2 History. It conveys to the student the impression that women don't really exist unless they are exceptional by men's standards. Women don't really exist unless we "make something of ourselves" in the public world. Phase 2 History or Literature or Science or Economics repeatedly features the famous or "notable" or salaried women. In the American Literature course on 19th Century America, Emerson's friend Margaret Fuller may get added to the syllabus but all the women of Emerson's family, as representative of the women whose unseen labor made possible that transcendental obliviousness to daily life, get left out. You never see in English courses anything about all the women who were preparing Emerson's meals while he wrote "Self Reliance." In Phase 2 History we particularly see consorts featured. Sometimes they are neutered consorts like Betsy Ross who is seen as a sort of asexual "forefather." Sometimes you see a woman who is both a public figure and a consort, like Cleopatra, or consort manqué, like Queen Elizabeth. But very rarely do you get a sense of all that substructure of the culture composed of women who didn't "make it" into the spheres of power, and who did not furnish material for myths. And almost always (or quite often) the women who

did "make it" are devalued in the historical record by being portrayed chiefly in terms of sexual relationships. Phase 2 thinking never recognizes "ordinary" life, unpaid labor, or "unproductive" phenomena like human friendship.

Phase 3 takes us further down from the pinnacles of power toward the valleys. It brings us in touch with most women, and makes us realize that curriculum change which addresses only discrimination against women or "barriers" to women hardly begins to get at the major problems we have faced and the major experiences we have had. Phase 3 introduces us to the politics of the curriculum. We can't simply "include" those who were left out, who were "denied opportunity" to be studied. It's not an accident we were left out. And as Marilyn Schuster, a Dean at Smith College, has said: "First you study women to fill in the gaps, but then it becomes more complicated because you see that the gaps were there for a reason."

Phase 3 curriculum work involves getting angry at the fact that we have been seen only as an absence, an anomaly or a problem for History, for English, for Biology, rather than as part of the world, part of whatever people have chosen to value. There is anger at the way women have been treated throughout history. We are angry that instead of being seen as part of the norm, we have been seen, if at all, as a "problem" for the scholar, the society, or the world of the powerful. People doing scholarship in Women's Studies get particularly angry at the fact that the terms of academic discourse and of research are loaded in such a way that we are likely to come out looking like "losers" or looking like pathological cases. A teacher at one of the Claremont Colleges has eloquently asked, "How can we alter the making and the finding of knowledge in such a way that difference needn't be perceived as deprivation?" Phase 3 work makes us angry that women are seen either as deprived or as exceptional. I think that the anger in Phase 3 work is absolutely vital to us. Disillusionment is also a feature of Phase 3 realizations, for many teachers. It is traumatically shocking to white women teachers in particular to realize that we were not only trained but were as teachers unwittingly training others to overlook, reject, exploit, disregard, or be at war with most people in the world. One feels hoodwinked and also sick at heart at having been such a vehicle for racism, misogyny, upper class power and militarism.

Phase 3 challenges the literary canon. We ask who defined greatness in literature, and who is best served by the definitions? We ask the same in Religion—who defined "major" theology, and "important" church history? In Music and Art, who defined greatness and whom do the definitions best serve? Both the definers and those best served by the definitions were Western white men who had positions of cultural power or who fared fairly well within cultural systems.

In Phase 3, scholars rankle against statements like this which as freshmen they might have taken for granted: "The quest for knowledge is a universal human undertaking." "Economic behavior is a matter of choice." "Man has mastered the environment and harnessed the resources of the planet." We may laugh today, but as freshmen, we didn't laugh. We just absorbed these ideas.

Once when I was a Freshman, the present personality in me, then a hidden part of the psyche, below the winning and losing part, spoke up—just once, six weeks into a freshman social science course on the History of the Church in Western Civilization. I suddenly blurted out something I hadn't meant to say at all. It was that voice which is now speaking to you directly today, briefly speaking then, 26 years ago. I was in a small discussion section which accompanied one of the Harvard lecture courses. The "section man," who was a graduate student, was running a discussion on fine points of theology, and on the governance of bishops and kings. Joined with him in this conversation were two dazzling freshmen; one was Reinhold Niebuhr's son, who knew all the fine points of theology; the other was from Pasadena, a tall, godlike man, with a tan and a tennis racket; I remember him as wearing a cream-colored cable sweater with the two blue and red stripes, **and** knowing all the fine points of theology, too. I couldn't understand what was going on in any of this course. I had not even begun to learn about the medieval feudal system until I took this course. Then suddenly one day, in the middle of a discussion, I blurted out: "I don't see why the serfs stood for it."

We hadn't even been talking about the serfs. You can imagine the dilemma of the teacher, hearing this utterly irrelevant freshman comment coming from someone who hadn't said anything for six weeks. He said gently, but in a very somber voice, "I think you had better see me in office

hours." I was of course too scared to go see him in office hours; as one who had not yet noticed how the pyramids of power work, I was afraid of those in authority, and I always hoped that the professors wouldn't notice me. I was humiliated by my comment. I assumed that the others in the class understood how the feudal system worked, and that I was the only one who didn't understand "why the serfs stood for it."

I went through four years at Harvard thinking that everyone else had understood medieval social systems, but then in later years, after I had done some teaching. I began to see further dimensions in that uncontrolled comment. It was coming from a "serf," a freshman girl who was asking not only "Where are the serfs, and where are the women?" but also "Where am I in this picture, and why am I standing for this picture that leaves me out, and this discussion which leaves me out?" Years later I began to see that, uncontrolled though that comment was, it was based on very important material which hadn't been covered in that course about the pinnacles. We never studied the peasant woman on her knees in Chartres: we only studied Abelard in the streets of Paris and discussed what various intellectual geniuses or power-holders were saying. And the discussion itself was only among the power-holders.

It seems to me now, in retrospect, that if my teacher had really been able to do the kind of systemic teaching which Women's Studies encourages and enables one to do, he could have quickly filled me in on a number of points which would have shed light on the stability of the pyramidal feudal system. He could have mentioned the psychological theory of identification with authority; there was more in it for the serfs to identify upward with the apparent protector than to identify laterally with people who couldn't help them. He could have reminded me that before the Industrial Revolution serfs didn't have telephones, newsletters or political movements to allow them to work for revolution. He could have mentioned the serfs' identification with the Kingdom of Heaven. Years later, I began to realize that all teachers are trained to isolate bits of knowledge and that this very training keeps their students in turn oblivious of the larger systems which hold pyramids of power in place. I was obediently oblivious; having been raised on the American myth of individuality. I thought that there were no social systems anywhere, and then couldn't imagine why a serf wouldn't assert that God-given gift of individuality and make his way out of what I considered to be "the bottom," in the first social system I had ever noticed.

This autobiographical vignette is important to me now, though it shamed me and gnawed at me for years at Harvard. For a long time I thought it was "the stupidist thing I ever said in college," but now that I have flip-flopped the pyramid, I think it was one of the smarter things I said in college. This inchoate and uncontrolled outburst of the serf against a Harvard education came from a voice which spoke for people and functions of personality which we are trained to disregard.

Phase 3 gives way to Phase 4 at the moment when all of those who were assigned to specialize in the functions of life below the fault line refuse to see ourselves only as a problem and begin to think of ourselves as valid human beings. Phase 4 vision construes the life below the break in the pyramid as the real though unacknowledged base of life and civilization. In the 4th phase we women say: "On our own ground, we are not losers; we have had half the human experience. The fact that we are different from men and diverse within our own group doesn't necessarily mean we are deprived." Those who embark on Phase 4 thinking find the accepted pyramidal modes of seeing and evaluating are inappropriate to our sense of worth. For within the pyramidal images we can be seen only as being "at the bottom." All of the first three phases of curricular revision which I have described omit that positive look at us which is the crucial healing ingredient of the 4th phase and the chief revolutionary ingredient of the 5th phase. In other words, I see Phases 1, 2 and 3 in varying degrees as misogynist. In Phase 1, we weren't in history; Phase 2 allows that only a few exceptional women were in history, and Phase 3 says we were in history problematically, messing up the purity of the historical model, or making demands and being victimized. Women or men who say only these things have internalized the view of women as problems, or as deviant people with "issues." Such people can demonstrate persistent internalized misogyny in the midst of their righteous and legitimate anger on behalf of wronged women.

Phase 4 is the development in which we see Women As History, and explore all the life existing below the public world of winning and losing.

Now I want to go back to the image of the broken pyramid and say that in the top part of the pyramid I drew, the only two alternatives are to win or to lose. But there is another whole domain of the psyche and of the public and private life that works on a different value system or ethical perception altogether. These are a value system and an ethical system which operate laterally on the principle that you work for the decent survival of all, and that this effort conduces to your own survival and your humanity as well. This value system is approved in the spheres we have called private, invisible, and domestic. I cannot claim that families actually work on a lateral model. But mothers are not specifically trained to do with their children something that would involve, for example, marking the children and grading them to see which will win and which will lose. The publicly sanctioned behavior of mothers, though it is partly to make the children adjust to the pyramids in the public spheres, is partly to work for the decent survival of all the children at once. Moreover, the idea of decent survival of all lies behind our friendships and our conversations and much of our daily life as we go about our ordinary business. Most of what we do is on this lateral plane of working for our own decent survival rather than "getting ahead."

Now, the assigned work of women in every culture has chiefly been in this unacknowledged, lateral network of life below the fault line, supporting the rest of the pyramid but really opposed to it, because lateral consciousness is at odds with the value system of winning versus losing. The two systems have been pitted against each other through projection onto two "opposite" sexes. The value system of winning and losing has particularly been projected onto white Western man, and men in power in all cultures, and the value system and the work of the part below the break involving decent survival of all has been particularly projected onto women and other lower caste people. However, in the pyramidal configuration, one system is subordinated to the other. The contest is not equal. In Phase 4 thinking, whether in daily life or in curriculum revision, you call into question whether all that work behind the scenes is the work of losers. You ask if it isn't the real work of civilization. And you may also ask whether it isn't the work of the "haves" rather than the "have-nots." That's the moment at which the pyramid in a social construct begins to be seen as the creation of a special interest group. The work of taking care of ourselves and other people can be seen as a role assignment in our society, carrying many rewards and gratifications as well as punishments. If it is seen only as the work of victims, then it is still seen. I believe, in a misogynist way. We who were assigned the work of domestic upkeep and maintenance for the human race and the making of ties and relationships have done in many ways a reasonably good job of it. The race hasn't blown itself up yet. We most need continued work for decent survival of all in a nuclear age. The collaborative values coming out of the base of the pyramid are the ones we desperately need in public policy-makers.

We cannot, by wishing, dismantle the upper parts of the pyramid, or bring the unseen base into compatibility with the upper part. The two types of existence are presently in enmity with each other, as two differing value systems of "mastery" and "decency" (or compliance) projected onto powerful men and onto lower caste people respectively. But we desperately need for the future to try to carry the values from the undervalued sphere into the public spheres, in order to change the behavior and the sense of reality of all of our public institutions and the people who control them. The study of women, like women themselves, can help to supply the vision, the information, and the courage needed for this task, and can thus increase our chances of global and personal survival. I hope you realize that I am not claiming that women are morally superior to men by birth, and hence able to save the world. It is just that we were assigned the task which Jean Baker Miller calls "developing ourselves through the development of others." And that has meant that we have developed skills in keeping the human race alive which are the basic indispensable skills in an age of nuclear weapons.

Curriculum work in Phase 4, when you have begun to construe women as the world majority and see women in some respect as the "haves," not simply the "have nots," breaks all the rules of ordinary research or teaching. One studies American literature of the 19th century not by asking, "Did the women write anything good?" but by asking "What did the women write?" One asks not "What great work by a woman can I include in my reading list?" but "How have women used the written word?" In Phase 4 one asks, "How have women of color in many cultures told their sto-

ries?" not "Is there any good third world literature?" Phase 4 looks not at Abelard but at that peasant woman who didn't have any "pure" theology or even understand the heresies, but who rather had an overlay of platitudes and "Old Wives' Tales" and riddles and superstitions and theological scraps from here and there and kitchen wisdom in her mind. In Phase 4, one looks at the mix of life, and instead of being scared by the impurity of the mix, notices that the impurities reflect the fact that we have been terribly diverse in our lives. Biology taught from a Phase 4 perspective does not define life in terms of the smallest possible units that may be isolated and then examined in isolation. When you are doing Phase 4 Biology, it seems to me you particularly teach reverence for the organism, identification with it, and you see in terms of large, interlocking and relational systems which need to be acknowledged and preserved or whose balance needs to be observed and appreciated.

Many of civilization's present emergencies suggest that we need wider constructions of knowledge in all fields than our present investigators have developed, with their exclusive methods of study, whether empirical or otherwise. All of Phase 4 work is highly speculative and experimental in its epistemology, for we have not yet learned to name unnamed experiences of the plural, the common, the lateral and the "ordinary" life. In Phase 4 curriculum development, it feels as though we are all making it up together. Teachers can look at each other's bibliographies, but this work is so new that we need people to invent their own ways of describing what they are finding, to invent new categories for experience, new ways of doing research, and new ways of teaching.

In Phase 4, most of the teaching materials are non-traditional. Moreover, the boundaries between disciplines start to break down, for scholars doing feminist work come to realize that boundaries between disciplines serve to keep our present political, economic and social arrangements in place. There are a number of other boundaries that break down also. The relationship between the teacher and the material changes in Phase 4 because the material is so nontraditional and includes so much that we have never studied before that the teacher becomes less of an expert. The relationship between the teacher and the student changes because the teacher now seems less "high" and the student less "low" in knowledge about the areas of life being studied. Then, in addition, there is less of a distinction between the "observer" and the "observed," and often the "subject" of study is treated, in Phase 4 work, as a primary authority on her own experience. That is, economists doing really good work on women will listen very seriously to what a housewife wants to say about spending and then borrow from Psychology and Religion and Sociology to analyze her spending patterns and perceptions, rather than trying to fit her into an intricate economic model already built, which could account for her behavior in terms of a number of variables which have already been identified but not by her.

The pinnacles of fragmented and isolated knowledge seem more and more abstract and irrelevant as you try to learn from within women's experience what women's experience has been like. Phase I reinforces vertical value systems; Phase 4 reveals systems of lateral values and relationships. One key hallmark of Phase 4 consciousness and curriculum is that the Other stops being considered something lesser to be dissected, deplored, devalued or corrected. The Other becomes, as it were, organically connected to one's self. Realities, like people, seem plural but unified. That fragmentation of knowledge which characterizes our disciplines at present begins to end if you descend to the valleys of civilization in Phase 4 and you start to study commonality, plural experience and the work of daily survival. You also come to realize that the valleys are in fact more suitable places to locate civilization than are the deoxygenated summits of the mountains. The heights of specialization, like the concentration of economic power in the hands of a few are seen to have questionable usefulness to our continued survival.

One danger of Phases 3 and 4 work is that scholars trying to alter the structures of knowledge or society make the mistake of thinking that all women are alike, so that the study of a few will suffice to fill in the picture. Minority women in particular have often stated that Women's Studies tends to fall into some of the same traps as the traditional curriculum in describing chiefly the elites and the worlds they control, or in polarizing the elites and non-elites along bipolar lines.

When well done, Phase 4 work honors particularity at the same time it identifies common denominators of experience. It stresses diversity and plurality, and for many people doing work on

women in Phase 4. William James's *Varieties of Religious Experience* seems like a model book. It takes the pluralistic view that there are many varieties of religious life, and that one needn't rank and judge them. It shows a cast of mind which also accompanies serious work on women.

Now, Phase 5 curriculum revision is the hardest to conceive. I said it was the phase in which History (or Knowledge) gets redefined, reconstructed to include us all. But how can this be done? At a conference in 1981 for college deans and presidents held at the Johnson Foundation's Wingspread Center in Wisconsin, Gerda Lerner gave the keynote address on "Liberal Education and the New Scholarship on Women." After her talk, I asked, "On the basis of all the work you have now done on American women's history and on the experience of Black Americans, how would you organize a basic text called *American History?*" She answered, "I couldn't begin to do that; it is too early. It would take a team of us, fully funded, two years just to get the table of contents organized— just to imagine how we would categorize it." And then she said, "But don't worry, we were 6,000 years carefully building a patriarchal structure of knowledge, and we've had only 12 years to try to correct it, and 12 years is nothing."

As Elizabeth Minnich has pointed out, there have been important movements, to do and to institutionalize women's scholarship in earlier decades, so this isn't only a 12-year effort. But Lerner's larger point is important. We have had only a little time to correct major paradigms. We don't know yet what reconstructed History would look like. In my view, the reconstructed curriculum not only draws a line around the vertical and lateral functions, examining all of human life and perception. It also puts these horizontal and vertical elements in a revolutionary new relation to one another, so that the pyramidal shapes of the psyche, the society, the world are discarded, seen as inaccurate and also incompatible with the decent, balanced survival of human psyches, institutions, and nations. Global shapes replace the pyramids. Human collaborative potential is explored and competitive potential subjected to a sustained critique. A genuinely inclusive curriculum, based on global imagery of self and society, would reflect and reinforce the common human abilities and inclinations to cultivate the soil of the valleys and to collaborate for survival.

A teacher doing work in Phase 5 develops inclusive rather than exclusive vision and realizes that many things hang together. A Phase 5 curriculum would help us to produce students who can see patterns of life in terms of systems of race, culture, caste, class, gender, religion, national origin, geographical location and other influences on life which we haven't begun to name. At the same time, Phase 5 curriculum promises to produce students who can carry with them into public life the values of the private sphere, because inclusive learning allows them to value lateral functions rather than discredit them in the context of paid or public life. Right now, Phase 2 thinking tends to work only for the promotion of individual values; it tends to advance a few women who can "make it in the public world." But I think that putting women's bodies into high places does little for people in the aggregate and little or nothing for women in the aggregate. It makes life nice for, or brings power to, a few women but it doesn't necessarily bring about social change. At present our so-called "leaders," women included, are mostly working from that misguided world view that says either you win or you lose. It's not true, and women in the aggregate know it's not true. And the conviction that you either win or lose is, as I have said, a very dangerous ethic and prescription to carry into public life and into leadership positions at a time when nuclear weapons are what you have to test the idea with.

We can't afford to have leaders who think only in terms of winning or losing. And so it seems to me critically important for us to develop a Phase 5 curriculum. But lest you think I am forgetting the educational world in my interest in world peace, let me say that the development of Phase 5 curriculum is also important to colleges and universities because of their own educational claims. The university claims to develop and to pass on to students and to the wider society an accurate and comprehensive body of knowledge. And in the words of Ruth Schmidt, the Provost of Wheaton College, and now President of Agnes Scott College, "If you claim to teach about the human race, and you don't know anything about half the human race, you really can't claim to know or teach much about the human race." The main argument for curriculum change is that it will help universities to fulfill their acknowledged primary responsibility: to develop and pass on to the

society and to students accurate bodies of knowledge. Since women are now left out, those bodies of knowledge are grossly inaccurate.

I want now to illustrate these five interactive phases of curriculum development in five specific disciplines. While I was writing this part of my talk, discipline by discipline, abstractly analyzing Psychology, English, and so on, I heard the voice of Florence Howe asking her familiar question. "Where are the women?" So I stopped organizing my ideas according to those fragmented peaks and pinnacles called "disciplines," and began mentally to follow a group of women like ourselves studying in a variety of curricula from the most exclusive to the most inclusive I could imagine, and then I watched the effects on their minds and their lives. These women are named Meg, Amy, and Jo, and Jo's children: Maya and Angela and Adrienne.

Meg feels extremely privileged to go to college and to sit at the feet of her professors. Her Phase One freshman English class is called "Man's Quest for Knowledge." She studies *Huckleberry Finn*, *Moby Dick*, Walt Whitman's poetry, Emerson on "Self Reliance," Thoreau's *Walden*, a Hemingway novel and Norman Mailer. Meg thinks it really is amazing when you think about it, how man has quested for knowledge: it's a universal trait! The expository essays are very difficult for Meg to write, and she cannot remember after she's handed them in what any of them were about. She gets middling grades: her professors find her indecisive. In Medieval History she studies bishops and kings. She wonders once or twice, but doesn't ask, why the serfs stood for the feudal system. Mostly she hopes that she will marry a strong man who will take care of her just as a bishop or a king must have taken care of the serfs.

In Psychology, Meg learns of a number of interesting complexes, and she feels particularly glad that she has studied the Oedipus complex because it will help her as a parent, some day, to understand her sons. In Freud's model of the personality she identifies strongly with the superego. She is very relieved that there is a part of the personality with which she can identify as a beautiful soul, one who has transcended the moiling, toiling world and the need to compete. She overlooks the fact that Freud did not think women had highly developed superegos. She is vulnerable, deluded, and ignorant about what Freud really said, since she has received no training in looking for herself in the curriculum.

In Biology, having been told that man has mastered nature and that knowledge is mastery, Meg dissects a frog. She finds this repulsive, but necessary for Science. After all, Scientists would have to take life apart in order to understand it, wouldn't they? Mostly she dreams of security, and will succeed in marrying, at the end of her junior year, her lab partner. In Art History, which is Meg's favorite course, she moves away from that bewildering world which really hasn't made much sense to her and looks at beautiful things. She really respects her art professor, a kindly man who is teaching her what to admire in the great masters' work. She hopes that when she and her husband have raised their children and have some extra money, they can themselves collect some beautiful works of art for the walls of their house. She would, however, not want to collect second-rate art, so that may be a problem.

Amy goes to college a few years after Meg. Amy talks a lot about role models. Amy intends to Make It. She says things like "My mother never did anything." Amy's freshman English course is called "The individual versus Society." She studies *Huckleberry Finn, Moby Dick,* Walt Whitman's poetry, Emerson's "Self Reliance," Thoreau's *Walden, The Autobiography of Frederick Douglass,* Hemingway, Kerouac and Sylvia Plath. This is a Phase 2 course; there is a black writer and a woman on the reading list. The curriculum has started to change to include a few "exceptional" members of minority groups who are considered capable of "making it" in the syllabus. Amy gets a lot of "ammunition" for her life from Sylvia Plath's character in *The Bell Jar* who says, "I didn't want to be the platform that the man shoots off from; I wanted to be the rocket myself and shoot off in all directions." Amy is fueled by Esther Greenwood's words to drive herself to exceptional heights. She doesn't notice that the speaker, like Plath herself, was suicidal. She is identifying upward, and she likes the Medieval/Renaissance course best when it moves from that static feudal system into the development of guilds, and the middle class, and upward mobility. She is psychologically tuned into the theme of individual autonomy that is running through that part of the course.

In her Women in Psychology course, Phase 2, she learns about women who "made it" in

Psychology. She learns nothing of their struggles nor of the many who have remained invisible to us. "They did it, I can too," Amy believes. "Women can do whatever they want; if they want anything enough to really work for it. Of course Biology isn't destiny." Amy is, however, very little interested in the psychology of women, and her courses don't give her anything to make her interested in her own psychology, or make her ask why she has switched from pre-law to art or wonder about any inner life in women which psychological research hasn't named.

In her Biology course, she is interested in Darwin's theories about competition and the "survival of the fittest." She thinks of herself as one of the "fittest." The losers will lose, but she, Amy, is going to make it in a man's world. She thinks of herself as a Frederick Douglass, "smart enough to get away," and as an organism ready to adapt to a particular niche in the environment, her niche; she intends to fight for her niche.

Amy's Art History work further demonstrates to her that women have now "arrived," because her Impressionists course includes Mary Cassatt and Berthe Morisot. Amy does not notice that they are called "Mary" and "Berthe" throughout the course, whereas the men are "Monet" and "Degas." All of Amy's eloquent papers in her freshman year in every course are variations on the theme of "The Individual vs Society." She never sees herself as "Society." Amy has been given the Phase 2 vision of herself as the unique woman rising up in history and leaving her mother behind where mothers really always were.

Jo comes to college later than Amy, tired and rather battered by certain personal episodes in her life. She comes reluctantly to college for further training; she is a "re-entry" woman. She finds to her surprise that college speaks to her condition. She comes alive in class. Other students like to be with Jo and Jo likes to be with them. She is somewhat older than most around her. In her freshman English course she reads Dale Spender's *Man Made Language* and she reads Nancy Henley and Barrie Thorne, and then she reads Emily Dickinson and is invited to take an interdisciplinary look at Emily Dickinson after having read five other feminist critics. She writes a paper she will never forget, on Emily Dickinson as a person working on many rebellions at the same time—against the social mores and axioms of her community, against patriarchal, public "authorities," against intellectual certainty, against the theology of her church, and against conventions of the sentence and of language itself. She will never forget this paper; it actually possesses her while she writes it. Somewhere in the curriculum she is finding something that speaks to her personally and directly about her own life.

In Medieval History, Jo's teacher introduces her to the essay by Joan Kelly-Gadol: "Did Women Have a Renaissance?" She gets mad, particularly when learning the answer is "No, not in the Renaissance," and she determines to mistrust periodization of history from then on. She has found something that fits with her sense of not having fitted in. She is being given the "doubled vision" which Joan Kelly refers to in one of her last works, of both fitting in and being alien and apart from a dominant culture. She is being given the enabling doubled vision that explains her life to her.

Then in Psychology Jo reads Naomi Weisstein on "How Psychology Constructs the Female," and Carol Gilligan. In a time warp, Jo has just received Gilligan's latest book, *In a Different Voice.* She reads that women don't fit the existing models of moral development and that they really seem to test out differently. She learns that Lawrence Kohlberg's "Six Universal Phases" are not after all universal but were based on a small white male sample. But because Jo is in a Phase 3 curriculum, she is also told that Gilligan's sample has its limits too. She learns that women are probably more diverse than most of the existing research shows. She reads Berger and Luckmann's *The Social Construction of Reality* and learns that the world of "knowledge" was constructed by cultural authority figures. She finds herself almost insouciant in starting to write a paper now.

In Biology, she reads Ruth Hubbard's essay, "Have Only Men Evolved?" She is shocked to learn that scientific knowledge is permeated with politics. She learns that accounts of evolution and of human propensities which she had taken as objective are completely androcentric. She learns that all forms of female life have been seen as defective or incapacitated versions of male life. She can hardly bear to think that even Science is not objective, but as her distress grows she finds herself grateful to Ruth Hubbard for a metaphor which explains her distress to her: she looks out the back window of a bus and sees that she is herself pushing the bus in which she is riding.

And then in her Art History course Jo, in another time warp, goes to New York City and sees Mary Beth Edelman's work, filled with anger and expressiveness and female nudity. Jo is shaken but not revolted. She invites Amy who lives in New York, to join her at the show. Amy is patronizing; Jo has nothing much to say but is moved by the show in ways she cannot express.

Some time later, Jo's children come to college. They are twins. She has named them Maya and Angela, not by accident. Their freshman English course isn't in English at all. It is in Spanish. They need Spanish for an oral history project they are doing. In my fantasy they are at college at Humboldt State. They are spending a great deal of time becoming proficient in Spanish, and moreover, their final exams in the Spanish Language and Composition course are not only on the way they read and write the language but also on their ability to elicit information from others in Spanish, their ability to understand what they have heard, and their ability to carry on a conversation in Spanish, linking on to previous things said rather than directing the talk or making statements.

In the History component of their curriculum, these twins have a project on which they are doing oral history research with six Spanish-speaking women. It started to be the history of migrant labor in a certain part of northern California but the students persuaded the professor not to label it a history of migrant labor before they had interviewed these women, lest they narrow the canvas too much. The students have decided that right now it will be an open-ended series of interviews and the topic will not be named. They will ask the women about their lives rather than asking them about migrant labor history; then they'll see where the women start.

In Psychology, Maya and Angela read Jean Baker Miller's *Toward a New Psychology of Women* and they feel they have been invited on an exploration with her, to try to name all of that women's experience in us that doesn't come under the public spotlight and hasn't yet been focused on or seen to exist. They also read Caroll Smith-Rosenberg's essay, "The Female World of Love and Ritual: Relations Between Women in Nineteenth Century America," and see what a rich world is revealed when you look at women's lives starting from women's own ground. They begin to care about their mother's letters and their mother's past in a new way, and begin to understand why their mother named their sister Adrienne.

In Biology, Maya and Angela take a course called "A Feeling for the Organism: Science Without Mastery," read Evelyn Fox Keller's book of this title and Barbara McClintock's work on genetics in a field of corn. The course syllabus opens with a remark of McClintock's on receiving the Nobel Prize: "It might seem unfair to reward a person for having so much pleasure over the years, asking the maize plant to solve specific problems and then watching its responses."

Last of all, in Art, Maya and Angela have a terrific project and they are having a lot of fun doing it. They have two assignments in Art. Humboldt State, in my fantasy, has a big art building whose front hall is decorated by a long mural made by art students. Every year a student replaces a part of the mural. Maya and Angela each have to replace a previous year's painting with a tempera painting of their own. But what are they to replace? This is where their teaching assignment comes in. In this Phase 4 curriculum every student is also a teacher. Therefore Maya and Angela have to spend part of every day teaching some young children in a subject which they are themselves "taking." Maya and Angela have a group of ten children working with them to decide whose work from the previous year's mural will be taken down and whose work will be replaced by Maya's and Angela's new work. How will the judgments be made? The children are doing a number of things, both talking and writing about the paintings that are to be replaced and also copying them with their own paints. Maya and Angela are teaching art at the same time they are studying art because this revised Phase 4 curriculum not only lowers the usual wall between the teacher and the taught but also alters the relationship radically. Moreover, art is construed in my fantastic Humboldt State as including decoration of all of the environment beyond walls and canvases and pieces of paper. Therefore the second art assignment which Maya and Angela and their students have is to take care of one of 30 gardens assigned to their art class and they are allowed to plant it as they like but they must then maintain it throughout the year. The children dislike this assignment very much. Maya and Angela have chosen succulents and shrubs which need pruning and cleaning up; those plants thrive in the cli-

mate of the campus. The children wish there were flowers. Maya and Angela explain why this isn't a flower garden. The children watch the flowers wilting in other people's beds and gradually learn that there is a reason to plant shrubs which strike them nevertheless as unpromising, unpretty, and unromantic.

Maya and Angela have an ambition for the years after college. Their father lives in New Hampshire. Whenever they visit him in the summers they are galled by the New Hampshire license plate. It has a slogan which reads "Live Free or Die." The more they read it, the more it annoys them. So they are going to spend their time after college working for a few years in New Hampshire. They'll earn a living, but their aim is to change that slogan. They have a slogan they are going to try to get put in its place: "Share Life or Perish." They'll learn the political ropes, work through the legislature or lobby, or work through the state's committee system or campaign, or run for office; this is partly a lark but they're in dead earnest, and they'll give it a good try for ten years or so, as they make a living in New Hampshire. They imagine they'll have several public and professional and perhaps several private lives as well, before they're through.

Now these phases of curriculum have socialized each woman differently. Meg has been socialized to "fit in," oblivious to and therefore very vulnerable to the forces at work on and around her. Amy has been socialized to kill herself trying to be, and dreaming that she is, exceptional, different from other women, and dreaming that she will be seen as different from other women. Jo has been socialized to understand the interlocking systems that work to produce Meg's illusions. Amy's internalized misogyny, and the dangers to all of learning systems that exclude them. Maya and Angela have been educated to be quite happy with the diversity of life and canny about systems; they are able to use their anger in a way that gives them pleasure. They are real to themselves and may well become real to larger groups: a legislature, or drivers on the roads of New Hampshire. Well, what of Adrienne? Phase 5 remains for her. I dream we invent for her a circular, multicultural, inclusive curriculum which socializes people to be whole, balanced, and undamaged, which includes rather than excludes most parts of life, and which both fosters a pluralistic understanding and fulfills the dream of a common language. This is the Phase 5 curriculum.

Ten years after graduation Meg, deserted, divorced, and still not knowing what hit her reenters college as a Continuing Education student and now again reads the Masterworks of Western Civilization. She finds them not so great. She has learned that the bishops and kings do not take care of the serfs. She is bewildered, amazed by Jo's girls, Maya and Angela. She is in one course with them. They say things she couldn't have imagined at their age. She admires them, she likes them, and to her amazement, she is learning from them.

Amy does all right in New York as an artist; she is tough as nails, lonely, and scornful of the women's groups. She hasn't joined any collective. She's furious that she hasn't had her own show yet. She thinks if you're good enough you'll get recognized and that if women would only pull "their" act together and stop bitching, her chances for recognition would improve. Jo feels more and more whole and effective as her life goes on. She is past her first self-directed anger and her years from 40 onward are her best; she has herself learned to see systemically and become a force for personal and for aggregate change.

Maya and Angela—will they change the New Hampshire license plate? But wait—they haven't yet gone to college. We haven't yet got the Phase 4 curriculum. And the Phase 5 curriculum has not yet been invented for Adrienne. So the answer about what Maya and Angela and Adrienne will be able to do lies in us, and in the work we do now for their future and for ours.

Class 9

Native Americans in the USA (Part I)

Chapter 14
Civic Literacy, Sovereignty, and Violence: Ojibwe Treaty Rights and Racial Backlash in the North Country

Senese Gaetano B.

"Guy" Senese provides a detailed view of the nation's treatment of the Native American from the contemporary social issues surrounding hunting and fishing rights to the more complicated and misunderstood issues of tribal sovereignty.

Civic Literacy, Sovereignty, and Violence: Ojibwe Treaty Rights and Racial Backlash in the North Country

Gaetano B. Senese

Associate Professor of Foundations and Educational Leadership in the Center for Excellence in Education at Northern Arizona University, "Guy" Senese has taught on the Navajo reservation at the Rough Rock Demonstration School, in Junea, Alaska, where he has worked with Tlingit-Haida Native American students. His writings focus on Native American educational policy and policy history, and on culture and education, as well as ethnicity, and social class identity. He is currently working on the history and development of Little Singer Community School (Navajo) in Birdsprings, Arizona.

This paper is intended to expand on some dimensions of education which have great consequence for teacher educators, particularly those who train teachers whose pedagogy will impact Native American students and students living in association with American Indian peoples. It focuses on the phenomenon of civic discord, especially on violence as an expression and outgrowth of ill-considered yet legitimate differences between Native people's rights and those of the dominant culture. In order to counteract the potential for social and civic misunderstanding which may lead to discord, it is especially important that teacher educators be familiar with the unique government-to-government relationship between Native Americans and the United States federal government.

First I will discuss the way in which the rationality of native life has been viewed and continues to be viewed by non-Native Americans. As a consequence of this view native life and tribal sovereignty have been driven to the periphery of American consciousness. Yet tribal sovereignty is the lifeblood of American Indians. The education of both the student with roots in the dominant European American culture and the American Indian student is characterized by the marginalization of Native rights. A number of forms of violence, both to property and to persons, is a result.

I will argue that this violence is the result of a socialization process that omits key points of information about tribal and Indian rights, particularly sovereign rights. I then discuss the role for curriculum in this socialization process and suggest a proper notion of "countersocialization" and the establishment of proper and complete information in curricula as well as the reestablishment of American Indian sovereignty as a key component of pluralist U.S. democracy.

Critical civic literacy, the ability of ordinary citizens to see and secure their legitimate self-determined social policy among competing and often conflicting considerations, plays a crucial role in this countersocialization process. It has far-reaching consequences for the development of both Native American social policy and for the relationship between American Indians and non-Natives.

Traditional socialization and curricula have led to misunderstanding between the Indian and non-

Senese, Guy (1998), University of Northern Arizona. Reprinted by permission of the author.

Indian interests and indirectly to social policy injurious to Native people and others as well. Donald Fixico (1989) describes well some of the roots of this misunderstanding. He discusses the way the radical individualism of colonial societies clashed with the corporatism of Native peoples. For Native Americans, lands were part of the nature with which individuals and collectivities identified. For settlers nature was an object to be respected but ultimately mastered (p. 13). He cites Reginald Horsman's *Race and Manifest Destiny* as a work which outlines the clash between the mechanistic European view of nature and the organic relationship kept by Native peoples. (p. 15)

Native people have fought, since the European American incursion, to maintain a land base upon which they might live out the meaning of their existence. Today, this dream is kept alive in the lands guaranteed them by treaties made between tribes and the federal government. These lands, reservation lands, are often viewed by non-Natives as concentration camps, holdovers from the 19th century when the military ran out of options for the Native peoples. There is a great deal of misunderstanding about the nature of these lands and their meaning. Indeed, that confusion must become the object of a healing education.

From the early 1980s until the early 1990s, counties in northern Minnesota, Michigan, and especially Wisconsin, were the scene of serious conflict between Native American, principally Ojibwe (Chippewa), fishermen and local European Americans. Serious, sometimes violent protests occurred. These protests were accompanied by racial baiting, racist effigies, rock throwing, and physical threats to Native fishermen. These fishermen were engaged in legal spearing of game fish, a right reserved to them by treaty. These "usufructory" rights enable the Ojibwe to use nonreservation lands for hunting and fishing. They retained these rights on territories they "ceded" to the States and the U.S. government, in exchange for these reserved rights, in 1837 (Wisconsin Advisory Committee, 1989). Indeed, Chippewa often reject the term "treaty rights" since it implies that these rights were awarded by treaty. They remind us that these rights **always** have belonged to the Chippewa and were simply "reserved" by treaty (Strickland, Hertzberg, & Owens, 1990, p. 10).

The following is a poster reprinted in a Northern Wisconsin Ojibwe newspaper, *News from Indian Country.* That it was hung during the mid-1980s reflects clearly the tension between the Ojibwe spearfishers and Wisconsin sportfishing interests. It also suggests the potential for violence in relations between Indian people and whites in this area, a violence which requires a better understanding of Native American civic prerogatives. The poster is a mock invitation to an "Indian Shoot" and reads as follows:

FIRST ANNUAL INDIAN SHOOT
Time: Early spring, beginning of walleye run
Place: Northern Wisconsin lakes
Rules: Open shoot, off hand position only, no scopes, no sling, no tripods, and no whiskey for bait!
OPEN TO ALL WISCONSIN
TAXPAYING RESIDENTS
Residents that are BLACK, HMONG, CUBAN or those on WELFARE, A.D.C. FOOD STAMPS or any other government give-a-way program are not eligible. Scoring:
PLAIN INDIAN—5 POINTS
INDIAN WITH WALLEYES—10 POINTS
INDIAN WITH BOAT NEWER THAN YOURS—20 POINTS
INDIAN USING PITCHFORK—30 POINTS
INDIAN WITH H.S. DIPLOMA—50 POINTS
SOBER INDIAN—75 POINTS
INDIAN TRIBAL LAWYER—100 POINTS
Judges: GOV. TOMMY THOMPSON, REV. JESSE JACKSON
Prizes: FILLET-O-FISH SANDWICHES AND SIX PACKS OF "TREATY BEER"

The contest goes on to offer "Save a Fish, Spear an Indian" bumper stickers as consolation prizes.

While it is wrong to dignify this poster in any way, it does point up the extent to which racist sentiment may develop as an adjunct to what is widely observed to be a violation of the rights of the dominant culture. In this case it is against the Chippewa fishermen, who have, by treaty right, the freedom to use traditional fishing methods for subsistence. This right is clear in all the extant Ojibwe treaties in North Wisconsin. Yet such a level of sovereignty is poorly understood by non-Natives, who have not been educated about the law. In 1984, responding to the escalating threat of violence, the Wisconsin Advisory Committee to the U.S. Commission on Civil Rights conducted a community forum in Superior, Wisconsin. As a result of this forum, the Committee found that non-Indians' lack of information about Indian treaty rights and their legal implications was a major problem. One of the solutions they proposed was the development of a curriculum in which Wisconsin students would be exposed to the concept of Native American sovereignty and to Ojibwe hunting and fishing treaty rights on "ceded" territories. As these materials were developed and piloted, they came with an encouragement, not a requirement, that the districts use them.

For Native Americans, as well as for the understanding of those in the European American culture, reactions to the Native American presence on the nation is of great consequence, and the point is not that sovereignty must be won. We must understand that what is rightfully held must be protected. Multicultural presence in the polity is clear, yet understanding the actual nature of cultural difference has the potential, operating at the edge of the dominant cultural consciousness, to be the scapegoat for violence against person and property. It is my argument that division and destruction are the result of a rationality which cannot accept plural presences and differences which demand positions and places separate from the functional demands of the "uniculture" of property prerogative.

What sort of education is available to help make sense of these issues? Teacher educators must all receive an education that allows them to alert their students to the inadequacies of standard texts in social education, history, civics, and related subjects. They must begin the process of equipping their students to become sensitive critical readers of the curricula they use and to argue for curricular changes and supplementation that give a more accurate picture of the complexities and uniqueness of the American Indian political presence.

In the 1990s several popular high school U.S. government and U.S. history texts were in use in Northern Wisconsin. *American Government Today* (Lewinski, 1980) was used in a high school near the Lac Du Flambeau Ojibwe reservation, Wisconsin. In 768 pages of text, one page is devoted to American Indians in the U.S. In a brief scan of the index I found hundreds of other topics considered more worthy of as much or greater treatment, for example: Calvin Coolidge, 5 pages; Connecticut, 5 pages; The U.S. Secret Service, 5 pages; Dade County, Florida, 2 pages; Dekalb County, Ga. 2 pages; The Export Import Bank, 3 pages; The Fair Credit Reporting Act, 2 pages; Gerald Ford, 16 pages. There is nothing in this civics text on Native American civics.

I examined several U.S. history texts and found only one with more than a few cursory mentions of American Indian people (Smith, 1977). In this text there is nothing about the sovereign nature of treaties. Rather, what little it does contain is misleading information. For example, there is the obligatory map of culture and land use, where tribes covering a territory from southern California to the Rockies are shown as collective "Seed Gatherers" (p. 229). In the obligatory summary section, after having literally no substantive discussion of the nature of tribal sovereignty, students are asked, "In your opinion should the U.S. honor treaty commitments?" It might as well ask in the section on the making of the Constitution, "In your opinion should the federal government follow the Constitution?"

Another text, in a section covering U.S. history since 1945, devotes one page to the changes in Indian America during that period. It mentions nothing of the momentous events at Wounded Knee in 1972, nor the treaty rights victories, the occupation of Alcatraz Island, the B.I.A. occupation, nor the Alaska Native Claims Settlement, the largest land deal since the Louisiana Purchase. Rather it talks about the American Indian Movement setting up "patrol" to protect "drunken Indians from harassment." It uses this negative stereotypical language without mentioning that such harassment came not from thugs but from the Minneapolis police (Nash & Jeffrey, 1986).

During this period, what would a white or a Chippewa student in St. Croix, Wisconsin, learn about themselves or about each other with such guides. There is simply no discussion of the nature of treaty rights that underlie traditional fishing in Northern Wisconsin waters, or of other treaty rights which exist in tribal communities across the nation. In response to the discord emerging during the late 1980s at boatlandings across Ojibwe land and the "ceded" territories, in 1991 the state of Wisconsin passed curriculum reforms as one provision of its Act 31. The Act required the State Superintendent of Public Instruction to develop treaty rights curricula. However, no **implementation** was required to follow this. In 1995 teacher education programs were notified that teaching licenses would not be granted to students who had failed to participate in programs that made the treaty rights materials available. While some teacher education programs were enthusiastic, compliance was left to the discretion of individual colleges, and apparently in several cases professors met their obligation by simply handing out booklets developed by the State Department. Standard L of this legislation requires districts to cover treaty rights twice in elementary school and once in high school. However, these requirements have not been followed by a commitment to fund compliance oversight and evaluation. Indeed, funding for statewide monitoring and compliance regarding curriculum use ended in 1995 (Leary, 1999).

Education in treaty rights is not only fascinating but indispensable for the civic education of Indian people and their neighbors. Yet the complexities are mostly absent from texts used by school districts serving significant Indian student populations or any other population. The progress of the trust relationship has been historically determined by the status of American Indian treaty title to land and compensation for lands used or taken. This compensation has taken a variety of forms, principal of which has been the provision of goods and services to tribal people. The trust relationship identifies the responsibility the federal government has to protect treaty rights in perpetuity. The following issues are central to any Native American multicultural education and should be the basis for any responsible teacher education program selecting, evaluating, and using curricular materials about American Indians.

Evidence for the extent of this trust is to be found in the myriad of treaties and agreements made with Indian peoples from colonial times through the latter half of the 19th century. This extremely large and complex body of law can be found speaking to issues which go beyond trusteeship over land to include education and social development. However, while the nature and extent of trust has been an issue, behind this lies the considerable power of the government to interpret the trust without consulting the beneficiary and, in some cases, to abrogate its responsibility over the protests of those whom the government is treaty-bound to serve.

Until the year 1871, the treaty was employed as the method of establishing the colonial European-Indian and, later, the U.S.-Indian relationship (Cohen, 1945, p.33). Although the method of dealing with tribes by this practice was abandoned with the adoption of the Indian Appropriation Act of 1871, treaties created prior to the Act were not abrogated by its passage (Cohen, 1945). Subsequent to this Act, Congress continued to treat tribes in a fashion similar to that of the Senate under the authority of Article II, Section I of the Constitution. "Agreements" were made and ratified by both Houses which de facto operated as the treaties had before. The only substantial change lay in the provision that now the House of Representatives would cooperate with the Senate in ratification of the new "agreements." Along with treaties and agreements, much of the relationship of the federal government to the tribes came by way of special statutes dealing with specific tribes or Indian people generally, and through the adoption of tribal constitutions and charters after the Indian Reorganization Act of 1934 (Cohen, 1945, p. x).

Between the General Allotment Act of 1887 and the Indian Reorganization Act of 1934, the federal government tended to impose regulations and laws upon Indians as a general entity rather than as individual tribes (Cohen, 1945, p. viii). That these overgeneralized statutes and other legal instruments ignored the individual treaty rights of specific tribes prompted a study to be undertaken by the Institute for Government Research. The results of its 1929 study, the "Problem of Indian Administration," helped fuel a decade of governmental, social, and educational "reform" which led to the development of the Indian Reorganization Act and corporatization of tribal entities (Cohen, 1945, p. ix). Regardless of the nature of legal instruments, laws, agreements, and resolutions made subsequent to 1871, however, they carry a concomitant legal weight equivalent to that of the treaties and vice versa. Whether treaties and laws related to Indians receive the same status as other legal instruments dealing with the "general public" is another question, for indeed, the unique place of American Indians in the United States renders problematic their legal status.

A central paradox exists with regard to the status of the Indian which throws Indian policy upon the winds of political fate. On the one hand, Indian people are United States citizens with full guaranteed rights, and with accompanying full responsibilities. On the other hand, the quasi-sovereign nature of the tribes and the recognition of this during the treaty years is ample evidence for special treatment of Native peoples as a polity. In addition, apart from any congressional or court recognition of tribal sovereignty, the Constitution gives Congress "plenary power" over the commerce with Indian people. This plenary power, along with the developing notion of the Indians as "wards" of the government, confuses and dilutes the seemingly polar positions of Indians as sovereign and Indians as full United States citizens. It allows Congress to decide Indian policy unilaterally. A third problem centers around the extent of the government's trust responsibility. While some argue the trust only extends to the protection of Indian material resources, others argue the trust extends to the development of Indian human capital, even to the extent of saying that sovereignty itself is to be protected.

This trust responsibility has itself been a problem for policy makers throughout history. The trust relationship has been called "patronizing" and means have been sought to give more control to Indians. However, when Indians have been shown to be capable of maintaining control, they have been "rewarded" with loss of federal assistance or termination of the relationship between tribe and federal government, including that of limited tribal sovereignty, and a great loss of tribal property through sale and hypothecation.

With all of this, nevertheless, government Indian programs have been geared to preparing Indians to do without special protection in achieving competency for 20th-century life. Indian policy has reflected a spectrum of interpretation, from full sovereignty, through dependence and wardship, to competence, and to citizenship. The discussion of tribal status has often centered on the argument over the degree of tribal sovereignty. Indian legal history turns less on the pull between sovereignty and citizenship than on the issue of "competence" leading to responsibility, with the United States government, from the Civilization Acts to the current era of self-determination, attempting to provide tribes with the social, economic, and educational competencies which will lead from tribal "status" to full citizenship, with all that implies: the responsibility to pay state, sales, and income tax, the abrogation of treaty rights, and the full termination of reservation status. Throughout history this process has been supported by political powers opposed to the legal nature of tribal status. Regardless of the logic supporting the legal status of treaty rights, the plenary power of Congress has been and can be invoked unilaterally to abrogate those treaties.

Federal Indian legal theory takes much of its form and substance from a set of landmark cases adjudicated in the 1830s. The cases began in conflict then as they often do today, although they operated at that time to set a precedent for interpreting dependent sovereign status (U.S. Commission on Civil Rights, 1981). The development of the dependent sovereign concept began with the decision of the Supreme Court in the case of *Cherokee Nation versus Georgia.* Georgia had attempted to impose its state laws on the Cherokee people. The Cherokee filed suit with the Supreme Court under Article III of the Constitution, which provides the court with original jurisdiction in cases involving foreign nations and states. At issue was whether the Cherokee constitute a foreign nation in the Constitutional sense. Chief Justice John Marshall held that the Cherokees and other tribes were not foreign nations but "domestic dependent nations" (U.S. Commission on Civil Rights, 1981).

The domestic-dependent nation concept is important, for it encompasses two key points: 1) that the tribes maintain nation-state, self-governing status, and 2) that they have a special, albeit dependent, relation to the United States government. Marshall relied partially for his opinion on the work of Emerich Vattel, the leading scholar of international law during this period. Vattel held that, "Weaker nations that submit themselves to alliances with more powerful nations are still Sovereign," and quoting Aristotle, "the more powerful [nation] is given more honor, and to the weaker, more assistance" (1860). Later, in *Worcester versus Georgia,* Marshall maintained that all power the federal government held over the tribes was limited to that which represented tribal consent, such as it is expressed in treaties.

In the *Cherokee Nation* case, Marshall argued for the sovereignty of the Cherokee Nation, while claiming that this sovereignty is partial and limited because of the "dependence" of the Cherokee on the United States government (Barsh & Henderson, 1980, p. 140). They are "acknowledged to have an unquestionable and, heretofore, unquestioned right to the lands they occupy, until that right shall be extinguished by a voluntary cession to our government" (Barsh & Henderson, 1980, p. 53). He goes on to argue the limits of this power as due to the "dependent" status of Indian Nations. In the case of *Worcester,* he went further in his determination of sovereign status. Samuel Worcester, a New England missionary, was imprisoned in the state of Georgia for trespassing on Cherokee land in Georgia. At issue was the right of the Cherokee to accept the presence of Worcester without the consent of Georgia. Marshall declared that the laws of Georgia in this regard were "repugnant to the Constitution" (Barsh & Henderson, 1981, p. 56). He argued that tribal status was based only on a "condition" of dependence, not on a decision. Thus, dependence was in no way construed to indicate abdication of inherent political rights. Although dependence of condition was an increasing reality in the 1830s, the "language" of dependence often accepted by the tribes in treaties during an earlier period was, Marshall implied, "A pretense, which tribes had tolerated out of ignorance of its legal implications." They were "not well acquainted with the words [that signify] dependence—nor did they suppose it to be material whether they were called subjects or the children of their father in Europe" (Barsh & Henderson, 1981, p. 57).

For Marshall, then, tribes were politically sovereign, limited by their dependence only to the extent of their admission of dependence at the time of treaty, not the **condition** of their dependence. In most cases, tribes had "never been conquered, but together with Europeans, had yielded and compromised in matters of mutual economic interest" (Barsh & Henderson, 1981, p. 57). They had not forfeited their tribal political authority. Tribes clearly had rights and possessions. In the case of *Worcester,* dependency was redefined as stated in *Cherokee Nation versus Georgia.* United States-Indian relations were clearly related to tribal consent and not to any **condition** of dependence (Barsh & Henderson, 1981, p. 57). These cases laid the groundwork for a relatively broad interpretation of tribal sovereignty and yet, ironically, solidified the "plenary power" of Congress, reinforcing its original jurisdiction over commerce with Indian tribes. However, only the doctrine of the plenary power of Congress survived into the years during which the frontier began rapidly to expand, from shortly before the Civil War into the late 19th century.

Marshall, the ardent federalist, had succeeded in establishing federal power over the state of Georgia with regard to the interpretation of tribal hegemony and immunity from state law. This strong federalist stand and the concomitant broad interpretation of Congressional plenary power are Marshall's legacy in the history of U.S.-Indian power relations from just before the Civil War to the present. Grant's Peace Policy, the Allotment Period after the Dawes Act, the Indian Reorganization Act and the "Indian New Deal," and postwar termination and self-determination were all major policy shifts. Each has a separate character springing from a changing constellation of political and reforming forces. Each, however, reaffirmed the power of the Congress to act with impunity and to impose unilaterally policy change in Indian affairs with little legal recourse on the part of tribes. This emphasis on congressional unilateral plenary power is exacerbated by the concept "dependent sovereign" which evolved from the earlier Cherokee decision, yet in a much weaker form. The **condition** of, rather than the **consent** to, dependence relationship became the leading concept. Sovereignty took a subordinate role in the political relationship due to the growing emphasis on congressional plenary power over its dependent ward, the Indian.

The years during which the European American expanded westward up to and beyond the Mississippi were not characterized by great federal toleration for tribal sovereignty. Tribal sovereignty and political self-determination also meant toleration of tribal custom and habit, along with tribal political will. These were clearly inconsistent with the aims of the European American and his "Manifest Destiny." For only a brief time after the *Worcester* decision were tribes treated as special political entities through the use of special legislation such as that exempting them from federal taxation. However, as early as 1802 and again in 1819, Congress began stipulating this special relationship be contingent upon a federal goal of assimilation—the aim to meld the American Indian, socially, economically, and morally, into the mainstream of the European American life in this country (U.S. Department of Health, Education and Welfare, 1979, p. 19). Indian policy makers began to see tribal dependency, and in some ways the limited sovereignty which remained, as a curable condition.

The "Civilization Acts" of 1802 and 1819 were the first Acts specifically codifying the responsibility of the federal government to provide for "Indian social and welfare programs—to help Indians make the transition from the life of the migratory hunter to that of the self-sufficient farmer" (U.S. Department of Health, Education & Welfare, 1979, p. 19). Prior to the Civilization Act of 1819, federal laws had dealt with or were intended to implement specific provisions of a treaty. The Act of 1819, however, dealt both with treaty and nontreaty tribes and thus established a basis for a federal-Indian relationship apart from, but including, the federal responsibility to treaty tribes.

The federal government's assumption of responsibility for Indian welfare, in addition to specific treaty provisions, begins perhaps in the Civilization Acts. Of paramount importance is the understanding that these government efforts reflect mainly a concern for welfare to the extent that welfare puts the Indian on a path of self-sufficiency and "civilization," or competence. This notion of providing welfare and education until competence is already evident in several early treaty provisions. As Vine Deloria wrote:

> While the removal of the Chippewas, Potawatomies, and Ottawas from the Chicago area was based on the explicit promise that the United States would provide educational services forever, most treaties promised schooling and other federal services for only a limited time. The Menominee (1831) and Pawnee (1833) treaties, for example, provided federal schools for 10 years; other treaties extended the period to 20 years. Officials in Washington believed that these relatively short periods would be adequate to prepare Indians to till the land, become self-sufficient, and be ready for assimilation into the general population. (U.S. Department of Health, Education and Welfare, 1979, p. 15)

The beginnings of Indian welfare as a part of the trust responsibility lay squarely in the effort to "civilize" and assimilate, these being preconditions for a satisfactory Indian social and economic policy. This effort to assimilate is buried not far beneath the surface of the Indian policy of self-determination, a policy promoted as an extension of tribal sovereignty on matters political, economic, social, and educational. Tribal political sovereignty as well as federal rather than state jurisdiction are the legacy of the precedent-setting Supreme Court decisions regarding the Cherokee. Indian material and human capital is held in trust by the federal government. This trust is, however, to be in force only as long as Indians remain in a dependent state as wards of the government. The plenary power of Congress is such that Congress may decide when the condition of dependence is weak enough for the trust to end.

Land is the part of the trust about which there is most agreement. "The U.S. holds technical legal title while equitable title or the right to use the land is held by the beneficiary—the Indian." (Cahn, 1970 p. 170) Indeed, in 1967–1968 fully 90% of the bills which came through the Subcommittee on Indian Affairs dealt with Indian land or land claims money. Regardless of the extent or nature of this trust, however, major Indian legislation has always been written around the notion that Indian material or human capital shall be protected, held in trust, until such time as Indian people gain the "competence" to manage these assets themselves, ending the trust relationship.

Worcester versus Georgia established the notion of treaty federalism with regard to Indian tribes. Tribes are not to be dealt with "within the scope of the federal-state compact, but relate to the United States through separate compacts authorized and enforced under the Treaty Clause: treaty federalism as opposed to constitutional federalism" (Barsh & Henderson, 1980, p. 59)—such as that with states. This interpretation limits the Congress to regulation of "commerce" with Indians, in the same way commerce is regulated with foreign governments. The political relationship flowing from this interpretation must follow a course of mutual agreement. After 1871, unilateral plenary power began to have a broader interpretation, and the government often adopted legislative "agreements" unilaterally. The United States government treated Indian peoples as limited sovereigns for forty years after *Worcester*. But, subsequently the government began to limit its recognition of the tribes to their status as wards rather than limited sovereigns. Indeed, the concept of treaty sovereignty, set by pacts of mutual agreement, became a moot point; in practice, a fiction, for with the total subjugation of the tribes, Indian ward status and capital held in trust through treaty became more and more subject to a broad interpretation of Congressional plenary power.

Because of the sensitive nature of the treaty-trust relationship, a clear education is required for its comprehension. Sadly, much of the requirements for such civic literacy are lacking in the standard curricula at every educational level. This paper points to a need for more study regarding the status of Indian sovereignty studies in our schools, particularly in those near tribal communities. It is particularly important for teacher educators to be conversant with these issues as a way to inoculate their students against the virus of ignorance concerning the special nature of Native American civil life.

It is indeed strange to delineate the strength and complexity of tribal sovereignty while remaining fully aware that neither members of the dominant culture nor most Indian students are educated to appreciate this issue. A recent issue of *News from Indian Country*, an Ojibwe paper, includes the headlines: "Wisconsin Counties Association to Spearhead National Coalition to 'modernize' Indian Treaties." The ensuing story discusses county efforts to begin the abrogation of treaties that allow for traditional Ojibwe fishing practices. It is no surprise, especially in light of the theme of this paper, that the story under that is headlined, "Federal Court Sentences Man for Boatlanding Pipe Bombing." What follows is a story of the indictment and sentencing of a man who ignited a pipe bomb to intimidate some Chippewa fishermen in Solon Springs, Wisconsin. One of the central concerns of this paper is the way political violence, and in this case violence with racial overtones may have roots in both perpetrators' and victims' misunderstanding of civic and economic conditions, of attendant rights and responsibilities.

Horkheimer and Adorno (1972) present an analysis of the nature of reason which works to explain this cultural conflict and begins to unpack some dimensions of the relationship between reason and violence here. They argue that law growing out of the Enlightenment cohabits poorly with realities such as tribal rights, or a Native presence that extends beyond traditional limited concepts of "Native" American which indigenous people do not share. Indeed tribalism itself, when set against the rational state, is mythic, and as such has a weak purchase on legitimacy, as does all reality which survives without an "objective measure." Horkheimer and Adorno argue that the legacy of law in the Enlightenment and after is an extension of power. Public policy is an extension

of power, and rights, because they can have no rationality beyond power, exist at the pleasure of the dominant polity, in this case not the tribe. (Horkheimer & Adorno, p. 16)

Harry Girvetz (1974) extends this argument to a notion of violence against property, a type of violence with grave consequences not just for Native property but personhood as well. He talks about economic violence stemming from need. Central to the political security of Indian people is their property. Yet this property, because it is often not recognized or understood, is in constant jeopardy. Tribal lands are held through covenants established between two sovereigns, the tribe and the federal government. This relationship is difficult for those in the dominant culture to understand, much less appreciate. Property ownership is likely to be an individual or family affair in European American culture. The only sovereign recognized is the nation-state because tribal reservation sovereignty is poorly understood, and when tribal rights to land or resources conflict with those of the surrounding communities, the perceived lack of legitimacy can be a source of conflict.

Sherman Stanage (1977), in discussing the nature of violence and civil life, notes that civic understanding is a process of dialogue toward mutual understanding. "Civilization" is **living** dialectically. He cites Collingwood's *New Leviathan* in his discussion of how civic life moves to violence when dialogue cannot happen. In the Native-dominant culture relationship, dialogue is severely restricted because the two sides are often speaking two different languages of reason when discussing property and national sovereignty (p. 212). Hannah Arendt (1970) suggests that we have avoided the study or discussion of violence because study implies a sequence of reason to which violence itself is extremely resistant. Violence, as unreason, refuses to submit to the clear analysis which constitutes reason itself.

Conclusion

It is not only the paucity of textbook information that indicts education, but also the lack of nerve on the part of the education community, including State Departments of Education, to meet the obligation to serve our students with rich material in a manner that promotes reflection. Catherine Cornbluth (1983), in a perceptive essay, cites a number of unsubstantiated myths about the student mind. She argues that these myths perpetuate the teacher's willingness to capitulate to the superficial treatment of a text. She cites fears about student readiness and ability to think critically, wariness about learning "styles," and supposed lack of maturity as convenient excuses to deprive students of a rich reflective experience (p. 175). The kind of education available in the schools and universities is, by its omissions, the precursor to distortion and attendant violence. Dullness and superficiality in the curriculum have more than inert consequences here. Students in the dominant culture have little understanding nor more than shallowly romantic sympathy for a notion of tribal holdings and property rights; American Indian students, unable to crack the codes of privileged literacy, will be helpless in the face of the complex nature of their rights to counter the socialization of their neighbors. What is required is a reemphasis on critical civic literacy both in skills and in material content.

Shirley Engle and Anna Ochoa (1988) have argued that we owe students in a democracy a "countersocialization." I would agree, particularly since latent structures of unexamined prejudice dominate the discourse of rights and do so from arguments of "fairness" and "equal treatment." The legacy of fairness to tribal semi-sovereignty plays poorly in the Enlightenment court where power is tantamount to a certain kind of reason. Indeed, James Leming (1989) has shown that ideals of participatory citizenship and civic literacy are the normal preoccupation of the curriculum theorist rather than the classroom teacher. He cites the two cultures of social studies curriculum—the "countersocialization" culture stemming as far back as Counts and Rugg and the "citizenship socialization" culture, particularly the one which makes its presence known in the National Commission on Social Studies in the School's *Charting a Course* outline for curriculum for the 21st century. Capitulation to a narrow view of civic literacy may well have vicious consequences in the not distant future. In any case this shows a clear path for the teacher educator. Equipping teachers to "countersocialize" is not only appropriate in many cases, but essential to counteract the misjudgments of ordinary curriculum producers.

If Arendt and others cited here are right, violence can be *expected* to follow on the heels of an education that in not "civic," that is, in Stanage's (1975) words, dialectical. We must have a civic education with full information, students who possess the resources to access that information, and the wisdom to make education dialectical, a dialogue across differences. Throughout the 1990s, Ojibwe leaders and concerned Wisconsin educators, have worked to provide supplemental curriculum materials for treaty rights education. Wildlife biologists have contributed to the effort to show data that indicates the tribal fishery take does not seriously impact the sportfishery. While anti-Indian groups sympathetic to the KKK and other white supremacists continue to organize in the north country, courageous educators have continued to disseminate the truth about treaties (Great Lakes Indian Fish and Wildlife Commission, 1998, p. 28). Public forums, letters to editors, boatlanding "witnesses" are evidence that citizens are exercising the power of peaceful resistance to racism (Masinaigan, 1991, p. 7). Given the lack of legislative support for curriculum reform and the tendency toward textbooks homogenized for the mass market, will appropriately revised textbooks be implemented across the United States or, minimally, in locales with a significant tribal presence? Perhaps educators will take advantage of advances in digital technology to flesh out for their students the historic particulars of tribal sovereignty. Tribes continue to fight to defend their civil rights in courts across the nation, and ongoing popular education is essential if Native Americans are to be equipped with sound information and heard by judges and peers in fairly informed courts of law.

The stakes for a tribal future may be higher than the question of how to prevent seasonal violence over tribal rights to fish and hunt. Felix Cohen (1945) argued that Native American sovereignty, since it is so delicately balanced by history and Supreme Court precedent, is the "miner's canary" of our democracy. Its health is, to invoke a second metaphor, the bellwether of the health of democracy itself. If tribal sovereignty is dissolved in the face of unexamined power, can pluralist democracy, American democracy, endure?

References

Arendt, H. (1969). *On violence,* New York: Harcourt, Brace, Jovanovich.

Barsh, L. R., & Henderson, J. Y. (1980). *The road: Indian tribes and political liberty.* Berkeley: University of California Press.

Cahn, E. (1970). *Our brother's keeper: The Indian in white America,* New York: World Publishing.

Cohen, F. (1945). *Handbook of federal Indian law.* Washington, DC: U.S. Government Printing Office.

Cornbluth, C. (1983). Critical thinking and cognitive processes. In W. B. Stanley (Ed.), *Review of research in social studies education: 1976–83* (pp. 11–64). #85. Washington, DC.

Costo, R., & Henry, J. (1977). *Indian treaties: Two centuries of dishonor.* San Francisco: The Indian Historian Press.

Engle, S. H, & Ochoa, A. O. (1988). *Education for democratic citizenship: Decision-making in the Social Studies,* New York: Teachers College Press.

Fixico, D. L. (1989). Indian and white interpretations of the frontier experience. In *Native views of Indian-White historical relations* (pp. 8–19). Occasional Papers in Curriculum Series, No.7. Chicago: The Newberry Library.

Girvetz, H. (1975). An anatomy of violence. In S. M. Stanage (Ed.), *Reason and violence: Philosophical investigations* (pp. 183–207). Totowa, NJ: Rowan & Littlefield.

Great Lakes Indian Fish and Wildlife Commission (GLIFWC). (1998). *Treaty rights.* Odanah, WI: GLIFWC Public Information Office.

Horkheimer, M., & Adorno, T. W. (1972). *Dialectic of Enlightenment.* New York: Herder & Herder.

Howe, I. (1991, February 18). The value of the canon. *The New Republic,* pp. 40–47.

Kammer, J. (1980). *The second long walk: The Navajo-Hopi land dispute.* Albuquerque: University of New Mexico Press.

Leary, J. P. (1999). [Telephone interview]. Madison, WI: Wisconsin Department of Public Information. Office of American Indian Programs.

Leming, J. (1989, October). The two cultures of social studies. *Journal of the National Council for Social Studies.*

Lewinski, M. (1980). *American government today.* Glenview, IL: Scott, Foresman.

Masinaigan, (1991, June, July). *Chronicle of the Lake Superior Chippewa,* p. 7.

Nash, G. B., & Jeffrey, J. R. (Eds.). (1986). *The American people: Creating a nation and a society.* New York: Harper & Row.

Smith, L. (1977). *The American dream.* Glenview, IL: Scott, Foresman.

Stanage, S. M. (Ed.). (1975). *Reason and violence: Philosophical investigations.* Totowa, NJ: Rowan & Littlefield.

Stanage, S. M. (1975). Violatives: Modes and themes of violence. In S. M. Stanage (Ed.), *Reason and violence: Philosophical investigations* (pp. 207–240). Totowa, NJ: Rowan & Littlefield..

Stanley, W. B. (Ed.). (1983). *Review of research in social studies education: 1976–83.* #85, Washington, DC.

Strickland, R., Hertzberg, S. J., & Owens, S. R. (1990). *Keeping our word: Indian treaty rights and public responsibilities.* Odanah, WI: Great Lakes Indian Fish and Wildlife Commission.

U.S. Commission on Civil Rights, (1981). *Indian tribes: A continuing quest for survival.* Washington, DC: U.S. Government Printing Office.

U.S. Department of Health, Education and Welfare, Office of Education, (1979). *A brief history of the federal responsibility to the American Indian.* Washington, DC: U.S. Government Printing Office.

Vattel, E. (1860). Law of Nations, or principles of the law of nature: applied to the conduct and affairs of nations and sovereigns. [Microform], New York: Printed for Messrs. Berry and Rogers, Hanover-Square.

Wisconsin Advisory Committee to the U.S. Commission on Civil Rights, (1989). *Discrimination Against Chippewa Indians in Northern Wisconsin.*

CLASS 10

Native Americans in the USA (Part II)

CHAPTER 15
Native Nations and American Indians, Culture, Curriculum, and Social Justice

James V. Fenelon

James Fenelon provides an overview of the history of contact between Native Nations, American Indians and the U.S.A. He also outlines some serious issues that need to be incorporated in our nation's curriculum for the purpose of promoting cultural understanding and social justice for all people.

Native Nations and American Indians: Culture, Curriculum, and Social Justice

James V. Fenelon

An Associate Professor in the Sociology Department at California State University, San Bernadino, James V. Fenelon teaches courses on race and ethnic relations and discrimination. He is the author of *Culturicide, Resistance and Survival of the Lakota "Sioux" Nation.* He is a member of the Standing Rock (Sioux) Nation and comes from Dakota and Lakota peoples.

"You, who are wise must know that different Nations have different Conceptions of things and you will therefore not take it amiss, if our Ideas of this kind of Education happen not to be the same as yours."

Canassatego, 1744
Leaders of the Six Nations
Lancaster, Pennsylvania

"Mitakuye Oyasin" is used by many Lakota and Dakota traditionalists, and increasingly other Native peoples, to express "all our relations" within "the people" as a whole, like a nation, related to all others. Native and non-Indian alike. As the 20th century ends, indigenous people have re-appropriated the term "nation" as used by leaders in the centuries around 1744 and have reverted to using both resistance and survival ideologies.

This essay illustrates these issues by emphasizing indigenous cultures, curricula, and conflicts over social justice, historical perspectives, and the current "voice" of Native Nations and people, all existing long before and certainly since Columbus and other Europeans first arrived in the Americas (Cleary & Peacock, 1998). Underlying themes underscore that previous forms of education in the United States and colonial North America were for the purposes of cultural destruction (Adams, 1995) and social domination that included institutional racism (Huff, 1997) and deep struggles over the

meaning of life itself (Locust, 1988). Therefore we begin an understanding of Native Americans and systems of Indian education, at the beginning of "contact" between western Europeans and indigenous peoples of the Americas.

Introduction

The Arawaks were a peaceful, well-organized society living in the area of present-day Haiti in 1492, when Christopher Columbus arrived and from the myopic view of the Europeans "discovered" them and other Caribbean people (Zinn, 1980). He promptly dubbed these indigenous peoples "Los indios" after his monumental miscalculation on where in the world he was (Josephy, 1994). The rest, as "they" say, is history.

But whose history is it? Are scholars and students aware that the indigenous people throughout the Americas, those whom Columbus carelessly dubbed "Indians," represent a great diversity in language and culture throughout the continent? Have we stopped to consider the implications of the fact that within fifty years after Columbus arrived in the "New World" the Arawaks on Hispaniola would be wiped out (Las Casas, 1974) and the great Aztecan empire of Mexico would be destroyed (Josephy, 1994): that within another three centuries whole nations such

Reprinted by permission of the author.

as the Cherokees would be struggling for existence and forcibly "removed" over half a continent (Dippie, 1982: Wallace, 1993), and that five hundred years later Lakota "Takini" (survivors) and other Natives would end the hundred years of mourning for the Ghost Dancers and families killed at Wounded Knee (Fenelon, 1998; Brown, 1970), symbolizing the end of the western "frontier" for the United States?

We must answer these and other questions in order to produce a more relevant and truthful curriculum about the make-up of American culture, what we teach in our schools as well as the research and knowledge presented in colleges and universities. In this light, we can view integrating Native American perspectives within four broad arenas: 1) history, 2) cultural understanding or world view, 3) contemporary sociological structures, and 4) the struggle for social justice and voice.

History

Integrating the history of Native American people more fully into the curriculum involves much more than including simple factual accounts. It is the **Indian perspective**, historical and philosophical, that requires inclusion whenever possible. What did the Wampanoags think about the Puritan enclave at Plymouth? Could they have tolerated and assisted the newcomers (Peters, 1987), only to be shocked at the barbarity of the New Englanders' response to religious differences? The United States history is replete with Indian Wars looked at only from the conqueror's point of view. Does the Trail of Broken Treaties, extending from one continent to the other, support the concept of Manifest Destiny or the power of the sword leading to the Termination Policy of the 1950s (Deloria, 1990, 1984)? In more recent history there are fewer indications of genocidal actions, and more of purposeful "culturicide" (Fenelon, 1998) through coercive assimilation that wipes out Native American cultures, especially through educational policy, as when:

> The (Navajo) children are caught, often roped like cattle, and taken away from their parents, many times never to return. They are transferred from school to school, given white people's names, forbidden to speak their own tongue, and when sent to distant schools are not taken home for three years. (Coolidge, 1977)

Most Native American families have stories from the boarding school period of Indian education policy (Hamley, 1994), the fall-out extending into modern times for reservation and urban Indian populations (Fixico, 1986: Prucha, 1978). A poignant example of historical perspective is the observance of the previously mentioned hundred years passing since the slaughter of the surrendered Ghost Dancers on Pine Ridge (Oglala "Sioux") Reservation in South Dakota. The military and frontier states recorded it as the last battle with "hostiles" in the name of civilization, while Lakota and other Native American Nations remember it as the purposeful killing of hundreds of women and children because they practiced an outlawed religion (Miller, 1985), because they wished to move about in cultural freedom, or perhaps because they had defeated Custer in battle over twenty years earlier (Fenelon, 1998).

Inclusion of Native American historical perspectives means a much broader horizon of who Indian people were and are—the accomplishments and contributions as well as the conflicts and conquests. The United States Constitution was at least partly based on the Iroquoian Confederacy of Nations (Johansen, 1982). Many states and other place-names are from indigenous languages, such as Chicago, Illinois. Small and mid-sized cities existed in the Ohio River Valley all the way westward to the upper Missouri (Forbes, 1998; Silverberg, 1986). Food, plant and animal lore, natural sciences, and even medicines are derived from Indian knowledge.

> Over the past five hundred years, human beings have sculpted a new worldwide society, a new political and economic order as well as a new demographic and agricultural order. Indians played the decisive roles in each step to create this new society. However, the modern world order came to be viewed as the product of European, not American, history. (Weatherford, 1988, p. 253)

In viewing the history of the United States, a key element of multicultural development is the inclusion of Native American contributions on every level. Besides bringing this history to the curriculum with equal weight—both in generic forms and in specific regional and community history, we need to include the Native American perspective of being conquered and cheated out of their lands (Deloria, 1984). This will benefit all students of our country's past, indigenous and "immigrant" Americans alike.

Cultural Understanding

Awareness, appreciation, and respect for cultural differences and similarities is critical to integrating any Native American perspective into the curriculum effectively. One way of addressing these needs is to use existing works, such as the book and guide *People of the Three Fires* (Clifton, Connell, & McCluken, 1986), which, through historical representation of the Ottawa, Potawatomi and Ojibway of the greater Michigan area, shows how the indigenous societies changed as they came into contact with Anglo Americans, and how the United States government ultimately possessed all their lands.

Even within distinct Native American groups, nations, or "tribes," cultural perspectives have many variations, including "traditional," bicultural or multicultural, coercively assimilated, and acculturated. Using local and regional materials or content allows students to see the sweep of these changes, and the connections to their own community development.

Another effective means for building cultural understanding is to present Native American philosophy and thought through the words of some of the many great indigenous orators of the past and present.

> The man who sat on the ground in his tipi meditating on life and its meaning, accepting the kinship of all creatures and acknowledging unity with the universe of things was infusing into his being the true essence of civilization. . . .
>
> The white man does not understand the Indian for [the] reason that he does not understand America. In the Indian the spirit of the land is still vested, it will be until other men are able to divine and meet its rhythm. (Standing Bear, 1933)

This approach has the additional benefit of developing discussion of the legitimacy of different "world views" (Whorf, 1956) on issues such as what civilization is or the relationship of peoples to the land and environment. Vine Deloria Jr. points out that "Traditional people preserve the whole vision and scientists generally reduce the

experience to its alleged constituent parts and inherent principles." (Deloria, 1990)

A third effort to make toward cultural understanding is to develop empathy by reading and talking to Native American artists and scholars, visiting nearby reservations or Indian centers, and attending Indian social and cultural events. This kind of contact, sought after by ethnographers and anthropologists, can lead to scientific and ecological insights remarkably similar to those of the academic community (Green, 1995; Willis, 1983).

> Native peoples view the world as complex, interconnected in non-linear relationships (heterarchic), dynamic, unknowable (indeterminant), changing/moving in several simultaneous cycles (mutual causality), growing as a whole (morphogenesis) and consisting of many perspectives. (Nichols, 1991)

Many of these qualities are the same needed in developing multicultural curricula for higher education and are the basis for research on whole mind, accelerated learning, and multiple intelligences theory (Gardner, 1987).

In developing and integrating Native American content into the curriculum, the problem of stereotyping surfaces again and again. With mainstream Americans, this stereotyping of Native peoples tends to fall into two categories: the romantic "warrior/princess" of the past and the wild "savage" associated with drunken laziness in modern times (Riding In, 1998). In an unpublished research study I conducted with Native American graduate students at Harvard University in 1991, the "Noble Savage" syndrome in conjunction with pan-Indian generalities (i.e. feathers and tipis, Custer and Crazy Horse, "chiefs" and "tribes") was stated most often to be the main problem with conventional curriculum. But culture refers to the mechanisms of social control and organization as much as clothing, singing, and dancing. "Culture" is 1) the cognitive paradigms through which people define and communicate the proper and the possible, and 2) the corresponding informal norms and implicit contracts by which a group of people reward and penalize each other (Cornell & Kalt, 1992).

When Western schools only address the surface features of culture and attempt to break down "deep" cultural interactions through forced assimilation to the dominant culture's secular institutions (Fuller, 1991; Fenelon, 1998), traditional communities are threatened and Indian children experience direct conflict with the modern, civic world (Hornett, 1990; Locust, 1998). Only through comprehensive and meaningful content sensitive to Native Americans can the "Indian" students' self-esteem and the Anglo students' sense of balance be maintained in today's diverse educational systems.

Sociological Structures

Native Americans represent an incredible diversity of indigenous nations, "tribal" societies, languages, cultural practices, local environments, and histories. Wide-ranging topics such as anthropology, architectural design, geography, sociolinguistics, and history can be drawn from simply studying a few reservations in the United States. For example, spatial and directional orientation are more common in Native American philosophy than hierarchy and binomialism (Deloria, 1979; Fenelon & Pugh, 1988; Hornett, 1990). From es-Chikag-o, let us look to the four directions of Native America: West, with the Puyallups, northwest coastal fisherman, living in longhouses when explorers met them, now an urban "tribe" recently winning their treaty settlement in Tacoma: North, the Lakota and Dakota "Sioux," hunters of the plains buffalo, living in tipis and earth lodges when fighting soldiers, and now defending arid reservation lands in the Dakotas in the shadow of the Black Hills; East, the Wampanoag, East Coast fishing and farming people, living in wickiyup longhouses when the Puritans arrived, now rebuilding on their island and peninsula areas of Massachusetts; and South, the "Navajo" Dine, ranchers and farmers of the southwest mountains and desert, living in hogans when pioneer wagon trains invaded, now managing the largest land-base reservation in the United States. "Curriculum should be localized to reflect the historical experience, culture and values of the local and regional Native communities" (Indian Nations at Risk, 1991).

Each Indian Nation and reservation has to deal with complex questions of sovereignty and cultural maintenance. Throughout many shifts of federal policy the belief of Native people has been that education should integrate goals of both cultural sustenance and self-sufficiency (Nichols,

1991), while non-Natives have viewed these goals as incompatible. In fact, both viewpoints are valid:

> There is much to be learned from a traditional education and we must see it as the prerequisite to any other kind of education or training. Traditional education gives us an orientation to the world around us, particularly the people around us, so that we know who we are and have confidence when we do things. (Deloria, 1990, pp. 12–18.)

In respect to the origination of the curriculum, the Indian Nations at Risk Task Force (INAR) has stated that "Native communities must be the producers of Native education materials that reflect the language and culture of the local area." INAR has noted the importance of working on language development, cultural background (history, curriculum change), partnerships with community organizations, and accountability (Demmert, 1991). These elements of Native American curriculum development are likewise needed for mainstream higher education.

Finally, in discussing such cultural paradigms as knowledge, Kalt and Cornell (1989) tell us that "Indian tribes can provide answers to such questions as whether or not public ownership of enterprises is acceptable, or whether a separation of political authority and judicial authority is appropriate . . . selecting for activities that best fit with indigenous conceptions of self and appropriate intragroup relations."

Social Justice and Voice

As explained in the previous passages, Native Americans as individuals, nations, and as peoples have lived through great injustices (Noriega, 1992). It is only through changing the dominant Anglo-Eurocentric curriculum content and perspectives that higher education, and then public schooling, can begin to redress these wrongs. The role of both U.S. government and "tribal" courts, the numbers and placement of Native Americans throughout the country, their sense of nationality, the causes of the dire poverty and victimization of Indian people, and their vast contributions to society should be noted in the curriculum whenever possible and appropriate. "The study of Native American language, law, history, culture, art, and philosophy should be required of students. . ." (Indian Nations at Risk, 1991).

Cultural capital theories (Shamai, 1990) demonstrate that monocultural curricula perpetuate inequality as a social hierarchy in the face of significant and lasting Native American contributions to the development of the United States (Weatherford, 1988). A direct connection exists between redressing issues of justice through curriculum and whose voices are heard in that dialogue. Native Americans deserve to be the authors of such curricula since it is their voices that have been missing and are needed. An excellent example of voice, based primarily on the oral tradition of storytelling found in nearly every Indian Nation is *Keepers of the Earth* (Caduto & Bruchac, 1990), which integrates natural science, tribal authenticity, regionalism, and Native American world views. When Indian-inspired curricula such as these are combined with local, regional and national histories of indigenous people, a comprehensive Native American curriculum becomes possible.

> If we redefine Indian education as an internal Indian institution, an educational process which moves within the Indian context and does not try to avoid or escape this context, then our education will substantially improve. It will originate as part of the tribal perspective about life and pick up additional information on its return to Indian life. (Deloria, 1990)

Curricular Integration

Out and out assimilation has proven to be disastrous for Native Americans (Deloria, 1984; Wax, 1971) and produces a very distorted picture of the United States for other Americans. We are at a point when we must integrate Native American content into the curriculum, not only for the self-esteem and continuance of Indian students (Hornett, 1990), but for the benefit of all students and all schools, especially in light of the multicultural world in which we live, in contrast to a hegemonic curriculum which legitimates only part of the overall cultures of our nation (Giroux, 1983). Inclusion of Native Americans will enhance oral traditions and identity, both personal and national, bringing forth rich and varied backgrounds in storytelling and cultural histories. As Cazden

(1987) points out, in educational institutions "spoken language is an important part of the identities of all the participants."

We can approach the integration of Native American curriculum from many entry points, including adding history and cultural knowledge to the established curriculum; replacing key areas with Native American perspectives; and infusing historical and cultural knowledge and perspectives as alternative ways to view "mainstream" perspectives (Banks, 1989). Adding to the curriculum has the problem of being "in addition to," an afterthought, the first element to be cut out under time or resource constraints. Replacing brings elements of the curricula into opposition with each other, a conflict the minority-culture perspective will either lose outright or that will cause resentment (Corrigan, 1988; Locust, 1988). Infusing, while healthier than the other two, continues with the world view of a "mainstream" and the implication of lesser tributaries (McCarthy, 1990), reinforcing cultural dominance (Smelser, 1992). While such an approach may be useful in the short run, it does not accord the respect and prominence that other cultural perspectives deserve, most pointedly Native American "Indian" Nations, the first stewards of North American lands (Snipp, 1989). Therefore, I propose we view Eurocentric curriculum as one stream, currently in dominance, that we need to balance with many other cultural streams, first and foremost with Native Americans. A more global curricular metaphor would be a "River of Nations and Cultures."

When I took Harvard Law School's, Federal Indian Law course, one intelligent yet perplexed student could not grasp the concept that enrolled American "Indians" were members of their respective tribe's National society, including its law and order system, and were both State and Federal citizens of the United States (Deloria, 1984) with all its sovereignty underpinnings (Fenelon, 1998). An either-or dichotomous mentality (Rosenblum & Travis, 1996) had been indoctrinated in him through his schooling, right on through to the graduate level. Realistic and effective multicultural education concerning Native American will take place when majority-culture students are brought to realize, first through the curriculum, that history, knowledge, and people can belong to more than one culture, (Cajete, 1994;

Cleary & Peacock, 1998) and that we are better off when more inclusive and diverse.

Conclusions

The first settlement within the present borders of the United States sees the first slave revolt. About five hundred Spaniards bring with them one hundred African slaves. The slaves revolt, and the Spaniards are so discouraged and beaten that they return to Haiti, leaving the Africans living with the indigenous population, the first of several black and native acts of solidarity. (Bennett, 1984; in Chicago Religious Task Force on Central America, 1991:95)

Within *Dangerous Memories, Invasion and Resistance since 1492,* developed by the Chicago Religious Task Force on Central America, (1991), these issues of differing "racial" histories literally show how knowledge, history, world view and intercultural understanding in higher education are constructed and then reinforced to the dominant group's interests. The title *Dangerous Memories* ". . . is meant to challenge us to understand and appreciate the last five hundred years in American history from vantage points to which many of us have not been privileged" (p. 9).

Native American content materials, with historical and cultural perspectives, must be integrated into the curriculum of all schooling in the United States, elementary through university. This should be done with Native American people as the primary resource specialists for the benefit of everyone. For the short term, this Native American curriculum should be infused into curricula already being taught. The final goal should be to develop, wherever appropriate, balanced "cultural streams" which minimally address the four major areas of history, cultural understanding, sociological structures, and issues of social justice and voice for Native American "Indian Nations" and people.

This integration will achieve four basic objectives:

- to reinforce and sustain Native American societies and culture: since these societies are more than just of value to their members, or to accurate history and ethnography, but can provide alternative world views useful in solving world problems, (Fishman, 1991);

- to make "Americans" in general more informed about their roots: since current monocultural histories increase the often isolated and, therefore, distorted perspectives Americans have about North America, (Wolf, 1982; Fenelon, 1998; Josephy, 1994);

- to build the basis for a truly multicultural society in the U.S.: since understanding the historical and current cultures of Native Americans assists the development of similar processes for other cultural, racial/ethnic groups in the United States, (Deloria, 1990; Weatherford, 1988; Crawford, 1995); and

- to provide equity and hope for the disenfranchised in "America": since recognizing the contributions of and injustices toward Native Americans through an intercultural understanding is the first step, in curriculum, on the path to equal opportunity through education, (Riding In, 1998; Wax, 1989; Begay, 1997).

Infusing, integrating, and ultimately streaming Native American cultures into curricula valid contributors to United States society will benefit all people in our country, not only indigenous people and "minority" groups. Basic understanding of slavery, genocide, domination, conquest, resistance, and survival ultimately liberates "us" all as Americans. When colleges and universities, and schools and communities, achieve this in the curriculum taught each and every learner. Native American people, other traditionally underrepresented groups and majority-culture students will all benefit with an increased awareness and more knowledge of the world we live in. Then we can truly say "Mitakuye Oyasin."

References

Adams, D. W. (1995). *Education for extinction: American Indians and the boarding school experience, 1875–1928.* Lawrence: University of Kansas Press.

Banks, J. (1989). *Multicultural Education: Issues and Perspectives,* Boston: Allyn & Bacon.

Begay, M. (1997). Leading by choice, not chance: Leadership education for Native chief executives of American Indian Nations. Doctoral dissertation. Harvard University.

Bennett, L., Jr. (1984). *Before the Mayflower.* New York: Penguin Books.

Brown, D. (1970). *Bury My Heart at Wounded Knee*. New York: Holt, Rhinehart and Winston.

Caduto, M., & Bruchac, J. (1988). *Keepers of the Earth*, (w/teacher's guide) Golden, CO: Fulcrum.

Cajete, G. (1994). *Look to the mountain: An ecology of indigenous education*, Durango Kavaki' Press.

Canassatego. (1744; 1971) In T. C. McLuhan (Ed.), *Touch the Earth*. New York: Simon & Schuster.

Cazden, C. (1987). *Classroom discourse: The language of teaching and learning*. Portsmouth. NH: Heinemann.

Chicago Religious Task Force on Central America. (1991). *Dangerous Memories: Invasion and Resistance Since 1492*, (Golden, McConnell, Mueller, Poppen, & Turkovich, Eds.), Chicago. IL: Author.

Cleary, L. M., & Peacock, T. D. (1998). *Collected wisdom: American Indian education* Boston: Allyn & Bacon.

Clifton, J., Cornell, G., & McCluken, J. (1986). *People of the three fires*, (w/guide & workbook). Grand Rapids: University of Michigan Press.

Coolidge, P. (1977). *"Kid catching" on the Navajo Reservation: 1930*. New York: Association on American Indian Affairs.

Cornell, S., & Kalt, J. P. (1992). *What can tribes do? Strategies and institutions in American Indian economic development*. Los Angeles: American Indian Studies Press.

Corrigan, P. (1988). Race/ethnicity/gender/culture: Embodying differences educationally; An argument. In J. Young (Ed.), *Breaking the Mosaic*, Toronto: Garamond Press.

Crawford, J. (1995, Winter). Endangered Native American languages: What is to be done and why? *The Bilingual Research Journal*, 19(1), 17–38.

Deloria, V. (1990, Autumn). Knowing and understanding 5(1): Traditional technology 5(2): 12–17: Transitional education 5(3): 10–15: Property and self-government as educational initiatives 5(4), 26–31. *Winds of Change*. Boulder, CO: American Indian Science & Engineering Society (AISES) Publishing.

Deloria, V. (1979). *The metaphysics of modern existence*, San Francisco: Harper & Row.

Deloria, V., Jr. (1984). 'Congress in its wisdom': The course of Indian legislation. In S. Cadwalader & V. Deloria, Jr. (Eds.). *The aggressions of civilization, federal Indian policy since the 1880s*. Philadelphia: Temple University Press.

Demmert, W. (1991, March). Status of the Indian Nations At Risk Task Force. Unpublished presentation at Harvard Graduate School of Education. (Also in INAR, 1991)

Dippie, B. W. (1982). *The vanishing American*. Middletown, CT: Wesleyan University Press.

Fenelon, J. (1998). *Culturicide, resistance and survival of the Lakota ("Sioux" Nation)*. New York: Garland Publishing.

Fenelon, J., & Pugh, S. (1988, January). Integrating learning, language and intercultural skills for international students. *Journal of Reading*, 31(4), 310–319.

Fishman, J. A. (1991). *Reversing language shift: Theoretical and empirical foundations of assistance to threatened languages*. (Clevedon) Philadelphia: Multilingual Matters.

Fixico, D. (1986). *Termination and relocation, federal Indian policy 1945–1960*. Albuquerque: University of New Mexico Press.

Forbes, J. (1998). The urban tradition among Native Americans. *American Indian Culture and Research Journal*, 22(4), 15–42.

Fuller, B. (1991). *Growing up modern*. London: Routledge.

Gardner, H. (1987). The theory of multiple intelligences. *Annals of Dyslexia*, 37, 19–35.

Giroux, H. (1983). Theories of reproduction and resistance in the new sociology of education: A critical analysis. *Harvard Educational Review*, 53(3).

Green, M. K. (1995). Cultural identities: Challenges for the twenty-first century. In M. K. Green (Ed.), *Issues in Native American cultural identity*. New York: Peter Lang Publishing.

Hamley, J. (1994). Cultural genocide in the classroom: A history of the federal boarding school movement in American Indian education, 1875–1920. Doctoral dissertation, Harvard University.

Hornett, D. (1990, Fall). Elementary-age tasks, cultural identity, and the academic performance of young American Indian children. *Action in Teacher Education*, 12(3).

Huff, D. J. (1997). *To live heroically: Institutional racism and American Indian education*. Albany: State University of New York Press.

Indian Nations at Risk. (1991, October). An Educational Strategy for Action. In M. Charleston & G. L. King (Eds.), *Final Report of the Indian Nations At Risk Task Force*. Conference Publishing Title: Indian Nations at Risk Task Force: Listen to the People. Washington, DC: U.S. Department of Education.

Johansen, B. E. (1982). *Forgotten founders*. Boston: Harvard Common Press.

Josephy, A. M. (1994). *500 Nations*. New York: Knopf.

Kalt, J., & Cornell, S. (1989, December). Pathways from poverty: Economic development and institution-building on American Indian reservations. Harvard Project on American Indian Economic Development. John F. Kennedy School of Government. Cambridge, MA.

(de) Las Casas, B. (1974). *The devastation of the Indies: A brief account* (H. Briffault, Trans.). New York: Seabury Press. (Original work published 1538)

Locust, C. (1988, August). Wounding the spirit: Discrimination and traditional American Indian belief systems. *Harvard Educational Review, 58*(3).

McCarthy, C. (1990). *Race and curriculum: Social inequality and. . . .* Philadelphia: Falmer Press.

Miller, D. (1985). *The ghost dance*. Lincoln: University of Nebraska Press.

National Advisory Council on Indian Education, (1989). Educating the American Indian/Alaska Native family. 16th Annual Report to the United States Congress. Author.

Niehardt, J. G. (1959). *Black Elk speaks*. New York: Pocket Books.

Nichols, R. (1991, October). Continuous evaluation of Native education programs for American Indian and Alaska Native students (#8). (U.S. Department of Education Task Force, Co-Directors W. Demmert & T. Bell) Indian Nations at Risk Task Force: Listen to the People Conference Publication. Washington, DC: U.S. Department of Education.

Noriega, J. (1992). American Indian education in the United States: Indoctrination for subordination to colonialism. In M. Annette Jaimes (Ed.). *The State of Native America*. Boston: South End Press.

Peters, R. (1987). *The Wampanoags of Mashpee*. Jamaica Plain, MA: Inter-tribal Press.

Prucha, F. P. (1978). *Americanizing the American Indian*. Lincoln: University of Nebraska Press.

Riding In, J. (1998). American Indians in popular culture. In C.R. Mann & M. Zatz (Eds.), *Images of color, images of crime* (pp. 15–29). Los Angeles: Roxbury.

Rosenblum, K. E., & Travis, T. M. (1996). *The meaning of difference*. New York: McGraw-Hill.

Shamai, S. (1990). Critical sociology of education theory in practice: The Druze education in the Golan. *British Journal of Sociology of Education, 11*(4).

Silverberg, R. (1986). *The mound builders*. Athens: Ohio University Press.

Smelser, N. (1992). Introduction. In R. Munch & N. Smelser (Eds.), *Theory of culture* Berkeley: University of California Press.

Snipp, M. C. (1989). *American Indians: The first of this land*. New York: Russell Sage Foundation.

Standing Bear, L. (1933). *Land of the Spotted Eagle*. Boston: Houghton Mifflin.

Wallace, A. (1993). *The long and bitter trail*. New York: Hill & Wang.

Wax, M. (1971). *Indian Americans: Unity and diversity*. Englewood Cliffs, NJ: Prentice Hall.

Wax, M. (1989). *Formal education in an American Indian community: Peer society and the failure of minority education*. Prospect Heights, IL: Waveland Press.

Weatherford, J. (1988). *Indian givers: How the Indians of the Americas transformed the world*. New York: Ballantine.

Whorf, B. L. (1956). *Language, thought, and reality*. Cambridge, MA: M.I.T. Press.

Willis, P. (1983). Cultural production and theories of reproduction. In L. Barton & S. Walker (Eds.), *Race, Class and Education*. London: Croom Helm.

Wolf, E. R. (1982). *Europe and the people without history*. Berkeley: University of California Press.

Zinn, H. (1980). *A people's history of the United States*. New York: Harper & Row.

CLASS 11

Hispanic/Latino Americans (Part I)

CHAPTER 16
Immigrant Latino Parents' Values and Beliefs
About Their Children's Education
Gallimore and Goldenberg
This study highlights the differences in the perceptions of Latino parents
in reference to their roles in child rearing and the role the schools should
play in the education of their children.

Immigrant Latino Parents' Values and Beliefs About Their Children's Education: Continuities and Discontinuities Across Cultures and Generations

Claude Goldenberg and Ronald Gallimore

A Professor of Psychology in the Department of Psychology & Bio-behavioral Sciences at the University of California, Los Angeles (Center for Culture & Health, previously known as the Sociobehavioral Group), Claude Goldenberg holds a second appointment in UCLA's Graduate School of Education and Information Studies. He has received numerous awards and recognition for his work and is the author of several books, chapters and articles.

A Professor in the Department of Psychiatry & Bio-behavioral Sciences, University of California, Los Angeles, Ronald Gallimore holds a second appointment in UCLA's Graduate School of Education and Information Studies. He is also co-director of the Latino Home-School Research Project.

Immigrants and Education

Immigration from Mexico and Central America continues to alter the demographic landscape of the United States. In 1980, little more than 2 million U.S. residents were Mexican-born. By 1990, the Mexican-born population had grown to 4.3 million; the Central American-immigrant population was at least 700,000. The Census Bureau estimates that Hispanic population growth in the United States will surpass the growth of any other group in the country. Much of this growth will be attributed to immigration—nearly 325,000 Hispanic immigrants are expected to arrive in the United States yearly during the next half century. The impact will continue to be especially profound in the Southwest U.S., which has received the lion's share of Latin American immigration (U.S. Bureau of the Census, 1992).

Schools have been especially affected by Latino immigration. The Hispanic population, both immigrant and U.S.-born, tends to be younger and have a higher birth rate than the U.S. population as a whole (U.S. Bureau of the Census, 1992; Hispanic Policy Development Project, 1990). The median age of Hispanics in the United States is 25.5 years in contrast to 32.2 years for the population as a whole; fertility rate for Hispanics is nearly 2.7 births per woman in contrast to slightly more than 2 per woman for the general population. As a result, many immigrants come with young or school-age children or give birth sometime after their arrival. Thus this first-generation[1] of Mexican- and Central American-descent students constitute an ever-growing portion of U.S. schools, particularly in the Southwest. In California, where Latin American immigration has had the greatest impact, almost 1 million students—*nearly one-fifth* of the total school-age population in the state—are limited English-speaking students from Spanish-language backgrounds (Macías, 1994).

This population of students poses particular challenges to U.S. schools. Not only is the number of Mexicans and Central Americans large and growing; in addition, these immigrants have lower levels of formal schooling than either native-born U.S. adults or other immigrant groups in the

From *Advances in Motivation and Achievement*, 9, pages 183-228, JAI Press, Inc. Reprinted by permission of the authors.

United States. Seventy-seven per cent (77%) of U.S.-born adults have at least a high school diploma; over 20 percent have a bachelor's degree or higher. Among non-Latin American foreign-born adults in the United States, almost 60 percent have at least high school degrees; slightly more that 20 percent have at least college degrees. In contrast, fewer than 25 percent of Mexican immigrants have the equivalent of at least a high school diploma and only 3.5 percent have a bachelor's degree or higher. Central American immigrants also have lower levels of schooling than the United States- or other foreign-born population: 46 percent have high school degrees or higher; fewer than 9 percent have college degrees (*Education Week*, 1993). The well-established link between parents' formal schooling and children's academic achievement and the widely-reported and persistent under achievement among Latino school-age youngsters (e.g., Valencia, 1991) suggest an urgent need to help schools confront the challenges this population poses for U.S. educators.

Yet as Rumbaut (1990) points out, we know very little about these students and their parents. One area in need of investigation, and of particular interest to us, has been families' educational values, goals, beliefs, and aspirations related to children's learning and achievement. Some writers and researchers have argued that differences, or discontinuities, between the educational values and beliefs of Latinos and the values and beliefs needed for success in U.S. schools are responsible for these students' low levels of academic achievement. One perspective, now widely discredited in the research and professional literature (although still heard informally), attributes Latino children's school failure to deficiencies in their socialization. Nearly thirty years ago Heller (1966), for example, wrote:

> The kind of socialization that the Mexican-American children generally received at home is not conducive to the development of the capacities needed for advancement in a dynamic industrialized society. This type of upbringing creates stumbling blocks to future advancement by stressing values that hinder mobility—family ties, honor, masculinity, and living in the present—and by neglecting values that are conducive to it—achievement, independence, and deferred gratification (pp. 33–34).

Other authors also cite discontinuities in values or beliefs between Latino families and schools, but interpret these discontinuities within a frame-work of cultural differences not *deficiencies* (e.g., Delgado-Gaitan, 1993; Delgado-Gaitan & Trueba, 1991; Laosa, 1982). The problem, according to these researchers, is that Latino family socialization patterns and values (e.g., greater emphasis on family cohesion and responsibility among Latino families) are inconsistent with—not inferior to—styles and values espoused by the school (e.g., individual effort and achievement), thus putting children at a disadvantage since they are required to adapt to norms and standards that are foreign to them.

Still others, such as John Ogbu and his highly influential theory of why "caste-like minorities" tend to do poorly in U.S. schools, argue that Hispanic students and parents (as well as other groups historically victimized by discrimination) develop attitudes and values—Ogbu calls it "low academic effort syndrome"—that are dysfunctional for optimal school achievement. Ogbu (Ogbu, 1978; Ogbu & Matute-Bianchi, 1986) hypothesizes that because of job ceilings and discrimination, Hispanics see little connection between school success and jobs or earnings and therefore see little point in expending great efforts in school. Latino immigrants as well, Ogbu argues, quickly understand the disadvantageous opportunity structures that exist for Latinos in the United States. These perceptions then give rise to differences in achievement-related values and beliefs: "Even young children will begin to form their image of the connection or lack of connection between school success and future employment or self-advancement" (Ogbu & Matute-Bianchi, 1986, p. 128).

These three perspectives, different as they are, have at least one thing in common: They attribute the difficulties Latino youngsters have in U.S. schools to discrepancies, or discontinuities, between family values and beliefs about schooling and the values and beliefs assumed to be important for school success in this country—high aspirations for educational attainment and a belief in the value of formal schooling for future success and well-being. Parent (and child) values and beliefs certainly matter for children's school achievement (Duran & Weffer, 1992; Hanson & Ginsburg,1988; Hess & Holloway, 1984), and to the extent Latino families (or any other group) have values that clash with those that facilitate achievement in U.S. schools, we have cause for worry.

But are the educational values and beliefs of Latino immigrant families entirely discordant with more mainstream U.S. values and beliefs, those presumably espoused by the schools and necessary for school success? We suspect not, and this skepticism provided a large part of the impetus for the program of research we will describe here. Despite differences in cultures and outlook, we have seen evidence of considerable commonality between values and beliefs of Latino immigrant parents and those of educators in our schools. Moreover, and despite clear attempts to maintain links with their native cultures, we have seen evidence of self-conscious attempts by immigrant parents to move away from the educational values espoused by their parents and provide greater educational opportunities for their children than they felt were provided to them. This complex portrait of commonalities and differences, continuities and discontinuities, is at the heart of this chapter.

CULTURAL MODELS, VALUES, AND BELIEFS

One focus of our research program has been parents' cultural models of learning and their education-related values, beliefs, and actions (Goldenberg, 1987, 1988, 1989; Goldenberg, Reese, & Gallimore, 1992; Reese, Balzano, Gallimore, & Goldenberg, in press). We have presumed that, like all cultural models (D'Andrade & Strauss, 1992), those that guide family management of children's learning and education represent a complex and interpenetrated set of assumptions and dispositions. Although they may be experienced by individuals as coherent and consistent, values and beliefs encoded in cultural models do not necessarily appear to others as internally consistent, nor consistently related to behavior (Strauss, 1992). Some features have motivating properties for individuals because they include elements with directive force—the kind of motivation that has moral or quasi-moral force, where the individual feels an obligation to carry out the behaviors the model directs (D'Andrade & Strauss, 1992). Others may be strongly endorsed, but not all elements of the model are acted on, or have directive force for every individual. Some features may be honored more in the breach than in the observance. For example, blue collar U.S. workers know, endorse, and even advocate to others the American occupational success and social mobility model, but seldom act on it in their own lives; they are guided instead by a "breadwinner" model that stresses stability of employment and

income over risky actions that could lead to higher income and status (Strauss, 1992).

Similarly, endorsing and talking about a cultural model for children's learning and education does not always translate into parental actions that might be predicted by a superficial analysis. Later in this chapter, we detail which beliefs encoded in our sample's cultural model of learning and education they act on and some reasons why they do not act on others. One significant implication of this analysis is its usefulness for program design, such as finding ways to improve home/school cooperation to promote student achievement. Knowing which beliefs in their model of child learning and education are linked to action provides a basis for designing programs that are more sensitively fitted to the family's culture and more likely to work effectively.

In this chapter we review what we have learned about Mexican and Central American immigrants' cultural models of learning and education from nearly a decade of work and research. Our studies have been guided by several questions about immigrant Latino parents' educational values and beliefs: To what extent do immigrant Latino parents value formal schooling for their children? What role do they see formal education playing in their children's future lives and well-being? To what extent is there discontinuity in values and beliefs that might work against children's academic achievement (e.g., "low academic effort syndrome")? Alternatively, to what extent is there continuity, or commonality, between parents' education-related values and beliefs and values and beliefs that support school achievement? What other discontinuities might exist that can interfere with these children's school success?

This review will be informed by the conclusions we have reached over the past decade of research:

1. Latino immigrant families from Mexico and Central America express a deep and abiding belief in formal education as a means toward social and economic mobility and stability.

2. Immigrant Latino parents want to be involved in their children's schooling, and they express considerable satisfaction when teachers make efforts to involve them in children's academic development; the possibility of productive home-school collaboration for this population of students is therefore considerable.

3. Parents' views of what education—or in Spanish, educación—comprises is much broader than formal schooling; it includes moral development and familial responsibility.

4. Although parents greatly value academic development in general and literacy development in particular, children in immigrant families from Mexico and Central America typically have relatively few experiences at home that promote text-based literacy development as it is defined in school.

Two seemingly paradoxical themes weave their way through our presentation. One theme is *discontinuity* across generations and cultures; the other is *continuity* across generations and cultures.

In some important respects, the beliefs and attitudes of the families do differ from that of the schools the children attend. These differences are important. Differences in beliefs and attitudes and differences between how children are socialized at home and taught at school can interfere with students' school adaptation and performance (California State Department of Education, 1986; Delgado-Gaitan & Trueba, 1991; Jacob & Jordan, 1987; Laosa, 1982). But in equally important respects, there can be common features across school and family cultures. These commonalities are perhaps just as important, since they offer potential avenues for cooperation and mutual benefit.

Similarly, the families represent important continuities with traditional features—including values and attitudes—of their natal cultures. But there are also important discontinuities, sometimes even self-conscious attempts to break with the past and with the values and attitudes of the older generation in the native country. Both continuity and discontinuity across generations are part of the process of cultural evolution, a complex dynamic that contributes to change and variability within cultures (Chibnik, 1981; Edgerton, 1992). These paradoxes—continuity *and* discontinuity across cultures and generations—will defy attempts to reach simplistic and reductionistic conclusions about parents' cultural models and the role they play in children's schooling and achievement.

DESCRIPTION OF STUDIES AND SAMPLES

The series of investigations we have carried out began in 1983 with a study of 9 first-grade children at risk for reading problems in first grade (Goldenberg, 1989). A principal focus of this project was parents' beliefs, attitudes, and actions that contributed to children's early literacy achievement (Goldenberg, 1987). As with the studies that followed, the participating children were mostly first-generation United States-born of immigrant parents, primarily from Mexico. A subsequent series of studies examined children's home literacy experiences, parents' beliefs and attitudes toward children's schooling and literacy development, and what schools could do to foster early literacy development in children's native language (Gallimore & Goldenberg, 1993; Goldenberg, 1994; Goldenberg & Gallimore, 1991; Goldenberg, Reese, & Gallimore, 1992; Reese, Goldenberg, Loucky, & Gallimore, in press).

We have used a combination of quantitative and qualitative methods in our studies.[2] One of our goals has been to try and understand "activity settings" at home and school that contribute—or fail to contribute—to children's emerging literacy development. The components of these activity settings include the persons available to engage in activities with children, the beliefs, values, and motivations of participants, materials available and in use, and the scripts used in carrying out activities (Gallimore, Goldenberg, & Weisner, 1993; Tharp & Gallimore, 1988). How parent beliefs and attitudes—their cultural models of learning and education—played themselves out in the activity settings of the home had important consequences for children's learning experiences, opportunities, and actual achievement. For example, the discovery of parents' interest in and commitment to children's school success led to a parent involvement component in a multi-faceted and successful attempt to improve early literacy achievement at one school (Goldenberg & Gallimore, 1991). However, when parents' culture-based theories about early literacy development are inconsistent with materials sent home from school, the resulting activities will not necessarily contribute to literacy development; in contrast, materials that are consistent with parents' theories promote in-home activities that support children's learning (Goldenberg et al., 1992; Gallimore & Goldenberg, 1993).

Most recently, in 1989 we randomly selected 121 kindergartners of Mexican and Central American origin—75 percent of whom were first-generation children—in two different Southern

California school districts and began a longitudinal study of them and their families. We have made at least twice-yearly contacts with the families (either by phone or in person) where we asked about their child's progress, their aspirations and expectations for children's future attainment, their beliefs about the role of schooling in children's future success, factors they considered important for student academic success, and about the role parents and teachers play in school achievement. We also obtained assessments of children's academic progress, both from teachers and from test scores. Within the Longitudinal Cohort (66 boys & 55 girls), a subset of 32 families were randomly selected for an Ethnographic Subset. For these families, fieldworkers undertook more in-depth, detailed, and interpretive interviews designed to reveal more subtle and complex aspects of parents' cultural models of schooling and education. Families were visited 12 times in three years to obtain extensive case data that enriched our interpretation of the Longitudinal data.

Among the cohort of 121 children, 91 live in Lawson, an unincorporated area of approximately 1.2 square miles in metropolitan Los Angeles. School enrollment in the Lawson District is over 90 percent Latino. A second group (N = 30) comprises immigrant Spanish-speaking families residing in a racially mixed neighborhood approximately 25 miles south of Lawson (Sandy Beach); these children attend school in a large urban district. The great majority (84%) of the parents in both communities came to the United States from Mexico; the rest are from Central America. The Mexican-origin parents in our sample tend to follow an earlier migration pattern identified by Cornelius (1989–1990): 55 percent of the women and over 60 percent of the men are from the states of Jalisco, Michoacan, and Zacatecas. Mothers in the sample average 9.6 years (range = 1–34) in the United States; fathers average 11.7 (range = 1–53). The average number of years of formal schooling for both mothers and fathers is 7 (range = 0–16 years).

Parents' occupations in our sample tend to cluster in the lower levels of occupation within each census category: Service (30%; e.g., cooks, waiters, maids, janitors, bartenders, bus boys, parking attendants, child care and cafeteria workers, teacher's assistants); Repair (23%; mechanics, electricians, carpenters, welders); and Laborer (34%; construction, assembly, packing, machine operation, and loading). Only 3 percent of the fathers reported being unemployed in 1989. Approximately 43 percent of the mothers work outside the home.

In contrast to their parents, who are all immigrants, the majority (75%) of the children were born in the United States, 94 percent of these in California. Close to 22 percent of the children were born in Mexico; 3 percent were born in Central America.

In all of our studies, we have worked through the schools and contacted parents of all Spanish-speaking children in kindergartens of participating teachers. The response rate has been consistently very high, with at least 85 percent of parents agreeing to be contacted to take part in our studies. We are thus confident that we have included a representative sampling from our target population.

The Families' Cultural Model of Child Education

Immigrants have typically expressed a strong faith in formal education's power to propel upward social mobility (Ogbu, 1978). The immigrant Latino parents whom we have studied and with whom we work are no exception. The parents in our study sample express uniformly high aspirations for their children's education. We asked two simple questions in the fall of each year, beginning in kindergarten: How far do you *want* your child to go in his/her formal schooling? and How far do you *think* your child will go in his/her formal schooling? For both questions, parents were asked to choose among: (1) finish elementary school, (2) finish middle school, (3) finish high school, (4) finish trade/vocational school, (5) attend college/university, or (6) finish college/university.

As we predicted, parents indeed had high aspirations and expectations for children's future schooling. When children began kindergarten, over 90 percent of parents wanted their children to attend university. Parents' expectations—what they actually thought would happen—were lower, although still relatively high. Slightly more than half (54%) of the parents expected college or university attendance. Virtually all the rest (except for 7 (5.8%) who did not answer) expected high school or vocational school completion.

These aspirations and the valuing of education are one element of the *cultural model* for child socialization and education held by virtually all members of our study sample (Reese, Balzano, et al., in press). By cultural models (D'Andrade & Strauss, 1992), we mean shared ways of organizing and understanding the social world and personal experience. Cultural models or schema make sense of the world, how things work, and what is the right and proper course of action. Many features of cultural models are relatively transparent to the individuals who hold them, because they are not just cognitive representations of reality, they are reality. They are the ways things are, the taken-for-granted view of the world (D'Andrade, 1992). The importance of education and the aspirations they express are good examples of cultural model features. But they are not the only ones.

In addition to the level of *formal schooling* parents aspire to for children, we identified other features of the their cultural model of child education. We describe three in this chapter:

1. The role of formal schooling in their children's future prospects

2. Parents' own educational experiences and opportunities

3. *Educación* and the foundations of formal schooling

1. THE ROLE OF FORMAL SCHOOLING IN CHILDREN'S FUTURE: "IF YOU'VE STUDIED, YOU HAVE MANY OPPORTUNITIES OPEN TO YOU."

The parents with whom we have worked view education in instrumental terms. Education is a means to economic security, the attainment of professional status, or both. Although they also express the hope that children will learn something useful as part of their schooling, they unquestionably believe that education is necessary for social mobility and economic success. In this regard, there is no doubt among parents that they want their children to go as far as possible in their formal schooling. Many speak explicitly of specific professional careers they hope their children would pursue. The following are representative quotations taken from interviews conducted with the parents of 30 kindergarten children (30 mothers and 24 fathers):

Yo quisiera después de la secundaria, que estudie medicina, leyes, algo grande, una carrera larga, pero . . . si no [se] puede . . . pues enfermera o dentista, una carrera corta, que gane bien que tenga con que vivir, que se desenvuelva sola. . . . si es demasiado caro acá pues mandarla a México y que termine su carrera. Si es demasiado caro y no podemos, inclusive yo donde trabajo tengo unos savings, estoy ahorrando para eso, ella tiene cinco años y yo ya empecá a ahorrar. Quiero darle algo a mis hijos para su educación. Para cuando terminen 'high school.' (After she [his daughter] finishes secondary school, I'd like her to study medicine, law, . . . a major career . . . [but if I can't afford that] then a nurse or a dentist, a shorter degree [one that doesn't take as long to complete] so that she can make a good living, do well on her own . . . If it's too expensive here, [we are thinking] we would send her to Mexico to finish her studies. Where I work, I have some savings for that, she is five years old and I have already begun to save. I want to give my children something for their education. For when they finish high school.) (202.7.1)[3]

Yo quiero que tenga una carrera, que tenga una educación mejor, aunque Ud. sabe ya cuando crecen a lo mejor es más difícil, pero si uro los va empujando desde chicos a que agarren una carrera o sea que empiezen a estudiar más fuerte, para que el día de mañana, uno diga 'Bueno ya no tengo nada que dejarles por lo menos darle el estudio para que tenga más oportunidades para ganarse la vida más fácil que uno'. (I want him to have a career, a better education, although you know that once they get older maybe it becomes more difficult. But you [can] start pushing them to have a career from the time they are young, that is, so they'll study harder; so that tomorrow one can say, 'Well, I don't have anything to leave them, but at least I gave them an education, so that they will have more opportunities and an easier time than [I] did.') (203.6.4)

Yo quisiera que llegara muy alto, por mi que termine el 'high school' y que siga con el colegio, según sus posibilidades de uno ¿verdád? Pero uno los alienta a que terminen la 'high school' y sigan con el colegio, los deseos que tiene uno . . . Mi esposo les dice que todos estudien para maestros (I would like him to go very high [in his education]. As far as I'm concerned, he should finish high school and continue with college, depending upon his abilities and possibilities, right? But one encourages them to finish high school and continue with college, that's what one wishes [for one's children] . . . My husband tells them all to study to become teachers.) (205.8.3)

Yo trato de inculcarles que ellos deben estudiar, porque ya todo lo que sirve es la preparación . . . porque cada día están pidiendo más cosas en los trabajos, depende de lo que dice uno hasta que fue a la escuela así le dan a uno el trabajo, es lo que yo siempre le digo a mi hijo. (I try to inculcate in them that they should study, because what is most valuable is your preparation . . . every day they require more and more at work. Whether they give you the chance of a job depends upon what you tell them—how far you went in school. This is what I always tell my son.) (206.10.2).

Uno puede abrirse camino teniendo muchos estudios. En cambio así, uno tiene que andar limpiando, pidiendo de gata porque no puede uno hacer otra cosa. (If you've studied, you have many opportunities open to you. Otherwise, you have have to clean houses or ask [for handouts] because you don't know how to do anything else.) (103.9.3).

Quantitative data from our sample of 121 children confirm what these quotes suggest. Parents see formal education as instrumentally related to socially desired outcomes. When asked whether doing well in school would help their particular child (1) have a better job, (2) make more money, and (3) be happier in his/her life, parents responded overwhelmingly in the affirmative. On a 1–7 scale (7 = definitely agree), mean parent responses for these 3 outcomes was 6.6, 6.3, and 6.0, respectively.

The views of these parents on the subject of education as a ladder of social and occupational mobility are indistinguishable from those of other U.S. residents and the teachers in their local school. Here is what the former president of the California Teachers' Association says on the subject: "The relationship between educational attainment and affluence is undeniable" (Foglia, 1988). Indeed this belief is part the American ideology about schooling and social mobility. It is a belief supported by social science research: "It is a well known fact that education is the single most

important means to economic stability" (Casas & Furlong, 1986, p. 45); "Education is the key to mobility . . . [and] Mexican-Americans are translating their educational achievement into occupational mobility" (McCarthy & Valdez, 1986, p. 58).

These views are also similar to previous generations of immigrants' hopes for their children. Journalist and author Theodore H. White, speaking of his mother's—the daughter of immigrants—ambitions for her children, wrote:

> What she wanted of life was security . . . she dreamed for her children . . . of a "good job," a "government job," perhaps even a schoolteacher's job, which was the farthest limit of her ambition. She wanted no factory job for [her children]. (White, 1978, p. 21)

Ironically, the parents in our sample, as did those from earlier immigrant groups (e.g., Sennett & Cobb, 1972, p. 128), want their children to be different—to be more educated, have higher status, and exert more social authority. As the next section shows, this generational discontinuity to which parents aspire parallels a discontinuity that parents only wish they had experienced. Indeed a strong motivation for wanting different educational outcomes for their children stems from parents' own sense of restricted opportunities.

2. Parents' Own Educational Experiences and Opportunities: "We Didn't Study, and Look at Us Here."

Parents expressed the view that education would permit their children "to be somebody" (*"ser alguien en la vida"*), something they feel was denied to them because of the limited education they received. Of the 54 mothers and fathers interviewed in the earlier study, all but one expressed dissatisfaction with their own educational attainment. And without exception, parents wanted their children to go further in school than they had gone. When one couple (the mother had gone to the sixth grade, the father ninth) was asked why they wanted their son to finish high school and attend university, the father answered, "We didn't study, and look at us here" (*Nosotros no estudiamos, y mírenos acá.*) (104.10.2).

Parents were virtually unanimous in the belief that their lack of formal education meant a harder life for them and greater difficulties in getting ahead. Their dissatisfaction with their own educational attainment stemmed from this belief:

Yo siento que no fue suficiente, yo habría [sic] querido estudiar más, ser alguien en la vida. Con este poquito que estudié no es suficiente. . . . . Y batalla uno mucho por lo que no sabe uno, de que no estudió batalla uno mucho para buscar trabajo. A veces no sabe una mi lo que dice cuando va uno caminando en la calle y no sabe ni dónde and ardi [I feel that [my formal schooling] was not sufficient. I would have liked to study more, to be somebody. With the little I studied, it's not enough. . . . One really struggles a lot because of what one does not know. Because of not having studied, one must really struggle to find a job. Sometimes you don't even know what they're saying when you go walking down the street, and you don't even know where you are going.) (204.8.3)

Papá no nos dejó estudiar más del sexto grado . . . así es que a todos nos dejaron cortos de escuela, como quien dice el sexto no es nada, porque yo ahora lo vengo viendo, porque yo he querido entrar a programas de inglés y no puedo adelantar en el inglés escrito y leído porque no tengo la base de los verbos y todo eso. Si apenas cuando sale uno de sexto, apenas si lo sabe uno. (Father did not let us go past sixth grade . . . so they left us short of schooling. [But] sixth grade is nothing, I now realize, because I have wanted to enter English programs, but I can't advance in oral and written English because because I don't have the foundation in verbs and all that. When you finish sixth grade you barely know all of that.) (206.11.1)

One mother, who had had no formal schooling, had taught herself to read and write. Yet she considered herself "illiterate," and attributed her failure "to be something" to her lack of formal schooling.

A pesar que yo no tuve estudios, yo me siento que he sido inteligente, porque yo sola he aprendido a leer y a escribir, sin haber podido ir a la escuela. A ellos les pongo de apariencia [sic] a mi. Yo les digo que no estén igual que yo de analfabeta, quiero que sean alguien en la vida. (Even though I did not study, I feel I have been intelligent, because I learned by myself how to read and write, even without having gone to school. [But] I use myself as an example

for them. I tell them not to be an illiterate like me. I want them to be something in this life.) (103.9.2,4)

This same parent described her own attempts to go to school:

A mi me gustaba mucho la escuela. En una ocasión que mi mamá se fue para un rancho y me dejó encargada con una señora, yo fui sola y me matriculé en una escuela, tenía como nueve años, y le dije al maestro que yo no tenía dinero pero que yo quería ir a la escuela, porque allá en México se cobra por inscribirse. El me dijo no importa, puedes venir a la escuela y cuando tu mamá venga me pagas. Yo me levantaba temprano y ayudaba a la señora con lo que me había encargado. . . . Pero no más fui una semana. A la semana vinieron por mi porque mi mamá necesitaba que me fuera para cuidar a los niños y ya no fui a la escuela. Por eso yo les digo a ellos que es muy importante ir a la escuela, que no porque yo no fui a la escuela van a dejar ellos de ir. (I liked school, and one time when my mother went away and left a lady to take care of me, I went alone and I enrolled in school. I was about nine years old. And I told the teacher that I didn't have any money but that I wanted to go to school. There in Mexico you have to pay to enroll. The teacher said it didn't matter, you can come to school and when your mother returns you can pay me. I would get up early and help the lady with whatever chores she had given me, and then I would go and run the errands. . . . But I only went [to school] for a week. At the end of the week they came and got me because my mother needed me to take care of the children, so I didn't go to school anymore. That's why I tell [my children] that it's important to go to school. Just because I didn't go, it doesn't mean they're not going.) (103.9.2)

Parents cited a variety of reasons for their own failure to secure higher levels of formal education. Many said their schooling was interrupted because of economic reasons. Either they had to work to support the family, or their own parents could not or would not pay fees and expenses required for school attendance. In other instances, there was no school close enough for them to attend, once they had finished elementary school. Most of the parents came from rural areas served by, at most, a primary school. In yet other instances, parents felt there had been insufficient value placed on education in their homes, and, as a result, they had left school prematurely.

In some cases, parents reported, the de-valuation of education in their own parents' homes was overt and explicit, especially for girls. Two mothers spoke of how their parents did not think it necessary for women to be educated:

> *Papá . . . decía . . . que las mujeres después del sexto año que ya se debía enseñar a los quehaceres de la casa, que porque nosotros crecíamos y nos íbamos a casar, y que con el estudio no le íbamos a dar de comer al esposo y esto y aquello. Y mi mamá también siguiéndole a mi papá el juego. Llegábamos al sexto año y todo [sic]mundo iba afuera.* (Father . . . would say that women, after the sixth grade, should learn about housework, because when we grew up we would get married, and education would not feed our husbands and so on and so forth. And my mother followed his line. [So] when we got to the sixth grade, everybody [was] out.) (206.11.1)

> *En México los padres no lo mandan a uno a la escuela, más si uno es mujer. Dicen que 'Al cabo se casan que va estar con el marido, entonces no necesitan escuela.'* (In Mexico, parents don't send you to school, especially if you are a woman. They say, 'She's going to get married, she will be with a husband. So she doesn't need to go to school.') (103.9.3).

In other cases, parents felt they had had insufficient support from their own parents, and this had hurt them. Parents directly or indirectly criticized their own parents for failing to pay sufficient attention to education. A father with an eighth-grade education, who had been raised by his grandparents, said his own schooling suffered because no one paid close enough attention to him, and he said he did not want the same to occur to his daughter:

> *Pues ya ve en México, según lo mandan a uno a la escuela y pues uno se va de vago y se la pintea porque uno no tiene el cuidado que tiene que tener. Y entonces yo pienso que tengo que dedicarle más a mi hija para que se sepa desenvolver porque sí tengo visiones de que sobresalga en sus estudios. No digo que uno no haya podido, porque uno siempre lo puede lograr, lo que me refiero es que nosotros nunca tuvimos los padres cerca como los puede tener ella. Y le*

> *digo a ella [madre] que tratemos de ayudarla y hacer lo que esté a nuestro alcanze . . . No me siento muy bien de la educación que tuve en la escuela, por eso trato de que la niña, pues ayudarla en lo que más pueda para (?) ella sí trate de sobresalir en los estudios.* (You know in Mexico, presumably they send you to school, but you really bum around and skip school because one [the parent] is not as careful as one should be. So I think that I have to devote more attention] to my daughter so she will develop completely, . . . I have hopes that she will excel in her studies. I am not saying I could not have [excelled in studies because one can always accomplish this [if he or she really wants to]. What I mean is that we never had our parents nearby, as she [his daughter] can have hers. And I tell her [the mother] that we should try to help her and do what is within our reach . . . I don't feel very good about the education I received in school, and that is why I try to help [my daughter] as much as I can, so that she will try to excel in her studies . . .) (106.4.1).

The parents' cultural model of learning and schooling is not an unamended version brought from the natal country to the United States. There is an explicit discontinuity with what they perceived to be their own parents' view of education for children, especially for females. This is a powerful reminder that cultural models are not static, dead-hands of custom and tradition. They evolve as challenges arise and conditions change. Note, for example, the parent quoted above (case # 206) who said "sixth grade is nothing, *I now realize* (emphasis added)." He had wanted to enter a program for more advanced English study, but lacked (in his estimation) a foundation in formal study of language forms and conventions. As was true of others, this parent had concluded (accurately or not) that the level of formal schooling deemed adequate for the *ranchos* in rural Mexico was insufficient for successful adaptation to urban United States. It is clear that these families are not members of a monolithic immigrant group that brought with them unchanging cultural rules and practices. In their comments and everyday talk one can see a dynamic process of cultural adaptation playing out.

For our purposes, the key point is this group of immigrant families has amended their cultural model of schooling to a form that is more continuous with the public school personnel that now teach their children. As a result, to this point we see more continuity than discontinuity between family and school models—valuing formal schooling and its instrumental relation to social and economic mobility, high aspirations, saving money for college, motivational speeches to children, and rejection of sex discrimination. These continuities point to a central conclusion of our ten years of research with this population: There are many continuities between the families and schools, often overlooked by teachers and school administrators and sometimes by researchers focused on identifying cultural differences and discontinuities to account for the differential achievement of Latino children with immigrant backgrounds.

However, there are discontinuities as well as continuities. In the next section, as we flesh out the model of learning and education of the families, significant discontinuities emerge between home and school that might help explain some of the educational difficulties some immigrant children experience. As these are identified, we will move in the final sections of this chapter to identify possibilities for family/school collaboration that are built on the continuities and are sensitive to the discontinuities. The immigrant families in our studies are culturally different, but they also share many things with other residents of this country.

3. EDUCACIÓN AND THE FOUNDATIONS OF FORMAL SCHOOLING[4]

On the surface, the Spanish *educación* appears to be a direct translation of the English word "education." Although they are clearly related etymologically, the Spanish term refers to beliefs and practices that are not generally referents of its English cognate. Whereas in English, someone who is "well-educated" is considered schooled, knowledgeable, and literate, in Spanish, *"bien educado"* has a different set of associations—respectful, dutiful, well-mannered. A well-educated person, in the English sense, might also be bien educado—but not necessarily; conversely, someone who is *bien educado* might have little formal schooling.

We found in earlier interviews (see Reese, Balzano et al., in press) that many parents did not spontaneously distinguish between education as schooling (academics) and education—or *edu-*

cación—as upbringing (morals and comportment). One mother, for example, when asked what she would like for her son's future occupation, replied:

> *Me gustaría que estudiara, y sobre todo que fuera recto, que tuviera buenas costumbres, que llegara a ser una persona de respeto y que también fuera respetuoso con las personas.* (I'd like him to study, and above all to be upright, to have good behavior, to become (literally: to arrive at being) a person of respect and to be respectful of others too.) (Case #91).

This interconnectedness of *formal study* and *moral rectitude* was so common in the conversational interviews that we added a direct question to our more structured interview protocol, in which we attempted to have parents distinguish between and assign priority in academic and moral aspects of education/*educación*. Even extended attempts to get parents to distinguish academics and morals and to speculate on which was more important to child's schooling success were unsuccessful in many cases. Twenty-eight per cent (28%) insisted academics and morals could not be separated, perceiving each as part of a larger whole leading to becoming a good person. One father's comments were typical:

> *Las dos cosas van de la mano. Uno tiene que estar siempre tratando de caminar un camino recto. Sería imposible llegar a la universidad si no tiene buenos modales, si no se enseñe a respetar a los demás. Llegaría a ser pandillero, si no.* (The two things go hand in hand. One always has to try to walk a straight path. It would be impossible to get to the university if one doesn't have good behavior, if one isn't taught to respect others. One would end up as a gang member otherwise.) (Case #64).

(The term *'buenos modales,'* often translated as 'good manners' has been translated here as 'good behavior' in an effort to convey accurately the usage of the parents who seem to be referring to fundamentally correct behavior more than just etiquette.) Another parent was explicit about the inseparability of academics and morals:

> *Si uno es una buena persona, va a ser un buen estudiante, y si no es buena persona no puede ser un buen estudiante. Son cosas que no se*

pueden separar (If one is a good person, you are going to be a good student. And if you are not a good person it is not possible to be a good student. These are things that cannot be separated.) (Case #64).

Nearly half—44 percent—of parents subordinated academics to moral development, but still maintained they were inextricably linked; moral development is seen as indispensable for school achievement. One parent said:

Es más necesario mas bien educarlos moralmente que académicamente. Para poder educar, si a un maestro le dan un niño que no tiene principios morales, ni está preparado moralmente, va a ser bien difícil de enseñarle cosas académicas. Un niño va a aprender más fácil si ya sabe respetar y tratar. (It's more necessary to educate children morally than academically. In order to educate, if a teacher is given a child who doesn't have moral principles, or who isn't morally prepared, it will be difficult to teach this child academic things. A child will learn more easily if he already knows how to respect and treat others.) (Case #33).

The Parent's Role

Many parents say explicitly that their principal responsibility is the rearing of a moral and responsible child, a child who will become what is often referred to as a *"persona de bien,"* a good person. For example, one father stated emphatically that the most important thing for his children is *"básicamente la moralidad, la honestidad. Son las cosas fundamentales de la familia, hacerlos personas de bien."* (" . . . basically morality, honesty. These are the fundamental things of the family, to make them good people." Case #63). A mother reaffirms, *"Tiene uno que enseñarles a ser buenos, aparte del estudio. Enseñarles a ser correctos. Enseñarles moralidad, enseñarles a ser buenos, pues pueden estar muy estudiados y todo, pero si uno no les enseña a ser correctos de últimas de nada les sirve."* ("One has to teach them to be good, aside from schooling. Teach them to be correct [in behavior]. Teach them morals, teach them to be good, because they can have studied a lot, but if one hasn't taught them correct behavior, in the end it (study) doesn't help them." Case #1).

Not only do parents feel they must teach children to distinguish between right and wrong, but they must also teach them to act accordingly, in other words, to demonstrate good behavior. Both the knowledge of right and wrong and knowing and practicing the behaviors and manners that are the result of such knowledge are key aspects of the concept of *educación*.

Teaching respect for parents and others is one of these behaviors and one which forms an essential part of *educación*. As one parent explains,

Todos nosotros, los mejicanos, venimos de una tradición antigua, de ranchos donde se respeta al padre y a la madre. Tratándose de hermanos, los menores respetan a los mayores. (All of us, we Mexicans, come from an old tradition, a tradition of the 'ranchos,' where the father and mother are respected. Regarding siblings, the younger ones respect the older ones. (Case #23)

Respect for all members of the family, taught by the parents and demonstrated by the children, is what causes one father to conclude that all is well with his family:

Ella, él (he gestures to the focal child's brother and sister) *son hermanos; es lo más importante. Respetar a los prójimos* (sic) *y a ellos mismos. Ahorita yo veo que mi familia va bien. No tengo problemas. Respetamos las opiniones de cada persona.* (She, he [he gestures to the brother and sister of the focal child] are siblings; that is the most important thing. Respecting others and themselves. Right now I see that my family is doing well. I don't have problems. We respect the opinions of each person.) (Case #2).

This same father describes the respect he was taught at home by his parents as a *"bonita herencia"* ("beautiful inheritance"), which he was given by his parents and which he is giving his own children. As they educate (*educar*) their children, then, these parents seek to pass on ethical values and behaviors learned from their own parents. At the same time, as we saw in the preceding section, *educación* for these immigrant parents has a much stronger component of "formal schooling." The immigrant parents in our sample clearly wish to maintain many of the traditional family values of responsibility and respect taught to them by their own parents, our target children's grandparents. But with its greater emphasis on formal schooling—for both boys and girls—these immigrant parents' cultural model of *educación* is itself undergoing change. It is adapting to the exigencies of life in a society where education—in the English sense of the word—matters.

Nonetheless, we have seen that the term *educación* encompasses but is not limited to formal academic training. *Educación* has a broader meaning than the English term 'education.' The term invokes additional, non-academic elements, such as learning the difference between right and wrong, respect for parents and others, and correct behavior, which parents view as the base upon which all other learning lies.

EL BUEN CAMINO—THE GOOD PATH

In talking about their model of child development and education, parents make statements indicating that the concept of *educación* is structured metaphorically according to the idea of a road down which children travel under parents' guidance. Parents see their responsibility as that of giving their children the knowledge necessary for them to follow the el *buen camino*—the "good path"—in life; however, children make the decision for themselves. Eighty-one per cent of the Ethnographic Subset families stated that children make these life-course decisions between the ages of 12 and 18.

Parents say about el *buen camino*, for example, "*Desde que son chiquitos, uno trata de encaminarlos. Ya cuando son más grandes, las malas compañías los echan a perder.*" ("From the time they [children] are young, one [as a parent] tries to put them on the right road. When they are older, bad company ruins them." Case #78). "*A la edad de doce años, muchas veces las criaturas se descarrilan.*" ("Sometimes, at the age of 12, children get derailed [go astray]." Case #53). "*Yo no fui criada 'a la moda', ni mi marido tampoco. Nosotros queremos enseñarles [a nuestros hijos] ese camino. Como nos criaron a nosotros.*" ("I was not brought up to follow the new wave, neither was my husband. We want to teach our children that road, the way we were brought up." Case #54).

As parents describe the characteristics of el *buen camino*, they place school on the good path and dropping out of school on the bad path. Thus, schooling and academic achievement are not seen as separate from moral development, but are rather imbued with virtue as part of the good life for which one aspires and prepares one's children.

We are not suggesting that Latino families are unique in their concern over raising morally

responsible children. Indeed, Azmitia et al., (1994) report similar priority given to children's moral development by European-American as well as Mexican-American parents. Our point is that for immigrant Latino parents, the counterpart to what we term in English "education"—*educación*—includes a number of dimensions encompassing many aspects of children's development—academics, morals, proper behavior, familial unity and responsibility, and in general staying on the right path in life, *el buen camino*. In the next section, we will show how this cultural model directs parents' actions in ways that significantly affect children's experiences before and after they enter public school. We will also show how the parents' model leads to continuities and discontinuities with the cultural model of the school.

Child Behavior and Moral Development: Continuities, Discontinuities in Cultural Models and Parents' Actions

THE IMPORTANCE OF TEACHING MORALS AND PROPER BEHAVIOR

Given the centrality of the cultural model of *educación* and the beliefs it encompasses, it is not surprising that parents describe taking actions for and with their children that feature issues of morality and proper behavior. When asked what actions parents should take to help their children succeed in school, only rarely do parents cite promoting early literacy, preschool preparation, or other academically-oriented activities (See below, "*Parents' Preschool Preparation of Children.*") Rather, the action most commonly reported by parents is to talk with or counsel their children concerning correct and incorrect behavior. One mother reports, "*Siempre le estoy diciendo: 'Tú tienes que ser un niño bueno y usar tu inteligencia en lo bueno y no en lo malo.'*" ("I'm always telling him: 'You have to be a good boy and use your intelligence for the right things and not for the wrong ones" (Case #26).

Use of dramatic examples is a common technique parents use to teach right and wrong and discourage misbehavior. One mother says that she uses books and magazines for this purpose. She reads a story to her children and then she says, for example, "Look what happened to that boy. He got run over because he didn't listen to his parents" (Case #111). Another mother reported pointing out a woman on the street as an example for her five-year-old daughter of what happens when you use drugs (Case #113).

Because children are believed to learn principally through example and imitation, a common strategy for ensuring proper behavior is restricting children's peer contacts and their play areas. For example, when parents in the longitudinal sample were asked what they do to minimize the dangers to their children of the neighborhood in which they live, of the 28 parents who rated their neighborhood as more dangerous than average, 57 percent reported that they kept their children inside the house (21% reported that they counseled their children about the dangers; 14% said that there was nothing that they could do.) One mother will only let her young daughters play outside of their one-room apartment when she sits in the window to watch them. She gives as an explanation of her behavior that children learn good things and bad things when they see them, *"sin que nadie haga nada en especial para enseñarles,"* ("without anyone doing anything special to teach them") and she wants to be very careful about what they are exposed to (Case #113).

An extreme example of restricting children's friends, but one that has been reported to us and that parents in our samples have told us sometimes happens, is to send a child who is having problems and following the "wrong path" to stay with relatives in Mexico. As one parent told us: *"Como Ud. sabe, al pueblo que fueres, hacer lo que vieres. Aquí ven puro cholo, pura cosa de esas, pues. Les hace mal. Donde no lo ven, pues, no lo hacen."* ("As you know, wherever you go, you do what you see the people there doing [referring to a well-known saying in Spanish]. Here they see only "cholos" and things like that. It is bad for them. If they don't see these things, they won't do them." (Case #53).

Keeping children inside and away from bad influences can have the additional benefit of supporting academic and learning activities. For example, one father tells a high-school-aged daughter to study so that she will not be interested in having a boyfriend. (Case #2) Other parents state that they wish the school would give more homework so that they can then keep the children

busy (*"entretenidos"*) inside the home (e.g., Cases #111 & 112).

The context of this *moral teaching* is a unified family that spends time together, values each other, and communicates. One father stated, *"Somos pobres pero tenemos nuestra familia."* ("We are poor but we have our family." Case #2) Another mother revealed,

Yo pienso que estar unidos, tanto mi esposo como mis hijos, tener la comunicación, es muy importante. Yo pienso que no hay otra cosa tan importante. Entonces, por buscar dinero, para tener dinero, para tener riqueza, uno trabaja y pierde uno lo que es lo más importante. Para mí, lo más importante es los hijos, el esposo, para mí. (I think that being together, with my husband as well as my children, having comunication, is very important. I don't think there is anything else as important. Because in order to seek money and riches one goes to work and loses sight of what is the most important thing. For me the most important thing is my husband and children.) (Case #92).

Thus, the teaching of morality takes place in the atmosphere in which the family, and the child's place in the family, is highly valued.

FAMILY AND SCHOOL DISCONTINUITIES IN PROMOTING MORALS AND GOOD BEHAVIOR

To the extent that mainstream U.S. educators value proper and respectful behavior by children, there is no incompatibility between the school and the families. On the contrary, given that 86 percent of teachers cite disruptive behavior as at least "somewhat" of a problem in their school (Carnegie Foundation for the Advancement of Teaching, 1990), we suspect that teachers would be extremely pleased if more children conformed to the behavioral norms held by the parents. Moreover, as we have already pointed out, Latino families are not unique in attaching great, perhaps even pre-eminent, importance to moral development (Azmitia et al., 1994). Thus there is probably considerable compatibility, or consistency, between Latino parents and the mainstream culture in terms of desires and expectations for children's behavior and their moral growth.

On the other hand, according to parents the achievement of children's proper moral development depends on consistent, vigilant, and sometimes harsh discipline. One form of discipline mentioned by some parents, and associated by some with *educación*, is the use of corporal punishment to keep children on the "right path." Although not all mentioned use of corporal punishment, most parents did say they are strict with their children. These beliefs and practices can bring the parents into direct conflict with the school. That this issue is of great concern to parents is indicated by the number of times it surfaced without prompting in the interviews and by the passion accompanying the views. Parents of both higher and lower achieving students express emotions ranging from concern to outrage about what they regard as school interference with family discipline practices.

These emotional reactions arise in part from instruction on child abuse that is currently required of students in California public schools. Florid tales about authorities removing children from their families circulate in the community. Parents are told by their children that they have been instructed to report to school authorities any time their parents hit them. Parents feel this directly undermines the respect they are trying to instill in their children.

As a result, many parents feel that they are or will be prevented from fulfilling their childrearing responsibilities by the very institution that they would have expected to support them and help achieve their aspirations. Whereas American school personnel often tell parents that they are the children's "first teachers," a common expression used by Latino immigrant parents is *"la maestra es la segunda mamá."* ("The teacher is the second mother"). It is, therefore, a source of confusion for parents, who cannot understand why the teacher/mother is calling into question a family's teachings about right and wrong. Far from viewing their own actions as child abuse, many parents see the school response as lack of concern for children's *educación* and an indication that the school is a threat to moral development, which they perceive as the foundation of all learning.

FAMILY AND SCHOOL MODELS OF THE EL BUEN CAMINO OF CHILD DEVELOPMENT

We propose that "discipline discontinuity" reveals two different cultural models of the course

of child development. The *educación* model of the families is an example of what LeVine and White (1986) termed an agrarian cultural model of human development, which they distinguished from an "academic occupational" model commonly held in the United States and by the school personnel in the communities where our study is conducted.

Agrarian societies, LeVine and White (1986) argue,

> evolve moral codes favoring filial piety and intergenerational reciprocity, gender-specific ideals of social and spiritual values rather than specialized intellectual ones, concepts of childhood learning that emphasize the acquisition of manners and work skills without competitive evaluations, and concepts of the adult years as the prime period for significant cognitive development (p. 3).

The values of *educación*—as is true of any set of cultural values—evolve and are passed on in socialization contexts where children observe and participate in the everyday activities of those around them. In contexts where the family works together as an economic unit and where child labor contributes to family subsistence in an interdependent social order—as is true of the societies from which these parents emigrated—the focus is the teaching and learning of the social and moral capacities a child will need to function as an adult in an *inter-dependent* context (LeVine, 1990). Strict discipline in such a context is intended to prevent the kind of social conflict and mischief that require its use. The emphasis in such a model is on the development of refined, sensitive social skills which parents believe prepare the child to do well in school and to stay on the *el buen camino*.

Different though their cultural model may be from the assumptions of school personnel in the United States, the values of *educación* are not irrelevant to the family's adaptive challenges in the United States. There is value in bending the agrarian values carried from Mexico and Central America to the adaptive challenges of United States urban life. We have some suggestive evidence that children are more successful academically when families manage to put into practice some of the values they carried with them to the U.S. (Reese, Balzano, et al., in press). Our case studies also document that those families who successfully implemented *educación* values into everyday routines have children who do better in school:

> In Case 26, the boy's mother and father are both very concerned about their children's moral upbringing. Although they arrived in the United States 20 years ago, the family has still strong cultural ties with the home country. Every summer, the whole family spends vacations in Mexico because the mother wants her children to learn and experience the Mexican traditions. From the parents' perspective, life in the United States provides many economic opportunities. However, they do not feel the United States provides an optimum environment for their children's moral instruction. To compensate, the mother tries to instruct the children in her traditional beliefs, among which the unity of and help within the family is one of her key values.
>
> The daily routines in this child's house are carefully organized. The father, who has been working in the same restaurant for 20 years, leaves early in the morning. The older sisters have to get up early in order to clean up and make their beds before going to school. Mother stays at home doing her chores until the children arrive from school. Then she leaves for a part-time job. From that moment on, the children are not allowed to leave the house. The sisters' obligations include not only helping with chores and childcare, but also supervising the target child's schoolwork. The boy and his three sisters excel in school and all have the reputation of being excellent students.

This family, with its strong commitments to *educación* values, and the admirable adjustment they've made, is led by parents who left their place of birth, the forge of their value system, for a place they feel is less supportive of those values. They return to Mexico for social and moral reasons; they remain in the United States for economic purposes.

These parents are similar in some respects to the descendants of earlier European immigrants living in Boston studied and described more than two decades ago by Sennett and Cobb (1972). In this case, the parents separated from the older generation by leaving the ethnic neighborhood for a distant suburb, and then almost immediately expressing their ambivalence by returning every weekend because social relations are more comfortable, available, secure, and satisfying. In the suburbs, they complain that no one interacts in the street, one is ignored, there is constant distancing, avoidance of supportive but entangling reciprocities, and no shared social control of youth (Sennett and Cobb, 1972).

In time and place the families in Sennett and Cobb's samples could hardly seem more different from the Latino families we have studied. And yet there are compelling similarities in their delicate reliance on some of the old, traditional ways for adapting to life's challenges and to the particular challenges of rearing children.

By stressing the adaptive functions of *educación* and the more "traditional" values and beliefs that inform parents' thinking and behaviors, we diverge sharply from previous commentators who saw what an "agrarian cultural model" as the source of Latino children's school problems (see, for example, Heller, 1966; cited above). We hypothesize that Heller's assessment (and the many others found in an older literature) does not fit the complexity we have observed in these immigrants' adaptive processes and pathways.

The precariousness of life in urban settings—no less than the precariousness of life in impoverished rural or less urbanized areas—demands adaptive behaviors such as the ones we have seen and heard from parents in our sample. To adapt successfully, Latino immigrants to the United States continue to rely on family unity, respect and interdependence, parental authority, kinship networks, and related adaptive tools. Thus, the agrarian cultural model in Latin American countries or for newly-arrived immigrants to the United States "is . . . a continuous source of meaning and guidance . . ." (LeVine & White, 1986). As parents in our cohort try to shape household values and activities to adapt to the exigencies of life in this country and better serve their and their children's long-term interests, cultural models from the home country continue to contribute significant strategies.

But how robust and resilient will these strategies be as the children enter adolescence? This is a period know to be problematic even for children not facing the adaptive challenges faced by immigrant parents and first-generation children (Anderman & Maehr, 1994). The adaptive challenges parents and children face in their new country are different in fundamental ways that will test the adaptive tools used when the children were in kindergarten-through-third grade.

Examples of discontinuity between home and school have begun to emerge with respect to assumptions about the ordinary course of child and adolescent development: Some parents complained that the schools in the United States are not in alliance with them regarding moral development. Teachers did not act as second parents, enforcing a moral code. There are the vague and some explicit threats from the school regarding the use of physical punishment in the home. Some of our informants are angry; some are confused as to why they are not supported in their efforts to teach moral values and to enforce them. They complain that the schools and teachers are too lax, that they do not discipline, nor control the youngsters in their charge. The schools themselves are sometimes described as havens for misconduct and immoral behavior, as being too permissive about gangs and drugs and sex.

We have heard and seen these conflicts manifest themselves with the older siblings of the children we have studied. Particularly in junior and high school, parents believe students are exposed to the bad influences of their peers ("*las malas amistades*"). Parents fear these influences can then lead to getting involved with gangs and drugs, dropping out of school, and generally making nothing of oneself—that is, getting on the "bad road," *el mal camino*. Some families take steps to remove children from these bad influences and prevent their derailment. For example, when one family's older son began to be involved in gang activities, his schooling was interrupted by his being sent to Mexico (Case #114). Another mother kept an older child out of school altogether rather than risk further involvement with the bad influences there (Case #53). There is the mother who prevented her eighth grade daughter from attending a special advanced math class because it meant she had to go to a local high school which they regarded as a haven of bad peer influence. This mother (Case #26) described her eleven-year-old daughter's selection for a special advanced math class at a local high school campus. The girl, at sixth grade in middle school, was already taking eighth grade level classes. Although she was very proud of her daughter, the mother stressed the undesirability of letting her be in contact with older children in a bigger, more distant school. She felt that, through interaction with older students,

Maria would be exposed to attitudes and behaviors that were contrary to home teachings, and that Maria was too young to distinguish clearly between right and wrong. Maria was not allowed to take the advanced class.

Not only is school the place where peers may influence the child for the worse, but it is the place where topics are taught and discussed that some parents feel are not appropriate for their children's level of moral development and are thus damaging to them. By the age of nine or ten, children begin receiving specific information about the deleterious effects of drugs and the danger of contagious diseases such as AIDS. Although parents agree that knowing about "drugs and sex" is necessary in this society, they often think that children are introduced too quickly to these matters:

> . . . *a veces esto los desorienta y la juventud no agarra la orientación correcta y se van para el otro lado . . . Porque no tienen su mente capaz de distinguir lo bueno y lo malo. Su mente no está tan preparada, tan capacitada, porque ellos son niños.* (. . . sometimes [these teachings] disorient them and young people don't take the right orientation and they go astray . . . Because their mind is not prepared enough, because they are still children. (Case #54).

To this point we have sketched a mixed picture of continuities and discontinuities between values and beliefs of the families and those of public school personnel. On the one hand, parents share with school personnel a belief in the importance of education and certain instrumental means to promote it. But on the other, parents reveal contradictory feelings with regard to the school's impact on their children's lives—as parents define and envision their children's lives. They do not share the view that children grow more independent and autonomous of families. They are less willing to risk what they see as the moral development of their children even if an experience promises academic gains—because they see the latter as growing from the former. We have no final answer at this point on how these discontinuities in cultural models of the child learning and education work out in the lives of pre- and adolescent youngsters. That remains to be explored.

In the next section, we explore another set of family/school continuities and discontinuities. In this case, we focus on child activities that specifically affect school-related learning, in particular early literacy development, and on the actions of parents that influence those activities. As we will attempt to show, the cultural model of the parents leads them to emphasize some activities that have a direct, positive effect on learning. We will also describe some discontinuities in activities and actions that must be accommodated in school-initiated programs.

Continuities and Discontinuities of Academic Learning and Preparation Models

PARENTS' PRESCHOOL PREPARATION OF CHILDREN

In contrast to teaching their children about right and wrong, good manners, respect for elders, and the other qualities that make an individual *"bien educado,"* parents report less emphasis on arranging or encouraging academic activities that might prepare a pre-school child for school. When Ethnographic Subset families were asked to rank in order of importance a set of twelve statements regarding parent responsibilities before a child enters school, 30 percent chose teaching respect for parents as the most important task. In order of frequency of choice, the other statements chosen most important were: teaching the child the difference between right and wrong (22%), teaching good manners and behavior (17%), and engaging in dialogue with the child (13%). Preparing the child for school by teaching such things as the alphabet and numbers was ranked ninth of the 12 statements and reading to the child was rated tenth (Reese, Balzano et al., in press).

The parents in our studies do relatively little during the preschool years that prepares children directly for the academic tasks of school. In an earlier study of 30 kindergarten children, parents reported (and subsequent observations have borne out) that 60 percent of the children had fewer than 5 books in their homes; over 40 percent had *no* children's books. When interviewed shortly after the middle of the school year, 77 percent of the parents reported their child had not been taken to the library (outside of school hours) since the beginning of kindergarten. Another 8 percent

reported that their child had been to the library only once. Not surprisingly, at the beginning of kindergarten only 25 percent of the families reported reading to their children. In contrast, in a nationally representative sample of parents of young children (from a range of socio-economic and ethnic groups) 96 percent reported reading to their child at least occasionally (West, Hausken, & Chandler, 1991).

Literacy activities and materials are certainly not absent; but neither are they plentiful nor do parents necessarily exploit those that do exist for the benefit of children's literacy development. For example, households send and receive an average of three or four letters per month. Both parent reports and direct observation indicate letter writing and reading often in the presence of children, who express considerable interest in the activity. But while adult letter-writing is a fairly common and familiar feature of children's home experiences, parents do not use it as an opportunity for children's literacy-learning. In one instance a fieldworker observed a mother writing a letter to her family of origin in Mexico. A five-year-old kept intruding, wanting his mother to play with him. To divert the child, the mother suggested he write letter to the grandmother. The mother wrote out two lines in Spanish for the child to copy, but there was never any mention of what the lines said. A critical element in learning was absent— the meaning of the message. However, the child later told a friend that he was writing to his grandmother to send her his picture, so clearly he did have an idea of the function and purpose of what he had copied.

In addition, children frequently attempt to write on their own, often (although not exclusively) when a parent is writing a letter or a sibling is doing homework. Children also show a great deal of interest in learning how to write their names, the names of family members, and the names of visitors. In many homes, children have little chalkboards on which they write or play school. We have observed many instances of children copying environmental print, such as labels on a Play-doh can, food packages, or folders. Virtually every parent we have interviewed reports their children make regular attempt to write something.

But young children's attempts at writing are considered amusing and not very meaningful. In the parents' minds, children are not doing anything particularly important; they are simply pretending. Parents do take more seriously children's attempts to practice writing their names or writing recognizable letters—particularly if it is part of the homework sent by teachers—but anything else is considered "pure scribbling" ("*puros garabatos*"). Parents do not, for the most part, attribute any communicative intent or significance to children's early attempts at writing. They focus on its formalistic aspects (e.g., shape and legibility of letters and words) and judge its meaningfulness by adult standards of communicative adequacy—that is, whether it "says" ("*dice*") anything.

As is true of writing, parents and direct observation suggest that children make frequent attempts at reading text or else asking about the meaning of print. Children ask about written texts. Very often, this involves environmental print, such as package labels and signs, notes and letters from school, and advertisements. Children also attempt to read on their own. We have observed, for example, a child picking a letter up from the floor and "reading" it: "*Querida mamá . . .*" ("Dear mother . . . .") Sometimes "emergent reading" of longer texts—books or magazines—were reported or observed. One mother said, for example:

> About 2 or 3 times a week he gets a book and leafs through it. According to him, he's reading. . . . It's as if he were reading. He moves his hand as if he were reading.

But again, as was the case with writing, parents do not take children's early reading attempts very seriously. Another mother said her daughter pretended to read "although she doesn't know anything." The mother said her daughter would get the older sister's school books and "read" them: "She talks to herself and makes it up," the mother said, laughing.

The relative absence of early literacy opportunities becomes manifestly clear when children enter school. We individually tested 179 Spanish-speaking entering kindergarten children at the beginning of our longitudinal study and found they had relatively few literacy skills. When presented with a prompt of 10 most frequently used letters (the five vowels and five common consonants), the average number recognized was 1 lower case letter and 1.5 upper case letters. Two-thirds of the children could not name or recognize

a single letter. When asked to write any letters they knew, the average was 2.3, but again the distribution was highly skewed: The majority—62 percent—could write no letters at all. The majority also could write no words, either correctly or attempted. With few exceptions, those who could write (about 30%) wrote or attempted to write their name only. About 10 percent of the children produced something that could be considered invented writing or spelling. On the Concepts about Print test (Clay, 1985; translated into Spanish), which gauges children's understanding of how print functions in a book, the average score was 4 (out of 24).

In contrast, we know that when children from homes with more text-based literacy experiences and opportunities arrive in kindergarten they can recognize more letters, and they can write letters, words, even phrases. They have more invented spelling and scribble writing; their scores on the Concepts about Print test are higher; some are even readers in a more conventional sense, although this is less common (Adams, 1990; Chall, 1983; Mason, 1977). The absence of many home literacy experiences for first-generation Latino children means that many do not come to school with many critical understandings about the nature of print and how it functions. This is a discontinuity that is almost certain to place them at a disadvantage as they begin to learn conventional literacy skills and knowledge.

PARENTS' RESPONSES TO THEIR CHILDREN'S SCHOOL EXPERIENCES AND TASKS

Once the children begin school, however, and the explicit agenda becomes learning the academic skills and knowledge for which parents send their children to school, parents assist children with homework and give additional practice on concepts taught at school. For example, by the spring of the first grade year, 91 percent report that children are assisted with homework (53% daily and 38% sometimes/often) and 61% (46% daily and 15% sometimes/often) report they review completed schoolwork with the child. (These percentages include help and reading provided by siblings, relatives, and non-relatives as well as by parents.)

By the end of first grade, 85 percent of the parents report that their children are read to (25%

report that this takes place "daily" and 60% report "sometimes" or "often.") In discussing the reasons that reading to children is important, none of the parents in the Ethnographic Subset families stated that he or she read to the child in order to help the child learn to read. One third of the parents stated that reading served to foster interest in the child's reading. Other common answers included entertaining the child (24%) and teaching the child about morals (20%). One parent saw that reading together was part of building family unity: "*Los niñs cuyos padres no les han leído se crían o se desarrollan un poquito retirados de sus padres o de su papá.*" ("Children who are not read to by their parents grow up or develop a little separated from their parents or their father." (Case #26). Other parents reported reading Bible stories to their children so that they would know the difference between right and wrong (Case #92) or reading magazine selections to their children and discussing what could be learned from the behavior of the characters in the stories (Case #111).

When literacy learning does become a goal for children (once they enter school), parents generally adopt what is sometimes called a "bottom up" view. Parents see learning to read as consisting, in essence, of learning to associate written language (letters, syllables, words, or passages) with the corresponding oral language. Parents do not attach nearly as much importance to children's hearing books read or to their having ample opportunities to read, "pretend-read," or talk about simple books. Parents place great emphasis on the accurate decoding and recitation of written passages. To them, this is the essence of learning to read. This view has its origins, at least partly, in how Spanish reading is typically taught in Mexico and Central America, particularly at the time these parents were in school. Although recent trends in Spanish literacy instruction promote holistic and constructivist perspectives (Ferreiro & Teberosky, 1982; Osuna, 1989), the parents in our studies experienced a very "bottom-up" approach: First you learn the letters, then you learn the sounds of the letters, then how letters (usually a consonant and a vowel) combine to form syllables and words. And then you can read. In effect, then, the parents' "theory of reading instruction" has a cultural origin (Goldenberg, 1988; Goldenberg et al., 1992). The following field-

note excerpt is from a study of kindergarten children who had received simple, predictable little books to take home and share with their families:

> Fernando's mother calls him over, "*Ven a estudiar este libro.*" ("Come and study this book.") He stands beside her as she sits on the bed with the baby on her lap. She reads a page and has Fernando repeat it. She's reading upside down, so when she reads "*miles de melones*" as "*melones de melones,*" that is how he repeats it.
>
> On the next page, Fernando reads what he knows. When he hesitates on a word, Mother tells him and he repeats it. This form of word-by-word repetition continues for the rest of the book.
>
> They finish the book, and Mother says, "*Otra vez*" ("Again"). She has him start again and they continue word-by-word as earlier. On one page, Fernando looks at the picture of the melons in the tree and asks, "*Mamá, ¿por qué se metieron aquí los melones?*" ("Mama, why are the melons put here?") She responds, "*¿Sabe?*" ("Who knows?") and immediately says the next word to cue him to continue with the repetition. (Goldenberg et al., 1992, p. 517).

In contrast to contemporary theories of literacy, which assign a role to meaning even in the earliest stages of literacy development (Clay, 1991), the scripts parents use when attempting to help children become literate almost exclusively focus on symbol-sound correspondences.

At the same time, however, we should note that parents' understandings of the literacy learning process are not without foundation. Spanish orthography is phonetically highly regular with a clear syllabic structure. When asked how children learn to read, parents generally respond that children need to learn letters, sounds, and "how to join them" (*como juntarlas;* Goldenberg, 1988). Learning the relations between letters and sounds does help children learn to read, although they need many other print-related experiences as well (Adams, 1990). Thus despite differences in how educators and parents might understand literacy development, at least some aspects of the activities parents spontaneously engage in probably can play a productive role in helping children learn to read. We will return in the following section to the opportunities for productive collaboration this presents.

The Parents' Cultural Model of Academic Preparation

The actions reported by the parents reflect their cultural model of child education and schooling, and in particular their perception of early literacy development. There are two key aspects to this cultural model of academic (literacy) preparation. First, during the pre-school years there is very little, if any, emphasis on literacy-enhancing opportunities for children; second, once literacy-learning becomes an important item, the kinds of activities parents are likely to promote and engage in with children are heavily laden with didactic instruction, repetition, and learning of letter-symbol correspondences. It is not a deficit nor a deficiency on their part, we believe, but a natural consequence of the shaping of the parents' cultural model by their own ecological and cultural (ecocultural) experiences. By their own reports, most of the parents come from families in which education was not a key to economic and social survival nor seen as a means for social mobility. Indeed, this fact of life was in large measure a reason why their own parents did not support their children's formal education, as the comments of parents in our samples clearly suggest. Family economic activities and parents' work influences the cultural model of child learning and education, including the kinds of experiences parents believe are needed to prepare the child for family life, schooling, peer relations, and adulthood.

For the families in our samples, a number of factors, including those related to family economic base and parents' work, influenced early literacy activities and experiences of the children. In an ethnographic study of 10 families we conducted in the community, Reese, Goldenberg, et al., (in press) grouped children into higher, middle, and lower achievers based on their performance on a battery of early literacy measures and the end of the kindergarten year.

The families of the three highest achieving children all had at least one adult in the home who had gone beyond an elementary school level of education. Their homes also appeared to contain more materials that children could incorporate into their own literacy activities. The homes of these three highest achievers included the following sources of literacy experiences for children: a father who wrote reports on his maintenance jobs

at home; a mother who took telephone orders for cosmetics sales in the home; a home in which women from the church met to read and discuss Bible lessons, and where children were read to from the Bible and encouraged to recite prayers and verses.

In contrast, the four lowest achieving children all had parents who had not gone beyond elementary school, who reported no use of literacy on their jobs, and who therefore were not observed by their children engaging in work-related literacy activities. In fact, in only one of these families of lowest achievers was reading material of any sort, except that provided by the school, observed on more than three occasions over the course of the year.

Interviews and observations from our subsequent longitudinal Ethnographic Subset provided some case examples of the impact the family's subsistence base (parents' job or other economic activity) had on children's literacy experiences. The following case materials provide some examples of what was reported for fathers who use literacy on the job, and who had children who scored well on our end-of-kindergarten literacy test (approximately one standard deviation above the group mean):

(Case # 2): The father must read and write orders in English at his job. He helps the child with homework and reads to her. In addition, he speaks English to her and demands good school performance. He is also the driving force behind other family members' activities with the child. For example, when she was sick with chicken pox, he sent the mother to school to pick up additional homework, and he made sure that the older sister helped her complete it. He has purchased a set of encyclopedias and other educational material, such as a chalkboard, for his children's use. His efforts have been described by the fieldworker as "choreographing" the family's efforts to help the target child achieve in school.

(Case #33): This father writes orders in English on the job and at home helps his child with homework.

In another case, the child scored slightly above the mean on the literacy tests, and the following was reported:

(Case #111): The father uses literacy at work and has been asked by the mother to assist the children with their homework on the days that she has to work late. He is taking classes in mechanics and English and was observed to study at the kitchen table in the afternoon when the children had the opportunity to observe him.

In homes in which the fathers are not required to use literacy and the children scored relatively low (one standard deviation below the mean), we see a different pattern:

(Case #113): This father does not use literacy on his job as a loader at a refinery. He works long hours and is rarely available to help his daughter with her schoolwork, although he is the one who speaks some English. (The child was placed in an English-only classroom at school). Mother asks him to write out phonetically some English words so that she can help the child. He does, but she can't read them well enough to use them. *"Mi viejo casi no escribe bien."* ("My old man doesn't write very well.") Later, however, she asks him to write phonetically the letters of the English alphabet. This she posted on the wall to help her as she worked with the target child.

(Case #114): This father does not make use of literacy on his gardening job. He could not understand why the mother (they are separated) spent money on a set of encyclopedias. He thought they were too expensive. *"¿Por qué compras esto? Es bastante caro,"* he is reported to have said. ("Why did you buy that? It's very expensive.") When the boy expressed a desire to become a policeman, the father is reported to have said that "in order to be a policeman one had to be big and strong." The boy replied that he'd eat a lot of potatoes in order to be strong. In discussing his son' future occupation, the father made no mention of educational requirements of the job. The mother also reported that the father is earning good money ($12/hr) as a gardener, as compared to his brother who finished school and works in an office but only earns $6/hr. On one occasion, she suggested to the father that he should continue his studies, because as the children got older and brought home homework or questions that their parents don't know, they'd think *"Mi papí no sabe"* ("My father doesn't know."). The mother reported that Father only laughed and said that he was doing fine on the job as it was and didn't need to study.

The case materials also illustrated how religious values as well as the family's subsistence base affects early experiences. In one case, the father does not use literacy in the workplace, but the child had high scores on our kindergarten literacy test and multiple literacy experiences created by the family's religious practices:

In Case 56, there is a strong religious orientation. Tuesday evenings and Sundays are days devoted to the Church. While parents attend the service, the target child attends the Church school where he has the chance to he exposed to literacy activities such as memorizing Bible verses or listening to stories about Jesus' life. What has been learned at school is always reinforced by his parents' asking about what he has done in the church school.

These cases provide some hint of the complex connections among job-related literacy, beliefs, and actions at home that directly affect children's experiences. They document that the parents' views and actions regarding early literacy are influenced by their ecocultural backgrounds and circumstances. In the Ethnographic Subset as a whole, there is a significant relationship between a fieldworker ratings of the *general education/literacy environment* and kindergarten reading achievement. This rating included such factors as the amount of printed material in the home, the opportunities that exist for children to observe or experience literacy activities of different types, and the responsiveness of adults and siblings to children's interests and initiation of literacy events. The rating of general home literacy environment correlated ($r = .42$, $p < .01$ with end of kindergarten literacy measures and with a teacher rating of the child's progress in reading during kindergarten ($r = .61$, $p < .001$).

We again conclude a section by noting a pattern of continuities and discontinuities between family and school. Despite generally low educational levels among parents, they value schooling, are available to the children, and are interested in and capable of providing literacy-enhancing experiences, particularly when children are younger. Activities involving literacy are more frequent than many stereotypes of low income Spanish-speaking families suggest. Without discounting the discontinuities and the challenges they pose and may yet pose as the children mature, therefore, it is our brief that there are sufficient continuities to allow collaboration and cooperation among families and schools.

On the other hand, children's home literacy activities and opportunities are not optimal for their literacy development. Children were either seen or reported to have relatively few experiences of the sort most conducive to early literacy growth: hearing, reading, and pretending to read children's books; writing or trying to write words, messages, or even stories in the presence of more competent individuals who attempt to render meaningful these immature attempts at literate behavior. When young children attempt to use or create "texts," parents' interaction scripts do not treat these efforts as forms of "emerging literacy." Parents do not use such events as occasions for "talk" about texts, reading, and the like. Such opportunities for "pretend reading" or "pseudo-reading," preferably in the presence of a responsive, more competent individual, represent an important step in young children's early literacy acquisition (Mason & Allen, 1986; Teale, 1978; Teale & Sulzby, 1986).

While the families, by their own report and our observations, do not always engage in the most optimal activities or provide enough frequency of certain experiences that are provided, they are still highly motivated to help their children once they begin school. With very few exceptions, parents will respond to materials, activities, and suggestions from their child's school. Consider this: In each of the ten homes included in an earlier study (Goldenberg et al., 1992; Reese, Goldenberg, et al., in press), the school had a major impact on the children's home literacy experiences and was largely responsible for the consistency in types of tasks observed. Over 40 percent of all observed learning activities involved use of materials from school. In two families, the flyers, calendars, homework, and booklets sent home by the school account for virtually all of the printed material in the home. Homework and homework-like drill initiated by parents were part of the literacy experience of all target children, and accounted for the majority of the learning activities in certain households. Paper and pencil activities reflecting activities taking place at school were also common. Indeed, several parents reported that they had waited to teach their child certain skills until the child went to school.

In other words, despite discontinuities in family and school cultural models of academic social-ization and preparation, parents are highly responsive to school-based literacy learning for their children, and therefore opportunities for productive collaboration exist. This collaboration can produce greater satisfaction for parents and substantial achievement benefits for the children. Although there are model discontinuities, there are more continuities than often recognized by educators (and researchers). By carefully unpacking the cultural model of the parents, and avoiding stereotyping, we can work for the benefit of the children and their families.

Continuities, Discontinuities, and Family/School Collaboration Opportunities

We next turn to the implications of our studies for educational interventions. What do our analyses of cultural models of schooling and *educación* suggest about improving the educational attainment of Latino children, particularly first-generation Latino children who will become increasingly prominent in our schools? Our two-pronged argument, in brief, is this:

On the one hand, schools should build on commonalities between schools and families—for example, beliefs about the value of formal schooling school achievement, good behavior, and parent support and involvement—to forge productive relationships with families. On the other hand, schools should be aware of potential discontinuities—for example, attitudes toward discipline, beliefs about how children learn, the nature and quality of learning experiences in the pre-school years—and design programs and interventions that will foster common understandings and complementarity of efforts. We will provide an example of each: first, using commonalities to forge productive relationships; second, designing programs that promote complementary efforts in the face of potential discontinuities. Finally we will cite an instance where looking beneath the surface of an apparent cultural discontinuity (mismatch between teacher and child ethnicity leading to lowered achievement) reveals the power of action based on continuities—teacher attempts to involve parents in children's learning improves achievement.

COMMONALITIES AND COLLABORATION

In an analysis conducted when our 1989 cohort was in kindergarten, we were interested in examining whether teachers' parent involvement efforts were related to (1) parents' satisfaction with the child's school experience and (2) children's early literacy achievement. Because of parents' great interest in their children's schooling and achievement and their willingness and ability to make positive contributions—particularly when children were just beginning school—we predicted that teachers' attempts to involve parents in children's literacy development would lead both to greater parent satisfaction and to enhanced student achievement. We in fact found this to be the case (Goldenberg & Arzubiaga, 1994). For example, the more teachers attempted to involve parents in children's academic learning—by sending home activities or through messages or phone calls home—the more satisfied parents were with both the academic content of their child's classroom and with the extent to which they felt involved in their children's learning.

In addition, teacher attempts to involve parents also predicted children's literacy development at the end of kindergarten. The more teachers attempted to involve parents in children's learning, the higher were children's end-of-year literacy scores. There was *no* relationship between teacher parent-involvement efforts and beginning of year achievement, so we can rule out the explanation that teachers were more likely to reach out to parents of higher achieving students. Furthermore, there was a striking relationship between teachers' parent involvement attempts and *changes* in child achievement in relation to other kindergartners across the year ($r = .58$; $p < .01$). In other words, the more the teacher attempted to involve a child's parents in his/her academic learning in kindergarten, the more a child *gained* in relative achievement standing from the beginning of the year to the end. Students whose teachers took the initiative to involve parents in children's learning gained ground in comparison to peers; students whose teachers did not take the initiative to involve parents, slipped back in their relative achievement standing.

These results illustrate an important continuity between Latino parents and children's teachers: An interest in children's academic achievement and a belief in the importance of parents' playing a productive role in promoting it. When teachers take advantage of this continuity by facilitating parent involvement, the results are greater parent satisfaction and improved learning by children.

Although we have not replicated parent involvement effects on achievement as children enter elementary school, we have found the relationships hold between teachers' parent involvement efforts and parents' satisfaction. We asked parents in our longitudinal sample of over 100 students (when children were in grades 1 and 2) how satisfied they were with the instruction their child received. We also asked a series of questions asking parents to rate various aspects of the school program, such as homework quality and quantity, the homework's effect on learning and motivation, whether parents felt informed about their child's schooling, and the academic emphasis of the classroom. As Table 1 shows, parents are more satisfied when their child receives homework they feel is of high quality and that promotes learning and motivation. Parents are also more satisfied when they feel informed of their child's progress and when the academic content of the classroom is high. The amount of homework, *per se*, was unrelated to parents' satisfaction.

At least in the first two grades of elementary school, then, parents are more pleased with their child's schooling when teachers extend and reinforce children's academic learning by sending quality homework and informing parents of their child's progress. Note in particular the strongest correlations in the table—between parent satisfaction and their perception of the classroom academic emphasis. This is clearly in keeping with the values and beliefs we have heard parents express for the past ten years. They want their child's school experience to be academically challenging. Indeed, as we have reported before, on occasion parents will comment that U.S. schools are less demanding than those in their native countries (Goldenberg & Gallimore, 1991).

DISCONTINUITIES AND COMPLEMENTARITIES

In an earlier study (Goldenberg et al., 1992), we created a set of simple, photocopied story books in Spanish (Libros) for children to take home and read with friends and family members.

Table 1. Spearman Correlations Between Parents' Satisfaction with Child's Schooling and their Perceptions of Aspects of Child's School Experience

Parents' report or rating of:	Parents' Reported Satisfaction with Instruction; Grade:	
	1	2
Homework (HW) quality	.37***	.42***
HW effect on learning	.25**	.37***
HW effect on motivation/interest	.20*	.31**
HW during vacations	.22*	ns
Parent informed of child's academic progress	.30**	.19†
Classroom academic emphasis	.45***	.44***

Notes: *** $p \leq .001$.
** $p \leq .01$.
* $p < .05$.
† $p = .06$.
n's = approximately 100.

Our hypothesis was that repeated opportunities to read or "pretend-read" these simple but interesting and meaningful little books would produce literacy-related talk between parents and children at home and help prepare children for more conventional literacy instruction by helping familiarize them with letters, words, and text in a meaningful context. Teachers showed parents a videotape at the beginning of the year and suggested to parents that they use the Libros just as they would any other children's books. Parents were told that repetitive reading accompanied by conversation with the child would be especially helpful. In comparison classrooms, teachers used the district readiness program, supplemented by project-supplied phonics worksheets. As part of our data-gathering, field workers went into the homes to observe how and how often the different types of materials (Libros and phonics worksheets) were used. We also tested all children on literacy knowledge at the end of kindergarten.

As expected, we found that children in kindergarten classrooms using the Libros (and accompanying materials) were more advanced in their literacy development than were children in comparison classrooms using the regular district readiness program (Goldenberg, 1994).

We were surprised, however, by a second finding regarding how the materials were used at home and how their use related to literacy development. Although children in the Libros classrooms had higher levels of early reading development than children in the "readiness" classrooms, observed use of the books at home was *unrelated* to children's literacy development. In contrast, use of the phonics worksheets (among the control students) was strongly related to individual children's literacy development (Goldenberg et al., 1992). In other words, use of Libros at home seemed to make no contribution to literacy achievement, but the more children used the phonics worksheets, the higher their end-of-kindergarten achievement. What explains these findings? We think it has to do with the parents' theories—perhaps culturally-based—of literacy development.

As we've previously discussed, this parent population has essentially a "bottom-up" view of how literacy learning takes place, that is, children learn letters, sounds, and how they form syllables and words. Families in our study introduced whatever materials the teacher sent in ways that made sense to them. Worksheets were used in a way that was consistent with their design and explicit purpose—to help children correctly and reliably relate symbols and sounds. The Libros were also used in a way that made sense to the parents (by practicing accurately associating written language with corresponding oral sounds); but it was a way that was incompatible with the nature of the materials themselves. The Libros made poor worksheets, since the sort of rote drill and repetition that we observed (see earlier example of Fernando reading with his mother) is unlikely to contribute to literacy development. However, drill and repetition at the level of letters, sounds, and blending—the level of the worksheets—is much more likely to contribute to literacy development. In short, the congruence between the worksheets and parents' beliefs led to their effective use in the home, and the more children used the worksheets at home, the higher their literacy attainment at the end of the school year.

Latino parents—indeed all parents—have their own views and theories ("cultural models") about child development and learning; these models will influence how parents implement activities or use materials sent home from school. The parents we have studied and worked with see learning to read as largely a matter of learning and mastering the orthographic code. Therefore, when attempting to help their children become literate, they are likely to interact with them in a way that emphasizes sound-symbol relations and synthetic phonics.

What, then, are the implications for intervention, given current popular models of literacy development (e.g., McLane & McNamee, 1990) suggesting that meaning-driven and communicatively-based activities with print are most supportive of learning to read? There are two possibilities. One is that intensive parent training needs to be undertaken in order for parents to understand fully and implement appropriately materials and activities sent home from school. The other is that schools should send home materials and activities that are a) beneficial for children's academic development but that are b) consistent with parents' cultural models of learning and development. The phonics worksheets, for example, satisfied both criteria. We do not know which of the two strategies will prove most efficient and cost-effective, but we would suggest this is a crucial issue for future exploration.

SURFACE AND REALITY IN CULTURAL CONTINUITIES AND DISCONTINUITIES

The third example we cite illustrates the paradoxical themes woven into our discussion—continuity and discontinuity between Latino children's homes and the schools they attend. Depending upon how we look, cultural differences between the families and the school might create *discontinuities* that must be bridged in order to help children succeed; alternatively, similarities between the families and the school suggest *continuities* that might provide productive avenues for mutual help. Distinguishing between the two possibilities is, in practice, more problematic than many might assume.

In our study on the effects of kindergarten teachers' parent involvement efforts on parent satisfaction and children's achievement (Goldenberg & Arzubiaga, 1994), half the teachers were Latinas who spoke Spanish fluently, and the other half were Anglos with varying degrees of skill in Spanish. When we compared the achievement change of children taught by Latinas and Anglos, there was a significant difference. Those taught by the Latina teachers improved from fall to spring, whereas the Anglo teachers' children declined. At first glance this seems consistent with a discontinuity interpretation—that is, the bridging of discontinuities between child and school cultures (in the form of Latina, fluent-Spanish teachers) improved children's school. When the discontinuity was not bridged, children made less progress. (These results, incidentally, are inconsistent with previous findings that teacher ethnicity is unrelated to Latino children's achievement. Vierra, 1984, reported that Chicano third- and fourth-graders children did as well with Anglo as with Latino teachers.)

However, further analyses suggested a more complex interpretation was required. It turned out that the Latina teachers were rated much higher than the Anglo teachers in their efforts to involve parents in their children's academic learning. A multiple regression analysis indicated that teacher attempts at parent involvement had very strong effects on achievement ($r = .67$; $p = .01$), and teacher ethnicity/language had no effect. This suggests that the critical variable affecting student progress was teachers' parent-involvement efforts, not teacher ethnicity and language *per se*. No doubt teacher ethnicity and language contributed to communication between teachers and parents, but it was not the fact of these shared qualities. It was what teachers *did* that mattered.

This finding provides a striking example of a central point of this chapter, particularly with respect to culturally diverse populations and home/school collaborations to improve student success: Culture does matter, and we must seek to accommodate cultural differences when they matter. But we can be surprised if we are not careful. The Latina teachers may have had a cultural edge, but it apparently was because they knew the parents like homework, are responsive to homework assignments, like being involved and informed about their child's school progress, and prefer a classroom emphasis on academics. None of these practices qualifies as an example of cultural accommodation to a major discontinuity. Quite the opposite: Teachers were simply engaged in what most people might assume are normal and important functions—for any group of young students. To be sure, there may be subtle factors at work that we did not assess, for example better or more comfortable communication between parents and teacher. But such qualifications included, there is a powerful generalization implied by these data. The Latina teachers' major advantage might have been that they knew there was a continuity between the families and the school regarding such matters as homework and having a strong academic orientation.

That the advantage of the Latina teachers was knowing there was a continuity between family and school is borne out by the comments one of the teachers, Ms. Delgado, made prior to the study. While recognizing that many children from certain backgrounds probably have less access to academic learning opportunities than others—a discontinuity of academic preparation discussed previously—Ms. Delgado also maintained a strong belief (supported by educational research), that these children, like other children, can be taught what they need to know in order to be successful in school—an instance of a continuity between children and schools:

> Teachers think these kids are deprived so we need to let them play all day here. That really makes me mad because I came from [immigrant Latino] background like this. . . . These kids can learn but they have to be taught. If more teach-

ers realized this and did what they were supposed to do, more of these kids would go on to college (Goldenberg, 1994, p. 185).

Conclusion

LATINO IMMIGRANTS IN U.S. SCHOOLS: MODELS, SCHEMES, AND ACTIONS

Over the past quarter-century, psychodynamic approaches to motivation and behavior have given way to cognitive perspectives (e.g., Anderman & Maehr, 1994; Bandura, 1986; Deci, 1975; Stipek, 1993; Weiner, 1980). "The study of needs and drives," Anderman and Maehr (1994) note, "became . . . the study of perceptions, thoughts, and beliefs (p. 290)." We think it particularly apt, then, to examine the thoughts and beliefs (including values) of Latino immigrant parents and other U.S. culture groups who experience difficulties with schooling. In the most general terms, a study of "perceptions, thoughts, and beliefs" of Latino and other culture groups helps understand the bases for their actions.

Introducing concepts of culture and cultural schema into motivation theory is a recognition that motivation is not solely a property of the individual. The beliefs and values that motivate action do not arise in a cultural and historical vacuum. Why the families in our studies behave as they do is traceable, in part, to cultural models they brought with them from their homelands. These models continue to serve as important adaptive resources in a new place. But they also undergo change in response to changed circumstances, as we saw from parents who express a commitment to helping their children achieve higher levels of formal schooling than their parents allowed them to achieve. D'Andrade (1992) puts it this way: " . . . to understand people one needs to understand what leads them to act as they do, and to understand what leads them to act as they do one needs to know their goals, and to understand their goals one must understand their overall interpretive system. . . ., which is provided by their culture (D'Andrade, 1992, p. 31)."

Our own motivation for studying the values, beliefs, and actions of the Latino parents had a more pragmatic aim, although we think the results are relevant to theory as well. We sought to discover whether beliefs and values underpinning family actions provide a foundation for productive school-home collaborations that could help students succeed in school. We believe such a foundation has been uncovered, at least in the elementary school years (although it might exist in high schools as well; Lucas, Henze, & Donato, 1990). In the case the of immigrant Latino families, this foundation consists of parents' deep and abiding belief in the value of formal schooling for children's social and economic mobility, parents' willingness to take an active role in their child's school achievement, and parents' responsiveness when teachers suggest they do so.

Parents' conception of *educación*, which emphasizes good and respectful behavior, and staying on the right path—being "well-educated" (*bien educado*) as well as well-schooled—also provides part of this foundation, although it is of a different order. Teachers with whom we have worked often comment (sometimes disparagingly) that Latino parents appear more interested in their children's comportment than their cognitive achievement. Our interviews reveal that this might well be true, but one of the reasons is that parents see good and proper behavior as the basis for academic and cognitive advance. Thus parents' emphasis on comportment and the schools' (at least overt) emphasis on academic learning complement, rather than conflict with, each other.

In contrast, parents' de-emphasis of pre-school academic learning opportunities in the home (both because literacy is not a fundamental activity for most families' economic activities and because parents emphasize morals and comportment in their socialization practices) translates into a relative scarcity of text-based literacy experiences for these children before they begin school. This leads to a fundamental discontinuity between schools and immigrant Latino homes, since when children begin school, even kindergarten, one of the main items on the agenda is to begin promoting literacy skills. Although literacy is not absent—families write and receive letters; ads, printed matter, and environmental print are often present; parents and older siblings do read, particularly if they are in school—the relatively little emphasis on literacy, or "emergent literacy," during the preschool years put Latino youngsters at risk for underachievement. However, as soon as children begin school, and learning literacy becomes an important goal, we see parents playing a more active role in helping children academically, particularly if parents receive encouragement and assistance from children's teachers.

The Latino parents' cultural models or schemas related to schooling and achievement thus present a mixed picture. On the one hand, values and practices exist that are at least complementary and at best fully compatible (even congruent) with school values. On the other hand, there are clear differences. In much of the current literature, there is a tendency for observers to feature the differences as the principal issue and to take one of three positions: Some argue success in U.S. schools will come only as immigrant families leave behind their "different" values that were adaptive in more traditional, non-technological contexts and adopt those of the academic occupational model. Others argue that for these children to succeed, schools must accommodate to differences in values, learning styles, and children's home experiences. Yet others contend that differences in U.S. opportunity structures mean that Latinos and other disenfranchised groups will inevitably devalue formal schooling as an avenue for social and economic mobility.

Our findings suggest a different interpretation. To the extent that the cultural schema we have described have motivational force, that is, they function as goals and instigate action (D'Andrade, 1992), there are *commonalities* that the Latino families and the schools share, which provide avenues for home-school collaboration. We cannot generalize to other groups, but we hypothesize that significant commonalities also exist between the schools and those for whom the schools have not worked well.

Our examples and analyses raise an intriguing possibility: Is accommodating to culturally different children mainly a matter of making fundamental changes in teaching, staffing, or curriculum? Or can we also accommodate to culturally different children by recognizing similarities and consistencies, as well as differences and discontinuities, across cultures? We suggest that cultural accommodation cuts both ways—making changes if needed but recognizing similarities when they exist. Ignoring one over the other is not in the best interest of children or families. As we confront the challenges posed by this most recent wave of immigrants to the United States, educators must be aware of discontinuities that must be skillfully and sensitively handled. But they must be equally sensitive to what the families, children, teachers, and administrators share.

Acknowledgment

The research reported was supported by a Spencer Fellowship from the National Academy of Education and grants from the Spencer Foundation, the National Institute of Child Health and Human Development, the Linguistic Minority Research Program of the University of California, and the Center for Cultural Diversity and Second Language, University of California, Santa Cruz. Continuing support has been provided at UCLA by the Sociohebavioral Research Group (Mental Retardation Research Center), the Division of Social Psychiatry, Department of Psychiatry and Biobehavioral Sciences, and the Urban Education Studies Center, Graduate School of Education, UCLA. Leslie Reese, Silvia Balzano, Carol Benson, James Loucky, and Angela Arzubiaga made major contributions to projects on which this chapter is based. We are deeply grateful to the parents, children, teachers, and administrators of the school districts where we conducted this research. Thanks also to colleagues who generously read and commented on earlier versions of this chapter. Jaime Calderón, Courtney Cazden, Concha Delgado-Gaitan, Jill Fitzgerald, Ronald Henderson, Hugh Mehan, and Deborah Stipek.

Notes

1. There is considerable inconsistency in the literature regarding the use of 1st and 2nd generation when referring to U.S.-born children of immigrant parents. McCarthy & Valdez, 1986, for example, use 1st-generation to refer to *U.S.-born* children of immigrant parents. Others use 1st generation to refer to the immigrants themselves, with their children then becoming 2nd generation. We use 1st-generation to refer either to *U.S.-born children of immigrant parents or children born in Mexico or Central America but who arrived in the U.S. during infancy or preschool.*

2. This combination of methods explains why our data reporting, below, might seem inconsistent. When we have quantitative data in the form of rat-ings, numbers, or percents, we report these. Similarly, when we have coded qualitative data and counted frequencies and percentages to make a point, these too are reported. However, our data sometimes come from comments or observations made by parents, which we have not coded and counted since exact frequencies were not relevant for making a point. When precise counts are not important in addressing a particular issue, for example, if parents cited numerous reasons for a certain belief, we simply report that "many" parents had reason A or "some" parents reported reason B.

3. Numbers following quotations refer to case numbers and locator information for the various samples used in this review.

4. Portions of this section are adapted from Reese, Balzano, Gallimore, & Goldenberg (in press). We gratefully acknowledge the substantial contributions of Leslie Reese and Silvia Balzano to the materials and ideas in this section.

References

Adams, M. (1990). *Beginning to read: Thinking and learning about print. Cambridge,* MA: MIT Press.

Anderman, E., & Maehr, M. (1994). Motivation and schooling in the middle grades. *Review of Educational Research, 64,* 287–309.

Azmitia, M., Cooper, C.R., Garcia, E.E., Ittel, A., Johanson, B., Lopez, E., Martinenz-Chavez, R., & Rivera, L. (1994). *Links between home and school among low-income Mexican-American and European-American families* (Educational Practice Report No. 9). Santa Cruz, CA: National Center for Research on Cultural Diversity and Second Language Learning.

Bandura, A. (1986). *Social foundations of thought and action: A social cognitive theory.* Englewood Cliffs, NJ: Prentice-Hall.

California State Department of Education (1986). *Beyond language: Social and cultural factors in schooling language minority students.* Los Angeles: Evaluation, Dissemination and Assessment Center, California State University, Los Angeles.

Carnegie Foundation for the Advancement of Teaching. (1990). *The condition of teaching: A state-by-state analysis, 1990.* Princeton, NJ: Carnegie Foundation for the Advancement of Teaching.

Casas, J., & Furlong, M. (1986). In search of an understanding and a responsible resolution to the Mexican-American educational dropout problem. *California Public Schools Forum, I,* 45–63.

Chall, J.S. (1983). *Stages of reading development.* New York: McGraw-Hill.

Chibnik, M. (1981). The evolution of cultural rules. *Journal of Anthroplogical Research, 37,* 3, 256–268.

Clay, M. (1985). *The early detection of reading difficulties* (Third edition). Portsmouth, NA: Heinemann.

Clay, M. (1991). *Becoming literate: The construction of inner control.* Portsmouth, NH: Heinemann.

Cornelius, Wayne A. (1989–1990). Mexican Immigrants in California Today. *ISSR Working Papers in the Social Sciences, Vol. 5.* No. 10. Los Angeles: Institute for Social Science Research, UCLA.

D'Andrade, R.G. (1992). Schemas and motivation. In D'Andrade, R.G. & Strauss, C. (Eds.), *Cultural models and human motives* (pp. 23–44). Cambridge: Cambridge University Press.

D'Andrade, R.G., & Strauss, C. (1992). *Cultural models and human motives.* Cambridge: Cambridge University Press.

Deci, E. (1975). *Intrinsic motivation.* New York: Plenum.

Delgado-Gaitan, C., (1993). Parenting in two generations of Mexican American families. *International Journal of Behavior Development, 16,* 409–427.

Delgado-Gaitan, C. & Trueba, H. (1991). *Crossing cultural borders.* New York: Falmer.

Duran, B. & Weffer, R. (1992). Immigrants' aspirations, high school process, and academic outcomes. *American Educational Research Journal, 24,* 163–181.

Edgerton, R.B. (1992). *Sick societies: Challenging the myth of of primitive harmony.* New York: Free Press.

Education Week (1993). Education and the foreign-born. Oct. 6, p. 3.

Ferreiro, E., & Teberosky, A. (1982). *Literacy before schooling.* Portsmouth, NH: Heinemann.

Foglia, E. (1988). One California minority group is especially poverty-stricken. *Los Angeles Times,* pt. II, p. 4

Gallimore, R., & Goldenberg, C. (1993). Activity settings of early literacy: Home and school factors in children's emergent literacy. In E. Forman, N. Minick, & C.A. Stone (Eds.), *Contexts for learning: Sociocultural dynamics in children's development* (pp. 315–335). Oxford: Oxford University Press.

Gallimore, R., Goldenberg, C., & Weisner, T. (1993). The social construction and subjective reality of activity settings: Implications for community psychology. *American Journal of Community Psychology, 21*(44), 537–559.

Goldenberg, C. (1987). Low-income Latino parents' contributions to their first-grade children's word-recognition skills. *Anthropology and Education Quarterly, 18,* 149–179.

Goldenberg, C. (1988). Methods, early literacy, and home-school compatibilities: A response to Sledge et al., *Anthropology and Education Quarterly, 19,* 425–432.

Goldenberg, C. (1989). Parents' effects on academic grouping for reading: Three case studies. *American Educational Research Journal, 26,* 329–352.

Goldenberg, C. (1994). Promoting early literacy achievement among Spanish-speaking children: Lessons from two studies. In E. Heibert (Ed.), Getting ready from the start: Effective early literacy interventions (pp. 171–199). Boston: Allyn and Bacon.

Goldenberg, C.N., & Gallimore, R. (1991). Local knowledge, research knowledge, and educational change: A case study of early Spanish reading improvement. *Educational Researcher, 20*(8), 2–14.

Goldenberg, C., & Arzubiaga, A. (1994, April). The effects of teachers' attempts to involve Latino parents in children's early reading development. Paper presented at the annual meeting of the American Educational Research Association, New Orleans, LA.

Goldenberg, C., Reese, L, & Gallimore, R. (1992). Effects of school literacy materials on Latino children's home experiences and early reading achievement. *American Journal of Education, 100,* 497–536.

Hanson, S., & Ginsburg, A. (1988). Gaining ground: Values and high school success. *American Educational Research Journal, 25,* 334–365.

Heller, C. (1966). *Mexican-American youth: Forgotten youth at the crossroads,* NY: Random House.

Hess, R.D., & Holloway, S. (1984). Family and school as educational institutions. In R.D. Parke (Ed.), *Review of child development research, 7: The family* (pp. 179–222). Chicago: University of Chicago Press.

Hispanic Policy Development Project (1990). *The Hispanic almanac.* New York: Author.

Jacob, E., & Jordan, C. (Eds.), (1987). Explaining the school performance of minority students (Theme issue), *Anthropology and Education Quarterly, 18* (4).

Laosa, L. (1982) School, occupation, culture and family: The impact of parental schooling on the parent-child relationship. *Journal of Educational Psychology, Vol. 74,* No. 6, 791–827.

LeVine, R. (1990). Infant environments in psychoanalysis: a cross-cultural view. In J.W. Stigler, R.S. Shweder, & G. Herdt (Eds.) Cultural psychology: Essays on comparative human development. Cambridge: Cambridge University Press, pps. 454–474.

LeVine, R., & White, M. (1986). *Human conditions: The cultural basis of educational development.* New York: Routledge & Kegan Paul.

Lucas, T., Henze, R., & Donato, R. (1990). Promoting the success of Latino language-minority students: An exploratory study of six high schools. *Harvard Educational Review, 60,* 315–340.

Macías, R. (1994). 1994 CA language census reflects continued LEP increase. *LMRI News, 4* (1), 2–3 (Available from University of California Linguistic Minority Research Institute, Building 402, Rm. 223, Santa Barbara, CA 93106).

Mason, J., & Allen, J. (1986). A review of emergent literacy with implications for research and practice in reading. *Review of Research in Education, 13,* 3–48.

Mason, J. (1977). *Reading readiness: A definition and skills hierarchy from preschoolers' developing conceptions of print* (T.R. No. 59). University of Illinois at Urbana-Champaign: Center of the Study of Reading.

McCarthy, K.F., & Valdez, R.B. (1986). *Current and future effects of Mexican immigration in California* (R-3365-CR). Santa Monica, CA: Rand.

McLane, J., & McNamee, G. *Early literacy.* Cambridge, MA: Harvard University Press, 1990.

Ogbu, J. (1978). *Minority education and caste.* New York: Academic Press.

Ogbu, J. & Matuti-Bianchi, M. (1986). Understanding sociocultural factors: Knowledge identity, and school adjustment. In *Beyond language: Social and cultural factors in schooling language minority students* (pp. 73–142). Los Angeles: Evaluation, Dissemination and Assessment Center, California State University.

Osuna, A. (1989). El lenguaje integral y la lectoescritura en la escuela primaria latinoamericana. [Whole language and literacy in Latin American schools.] *Lectura y Vida, 10*(4), 5–11.

Reese, L., Balzano, S., Gallimore, R., & Goldenberg, C.N. (in press). The concept of Educación: Latino family values and American schooling. *International Journal of Educational Research.*

Reese, L., Goldenberg, C.N., Loucky. J., & Gallimore, R. (in press). Ecocultural context, cultural activity, and emergent literacy of Spanish-speaking children. In S.W. Rothstein (ed.), *Class, culture and race in American schools: A Handbook.* Westport, CT: Greenwood Press.

Rumbaut, R. (1990). *Immigrant students in California public schools: A summary of current knowledge* (Report No. 11). Baltimore, MD: Center for Research on Effective Schooling for Disadvantaged Students, The Johns Hopkins University.

Sennett, R., & Cobb, J. (1972). *The hidden injuries of class.* New York: Norton.

Stipek, D. (1993). *Motivation to learn: From theory to practice* (2nd edition). Needham Heights, MA: Allyn & Bacon.

Strauss, C. (1992). What makes Tony run? Schemas a motives reconsidered. In R.G. D'Andrade & C. Strauss, (Eds.), *Cultural models and human motives.* Cambridge: Cambridge University Press, pps. 197–224.

Teale, W., & Sulzby, E. (Eds.). (1986). *Emergent literacy: Writing and reading.* Norwood, NJ: Ablex.

Teale, W.H. (1986). Home backgrouud and young children's literacy development. In W.H. Teale & E. Sulzby (Eds.), *Emergent literacy: Writing and reading* (pp. 173–206). Norwood, NJ: Ablex.

Teale, W. (1978). Positive environments for learning to read: What studies of early readers tell us. *Language Arts, 55,* 922–932.

Tharp, R., & Gallimore, R. (1988). *Rousing minds to life: Teaching, learning, and schooling in social context.* Cambridge: Cambridge University Press.

U. S. Bureau of the Census. (n.d.). *The foreign born population in the United States: 1990.* (CPHL-98). Washington, DC.

U. S. Bureau of a the Census (1992). *Population projections of the United States, by age, sex, race, and Hispanic origin: 1992 to 2050.* (Current population reports, P25–1092). Washington, DC.

Valencia, R., Ed. (1991). *Chicano school failure and success: Research and policy agendas for the 1990s.* New York: Falmer Press.

Vierra, A. (1984). The relationship between Chicano children's achievement and their teachers' ethnicity. *Hispanic Journal of Behavioral Science, 6*, 285–290.

Weiner, B. (1980). *Human motivation.* New York: Holt, Rinehart and Winston.

Weisner, T., & Garnier, H. (1992). Stability of family structure and student learning in elementary school. *American Journal of Educational Research, 29*, 605–632.

West, J., Hausken E., & Chandler, K. (1991). *Home Activities of 3- to 8- Year Olds: Findings from the 1991 National Household Education Survey.* Washington, D.C.: National Center for Education Statistics.

White, T. (1978). *In search of history.* NY: Harper & Row.

CLASS 12

Hispanic/Latino Americans (Part II)

CHAPTER 17
The Cultural Patterning of Achievement Motivation: A Comparison of Mexican, Mexican Immigrant, Mexican American, and Non-Latino White American Students

Marcelo Suárez-Orozco and Carola E. Suárez-Orozco

Marcelo and Carola Suárez-Orozco's chapter examines the research on Latino populations in the U.S.A. It seeks to explain the various psychological behaviors of this group as it relates to how they immigrated to this nation and/or how long they have been in this country. Their work also reveals some insights as to why these students perform the way they do academically.

CHAPTER 17

The Cultural Patterning of Achievement Motivation: A Comparison of Mexican, Mexican Immigrant, Mexican American, and Non-Latino White American Students

Marcelo M. Suárez-Orozco and Carola E. Suárez-Orozco

A psychological anthropologist whose area of expertise includes immigration in the areas of cultural psychology and psychological anthropology with special reference to populations coming from Latin America, Marcelo Suarez-Orozco is the co-director of Harvard's Longitudinal Immigrant Student Adaptation Project. Some of his publications include *Children of Immigration, The New Immigration,* and *Cultures Under Siege: Collective Violence and Trauma.* He received his doctorate from the University of California, Berkeley.

A Senior Research Associate and Lecturer in education in the area of human development and psychology, Carola E. Suarez-Orozco is the co-director of Harvard Immigration Projects. She has published in the areas of cultural psychology, academic engagement, immigrant children, and identity formation. Her focus in recent years has been on the intersection of cultural and psychological factors in the adaptation of immigrant and ethnic minority children. She received her doctoral degree from the University of California, Berkeley.

This chapter examines some important themes in the cultural psychology of Mexican, Mexican immigrant, Mexican American, and non-Latino white American students. We explore central aspects of the immigrant experience among first- and second-generation individuals and families. We refer to some very interesting findings by our colleagues who work with Mexican immigrants, Mexican Americans (the largest Latino group in the United States), as well as to our research findings among Mexican students in Mexico, Mexican immigrant students, Mexican American students, and a control sample of non-Latino whites. We consider how certain enduring psychocultural features in the Latino experience may be of importance to understand-ing—and ameliorating—the educational condition of these subgroups:

It is impossible to discuss the Latino condition as if it were a monolithic phenomenon. Mexican Americans, Cuban Americans, mainland Puerto Ricans, and immigrants from Central and South America are distinct populations although they share a number of unifying characteristics. These include various degrees of familiarity with the Spanish language and such cultural traits as the importance of the extended family ("familism"), an emphasis on spiritual and interpersonal relationships, respect for authority, and an emphasis on the "here and now" rather than the future-time orientation valued by the dominant American culture.

From *California's Immigrant Children: Theory, Research, and Implications for Educational Policy.* Center for US Mexican Studies: University of California. Used with permission.

It is important to emphasize that Latinos in the United States are a demographically and socioculturally diverse population. Latinos come from many different countries and different socioeconomic, educational, and professional backgrounds. Many have been in the United States for several generations. In the case of immigrants, we find special problems relating to whether they entered the United States as "documented" or "undocumented" migrants (see Leo Chávez 1992), whether they came voluntarily or involuntarily (many recent arrivals from Central America migrated to escape political persecution; see M. Suárez-Orozco 1989), whether they are seasonal migrants who plan to return home or migrants with plans to stay in the United States more or less permanently, and whether they came to the United States as a family unit or as individuals. All of these factors greatly impact opportunities and the migration experience. If we were to search for a common denominator in the experiences of Latino immigrants, it is that most are coming (or came) from relatively impoverished "developing" countries, and typically from the lower socioeconomic strata, into a more affluent, industrialized society.

The Immigrant Paradox: Instrumental Gains and Affective Losses

It is well recognized that immigrants often come as pioneers with a dream of making a better life for themselves and their children. Their objectives are relatively clear: to get a job, earn money, learn a new language, educate their children, and improve their lot in life. The obvious difficulties that most immigrants face include language inadequacies, a general unfamiliarity with the customs and expectations of the new country (what anthropologists refer to as "cultural discontinuities"), limited economic opportunities, poor housing, discrimination, and what psychologists term the "stresses of acculturation" (Rogler, Cortés, and Malgady 1991: 585–97).

Although from the perspective of the host country the immigrants' living circumstances may seem "poor" and "disadvantaged," in many cases immigrants see their lot as having improved from what it was in their country of origin (M. Suárez-Orozco 1989). As a result, immigrants may fail to

internalize the negative attitudes that the host country holds toward them, maintaining their country of origin as a point of reference. Hence immigrants commonly view and experience their current situation not in term of the ideals and expectations of the majority society but rather in terms of the ideals of the "old culture."

This part of an interesting immigrant orientation that we have termed "the immigrant's dual frame of reference" (M. Suárez-Orozco and C. Suárez-Orozco 1993). That is, immigrants are constantly comparing and contrasting their current lot in the host society against their previous experiences and expectations in their respective country of origin. During the earliest phases of immigration, the new arrivals may come to idealize the host country as a land of unlimited opportunities. Many new arrivals may at the same time concentrate on the negative aspects of life in the land left behind. After the initial excitement and idealization, there may be a period of letdown accompanied by a realization of the hardships that immigrants face in the host society.

It is important to note that first-generation immigrants may increase not only their own standard of living but also (and perhaps more importantly) the standard of living of family members left behind. Latino immigrants almost universally assist their relatives in the home country with regular and substantial remittances from the United States (see Gamio 1971).

We would also like to explore the psychological toll that individuals pay when they migrate to another country and how this affects immigrant children in schools. Although immigration may bring about an improvement in economic conditions, migration also ruptures the "immigrant's supportive interpersonal bonds" (Rogler, Malgady, and Rodríguez 1989: 25), well recognized to be crucial for psychological well-being. Psychologically, migration may represent a cumulative trauma; it often results in multiple losses whose effects are not always immediately apparent (Grinberg and Grinberg 1989).

Rogler, Cortés, and Malgady summarized their recent overview of the literature on acculturation and mental health status among Hispanics in the United States as follows:

> Migration is likely to disrupt attachments to supportive networks in the society of origin and to impose on the migrant the difficult task of incor-

poration into the primary groups of the host society. The migrant is also faced with problems of economic survival and social mobility in an unfamiliar socioeconomic system. These uprooting experiences are accompanied by problems of acculturation into a new cultural system, of acquiring the language, the behavioral norms and values characteristic of the host society (1991: 585).

In those individuals who possess sufficient psychological resources to withstand the trauma and who have adequate available social support, the migration experience can result in personal enrichment and psychological growth. For many, however, the losses result in an exacerbation of psychological traits and problems. Rogler, Cortés, and Malgady report that those immigrants "with fewest psychological resources for coping with the new environment reported the worst stress outcomes" (1991: 593).

Grinberg and Grinberg (1989) outline three typical patterns of psychological problems that may occur after migration. These include problems with "persecutory anxiety" (whereby the host environment is experienced as hostile and persecutory in nature), "depressive anxiety" (when the individual is preoccupied with his or her losses due to migration), and "disorienting anxiety" (which results from disorientation about the "old" and the "new" ways of being, time, and space).

Persecutory anxieties may be manifested in the form of irrational fears of aspects of life in the host society. During the first days of the 1991 Persian Gulf War, a rumor spread rapidly among Mexican migrants in Southern California that all "undocumented" persons captured by the Border Patrol would be sent to fight in the front lines! The (undocumented) immigrants' well-grounded fear of persecution by the Border Patrol metamorphosed into an irrational fear of being sent to war. Immigrants may also feel disappointment after realizing that their initial idealization of life in the new land was erroneous and that life in the new country may well be very difficult.

A sense of "depressive anxiety" is characterized by migrants' excessive preoccupation with psychological losses. A young Latino immigrant speaks of the tremendous sense of loss he feels in the new land:

> Here I have no family, I have no home. If I had my family and a home here I would be more

optimistic. Now I feel tired. I am sure that if I had a home here, my mother would be waiting for me with my food ready. Now I come back home, and I have to make my own food. I get up in the morning to go to school, and I am all by myself. I make my own coffee, iron my clothes, do everything alone. I come back from work at night and I am all alone. I feel very low. I sit in bed all alone, and I lose morale. I think about my future and about being all alone. This depresses me a lot; I feel desperate (Grinberg and Grinberg 1989).

The sense of anxious "disorientation" that Grinberg and Grinberg found among new immigrants is related to what anthropologists have termed the sense of "culture shock" one typically experiences entering a radically different way of life. The children of Mexican immigrants may become the repositories of the parents' anxieties, ambitions, dreams, and conflicts (Trueba et al. 1993; Trueba 1989; Delgado-Gaitán and Trueba 1991). They are frequently vested with responsibilities (such as translating and sibling care) beyond what is normal for their stage of psychological development. Due to a lack of linguistic skills, Latino immigrant parents are often unable to help their children in school-related tasks. This may bring about further anxieties and a sense of inadequacy in the parents. At the same time, and perhaps related to the last point, Latino immigrant parents typically over-restrict the activities of their children and attempt to minimize the host country's influence.

The losses and disruptions of migration and the poisons of discrimination may undermine immigrant children's self-confidence and development (Padilla, Alvarez, and Lindholm 1986). Feelings of inadequacy and inferiority may reduce a child's faith in his or her ability to succeed in the new setting (Grinberg and Grinberg 1989). A psychological choice for young adults seems to emerge: either "dropping out" or overcompensating by overachieving.

The Second Generation: "Multiple Marginalities" and Ethnic Identity

The children of immigrants born in the new land (the second generation) do not share their parents' dual frame of reference. Not being immigrants themselves, they cannot frame their current experiences in terms of the old country's ideals, standards, and expectations. They are less likely to send remittances to relatives in the old country. Rather than seeing themselves as better off vis-à-vis the old country (as their parents did), the second generation often views their situation as one of deprivation and marginality vis-à-vis the majority culture's (American) "dream" (Horowitz 1983). Thus the second generation often faces the same discrimination and economic difficulties as their parents but without the perceived benefits.

Rogler, Cortés, and Malgady explore the psychosocial consequences of an important generational discontinuity between Mexico-born parents and their California-born children that relates to the immigrants' dual frame of reference. They write:

> The selectivity of the migration stream from Mexico to California tends to create a psychologically robust first-generation immigrant population who feels less deprived because migration has increased their standard of living; in contrast, the Mexican Americans born in the United States feel more deprivation because of their much higher but unrealized aspirations (1991: 589).

Ongoing discrimination and ethnic tension have an erosive effect particularly in the more vulnerable *children* of immigrants.

De Vos (1980) and Ogbu (Ogbu 1978; Gibson and Ogbu 1991) have argued that the specific problems facing immigrants and minority groups in general must be seen in the context of the distinct psychosocial experiences of each group as it enters a majority dominant society. Ogbu (1978) describes what he terms "involuntary minorities." These are minorities that have been initially incorporated into a dominant society against their will (such as African Americans through slavery, or American Indians and the original Mexican Americans through conquest). In addition to their original subordination, these groups have been subjected to a "job ceiling." Ogbu maintains that many of the involuntary minorities were traditionally channeled into the least desirable jobs in the opportunity structure and could not rise above these menial positions regardless of talent, motivation, or effort.

We would add that in addition to "instrumental exploitation" for economic purposes (for example, to maintain a pool of low-skilled, low-paid workers to do undesirable but necessary jobs),

these minorities are also used for "psychological exploitation." That is, they may also be the target of psychological abuse such as stereotyping as "innately inferior," "lazier," and therefore less deserving of sharing in the dominant society's "dream." Economic exploitation and psychological exploitation are, in a sense, two sides of a coin: psychological exploitation and disparagement help the dominant society rationalize its economic treatment of these groups.

In some cases the children of immigrants raised in a context of ethnic disparagement may "identify" with an oppressing dominant group and attempt to join them, leaving their own ethnic group behind (see Rodriguez 1983). In other cases they may creatively navigate antagonistic cultural and ethnic borders, creating their own syntheses of traditions and acting as cultural translators and facilitators between groups. In yet other cases the children may resolutely reject the society that rejects them and turn to others sharing their predicament—their peers. From this last situation typically emerge countercultural groups or gangs that reject the dominant society and affirm their own ethnic identity.

Poor achievement in school tends to be a serious problem among Latinos (Pathey-Chávez 1993; M. Suárez-Orozco and C. Suárez-Orozco 1993; C. Suárez-Orozco and M. Suárez-Orozco n.d.; Trueba 1989). The reasons for this are complex. Vigil (1988a and 1988b) attributes this to the fact that many Latino immigrant parents have not had much education themselves and yet have attained a modest degree of prosperity (relative to whence they came). Hence some parents may be sending the following message to their children, "We made it without a formal education; so can you." Latino families facing economic hardships may encourage youths to seek early employment. There are also cultural expectations regarding marriage and child bearing which may divert some youths from investing in formal education.

A problem with this line of argument, as Trueba and his associates have eloquently demonstrated, is that Latino parents typically say they *want* their children to have the formal education they themselves could not have (Trueba et al. 1993; Trueba 1989; Delgado-Gaitán and Trueba 1991). Ogbu (1978) has approached the problem of poor Latino performance in school from a different but related perspective. According to Ogbu there is a perception among some Latinos, particularly Mexican Americans and mainland Puerto Ricans, that high school graduates are not much more successful financially than those who dropped out of school to work. Hence these Latino youths may not invest in school because they do not see that they will get any additional rewards in the posteducational job market.

School personnel are often indifferent, or even hostile, to the linguistic and other cultural needs, as well as the special circumstances, of immigrant Latino families (Pathey-Chávez 1993; M. Suárez-Orozco 1989). This indifference, coupled with the economic pressures of providing for a large family, may lead to Latinos' ambivalent attitudes toward school and the value of education. Consequently, a high dropout rate from school continues to be a severe problem in the Latino community (Horowitz 1983; Pathey-Chávez 1993; M. Suárez-Orozco 1989; Vigil 1988a, 1988b).

Grinberg and Grinberg (1989) and Vigil (1988a) maintain that a critical issue facing the children of immigrants is that of developing a sense of "identity." According to Erikson (1964), evolving a sense of identity is the critical task in development during adolescence. In order to develop "ego-identity" (a healthy sense of who one is), there must be a certain amount of complementarity between the individual's sense of self and the social milieu. If there exists too much cultural dissonance and role confusion, there may be difficulties in developing a strong sense of identity.

Children of Latino immigrants may suffer from what Vigil terms "multiple marginalities," which in some cases compromise the development of a sense of identity. Vigil and others have noted that children in these contexts are likely to experience intense culture conflict on both an individual and group level. For many second-generation Latino youths:

> Language inconsistency at home and school, a perceived gap in the status of their parents and the quality of their environment and those of the larger society, and the dangers and attractions of *barrio* streets create an ambiguity in their ethnic identity. Parents and older siblings are often unable to effectively guide youngsters in ways to reconcile the contrasting cultural worlds, and this results in an uneven adoption of acculturative strategies (Vigil 1988a: 41).

In some cases, youths attempt to resolve identity issues by embracing total assimilation and a wholesale identification with mainstream American values. In other cases, a new ethnic identity is forged, incorporating both Latino and dominant American culture (in which cases bilingual fluency is often achieved). Yet in other cases the adaptation is not smooth, and a "subculture of cultural transitionals" develops (Vigil 1988a: 39). These "transitional" youths are sometimes called *cholos*. Within the same family each child may adopt his/her own way individually, resulting in various siblings occupying very different sectors of the spectrum—from *cholo* to "anglicized," and from bilingual to "Spanglish" speaking, to English-only speaking (Vigil 1988a).

It is precisely such identity issues that propel many second-generation Latino youths to join gangs. In fact, Vigil (1988a, 1988b) contends that gangs are largely a second-generation immigrant phenomenon. In his perceptive studies, Vigil traces the historical pattern of gang formation in urban areas beginning with the large-scale Mexican immigration to the United States before the turn of this century. He accounts for several key factors in the development of Latino gangs: low socioeconomic status, urban poverty, and limited economic mobility; ethnic minority status and discrimination; lack of training, education, and constructive opportunities; and a breakdown in the social institutions of school and family.

Vigil also points out major causal factors in "a first- and second-generation conflict within each ethnic group, which creates loyalty discord and identity confusions; and a noted predisposition among youths to gravitate toward street peers for sources of social associations and personal fulfillment" (Vigil 1988a: 4). All of these factors hold particularly true for many second-generation Latino youths. In addition, we must note that *"cholo gangs"* have been a long-lasting, rather than transitory, phenomenon due to a unique situation of continuous migration from Mexico which brings in reinforcements of the traditional culture, and new cycles of "marginality," on an ongoing basis.

Gangs provide a "mechanism of adaptation for many youths who need a source of identification and human support." The gang provides a "reforging of Mexican and American patterns . . . creating a culture [and language] of mixed and blended elements" (Vigil 1988a: 6–7). Vigil maintains that "although *cholos* are Americanized, either by accident or design, they refuse or are unable to be totally assimilated" (1988a: 7). They retain certain Mexican customs, sometimes in caricature form, and a strong sense of peer (gang) group as family, daring/bravado male patterns of *machismo*, and an ambivalent attitude toward authority (Horowitz 1983; Vigil 1988a, 1988b).

At the same time, youths in gangs may not feel "Mexican," and in some cases they may experience considerable antipathy toward Mexican visitors (Dayley 1991) and disparage "wetbacks" (first-generation undocumented immigrants) (Vigil 1988a). Often there is a perception of "limited good" and competition over scarce resources (such as jobs, education, housing, and so forth) with the newer arrivals. Psychologically, the second generation may view the new arrivals as embodying aspects of themselves that the second generation may wish to disclaim.

Both Vigil (1988a) and Horowitz (1983) have found that the individuals who are most heavily involved in gangs come from the most troubled families: with absent parents and with a history of alcohol or drug addiction and child neglect and/or abuse. Vigil (1988a) estimates that 70 to 80 percent of the heavily involved gang members come from such family situations. For those individuals, in the absence of more appropriate role models, gang membership becomes incorporated into their sense of identity. Gangs offer their members a sense of belonging, solidarity, and support. Although many second-generation youths may look toward gangs for cues about dress, language, and attitude, most remain on the periphery and eventually outgrow the gang mystique after passing through adolescence. Nevertheless, the gang ethos provides a sense of identity and cohesion for marginal youths during a turbulent stage of development.

Second-generation Hispanics who have the opportunity and choose to join mainstream American culture face very different day-to-day experiences but may continue to suffer from a marginal status:

> Individuals who choose to measure their competency in terms of the wider society rather than in terms of local identity risk a loss of emotional support from peers and kin. Trusting and close relationships must be developed with new people and on different terms. The movement away from the traditional sources of support and the traditional basis of social relationships can create feelings of acute loneliness. Little within the Chicano community prepares them for the competitive, individualistic Anglo world of social relationships in which they must face lack of acceptance and some degree of discrimination. They become caught between two worlds (Horowitz 1983: 200–01).

Some of those who choose to leave their ethnic group behind may even refuse to speak Spanish and reject bilingual education (see Rodriguez 1992, 1983; Linda Chávez 1991). The issue of language and identity deserves some further comment. Certainly it is true that by using "non-mainstream" English (such as Spanglish, Black English, lower-class English) one is at a disadvantage, as evaluations are constantly being made about oneself based on language usage. However, we would question whether it is indeed necessary to give up one's native language, one's affective language (along with all the resulting accompanying losses), in order to "make it." In ideal circumstances, it should not be an either/or situation.

Language has both a symbolic and an affective value. To see language as a mere instrumental tool for communication is to miss its deep affective roots. To give up Spanish to acquire English represents a symbolic act of ethnic renunciation: it is giving up the mother tongue for the instrumental tongue of the dominant group. It is in such contexts, when learning the language of a dominant group is symbolically equated with giving up one's own ethnic identity, that language acquisition becomes a problem. The Dutch can speak English very effectively at no emotional cost. In contrast, the Flemish-speaking people in Belgium have faced historical difficulties in learning French—the language of the once dominant and oppressive Walloons. An understanding of affective aspects of language also helps to explain why minority ethnic rights movements often pick up language as a symbolic banner of belonging vis-à-vis dominant groups (e.g., the Basques in Spain, the push for bilingual education in the United States, the insistence that Black English be given equal value to standard English, and so forth).

Empirical Findings

Our most recent study investigated how concerns regarding achievement and family orientation differ between Mexican, Mexican immigrant, Mexican American second-generation, and white non-Latino American (the majority American culture) youth. Hence our study attempts to address both differences between cultures (Mexican and American) *and* generational discontinuities associated with the immigration process (nonimmigrants, first-generation immigrants, and children of immigrants). Past research had suggested that it was likely that there would be significant differences between groups on the dimensions under consideration.

It must be emphasized at the outset that cross-cultural research is fraught with methodological limitations. The challenge involves both the difficulties of static-group comparisons (and hence of having group equivalence) and finding "culture free" or culturally equivalent measures. Regarding the concern about group equivalence, in our research we attempted to make the groups as representative and equivalent as possible on what were thought to be key dimensions. In contending with the second concern of using culturally equivalent measures, this study used a variety of techniques to elicit the information needed to answer the research questions. These techniques included structured ethnographic interviews, objective measures, and projective measures. A particular effort was made to strengthen the psychometric properties of the Thematic Apperception Test (TAT), as it has been both highly proclaimed and severely criticized as a tool for cross-cultural research.

One hundred and eighty-eight students were evenly distributed between the groups. There was no significant difference between groups in terms of gender distribution. Participants were restricted to adolescents between the ages of thirteen and eighteen. The phase of the research dealing with Mexican students was conducted in Guanajuato, Mexico, in 1990–1991. Research with the other three groups—Mexican immigrant, Mexican American, and non-Latino white American students—was conducted in Southern California in 1992–1993.

The groups were significantly different from one another on the dimension of socioeconomic status. Mexican immigrant and Mexican American students were of significantly lower socioeconomic status than either the Mexican or the American students. This is not surprising given that the measure of socioeconomic status used for this study (the Hollingshead [1975] four-factor scale) takes into consideration both a rating of the parents' occupation and years of education.

The limited English-speaking abilities of the parents of many of the immigrant students tended to relegate them to positions in the laboring and service sectors. Furthermore, many of the parents of the Mexican immigrant and Mexican American students had very limited education; the educational levels of the American and Mexican students were, on the whole, higher. This finding indicates that the sample is representative of the groups under examination in the respective societies as a whole. Although an attempt could have been made to make the groups more equivalent in socioeconomic status, the resulting sample would not have been representative of the majority of Mexican immigrants to the United States.

Let us now consider each of the research questions and how they were answered using the quantitative methods employed in this study. Our findings confirm the general observation that Mexico-origin populations tend to be more family oriented than are other populations (see Becerra 1988; Karrer 1987; Vernon and Roberts 1985; Falicov 1982; Sabogal et al. 1987; Keefe, Padilla, and Carlos 1979; Murillo 1971; Montiel 1970; Hayner 1954). Further, our findings indicate that members of immigrant families become increasingly dependent on one another in the context of resettling in a foreign land (immigrants received higher scores on Sabogal et al.'s [1987] Familism scale than did Mexicans in Mexico, second-generation Mexican Americans, and the non-Hispanic white students).

There may be several factors to account for this important finding. The community networks of support that are important in daily life prior to migration (e.g., relying on neighbors, friends, and extended family to resolve everyday problems) are typically not available to newly arrived migrants in a foreign land. It would appear that migrant families turn inward as a result of this social fact. Additionally, it can be suggested that members of migrant families compensate for the individual losses accompanying migration by intensifying their affective ties with accompanying relatives (Grinberg and Grinberg 1989). Lastly, "culture shock"—the general sense of disorientation to a novel and culturally distinct setting—may also lead migrants to what is most familiar to them (i.e., members of their own family).

It is worth noting that the second-generation students fall in between the Mexican and Mexican immigrant subsamples, on the one hand, and the white non-Latino American group, on the other, in the degree of concern with familism as measured by this scale. This means that the concerns of second-generation Mexican American students are similar in many respects to those of both Mexicans and non-Latino white Americans. As could be anticipated, these students are bicultural, sharing concerns of two cultures along with their own unique configuration.

White non-Latino American students demonstrated significantly less perceived obligation to provide emotional or material support to the family than did students from any of the Latino groups. The immigrant group demonstrated the greatest concern about this dimension, followed closely by the Mexican American group. This finding again confirms the observations regarding the cultural patterning of family interdependence in Mexico-origin populations discussed above.

In the results of the TAT stories, as with the objective Familism scale (Sabogal et al. 1987), Mexico-origin individuals reveal a greater willingness than do non-Latino white Americans to provide material and emotional support to family members. A most interesting finding is that the Mexican immigrant and second-generation Mexican American youths revealed the highest concern with a sense of obligation to the family (e.g., more than white non-Latino Americans or Mexicans). Several observations could be made to account for this pattern. The Mexican immigrant and second-generation youths share an important characteristic: both have immigrant parents. The process of migration typically entails great emotional and material sacrifices on the part of the parents. It has been noted that immigrants rationalize the material sacrifices and affective losses by anticipating a better future in the new land; this future is, of course, the children. Children of immigrant parents may perceive the hardships endured by their parents as a sacrifice made so that they could have a better future. Beyond the normative difference between the Anglo and Mexican sense of obligation vis-à-vis family members, there might also be an immigrant aspect to the sense of obligation to repay parents for the sacrifices they made.

As noted earlier, the children of immigrants in some respects become "cultural translators" for their parents. These children generally speak the language of the host culture and may have a better understanding of the cultural process in the new setting than do their parents. Immigrant parents often turn to their children to help them in ways that they would not in their country of origin. Children help to translate, to open bank accounts, to intervene in emergencies, and to deal with the non-Spanish-speaking world in general. The children, aware of their parents' lack of relative competence in cultural matters, may come to feel a special sense of responsibility toward them.

The issue of whether family conflict would increase within the Mexican American second generation, as clinical observations had indicated, was also assessed. The fact that the Mexican American group did not score higher on either the objective (Beavers, Hampson, and Hulgus 1985) or TAT family conflict subscales disconfirmed this hypothesis. It should be noted that this hypothesis was developed after reviewing the clinical literature (e.g., Falicov 1982; Sluzki 1979; Vega 1990) that discusses the "cultural dissonance" and the "culture gap" that may arise between immigrant parents and their children. The sample used for this study consisted of "normals" (adolescents in high school not involved in individual or family therapy), while the clinical literature is based on patient cases seen by the clinicians. Clearly these samples are not comparable. One important finding of this study is that the so-called cultural gap does not necessarily lead to increased parent and child conflict in nonclinical adolescent children of immigrants.

Our study also considered the issue of peer influences. It was predicted, based on our reading of the relevant literature, that the Mexican American second generation and the white non-Latino American youths would express greater concerns with turning toward peers as behavioral and attitudinal referents than would either the Mexican or Mexican immigrant youths. The analysis of these data revealed that the white non-Latino American youths demonstrated the highest overall concerns with turning toward their peers for opinions regarding behaviors and attitudes. Contrary to prediction, however, the Mexican American group was very close to the Mexican and Mexican immigrant groups on this dimension.

This brings us to question the notion that adolescence is normatively a time of peer orientation and a pushing away of the family. While this may be true of white non-Latino American adolescents, it may not be true across cultures and nationalities. In his classic study of American culture,

Gorer emphasized the American tradition of "the moral rejection of authority" (1963: 53) which began historically and has been perpetuated in the social and political structure of American society. Gorer discussed at length how the parent is rejected as a guide and model and how peers take on a central role in affirming self-esteem "with a feeling of far greater psychological urgency than is usual in other countries" (p. 108). In contrast, it is apparent that the family retains a key role for Mexico-origin adolescents, and peers may not necessarily achieve the same powerful degree of influence that they do for white non-Latino adolescents.

Our study also addressed questions about achievement orientation. The literature had suggested that achievement motivation may be based on different dynamics for different cultural groups (M. Suárez-Orozco 1989). This study explored this issue using the Thematic Apperception Test (as done previously by De Vos [1973]; McClelland [1961]; M. Suárez-Orozco [1989], and others). Did the achievement motivations of white non-Latino American and Mexican youths differ from one another? Did concerns with achievement shift in relation to immigration and in the second generation? Would second-generation immigrants demonstrate achievement concerns like their parents, or would they be closer on this dimension to white non-Latino American youths? Or, alternatively, would second-generation youths significantly turn away from concerns with achievement?

It was hypothesized that both Mexican and Mexican immigrant youths would express more concern with compensatory achievement (i.e., achievement as a means to compensate for relative deprivation and poverty) than either second-generation Mexican American or white non-Latino American youths. The fact that the differences between the groups on the TAT Compensatory Achievement subscale did not reach statistical significance indicates that this hypothesis was not confirmed. However, the supplemental qualitative analysis indicated that Mexican youths voiced greater concerns with poverty than did any of the other subgroups.

Prior research with Central American adolescents (M. Suárez-Orozco 1989) had led to the hypothesis that Latinos in general, and Mexicans in particular, would construct TAT narratives in which achievement motivation would be within a framework of social obligations and mutual interdependence (i.e., achieving to help others or with the help of others). It was assumed that Mexican and Mexican immigrant youths would express more concern with affiliative achievement than would white non-Latino American youths and Mexican American youths.

However, the Mexican and Mexican immigrant youths did not in fact demonstrate higher TAT Affiliative Achievement subscale scores. Hence this hypothesis was not confirmed. After scoring the data, however, it became clear that overall affiliative concerns were differentially voiced between the groups. It was deduced that this scale was somewhat confounded as it incorporated two separate concepts (affiliation and achievement), both of which had to occur in a specific manner in order to be scored. As will be described in greater detail in the next section, there were in fact significant differences between the groups in affiliative concerns.

It was postulated that Mexican American youths would express more concerns regarding avoiding challenging tasks than would each of the other three groups. The fact that the Mexican American youths demonstrated statistically lower scores on the TAT Avoiding/Engaging Tasks subscale than did any other group confirms this hypothesis. Therefore, second-generation Mexican American youths related more narratives in which the protagonist is depicted as avoiding or giving up on the task at hand. This finding can be interpreted as follows: whereas the immigrant generation typically demonstrates high expectations and an optimism that they can achieve status mobility through schooling, the second generation may develop a less enthusiastic faith in the educational system.

Our finding is consistent with the observations of such researchers as Ogbu (1978), Matute-Bianchi (1991), and Pathey-Chávez (1993). According to these researchers, second- and third-generation Mexican American youths may respond to ongoing patterns of discrimination and cultural alienation in schools by giving up on education. As Pathey-Chávez poignantly puts it:

> Latino adolescents are highly motivated, but their expectations of success are colored by experiences of hostility and discrimination from the society at large. They question whether school is working in their interest. . . . They find

it difficult to cooperate in the educational enterprise. Many of them simply leave it altogether (1993: 56).

Interestingly, the Independent Achievement scale reached significance, but in a direction that was unexpected. Analysis of this scale revealed that the Mexican subjects demonstrated significantly greater concerns with achievement in a self-initiated manner than did the Mexican American and non-Latino white American subjects. There was no significant difference on the Independent Achievement scale between Mexican and Mexican immigrant subjects.

The finding that non-Hispanic white Americans revealed less concern with self-initiated achievement than did the Mexican youths is in keeping with neither cultural stereotypes nor expectations based on the literature. Carter and Segura, for example, reviewed a number of studies that assessed teachers' views regarding "Mexican American cultural values and orientations" (1979: 83). Traits that were frequently imputed by educators to Mexican American students included fatalism, present-time orientation, low level of aspiration, and noncompetitiveness. Additionally, McClelland's (1961) pioneering studies had established that self-initiated achievement motivation was the predominant achievement pattern among his non-Hispanic white subjects.

In our research, both the Independent Achievement *a priori* scale and the Internally Motivated supplemental scale demonstrated that achievement motivation was more self-initiated in the sample of Mexican youths than in that of the white non-Hispanic American youths. This last finding is particularly important when we take into consideration Ogbu's (1987) contention that "in general American social scientists . . . tend to assume explicitly or implicitly that the main cause of school failure lies in the background of the children." By "background" Ogbu is referring to genetic, linguistic, cultural, psychological, and social characteristics. The "cultural deprivation" model articulated by Bloom, Davis, and Hess asserted that school failures can be attributed to "experiences in the home which do not transmit the cultural patterns necessary for the types of learning characteristic of the schools and larger society" (1965: 4). In the case of Latino—and, more specifically, Mexico-origin—populations, some observers have argued that cultural background is somehow responsible for the relatively high levels of school failure and dropout. For example, Heller argued that Mexican American socialization emphasizes such values as "family ties" and "living in the present," all the while "neglecting the values that are conducive to [mobility], achievement, independence and deferred gratification" (1966: 34–35).

The findings of our study do not support these contentions. Our findings suggest that the Mexican cultural background does indeed emphasize self-initiated achievement and values the notion that hard work is critical for success, although it stresses interdependence, familism, and obtaining help from others more than does the cultural background of non-Hispanic Americans (see also Trueba et al. 1993; Trueba 1989; Delgado-Gaitán and Trueba 1991). We must conclude that a shift seems to occur in the psychosocial patterning of achievement motivation of Mexico-origin populations after moving into minority status in the United States. The narratives told by the Mexican students reveal that a pattern of self-initiated achievement orientation is fostered within the Mexican psychocultural background. Likewise, the immigrant subsample also reveals more concern with self-initiated achievement motivation than either the second-generation Mexican American or the non-Hispanic white subsample.

These findings suggest that problems in the motivational dynamics and schooling experiences of Mexico-origin second-generation youths cannot be attributed to cultural background per se. Other factors such as the stresses of minority status, discrimination, alienating schools, economic hardships, and pressures to work may all contribute to the elevated school dropout rate in this population. Further studies will be required to examine carefully the nature of this generational discontinuity.

Playing the Violin in Four Cultures

A large body of data was gathered for this project. An analysis of the entire data base goes far beyond the specific considerations and scope of this paper. It is, however, particularly instructive to delve into the most significant themes emerging from Card 1 of the Thematic Apperception Test. This card depicts a latency-age boy, pensively gazing at a violin on a table before him. This card tends to pull for the themes under consideration— achievement orientation and parent-child relations (Henry 1956). The comparative materials on Card 1 illustrate in rich and subtle detail many of the issues we have already discussed.

All of the stories on Card 1 were grouped by subsample (i.e., white non-Hispanic American, Mexican, Mexican immigrant, and Mexican American), and all of the responses for each group were read separately. In reading through the TAT responses to Card 1, it became evident that different themes seemed to predominate for each group. A list of recurring themes was compiled. All of the stories for Card 1 were then placed together randomly. The stories were read, analyzed, and discussed by two raters who were blind to the group membership of the storyteller. Each story was rated for the presence or absence of each of the themes under consideration. The incidence of each theme was tallied for each group. Chi-square analyses were then conducted to check for significant differences between groups. A number of findings resulted from this analysis (see table 1). Only the most significant of these will be discussed.

WHITE NON-HISPANICS

The predominant theme that emerges in analyzing the white non-Hispanic adolescents' responses to Card 1 of the TAT is that of frustration (in fully 50 percent of these narratives, contrasting with only 2 percent of the Mexican sample). In the majority of these narratives, frustration seems to be the outcome of either the difficulties and challenges of the task (learning to play the violin) or the pressures of the parental figure imposing the task on the unwilling child. Adolescents in this subgroup related narratives of pressuring parents far more frequently (in 36 percent of the cases) than did Mexican and Mexican immigrant youths (8 and 10 percent, respectively). The narratives told by the white non-Hispanic adolescents reflected concerns with independence and gave some indication that for these youths adolescence is a period of significant turmoil, which is particularly revealed by tensions with parental figures. Themes of individuation and independence are prominent within this group. Themes of turning to others for help occur very rarely in this group (4 percent). Here are some representative stories told by non-Hispanic white American adolescents:

His parents want him to take violin lessons and they sent him to his room to practice until he got good. He doesn't like the violin and is sitting there looking at it, thinking that maybe he should play it to get out of his room. But he really doesn't want to. He stares at it. He has played it and doesn't like it. Eventually his parents come up and see that he hasn't played it at all. They make him play it anyway. He feels frustrated that he can't do what he wants, but he has to do what his parents say, no matter how stupid it seems (female, age 16).

There is a boy, and for his birthday he is given a violin. His parents expect him to learn to play it but he becomes frustrated and never plays it. His mom has a party and expects him to play it there. He sits at his desk and stares at it. The day before the party, he tells his Mom the truth. She understands and forgives him. He asks if he can play a different instrument and she says that she will be just as proud. In the picture he is confused and mad that he can't play it. He feels like a disappointment to his parents (male, age 13).

This boy is sad because his parents want him to play the violin. He wants to be something else. He is sitting there and is looking at the violin and is trying to think what to say to his parents. He throws his violin and breaks it. His parents get mad and so he tells them he wants to play baseball. He is sad and angry and feels forced into something. He gets mad and they finally realize that it is his life and they encourage him to do what he wants (male, age 16).

MEXICANS

In the Mexican sample, the most significant feature of the stories told by the students is a concern with self-motivated achievement orientation (54 percent versus 14 percent of American students). Themes of frustration and of the task having been imposed by others rarely occurred. Concerns with adequacy (28 percent) were frequently voiced, as was the notion that hard work was required for success (34 percent versus 10 percent of the American students). These adolescents told the most stories in which inherent pleasure derived from the activity. They also told many more stories in which the protagonist engaged in daydreaming and imagination than did any of the other groups (32 percent versus 4 percent of

Table 1. Responses to TAT Card 1

Theme	White Non-Hispanic		Mexican		Mexican Immigrant		American		Chi-square
	N	%	N	%	N	%	N	%	Probability
Parental pressure to perform	18	36	0	0	3	6	15	30	.001***
Internally motivated	7	14	27	54	16	32	9	18	.001***
Succumbing to pressure	7	14	3	6	2	4	4	8	.274
Avoiding pressure	8	16	1	2	5	10	8	16	.114
Hard work	5	10	17	34	5	10	8	16	.005**
Instant gratification	3	6	2	4	2	4	1	2	.789
Success as a result of efforts of self	5	10	15	30	10	20	5	10	.026*
Success as a result of efforts of others	3	6	3	6	5	10	3	6	.813
Success as a result of efforts of self and others	7	14	4	8	5	10	4	8	.707
Achievement motivated for self	0	0	2	4	0	0	0	0	.007**
Achievement motivated for others	1	2	4	8	5	10	4	8	.429
Achievement motivated—self and others	0	0	2	4	0	0	0	0	.707
Concerns with adequacy	8	16	14	28	17	34	9	18	.013**
Concerns with failure	2	4	1	2	1	2	14	28	.001**
Boredom	3	6	1	2	1	2	7	14	.134
Frustration—resolved	17	34	0	0	3	6	3	6	.001***
Frustration—unresolved	8	16	1	2	1	2	4	8	.016
Broken violin—purposeful	5	10	0	0	0	0	1	2	.008**
Broken violin—accidental	4	8	0	0	7	14	4	8	.063
Mad	7	14	0	0	3	6	10	20	.004**
Sad	16	32	8	16	33	66	17	34	.001***
Searching out help	2	4	6	12	13	26	6	12	.012**
Pleasure	3	6	9	18	8	16	3	6	.115
Financial deprivation	2	4	6	12	3	6	3	6	.451
Daydreaming/imagining	2	4	16	32	5	10	1	2	.001***
What do I want to do?	6	12	0	0	0	0	1	2	.002**
Parenting style—pressuring	18	36	4	8	5	10	5	10	.001***
Parenting style—nurturing	5	10	8	16	4	8	4	8	.541
Parenting style—punitive	2	4	1	2	1	2	3	6	.644

* p> .05
** p>.01
*** p>.001

Americans and 2 percent of Mexican Americans). Another interesting occurrence in the Mexican stories is the number of narratives in which the parental dramatis personae are depicted as nurturing, warm, and supportive. This contrasts with the white non-Hispanic subsample, in which the parental figures were typically depicted as pressuring. A related concern in the Mexican subsample is actively seeking help from a competent person to aid the protagonist in accomplishing the difficult task at hand. Rather than fighting off intrusive parents, Mexican students tell stories in which the protagonist is searching for an adult figure to help him with his task. Representative stories follow:

> This is a young boy who is concentrating on the violin. He's thinking that he's not going to be able to learn the notes of the melody that he wants to learn to play. But with time he keeps trying and he eventually learns to play the melody. It comes out really well because of all his efforts, and when he gets it perfect he calls his friends to show them what he has learned. They listen to him and they tell him how beautiful the music is. They tell him his success is due to all his hard work (female, age 14).

> There was a boy who wanted to learn to play the violin but he did not know how. He is sitting there thinking and contemplating about the future. He's thinking about whether he will be able to learn to play and become a great violinist. Just now he is imagining that he is in a concert hall giving a concert. After thinking about it, he tells himself that he needs to put a lot of effort and enthusiasm into learning so that he will be able to achieve his dreams in the future (male, age 14).

> This boy is looking at his violin that he inherited from his father. He doesn't have anyone to help him learn to play the violin. He is very sad and he realizes that he doesn't know how to play the violin. His mother is going to help him find someone to help him learn to play. His family doesn't have any money to get anyone to help. She manages anyway, and when he gets to be older he has learned how to play. He learns to play very well. He learned when he was fifteen years old and he began working, and with the money that he earned he took more and more lessons in order to become a better musician (male, age 14).

MEXICAN IMMIGRANTS

Within the Mexican immigrant subsample, the most frequently voiced theme is that of a sense of sadness or of "feeling bad" attributed to the protagonist (fully 66 percent of this sample, double the white non-Hispanic sample and Mexican American sample and four times the Mexican sample). This theme of sadness found in stories told by the Mexican immigrants is highly consistent with previous findings of depression resulting from immigration losses (see Padilla and Durán, this volume; Brenner 1990; Grinberg and Grinberg 1989).

As with the Mexican subsample, the immigrant youths articulated a preoccupation with self-motivated achievement orientation along with concerns with adequacy. However, rather than achieving the important large-scale successes recounted in the stories of the Mexican students, the narratives told by the immigrant adolescents reveal a smaller scale of success. Rather than playing in orchestras all over the world or being widely applauded (as in many of the narratives of the Mexican students), the protagonist of the immigrant stories, when he succeeds, merely learns how to play. Hence, the expected successes seem to be significantly scaled back. A greater number of the Mexican immigrant youths mentioned seeking help from others (26 percent versus 12 percent of Mexican and Mexican American youths and 4 percent of American youths) than did any of the other subsamples. Here are some representative stories illustrating these themes:

> He is sad because he is not able to play the violin and he doesn't know who he can ask to help him. He is trying to figure out how he might be able to play it. His mom is sad also because she asked him if he could play and he said no. She decided that he needed to get someone to help him. She finds someone to help him and teach him how to play and he learns how to play and he feels really happy about it (female, age 13).

> He is looking at it, trying to use it—what parts it has. He feels worried and preoccupied because he is still unable to use it well. He will find out how to play this. He doesn't have help. He does it alone. He feels sad and thinks that he needs someone who can help him, show him how to use it. He will be happy when he knows how to use it (male, age 17).

> This is a boy who liked to play the violin but he didn't know how. He is sad but he takes classes on how to learn. After a time he learns to play and he is happy (female, age 14).

SECOND-GENERATION MEXICAN AMERICANS

In the case of the second-generation Mexican Americans, we encountered some characteristics that are also present in other subsamples. For example, like the themes emerging in the white non-Hispanic sample, an important feature of the narratives articulated by the second generation is that of parental figures (including teachers and other authority figures in society) depicted as pressuring the protagonist to perform the task (in 30 percent of the stories). Likewise, the percentage of stories in which the predominant theme is self-motivated achievement orientation is comparable to the American subsample (14 and 16 percent, respectively). In many of these stories, the self-motivated orientation leads to success in an atmosphere of social interdependence (e.g., success is due to the inspiration of the grandfather, is achieved by a parent teaching him or by the parents providing emotional support). In these stories, hard work is involved but success is socially mediated; help or inspiration from others is crucial.

A very striking theme found in the second-generation narratives is a concern with failure. In 28 percent of the Mexican American stories, there is reference to a concern with threatened failure to achieve the task at hand. This contrasts with 2 percent among the Mexican and immigrant groups and 4 percent among the white non-Latino Americans. Whereas concerns with adequacy are voiced in many of the stories told by the Mexican and Mexican immigrant subsamples, there is a strong sense of hope and optimism for the future (i.e., the initial inadequacy is overcome and success is finally achieved through hard work). In a number of the stories told by the second generation, however, a disturbing preoccupation with failure and a sense of hopelessness emerge. In many such stories, the future looks bleak. The following are some representative stories.

> The child was very interested in playing the violin in the beginning. Now he doesn't know what to do without any help. Now he is going through stages where he puts too much effort and nothing is happening. So he is feeling depressed. He loses his interest in music and now has a mental block in himself. He can't solve other problems. He gives up all interest in music and has a mental block. He loses confidence in solving problems (male, age 18).

> He probably went to try out for a music class and he didn't make it. So he is sad. He looks sad because he didn't make it. He goes home and tells his Mom what happened—that he didn't get to make it (female, age 18).

> There was this little boy who wanted to play the violin. He had the violin but no money to take classes. He got a job and worked and worked for days. Finally he got money but he couldn't find where to go to take classes. He looked and found some place to go and learn. He took classes but couldn't learn how to play it. One day he was playing in the park with some friends and he kicked a ball and broke a window. He went to his parents and told them and asked them to pay for the window. They said "no." He either would have to work or sell his violin, they told him. He went to his room and sat down and stared at it and thought about it. He decided to sell it. He feels sad because he was starting to learn to play it and he had to let it go (female, age 14).

In some of these stories told by second-generation youths, the protagonist attempts to engage with the task; he tries to play the violin but eventually quits, realizing that he is not competent. In others, the protagonist cannot learn without help or simply tries but is unable to play adequately and is disheartened. In yet other narratives, the concern with failure is more specifically related to obstacles in the environment that prevent the protagonist from taking on the challenge. In these stories, the boy is trying to learn the violin but must give it up due to factors outside of his control. In some cases, though, the protagonist struggles with the threat of failure and eventually finds a solution by asking for help from others.

It is particularly poignant to note the discontinuities in the narratives told by the Mexicans in Mexico, the Mexican immigrants, and the second-generation Mexican Americans. Whereas Mexicans and immigrant students revealed a faith that success was possible through hard work, many of the second-generation youths told stories in which failure was a significant preoccupation. The energy and faith in "making it" that are characteristic of the Mexican and immigrant students seem to have significantly diminished by the second generation.

These findings may be related to the vicissitudes in the path from immigration to minority status. Immigrants typically endure their affective losses by concentrating on the material gains to be made by exploiting new opportunities in a host country. Members of the second generation, on the other hand, may not measure their current state in terms of their former life in Mexico. Rather, they use as their standard the ideals and expectations of the majority society (M. Suárez-Orozco and C. Suárez-Orozco 1993). Using this standard, many Mexican Americans may fall, short of their aspirations. Racism, disparagement, and lack of equal opportunity may compromise the faith of at-risk youths in their ability to succeed. This may well be related to the disturbingly elevated school dropout rates among second- and third-generation Mexican American youths (Bean et al. 1994; Chapa 1988; Kantrowitz and Rosaldo 1991).

Conclusion

A premise of this project, stated at the outset, was that Latinos are far from a homogeneous group. This study focused on the specific experiences of Mexican immigrants and Mexican Americans (and compared them to non-Latino whites and to Mexicans in Mexico). Differences in the characteristics of each subgroup were found. Perhaps the most significant finding of this study is the important discontinuity in the psychosocial profile of Mexican immigrants and second-generation Mexican Americans.

Educators working with immigrants would be wise to take into account the psychosocial consequences of the affective ruptures involved in immigration. Of particular relevance is the normative preoccupation with losses and the mourning endured in the context of immigration. Not only are immigrant youths preoccupied with their own losses, but the stresses and losses of their immigrant parents affect their psychological availability to help their children navigate the dual challenges of adolescence and the adjustment to a new cultural context. As parents' psychological resources are absorbed by their own losses, culture shock, and the need to earn a living in the new country, it is to be expected that they may have less time and energy to devote to the adolescent.

In terms of familial conflict, educators may benefit by paying attention not only to how conflicts may be age-specific (related to the adolescent phase of development in the United States) but also how they may be the product of specific acculturation stresses and discontinuities separating immigrant parents from their children. In working with the second generation (as with immigrant adolescents), it is important to take into account their (immigrant) parents' relative unavailability (due to their own losses and economic pressures), which may lead the youths to turn elsewhere for satisfaction of their affective needs. Many minority youths residing in conflict-ridden inner cities turn to peer groups for the instrumental and affective supports that help them endure their difficult surroundings (Vigil 1988a, 1988b).

The most obvious characteristic of the second-generation Mexican Americans is their participation in two distinct psychocultural universes. Not surprisingly, they operate in two cultural realms and are preoccupied with issues concerning adolescents in each of the two cultures. Issues facing the second generation are in some respects very different from the issues facing the immigrant generation. A significant proportion of second-generation youths revealed in their narratives a disturbing preoccupation about an inability to "make it." A compromised sense of self-esteem seems to be a corollary of the second generation's minority status (see Padilla and Durán, this volume; Carter and Segura 1979). Clinically, the second-generation youths reveal less concern with sadness, but issues of frustration and self-esteem appear to be significant. Providing successful role models may be an especially effective intervention in conveying hope to second-generation youths who seem concerned with failure.

In essence, second-generation children must navigate between Latino familism and the American cultural ideal of independence and making it in one's own way. Educators working with second-generation youths should locate psychological problems and conflicts in the context of the stresses facing immigrant families and their minority status youths. Given that familism is an enduring trait for the Mexican and Mexican American youths, educators should try, whenever possible, to involve the family in their interventions.

The school, perhaps more than any other social institution, is an arena in which many of the problems facing Hispanics—both first and second generation—are played out. Educators working with Latino immigrant children are often surprised to see how vigorously the new arrivals pursue their dream of a better tomorrow through education. These same educators seem puzzled to see how, contrary to common expectations rooted in a simplistic notion of "assimilation," many second- and third-generation children of Latino descent grow disaffected with the school system. Educators watch as large numbers of these youths fail to thrive in school environments, turning to gangs or "dropping out."

Educators working with Latino youths should understand that there are class, gender, and generational factors that shape experience and expectations differently across groups. They should consider the burdens (affective losses, psychological disorientation, cultural discontinuities, etc.) that immigrant children carry. Sensitive educators may emerge as "cultural brokers" bridging some of the generational discontinuities between immigrant children and their parents and between immigrants and the dominant culture.

With respect to newly arrived immigrant children, educators are placed in a strategically important position to capitalize on their dynamic of positivism, hope, and desire to succeed. Understanding motivation is at the heart of pedagogy. Yet the assumptions that have guided pedagogical practice and curriculum strategies to date are based on an understanding of motivation relevant largely to white, middle-class students from the dominant culture. As we discussed above, the cultural paradigm of individualism that defines and patterns motivation among members of the dominant culture does not apply to Latino students. Latino students, we have argued, typically achieve in the context of family and peer obligation, not in the context of individualistic self-advancement.

It is clear that the Latino immigrant experience is a rich and diverse tapestry. Gender, country of origin, socioeconomic status, legal status, level of "acculturation," generational differences, and psychological resources must all be taken into account when considering the Latino experience. Only when such issues are considered can we begin to understand, and be of service to, the various Latino groups in the United States.

References

Bean, Frank D., Jorge Chapa, R. Berg, and Kathryn Sowards. 1994. "Educational and Sociodemographic Incorporation among Hispanic Immigrants to the United States." In *Immigration and Ethnicity: The Integration of America's Newest Arrivals*, edited by Barry Edmonston and Jeffrey S. Passel. Washington, D.C.: Urban Institute Press.

Beavers, W. Robert, Robert B. Hampson, and Y.F. Hulgus. 1985. "Commentary: The Beavers System Approach to Family Assessment," *Family Process* 24:398–405.

Becerra, Regina M. 1988. "The Mexican American Family." In *Ethnic Families in America: Patterns and Variations*, edited by Charles H. Mindel, Robert W. Habenstein, and Roosevelt Wright. 3d ed. New York: Elsevier.

Bloom, Benjamin S., Allison Davis, and Robert Hess. 1965. *Compensatory Education for Cultural Deprivation*. New York: Holt, Rinehart, and Winston.

Brenner, E. 1990. "Losses, Acculturation and Depression in Mexican Immigrants." Ph.D. dissertation, California School of Professional Psychology.

Carter, Thomas P., and Roberto D. Segura. 1979. *Mexican Americans in School: A Decade of Change*. New York: College Entrance Examination Board.

Chapa, Jorge. 1988. "The Question of Mexican American Assimilation: Socioeconomic Parity or Underclass Formation?" *Public Affairs Comment*. Austin: Lyndon B. Johnson School of Public Affairs, University of Texas at Austin.

Chávez, Leo R. 1992. *Shadowed Lives: Undocumented Immigrants in American Society*. Fort Worth, Tex.: Harcourt, Brace, Jovanovich.

Chávez, Linda. 1991. *Out of the Barrio: Toward a New Politics of Hispanic Assimilation*. New York: Basic Books.

Dayley, J. 1991. "One Big Happy Family," *Reader* (San Diego) 20 (17): 5–8.

Delgado-Gaitán, Concha, and Henry Trueba. 1991. *Crossing Cultural Borders: Education for Immigrant Families in America*. London: Falmer.

De Vos, George A. 1973. *Socialization for Achievement*. Berkeley: University of California Press.

———. 1980. "Ethnic Adaptation and Minority Status," *Journal of Cross-Cultural Psychology* 11 (1): 101–25.

De Vos, George A., and Marcelo Suárez-Orozco. 1990. *Status Inequality: The Self in Culture*. Newbury Park, Calif.: Sage.

Erikson, E. 1964. *Childhood and Society*. New York: W.W. Norton.

Falicov, Celia J. 1982. "Mexican Families." In *Ethnicity and Family Therapy*, edited by Monica McGoldrick, John K. Pearce, and Joseph Giordano. New York: Guilford.

Gamio, Manuel. 1971. *Mexican Immigration to the United States: A Study of Human Migration and Adjustment*. New York: Dover.

Gibson, Margaret A., and John U. Ogbu, eds. 1991. *Minority Status and Schooling: A Comparative Study of Immigrant and Involuntary Minorities.* New York: Garland.

Gorer, Geoffrey. 1963. *The American People: A Study in National Character.* Rev. ed. New York: W.W. Norton.

Grinberg, Leon, and Rebecca Grinberg. 1989. *Psychoanalytic Perspectives on Migration and Exile.* New Haven, Conn.: Yale University Press.

Hayner, Norman S. 1954. "The Family in Mexico," *Marriage and Family Living* 11:369–73.

Heller, Celia. 1966. *Mexican-American Youth: The Forgotten Youth at the Crossroads.* New York: Random House.

Henry, William. 1956. *The Analysis of Fantasy.* New York: J. Wiley and Sons.

Hollingshead, August B. 1975. "Four-Factor Index of Social Status." Working paper. New Haven, Conn.: Yale University.

Horowitz, Ruth. 1983. *Honor and the American Dream: Culture and Identity in a Chicano Community.* New Brunswick, N.J.: Rutgers University Press.

Kantrowitz, B., and L. Rosado. 1991. "Falling Further Behind," *Newsweek,* August 19, p. 60.

Karrer, Betty M. 1987. "Families of Mexican Descent: A Contextual Approach." In *Urban Family Medicine,* edited by Richard B. Birrer. New York: Springer-Verlag.

Keefe, Susan E., Amado M. Padilla, and M.L. Carlos. 1979. "The Mexican-American Extended Family as an Emotional Support System," *Human Organization* 38:144–52.

Lindzey, Gardner. 1961. *Projective Techniques and Cross-cultural Research.* New York: Appleton-Century-Crofts.

Matute-Bianchi, Maria E. 1991. "Situational Ethnicity and Patterns of School Performance among Immigrant and Nonimmigrant Mexican-descent Students." In *Minority Status and Schooling: A Comparative Study of Immigrant and Involuntary Minorities,* edited by Margaret A. Gibson and John U. Ogbu. New York: Garland.

McClelland, David. 1961. *The Achieving Society.* Princeton, N.J.: Van Nostrand.

McClelland, David, John W. Atkinson, R.H. Clark, and E.L. Lowell. 1953. *The Achievement Motive.* New York: Appleton-Century-Crofts.

Montiel, Miguel. 1970. "The Chicano Family: A Review of Research," *Social Work* 18 (3): 22–31.

Murillo, N. 1971. "The Mexican American Family." In *Chicanos: Social and Psychological Perspectives,* edited by Nathaniel Wagner and Marsha Haug. St. Louis: C.V. Mosby.

Ogbu, John U. 1978. *Minority Education and Caste: The American System its Cross-cultural Perspective.* Orlando, Fl.: Academic Press.

———. 1987. "Variability in Minority School Performance: A Problem in Search of an Explanation," *Anthropology and Education Quarterly* 18 (4): 312–34.

Padilla, Amado M., M. Alvarez, and Kathryn J. Lindholm. 1986. "Generational Status and Personality Factors as Predictors of Stress in Students," *Hispanic Journal of Behavioral Sciences* 8 (3): 275–88.

Pathey-Chávez, G. 1993. "High School as an Arena for Cultural Conflict and Acculturation for Latino Angelinos," *Anthropology and Education Quarterly* 24 (1): 33–60.

Rodriguez, Richard. 1983. *Hunger of Memory: The Education of Richard Rodriguez— An Autobiography.* New York: Bantam Books.

———. 1992. *Days of Obligation: An Argument with My Mexican Father.* New York: Viking.

Rogler, Lloyd, D. Cortés, and Robert Malgady. 1991. "Acculturation and Mental Health Status among Hispanics," *American Psychologist* 46 (6): 585–97.

Rogler, Lloyd H., Robert G. Malgady, and Orlando Rodríguez. 1989. *Hispanics and Mental Health: A Framework for Research.* Malabar, Fl.: Robert E. Krieger.

Sabogal, Fabio, Gerardo Marín, Regina Otero-Sabogal, Barbara V. Marín, and Eliseo Pérez-Stable. 1987. "Hispanic Familism and Acculturation: What Changes and What Doesn't?" *Hispanic Journal of Behavioral Sciences* 9 (4): 397–412.

Sluzki, Carlos E. 1979. "Migration and Family Conflict," *Family Process* 18 (4): 379—90.

Suárez-Orozco, Carola. 1993. "Generational Discontinuities: A Cross-cultural Comparison of Mexican, Mexican Immigrant, Mexican American and White Non-Hispanic Adolescents." Ph.D. dissertation, California School of Professional Psychology.

Suárez-Orozco, Carola, and Marcelo Suárez-Orozco. n.d. "The Cultural Psychology of Hispanic Immigrants." In *The Handbook of Hispanic Cultures in the United States,* edited by T. Weaver. Houston: Arte Público Press. In press.

Suárez-Orozco, Marcelo. 1989. *Central American Refugees and U.S. High Schools: A Psychosocial Study of Motivation and Achievement.* Stanford, Calif.: Stanford University Press.

Suárez-Orozco, Marcelo, and Carola Suárez-Orozco. 1993. "La psychologie culturelle des immigrants hispaniques aux Etats-Unis: implications pour la recherche en éducation," *Revue Française de Pédagogie* 101 (4): 27–44.

Trueba, Henry T. 1989. *Raising Silent Voices: Educating Linguistic Minorities for the 21st Century.* Cambridge: Newbury House.

Trueba, Henry T., C. Rodríguez, Yali Zou, and José Cintrón. 1993. *Healing Multicultural America: Mexican Immigrants Rise to Power in Rural California.* London: Falmer.

Vega, William A. 1990. "Hispanic Families in the 1980's: A Decade of Research," *Journal of Marriage and the Family* 52 (11): 1015–24.

Vernon, S.W., and R.E. Roberts. 1985. "A Comparison of Mexicans and Americans on Selected Measures of Social Support," *Hispanic Journal of Behavioral Sciences* 7:381–99.

Vigil, James D. 1988a. *Barrio Gangs: Street Life and Identity in Southern California.* Austin: University of Texas Press.

———. 1988b. "Group Processes and Street Identity: Adolescent Chicano Gang Members," *Ethos* 16 (4): 421–45.

CLASS 13

African Americans (Part I)

CHAPTER 18
What Ever Happened to Integration?
Tamar Jacoby.
Tamar Jacoby poses some serious questions about the progress of social integration in this country. She challenges both blacks and whites as well as the government's resolve to create a society that reflects social justice and equity.

CHAPTER 19
U.S. News Media:
A Content Analysis and Media Case Study
Pearlie Strother-Adams
Pearlie Strother-Adams conducts a content analysis using both broadcast and print media, which looks at the reportage of crimes committed by African American males against European Americans as well as the reportage of crimes committed by European American males. This study gives readers a candid look into the way media can either promote understanding and sympathy for an accused perpetrator, thus allowing in extenuating circumstances, or assist in creating a climate of hostility that indicts not only the alleged perpetrator but the whole group of which he belongs.

CHAPTER 18

What Ever Happened to Integration?

Tamar Jacoby

A journalist formerly on staff at *The New York Review of Books, Newsweek* and *The New York Times*, where she was deputy editor of the op-ed page, Tamar Jacoby is a senior fellow at the Manhattan Institute for Policy Research. She writes frequently about race and other social issues for *The Wall Street Journal, The New Republic, Commentary, Dissent* and other publications. She lives in Montclair, New Jersey.

It was late one night at *Newsweek,* and I was filing my story at the last minute, rushed and a little bleary-eyed. *Newsweek* in the late 1980s was not a happy place to work. Much of the editorial staff was disgruntled—hemmed in by editors, frustrated by the corporate culture, resentful of a schedule that required us to work till midnight and beyond most Friday nights. Many writers vented their unhappiness in e-mail messages: this editor cut my lead paragraph to shreds, that new layout leaves no room for my story. Sometimes the collective malaise got so bad, one colleague claimed, you could use it to power the computer system.

That Friday night, as I was finishing up, I stopped by my researcher's empty desk to look something up in a reference book. In those days, *Newsweek* writers were assisted by researchers, and I was working with a young black woman: attractive, able, personable, making her way up through the ranks at the magazine. I sat down in her chair to use the heavy volume and found myself staring at her computer screen, where she had left her e-mail open. The words jumped out at me, and though I knew I shouldn't, I couldn't stop myself from reading on. There were about two dozen messages sent and received over the past few weeks: another *Newsweek* litany of discontentment. The difference was that, unlike my own stored mail, virtually all of hers made some mention of color: that white editor won't give me an

assignment, that white scheduler put me on the late shift, that white librarian was rude to me, the white system will never be fair—to me or to us.

Like everyone in my generation, I had grown up hearing blacks talk about their anger at white society. As a student in the sixties and seventies, I'd met my share of black activists. More recently, as *Newsweek*'s law reporter, I had spent several weeks visiting juvenile detention centers and had been struck by the alienation I encountered among black inmates: kids who seemed to fed no sense of connection with the society whose laws they had broken. But my researcher was neither an activist nor an impoverished outsider. On the contrary, she seemed to be a privileged insider. The racial changes of the past few decades had opened doors for her at school and in the workplace. As far as I could tell from her lifestyle, there was little to distinguish her from other middle-class professionals her age, and already on a fast track at a national magazine, she faced a promising career in mainstream journalism. Besides, we all felt put upon by the system at *Newsweek.* Why had she come to see this common professional problem in racial terms, and why did she feel so irreparably cut off from her white peers?

The young woman's alienation stayed with me in the weeks to come, the kind of glimpse few of us ever get into how someone else sees the world, and the more I thought about it, the more I wondered: what exactly is the goal of race relations in

America today—and is there any hope of achieving it if even this successful young journalist still does not feel she belongs?

Like most whites of my generation, I had always thought the goal was integration. I came of age politically in the years when the very word had a kind of magic to it—a vague but shining dream of social equality and fairness for all. In the years that followed, I watched as both blacks and whites fought for the ideal on a variety of fronts: first taking the signs off water fountains, then securing the right to vote, desegregating local school systems, bringing blacks into the corporate world, struggling to create a sense of political cohesion between cities and their suburbs. Inclusion turned out to be a delicate, time-consuming process; the front keeps moving, and the challenges grow more and more subtle. But blacks as a group have made enormous progress in three or four decades. The middle class has quadrupled, education levels have soared, blacks are increasingly well represented in electoral politics and other influential realms of national life.

Still, as I thought about my *Newsweek* researcher, I had to wonder if full integration was really possible. Like a growing number of blacks in America, she was leading an integrated life, but for her this hard-won achievement seemed all but meaningless. Accomplished as she was, she still felt deeply alienated, an uncomfortable and unwelcome visitor in someone else's house. "I've seen plenty of physical integration," a black college student said to me a few weeks later. "That doesn't guarantee integration of the heart." Like my researcher, he seemed to feel irreparably cut off from what he saw as the white world, and the more I thought about them both, the larger the question loomed: how close have we come to integration, and can we ever hope to bridge the remaining gap?

If integration is still most Americans' idea of the goal, few of us talk about it any more. The word has a quaint ring today—like "gramophone" or "nylons," it is a relic of another era—and the ideal, under any name, has just about fallen out of most discussions about race. The focus now is on diversity, and few of us stop to ask if it is really compatible with the goals of the civil rights movement. We reflexively honor Martin Luther King, Jr., but not many still pursue the vision he called "the beloved community": a vision of a more or less race-neutral America in which both blacks and whites would feel they belong. Today, the word "community" means not one integrated nation but a minority enclave, as in "the black community." "Brother" evokes not the brotherhood of man but the solidarity of color. "*It's a black thing, you wouldn't understand,*" the T-shirts say—and few of us question the underlying assumption.

Only a tiny minority, black or white, have repudiated integration outright, but increasingly on both sides there is a new contrary mood. Some whites, tired of the issue and the emotion that comes with it, have grown indifferent to blacks' problems. Others, black and white, think of integration as a sentimental notion, more or less irrelevant to the real problems of race in America—black poverty, black joblessness, black advancement. Still others, particularly blacks embittered by a long history of exclusion, view the old color-blind dream as a pernicious concept, rightly superseded by identity politics. Left, right, poor and middle class all have their own reasons: everything from anger to callused neglect. But together, wittingly or not, we as a nation are dropping the flag, turning our backs on the great achievement of the civil rights era—the hopeful consensus that formed in the 1960s around King's vision of a single, shared community.

In fact, since Emancipation, most blacks with any realistic hope of inclusion have chosen to try to make their way into the political and economic mainstream. The first nationally known black spokesman, Frederick Douglass, was an ardent integrationist, and the popular thrust from the nineteenth century onward was for incorporation in the body politic. Of course, there was always another tendency, too: the proud and often angry separatism that flourished in the ghetto in periods, like the 1930s, when integration looked least likely. Yet even when the prospects were bleakest, most blacks nourished some long-term hope and pursued every chance they got to participate in the mainstream. Eventually, in the early 1960s, a critical mass of whites espoused the ideal, and the nation set out on the difficult course of trying to accelerate the long-delayed process. But paradoxically, even as America moved toward full inclusion, more and more younger blacks began to turn away, embracing a modern-day variant of separatism.

This new insularity has emerged starkly for everyone to see in the years since I stumbled on my researcher's e-mail. Unlike the street-corner chauvinism popularized by Marcus Garvey and others in the 1930s, today's separatism does not dream of a return to Africa. Unlike the Nation of Islam, it involves few rituals or regimens. Following in the path set by these predecessors, its first tenet is self-respect, although like both of them it also has a sharper edge. More an attitude than an ideology or even a political program, it is part pride, part disappointment with whites, part diffidence—an uneasiness about competing in the mainstream—part defensiveness and part resentful defiance. It shows up most plainly in Afrocentric curriculums and celebrations of black culture, but also in the NAACP's public ambivalence about school desegregation and the widespread feeling among black youth that to do well in class is somehow shameful—"acting white."

This new, "soft" form of the old separatist vision is capturing poor and better-off blacks alike. It caught on first on the left, among movement veterans, but then spread through the moderate middle and on to the new black right, where prominent conservatives like Clarence Thomas now doubt the value of mixed schooling and maintain that only blacks can help less privileged blacks out of poverty. Gangsta rap, Louis Farrakhan's Million Man March, Spike Lee's film *Malcolm X* and the reverential following it awakened all reflect and enshrine the credo—that the system is inherently prejudiced, that blacks are somehow fundamentally different from whites, that they will never be fully at home in America, that they are right to be angry and that only good can come of cultivating this bitterness.

Unlike old-fashioned black nationalism, the new separatism often coexists with functional integrationism. Young black professionals are making their way into the system and up the ladders of mainstream success, but a large number of them cling to their mistrust even as they enjoy the fruits of the "white world." Accomplished as they are, many seem to feel the system is rigged against them and that as long as racism exists, their abilities will carry them only so far. After decades of effort, some of their parents too have managed to create comfortable, middle-class lives, all but indistinguishable from those of white

middle-class families. Yet even these prosperous citizens, wary of prejudice, often prefer to live in a realm apart: to buy homes and worship and spend their leisure time in the racial comfort zones of self-segregated suburbs.

Strangest of all, the white mainstream is encouraging this clannishness—in the name of integration. The government fosters color-coded hiring, voting and school admissions. Businesses like Time Warner lead the way in promoting gangsta rap; others have remade their corporate cultures to nourish a sense of diversity and color consciousness. Philanthropic institutions like the Ford Foundation fund the development of black curriculums. Magazines like *The New Yorker* publish profiles of black figures—intellectuals, celebrities, sports heroes and others—that make a shibboleth of "how black" they are. In the name of racial justice, of accommodation and respect, the mainstream culture has embraced the new black separatism. The idea is to make blacks feel more welcome, to honor their historical grievances and incorporate their culture into the mainstream. But in the long run, this well-meaning endorsement of separatism can only help prevent the realization of the civil rights vision.

Even under the best of circumstances, nationalism of the kind coursing through the black community would be difficult for Americans to accommodate—hard to square with our universalist values and our sense of a nation based not on blood but on political principle. But whatever the benefits of the new separatism in promoting pride and self-esteem, the overlay of anger and alienation that comes with it is poisoning our lives, both black and white.

Underclass youths ruin their own futures by declining to make an effort in "the white man's school." Others refuse to obey the "white" law. Even the most promising, middle-class black students are encouraged to feel put upon, different and forever apart. In the image of Malcolm X, they embrace anger as their identity—and then spend the rest of their lives trying to deal with its corrosive side effects. As for whites, the conventional wisdom that there are two separate and different communities has become an excuse for ignorance, indifference and worse. Increasingly resentful and put off by racial rhetoric, many feel little responsibility for even neighboring black poverty. Others—including those who believe themselves free of prejudice—still harbor half-conscious notions of black inferiority. Cut off from all but superficial contact and encouraged to think that black culture is different, their stereotypes only grow worse.

When did this happen? How and why? Have we Americans really agreed to give up on a common humanity? I don't think so. I believe most people still feel that what blacks and whites have in common is more important than their differences. Despite their anger and alienation, most blacks still want in—and most whites still want to do what they can to make this the land of opportunity they have been taught to believe it is. But if most Americans still believe in integration, they don't know how to reconcile it with diversity and identity politics—and meanwhile the nation is sliding haplessly toward a future that leaves less and less room for commonality.

What ever happened to integration? Do we as a nation recognize how dramatically we have changed course? What consequences will this unexamined turn hold for the future of black and white America? The answers to all these questions lie in the history of the past few decades and in choices made on the ground, at the local level, by individuals.

The failure of integration is a national failure, but as with politics, all race relations are local. The dynamics of our misunderstandings are invariably personal and shaped in some way by context—by a region's past, by its changing economy, by the quality of its civic leadership. Besides, wherever the mistakes begin, the tragedy usually plays out at the local level: in the streets; at City Hall; in a schoolyard or a downtown boardroom where blacks and whites encounter each other, both trying awkwardly to readjust their relationship, and end up talking past each other or worse. On the theory that the best way to see what went wrong is to look up close, this book traces race relations in three cities: New York, Detroit and Atlanta.

Why chart the history of a largely failed initiative? Integration's most convincing critics base their argument on history. We tried it, they say, and it didn't work. To a degree, the skeptics are right. Much of what we've tried in the past few decades hasn't worked. For all the progress made, the crusade has failed. But it failed, I am convinced, because we as a nation went about it wrong—and

if we could learn from these years of mistakes, we could still, I believe, achieve real integration. That is why what follows is a work of history: an effort to disentangle the ideal from the flawed means used to pursue it. What dead ends did we turn down? What doubts led us to lose sight of the goal? What well-meaning efforts led in exactly the opposite direction, not toward a sense of community but toward ever more angry divisiveness?

In New York in the 1960s, as at the federal level in Washington, hopes ran high. Race relations, it was thought, were something white society could fix: with the right strategy and enough money, government could solve the problem. A handsome young mayor, John Lindsay, teamed up with the brilliant new president of one of the nation's most powerful foundations, Ford's McGeorge Bundy, and together they set out to make the city an experimental laboratory. "Little City Halls," neighborhood empowerment, community control of schools: all were tested in New York, as Lindsay, Bundy and their allies in the city's liberal elite moved to translate the integrationist ideal into a practical agenda. What can the government do to spur integration? How much can be ameliorated by caring and charisma like Lindsay's? The New York chapters are a lesson in the limits of white goodwill and sixties-style top-down engineering.

In Detroit, it was the election of a black mayor that made the city an important test case: just what difference can black leadership make? Already by the late 1960s, race relations were worse than almost anywhere else in the country. Blacks and whites reacted to the nation's most destructive riot by flatly giving up on integration. Whites moved to the suburbs; few blacks seemed sorry to see them go. A long court battle over busing between city and suburb only reinforced both sides' prejudices, and angry attitudes were still hardening when Coleman Young was elected in 1973. Could a longtime militant like Young come in from the cold and function successfully inside the system? Or would he see his mayoralty as a chance to create Black Power in one city, defying white suburbanites and alienating them further? Young's Detroit is a study in the consequences of choosing against integration.

If Detroit is a worst case—the failure of integration at its most stark—Atlanta is often celebrated as a model of racial harmony. The success story of the civil rights movement, now the jewel in the crown of the New South, it is a city where both blacks and whites prosper. Blacks have taken over local government but whites have stayed; a highly regarded affirmative action program has helped spawn a new middle class, and both blacks and whites feel they have a stake in a booming future. But even boosterish Atlantans have to admit that integration is eluding them. Whites live on one side of the city, blacks on the other, their tree-lined neighborhoods often indistinguishable but still color-coded—voluntarily so. Relations between black and white rarely go beyond workaday formality and, if anything, are said by many to be getting worse. "Race relations?" asked one man in the mid-1990s. "We don't have race relations in Atlanta any more." This half-success makes Atlanta a critical test: Is real integration possible in America today? Or is peaceful coexistence as good as it gets?

It's not a good record for three decades of effort. Yet most people still seem to believe in inclusion—still assume that's where we're headed in the long run. Corporations that insist on diversity training hope it will bring workers together. Middle-class blacks in segregated suburbs devote their lives to making it easier for their kids to join and prosper in the mainstream. Even whites who feel that race is no longer their problem, that there is nothing they or the government can do to help, assume that the field has been leveled and that most blacks are making it on their own. Ambivalent, inconsistent, hypocritical as we sometimes sound, the enduring moral power of integration still holds most of us in its sway, challenging us with the hope we once shared to return to the path we've lost.

What the past shows, more than anything, is that for thirty-five years we have been pursuing the vision with flawed means. Wholesale social engineering, color-coded double standards, forced interaction between people who are not social or economic equals; one after the other, the old stratagems have proved bankrupt or worse. But that does not mean the nation must give up its long-cherished ideal. Integration is in decline as a goal not so much because we don't believe in it but because we've failed to get there. The means haven't worked, or have made the problem worse, and when one road after another leads to a dead end, it's natural to start believing we can't get there from here. Devising new strategies will

not be easy, but history can guide us, if we know how to listen.

Some readers will argue that I've made things too complicated. " 'What ever happened to integration?' " they'll ask "The answer is obvious. It was sandbagged by racism." They aren't wrong. The reason inclusion is a problem to begin with clearly traces back to bigotry: hundreds of years of shameful practice and attitudes with continuing consequences, painful and dehumanizing, for whites as well as blacks. Nor is racism dead. For all the whites who care about integration, there are plenty who don't—who never backed it, or who gave up long ago. Even whites who would like to think well of blacks and treat them fairly harbor all kinds of prejudices: irrepressible preconceptions and patronizing impulses. No honest white can pretend otherwise. Still, to say it was white racism that killed integration is not exactly right. Black alienation and black bigotry have played a part too, and though they may be rooted in white mistreatment, they have taken on lives of their own. No change in white attitudes alone, however dramatic, is going to solve the problem.

In fact, white attitudes have shifted significantly in recent years. As recently as 1940, more than two-thirds of whites believed blacks were less intelligent. Today, under 6 percent think so. Before World War II, no more than 40 percent, even in the North, endorsed desegregation of any kind. Today, it's hard to find a white person who will tell a pollster he does not believe blacks belong in the mainstream. Whites of all ages look back on the civil rights movement as one of the high points of American history, and more whites than blacks—in the 95 to 100 percent range— defend the idea of integration. Still, for all the progress, there is no denying that resentment persists. Large numbers of whites—40 to 60 percent—tell pollsters that blacks could do better if they tried harder. Whites from all regions bitterly condemn what they see as black demands for special treatment. And this anger often spills over into what sounds like old-fashioned prejudice—in corporate offices, on campus, in a resurgence of racial jokes.

Just what accounts for this new resentment is not easy to untangle, but it is not always the same as out-and-out bigotry. A white man who thinks a black woman on welfare should get a job may in fact be responding to her color, voicing an ugly and unthinking assumption about black attitudes toward work. Or he may be reacting to something he didn't like in the racial rhetoric of recent decades: the claim that white society is responsible for the problems blacks face. Thirty-five years of color-coded conflict have taken a huge toll on both sides, and fairly or not the showdown has left many whites embittered. Their feelings may be an obstacle to harmony, but they are not necessarily prejudice in the conventional sense.

Far more damaging today than the old bigotry is the condescension of well-meaning whites who think that they are advancing race relations by encouraging alienation and identity politics. After three hundred years of unfulfilled promises, it's not surprising that even the most successful blacks mistrust whites and that many hesitate to cast their lot with the system that held their people back for so long. But no one is served by a mainstream culture that spurs this estrangement, encouraging blacks to believe that the system is inherently racist and that all responsibility for change lies with whites. Well-intentioned as such deference is, it will not lead to inclusion. It will not empower blacks or make them feel more welcome. On the contrary, it can only delay the kind of push that is still needed to bridge the gap, particularly for the poorest blacks with the fewest chances and most meager skills.

As a white woman writing about race, I know my own color will be an issue for some readers. What do I know about how black people feel? How dare I presume to speak for them? How could I possibly describe what goes on between blacks and whites in a fair or objective way? I can only reply that this is what writers do. They tell stories about other people, usually different in some way from themselves, and they do their best to imagine those people's feelings, to recreate their thoughts and points of view. The racial perception gap may sometimes make this task a little harder. But as someone who believes that blacks and whites have more in common than what separates us, I don't think the difficulty is as great as some racial absolutists suggest, and I refuse to concede that racial inclusion is somehow a "black" subject. On the contrary, I believe it is a challenge for all Americans—the ultimate test we face as a nation. As for objectivity, readers will have to judge for themselves. This book contains heroes and villains on both sides of the color line. A small note tacked

to the bulletin board above my desk reminds me daily: "If you can't call a black thug a thug, you're a racist." It is an idea I stand by.

Can the integrationist ideal be revived and reshaped to make sense in the racially jaded 1990s and beyond? I don't see any alternative.

Seductive as the other path may sometimes seem, it would soon lead into unlivable territory. How would the social contract hold in a nation where separate communities no longer felt bound or responsible to each other? Why should people pay taxes for social services to help others with whom they feel they have nothing in common? The rising indifference between city and suburb is already taking its toll, and it would only get worse if we were to give up all hope of a shared community. Then there's the law: the social order. The estrangement of my integrated, middle-class researcher is nothing compared to the alienation one hears from young people in prisons and reformatories. Poorer, less privileged black youth don't just feel like unwelcome guests in a white world; they believe they are trapped in an enemy camp. When they break the law—the rules of a game they feel they're excluded from—many express little or no remorse, and this in turn only erodes what white concern remains for blacks' problems.

In the end, we have no choice. The alternative to integration is not, as many hope, a rich feast of diversity. Far more likely, given America's history and the enduring problems many blacks face, a decision to give up on inclusion would leave us with a permanent, festering sore: a bitter juxtaposition of inside and outside that would consume all our energies and sap our morale. Neither blacks nor whites would benefit, and no one could escape the moral corruption, which would eventually spread to all realms of national life. The political values we've inherited could not survive in a nation divided. If the civil rights era taught us anything, it was that—and slow as we were to grasp the lesson, it is not something we can forget now.

The corrosive effects of division—of living next door to someone with whom you feel no connection—are already all too evident in too many communities. Many of the people I spoke to in the suburbs of Atlanta and Detroit feel regretful about the way they've chosen to live: guilty, concerned— but, because of the gulf, often helpless to make a difference. Others live in denial, nostalgic for their cities but not sure exactly what it is they miss. Still others are simply hardened, and although they don't know it, they make the most powerful case for recovering a sense of shared community. By accepting the partition of city and suburb, giving up all sense of concern and responsibility, they have abandoned not just the poor blacks in their midst but also the ideals on which the nation is based. As for those blacks who choose separatism, it's hard to see how they benefit in the long run, cut off from the possibilities that the mainstream has to offer.

Just what would real integration mean? What would it look like? It's difficult to say from here. By definition, inclusion is an ideal—more a beacon than a concrete prescription. The closer we've come over the years, the more specifically and realistically we've envisioned the goal. We know now that it will take more than physical mingling; we know it starts but doesn't end with equal opportunity, and we know it won't look like the monotone conformity some people imagined in the 1950s. As my alienated *Newsweek* researcher makes all too clear, ultimately inclusion is about feeling you belong, but we still do not know much about how to foster that sense of a shared society. The government policies of the last three decades have met with mixed results, often unleashing more harm than good, though that does not mean, as some conservatives argue, that there is nothing the state can do.

Government, business, media, popular culture and activists on both sides of the color line: we have all contributed to the failure of integration, and we must all be part of a renewed effort. The best place to pick up the trail is where we lost it, bit by bit over the last few decades. Only by looking at the past can we see how much the turn away from integration has cost us. Only by understanding our failures can we hope to do better in the future—finding new, more workable ways to achieve the community most Americans long for.

CHAPTER 19

U.S. News Media:
A Content Analysis and Media Case Study

Pearlie Strother-Adams

Introduction

Media representation can either promote attitudes of acceptance or encourage fear and/ or hostility. When possible, educators might consider incorporating content analysis of media into their classroom activities to give students an opportunity to see how both print and broadcast media work to create, shape, and promote cultural trends, thus influencing the formation and spreading of stereotypical cultural concepts and conclusions.

In the midst of such media images as Willie Horton (1988, George Bush presidential campaign) and Susan Smith's phantom kidnapper/car jacker (1994). I began to wonder how often such images are featured in the media and to what end. In essence, how effective are such representations and for what purpose? Hopefully, this study of media images of African American males, though not exhaustive, will provide students with some insight into conducting a media content analysis. I focus on coverage of crimes, allegedly committed by African American and European American male offenders, that involve race. I include an analysis of the media of the late 1800s to mid 1900s that reveals media's role in promoting and perpetuating racism and a spirit of mob violence that, I contend, echoes in the U.S. today.

George Simpson (1936), in a study of the Philadelphia press, discussed the invisibility of African Americans in the mainstream press except for their stereotypical portrayals as perpetrators of violent crimes, and, in a report of the National Advisory Commission on Civil Disorder (Kerner, 1968), the Kerner Commission criticized main-stream media's tendency to focus on negative images of African Americans as a contributing factor to racism.

Selected Literature Review

While many studies (see Ginzburg, 1988; Raper, 1969; Howard, 1995, for further examples) have examined the effects of mainstream media coverage of African Americans, few have touched upon the relationship between the stereotypical, provocative "lynch mob" style of language created and popularized by U.S. media and key political figures in the period from the late 1800s to the mid 1900s that are still used today to describe African American males alleged to have committed crimes against whites, particularly white women. The negative descriptors or depictions used in today's media echo the earlier sentiments and language when such crimes are reported. Though little research draws a direct correlation between the language of the late 1800s to mid 1900s and that of today, a body of evidence supports this claim. More literature that better synthesizes, interprets, and explains this evidence, however, is needed. Further explanation of this continuing phenomenon of negative images and its evolution are also needed.

Corea (1990) examined media portrayals of African Americans in television news and their impact on white perceptions of African American offenders as well as on the African American community. Corea also studied the limited positions of power African Americans have in the media and how negative portrayals are in part due to this. Corea looked specifically at television coverage of two highly publicized cases of rape and violence and in one instance, murder. According to Corea, the television coverage of the 1989 attack (beating and rape) of a young white woman, known as the "Central Park Jogger," by African American males and a Hispanic male, assumed that all African American men are liable to be violent, cruel, and vicious. Unlike white males who commit similar crimes or worse, Corea pointed out, these male offenders were not afforded any extenuating circumstances to excuse their behavior. In essence, growing up in a deprived situation and coming from low socioeconomic backgrounds were used against them. They were assailed by the press, leading the white community to suggest they be castrated, locked up with no hope of parole, and eventually sentenced to death. This contrasted sharply with what the press deemed the "Preppie Murder," said Corea, where a young, wealthy, white male raped and murdered a young, white woman in Central Park in 1987. The white male was represented in the press as a "Preppie" behaving out of character. In short, society was asked to forgive him. His victim, the young white woman, was treated as a "quasi prostitute"; her fate, the media suggested, was her own fault as they hinted she was a bit wild.

Corea concluded media promote the belief that white males are not prone to violence and are coerced to commit such acts only under extenuating circumstances, while African Americans have an "inherent tendency to mug, rape, and otherwise disrupt the normal orderly processes characteristic of white society" (p. 261). Corea's findings are noteworthy; however, a larger sample of cases would prove more conclusive. Corea used two cases from the same area, using the same media, one of the strengths of her study. Though she provides no samples from other areas of the country, her research is a valuable, concise, analytical work comparing and contrasting the coverage of African American and white male offenders in situations involving crimes committed in the same location against white women and adds a great deal to media study. Ironically, as Corea put it, the white male offender, who raped and murdered his female, white victim, is shown compassion in the press, while the African American offenders, who raped and beat their female, white victim are demonized.

A more extensive scholarly study (Gomes & Williams, 1990) challenged the accuracy of media portrayals of the relationship between race and crime, primarily using *Boston Globe* and *Boston Herald* accounts of the 1989 Charles Stuart case. Stuart, a furrier earning over $100,000 a year, accused a phantom black man of shooting and wounding him severely and killing his pregnant, attorney wife. The press, according to the study, generated disgust for the accused man but also raised questions about a community that could produce such a "gruesome" murderer. Press accounts of a community "run wild," populated with "animalistic" people, became common. Once a suspect was arrested, he was described as uneducated, mentally deficient, and "monstrous," with the press usually identifying him as "the killer" rather than a suspect (Gomes & Williams, p. 58). Elected officials called for a reinstatement of the death penalty, and Mission Hill's black residents were subjected to indiscriminate police harassment such as "stop and search" procedures. Stuart himself was later accused of the crime by his brother who confessed to being an unwitting accomplice. Charles Stuart's understanding of the potency of blaming an African American man, Gomes and Williams assert, was grounded in a long history of media popularization of an existing relationship between crime and race. They concluded: "African American perpetrators of crime tend to receive exaggerated coverage, especially when the victim is white" (p. 59). This study is crucial in investigations of the 1994 Susan Smith case.

Susan Smith, a young white mother first claimed her two sons were kidnapped when a black man, waving a handgun and wearing a knit cap and a flannel shirt, car jacked her vehicle and order her to get out, while refusing to let the children go. Smith later admitted to strapping her two sons into her car and drowning them. The Gomes and Williams study pointed out the dynamics of such uses of negative perceptions of African American males: having a white woman yell "black man" can work today as it did in the 1800s and in 1923 in Rosewood, Florida, when African Americans were run out of their homes, and many of them killed, when a white woman accused a "Negro" of attacking her (see Tolnay & Beck, p. 211).

Stereotypical depictions of African American males in the late 1800s to mid 1900s are strikingly similar to those prevalent in media today. Brundage (1988) looked at lynching in Georgia and Virginia from 1880 to 1930. According to his study, one of the loudest political expressions of racist dogma came from a Governor Hoke Smith, editor of the *Atlanta Journal* when he referred to the "Negro" as "beast rapists" who needed to be held down by force as they "degenerated towards extinction" (p. 198). Character assassination was central in the media's early campaign against African American men (see Raper 1969; Smead, 1986; Howard, 1995), but Brundage's work is supremely valuable in that it examined lynch mob violence as communal. Through a comparison of lynching statistics in Virginia and Georgia, Brundage connected the systemic violence perpetrated upon African Americans between 1880 and 1930 in southern Georgia to the white man's need to control and suppress African Americans in the "cotton belt" (p. 108). He concluded that the seriousness with which Southern whites viewed the need to subordinate African American sharecroppers often resulted in a communal quality of lynching. Like Corea, Brundage provided evidence of the use of provocative, stereotypical language in the press from the early 1800s to the 1930s as well as evidence to support the media's effectiveness in promoting a lynch mob mentality.

In a historical study Tolnay and Beck (1995) analyzed Southern newspaper accounts of lynch mob violence perpetrated on African Americans between 1882 and 1930 and found that editorials in the mainstream Southern press supported a "Doctrine of Radical Racism," ascribing to black behavior urges and instincts more characteristic of lower animals than humans. This study substantiates Gomes and Williams' research and ties the term "animalistic," which was used to describe the phantom killer in the Stuart case, directly to the description of African American males dating back to the early 1800s,

Tolnay and Beck document a change from a view of the African American slave as a childlike creature in need of a paternal master to the more malignant image of a subhuman, animalistic creature (p. 89). African American males were described as "beastly and loathsome" while also being characterized as strangely attracted to the white woman. The rape of a white woman by a "Negro" was the most "malignant atrocity" having no "reflection" in the "whole extent of the natural history of the most bestial and ferocious criminals" (Tolnay & Beck, pp. 89–90). In short, rape by a black man was described as a crime more vicious than rape itself. This recalls Corea's (1990) conclusion that African American men suspected of raping a white woman are viewed more harshly than a white man who committed both rape and murder (Central Park jogger-rape and Preppie Murder).

Finally, Ginzburg (1988) provides scholars with a much needed reference to specific cases of lynch mob violence over a period of 100 years. Typical of the news accounts he assembled is a story of the lynching of Sam Holt in Georgia. The *Kissimee Valley Florida Gazette* picked the story up on April 28, 1899. Holt, burned at the stake for the alleged crimes of killing a white man and raping the victim's wife, is described as being as brave as a man could be in such a matter, only murmuring a sound when knives plunged into his flesh and his "life blood sizzled in the flames" (p. 11). His lynching, like many others, was attended by as many as 2000, a crowd of both townspeople and others who came from good distances to see the affair. Ginzburg reports that a placard placed on the hanging tree read: "We must protect Southern women at all costs." Another sign warned "darkies" to beware (pp. 13–21). Such a warning was common in the case of violence perpetrated against African Americans during the period. This is demonstrated in many of the articles featured in Ginzburg's collection. The events are depicted as the root of what Corea and Gomes and Williams discuss in their studies as the tendency of mobs, with encouragement from the media, to hold the whole African American community hostage when a crime is reportedly committed by one. Ginzburg's collection of articles extends into the 1960s and includes stories from a variety of newspapers, both liberal and conservative, both black and white. While not an analytical study, Ginzburg's selections make apparent the stereotypical, provocative language so often used and allow for an analysis of the coverage of events from different angles and perspectives.

Research Overview

My study examined several primary sources using textual analysis and led me to themes and patterns evident through linguistic and qualitative analysis.

Although I examined many news articles and editorials as well as broadcast transcripts in this study. I will feature only news coverage here. The particular news programs I used are CNN's "Larry King Live" and ABC's "20/20." The print media are newspapers: the *New York Times, Los Angeles Times, Boston Globe,* and *USA Today.* The cases were selected because they were high profile and received a great deal of media attention. All involve a racial element except one. the "Sam Manzie" case, which added a much needed element in that Manzie is a white male accused of a crime against a white child. A comparison of Manzie's treatment in the media to the treatment of African American males proved valuable in two ways: as an example of a white male being vindicated in the murder of a white child (a case that deserves study along class lines) and as an indication that white males are often protected in the system and are not harshly treated even if the victim is white. More study in this area is greatly needed. The cases I used are:

- Susan Smith's,
- Sam Manzie's,
- Charles Stuart's and
- the rape and murders of Sherrice Iverson and the Central Park Jogger.

ACTUAL EXCERPTS FROM BROADCAST TRANSCRIPTS

Case 1: The Susan Smith alleged car jacking and kidnapping in South Carolina.

Larry King: . . . If you drive a car, listen up. You don't want to be the victim of a car jacking. Take it from Susan Smith. Her worst nightmare began 48 hours ago. . . .

Asking about the sketch of the phantom black man, the alleged kidnapper, car jacker: Larry King: Can you put that up closer to—put it right on camera. Let's see what it looks like . . . Hold it up a little. Hold the paper up a little. [Shows pic-

ture of alleged assailant]. After a commercial: Welcome back to . . . . And joining us are two who know how to throw the book at car jackers. Representative Charles Schumer wrote the first federal car jacking law and co-sponsored a bill signed last month by President Clinton, making car jacking a death-penalty offense. . . .

Rep. Charles Schumer:. . . There are various degrees depending on the harm done to the person. The recent crime bill reintroduced capital punishment . . . in the most heinous of offenses.

"Larry King Live" CNN Report on October 27, 1994

Case 2: Sam Manzie. accused murderer of 11-year-old Eddie Werner

Hugh Downs: The parents of Sam Manzie tell their story. Sam Manzie, 15, killed an eleven-year-old boy who came to his home selling candy and gift wrapping paper. Prior to the murder, Manzie was seduced via the Internet by a white male pedophile. . . . You have seen the dark side of the new computer technology.

Barbara Walters: . . . What the country heard about was the murder of an 11-year-old boy, killed while selling candy door-to-door in the neighborhood. . . . Sam Manzie's parents. . . talk publicly about what went wrong when they were trying to do everything right. Their story is heartbreaking. It is also a powerful warning to all young people and the parents who love them. . . . A nightmare with terrifying images. The 43-year-old who lures a 14-year-old Internet buddy into unimaginable depravity. An innocent 11-year-old who becomes the victim of the other boy's torment. . . . When the secret came out, . . . Sam apparently snapped, and this 11-year-old, Eddie Werner, became the target of Sam's rage and shame. How could this tragedy happen in a family that seemed so filled with affection, where parenting was taken so seriously? . . . Manzie was the perfect target for the sexual predators who freely roam the Internet . . . confused about his sexual identity, tortured by it, and he was lonely . . . grades, mostly A's until then, plummeted . . . behavior . . . erratic. . . .

Hugh Downs: It's a story not only about the Internet . . ., but about how the system failed a family in need and the community. . . .

"Sam's Story," ABC's "20/20,"
October 31, 1997

Case 3: The murder of 7-year-old Sherrice Iverson in a casino

ABC's "20/20," with an introduction from Barbara Walters and a special ABC News report from Antonio Mora, September 12, 1997: "Where are Their Parents? Children Roam Casinos while Their Parents Gamble." A seven-year-old girl is molested and murdered in a casino. The focus of this story, however, is the neglect of children, in general, in casinos. The murdered child is mentioned once on page four of the twenty-eight-page transcript.

Barbara Walters: Antonio Mora has startling footage of a growing and outrageous trend. As you'll see, when the chips are down the children have the most to lose.

Antonio Mora (voice-over): It looks like every child's fantasy land—medieval castles, side by side with Egyptian pyramids, battling pirate ships next door to a lava-spewing volcano. And down the street, towering buildings that scrape the sky . . . the perfect place for baby boomers to bring their kids. . . . But what happens to the kids after the roller coaster and the pools shut down? "20/20" decided to investigate. . . . Young kids, . . . in the wee hours of the morning, loitering just off the casino floors, waiting for their parents to quit gambling. . ., a tired 14-year-old holding her more tired five-year-old brother. At 2:00 a.m. . . .

Philip Coltoff, Children's Aid Society: It's neglect. It's wrong. It's dangerous . . . something at some point very bad is going to happen to children. Very dangerous.

Antonio Mora (voice over): Something very bad did happen this spring to little Sherrice Iverson (photo) at a casino just outside Las Vegas. At about 3:45 am., casino security cameras show the seven-year-old running into a bathroom with a young man following. There, he allegedly sexually assaulted Sherrice and then snapped her head. breaking her neck. At the time of the murder Sherrice's father was

gambling. . . . Months later, we still found dozens of parents like him, willing to play the slots, even if it meant playing roulette with their children's safety. . . . The law, as far as I can tell, is being violated right here, right now. . . . Some casinos are trying to address the problem of neglected children. . . .

ABC's "20/20." October 31, 1997

EXCERPTS FROM NEWSPAPER ARTICLES

Case 1: Susan Smith: Alleged kidnapping and car jacking

The majority of articles examined in print media were done with extreme caution and are discussed below.

Case 2: Sam Manzie, fifteen-year-old accused murderer of eleven-year-old Edward Werner

'Suspect in New Jersey Strangling was Reportedly Sex-Case Victim: Fifteen-year-old Sam Manzie murderer of eleven-year-old, Edward P. Werner, was seduced via the Internet by Stephen P. Simmons, 43, Holbrook, N.Y." ". . . Just as the slaying raised concerns about the safety of children venturing to the doors of strangers, the latest revelations raised new concerns about the safety of children roaming the Internet."

Robert McFadden, *New York Times*
Oct. 3, 1997

"Days Before Slaying, Parents of Suspect Pleaded for Help." "Three days before . . ., a state judge refused to order that the 15-year-old be committed. . . ."

Robert Hanley, *New York Times*,
Oct. 4, 1997, p. 5

Case 3: The murder of 7-year-old Sherrice Iverson in a casino

Casino Surveillance Footage Tells Story of Girl's Killing; Crime: Man follows her into restroom, emerges later. Officials warn children shouldn't be left alone in arcades. . . . It was there, next to an arcade with pinball games and Homer Hippo and Ms. Pac-Man, that 7-year-old Sherrice Iverson was killed in the wee hours of Sunday morning. Her strangled body was found seated on a toilet in a restroom stall. The father then demanded that the casino give him a six-Pack of beer and $100, pay for the girl's funeral, fly the girl's mother to Las Vegas from Los Angeles and provide him and the mother a room for the night, the source said. At 1:33 a.m. hotel security officials had noticed that the little girl was unattended . . . left alone . . . she played in the arcade . . . her father in the upstairs casino.

> Tom Gorman, *Los Angeles Times*,
> May 28, 1997, p.5

"Suspect told two classmates of the casino crime, and their parents called police. He is described as a smart but troubled youth . . . Jeremy Joseph Stromeyer, a once-promising 18-year-old high school senior . . . was behind bars . . . as the suspected killer of 7-year-old Sherrice Iverson, who was raped and slain this week at a Nevada state-line casino. . . .

> Jeff Leeds & James Rainey,
> the *Los Angeles Times*, May 30, 1997, p.2

"Officials Call Girl's slaying a Tragic example of Neglect; Children: Authorities in O.C. say many parents leave kids unsupervised and in periling malls, theaters and parks."

> Bonnie Hayes & Emily Otani,
> the *Los Angeles Times*, May 29, 1997

"Slaying Fuels Debate Over Children's Safety in Casinos; Crime: Unattended youngsters are major problem."

> Tom Gorman & John Mitchell,
> the *Los Angeles Times*, May 29, 1997, p.1

"Supervision of children can't Be a Sometime Thing; slaying raises Questions About parental and casino oversight.

> Editorial, the *Los Angeles Times*,
> May 29, 1997

"Suspect in girl's slaying at casino in custody." "Jeremy Joseph Stromeyer, . . . under suicide watch in a Long Beach, Calif., jail. Sherrice Iverson had been left alone in the casino's arcade while her father gambled, police said.

> *USA Today*, May 30, 1997, p.6

"Children die just out of focus." In this commentary, Smith did refer to Sherrice Iverson's alleged assailant as a "monster" but later in the commentary she says of the father, "He gambles her away."

> Patricia Smith, *Boston Globe*, June 2, 1997, p.1

Promotion of Gross Generalities

Historically, the mainstream press has perceived minorities as a people outside of the American system, thus representing them as a problem people (see Martindale, 1997; West, 1996). The Susan Smith case is perhaps the best example of the widely held view of African Americans as criminals. "Susan Smith knew what a kidnapper should look like," said Richard Lacayo in an article in *Time* (1994). "He should be a remorseless stranger with a gun." However, Lacayo added, "But the essential part of the picture—the touch she must have counted on to arouse the 'primal sympathies' of her neighbors and to cut short any doubts—was his race. The suspect had to be a black man." Better still, said Lacayo, he had to be a black man in a knit cap, "a bit of a hip-hop wardrobe" that can be "menacing" in [many] minds. Lacayo further asked, "Wasn't that everyone's most familiar image of the murderous criminal?" As was demonstrated by Gomes and Williams in their examination of the Stuart case of Boston, the African American male as "criminal" is deeply embedded in the U.S. psyche due in large part to the media. Further, the mainstream media reflect the racism prevalent in the United States and are themselves a racist institution (Martindale, p. 91).

MEDIA'S TENDENCY TO PROVOKE ANGER AND HOSTILITY TOWARDS AFRICAN AMERICANS

Susan Smith's allegation resulted in an uproar in Union, South Carolina. Perhaps, the Charles Stuart case of Boston and "her [Susan Smith's] own not quite right account of the kidnaping" cautioned the press, the U.S. on the whole, and Union residents (p. 47). One Union resident said, "This whole idea of her labeling a black man as the criminal sends a message of the black male as savage and barbarian" (Lacayo, p. 48).

The CNN "Larry King Live" transcript (Case 1, broadcast) shows King and a guest discussing the death penalty for the alleged "car jacker/kidnapper." Changes in the law are also discussed. Just as Southern lynch mobs justified mob violence as a "necessary response to black crime and an inefficient legal system for virtually any perceived transgression of the racial boundaries or threat to the system of white supremacy, King and his guest, Rep. Charles Schumer, concurred that something of a more drastic nature had to be done since car jackings had increased dramatically:

> Schumer: ". . . The recent crime bill reintroduced capital punishment . . . in the most heinous of offenses. . . .

Further, listeners were continually told in the report that the crime of car jacking was increasing. This gave the impression, since the African American male had been associated with car jacking and with the Susan Smith case, that African American males were dangerous and likely to commit such acts often. Larry King began his report announcing, urgently:

> If you drive a car, listen up, you don't want to be the victim of a car jacking. Take it from Susan Smith. Her worst nightmare began 48 hours ago and she's living it right now. . . . An armed car jacker pushed his way into her car. . . . He's still on the loose (p. 1).

In both the Charles Stuart and the Central Park rape cases, media indicted the whole black community. In both instances, as Corea explained, the African American male was cast in a subhuman light as the media referred to him in harsh terms and language. Corea's examination of broadcast media revealed the use of such terms as "brutally beaten, gang raped, and left to die" by the "cruel" African Americans and Latino "thugs" who were referred to as "animals." Thus, the terms "beast and brute" used in early media became "animal or vicious animal and thug." Only one young man is singled out as having come from a "good family" and once having prospects of a promising future, now dashed. Corea concluded, information about these young men's community and living conditions flowed into the airwaves of broadcast news and onto the pages of newspapers, painting a picture of African American males, in general, as violent, cruel and vicious (p. 259).

The same trend was seen in the Susan Smith case. Both Larry King and his guest agreed the death penalty should be a consideration when it was thought the assailant was African American (p. 5). In the Central Park jogger case, Corea explained, viewer outrage and a "hang 'em high" response ranged from a call for castration to life imprisonment to the death penalty (p. 260). A study of *New York Times* coverage of the case substantiates Corea's findings. In one article, the boys, said to be ages 13 to 15, were out "wilding" and had attacked several people. They are described as "calculating and menacing attackers who were lying in wait for their next prey," part of a "loosely organized gang of 32 who . . . terrorized at least eight other people." In the same article readers are told the youths probably attacked the woman because she was at an economic level they could not hope to attain. In another article, the attack is described as being an "especially ferocious version of group delinquency" (*New York Times*, 1987). Despite these depictions the *New York Times* seems oblivious it might be responsible in part for the African American community's fear that the crime will "further fuel a misconception that African Americans, particularly, young males, will be subjects of fear and scorn."

In the case of Charles Stuart, Lacayo (1994) observed, the police, and other officials, with the assistance of the media, bought his story and placed Boston's Mission Hill residents under siege. Referring to the Stuarts as the "Camelot couple," both the *Boston Globe* and the *Boston Herald* played the role of instigator as police rounded up and interrogated scores of African American men and eventually arrested a suspect (pp. 46–47). Gomes and Williams (1990) point out the press even raised questions about a community that could "produce such a vicious animal." The suspect was labeled a monster (p. 57). Likewise, viewers are told that both Susan Smith and her husband were from good family backgrounds and had good upbringing. Both the Smith and Stuart cases provide further evidence of the African American man's crimes being viewed more harshly than similar acts committed by white offenders.

FRAMING TO EXCUSE WHITE CRIMINAL BEHAVIOR

The murder of Edward Werner and the Casino murder, provide evidence white males are often handled with "kid gloves" when they commit crimes while African Americans are often vilified. Both the defendant and the victim in the Werner case are white.

Sam Manzie's parents, Delores and Nick Manzie, discussed their family in the "20/20" (1997) special report, with Barbara Waiters telling listeners the Manzies were a "family filled with affection. . . . Parenting was taken seriously" (p. 3). Manzie is said to be a victim of a sex offender who seduced him through the Internet. The Internet is blamed:" . . . Manzie was the perfect target for the sexual predators who roam the Internet . . . confused about his sexual identity, tortured by it, and he was lonely" (p. 10). His mother discusses his "isolation" and describes his "violence" as his crying out in pain (p. 15). Eddie Werner becomes a metaphor and is described as the "innocent trip wire for all of his rage" (p. 24). He is mentioned for the first time on page 18 of the transcript. We are told that he was "brutally" murdered and raped, but Waiters explains that Manzie was in therapy almost until that day (p. 18). We are told Werner's mother deserves sympathy but that we cannot bring Eddie back and Manzie really needs support now.

Downs refers to Manzie as a "child who is in desperate need of some kind of help" (p. 27). In the end we are told "It's a story not only of the dangers of the Internet but about how the system failed a family in need and a community" (p. 28) since the Manzie family reportedly tried to get their son committed. Such references to Sam Manzie as "a child" and an "innocent victim" are in direct contrast to the labeling of African Americans who are accused of similar crimes, i.e., the Stuart case and Central Park jogger cases. The offenders the Central Park jogger case might be more applicable here since they and Manzie are in similar age category. Corea asserts, such crimes, when committed by whites, are regarded as out of character and are treated as unreal while the media communicate the notion that African American males should know better and sidestep any discussion of their possible psychological needs (p. 260), thus no such calming devices of language or circumstance are used to garner sympathy.

In the Casino murder case, the African American father and the casino are blamed for the death of his daughter, Sherrice Iverson. The arcade within the casino where she is murdered is a monster, not the young, white man who killed her. Again, "20/20" (1997) sports on the case; how-

ever, the focus of the report is child neglect at casinos. The headline reads "Where Are Their Parents? Several incidents of children found without their parents are discussed and described as a roving reporter scans casinos nationwide. Sherrice Iverson as briefly mentioned on page 4 of the transcript as simply one of many cases. Her father is lamed for her murder. Her killer is said to have "snapped her head, breaking her neck . . . while Sherrice's father was gambling" (p. 4). Antonio Mora, the commentator, asserts, ". . . dozens of parents like him, [are] willing to play the slots, even . . . playing roulette with their children's safety" (p. 4). The killer's name, Jeremy Joseph Stromeyer, is not even mentioned in the transcript. He is removed from blame altogether. The father is said to be the greatest culprit; casino security is mildly blamed; and the arcade pinball games, Homer Hippo and Ms. Pac-Man, are identified as the real dangers parents should look out for p. 4). The print media provided similar coverage, showing very little sympathy for the family of the victim. Even though the father was surely careless and negligent, he did not. commit murder, but he is tried and convicted in the media and treated as if he did, while the actual murderer is said to be a good student with a once promising future. The irony is that the media, in setting an agenda that concentrated on the dangers of leaving children unattended in casinos and arcades failed to alert the public to the potential dangers posed by strangers, even white strangers.

Implications for Today's Media

"Mass media set the agenda for the public. News coverage is framed in such a way as to support the accepted societal order. Given this, it is crucial that mass media use their role responsibly—to bring the country together as a national community, taking into account its diverse audience and recognizing the damaging and divisive effects of its negative coverage of African Americans. Not only does such negative reporting damage the psyches of African Americans, but it also creates disturbing images in the minds of white citizens. Whites who commit heinous acts must not be given special treatment in the press and excused from their crimes. Media must see the importance of respecting victims' rights and their families' rights as well. To devalue the murder of an innocent, seven-year-old African American child or an innocent eleven-year-old white child because they are murdered by white males is not indicative of a press fighting for the good of the whole society and the humanity of all of us people.

While the research I've used here is not extensive, it does scratch the surface and can serve as a model and a catalyst for further research in this area. Media journalists and executives as well as scholars and students must explore the prejudices and stereotypes they have bought into as well as the dynamics of unbalanced reporting. They impact all Americans: those who fall victim to the press as well as everyone else in society who buys into the biased accounts and, even if unwittingly, bases his or her judgments and actions on them. Content analysis provides us with an excellent tool for studying past and present media representations, a first step in understanding and countering the negative images that have been, as the Kerner Commission (Kerner, 1968) found, a contributing factor to racism.

References

PRIMARY SOURCES:

Broadcasting

Car jacking and kidnaping in South Carolina. (1994, October 27). *Larry King live*. Special CNN Report.

Sam's story. (1997, October 31). *20/20*. ABC Special Report.

Where are their parents? Children roam casinos while their parents gamble. (1997, September 12). *20/20*. ABC Special Report.

Newspapers

Boston Globe. (1989, October 27).

Gibbs, N. (1994, November 14). Death and deceit. *Time, 144,* 43–45.

Gorman, T. (1997, May 28). Casino surveillance footage tells story of girl's killing. *Los Angeles Times*, p. 5.

Gorman, T., & Mitchell, J. (1997, May 29). Slaying fuels debate over children's safety in casinos. *Los Angeles Times*, p. 1.

Hayes, B., & Otani, E. (1997, May 29). Officials call girl's slaying a tragic example of neglect. *Los Angeles Times*.

Lacayo, R. (1994, November 14). Stranger in the shadow. *Time, 144,* 46–48.

Leeds, J., & Rainey, J. (1997, May 30). Suspect told two classmates of the casino crime. *Los Angeles Times*, p. 2.

Mariott, M. (1989, April 24). Harlem residents fear backlash. *New York Times*, p. B4.

McFadden, R. (1997, October 3). Suspect in New Jersey strangling was reportedly sex-case victim. *New York Times*, p. 5.

Police say youths were part of loosely organized gang. (1987, April 22). *New York Times*, p.2.

Smith, P. (1997, June 2). Children die just out of focus. *Boston Globe*, p. 1.

Suspect in girl's slaying at casino in custody. (1997, May 30). *USA Today*, p. 6.

Wolff, C. (1989, April 21). Group of youths rape and severely beat young woman jogger. *New York Times*, p. B1.

SECONDARY SOURCES:

Baker, J. F., Reid, C., & O'Brien, M. (1992, September 28). Willie Horton in print?: Big time politics. *Publisher's Weekly*, 239, 9.

Brundage, F. W. (1988). *Lynching in the new south: Georgia and Virginia, 1880–1930* Chicago: University of Illinois Press.

Corea, A. (1990). Racism and the American way of media. In J. Downing, A. Mohammadi, & A. Sreberny-Mohammadi (Eds.), *Questioning the media* (pp. 345–361). Thousand Oaks, CA: Sage.

Duster, A. M. (Ed.). (1970). *Crusade for justice: The autobiography of Ida B. Wells*. Chicago: University of Chicago Press.

Ginzburg, R. (1988). *100 years of lynching*. Baltimore: Black Class Press.

Gomes, R., & Williams, L. F. (1990, Summer). Race and crime: The role of the media in perpetuating racism and classism in America. *Urban League Review*, 14(1), pp. 57–69.

Howard, W. (1995). *Lynching*. Cranbury, NJ: Associated University Press.

Kerner, O. (1968). *Kerner report: The 1968 report of the National Advisory Commission on Civil Disorder*. Washington, DC.

Martindale, C. (1986). *The white press and black America*. New York: Greenwood.

Peyser, M., & Carroll G. (1995, July 17). Southern Gothic on trial. *Newsweek, 126,* 29.

Raper, A. F. (1969). *The tragedy of lynching.* Montclair, NJ: Patterson Smith.

Simpson, G. (1936). *The Negro in the Philadelphia press.* Philadelphia: University of Philadelphia Press.

Smead, H. (1986). *Blood justice: The lynching of Mack Parker.* New York: Oxford.

Timbs, L. (1994, December 17). To print or not to print. *Editor and Publisher, 239,* 12–14.

Tolnay, E., & Beck, E. M. (1995, July 17). *A festival of violence: An analysis of southern lynching, 1882–1930.* Chicago: University of Illinois Press.

Wulf, S. (1995, July 31). Elegy of lost boys. *Time, 146,* 36.

CLASS 14

African Americans (Part II)

CHAPTER 20
The Essentials of Kwanzaa: A Summary
Maulana Karenga

Maulana Karenga, the father of Kwanzaa, provides a brief overview of the essential elements of the holiday he created in 1966. Kwanzaa is now celebrated by more than 20 million people around the world.

CHAPTER 21
Afrocentricity and Multicultural Education: Concept, Challenge and Contributions
Maulana Karenga

Maulana Karenga offers a detailed discussion on why the Afrocentric vision should be a necessary component in the educational system within the U.S.A. Karenga argues that this nation prospers when minority as well as majority views are included in the nation's history.

CHAPTER 22
The Silenced Dialogue: Power and Pedagogy in Educating Other People's Children
Lisa Delpit

Lisa Delpit develops a model for understanding "the culture of power" that exists within the domain we call the American educational system. she explains the five aspects of power that are in operation in our nation's schools. Delpit also discusses the difficulty educators have communicating these aspects so as to engage all participants in meaningful dialogue regardless of race, class, or gender.

CHAPTER 23
Reframing the Affirmative Action Debate
Lani Guiner

Lani Guiner uses the analogy of the "Miner's Canary" as a way of communicating the state of affairs of people of color in the U.S.A. This article is a powerful warning and a blueprint for the changes needed to create a society that promotes both equity and social justice.

CHAPTER 20

The Essentials of Kwanzaa: A Summary

Maulana Karenga

The creator of Kwanzaa and the Nguzo Saba (The Seven Principles) and the author of Kawaida philosophy out of which they are created, Maulana Karenga is an internationally recognized social theorist and ethical philosopher in African Culture. Karenga, an activist-scholar, is professor and chair of the Department of Black Studies at California State University, Long Beach and the chair of The Organization US and the National Association of Kawaida Organizations (NAKO). He is also author of numerous books and articles including *Introduction to Black Studies, Selections From The Husia: Sacred Wisdom of Ancient Egypt, The Book of Coming Forth By Day: The Ethics of the Declarations of Innocence* and *Kawaida: A Communitarian African Philosophy.*

The Origins

KWANZAA IS AN AFRICAN AMERICAN HOLIDAY celebrated from 26 December thru 1 January. It is based on the agricultural celebrations of Africa called "the first-fruits" celebrations which were times of harvest, ingathering, reverence, commemoration, recommitment, and celebration. Therefore, Kwanzaa is a time for ingathering of African Americans for celebration of their heritage and their achievements, reverence for the Creator and creation, commemoration of the past, recommitment to cultural ideals and celebration of the good.

Kwanzaa was created out of the philosophy of Kawaida, which is a cultural nationalist philosophy that argues that the key challenge in Black people's life is the challenge of culture, and that what Africans must do is to discover and bring forth the best of their culture, both ancient and current, and use it as a foundation to bring into being models of human excellence and possibilities to enrich and expand our lives.

It was created in the midst of our struggles for liberation in the 1960's and was part of our organization Us' efforts to create, recreate and circulate African culture as an aid to building community, enriching Black consciousness, and reaffirming the value of cultural grounding for life and struggle.

Kwanzaa is celebrated by millions of people of African descent throughout the world African community. As a cultural holiday, it is practiced by Africans from all religious traditions, all classes, all ages and generations, and all political persuasions on the common ground of their Africanness in all its historical and current diversity and unity.

The Fundamental Activities

Kwanzaa, like other African first-fruits celebrations, is organized around five fundamental activities. And these activities are informed by ancient views and values which reaffirm and reinforce family, community and culture.

INGATHERING OF THE PEOPLE

First, Kwanzaa is a time of ingathering. Based on African first-fruits celebrations, it is a harvesting of the people; a bringing together of the most valuable fruit or product of the nation, its living human harvest, i.e., the peo-

From *Kwanzaa: A Celebration of Family, Community and Culture*, 1998. Reprinted by permission of University of Sankore Press, Los Angeles.

ple themselves. It is a time of ingathering for the family and of the entire community to renew and reinforce the bonds between them. Kwanzaa promotes rituals of communion, of sharing and renewal of peoplehood bonds which strengthen mutual concern and commitment. And it stresses the need to constantly seek and stand together on common ground in the midst of our differences and diversity.

SPECIAL REVERENCE FOR THE CREATOR AND CREATION

Secondly, Kwanzaa is a time of special reverence for the Creator and creation. It is a time of thanksgiving for the good in life, for life itself, for love, for friendship, for parents and children, the elders and youth, man and woman, and for family, community and culture. As a harvest celebration, Kwanzaa is also a time of thanksgiving for the earth and all that is on it, humans, birds, animals, plants and all living things, water, air, land and all natural resources. At the same time it is a time for recommitment to protect and preserve the earth and relate rightfully to the environment

COMMEMORATION OF THE PAST

Thirdly, Kwanzaa is a time of commemoration of the past. It is a time of honoring the moral obligation to remember and praise those on whose shoulders we stand; to raise and praise the names of those who gave their lives that we might live fuller and more meaningful ones. It is also a time to appreciate our role as "heirs and custodians of a great legacy" and to recommit ourselves to honoring it by preserving it and expanding it. We are, as African people, fathers and mothers of humanity and human civilization, sons and daughters of the Holocaust of Enslavement and authors and heirs of the reaffirmation of our Africanness and social justice tradition in the 60's. Each period leaves a legacy of challenge, struggle and achievement. We honor each by learning it and living it. And Kwanzaa is a focal point for this.

RECOMMITMENT TO OUR HIGHEST IDEALS

Fourthly, Kwanzaa is a time of recommitment to our highest ideals. It is a time of focusing on thought and practice of our highest cultural

vision and values which in essence are ethical values—values of the good life, truth, justice, sisterhood, brotherhood and respect for the transcendent, for the human person for elders and for nature. It is here that the Nguzo Saba (The Seven Principles) serves as the central focus of Kwanzaa in thought and practice.

CELEBRATION OF THE GOOD

Finally, Kwanzaa is a time for celebration of the Good, the good of life, community, culture, friendship, the bountifulness of the earth, the wonder of the universe, the elders, the young, the human person in general, our history, our struggle for liberation and ever higher levels of human life. The celebration of Kwanzaa, then, is a ceremony of bonding, thanksgiving, commemoration, recommitment, a respectful marking, an honoring, a praising, and a rejoicing.

In terms of inclusion, Kwanzaa has two basic kinds of celebrations, family-centered and community-centered, although public celebrations are also held. Family-centered celebrations may be any activities that the family chooses to introduce, reaffirm, teach and express the Nguzo Saba (The Seven Principles) in particular and African cultural values and practices in general. For example, at a chosen meal, one or more members can explain the principle for the day and say how s/he practiced it, or discuss an issue, event, or person of African history and culture, or organize an activity around the principles or other cultural focus.

Community-centered activities can be the collective African karamu (feasts) especially on 31 December, various school activities or any other collective activity which calls for ingathering of the people, reinforcing their cultural values and the bonds between them as a people, and sharing the beauty, richness and meaningfulness of African culture.

The Essential Values

Kwanzaa was created to introduce and reinforce seven basic values of African culture which contribute to building and reinforcing community among African American people as well as Africans throughout the world African community. These values are called the Nguzo Saba (in-goo'-zo sah'-bah) which in the Pan-African language of Swahili means the Seven Principles. These principles stand at the heart of the origin and meaning of Kwanzaa, for it is these values which are not only the building blocks for community but serve also as its social glue.

The Nguzo Saba, first in Swahili and then in English are:

1. **Umoja (Unity)**

   To strive for and maintain unity in the family, community, nation and race.

2. **Kujichagulia (Self-Determination)**

   To define ourselves, name ourselves, create for ourselves and speak for ourselves.

3. **Ujima (Collective Work and Responsibility)**

   To build and maintain our community together and make our brother's and sister's problems our problems and to solve them together.

4. **Ujamaa (Cooperative Economics)**

   To build and maintain our own stores, shops and other businesses and to profit from them together.

5. **Nia (Purpose)**

   To make our collective vocation the building and developing of our community in order to restore our people to their traditional greatness.

6. **Kuumba (Creativity)**

   To do always as much as we can, in the way we can, in order to leave our community more beautiful and beneficial than we inherited it.

7. **Imani (Faith)**

   To believe with all our heart in our people, our parents, our teachers, our leaders and the righteousness and victory of our struggle.

The Symbols

Kwanzaa has seven basic symbols and two supplemental ones. Each represents values and concepts reflective of African culture and contributive to community building and reinforcement.

The basic symbols in Swahili and then in English are:

Mazao (The Crops)
Symbolic of African harvest celebrations and of the rewards of productive and collective labor.

Mkeka (The Mat)
Symbolic of our tradition and history and thus, the foundation on which we build.

Kinara (The Candle Holder)
Symbolic of our roots, our parent people—continental Africans.

Muhindi (The Corn)
Symbolic of our children and thus our future which they embody.

Mishumaa Saba (The Seven Candles)
Symbolic of the Nguzo Saba, the Seven Principles, the matrix and minimum set of values which Black people are urged to live by in order to rescue and reconstruct their lives in their own image and according to their own needs.

Kikombe cha Umoja (The Unity Cup)
Symbolic of the foundational principle and practice of unity which makes all else possible.

Zawadi (The Gifts)
Symbolic of the labor and love of parents and the commitments made and kept by the children.

The two supplemental symbols are:

Bendera (The Flag)
The Black, Red and Green colors are based on the colors of the national flag given by the Hon. Marcus Garvey as a flag for African people throughout the world and used by numerous African countries. The meaning of these colors in the Kwanzaa bendera are black for the people, red for their struggle, and green for the future and hope that comes from their struggle.

Nguzo Saba Poster (Poster of The Seven Principles)
(see posters on pages 34, 68 and 125)

Greetings

The greetings during Kwanzaa are in Swahili. Swahili is a Pan-African language and is thus chosen to reflect African Americans' commitment to the whole of Africa and African culture rather than to a specific ethnic or national group or culture. The greetings are to reinforce awareness of

Kwanzaa Greetings

Day	Greeting	Response
December 26	**Habari gani?** *(hah-bah'-ree gah'-nee)*	**Umoja.** *(oo-mo'-jah)* **Habari gani?**
December 27	**Habari gani?** *(hah-bah -ree gah '-nee)*	**Kujichaguhia.** *(koo-jee-chahgoo-/ee'-ah)* **Habari gani?**
December 28	**Habari gani?** *(hah-bah'-ree gah'-nee)*	**Ujima.** *(oo-jee'-mah)* **Habari gani?**
December 29	**Habari gani?** *(hah-bah'-ree gah'-nee)*	**Ujamaa.** *(oo-jah-mah~ah)* **Habari gani?**
December 30	**Habari gani?** *(hah-bah'-ree gah'-nee)*	**Nia.** *(nee'-ah)* **Habari gani?**
December 31	**Habari gani?** *(hah-bah'-ree gah'-nee)*	**Kuumba.** *(koo-oom'-bah)* **Habari gani?**
January 1	**Habari gani?** *(hah-bah'-ree gah'-nee)*	**Imani.** *(ee-mah'-nee)* **Habari gani?**

and commitment to the Seven Principles. The greeting is: *"Habari gani?"* and the answer is each of the principles for each of the days of Kwanzaa, i.e., *"Umoja,"* on the first day, *"Kujichagulia,"* on the second day and so on. Celebrants also greet by saying *"Heriza Kwanzaa"* or *"Happy Kwanzaa."*

Swahili Pronunciation

Swahili pronunciation is extremely easy. The vowels are pronounced like those of Spanish and the consonants, with only a few exceptions, like those of English. The vowels are as follows:

a = *ah* as in *father*
e = *a* as in *day*
i = *ee* as in *free*
o = *o* as in *go*
u = *oo* as in *too*

The accent is almost always on the penultimate, i.e., next to the last, syllable except for a few words borrowed from Arabic which are not relevant here.

Other Kwanzaa Greetings and Phrases

Greeting	Definition
Kwanzaa yenu iwe na heri *(kwahn'-zah yay'-noo ee'-way nah hay'-ree)*	May y'all's Kwanzaa be with happiness
Her za Kwanzaa *(hay'ree zah kwahn'-zah)*	Happy Kwanzaa
Harambee *(ha-rahm-bay'-ay)*	Let's all pull together
Asante sana *(a-sahn'-tay sah'-nah)*	Thank you very much

Gifts

Gifts are given mainly to children, but should always include a book and a heritage symbol. The book is to emphasize the African value and tradition of learning stressed since ancient Egypt, and the heritage symbol to reaffirm and reinforce the African commitment to tradition and history.

Colors and Decorations

The colors of Kwanzaa are black, red and green as noted above and can be utilized in decorations for Kwanzaa. Also decorations should include traditional African items, i.e., African baskets, cloth, patterns, art objects, harvest symbols, etc.

CHAPTER 21

Afrocentricity and Multicultural Education: Concept, Challenge, and Contribution

Maulana Karenga

Introduction

GENERATIVE ASSUMPTIONS

The current debate on the character and content of quality education in a multicultural context offers new possibilities not only for the reconception and reconstruction of public and higher education but also for society itself. For the debate is in essence about power and place, standards of relevance, and the quality of relations among the various cultural groups which compose society.

This chapter is offered as a contribution to this discourse and is based on and informed by several interrelated assumptions: (1) that both our society and the larger human community are fundamentally characterized by diversity and that human diversity is human richness; (2) that to benefit from this rich diversity, we must not simply tolerate it but embrace and build on it; (3) that each people has the right and responsibility to speak its own special cultural truth and make its own unique contribution to the forward flow of societal and human history; (4) that the search for truth in the service of a fuller and freer humanity must include travel on paths opened and paved in history by humanity in all its rich, complex, and instructive diversity; (5) that given these realities, multicultural education is at the heart of any meaningful concept of quality education; (6) that the imperative of a truly multicultural education rests on substantive moral, intellectual and social grounds, and (7) that the Afrocentric vision of quality education offers in content, perspective, and methodology an important contribution to this urgent quest for both quality education and a just and good society.

GROUNDING OF MULTICULTURAL EDUCATION

It is important to stress, as stated earlier, that the thrust for a multicultural education rests on solid moral, intellectual, and social grounds. The moral grounds pertain to a real respect for the concrete human person in all her or his diversity. The student and teacher are not abstracted from concrete conditions for critical understanding but are engaged from the vantage point of their own experience. They speak from their own experience and location in history and culture and thus enrich educational discourse and express a democratic public life rooted in cooperative forms of participation and exchange.

The intellectual grounding of multicultural education is revealed, as I (Report 1991: 3) have argued elsewhere, in its use and value as (1) "a necessary corrective for the conceptual and content inadequacy of the exclusive curriculum which omits and diminishes the rich (and instructive) variety of human cultures"; (2) an equally important corrective for racist, sexist, classist, and chauvinistic approaches to knowledge and education which deny, demean, or diminish the meaning, experience, and voice of the other; (3) a necessary reflection of the multicultural society in which we live; and (4) a creative challenge to the established order of things. For it is in the established order of things that the university is reduced to a ware-

Reprinted by permission of the author.

house of Eurocentric goods to be authoritatively transmitted and imposed as a sacrosanct canon or unproblematic body of deference-deserving knowledge. Multicultural education, especially in its Afrocentric form, comes into being and establishes its raison d'être as an uncompromising and relentless critique of the established order. It then offers correctives pointed toward creating a richer and more varied educational experience as well as a just and good society.

The social grounds of multicultural education rise from its function as (1) a just response to the demand of marginalized and excluded peoples for an education relevant to their own life experience; (2) an indispensable preparation of students and teachers for the world in which they live, work, study, and interact with others; (3) preparation of youth for the burden of support of an older and different population based on principles of appreciation for diversity, mutuality and interdependence, and (4) "part and parcel of the thrust to create a just and good society, to avoid civil strife, and to enhance the quality of social life . . ." (Report 1991: 4).

If quality education is of necessity multicultural education, the challenge is not to provide an Afrocentric paradigm for the entire curriculum of schools and universities. Rather it is to propose an Afrocentric contribution which will become a constitutive part of the overall movement toward a genuinely multicultural university. For in a multicultural context, the curriculum cannot be totally Afrocentric or it will become hegemonic as is the current Eurocentric model, which dismisses and devalues other cultures. On the contrary, the curriculum will be multicultural with various cultural visions, including the Afrocentric vision, as fundamental constitutive parts of the educational process. This position in no way suggests that Africana studies departments and programs should not be Afrocentric. On the contrary, they must be Afrocentric; otherwise the distinctiveness of their contribution to multicultural discourse is called into question and ultimately undermined.

Toward Defining Afrocentricity

A successful delineation of the Afrocentric vision of quality education and its contribution to multicultural education requires several interre-

lated tasks. First, Afrocentricity, the central concept in the Afrocentric vision, must be explained in its own terms (Asante 1990; Karenga 1988). In this way the concept is freed from the imprecise descriptions of some of its adherents and from the hysteria of the media and Eurocentric academicians, who often seem more interested in preserving privileged position and canon rather than facilitating and clarifying discourse (Ravitch 1990; Schlesinger 1991).

Second, the successful delineation of an Afrocentric vision of quality education requires that it be distinguished from the established-order Eurocentric educational process in its most negative form. Third, such a delineation must present and explain the value of the areas of fundamental focus and practice of such an educational project. This includes simultaneous discussion of the pedagogy which informs and implements the basic demands of the paradigm.

DEVELOPMENT OF THE CATEGORY

Afrocentricity as an intellectual category is relatively new in the discourse of Africana studies, beginning with its introduction in the late 1970s by Molefi Asante (1980). It is Asante who attempted to unify conceptually the varied African-centered approaches to Africana Studies by designating them as Afrocentric. This is not to suggest that Afrocentric study and teaching are, themselves, new, for there are important works in African intellectual history which represent a long-term stress on the need for African-centered thought and practice. For example, one can cite, among others, works on education by W. E. B. Du Bois (1975), Anna Julia Cooper (1988), and Carter G. Woodson (1969).

Asante's (1980, 1987, 1990) essential contribution to this orientation in Africana studies is the provision of the category Afrocentricity itself and an accompanying literature which contributes definitively to the delineation of a conceptual framework for a self-conscious, unified, and effective way of understanding, appreciating, and utilizing the rich and varied complexity of African life and culture. Since the introduction of the category, the discourse around it and within its conceptual framework has been extensive and varied. Therefore, when one speaks of the Afrocentric project, one should always keep in mind that one is not talking about a monolithic position but rather a general conceptual orientation among Africana studies scholars whose fundamental point of departure and intellectual concerns and views are centered in the African experience.

Within Afrocentric discourse, two nominal categories are given from which the adjectival category, Afrocentric, is derived: Afrocentricity and Afrocentrism. In my contribution to discipline discourse, I prefer and use Afrocentricity for several reasons: (1) to stress its intellectual value as distinct from its ideological use; (2) to distinguish it clearly from Eurocentricism, which is an ideology of domination and exclusion; and (3) to establish it as a quality of thought and practice rather than thought and practice itself. The need to stress its intellectual value as opposed to or distinct from its ideological use appears obvious. For if it is to fulfill its educational potential and promise, it must prove itself essentially an intellectual category. Second, Afrocentricity rather than Afrocentrism is used here because of the equally obvious need to distinguish the category from uninformed or manipulative associations of it with Eurocentrism. In this respect, it is important that the specific cultural and general human character of Afrocentricity be stressed. For Afrocentricity must never be conceived of or employed as a reaction to or an African version of Eurocentrism, with its racist and structured denial and deformation of the history and humanity of peoples of color. As I (1988: 404) have stated, "Afrocentricity, at its best, is a quest for and an expression of historical and cultural anchor, a critical reconstruction that dares to restore missing and hidden parts of our historical self-formation and pose the African experience as a significant paradigm for human liberation and a higher level of human life." Moreover, "to be no more than an 'obscene caricature of Europe'—to use Fanon's phrase- is to violate historical memory and vitiate historical possibilities inherent in the special truth Africans can and must speak to the world, given their ancient, rich and varied experience."

The Afrocentric vision, critically defined and developed, demands that Africana studies root itself in the African experience and in the world view which evolves from and informs that experience. For inherent in the assumption of the legitimacy and relevance of the discipline is the conception of the validity and value of studying Africans in understanding humanity as a whole. Having rooted itself in the African experience, which is the source and substance of its raison d'être, Africana studies expands outward to acquire knowledge based on other human experiences. African humanity is thus enriched and expanded by knowledge of and mutually beneficial exchanges with others. Moreover, in understanding human history as a whole, Africans can even more critically appreciate their fundamental role in the origins of human civilization and in the forward flow of human history.

Third, the category Afrocentricity is preferred in order to focus on the cultural and human quality of the thought and practice rather than on the thought and practice as ideological conception and conduct. As a quality of thought and practice defined by its particular African and shared human character, it allows for greater intellectual use and value and again avoids reductive translation as just another ideological posture. It is, in a word, a category of African culture and shared human interests and thus fits within the particular and universal demands of multicultural education and exchange.

DEFINITION AND IMPLICATIONS

Afrocentricity can be defined as a methodology, orientation, or quality of thought and practice rooted in the cultural image and human interests of African people. To be rooted in the cultural image of African people is to be anchored in the views, values, and practices of African people. To be rooted in the human interests of African people is to be informed of and attentive to the just claims on life and society that Africans share with other peoples, such as respect and concern for truth, justice, freedom, and the dignity of the human person.

Afrocentricity as a culturally rooted approach to thought and practice brings both a particular and universal dimension. It contributes a particular cultural insight and discourse to the multicultural project and in the process finds common ground with other cultures which can be cultivated and developed for mutual benefit. In fact, Afrocentric thought shelters the assumption that the rich, varied, and complex character of African culture is a critical resource in understanding and engaging the human community. Moreover, in an educational context, Afrocentric contributions to research and teaching not only challenge established-order discourse but contribute to the broadening and deepening of the educational process.

It is important to state that my use of the terms *African-centeredness* and *Afrocentric* does not intend to suggest any more for the conceptual category African than is indicated by the terms European (Western), Asian (Oriental), or Latin American. The categories African philosophy, world view, values, etc., simply suggest shared orientations born of similar cultural experiences. As Gyekye (1987: x) notes, "it is the underlying cultural unity or identity of the various individual thinkers that justifies references to varieties of thought as wholes, such as Western, European or Oriental philosophy." In other words, Gyekye continues, "even though the individual thinkers who produced what is known as Western philosophy are from different European or Western nations, we nonetheless refer to such body of philosophical ideas as western philosophy (in addition to, say, French, German or British philosophy)." One can justifiably conclude that "the real reason for this is surely the common cultural experience and orientation of those individual thinkers."

Likewise, in spite of the obvious differences between Indian, Chinese and ancient Persian philosophy as well as the difference between Hindu, Buddhist, Confucian and Taoist thought, they are generally called Asian philosophy. And as Tu Wei Ming (1985: 7) states, Asian philosophy is based on the notion of "shared orientations." Therefore, to say African philosophy, world view, or values is to assume certain shared orientations based on similar cultural experiences. Among these shared orientations are (1) the centrality of community; (2) respect for tradition; (3) a high level spirituality and ethical concern; (4) harmony with nature; (5) the sociality of selfhood; (6) veneration of ancestors; and (7) the unity of being. This list is obviously selective, and there are other African core values which one can focus on as central to the Afrocentric vision. However, these are a conceptual and indispensable minimum regardless of other additions one might make. Having identified these basic components of the African world view, the task now is to demonstrate how these inform the conceptual contributions of Africana studies to the multicultural educational enterprise.

Afrocentric Conceptual Contributions

There are several Afrocentric conceptual contributions which can enrich multicultural discourse and education. Among these are (1) centeredness or groundedness and insight from one's own culture (this is also called location or orientation); (2) the wholistic approach to knowledge; (3) critique and corrective as a joint project in the educational enterprise; (4) the essentiality of a historical perspective; and (5) the centrality of the ethical dimension of the educational project, a self-conscious directed process in which there is a reaffirmation of the worth and dignity of the human person and the importance of knowledge in the service of humankind. All of these contributions are interrelated and mutually reinforcing and offer a paradigm of difference as possibility within a multicultural context.

THE CONCEPT OF CENTEREDNESS

Certainly, the first and most fundamental contribution an Afrocentric project brings to multicultural education is its stress on centeredness, which is also called place, location and orientation. This is a particularly challenging and, at times, even problematic concept, given the current stress in academia on decentering and deconstructionism as both an aid to more critical learning and greater social exchange (Hassan 1987; Hooks 1990). However, Afrocentric scholars as well as many feminists and Marxists also recognize the problems of unlimited deconstruction. It subverts the emancipatory possibilities in ethnic, national, gender, and class theory and practice and undermines human agency by decentering the subject and denying difference its oppositional, enriching, and essential role in both education and social practice (Ferguson et al. 1990; Giroux 1992; Hooks 1990; Karenga 1986).

History and culture are essential points of rootedness and departure for Afrocentric studies. Thus, in an Afrocentric vision of learning, one does not step out of one's history to learn or practice but rather engages in it to ground oneself and grasp both the particular and the universal. As Asante (1990: 5) argues, "One steps outside one's history [only] with great difficulty. . . . In fact, the act itself is highly improbable from true historical consciousness." Moreover, he continues, "There is no anti-place, since we are all consumers of space and time." Given this, he states, "the Afrocentrist seeks knowledge of this 'place' perspective as a fundamental rule of intellectual inquiry." Moreover, Asante maintains that "all knowledge results from an occasion of encounter in place," and that such a "shaped perspective [then] allows the Afrocentrist to put African ideals and values at the center of inquiry."

Asante (1990: 12) defines centeredness as "the groundedness of observation and behavior in one's own historical experiences." This concept, he maintains, shapes the Africana studies project but allows for a similar posture and process for all other cultures. Thus, he states, Africana studies "secures its place alongside other centric pluralisms without hierarchy and without seeking hegemony." Here Asante answers critics who incorrectly contend that Afrocentricity claims a privileged and hegemonic racial position for Africans in human history and culture. He does this by posing centeredness as an essential and effective orientation and point of departure for all cultures. In this stress on the value of location, place, or orientation. Asante reaffirms the contentions of earlier African scholars like W. E. B. Du Bois (1975), who argued against simply teaching of what he called general and disembodied knowledge of science and human culture.

Du Bois (1975: 98), in his seminal essay. "The Field and Function of the Negro College," argued for an education located in and oriented toward the concrete experience of the students. "No teacher, Black or White, who comes to a university like Fisk, filled simply with general ideas of human culture or general knowledge of disembodied science, is going to make a university of this school," he stated. For "a university is made of human beings, learning of things they do not know from things they do know in their own lives." Du Bois criticizes the assumption of the effectiveness of transmission of simply "general ideas of human culture or general knowledge of disembodied science." Du Bois' position, which informs the Afrocentric vision of quality education, is that there is no real substitute for an embodied knowledge, a knowledge rooted in and reflective of the concrete situation of the student. This essentially means starting from what students know to teach them and assist their learning what they do not know. Thus, he advocated use of the familiar as an instrument to discover the

unknown and the unfamiliar and as a rich resource for understanding the universal (i.e., humanity as a whole).

The point which Du Bois (1975: 96) makes is that a quality education is especially attentive to the process of "beginning with the particular and going out to universal comprehension and unhampered expression." Thus, he criticizes much of the literature of the Harlem Renaissance, which was, he contends, "written to the benefit of white readers, and starting out primarily from the white point of view." Therefore, the movement eventually declined for "it never had a real [black] constituency and it did not grow out of the inmost heart and frank experience of [Blacks]; . . . [and] on such an artificial basis no real literature can grow." Again, the point is that a disembodied knowledge, an abstract discourse on humans cannot and does not produce a quality education. The need is to begin with each culture's experience and then translate it into a process of understanding others' experience as well as the varied and collective experience of society and humankind.

THE WHOLISTIC APPROACH TO KNOWLEDGE

A second contribution that Afrocentric methodology brings to the enterprise of multicultural education is the stress on the wholistic approach to knowledge. As James Stewart (1984: 296–97) remarked, this focus is both a source of intellectual challenge and a mark of uniqueness of the Africana studies enterprise. At its inception Africana studies conceived of itself as an interdisciplinary project. As I (1993: 21) have stated, "the scope of Africana studies was established by its self-definition and by the parameters it posed for itself as a multidisciplinary discipline." More precisely, however, Black studies is a single discipline with many fields which seeks to grasp the totality of black life from its various constituent dimensions (i.e., history, religion, sociology, politics, economics, creative production, psychology, etc.).

By definition, Africana studies is a systematic and critical study of the totality of black thought and practice in their current and historical unfolding. The use of the term *totality* is intended to suggest a wholistic approach to the study of black life. This means, first, an intellectual engagement which stresses totality as an inclusive social dimension and invites study in all fields. But it also is designed to stress the importance of totality in time. This is what is meant by "the study of black life in its current and historical unfolding." This inclusive approach of Black studies stresses the wholistic character of knowledge and integrates various subject areas into a coherent discipline, reaching across what James Turner (1984: xi) calls "the voids that have inevitably occurred as a result of artificial disciplinary demarcations."

In addition, Africana studies is also informed by an African ontology that argues the unity of being and an epistemology that sees both being and truth about it as whole. Speaking of classical African ontology as expressed in ancient Egypt, Finnestad (1989: 31ff) notes its stress on "the affinities and connections" rather than differences in its conception of reality and being. In such a conception, human life "merges with that of the entire world and being is conceived as an "integrated whole." The logic of such a position leads to the epistomological assumption that the truth of being is also whole, and any partial approach to it must yield only a partial understanding of it.

It is important to note, however, that such an approach does not deny the value of the temporary analytical decomposition of subjects of study for a more internal or detailed study. But a wholistic approach stresses the need to guard against losing sight and understanding of affinities, connections, or the interrelatedness of each part to the other and to the whole. The implications of such a view for both social study and practice are numerous and important. Such a wholistic approach moves away from Cartesian dualism and rigid lines of demarcation in both conception of the world and approaches to it. And it is becoming increasingly important in social and intellectual discourse in various other alternative critical perspectives. In addition to Africana studies, other ethnic studies. Women's studies, and some socialist studies also assume such a wholistic position. This offers an excellent opportunity for creative dialog and challenge to the dualistic conception of the established order and promises a useful and ongoing discourse.

THE JOINT PROJECT OF CRITIQUE AND CORRECTIVE

A third conceptual contribution that Afrocentric studies offers to multicultural education is its stress on critique and corrective as a joint project in the educational enterprise. This stress is rooted in the very conception and earliest practice of Black studies as a discipline. From its inception, Africana or Black studies has had both an academic and social dimension which involved critique and corrective as essential to the meaning and mission of the discipline (Karenga 1993: Chap. 1). Black studies evolved out of the emancipatory struggles of the 60's which linked intellectual emancipation with political emancipation, campus with community, intellectuals and students with the masses, and knowledge in the academy with power in society (Hare 1969). What emerged in the process of both struggles on campus and in society was a paradigm of critique and corrective which sought to end domination, to expand the realm of freedom, and to create a just and good society.

THE CRITICAL DIMENSION

The Afrocentric stress on critique as essential to the educational enterprise emerges from the actual conditions in and under which Africana studies comes into being. The Afrocentric critique is concerned with the distortion and deficiency of what is present in the curriculum and larger social discourse and about the abundance and emancipatory possibilities of that which is absent. It seeks to rescue and reconstruct black history and culture in order to define more correctly black humanity. Thus, the Afrocentric critique can be defined as "a systematic unrelenting battle against both ignorance and illusion, the struggle against the poverty of knowledge as well as the perversion of truth" (Karenga 1988: 410). Moreover, it involves realizing that the greatest part of truth is hidden beneath the surface. Therefore, there is a constant need to reach beyond and below the surface manifestations of society and the world to penetrate and grasp the relations which give them their motion, meaning and character. Moreover, the Afrocentric critique requires focus on contradictions in society, especially ones of race, class and gender. This requires looking again not only for what is present and distorted in the discourse but also for what is absent and undiscussed.

Such an approach not only contributes to the encouragement of critical thinking about the present and absent, the given and the possible, but it also calls for a redefinition in practice of the university itself, which has historically been the brain and an apologist for the established order. In such a context the university became, through the struggles of the 1960's not simply a place to transmit authoritative views and values but a ground of contestation, a framework for struggle over intellectual issues as well as over the structure and meaning of the university and society. Contestation continues to be posed in Africana studies as a fundamental mode of understanding self, society, and the world. In such a process Africana studies seeks to create a space and a process for students to recover, discover, and speak truth and meaning of their own experience. This means that they locate themselves in social and human history and, having oriented themselves, bring their unique contribution to multicultural exchange in the academy and society. Ideally what results from this critique of established-order discourse and contestation over issues of intellect and life is the multicultural cooperative production of knowledge rather than its Eurocentric authoritative allocation.

Several paths are pursued in the process of bringing one's own experience and unique cultural contribution to the educational process. First, one is compelled to create both a different language and logic. For the established-order language and logic are not conducive to the emancipatory project which Africana studies represents and nurtures. As Malcolm X (1968: 133) argued in a lecture at Harvard, "the language and logic of the oppressed cannot be the language and logic of the oppressor" if an emancipatory project is to be conceived and pursued. Thus, Africana Studies began to develop and use new categories and modes of analysis and give new definition to old terms and concepts. For example, within Africana studies classics is no longer an exclusive category of European achievement but rather a category of achievement for humans in general. Stripped of all its Eurocentric pretensions, the term classics can be defined as works whose level of creativity and achievement deserve and demand both preservation and emulation. Thus, classical music, art, literature, civilizations, etc., are present in African, Native Americans, Latino, and Asian cultures as well as in Europe.

Second, the Afrocentric critique demands that one moves beyond the Eurocentric self-congratulatory narratives in various disciplines and engages in a multicultural discourse. Such a discourse reveals the rich variousness of human culture and poses a necessary creative challenge to European hegemonic discourse and practice. Using political science as an example, the Afrocentric critique demands that one looks before and beyond Plato to include the study of classical African texts from ancient Egypt such as *The Book of Ptahhotep,* which offers a discourse on leadership as a moral vocation (Lichtheim 1975: 61ff; Simpson 1973: 159ff) and *The Book of Khun-Anup*, the oldest treatise on social justice (Lichtheim 1975: 97ff; Simpson 1973: 31ff). Likewise, the study of literature would include both ancient and modern African classics, such as the classical praise poetry of the Zulu, *Izibongo*, (Cope 1968), of the Tswana, Maboko (Schapera 1965), as well as selected literature of the Harlem Renaissance and the 1960s. Finally, discourse on ethics need not begin or end in Judaism and Christianity but extend back before such frameworks to Maatian ethical texts of ancient Egypt, which offer both parallels and sources of Jewish and Christian concepts and practices (Breasted 1934; Karenga 1988; Morenz 1973: Chap. 6). It is important to note that the use of African classics and other achievements to enrich multicultural education and discourse must and does assume and require a similar and equal contribution of other cultures.

Third, within the framework of developing a new language and logic, one can pose different points of departure for understanding social and human reality. From an Afrocentric view, one studies society from a communitarian rather than an individualistic view (Mbiti 1970; Menkiti 1984). In addition, one poses the study of politics not simply as a struggle for power but also, as in Maatian ethical texts (i.e., the *Sebait*), as a collective vocation to create a just and good society (Karenga 1988). Likewise, one can pose communal and substantive democracy against "herrenvolk" and procedural democracy and then engage Malcolm X's (1965: 26) concept of being a "victim of democracy" for all its "fruitful ambiguity." For in an age of praise and pursuit of democracy as a central human good, one is challenged to understand and explain why Malcolm claims, in this particular case, such a negative role for it.

Finally, the Afrocentric approach challenges the parameters, focus, and central categories of intellectual discourse in the social science and humanities. For example, one talks of the "Holocaust of Enslavement" rather than "slave trade" as the most instructive and correct way of discussing the genocidal tragedy which marked the loss of millions of African lives. One poses enslavement as primarily an ethical issue rather than a commercial one and defines *holocaust* as an act of genocide so morally monstrous that it is not only against the people themselves but also against humanity. Such a redefinition of the experience of enslavement as a holocaust invites a rich comparative and contrastive discourse on other holocausts—Native American, Native Australian, Jewish, Romani, Palestinian, Armenian, Kurdish, and so on. In conclusion, the practice of critique and corrective means that suppressed and marginalized voices of various cultures will bring an enriched and enlarged agenda to the educational table. Various ways of viewing and approaching human reality will challenge and change Eurocentric hegemony and pose in its place a democratic and multicultural education which prefigures and points to the possibility of a truly democratic and multicultural society.

THE CORRECTIVE DIMENSION

The corrective dimension of the Afrocentric conception of education emanates from both the emancipatory role assigned to education and to the educated by earlier African scholars and leaders and from the emancipatory struggles of the 1960s which assigned Africana studies both an academic and social mission. Moreover, such an Afrocentric concept of education grows out of the African communitarian world view, with its interrelated concepts of the centrality of the community and the sociality of selfhood. This communitarian African world view, as Gyekye (1987: 157) states, contains within it "such social and ethical values as social well-being, solidarity, interdependence, cooperation and reciprocal obligations—all of which conduce to equitable distribution of resources and benefits of society." In such a context, "inherent in the communal enterprise is the problem of contribution and distribution." This translates in an educational context as recognition of the fact that instead of conceiving of education as knowledge for knowledge sake, one approaches education within a concept of knowledge for humans' sake. This means that knowledge as a key social value is conceived as belonging not simply to the student and intellectuals but also to the community and that both the mission of students and the university must relate to and con-

tribute to the historical vocation of human flourishing in the context of a just and good society.

Inherent in this communitarian concept of education is the concept of mission, which has long been a central theoretical pillar in Africana studies' conception of itself. W. E. B. Du Bois' conception of the Talented Tenth stands as a classic example of mission as an inherent aspect of the educational project. Education, he argued, is "a difficult and intricate task" whose "technique is a matter for educational experts, but its object is for the vision of seers" (Paschal 1974: 31ff). The fundamental challenge of education was for him at that time to "develop the Best" to guide the community, and to avoid focus simply on career preparation. The task is not to develop moneymakers or even artisans but men and women of intelligence and character, with knowledge of the world that was and is, and commitment to community. Although he later modified stress on the Talented Tenth to deal with its class problem, he still maintained that service to the people was key to any viable and valuable concept of education (Stewart 1984: 306ff).

One can see the concept of mission in Mary McLeod Bethune's (1939: 9) concept of education as a process of searching for truth, critically interpreting it, and then spreading it. In a word, she (1938: 10) says truth is "to discover the dawn and to bring this material within the understanding of the child and the masses of our people." For, she continues, although "we are living in a great age of science and invention . . . we still have the human problem of distribution of natural resources and of seeing that the fruits of science and invention are within the reach of the masses who need it most." The need, she concludes, is an ethically focused education which teaches one obligations not simply to self but to community, society, and humanity and to look forward at the end of one's life to standing tall "on the platform of service" (Bethune 1939: 46).

The stress on the academic and social nature of the educational project was also expressed in the relationship of the university to the community. Early in Black studies history, the relationship of the university to the community was defined as important and even indispensable by Nathan Hare, one of the founders of the discipline. Hare (1969, 1972, 1975), who established the first Black studies program, made essential to his conception of the discipline the joining of the university and the community in a mutually beneficial ongoing relationship. His conception was summarized in the idea, bring the community to the campus and take the campus to the community.

This mutually beneficial exchange between community and campus would involve, at a minimum, several aspects. First, it would require the university to recognize and reaffirm in practice its obligation to serve the communities in which it is located and those from which its students come. This implies not only the teaching of students but also joining with the community in cooperative projects to address critical issues and challenges. Second, such a relationship would necessitate the community's active involvement in the determination of what constitutes quality education. It would also require involvement in ongoing campus-sponsored educational projects and any other projects of mutual benefit. And finally, such an exchange would mean that students again, as Du Bois argued, would use their own experience to understand social and human reality and to enrich the educational process with it.

In such a process of reciprocal engagement on and off campus, students are challenged to frame questions and projects from their own experience and for their own future. They raise and seek to answer questions about the meaning, quality, and direction of their lives, not as abstracted individuals but as persons in community. Therefore, their efforts becomes not simply to understand self, society and the world but to change it. In this education and the corrective social practice it encourages, one discovers a practice of freedom.

Thus a joining of critique and corrective, in both the intellectual and practical sense, poses an important model which contains several components. First, the model focuses on critical thinking, on challenging the given and posing plausible alternatives to the established order of things. Second, this means that the university can no longer be seen and posed as simply a place for the authoritative transmission of sacrosanct knowledge of the Eurocentric world. On the contrary, it becomes a context for contestation and the cooperative discovery and production of knowledge of the real multicultural world. Third, this model encourages the creation of space and process for students to discover and speak the truth and meaning of their own cultural experience. This requires that they locate themselves in social and human history and having oriented themselves,

project possibilities of where they wish to go. Fourth, the concept of mission and social obligation removes education from the role of simple transmission of canon and job preparation to one of preparation for a quality life. And it reaffirms the imperative of critical thinking (i.e. below-the-surface searching for new and more ethically and culturally sensitive conceptions of society and human life). Finally, the university defined as a partner with the communities it serves creates the concept of joining the intellectual and practical in a project to create and sustain the just and good society.

THE HISTORICAL PERSPECTIVE

Another contribution which the Afrocentric vision of a quality education offers is its emphasis on the indispensability of the historical perspective in understanding social and human reality (Keto 1991). Africana studies is not to be equated with history, but it is considered within this framework as the key social science, given each discipline's dependence on it for grounding (Karenga 1993: 70). As Malcolm X (1965: 8) noted, "of all our studies history is best qualified to reward our research." For history is the central discipline of contextualization and orientation, and the Afrocentric stress on centeredness is both a historical and cultural concept. Thus, the first value and use of such historical stress is its function as a mode and means of centering.

Second, history for Africana studies has been the key means in the central and ongoing project of rescue and recovery. In a multicultural context, this means that African and other cultures are prized as treasure troves of rich and varied experiences, narratives, knowledge, and ways of being in the world. Thus, one rescues and reconstructs one's history as a part of the process of rescuing and reconstructing one's humanity. The study, writing, and discussion of history become ways of giving freedom to suppressed voices. Reconstructing a lost history is, as the ancient Egyptian texts teach, a process of "restoring that which is found in ruins, repairing what is found damaged and replenishing what is found lacking" (Lichtheim 1988: 43).

Central to Africana studies and the Afrocentric concept of education in this respect is the concept of *Sankofa*, an Akan concept of historical recovery. As Niangoran-Bouah (1984 Vol. I: n.p.) notes,

Sankofa "is made of the words san (to return), ko (to go) and fa (to take). The literal translation is: come back, seek and take or recover." The *Sankofa* ideogram is a bird reaching back with its beak into its feathers and "is a symbol representing the quest for knowledge and the return to the source." Niangoran-Bouah (1984 Vol. I: 210) further states that the ideogram implies that the resulting knowledge "is the outcome of research, of an intelligent and patient investigation." This concept of *Sankofa* with its dual emphasis on the quest for knowledge and return to the source has become a central concept in Africana studies in all its fields (i.e., history, religion, sociology, political science, economics, creative production, psychology, etc.). But the concept of *Sankofa* gets its greatest use in reference to the quest for historical paradigms to place in the service of the present and future.

Such a function of historical knowledge and paradigm is evident in the identification and beginning restoration of ancient Egypt (Kemet) as a paradigmatic classical African civilization. It is Cheikh Anta Diop (1982: 12), the Imhotepian or multidisciplined scholar, who posed ancient Egypt as the essential paradigmatic African civilization, arguing that "a look toward ancient Egypt is the best way of conceiving and building our culture future." In fact, he maintains that "Egypt will play, in a reconceived and renewed African culture, the same role that ancient Greco-Latin civilization plays in western culture." In a word, he concludes, for African peoples "the return to Egypt in all fields is the necessary condition to reconcile African civilizations with history, to build a body of modern human sciences and renew African culture." Afrocentric scholars have accepted the validity and urgency of this task and have begun to do work important to its completion (Asante 1990; Carruthers 1984; Karenga 1984, 1990a, 1990b; Karenga and Carruthers 1986).

The African rescue and recovery of ancient Egypt as a paradigm, which precedes and parallels in intellectual function as well as contributes to the Greek paradigm for Europe, has created an important source of contestation in the academy (*Arethusa* 1989: Bernal 1987; Diop 1982). The importance of this contribution lies in several areas. First, it provides an important creative challenge to Africana scholars who, in presenting and defending the paradigm and the work surrounding it, challenge and are challenged by Eurocentric

scholars. Second, the contestation becomes for Africana studies another opportunity to critique domination. For it challenges the cultural hegemony, an exclusive canon, and denial of the historical capacity and achievement of Africans and other peoples of color. In such a struggle, the falsification of African history becomes a metaphor for the falsification of human history. For central to Europe's falsification of human history was its removal of Africa from Egypt, Egypt from Africa, and Africa from human history.

Likewise, the emancipatory, intellectual, and practical struggles to return African to its own history and to human history become a metaphor and model of a similar return of all people to their history as well as to human history. Diop's concept of reconciling African civilization with human history becomes a metaphor and impetus for reconciling all excluded civilizations and cultures with human history. This process of reconciliation returns them to their rightful place, restoring the rich variousness of their voices and learning the complex and often contradictory messages they offer to teach. Such a contestation as both paradigm and process reaffirms the value and function of critical thinking in its demand for intellectual skill and human and ethical sensitivity.

Finally, the Afrocentric conception of history reveals history as a living concreteness. History, as I (1993: 70) argued elsewhere, is not simply a record but rather a struggle and record of specific peoples and humanity as a whole in the process of shaping their worlds and the world in their own image and interest. Here one sees the dynamic and dialectic of the particular and the universal, for as each people shapes its own world, it contributes to the shaping of the wholeworld. In this process it is important that no people impose their world view and practice on others or in a rationalized illusion of superiority assert themselves as the single paradigm for human thought and practice. Such has been the history of Europe in its drive for political and cultural hegemony. The history of peoples of color reveals liberational struggles in society and in the academy to challenge, check and end this hegemony.

At this point one sees how history, for Afrocentric scholars (as their critics charge) is not simply a neutral record. On the contrary, it is neither neutral nor simply a record. It is above all a struggle, a lived concreteness. At the heart of this process called history is the struggle to clear and create space for human freedom and human flourishing. Such is the history of Africans, for them history cannot be an abstract intellectual process. It is their lives unfolding or being checked, their perceptions given wings or restrained, and their struggle to be free and productive through emancipatory thought and practice. Such a conception of history offers multicultural education a mode of critical engagement in discourse and practice essential to the concept and process of quality education. For again students are challenged to discover, recover and speak the truth and meaning of their own experience, locate themselves in the larger realm of social and human history, and pose paradigms of human culture and society which contribute not only to our critical understanding of the world but also to our thrust to change it in the interest and image of human good. This, in turn, encourages and cultivates critical thinking, below-the-surface searching, and ethical concerns and conceptions of human life and society.

THE ETHICAL DIMENSION

A final contribution of the Afrocentric concept of education to the paradigm of a quality and multicultural education is the centrality of the ethical dimension. Again, since its inception, Africana studies has stressed the centrality of ethics to a quality education. This stress has its roots in several basic factors. First, it evolves from the emancipatory nature of the Africana studies project itself, which has at its central thrust a critique and corrective of domination and the posing of paradigms of human freedom and human flourishing. As mentioned earlier, the critique is essentially a moral critique of constraints on human freedom, and the correctives are always undergirded by the moral project of creating a just and good society.

Second, the focus on the ethical evolves from the definition of the dual mission of Black studies (i.e., academic excellence and social responsibility), a social responsibility which conceptually and practically is an ethical obligational task. It is an ethical responsibility to create the kind of community which practices and promotes human freedom and human flourishing. Moreover, one is obligated to create the kind of moral community one wishes to live in. In the earliest stage of Black

studies in the United States, Du Bois (1971: 61) argued that education was "primarily scientific, a careful search for truth conducted as thoroughly, broadly and honestly" as possible. However, he noted that in its more expansive form, the educational process was "not only to make the truth clear but [also] to present it in such shape as will encourage and help social reform."

Third, the very practice of generating reflective problematics and correctives from the African experience continuously raises critical ethical questions. For that experience is defined by oppression, resistance, and the creation and maintenance of free space for proactive practices in spite of social oppression. Both oppression and resistance unavoidably generate ethical questions, and thus much of Africana studies discourse revolves around issues of right and wrong and the grounds and meaning of human freedom and human flourishing.

Fourth, the stress on the ethical dimension evolves from an ancient tradition of emphasis on civic moral education. This tradition extends back to ancient Egypt with its concern for moral leadership and a just and good society (Carruthers 1984; Karenga 1989, 1994). Classical African philosophy in ancient Egypt posed the human ideal as a reflection of the universe which was grounded in and ordered by the principle of *Maat*. *Maat* was rightness in the social, nature, and divine sphere and translated as truth, justice, propriety, harmony, balance, reciprocity, and order.

Also key to this is the African world view in general with stress on freedom as responsible personhood in community. It stresses persons in community acting with shared initiative and responsibility to collectively conceive and create a social context for maximum social solidarity and human flourishing (Gyekye 1987; Wright 1984). This communitarian philosophy and emphasis of African culture serves as an essential framework for the conceptualization and pursuit of the just and good society. Such a society is defined by civility, reciprocity, and equality in all areas of human life and practice.

The contribution of this discourse to a quality multicultural education begins with its encouraging students and faculty to frame questions and generate problematics around the quality, purpose, and direction of social and human life. It cultivates an appreciation for framing and discussing issues of life and death in ethical terms rather than vulgarly pragmatic and egoistic ones. Second, such an ethical dimension to the educational process also encourages critical thinking, because only in matters of faith are such issues of life and death exempt from complexity and most often ambiguity. One is compelled to do below-the-surface thinking to confront and be confronted in a mutually benefiting process.

The Afrocentric stress on ethics also becomes a way to begin to integrate the disciplines. For it rightly raises questions about the relevance of knowledge and its pursuit to the human person and the human community. This means that ethical questions about the world or ethical questions of life and death are no longer safely assigned to religion. Rather each discipline raises its own ethical questions as well as participates in discourse on general ethical issues. This would include the hard sciences, which often conceive of themselves as exempt from and beyond valuative discourse and ethical judgment. However, it is the hard sciences—physical and technical—which have produced products and processes of the greatest threat to humankind and the environment. Thus, neither they nor their practitioners can be exempt from discussion of how they conceive, approach, and affect the world.

Finally, the Afrocentric stress on ethics as a fundamental component of a quality education brings to the multicultural process of exchange support for the concept of pursuit of the common good. For pursuit of the common good is at heart an ethical project in the philosophical and practical sense. It translates as democratic multicultural discourse on and pursuit of social policies aimed at creating a context of maximum human flourishing.

African Americans have played a historical and current vanguard role in setting and pursuing the moral and socially progressive agenda in this country. Therefore, it is only logical that they would play a vanguard role in creating space and impetus for a generalized and deepened ethical discourse in the academy. Not only does African culture have the oldest ethical texts in the world, but it is the African American struggle which has been at the heart of fundamental changes in the quality of life in this country. Moreover, this straggle for a just and good society has posed a paradigm which has been both instructive and inspiring to other people of color, women, the dis-

abled, the seniors, and other marginalized groups in this country, as well as peoples in South Africa, South America, the Philippines, China, Eastern Europe, and the Palestinian and Israeli peace movement. In these struggles, the participants borrowed from and built on the moral vision and moral vocabulary of the African American struggle and embraced it as a paradigm for the struggle of human liberation.

Jesse Jackson (1989: 14) contends rightly that the "greater good is the common good," which is clearly "a good beyond personal comfort and position." It is a good created out of the common aspirations of many peoples, groups, and cultures who share this society and want and are willing to cooperate in building a just and good society. This aspiration finds itself needing a public philosophy beyond liberal myths of melting pots and Eurocentric concepts of universality. It seeks and must be grounded in a public philosophy which teaches above all (1) the reality that U.S. society is not a finished white product but rather an ongoing multicultural project, and (2) that each person and people has both the right and responsibility to speak their own special cultural truth and make their own unique contribution to the forward flow of societal and human history. Moreover, such a public philosophy will build on the best ethical traditions of the many cultures that constitute the U.S. social project. These traditions will, of necessity, contain the values of civic virtue, voluntarism, reciprocity, cooperativeness, and social justice. They will stress creative resolution of tensions between the personal and the collective, community and society, the private and the public, and different and common.

Finally, these traditions must merge in the public sphere in redefining politics in the classical African sense as an ethical and collective vocation to create a just and good society. Such an ethical vocation will be one of shared responsibility in a shared public life of mutual benefit and cooperation. Such a vocation will also seek to create a democratic political and economic sphere. All this, of course, requires public debate and discourse, and the academy becomes an indispensable context for conception and discourse based on civility, reciprocity, and equality. The challenge is to initiate and sustain such a discourse and the companion practical project which gives such discourse its relevance and ultimate reality.

References

Arethusa. 1989. Special issue (Fall).

Asante, Molefi. 1980. *Afrocentricity: The Theory of Social Change.* Buffalo: Amulefi.

Asante, Molefi. 1987. *The Afrocentric Idea.* Philadelphia: Temple University Press.

Asante, Molefi. 1990. *Kemet, Afrocentricity and Knowledge.* Trenton, NJ: Africa World Press.

Bernal, Martin. 1987. *Black Athena: The Afro-Asiantic Roots of Classical Civilization.* Vol. I. London: Free Association Books.

Bethune, Mary McLeod. 1939. "The Adaptation of the History of the Negro to the Capacity of the Child." *Journal of Negro History* 24: 9–13.

Blassingame, John. 1973. *New Perspectives on Black Studies.* Chicago: University of Illinois Press.

Breasted, James. 1934. *The Dawn of Conscience.* New York: Charles Scribner's.

Brisbane, Robert. 1974. *Black Activism.* Valley Forge, PA: Judson Press.

Carruthers, Jacob H. 1984. *Essays in Ancient Egyptian Studies.* Los Angeles: University of Sankore Press.

Cooper, Anna Julia. 1988. *A Voice from the South.* New York: Oxford University Press.

Cope, Trevor. 1968. *Izibongo: Zulu Praise Poems.* New York: Oxford University Press.

Diop, Cheikh Anta. 1982. *Civilization ou Barbarie.* Paris: Presence Africaine. English translation, *Civilization or Barbarism.* Brooklyn, NY: Lawrence Hill, 1990.

Du Bois, W. E. B. 1971. *The Dusk of Dawn.* New York: Schocken Books.

Du Bois, W. E. B. 1975. *The Education of Black People: Ten Critiques, 1906–1960.* New York: Monthly Review Press.

Ferguson, Russell, Martha Gever, Trinh T. Minha, and Cornel West. eds. 1990. *Out There: Marginalization and Contemporary Cultures.* Cambridge, MA: MIT Press.

Finnestad, Ragnhild B. 1989. "Egyptian Thought about Life as a Problem of Translation." In *The Religion of the Ancient Egyptians: Cognitive Structures and Popular Expressions,* Gertie Englund, ed. Uppsala: Acta Universitatis Upsaliensis.

Giroux, Henry. 1992. *Border Crossings: Cultural Workers and the Politics of Education.* New York: Routledge.

Gyekye, Kwame. 1987. *An Essay on African Philosophical Thought: The Akan Conceptual Scheme.* New York: Cambridge University Press.

Hare, Nathan. 1969. "What Should be the Role of Afro-American Education in the Undergraduate Curriculum?" *Liberal Education* 55(March): 42–50.

Hare, Nathan. 1972. "The Battle of Black Studies." *Black Scholar* 3(May): 32–37.

Hare, Nathan. 1975. "A Black Paper: The Relevance of Black Studies." *Black Collegian* 6(September/October): 46–50.

Hassan, Ihab. 1987. *The Post Modern Turn: Essays in Postmodern Theory and Culture.* Columbus, OH: State University Press.

Hicks, Florience J., ed. *Mary McLeod Bethune: Her Own Words of Inspiration.* Washington, DC: Nuclassics and Science Publishing Company.

Hooks, Bell. 1990. *Yearnings: Race, Gender and Culture Politics.* Boston: South End Press.

Hornung, Erik. 1985. *Conceptions of God in Ancient Egypt.* Ithaca, NY: Cornell University Press.

Jackson, Jesse. 1989. "A Call to Common Ground." *Black Scholar* 20(1): 12–18.

Karenga, Maulana. 1984. *Selections from the Husia: Sacred Wisdom of Ancient Egypt.* Los Angeles: University of Sankore Press.

Karenga, Maulana. 1988. "Black Studies and the Problematic of Paradigm: The Philosophical Dimension." *Journal of Black Studies* 18, 4(June): 395–414.

Karenga, Maulana. 1989b. "Towards a Sociology of Maatian Ethics: Literature and Context." *Journal of African Civilizations* 10, (Fall): 352–395.

Karenga, Maulana. 1990a. *The Book of Coming Forth By Day: The Ethics of the Declarations of Innocence.* Los Angeles: University of Sankore Press.

Karenga, Maulana, ed. 1990b. *Reconstructing Kemetic Culture.* Los Angeles: University of Sankore Press.

Karenga, Maulana. 1993. *Introduction to Black Studies.* 2nd ed. Los Angeles: University of Sankore Press.

Karenga, Maulana. 1994. *Maat, The Moral Idea in Ancient Egypt: A Study in Classical African Ethics.* 2 Vols., Ph.D. Dissertation. University of Southern California.

Karenga, Maulana, and Jacob H. Carruthers, eds. 1986. *Kemet and the African World View.* Los Angeles: University of Sankore Press.

Keto, C. Tsehloane, 1991. *The Africa Centered Perspective of History: An Introduction.* Laurel Springs, NJ: K. A. Publishers.

Lichtheim, Miriam. 1975. *Ancient Egyptian Literature,* Vol. I. Berkeley: University of California Press.

Lichtheim, Miriam. 1988. *Ancient Egyptian Autobiographies Chiefly from the Middle Kingdom.* Feiburg, Switzerland: Universitatsverlag.

Locke, Alain. 1968. *The New Negro.* New York: Atheneum.

Malcolm X. 1965. *Malcolm X Speaks.* New York: Merit Publishers.

Malcolm X. 1968. *The Speeches of Malcolm X at Harvard,* Archie Epps, ed. New York: William Morrow and Co.

Mbiti, John. 1970. *African Religion and Philosophy.* Garden City, NY: Anchor Books.

Menkiti, Ifeanyi. 1984. "Person and Community in African Traditional Thought." In *African Philosophy: An Introduction,* 3rd ed. Richard Wright, ed. Lanham, MD: University Press of America.

Ming, Tu Wei. 1985. *Confucian Thought: Selfhood as Creative Transformation.* Albany: State University of New York Press.

Morenz, Siegfried. 1973. *Egyptian Religion.* Ithaca, NY: Cornell University Press.

Niangoran-Bouah, G. 1984. *The Akan World of Gold Weights: Abstract Design Weights,* Vol. I. Abidjan, Ivory Coast: Les Nouvelles Editions Africaines.

Paschal, Andrew, ed. 1974. *A W. E. B. Du Bois Reader.* New York: Macmillan.

Ravitch, Dianne. 1990. "Multiculturalism." *American Scholar* (Summer): 337–354.

Report. 1991. *The Challenge of Diversity and Multicultural Education: Report of the President's Task Force on Multicultural Education and Campus Diversity.* Long Beach: California State University.

Robinson, Armstead, C. Foster, and D. Ogilvie. 1969. *Black Studies in the University.* New York: Bantam Books.

Schapera, I., ed. 1965. *Praise Poems of Tswana Chiefs.* New York: Oxford University Press.

Schlesinger, Arthur. 1991. *The Disuniting of America: Reflections on a Multicultural Society.* Knoxville, TN: Whittle Direct Books.

Simpson, William K., ed. 1973. *The Literature of Ancient Egypt.* New Haven, CT: Yale University Press.

Stewart, James. 1984. "The Legacy of W. E. B. Du Bois for Contemporary Black Studies." *The Journal of Negro Education* 53:296–311.

Turner, James. ed. 1984. *The Next Decade: Theoretical and Research Issues in Africana Studies.* Ithaca, NY: Africana Research and Studies Center, Cornell University.

Woodson, Carter G. 1969. *Mis-Education of the Negro.* Washington, DC: Associated Publishers.

Wright, Richard. 1984. *African Philosophy.* 3rd ed. New York: University Press of America.

CHAPTER 22

The Silenced Dialogue: Power and Pedagogy in Educating Other People's Children

Lisa Delpit

Lisa Delpit currently holds the Benjamin E. Mays Chair of Urban Educational Leadership at Georgia State University in Atlanta, Georgia. She received the award for Outstanding Contribution to Education in 1993 from the Harvard Graduate School of Education, which hailed her as a "visionary scholar and woman of courage."

A black male graduate student who is also a special education teacher in a predominantly black community is talking about his experiences in predominantly white university classes:

> There comes a moment in every class where we have to discuss "The Black Issue" and what's appropriate education for black children. I tell you, I'm tired of arguing with those white people, because they won't listen. Well, I don't know if they really don't listen or if they just don't believe you. It seems like if you can't quote Vygotsky or something, then you don't have any validity to speak about your *own* kids. Anyway, I'm not bothering with it anymore, now I'm just in it for a grade.

A black woman teacher in a multicultural urban elementary school is talking about her experiences in discussions with her predominantly white fellow teachers about how they should organize reading instruction to best serve students of color:

> When you're talking to white people they still want it to be their way. You can try to talk to them and give them examples, but they're so headstrong, they think they know what's best for *everybody*, for *everybody's* children. They won't listen; white folks are going to do what they want to do *anyway*.

> It's really hard. They just don't listen well. No, they listen, but they don't *hear*—you know how your mama used to say you listen to the radio, but you *hear* your mother? Well they don't *hear* me.

> So I just try to shut them out so I can hold my temper. You can only beat your head against a brick wall for so long before you draw blood. If I try to stop arguing with them I can't help myself from getting angry. Then I end up walking around praying all day "Please Lord, remove the bile I feel for these people so I can sleep tonight." It's funny, but it can become a cancer, a sore.

> So, I shut them out. I go back to my own little cubby, my class room, and I try to teach the way I know will work, no matter what those folk say. And when I get black kids, I just try to undo the damage they did.

> I'm not going to let any man, woman, or child drive me crazy—white folks will try to do that to you if you let them. You just have to stop talking to them, that's what I do. I just keep smiling, but I won't talk to them.

A soft-spoken Native Alaskan woman in her forties is a student in the Education Department of the University of Alaska. One day she storms into a black professor's office and very uncharacteristically slams the door. She plops down in a chair and, still fuming, says, "Please tell those people, just don't help us anymore! I give up. I won't talk to them again!"

And finally, a black woman principal who is also a doctoral student at a well-known university on the West Coast is talking about her university experiences, particularly about when a professor lectures on issues concerning educating black children:

> If you try to suggest that's not quite the way it is, they get defensive, then you get defensive, then they'll start reciting research.
>
> I try to give them my experiences, to explain. They just look and nod. The more I try to explain, they just look and nod, just keep looking and nodding. They don't really hear me.
>
> Then, when it's time for class to be over, the professor tells me to come to his office to talk more. So I go. He asks for more examples of what I'm talking about, and he looks and nods while I give them. Then he says that that's just *my* experience. It doesn't really apply to most black people.
>
> It becomes futile because they think they know everything about everybody. What you have to say about your life, your children, doesn't mean anything. They don't really want to hear what you have to say. They wear blinders and earplugs. They only want to go on research they've read that other white people have written.
>
> It just doesn't make any sense to keep talking to them.

Thus was the first half of the title of this text born: "The Silenced Dialogue." One of the tragedies in this field of education is that scenarios such as these are enacted daily around the country. The saddest element is that the individuals that the black and Native Alaskan educators speak of in these statements are seldom aware that the dialogue *has* been silenced. Most likely the white educators believe that their colleagues of color did, in the end, agree with their logic. After all, they stopped disagreeing, didn't they?

I have collected these statements since completing a recently published article, a somewhat autobiographical account entitled "Skills and Other Dilemmas of a Progressive Black Educator," in which I discuss my perspective as a product of a skills-oriented approach to writing and as a teacher of process-oriented approaches. I described the estrangement that I and many teachers of color feel from the progressive movement when writing process advocates dismiss us as too "skills oriented." I

ended the article suggesting that it was incumbent upon writing process advocates, or indeed, advocates of any progressive movement, to enter into dialogue with teachers of color, who may not share their enthusiasm about so-called new, liberal, or progressive ideas.

In response to this article, which presented no research data and did not even cite a reference, I received numerous calls and letters from teachers, professors, and even state school personnel from around the country, both black and white. All of the white respondents, except one, have wished to talk more about the question of skills versus process approaches—to support or reject what they perceive to be my position. On the other hand, *all* of the nonwhite respondents have spoken passionately on being left out of the dialogue about how best to educate children of color.

How can such complete communication blocks exist when both parties truly believe they have the same aims? How can the bitterness and resentment expressed by the educators of color be drained so that the sores can heal? What can be done?

I believe the answer to these questions lies in ethnographic analysis, that is, in identifying and giving voice to alternative worldviews. Thus, I will attempt to address the concerns raised by white and black respondents to my article "Skills and Other Dilemmas." My charge here is not to determine the best instructional methodology; I believe that the actual practice of good teachers of all colors typically incorporates a range of pedagogical orientations. Rather, I suggest that the differing perspectives on the debate over "skills" versus "process" approaches can lead to an understanding of the alienation and miscommunication, and thereby to an understanding of the "silenced dialogue."

In thinking through these issues, I have found what I believe to be a connecting and complex theme: what I have come to call "the culture of power." There are five aspects of power I would like to propose as given for this presentation:

1. Issues of power are enacted in classrooms.

2. There are codes or rules for participating in power; that is, there is a "culture of power."

3. The rules of the culture of power are a reflection of the rules of the culture of those who have power.

4. If you are not already a participant in the culture of power, being told explicitly the rules of that culture makes acquiring power easier.

5. Those with power are frequently least aware of or least willing to acknowledge—its existence. Those with less power are often most aware of its existence.

The first three are by now basic tenets in the literature of the sociology of education, but the last two have seldom been addressed. The following discussion will explicate these aspects of power and their relevance to the schism between liberal educational movements and that of non-white, non-middle-class teachers and communities.

1. Issues of power are enacted in classrooms.

These issues include: the power of the teacher over the students; the power of the publishers of textbooks and of the developers of the curriculum to determine the view of the world presented; the power of the state in enforcing compulsory schooling; and the power of an individual or group to determine another's intelligence or "normalcy." Finally, if schooling prepares people for jobs, and the kind of job a person has determines her or his economic status and, therefore, power, then schooling is intimately related to that power.

2. There are codes or rules for participating in power; that is, there is a "culture of power."

The codes or rules I'm speaking of relate to linguistic forms, communicative strategies, and presentation of self; that is, ways of talking, ways of writing, ways of dressing, and ways of interacting.

3. The rules of the culture of power are a reflection of the rules of the culture of those who have power.

This means that success in institutions—schools, workplaces, and so on—is predicated upon acquisition of the culture of those who are in power. Children from middle-class homes tend to do better in school than those from non-middle-class homes because the culture of the school is based on the culture of the upper and middle classes—of those in power. The upper and middle classes send their children to school with all the accoutrements of the culture of power; children from other kinds of families operate within perfectly wonderful and viable cultures but not cultures that carry the codes or rules of power.

4. If you are not already a participant in the culture of power, being told explicitly the rules of that culture makes acquiring power easier.

In my work within and between diverse cultures, I have come to conclude that members of any culture transmit information implicitly to co-members. However, when implicit codes are attempted across cultures, communication frequently breaks down. Each cultural group is left saying, "Why don't those people say what they mean?" as well as, "What's wrong with them, why don't they understand?"

Anyone who has had to enter new cultures, especially to accomplish a specific task, will know of what I speak. When I lived in several Papua New Guinea villages for extended periods to collect data, and when I go to Alaskan villages for work with Native Alaskan communities, I have found it unquestionably easier, psychologically and pragmatically, when some kind soul has directly informed me about such matters as appropriate dress, interactional styles, embedded meanings, and taboo words or actions. I contend that it is much the same for anyone seeking to learn the rules of the culture of power. Unless one has the leisure of a lifetime of "immersion" to learn them, explicit presentation makes learning immeasurably easier.

And now, to the fifth and last premise:

5. Those with power are frequently least aware of or least willing to acknowledge its existence. Those with less power are often most aware of its existence.

For many who consider themselves members of liberal or radical camps, acknowledging personal power and admitting participation in the culture of power is distinctly uncomfortable. On the other hand, those who are less powerful in any situation are most likely to recognize the power variable most acutely. My guess is that the white colleagues and instructors of those previously quoted did not perceive themselves to have power over the nonwhite speakers. However, either by virtue of their position, their numbers, or their access to that particular code of power of calling upon research to validate one's position, the white educators had the authority to establish what was to be considered "truth" regardless of the opinions of the people of color, and the latter were well aware of that fact.

A related phenomenon is that liberals (and here I am using the term "liberal" to refer to those whose beliefs include striving for a society based upon maximum individual freedom and autonomy) seem to act under the assumption that to make any rules or expectations explicit is to act against liberal principles, to limit the freedom and autonomy of those subjected to the explicitness.

I thank Fred Erickson for a comment that led me to look again at a tape by John Gumperz on cultural dissonance in cross-cultural interactions. One of the episodes showed an East Indian interviewing for a job with an all-white committee. The interview was a complete failure, even though several of the interviewers appeared to really want to help the applicant. As the interview rolled steadily downhill, these "helpers" became more and more indirect in their questioning, which exacerbated the problems the applicant had in performing appropriately. Operating from a different cultural perspective, he got fewer and fewer clear clues as to what was expected of him, which ultimately resulted in his failure to secure the position.

I contend that as the applicant showed less and less aptitude for handling the interview, the power differential became ever more evident to the interviewers. The "helpful" interviewers, unwilling to acknowledge themselves as having power over the applicant, became more and more uncomfortable. Their indirectness was an attempt to lessen the power differential and their discomfort by lessening the power-revealing explicitness of their questions and comments.

When acknowledging and expressing power, one tends towards explicitness (as in yelling at your ten-year-old, "Turn that radio down!"). When deemphasizing power, there is a move toward indirect communication. Therefore, in the interview setting, those who sought to help, to express their egalitarianism with the East Indian applicant, became more and more indirect—and less and less helpful—in their questions and comments.

In literacy instruction, explicitness might be equated with direct instruction. Perhaps the ulti-mate expression of explicitness and direct instruction in the primary classroom is Distar. This reading program is based on a behaviorist model in which reading is taught through the direct instruction of phonics generalizations and blending. The teacher's role is to maintain the full attention of the group by continuous questioning, eye contact, finger snaps, hand claps, and other gestures, and by eliciting choral responses and initiating some sort of award system.

When the program was introduced, it arrived with a flurry of research data that "proved" that all children—even those who were "culturally deprived"—could learn to read using this method. Soon there was a strong response, first from academics and later from many classroom teachers, stating that the program was terrible. What I find particularly interesting, however, is that the primary issue of the conflict over Distar has not been over its instructional efficacy—usually the students did learn to read—but the expression of explicit power in the classroom. The liberal educators opposed the methods—the direct instruction, the explicit control exhibited by the teacher. As a matter of fact, it was not unusual (even now) to hear of the program spoken of as "fascist."

I am not an advocate of Distar, but I will return to some of the issues that the program, and direct instruction in general, raises in understanding the differences between progressive white educators and educators of color.

To explore those differences, I would like to present several statements typical of those made with the best of intentions by middle-class liberal educators. To the surprise of the speakers, it is not unusual for such content to be met by vocal opposition or stony silence from people of color. My attempt here is to examine the underlying assumptions of both camps.

"I want the same thing for everyone else's children as I want for mine."

To provide schooling for everyone's children that reflects liberal, middle-class values and aspirations is to ensure the maintenance of the status quo, to ensure that power, the culture of power, remains in the hands of those who already have it. Some children come to school with more accoutrements of the culture of power already in place—"cultural capital," as some critical theorist refer to it—some with less. Many liberal educators hold that the primary goal for education is for children to become autonomous, to develop fully who they are in the classroom setting without having arbitrary, outside standards forced upon them. This is a very reasonable goal for people whose children are already participants in the culture of power and who have already internalized its codes.

But parents who don't function within that culture often want something else. It's not that they disagree with the former aim, it's just that they want something more. They want to ensure that the school provides their children with discourse patterns, interactional styles, and spoken and written language codes that will allow them success in the larger society.

It was the lack of attention to this concern that created such a negative outcry in the black community when well-intentioned white liberal educators introduced "dialect readers." These were seen as a plot to prevent the schools from teaching the linguistic aspects of the culture of power, thus dooming black children to a permanent outsider caste. As one parent demanded, "My kids know how to be black—you all reach them how to be successful in the white man's world."

Several black teachers have said to me recently that as much as they'd like to believe otherwise, they cannot help but conclude that many of the "progressive" educational strategies imposed by liberals upon black and poor children could only be based on a desire to ensure that the liberals' children get sole access to the dwindling pool of American jobs. Some have added that the liberal educators believe themselves to be operating with good intentions, but that these good intentions are only conscious delusions about their unconscious true motives. One of the black anthropologist John Gwaltney's informants in *Drylongso* reflects this perspective with her tongue-in-cheek observation that the biggest difference between black folks and white folks is that black folks *know* when they're lying!

Let me try to clarify how this might work in literacy instruction. A few years ago I worked on an analysis of two popular reading programs, Distar and a progressive program that focused on higher-level critical thinking skills. In one of the first lessons of the progressive program, the children are introduced to the names of the letters *m* and *e*. In the same lesson they are then taught the sound made by each of the letters, how to write

each of the letters, and that when the two are blended together they produce the word *me*.

As an experienced first-grade teacher, I am convinced that a child needs to be familiar with a significant number of these concepts to be able to assimilate so much new knowledge in one sitting. By contrast, Distar presents the same information in about forty lessons.

I would not argue for the pace of Distar lessons—such a slow pace would only bore most kids—but what happened in the other lesson is that it merely provided an opportunity for those who already knew the content to exhibit that they knew it, or at most perhaps to build one new concept onto what was already known. This meant that the child who did not come to school already primed with what was to be presented would be labeled as needing "remedial" instruction from day one; indeed, this determination would be made before he or she was ever taught. In fact, Distar was "successful" because it actually *taught* new information to children who had not already acquired it at home. Although the more progressive system was ideal for some children, for others it was a disaster.

I do not advocate a simplistic "basic skills" approach for children outside of the culture of power. It would be (and has been) tragic to operate as if these children were incapable of critical and higher-order thinking and reasoning. Rather, I suggest that schools must provide these children the content that other families from a different cultural orientation provide at home. This does not mean separating children according to family background, but instead, ensuring that each classroom incorporate strategies appropriate for all the children in its confines.

And I do not advocate that it is the school's job to attempt to change the homes of poor and non-white children to match the homes of those in the culture of power. That may indeed be a form of cultural genocide. I have frequently heard schools call poor parents "uncaring" when parents respond to the school's urging, saying, "But that's the school's job." What the school personnel fail to understand is that if the parents were members of the culture of power and lived by its rules and codes, then they would transmit those codes to their children. In fact, they transmit another culture that children must learn at home in order to survive in their communities.

"Child-centered, whole language, and process approaches are needed in order to allow a democratic state of free, autonomous, empowered adults, and because research has shown that children learn best through these methods."

People of color are, in general, skeptical of research as a determiner of our fates. Academic research has, after all, found us genetically inferior, culturally deprived, and verbally deficient. But beyond that general caveat, and despite my or others' personal preferences, there is little research data supporting the major tenets of process approaches over other forms of literacy instruction, and virtually no evidence that such approaches are more efficacious for children of color.

Although the problem is not necessarily inherent in the method, in some instances adherents of process approaches to writing create situations in which students ultimately find themselves held accountable for knowing a set of rules about which no one has ever directly informed them. Teachers do students no service to suggest, even implicitly, that "product" is not important. In this country, students will be judged on their product regardless of the process they utilized to achieve it. And that product, based as it is on the specific codes of a particular culture, is more readily produced when the directives of how to produce it are made explicit.

If such explicitness is not provided to students, what it feels like to people who are old enough to judge is that there are secrets being kept, that time is being wasted, that the teacher is abdicating his or her duty to teach. A doctoral student of my acquaintance was assigned to a writing class to hone his writing skills. The student was placed in the section led by a white professor who utilized a process approach, consisting primarily of having the students write essays and then assemble into groups to edit each other's papers. That procedure infuriated this particular student. He had many angry encounters with the teacher about what she was doing. In his words:

> I didn't feel she was teaching us anything. She wanted us to correct each other's papers and we were there to learn from her. She didn't teach anything, absolutely nothing.
>
> Maybe they're trying to learn what black folks knew all the time. We understand how to improvise, how to express ourselves creatively. When I'm in a classroom, I'm not looking for

that, I'm looking for structure, the more formal language.

> Now my buddy was in [a] black teacher's class. And that lady was very good. She went through and explained and defined each part of the structure. This [white] teacher didn't get along with that black teacher. She said that she didn't agree with her methods. Buy *I* don't think that white teacher *had* any methods.

When I told this gentleman that what the teacher was doing was called a process method of teaching writing, his response was, "Well, at least now I know that she *thought* she was doing *something.* I thought she was just a fool who couldn't teach and didn't want to try."

This sense of being cheated can be so strong that the student may be completely turned off to the educational system. Amanda Branscombe, an accomplished white teacher, recently wrote a letter discussing her work with working-class black and white students at a community college in Alabama. She had given these students my "Skills and Other Dilemmas" article to read and discuss, and wrote that her students really understood and identified with what I was saying. To quote her letter:

> One young man said that he had dropped out of high school because he failed the exit exam. He noted that he had then passed the GED without a problem after three weeks of prep. He said that his high school English teacher claimed to use a process approach, but what she really did was hide behind fancy words to give herself permission to do nothing in the classroom.

The students I have spoken of seem to be saying that the teacher has denied them access to herself as the source of knowledge necessary to learn the forms they need to succeed. Again, I tentatively attribute the problem to teachers' resistance to exhibiting power in the classroom. Somehow, to exhibit one's personal power as expert source is viewed as disempowering one's students.

Two qualifiers are necessary, however. The teacher cannot be the only expert in the classroom. To deny students their own expert knowledge *is* to disempower them. Amanda Branscombe, when she was working with black high school students classified as "slow learners," had the students analyze rap songs to discover their underlying patterns. The students became the experts in explaining to the teacher the rules for creating a new rap song. The teacher then used the patterns the students identified as a base to begin an explanation of the structure of grammar, and then of Shakespeare's plays. Both student and teacher are expert at what they know best.

The second qualifier is that merely adopting direct instruction is not the answer. Actual writing for real audiences and real purposes is a vital element in helping students to understand that they have an important voice in their own learning processes. E. V. Siddle examines the results of various kinds of interventions in a primarily process-oriented writing class for black students. Based on readers' blind assessments, she found that the intervention that produced the most positive changes in the students' writing was a "mini-lesson" consisting of direct instruction about some standard writing convention. But what produced the *second* highest number of positive changes was a subsequent student-centered conference with the teacher. (Peer conferencing in this group of black students who were not members of the culture of power produced the least number of changes in students' writing. However, the classroom teacher maintained—and I concur—that such activities are necessary to introduce the elements of "real audience" into the task, along with more teacher-directed strategies.)

"It's really a shame but she (that black teacher upstairs) seems to be so authoritarian, so focused on skills and so teacher directed. Those poor kids never seem to be allowed to really express their creativity. (And she even yells at them.)"

This statement directly concerns the display of power and authority in the classroom. One way to understand the difference in perspective between black teachers and their progressive colleagues on this issue is to explore culturally influenced oral interactions.

In *Ways with Words,* Shirley Brice Heath quotes the verbal directives given by the middle-class "townspeople" teachers:[7]

—"Is this where the scissors belong?"

—"You want to do your best work today."

By contrast, many black teachers are more likely to say:

—"Put those scissors on that shelf."

—"Put your name on the papers and make sure to get the right answer for each question."

Is one oral style more authoritarian than another?

Other researchers have identified differences in middle-class and working-class speech to children. Snow and others, for example, report that working-class mothers use more directives to their children than do middle- and upper-class parents. Middle-class parents are likely to give the directive to a child to take his bath as, "Isn't it time for your bath?" Even though the utterance is couched as a question, both child and adult understand it as a directive. The child may respond with "Aw, Mom, can't I wait until . . .," but whether or not negotiation is attempted, both conversants understand the intent of the utterance.

By contrast, a black mother, in whose house I was recently a guest, said to her eight-year-old son, "Boy, get your rusty behind in that bathtub." Now, I happen to know that this woman loves her son as much as any mother, but she would never have posed the directive to her son to take a bath in the form of a question. Were she to ask, "Would you like to take your bath now?" she would not have been issuing a directive but offering a true alternative. Consequently, as Heath suggests, upon entering school the child from such a family may not understand the indirect statement of the teacher as a direct command. Both white and black working-class children in the communities Heath studied "had difficulty interpreting these indirect requests for adherence to an unstated set of rules."

But those veiled commands are commands nonetheless, representing true power, and with true consequences for disobedience. If veiled commands are ignored, the child will be labeled a behavior problem and possibly officially classified as behavior disordered. In other words, the attempt by the teacher to reduce an exhibition of power by expressing herself in indirect terms may remove the very explicitness that the child needs to understand the rules of the new classroom culture.

A black elementary school principal in Fairbanks, Alaska, reported to me that she has a lot of difficulty with black children who are placed in some white teachers' classrooms. The teachers often send the children to the office for disobeying teacher directives. Their parents are frequently called in for conferences. The parents' response to the teacher is usually the same. "They do what I say; if you just *tell* them what to do, they'll do it. I tell them at home that they have to listen to what you say." And so, does not the power still exist? Its veiled nature only makes it more difficult for some children to respond appropriately, but that in no way mitigates its existence.

I don't mean to imply, however, that the only time the black child disobeys the teacher is when he or she misunderstands the request for certain behavior. There are other factors that may produce such behavior. Black children expect an authority figure to act with authority. When the teacher instead acts as a "chum," the message sent is that this adult has no authority, and the children react accordingly. One reason that is so, is that black people often view issues of power and authority differently than people from mainstream middle-class backgrounds. Many people of color expect authority to be earned by personal efforts and exhibited by personal characteristics. In other words, "the authoritative person gets to be a teacher because she is authoritative." Some members of middle-class cultures, by contrast, expect one to achieve authority by the acquisition of an authoritative role. That is, "the teacher is the authority because she is the teacher."

In the first instance, because authority is earned, the teacher must consistently prove the characteristics that give her authority. These characteristics may vary across cultures, but in the black community they tend to cluster around several abilities. The authoritative teacher can control the class through exhibition of personal power; establishes meaningful interpersonal relationships that garner student respect; exhibits a strong belief that all students can learn; establishes a standard of achievement and "pushes" the students to achieve that standard; and holds the attention of the students by incorporating interactional features of black communicative style in his or her teaching.

By contrast, the teacher whose authority is vested in the role has many more options of behavior at her disposal. For instance, she does not need to express any sense of personal power because her authority does not come from anything she herself does or says. Hence, the power she actually holds may be veiled in such questions/commands as "Would you like to sit down now?" If the children in her class understand authority as she does, it is mutually agreed upon that they are to obey her no matter how indirect,

soft-spoken, or unassuming she may be. Her indirectness and soft-spokenness may indeed be, as I suggested earlier, an attempt to reduce the implication of overt power in order to establish a more egalitarian and nonauthoritarian classroom atmosphere.

If the children operate under another notion of authority, however, then there is trouble. The black child may perceive the middle-class teacher as weak, ineffectual, and incapable of taking on the role of being the teacher; therefore, there is no need to follow her directives. In her dissertation, Michelle Foster quotes one young black man describing such a teacher:

> She is boring, boring. She could do something creative. Instead she just stands there. She can't control the class, doesn't know how to control the class. She asked me what she was doing wrong. I told her she just stands there like she's meditating. I told her she could be meditating for all I know. She says that we're supposed to know what to do. I told her I don't know nothin' unless she tells me. She just can't control the class. I hope we don't have her next semester.[11]

But of course the teacher may not view the problem as residing in herself but in the student, and the child may once again become the behavior-disordered black boy in special education.

What characteristics do black students attribute to the good teacher? Again, Foster's dissertation provides a quotation that supports my experience with black students. A young black man is discussing a former teacher with a group of friends:

> We had fun in her class, but she was mean. I can remember she used to say, "Tell me what's in the story, Wayne." She pushed, she used to get on me and push me to know. She made us learn. We had to get in the books. There was this tall guy and he tried to take her on, but she was in charge of that class and she didn't let anyone run her. I still have this book we used in her class. It has a bunch of stories in it. I just read one on Coca-Cola again the other day.

To clarify, this student was *proud* of the teacher's "meanness," an attribute he seemed to describe as the ability to run the class and pushing and expecting students to learn. Now, does the liberal perspective of the negatively authoritarian black teacher really hold up? I suggest that although all "explicit" black teachers are not also good teachers, there are different attitudes in different cultural groups about which characteristics make for a goad teacher. Thus, it is impossible to create a model for the good teacher without taking issues of culture and community context into account.

And now to the final comment I present for examination:

"Children have the right to their own language, their own culture. We must fight cultural begemony and fight the system by insisting that children be allowed to express themselves in their own language style. It is not they, the children, who must change, but the schools. To push children to do anything else is repressive and reactionary."

A statement such as this originally inspired me to write the "Skills and Other Dilemmas" article. It was first written as a letter to a colleague in response to a situation that had developed in our department. I was teaching a senior-level teacher education course. Students were asked to prepare a written autobiographical document for the class that would also be shared with their placement school prior to their student teaching.

Onc student, a talented young Native American woman, submitted a paper in which the ideas were lost because of technical problems—from spelling to sentence structure to paragraph structure. Removing her name, I duplicated the paper for a discussion with some faculty members. I had hoped to initiate a discussion about what we could do to ensure that our students did not reach the senior level without getting assistance in technical writing skills when they needed them.

I was amazed at the response. Some faculty implied that the student should never have been allowed into the teacher education program. Others, some of the more progressive minded, suggested that I was attempting to function as gatekeeper by raising the issue, and had internalized repressive and disempowering forces of the power elite to suggest that something was wrong with a Native American student just because she had another style of writing. With few exceptions, I found myself alone in arguing against both camps.

No, this student should not have been denied entry to the program. To deny her entry under the notion of upholding standards is to blame the victim for the crime. We cannot justifiably enlist

exclusionary standards when the reason this student lacked the skills demanded was poor teaching at best and institutionalized racism at worst.

However, to bring this student into the program and pass her through without attending to obvious deficits in the codes needed for her to function effectively as a teacher is equally criminal—for though we may assuage our own consciences for not participating in victim blaming, she will surely be accused and convicted as soon as she leaves the university. As Native Alaskans were quick to tell me, and as I understood through my own experience in the black community, not only would she not be hired as a teacher, but those who did not hire her would make the (false) assumption that the university was putting out only incompetent Natives and that they should stop looking seriously at any Native applicants. A white applicant who exhibits problems is an individual with problems. A person of color who exhibits problems immediately becomes a representative of her cultural group.

No, either stance is criminal. The answer is to *accept* students but also to take responsibility to *teach* them. I decided to talk to the student and found out she had recognized that she needed some assistance in the technical aspects of writing soon after she entered the university as a freshman. She had gone to various members of the education faculty and received the same two kinds of responses I met with four years later: faculty members told her either that she should not even attempt to be a teacher, or that it didn't matter and that she shouldn't worry about such trivial issues. In her desperation, she had found a helpful professor in the English Department, but he left the university when she was in her sophomore year.

We sat down together, worked out a plan for attending to specific areas of writing competence, and set up regular meetings. I stressed to her the need to use her own learning process as insight into how best to teach her future students those "skills" that her own schooling had failed to teach her. I gave her some explicit rules to follow in some areas; for others, we devised various kinds of journals that, along with readings about the structure of the language, allowed her to find her own insights into how the language worked. All that happened two years ago, and the young woman is now successfully teaching. What the experience led me to understand is that pretending that gatekeeping points don't exist is to ensure that many students will not pass through them.

Now you may have inferred that I believe that because there is a culture of power, everyone should learn the codes to participate in it, and that is how the world should be. Actually, nothing could be further from the truth. I believe in a diversity of style, and I believe the world will be diminished if cultural diversity is ever obliterated. Further, I believe strongly, as do my liberal colleagues, that each cultural group should have the right to maintain its own language style. When I speak, therefore, of the culture of power, I don't speak of how I wish things to be but of how they are.

I further believe that to act as if power does not exist is to ensure that the power status quo remains the same. To imply to children or adults (but of course the adults won't believe you anyway) that it doesn't matter how you talk or how you write is to ensure their ultimate failure. I prefer to be honest with my students. I tell them that their language and cultural style is unique and wonderful but that there is a political power game that is also being played, and if they want to be in on that game there are certain games that they too must play.

But don't think that I let the onus of change rest entirely with the students. I am also involved in political work both inside and outside of the educational system, and that political work demands that I place myself to influence as many gatekeeping points as possible. Ant it is there that I agitate for change, pushing gatekeepers to open their doors to a variety of styles and codes. What I'm saying, however, is that I do not believe that political change toward diversity can be effected from the bottom up, as do some of my colleagues. They seem to believe that if we accept and encourage diversity within classrooms of children, then diversity will automatically be accepted at gatekeeping points.

I believe that will never happen. What will happen is that the students who reach the gatekeeping points—like Amanda Branscombe's student who dropped out of high school because he failed his exit exam—will understand that they have been lied to and will react accordingly. No, I am certain that if we are truly to effect societal change, we cannot do so from the bottom up, but we must push and agitate from the top down.

And in the meantime, we must take the responsibility to *teach*, to provide for students who do no already possess them, the additional codes of power.

But I also do not believe that we should teach students to passively adopt an alternate code. They must be encouraged to understand the value of the code they already possess as well as to understand the power realities in this country. Otherwise they will be unable to work to change these realities. And how does one do that?

Martha Demientiell, a masterful Native Alaskan teacher of Athabaskan Indian students, tells me that her students, who live in a small, isolated, rural village of less than two hundred people, are not aware that there are different codes in English. She takes their writing and analyzes it for features of what has been referred to by Alaskan linguists as "Village English," and then covers half a bulletin board with words or phrases from the students' writing, which she labels "Our Heritage Language." On the other half of the bulletin board she puts the equivalent statement in "Standard English," which she labels "Formal English."

She and the students spend a long time on the "Heritage English" section, savoring the words, discussing the nuances. She tells the students. "That's the way we say things. Doesn't it feel good? Isn't it the absolute best way of getting that idea across?" Then she turns to the other side of the board. She tells the students that there are people, not like those in the village, who judge others by the way they talk or write.

> We listen to the way people talk, not to judge them, but to tell what part of the river they come from. These other people are not like that. They think everybody needs to talk like them. Unlike us, they have a hard time hearing what people say if they don't talk exactly like them. Their way of talking and writing is called "Formal English."
>
> We have to feel a little sorry for them because they have only one way to talk. We're going to learn two ways to say things. Isn't that better? One way will be our Heritage way. The other will be Formal English. Then, when we go to get jobs, we'll be able to talk like those people who only know and can only really listen to one way. Maybe after we get the jobs we can help them to learn how it feels to have another language, like ours, that feels so good. We'll talk like them when we have to, but we'll always know our ways is best.

Martha then does all sorts of activities with the notions of Formal and Heritage or informal English. She tells the students.

> In the village, everyone speaks informally most of the time unless there's a potlatch or something. You don't think about it, you don't worry about the following any rules it's sort of like how you eat food at a picnic nobody pays attention to whether you use your fingers or a fork, and it feels *so* good. Now, Formal English is more like a formal dinner. There are rules to follow about where the knife and fork belong, about where people sit, about how you eat. That can be really nice, too, because it's nice to dress up sometimes.

The students then prepare a formal dinner in the class, for which they dress up and set a big table with fancy tablecloths, china, silverware. They speak only Formal English at this meal. Then they prepare a picnic where only informal English is allowed.

She also contrasts the "wordy" academic way of saying things with the metaphoric style of Athabaskan. The students discuss how book language always uses more words, but in Heritage language, the shorter way of saying something is always better. Students then write papers in the academic way, discussing with Martha and with each other whether they believe they've said enough to sound like a book. Finally, students further reduce the message to a "saying" brief enough to go on the front of a T-shirt, and the sayings are put on little paper T-shirts that the students cut out and hang throughout the room. Sometimes the students reduce other authors' wordy texts to their essential meanings as well.

The following transcript provides another example. It is from a conversation between a black teacher and a Southern black high school student named Joey, who is a speaker of Black English. The teacher believes it very important to discuss openly and honestly the issues of language diversity and power. She has begun the discussion by giving the student a children's book written in Black English to read.

TEACHER: What do you think about that book?
JOEY: I think it's nice.
TEACHER: Why?
JOEY: I don't know. It just told about a black family, that's all.

TEACHER: Was it difficult to read?
JOEY: No.
TEACHER: Was the text different from what you have seen in other books?
JOEY: Yeah. The writing was.
TEACHER: How?
JOEY: It use more of a southern-like accent in this book.
TEACHER: Uhm-hmm. Do you think that's good or bad?
JOEY: Well, uh, I don't think it's good for people down this-a-way, cause that's the way they grow up talking anyway. They ought to get the right way to talk.
TEACHER: Oh. So you think it's wrong to talk like that?
JOEY: Well . . . {Laughs}
TEACHER: Hard question, huh?
JOEY: Uhm-hmm, that's a hard question. But I think they shouldn't make books like that.
TEACHER: Why?
JOEY: Because they are not using the right way to talk and in school they take off for that, and li'l chirren grow up talking like that and reading like that so they might think that's right, and all the time they getting bad grades in school, talking like that and writing like that.
TEACHER: Do you think they should be getting bad grades for talking like that?
JOEY: {Pauses, answers very slowly} No . . . no.
TEACHER: So you don't think that it matters whether you talk one way or another?
JOEY: No, not long as you understood.
TEACHER: Uhm-hmm. Well, that's a hard question for me to answer, too. It's, ah, that's a question that's come up in a lot of schools now as to whether they should correct children who speak the way we speak all the time. Cause when we're talking to each other we talk like that even though we might not talk like than when we get into other situations, and who's to say whether it's—
JOEY: {Interrupting} Right or wrong.
TEACHER: Yeah.
JOEY: Maybe they ought to come up with another kind of . . . maybe Black English or something. A course in Black English. Maybe Black folks would be good in that cause people talk, I mean black people talk like that, so . . . but I guess there's a right way and wrong way to talk, you know, not regarding what race. I don't know.
TEACHER: But who decided what's right or wrong?
JOEY: Well that's true . . . I guess white people did. {Laughter End of tape.}

Notice how throughout the conversation Joey's consciousness has been raised by thinking about codes of language. This teacher further advocates having students interview various personnel officers in actual workplaces about their attitudes toward divergent styles in oral and written language. Students begin to understand how arbitrary language standards are, but also how politically charged they are. They compare various pieces written in different styles, discuss the impact of different styles on the message by making translations and back translations across styles, and discuss the history, apparent purpose, and contextual appropriateness of each of the technical writing rules presented by their teacher. *And* they practice writing different forms to different audiences based on rules appropriate for each audience. Such a program not only "teaches" standard linguistic forms, but also explores aspects of power as exhibited through linguistic forms.

Tony Burgess, in a study of secondary writing in England by Britton, Burgess, Martin, McLeod, and Rosen, suggests that we should not teach "iron conventions . . . imposed without rationale or grounding in communicative intent," but "critical and ultimately cultural awareness." Courtney Cazden calls for a two-pronged approach:

1. Continuous opportunities for writers to participate in some authentic bit of the unending conversation . . . thereby becoming part of a vital community of talkers and writers in a particular domain, and

2. Periodic, temporary focus on conventions of form, taught as cultural conventions expected in a particular community.

Just so that there is no confusion about what Cazden means by a focus on conventions of form, or about what I mean by "skills," let me stress that neither of us is speaking of page after page of "skill sheets" creating compound words or identifying nouns and adverbs, but rather about helping students gain a useful knowledge of the conventions of print while engaging in real and useful communicative activities. Kay Rowe Grubis, a junior high school teacher in a multicultural school, makes lists of certain technical rules for her eighth graders' review and then gives them papers from a third grade to "correct." The students not only have to correct other students'

work, but also tell them why they have changed or questioned aspects of the writing.

A village teacher, Howard Cloud, teaches his high school students the conventions of formal letter writing and the formulation of careful questions in the context of issues surrounding the amendment of the Alaska Land Claims Settlement Act. Native Alaskan leaders hold differing views on this issue, critical to the future of local sovereignty and land rights. The students compose letters to leaders who reside in different areas of the state seeking their perspectives, set up audioconference calls for interview/debate sessions, and, finally, develop a videotape to present the differing views.

To summarize, I suggest that students must be *taught* the codes needed to participate fully in the mainstream of American life, not by being forced to attend to hollow, inane, decontextualized subskills, but rather within the context of meaningful communicative endeavors; that they must be allowed the resource of the teacher's expert knowledge, while being helped to acknowledge their own "expertness" as well; and that even while students are assisted in learning the culture of power, they must also be helped to learn about the arbitrariness of those codes and about the power relationships they represent.

I am also suggesting that appropriate education for poor children and children of color can only be devised in consultation with adults who share their culture. Black parents, teachers of color, and members of poor communities must be allowed to participate fully in the discussion of what kind of instruction is in their children's best interest. Good liberal intentions are not enough. In an insighful 1975 study entitled "Racism without Racists: Institutional Racism in Urban Schools," Massey, Scott, and Dornbusch found that under the pressures of teaching, and with all intentions of "being nice," teachers had essentially stopped attempting to teach black children.[16] In their words: "We have shown that oppression can arise out of warmth, friendliness, and concern. Paternalism and a lack of challenging standards are creating a distorted system of evaluation in the schools." Educators must open themselves to, and allow themselves to be affected by, these alternative voices.

In conclusion, I am proposing a resolution for the skills/process debate. In short, the debate is fallacious; the dichotomy is false. The issue is really an illusion created initially not by teachers but by academics whose worldview demands the creation of categorical divisions—not for the purpose of better teaching, but for the goal of easier analysis. As I have been reminded by many teachers since the publication of my article, those who are most skillful at educating black and poor children do not allow themselves to be placed in "skills" or "process" boxes. They understand the need for both approaches, the need to help students establish their own voices, and to coach those voices to produce notes that will be heard clearly in the larger society.

The dilemma is not really in the debate over instructional methodology, but rather in communicating across cultures and in addressing the more fundamental issue of power, of whose voice gets to be heard in determining what is best for poor children and children of color. Will black teachers and parents continue to be silenced by the very forces that claim to "give voice" to our children? Such an outcome would be tragic, for both groups truly have something to say to one another. As a result of careful listening to alternative points of view, I have myself come to a viable synthesis of perspectives. But both sides do need to be able to listen, and I contend that it is those with the most power, those in the majority, who must take the greater responsibility for initiating the process.

To do so takes a very special kind of listening, listening that requires not only open eyes and ears, but open hearts and minds. We do not really see through our eyes or hear through our ears, but through our beliefs. To put our beliefs on hold is to cease to exist as ourselves for a moment—and that is not easy. It is painful as well, because it means turning yourself inside out, giving up your own sense of who you are, and being willing to see yourself in the unflattering light of another's angry gaze. It is not easy, but it is the only way to learn what it might feel like to be someone else and the only way to start the dialogue.

There are several guidelines. We must keep the perspective that people are experts on their own lives. There are certainly aspects of the outside world of which they may not be aware, but they can be the only authentic chroniclers of their own experience. We must not be too quick to deny their interpretations, or accuse them of "false consciousness." We must believe that people are rational beings, and therefore always act rationally. We may not understand their rationales, but that in no way militates against the existence of these rationales or reduces our responsibility to attempt to apprehend them. And finally, we must learn to be vulnerable enough to allow our world to turn upside down in order to allow the realities of others to edge themselves into our consciousness. In other words, we must become ethnographers in the true sense.

Teachers are in an ideal position to play this role, to attempt to get all of the issues on the table in order to initiate true dialogue. This can only be done, however, by seeking out those whose perspectives may differ most, by learning to give their words complete attention, by understanding one's own power, even if that power stems merely from being in the majority, by being unafraid to raise questions about discrimination and voicelessness with people of color, and to listen, no, to *hear* what they say. I suggest that the results of such interactions may be the most powerful and empowering coalescence yet seen in the educational realm—for *all* teachers and for *all* the students they teach.

CHAPTER 23

Reframing the Affirmative Action Debate

Lani Guinier

A Professor of Law at Harvard University, Lani Guinier has lectured and written on a variety of topics, including affirmative action and other issues involving equity. Her publications *Lift Every Voice: Turning a Civil Rights Setback into a New Vision of Social Justice; Becoming Gentleman: Women, Law School and Institutional Change;* and *The Tyranny of the Majority: Fundamental Fairness in Representative Democracy.* She received her J.D. from Yale Law School.

Affirmative action has, at least in contemporary terms, been thought of as an issue exclusively concerning blacks and women, and, if we were to think about the most recent debate - particularly in California - only about blacks. My goal in what follows is to try to reframe that debate so that all of us can begin to see the conversation about affirmative action not as a wedge, but as a platform and an opportunity to start a much bigger conversation about democracy, justice, and fundamental fairness. To do this, I would like to use the image of the miner's canary.[1]

It is my understanding that miners used to take a canary with them into the mine to alert them when the atmosphere in the mine was beginning to get dangerous—poisonous. The canary's more fragile respiratory system was a signal to the miners, not just that it was dangerous for the canary to remain in the mine, but that the miners had better leave the mine, too. My central claim is that the experience of blacks and women in this country is the experience of the miner's canary. Let me explain what I mean by this.

Unfortunately, the way the present affirmative action conversation is framed, we talk about fixing the so-called beneficiaries of affirmative action - namely, black men and women of various ethnicities and races. But this is analogous to talk about fixing the miner's canary. Perhaps we should provide a lung transplant or some other medical intervention for the canary, or maybe we should outfit the canary with a pint-sized gas mask so it can continue to survive in its deadly environment.[2] But we know it is not the canary that needs to be fixed; it is the atmosphere in the mines that is poisoning not just the canary, but eventually all of us. The same is true when we talk about race and gender in our society. That is, women and blacks need to be understood as our miners' canaries—their experiences signal us about the health of our social environment. In particular, the experiences of members of these groups make visible to us fundamental flaws in the way we are distributing opportunity to everyone, but we can't see the flaws except as they are revealed in the canary. Let me give you an example.

In 1976, the percentage of black high school graduates who went on to college was beginning to approximate the percentage of white high school graduates who went on to college - not the same number, but the same percentage.[3] That is, of blacks who graduated from high school, approximately the same percentage went on to college as the percentage of whites who graduated from high school. By 1986 that was no longer true. What happened between 1976 and 1986? One significant event was the election of Ronald Reagan as President. The Reagan administration decided to change the way college education was funded through something called the "Pell Grant."[4] In 1976, the Pell Grant provided scholar-

From *Kentucky Law Journal*, 86, 3, pp.505-525. 02138. Used with permission of Charlotte Sheedy Literacy Agency.

ship aid to needy students. In an effort to broaden the constituency that would be supported by Pell Grants and consistent with its "self-help" philosophy, the Reagan administration pushed to change Pell Grants from scholarships to primarily loans.[5]

Now, this may appear on its face as a race-neutral effort to expand the constituency for higher education. But it had a very distinct racial effect because the median net worth, or financial assets, of a black family is significantly less than the median net worth of a white family.[6] This is the cumulative effect of discrimination. We are not talking now about income; we are not talking about the amount of money coming in through salary. We are talking about the assets that a family has. In 1988, the net financial worth for a white family averaged about $43,000; for a black family, it averaged about $3700.[7] Assets have a significant effect on one's ability to get a loan, and the consequence of this difference in financial status between black and white families was that many black families could not compete for Pell Grants. So the fact that the Pell Grant program appeared to be race-neutral masked the way in which the Pell Grants were having a very specific racial effect, namely, lessening the percentages of black high school students going to college. That's the miner's canary.

In this case, college-aged blacks provide us a visible sign that there is something wrong. The something wrong is manifested in terms of black families, but it is not only black families who have a net financial worth of $3700. There are many white families whose net financial worth is only $3700.[8] Part of the masked problem here is that the poverty of whites is hidden by the great affluence of other whites. It is only when we look at the effect of the Pell Grant on blacks that we begin to see that this decision, which initially appeared to be so neutral, actually had a very significant effect in determining who had access to higher education. By race? Yes[9] But not only by race, also by class. What is more, this process of making wealth or making financial assets a pre-condition for college is not just limited to the way we fund a college education. Consider the example of Cheryl Hopwood.

Cheryl Hopwood is a white woman who applied to the University of Texas Law School ("UTLS") but was denied admission. She claimed that the reason she didn't get in is that a number of black and Mexican-American students with lower Texas index scores were admitted pursuant to an affirmative action program then in place in the University of Texas Law School. Now, it is true that sixty-three of the ninety-two black and Mexican-American students who were admitted to UTLS did have lower Texas index scores than Cheryl Hopwood. But so did 140 white students who also got into UTLS when Cheryl Hopwood was denied admission. This fact consistently goes unnoticed discussions of the case, but it turns out to be crucial in understanding it.[10]

Why was Cheryl Hopwood denied admission? Part of the reason she wasn't admitted goes back to the issue of using wealth or class or financial status as a credential. It turns out that Cheryl Hopwood had gone to both a state and a community college in Texas, and because of this, she was given a lower Texas index score than candidates who had gone to private colleges. Now, you may think that's odd since the University of Texas Law School is also a state institution. Nonetheless, it is a state institution that discounts the credentials of people who went to other state institutions. Points were taken off of Cheryl Hopwood's application because she went to both a state and a community college.[11] She went to those institutions in part because she is a working-class woman who couldn't afford a private institution. Yet the admissions protocol at UTLS discounted her degrees from public colleges in Texas as part of the process for denying her admission, as if going to a state or community college is not about class (although it was) but about competence. But commentators never talk about that. Instead, they talk simply about her Texas index scores in some abstract way, and look only at the black and Chicano students who got in with lower scores. But what do those scores actually tell us about the ability of any of these students to do well in law school? How do those scores relate not only to Cheryl Hopwood's class status, but to the class status of all the students who are applying to UTLS?

As it turns out, if we look at the SAT, the LSAT, and the GRE, within every race and ethnic group scores go up as income goes up-there is a direct correlation between family income and scores on these tests.[12] Part of that is because these are coachable tests. You can learn how to take them and you learn best how to take them if your parents can afford to send you to a review course that coaches you how to take them.[13] You also do very well on these tests if you have gone to a school that teaches for a long period of time how to start doing the kind of strategic quick guessing that is rewarded on these tests. Yes, guessing! A case in point: Twins in Florida scored a perfect 800 on their SATs; they were the first set of siblings to take the SAT at the same time and each get an 800. The *New York Times* interviewed their mother, who was asked, "Aren't you proud that you have two kids both of whom got perfect scores?" She said she was proud. The *Times* interviewer then asked, "To what do you attribute this great success?" Her answer? They'd been practicing taking the SAT since the seventh grade.[14] Examples like these show clearly that we're using certain aptitude tests to credentialize a social oligarchy and we're mistakenly calling it merit. Then, when some working class or poor people don't have the attributes that we assume are part of the social oligarchy, we don't say, "Well, it's too bad you're poor," we say, "It's too bad you're stupid."

Once we begin to see these things, we have an opportunity to have a different kind of conversation. This conversation has taken place in the most polarized and divisive way in California. One of the reasons it began there was that California used to have one of the premier systems of higher education in the country. In 1984, California spent more than two-and-one-half times as much money on higher education as it spent, for example, on prisons.[15] Ten years later, California spent the same amount on higher education as it spent on prisons. In 1995, California spent more on prisons than it did on higher education. Now, 140 years ago Victor Hugo said that "every time we build a prison we close a school."[16] He was right. For the cost of imprisoning one person for one year, California could educate ten community college students, five California state university students, or two University of California students. But instead, California decided to pass a "three-strikes-and-you're-out" policy.[17] The decision to imprison a third-strike burglar for forty years means the state is foregoing the opportunity to educate two hundred community college students for two years.[18]

It is not surprising, when higher education becomes such a scarce resource, that people begin fighting over who can get in. As they begin fighting over who can get in, they also start looking around at who seems to be getting in, but they don't look at those like the 140 students with lower Texas index scores or lower SAT scores in California - they look instead at the vulnerable canary. They question the admission of minorities to their schools. They start saying, "Look, these people can't even do well on the SATs." They blame the canary. I've been on a number of television debates in which I was told, "You know, these black and Chicano students, they don't do well on the SAT." And I say, "Yes. Well?" And then I pull out an SAT question, and I say, "Melodian is to organist as (choose one) reveille is to bugler, solo is to accompanist, crescendo is to pianist, anthem is to choir master, kettle drum is to timpanist."[19] I asked that question, for example, of Professor Lino Graglia of the University of Texas Law School, who was making this argument, and he said, "Are you asking me if that question is on the SAT?" I said, "No, I'm telling you it's on the SAT and I want to know the answer." He didn't know the answer. And so what? What difference does it make whether you know the answer to that question? It makes no difference unless, perhaps, you are going to be a musician.

Now, I am not saying we don't want to have and maintain standards of excellence. I am committed to standards of excellence. I am committed to high expectations for all students. All I am questioning is whether performance on a single paper-and-pencil test in which the stakes are high, and in which a large part of what we measure is quick strategic guessing, represents excellence or whether it, in fact, represents wealth.[20] If you look, for example, at those black and Chicano students in California who weren't doing as well on the SAT, thirty-six percent of them came from households with incomes of less than $15,000 a year.[21] On the other hand, sixty percent of the white students taking the SAT in California came from households with incomes of more than $60,000 a year.[22] We use these scores to determine merit but they are in many ways functioning as a wealth test. This is important because higher education has become a gateway to democratic citizenship: It is difficult to get a secure job without a college degree, and without a job, you are not treated as a contributing member of this society.[23] Yet, the gateway to citizenship is controlled by tests that tell us more about how much money your parents make than what kind of citizen you are ultimately going to be.

Now, we defend these tests by saying that they are efficient and, in any event, they predict first-year performance in college or graduate school. Well, they may be efficient, but they don't necessarily predict first-year performance. The average correlation between SAT scores and first-year college grades is about thirty percent.[24] In terms of the LSAT (and going back to those black and Chicano students at the University of Texas), Martin Shapiro, a statistician, did an affidavit in the *Hopwood* case in which he said that the correlation between black students' LSAT scores and first-year UT law school grades was negative.[25] In other words, if we wanted to figure out how the students were going to do using the Texas index, we would have to assign a negative number to their undergraduate GPAs. There simply was no correlation that was worth considering. I've spoken to many people, including people at the Law School Admissions Council, who say that nationwide the LSAT is about nine percent better than random in predicting the variation in first year law school grades. Nine percent! Not even ten percent.

I did a study of women and legal education with Michelle Fine and Jane Balin. We got the academic performance records of 981 students, and we also looked at their undergraduate GPAs and their LSAT scores.[26] We found that at the University of Pennsylvania Law School the LSAT did a little better-fourteen percent better than random.[27] However, that still means eighty-six percent of the variance in Penn's first-year grades is not explained by the LSAT scores. When we plotted out these scores on a graph they were all over the map. There were students with perfect LSAT scores who were among the students with the lowest course grades in the first-year class.

Now, if LSAT or SAT scores do not predict first-year grades, do they measure success in some other way? For example, do they measure success in life which, after all, seems a more important measure? A group at Harvard actually decided they were going to investigate this. They did a study of three different classes of alumni over a thirty-year period. They wanted to know what correlates with success. The researchers measured success as financial satisfaction, professional satisfaction, and contribution to the community. Within these three different classes of alumni the researchers found two things that did correlate with their criteria of success: low SAT scores and a blue-collar background. Part of the explanation, they said, is that the SAT does not account for a very important ingredient in achievement - ambi-

tion, drive, motivation, hunger to succeed.[28] Other variables that correlate with success, such as intense involvement in extracurricular activities,[29] willingness to ask for help,[30] the tendency to reflect on one's work and revise it,[31] the ability to prioritize and juggle tasks,[32] are not measured by the SAT. We do not measure these things when we give people a paper-and-pencil test and ask them to guess whether "melodian" is to "organist" as "kettle drum" is to "timpanist." And yet we are taking performance on these paper-and-pencil tests to be an accurate predictor of success. The discrepancy between test scores and actual performance in law school or ultimate success after graduation serves as the miner's canary. It is the miner's canary because black and Chicano students, despite their weak performance on the these timed paper-and-pencil tests, have the capacity to succeed.[33] Their experience is the miner's canary because it is telling us that we are using the wrong instrument to measure *everyone's* capacity to succeed, not just theirs.

It's not just race that's the miner's canary, but also gender. The study I did with Michelle Fine and Jane Balin of women at the University of Pennsylvania Law School started when one of my students wanted to do a video. I told her I didn't know anything about video, but it seemed to me that the first thing she should do would be to write a script. So she did. She wrote a script about various incidents of harassment that she had experienced. When she showed me the script, I said to her, "Ann, I don't doubt that all of this has happened. But you are the central figure in each of these incidents and if this is going to be a video that other people are going to learn from, perhaps it would help if you found out whether your experiences are representative of your classmates." So she did a survey. She distributed her survey to all the students. We got back some very discouraging results. On the one hand, over one-half of the students responded to the survey; on the other hand, disproportionate numbers of the women students who answered the survey were unhappy. They weren't speaking up in class and they felt alienated from their law school experience. One woman said, "Guys think law school is hard; we think we're stupid." Such comments revealed that they were internalizing their experiences. It reminded me of the razor company that was trying to conduct a study in which they observed (through a one-way mirror) men and women using defective razors. The men took the razor, shaved, cut themselves, declared the razor no good and threw it away. The women used the defective razor, shaved, cut themselves, and started to worry about what was wrong with their technique. So, like the razor study, part of what our study told us was that the women in our law school were internalizing something that everybody was experiencing. We then went from the self-reporting survey to the academic performance data, and we found that the women, despite identical entry level credentials - virtually the same GPAs, LSAT scores, and undergraduate majors - simply were not doing as well in law school.

I brought this information to some of my colleagues, one of whom said, "Varsity sports." "Well," I said, "that's an interesting theory. Play it out for me; what is it that you're saying?" He said, "Well, perhaps the men who attend law school were all very active in varsity sports as undergraduates. And maybe they were so distracted by their efforts in varsity sports that they didn't perform up to their potential in college so their undergraduate GPAs understate their capacity to perform in law school where there are no varsity sports." I did not pursue the theory.

On the other hand, my colleague may have had a point. Many of the men we interviewed said that they basically looked at law school as a game. Now, what do you do when you play a game? In our culture, you play to win. And if you're playing the game of law school and you're playing the game of winning in a law school class, you win by raising your hand first. You are the agenda setter. You get to talk and control how the rest of the class has to respond. The women, however, said that they did not look at law school as a game. Rather, they saw it as a conversation, and they wanted to say something relevant within that conversation. Part of this approach involves building on what the person before has said. So we found that women commonly edit their remarks. They want to make sure what they are saying is right. By the time they feel confident in what they have to say, however, the class has moved on. Or, they have been so efficient at editing their remarks that when they raise their hands, they essentially deliver a haiku poem. It can take many days to really figure out the significance of their comments.

Now, what does all of this have to do with affirmative action? And what does this have to do with the miner's canary? I think the women at Penn. Law School are a miner's canary. They are telling us that there may be something wrong with an academic style of discourse in which we, the professors, are sages on the stage. We engage in a dialogue with students where we have complete information. But we purposely edit student casebooks so that our students have less-than-perfect information. This method of teaching demonstrates to students that they, unlike their professors, do not know the answer because students, of course, have not read the entire case with all its footnotes, and the cases that came before it and the cases that came after it. As one of my law school colleagues observed, the law school process is too often like learning how to ask rude questions. That is, in normal contexts when you ask a question, you ask it because you want to know the answer. That's the reason you ask the question. Lawyers are trained *never* to ask a question to which they don't already know the answer. Thus, law professors ask questions of students, but the professors already know the answer. It's an intimidating environment. Some people learn by intimidation. But not everyone does. And the women were our miner's canary. Their doing less well than their male counterparts suggests that we are using a one-size-fits-all pedagogy that may impair some students' capacity to perform and denies *all* of the students the value of genuine conversation.

Now why do I say that lawyers, of all people, need to know the value of genuine conversation? Think about lawyers in the Twenty-first Century, even lawyers in the late Twentieth Century. Put out of your mind some of the lawyers on television, because they are exceptions. Most lawyers do not go to court, most lawyers do not litigate, most lawyers are not solo practitioners, most lawyers must function in a team.[34] And those who function in a team have to know how to cooperate, they have to know how to listen, they have to know how to build on what other people have said. These are skills that are valuable, not just for women lawyers, but for lawyering generally. So the model of advocacy that we are using as the singular frame to teach how to be a lawyer - learning how to ask rude questions - probably isn't the best way to teach all potential lawyers. The Penn. women students provide an opportunity to start re-thinking the educational process for *everybody*. The women are the miner's canary - their experiences suggest that we can do better. We can do better by the women and we can do better by the men. We can make better lawyers.

I've said that there are certain skills that are valuable to lawyers in the Twenty-first Century, but I know that not everybody is going to be a lawyer. Uri Treisman had some African-American students who were studying math; they were studying calculus. They weren't doing as well as some of his Chinese-American students, and he wanted to know why.[35] He asked some of the other math professors at his college about this, and they offered all sorts of classic stereotypes: they came from single-parent households, they didn't study as hard, they weren't as motivated. But none of that was true. In fact, the African-American students were studying harder, longer than the Chinese-American students. The difference was that the Chinese-American students were studying as a group. They would talk calculus on their way to lunch. They would talk calculus on their way to the library. They would work through problems together. They engaged in a conversation about calculus and as a result of that conversation, they became better mathematicians. So the notion of engaged conversation, a communication of learning how to cooperate, is not just something that is good for lawyers. It's also something that is good for calculus students. When Uri Treisman designed a peer workshop in which he adapted some of the techniques he had seen his Chinese-American students use, he invited the African-American students into the workshop. These students drew some of the highest scores in his calculus class the next semester. The lesson was simple, easy to learn, easy to use-Chinese-American students had a better way of learning calculus. We can learn from bringing in new perspectives and new ways of thinking about old jobs. The miner's canary signals us that the atmosphere in the mine is dangerous, but the warning also tells us to start thinking about new ways of fixing not the canary but the mine.

One final example involves women. The New York City Police Department used to have a height requirement. One had to be almost six feet tall in order to be a police officer. A group of women challenged this, since there aren't many women who are six feet tall. Their challenge to the height requirement was successful. More women became cops; more Latino men became cops; more Asian men became cops; more short white men became cops.[36] Women of average height executed the first role of the canary - to signal that the standard didn't really make a lot of sense; it was arbitrary. But they also executed the second role of the canary - they became the instigators of a different kind of thinking about police work.[37] This was especially true of the black and Puerto Rican women who lived near some of the housing projects in New York. They made the projects safer by approaching the young, primarily African-American and Puerto Rican teenage males, who were the likely trouble-makers, as mentors.[38] They offered these young men respect, and the young men, grateful for the attention of an adult, constrained their old behaviors so they could continue to earn that respect.[39] These women were developing a different style of policing. This is not to say that we want all police officers to become mentors, but it wouldn't hurt if more officers knew how to modify their command and control approach when appropriate. When the Los Angeles Police Department commissioned a study (headed by Warren Christopher, the former Secretary of State) to find out what they should do about excessive use of force by police officers, the answer that came back was, "Hire more women." Hire more women. Women, the study showed, were not reluctant to use force, but they didn't resort to force as their initial reaction to a situation involving conflict.[40]

Now, I have to say I'm optimistic about conversations in which we think about the miner's canary as a signal and as a lesson. I am optimistic as more people begin to see diversity as something that benefits the entire society - in other words, as more people learn the lessons of the miner's canary. To summarize, these lessons include:

(1) the value of democratic legitimacy - that all taxpayers feel they have an opportunity to pursue the benefits they are subsidizing;

(2) the value of diversity as an important tool for solving complex problems in the information economy when no single individual can memorize all the available information (nor do we need anyone to memorize it when it keeps changing, yet is quickly accessible. In other words, what we really need is synthesis of information - being able to take information from diverse sources, then put it together in innovative and creative ways to solve problems; and

(3) that bringing in previously underrepresented or marginalized groups can help all of us rethink the nature of the job or the task (for example, the lesson of the women cops and Uri Treisman's Chinese-American calculus students).

I'm optimistic as well because of my own experience raising my nine-year-old son, Nikolas. When Nikolas was seven he was in second grade, and the teacher had him keep a journal. (I asked him if it was okay to share with you his journal, and he said it was okay as long as I told you it was written when he was in second grade. He's now in fourth grade.) The teacher said, "Tell us what your family does, you know, what does your mother do? What does your father do?" Nikolas talked about his mom. "My mom is a professor," he said. "I think it's boring. I think it's boring because you get to sit in front of a computer and you don't get to play games. On the other hand, I think it's fun because you get to stand in front of a class and you're the boss." I could hear in my son's journal an echo of conversations with a lot of the men in my Penn. Law School classes who also see things as a game; the goal is to win, to be powerful. On the other hand, my son also showed me that he, too, can learn to look at the world differently. His second-grade teacher subsequently told me that they were sitting around talking about what each of their parents did, and one of Niko's classmates said that his mom is the vice-president of a bank. At which point my son just looked at him and blurted out, "Well, why isn't *she* president?"

Endnotes

1. *See* Lani Guinier & Gerald Torres, The Miner's Canary: *Race, Representation and the USA Experience; Understanding the Meaning and Uses of Political Synecdoche* (1997) (unpublished manuscript, on file with the author) (citing Felix S. Cohen, *The Erosion of Indian Rights, 1950–1953: A Case Study in Bureaucracy*, 62 Yale L.J. 348, 390 (1953) (Race functions like the miner's canary, "mark[ing] the shift from fresh air to poison gas in our political atmosphere . . . .")).

2. After I delivered this lecture at the University of Kentucky, a gentleman approached me at the lecturn to advise me that he found great irony in my application of the miner's canary metaphor to issues of racial justice. After all, he reminded me, a black man from Kentucky had invented the gas mask to replace the canary but because of racism

had trouble marketing it until the U.S. Army began using the same design in its gas masks during World War I. *See* BLACK FIRSTS: 2,000 YEARS OF EXTRAORDINARY ACHIEVEMENT (Jessie Carney Smith et al. eds., 1994) ("Garret Morgan (1875–1963) was the first black to receive a patent for a safety hood and smoke protector. . . . Born on a farm near Paris, Kentucky, Morgan became a very astute businessman and inventor in Cleveland. In 1923 he patented a three-way automatic traffic signal, which he sold to General Electric."). *See also Who Invented the First Traffic Light and Gas Mask?*, N.Y. BEACON (New York, N.Y.), Feb. 12, 1997, at 3.

> In 1916, [Garret] Morgan came to public attention in a big way when, using a breathing device he had invented two years earlier, he took part in a dramatic rescue. A disastrous explosion had occurred in a tunnel below Lake Erie [in Cleveland, Ohio], trapping nearly thirty [city waterworks] workers. Morgan and his brother, wearing his newly invented device, which he called a "Safety Hood," went into the smoke-filled shaft and pulled the workers to safety.
>
> When they heard about the rescue, fire officials around the country placed orders for the Safety Hood, but many canceled them when they learned that Morgan was an African-American. At this point, the army saw the value of Morgan's invention, made some improvements on it, and the Safety Hood became the gas mask that saved thousands of lives in World War I.

3. *See* A COMMON DESTINY: BLACKS AND AMERICAN SOCIETY 377–79 (Gerald David Jaynes & Robin M. Williams, Jr. eds., 1989). In a comprehensive study, Jaynes and Williams found that blacks' status in higher education worsened or stalled since the mid-1970s. "After the mid-1970s, the college-going chances of black high school graduates have declined . . . ." *Id.* at 378.

4. "The purpose of the [Pell Grant] is to assist students from low-income families who would not otherwise be financially able to attend a post secondary institution." MARGOT A. SCHENET, CRS REPORT FOR CONGRESS: PELL GRANTS: BACKGROUND AND ISSUES (Apr. 4, 1997). The Pell Grant program was established to be the foundation of federal student aid to further the goal of access and to provide students with more choice among institutions. *See id.* at 16.

5. President Reagan introduced budget proposals throughout the 1980s to cut Pell Grants and other higher education subsidies. *See, e.g.,* Macon

Morehouse, *House, Senate Bills Compared: Bills to Curtail Loan Defaults Would Also Expand Aid Rolls,* 46 CONGRESSIONAL QUARTERLY, Sept. 3, 1988, *available in* 1988 WL 2835183. "Pell Grants authorizations used to be open-ended. After Reagan came into office, however, the authorization was limited to a specific amount-$2.65 billion for that year." Also under the Reagan administration, the House proposed an expansion of budget authority for loans and other policies more likely to benefit students from middle income families. *See id.* (referring to H.R. 4986, 100th Cong. (1988)). In each of his budget proposals, President Reagan proposed a major parental and student contributions as the basis of meeting college costs. *See* U.S. DEP'T OF EDUC., REVISED FISCAL YEAR 1982 BUDGET 3 (1981):

> The 1982 budget includes reforms of the major post-secondary student assistance programs to focus the aid on students who need it for the costs of attending college while controlling the rapidly escalating growth in Federal costs. In proposing these reforms, the Administration assumes that families and students - not the Federal government - should be the first source of funds for educational expenses.

President Reagan attempted to implement this goal by limiting grant aid and other federal subsidies and by increasing "self-help aid." In his 1982 proposal, Reagan attempted to underscore his "self-help" philosophical approach by proposing a slight reduction in Pell Grant aid while increasing National Direct Student Loans from $186 million to $286 million. *See id.* at 4; *see also* U.S. DEP'T OF EDUC., THE FISCAL YEAR 1984 BUDGET 6 (1983) ("Under the new proposal, self-help would come first. Students would be required to provide a minimum of 40 percent (or a minimum of $800) of their educational expenses through work or loans before obtaining any grants."). Reagan's 1988 budget proposal sharply cut back the Pell Grant program from $4.2 billion in 1987 to $2.7 billion. *See* David Rapp, *Education: Reagan Targets Student Aid for Deep Spending Cuts,* CONGRESSIONAL QUARTERLY, Jan. 10, 1987, at 59, *available in* 1987 WL 2647837. This budget proposal would have made up the difference in student aid by expanding "income-contingent" loans from their 1987 level of $5 million to $600 million in fiscal year 1988. Under this program, "borrowers . . . would have to repay the loan without the benefit of federal interest subsidies, though on a repayment schedule geared to income after graduation." *Id.; see also* U.S. DEP'T OF EDUC., THE FISCAL YEAR 1988 BUDGET, SUMMARY AND BACKGROUND INFORMATION 2 (1987).

6. *See generally* MELVIN L. OLIVER & THOMAS M. SHAPIRO, BLACK WEALTH, WHITE WEALTH (1995).

7. *See id.* at 86. To compare median net worth over time, see U.S. BUREAU OF THE CENSUS, CURRENT POPULATION REPORTS, SERIES P-70, NO. 7, HOUSEHOLD WEALTH AND ASSET OWNERSHIP: 1984, 22 (1986) (stating that in 1984, white families had a median net worth of $39,135, black families had a median net worth of $3397, while families of Spanish origin had a median net worth of $4913); U.S. BUREAU OF THE CENSUS, CURRENT POPULATION REPORTS, SERIES P-70. NO. 22, HOUSEHOLD WEALTH AND ASSET OWNERSHIP: 1988, at 8 (1990) (stating that in 1988, white households had a median net worth of $43,279, while median net worth of black households was $4169; the median net worth for families of Hispanic origin was $5524); U.S. BUREAU OF THE CENSUS, CURRENT POPULATION REPORTS, SERIES P-70, NO. 47, ASSET OWNERSHIP OF HOUSEHOLDS: 1993, at 8 (1995) ("In 1993, White households had a median measured net worth of $45,740, while the figure for Black households was $4418. Hispanic households had median holdings of $4656."). This census data is the result of the Survey of Income and Program Participation ("SIPP") that was first used in 1984. For a description of SIPP, see OLIVER & SHAPIRO, *supra* note 6, at 55–58.

8. In 1984, the total number of households with a white householder was 75,343,000. U.S. BUREAU OF THE CENSUS, CURRENT POPULATION REPORTS, SERIES P-70, NO. 7, HOUSEHOLD WEALTH AND ASSET OWNERSHIP: 1984, at 18 (1986). Fourteen percent of these households, or 10,548,020, had a net worth of between $1 and $4999. *See id.* In 1984, the total number of households with a black householder was 9,509,000. *See id.* Of those, 23.9%, or 2,272,651, had a net financial worth between $1 and $4999. *See id.*

9. See OLIVER & SHAPIRO, *supra* note 6, at 37–45, for a discussion of racial effects of "neutral" policies. The current application of the tax code, the authors argue, is another form of the racialization of state policy. *See id.* at 43. They argue that the "*lower tax rates on capital gains* and the *deduction for home mortgages and real estate taxes* . . . flow differentially to blacks and whites because . . . blacks generally have fewer and different types of assets, than whites with similar incomes." *Id.* at 43. The effect of this "'fiscal welfare' is to limit the flow of tax relief to blacks and to redirect it to those who already have assets. The seemingly race-neutral tax code thus generates a racial effect that deepens rather than equalizes the economic gulf between blacks and whites." *Id.* Oliver and Shapiro also discuss the FHA program under which the federal govern-

ment places its credit behind private loans to homebuyers. *See id.* at 39. They explain that the "FHA's conscious decision to channel loans away from the central city and to the suburbs has had a powerful effect on the creation of segregated housing in post-World War II America." *Id.* The FHA even provided restrictive covenants that would be upheld in court to assist in the exclusion of blacks from white neighborhoods. *See id.* at 39. Though now unconstitutional, this "legacy of the FHA's contribution to racial residential segregation lives on in the inability of blacks to incorporate themselves into integrated neighborhoods in which the equity and demand for their homes is maintained." *Id.* When blacks move into white neighborhoods, white flight occurs, commencing the segregation process. This causes housing prices to fall, and the home appreciation seen by black homeowners slows relative to that of white homeowners in white areas. *See id.; see also* Michael Janofsky, *Report Finds Bias in Lending Hinders Home Buying in Cities,* N.Y. Times, Feb. 23, 1998, at A13 (citing report by the United States Conference of Mayors on discriminatory lending practices that disproportionately affect both urban dwellers and minorities; 71.3% of whites are homeowners, while only 43.6% of blacks and 41.7% of Hispanic Americans own homes). These figures are often the result of redlining.

Blacks also paid disproportionately more into the social security system and received less. *See* Oliver & Shapiro, *supra* note 6, at 38. Oliver and Shapiro note that "[b]ecause social security contributions are made on a flat rate and black workers earn less . . . 'black men were taxed on 100 percent of their income, on average, while white men earned a considerable amount of untaxed income.'" *See id.* (quoting Jill Quadagno, The Color of Welfare (1994)). They also point out that black workers earn lower retirement benefits which do not last as long as those enjoyed by whites due to the shorter average life span for blacks. *See id.* Finally, they argue that the "tax contributions of black working women 'subsidize the benefits of white housewives.'" *Id.* (quoting Quadagno, *supra*). More black women are single, divorced, or separated. They must work now and many of them will not be able to one day share a spouse's retirement benefit. For these reasons, African-Americans have paid more to Social Security but receive less.

10. *See* Susan Sturm & Lani Guinier, *The Future of Affirmative Action: Reclaiming the Innovative Ideal,* 84 Cal. L. Rev. 953, 961–62 (1996).

11. *See id.* at 990. Many law schools do this by creating an admissions index based on the applicant's GPA and LSAT and then adding in the median LSAT of the college from which the applicant graduated. The rationale for including the median LSAT score of all those who took the LSAT from the applicant's college is to provide a uniform standard from which to assess the value of the applicant's GPA. Since there is a strong relationship between LSAT scores and parental income, however, applicants applying from prestigious private institutions (that also cost more to attend) are advantaged by the fact that they attended college with peers who test well, many of whom, not surprisingly, are also upper middle class students. *See infra* note 12.

12. There is a correlation between income and SAT scores. *See* Sturm & Guinier, *supra* note 10, at 987–92. Generally, with each 100-point increase in SAT scores, average family income rises. *See id.* at 988 (citing Table 6.1, James Crouse & Dale Trusheim, The Case Against the SAT 125 (1988)); *see also id.* at 988 n. 152 ("'There is a positive correlation between income level and standardized test scores.'") (quoting Robert G. Cameron, The Common Yardstick: A Case for the SAT 11 (1989)) [N/A]; Michael Scott Moore, *Three Hours on a Saturday Morning: UC May Drop the Flawed SAT as an Admission Requirement. But Are the Other Options Any Better?*, San Francisco Weekly, Dec. 10, 1997 ("The correspondence between family income and test scores has historically been as high as 80 percent. So choosing between scores of, say, 1100 and 1000 on the SAT is likely to amount to a decision based on class, not potential"); David K. Shipler, *A Leg Up: My Equal Opportunity, Your Free Lunch,* N.Y. Times, Mar. 5, 1995, at 4, p. 1 (noting that within each racial or ethnic group, SAT scores increase as income rises); *University of California Weighs Optional S.A.T's,* N.Y. Times, Sept. 21, 1997, at 32 ("'The only thing the S.A.T. predicts well now is socioeconomic status.'") (quoting Eugene Garcia, Dean of the Graduate School of Education, University of California at Berkeley).

There is also a correlation between race and SAT scores. *See* Sturm & Guinier, *supra* note 10, at 992–97. "Blacks on average score 110 points below whites on the math portion of the SAT and 92 points below whites on the verbal portion." *Id.* at 992 (citing Robert B. Slater, *Ranking the States by Black-White SAT Scoring Gaps,* J. BlacksHigher Educ., Winter 1995/1996, at 71). *See also* Larry P. v. Riles, 495 F. Supp. 926, 954–60 (N.D. Cal. 1979) (noting persistent disparate impact of so-called aptitude or intelligence tests on blacks and noting existence of cultural bias), *aff'd in part and rev'd in part,* 793 F.2d 969 (9th Cir. 1984).

13. *See, e.g.,* Neil L. Rudenstine, *The Uses of Diversity,* HARV. MAG., Mar.–Apr. 1996, 48, 57 ("Students who have had less consistent access to good education (and who lack the money to pay for extra 'prepping') will frequently do less well on standardized tests."). It is important to note the differrence here between standardized achievement tests (which give diagnostic information and feedback to the teacher and the students) and aptitude tests, which seek to predict future performance. It is the aptitude test format that I challenge in this lecture. *See infra* note 20.

14. *See* Peter Applebome, *For Twins, Double Jackpot on the S.A.T.,* N.Y. TIMES, Nov. 10, 1995, at A16 (Mrs. Salthouse, the mother of fraternal twins who scored simultaneous 1600s - the highest possible score - said her children had benefited from taking the SAT repeatedly over time. Mrs. Salthouse said, "The best preparation for taking the S.A.T. . . . is taking the S.A.T.").

15. Troy Duster, *The New Crisis of Legitimacy in Controls, Prisons, and Legal Structures,* THE AMERICAN SOCIOLOGIST, Spring 1995, at 20, 24–25.

16. *Id.* at 25 (paraphrasing Victor Hugo).

17. *See* CAL. PENAL CODE § 667 (West 1998). This statute reads:

It is the intent of the legislature in enacting subdivisions (b) to (i), inclusive, *to ensure longer prison sentences and greater punishment* for those who commit a felony and have been previously convicted of serious and/or violent felony offenses.

. . .

For purposes of subdivisions (b) to (i), inclusive, and in addition to any other enhancement or punishment provisions which may apply, the following shall apply where a defendant has a prior felony conviction:

(1) If a defendant has one prior felony conviction that has been pled and proved, the determinate term or minimum term for an indeterminate term shall be twice the term otherwise provided as punishment for the current felony conviction.

(2) (A) If a defendant has two or more prior felony convictions as defined in subdivision d) that have been pled and proved, the term for the current felony conviction shall be an indeterminate term of life imprisonment with a minimum

term of the indeterminate sentence calculated as the greater of:

(i) Three times the term otherwise provided as punishment for each current felony conviction subsequent to the two or more prior felony convictions.

(ii) Imprisonment in the state prison for 25 years.

(iii) The term determined by the court pursuant to Section 1170 for the underlying conviction, including any enhancement applicable to under Chapter 4.5 (commencing with Section 1170) of Title 7 of Part 2, or any period prescribed by Section 190 or 3046.

Id.

18. *See* Duster, *supra* note 15, at 25. This costs all taxpayers, not just those unlucky to be tracked to prison. In 1995, California spent more money on prison construction than on building colleges for the first time. Between 1984 and 1994, California built 16 new prisons; in the same decade, the state built only one new campus for the California State University system. Furthermore, the Department of Corrections increased its personnel by 25,864 while higher education personnel dropped by 8082. *See id.*

19. ASA G. HILLIARD III, TESTING AFRICAN AMERICAN STUDENTS 95 (1991) (providing examples of questions from recent SATs).

20. Of course, this is an oversimplification. The SAT and other "norm-referenced" aptitude tests do tell us something about one's capacity to do analytic thinking. The problem is that such capacity is often improved by practice, which comes from coaching (which costs money), from taking practice tests (which means exposure to the opportunity of learning from previous mistakes), and from other kinds of exposure to travel, books, and unusual vocabulary words. Thus, while the tests do tell us something about those who do well, they often tell us less about those who do poorly; i.e., they do not tell us what a poor performer is actually capable of doing, only what that person has already learned or not learned to do. *See, e.g.,* Michael Feuer, *The Changing Science of Assessment: Issues and Implications* (remarks at Symposium held Jan. 30, 1998); *Rethinking Law in the 21st Century Workplace,* U. PA. J. LAB. & EMP. LAW. (forthcoming 1998) (stating there is a non-trivial proportion of people who would be excluded from employment opportunities because of performance on a test who could nevertheless do the job; low-scoring test takers are more likely to be misclassified; and black appli-

cants, in particular, are more likely to be misclassified). Feuer, who is Director of the Board of Testing and Assessment at the National Academy of Sciences, explained that for many low-scoring individuals, differences in performance on a job are less than the differences in their test performance. This is because the tests only measure certain quantifiable traits and ignore "context, situation, training, teams and prior performance," which also affect job performance. *Id.* Feuer mentioned that the Academy supported research, published as "Fairness in Employment Testing," which included a study of the performance of 3500 Air Force pilots. The study found that previous performance of the pilots was the best predictor of their future performance. Feuer also gave the example of research on milk truck delivery drivers in New York who were able to do sophisticated mathematical calculations as part of their job, but the same drivers would not have been able to perform comparable calculations had they been asked first to take a test. Feuer concludes that some test-driven decisionmaking confuses prediction with merit, especially in light of research regarding the important role of practice and skill acquisition in the workplace itself. *See id.; see also* Sturm & Guinier, *supra* note 10, at 974 n.82 and accompanying text. A study of 300,000 recruits who failed the Army battery of tests in 1976, but because of a calibration error were admitted, was done. Longitudinal study of their subsequent performance showed little difference in re-enlistment and promotion rates compared to those who actually passed the test. *See id.*

21. *Cf.* Stephanie Simon, *Education/An Exploration of Ideas, Issues and Trends in Education; Working to Compete; Latino Students Preparing for the SAT Want the Opportunity to Show They Can Succeed,* LOS ANGELES TIMES, Oct. 1, 1997 (citing THE COLLEGE BOARD, 1997. "SAT tests taken in California show that scores rise with the income of students' families. Two-thirds of Mexican-American high school graduates come from families with incomes of less than $25,000 annually.") The article includes a table showing that students from families with a total annual income between $10,000 and $20,000 had an average combined SAT score of 906 (437 verbal and 469 math) and students whose family income was under $10,000 annually had an average combined SAT score of 859 (409 verbal and 450 math). *See id.* Meanwhile, students from families with income of $80,000 to $100,000 had an average combined SAT score of 1082 (535 verbal and 547 math). *See id.*

22. *See* Fair Test, 1996 California SAT Statistical Data (comparing household income in thousands of dollars with the percentage of Mexican-American, black, and white test-takers) (Fair Test National Center for Fair & Open Testing, Cambridge, Mass., Jan. 1998) (unpublished analysis on file with author). The data analysis was compiled from the Educational Testing Service's Profile of College-Bound High School Seniors data from 1996.

23. *See, e.g.,* Robert B. Westbrook, *Public Schooling and American Democracy, in* DEMOCRACY, EDUCATION AND THE SCHOOLS 125 (Roger Soder ed., 1996). Westbrook asserts

The relationship between public schooling and democracy is a conceptually tight one. Schools have become one of the principal institutions by which modern states reproduce themselves, and insofar as those states are democratic, they will make use of schools to prepare children for democratic citizenship.

Id. Some might argue that the exclusive or at least primary aim of schools should be to educate students "for the market." In President Clinton's 1994 State of the Union address, he declared, "We measure every school by one high standard: Are our children learning what they need to know to compete and win in the global economy?" *Id.* at 126. Others, such as Benjamin Barber, suggest the important yet neglected goal of "'civic literacy,'" meaning "'the competence to participate in democratic communities, the ability to think critically and act with deliberation in a pluralistic world, and the empathy to identify sufficiently with others to live with them despite conflicts of interest and differences in character.'" *Id.* at 125 (quoting Benjamin Barber, *America Skips School,* 287 HARPER'S MAG. 39, 44 (Nov. 1993)). Westbrook agrees with Barber that public schools are public not just because they are supported by public monies but because they educate every student for the responsibilities and benefits of participating in public life. *See* Westbrook, *supra.* Professor Susan Sturm and I argue that both goals (of educating citizens for employment opportunities and for democratic participation) are critical although we might restate them differently. *See generally* Susan Sturm & Lani Guinier, *From Triage to Transformation: The Role of Multiracial Learning Communities* (arguing that learning how to collaborate with people who are different is an essential mission of education both because the workplace of the twenty-first century will demand such "teamwork" and because complex problems are often only solved when diverse perspectives are taken into account through the process of constructive conflict) (unpublished manuscript, on file with author). *See also infra* text following note 40 (summarizing values of democratic diversity).

24. *See* Sturm & Guinier, *supra* note 10, at 971 ("A recent study of the correlation of SAT scores with freshman grades showed correlations ranging from .32 to .36") (citing WARREN W. WILLINGHAM ET AL., PREDICTING COLLEGE GRADES: AN ANALYSIS OF INSTITUTIONAL TRENDS OVER TWO DECADES 43 (1990)); *see also* Moore, *supra* note 12 ("According to most independent studies, the SAT's accuracy in predicting first-year college grades hovers around 30 percent, odds Ralph Nader once described as 'a little better than throwing dice.'").

25. *See* Sturm & Guinier, *supra* note 10, at 972–73 nn. 69–70 (citing Shapiro's affidavit that found weak correlations between LSAT scores and first-year law school performance for everyone, but particularly for African-American students).

26. *See* LANI GUINIER ET AL., BECOMING GENTLEMEN: WOMEN, LAW SCHOOL, AND INSTITUTIONAL CHANGE 31 (1997).

27. *See id.* at 8 ("For students in their first and second years, the LSAT explains even less: 14% and 15% [of performance] respectively."); *see also id.* at 124 n.74 ("In other words, when LSAT is the only variable in a bivariate regression equation, it explains 14% of the variance in first-year law school GPA.").

28. *See id.* at 10. According to Marilyn McGrath Lewis, director of admissions for Harvard and Radcliffe, "We have a particular interest in students from a modest background . . . . We know that's the best investment we can make: a kid who's hungry."

29. *See id.*

   Intense extracurricular involvement in high school reflects qualities of student leadership as well as initiative, and also usually means that the student has developed a long-term relationship with an adult mentor. The mentoring relationship is critical. It usually means an adult has expressed confidence in the student's ability and provides emotional and other support even after high school graduation.

   Id. at 10 n.17.

30. Other capacities associated with success that are not evaluated by high-stakes test include willingness to seek help. *See* National Commission on Testing and Public Policy, *From Gatekeepers to Gateway: Transforming Testing in America* 7–8 (Boston College, Chestnut Hill, MA 1990).

31. *See generally* DAVID N. PERKINS, OUTSMARTING IQ: THE EMERGING SCIENCE OF LEARNABLE INTELLIGENCE (1995); THE NATURE OF EXPERTISE (Michelene T.H. Chi et al. eds., 1988); TOWARD A GENERAL THEORY OF EXPERTISE: PROSPECTS AND LIMITS (K. Anders Ericcson & Jacqui Smith eds., 1991).

32. In addition to the ability to prioritize and juggle tasks, it is important to understand and be able to do what is valued within one's environment. *See* Robert J. Sternberg & R.K. Wagner, *The G-ocentric View of Intelligence and Job Performance is Wrong,* 2(1) CURRENT DIRECTIONS IN PSYCHOL. SCI. 1–5 (1993); Robert J. Sternberg & Wendy M. Williams, *Does the Graduate Record Examination Predict Meaningful Success in the Graduate Training of Psychologists?: A Case Study,* 52 (6) AM. PSYCHOLOGIST 630 (1997); *see generally* Mindy Kornhaber, *Some Means of Spurring the Equitable Identification of Students for Selective Higher Education* (Nov. 17, 1997) (unpublished manuscript on file with author).

33. Indeed, this is Michael Feuer's point: that high-stakes aptitude tests may disadvantage low-scoring test-takers unfairly because the test results fail to tell us whether the person has the capacity to do the job, yet we rely on the tests to deny the applicant the chance to prove what he or she can in fact do. *See supra* note 20.

34. *See* Lani Guinier, *Lessons and Challenges of Becoming Gentlemen,* N.Y.U. J. L. & SOC. POL'Y 18 (forthcoming 1998) (citing LAW SCHOOL ADMISSION COUNCIL/LAW SCHOOL ADMISSION SERVICES, LAW AS A CAREER: A PRACTICAL GUIDE 17 (1993) (stating that many lawyers do not litigate at all)); Gary L. Blasi, *What Lawyers Know: Lawyering Expertise, Cognitive Science, and the Functions of Theory,* 45 J. LEGAL EDUC. 313, 322, 325 (1995) (asserting that even in litigation what counts is judgment and experience, and many lawyers work as members of teams representing large organizations in multiparty transactions and disputes and only rarely go to court)). "Lawyering is a 'bundle of skills' including the lawyer's ability to 'integrate factual and legal knowledge and to exercise good judgment in light of that integrated understanding.'" *See* GUINIER ET AL., *supra* note 26, at 107 n.27 (quoting Blasi, *supra,* at 326). For example,

   [o]ften lawyers work as members of teams representing large organizations in multiparty transactions or disputes and only rarely go to court. The lawyer as aggressive litigator representing a single client may be outmoded in terms of what most lawyers actually do, and this paradigm may be dysfunctional in terms of 'the collection of competencies' lawyers need to possess in order to do their job well.

   Id. at 15–16.

A study . . . found that the three most important qualities of lawyers were oral communication, written communication, and "instilling others' confidence in you." After these, the skills or areas of knowledge considered most important were, in order, "ability in legal analysis and legal reasoning, drafting legal documents, and *ability to diagnose and plan solutions for legal problems.*"

Id. at 107 n.27 (quoting Bryant G. Garth & Joanne Martin, *Law Schools and the Construction of Competence*, 43 J. LEGAL EDUC. 469, 473 (1993)).

35. *See* GUINIER ET AL., *supra* note 26, at 103 n.2 (citing Uri Treisman, *Studying Students Studying Calculus: A Look at the Lives of Minority Mathematics Students in College*, 23 C. MATHEMATICS J. 362, 364–65 (1992), and PHILIP URI TREISMAN, A STUDY OF THE MATHEMATICS OF BLACK STUDENTS AT THE UNIVERSITY OF CALIFORNIA, BERKELEY 13–15, 46 (1985)). Uri Treisman found that the

collaborative approach of Chinese American students "provided them with valuable information that guided their day-to-day study"; these students "routinely critiqued each other's work" and thus discovered when studymates also found problems unusually difficult; as a result, students learned that their failure "was not one of simple oversight" but could be addressed by asking a teaching assistant "without fear of appearing incompetent or ill-prepared."

Id. (quoting TREISMAN, *supra*).

36. *See id.* at 18 ("New York City once a height requirement pegged to all men to select police officers. This discriminated against women, Asian men, some Latino men, and short white men . . . and normalized a particular type of officer-tough, brawny, macho."). The Los Angeles Police Department had similar policies. *See* Sturm & Guinier, *supra* note 10, at 985 n.136 (citing Mary Anne C. Case, *Disaggregating Gender from Sex and Sexual Orientation: The Effeminate Man in the Law and Feminist Jurisprudence*, 105 YALE L.J. 1, 87 (not-

ing report finding that LAPD training officers criticized female officers for a perceived lack of "stereotypically masculine qualities")).

37. *See* Sturm & Guinier, *supra* note 10, at 984–85 n.134 (citing Telephone Interview with J. Phillip Thompson, Director of Management and Operations, New York City Housing Authority, 1992–93 (Jan. 25, 1996)).

Thompson . . . recounted that an internal evaluation conducted by the Housing Authority revealed that women housing authority officers were policing in a different, but successful, way. As a result of this evaluation, the authority sought to recruit new cops based on their ability to relate to young people, their knowledge of the community, their willingness to live in the housing projects, and their interest in police work. They also offered free housing to any successful recruit willing to live in the projects.

Id.

38. *See supra* note 29 (describing importance of mentoring relationship with an adult during adolescence).

39. *See* Sturm & Guinier, *supra* note 10, at 985 n.135 (noting that the "women officers showed the young men respect, which was critical to the social status needs of these males; and that the men in turn checked their own behavior, out of mutual respect for the women officers") (citing Telephone Interview with J. Phillip Thompson, *supra* note 37).

40. *See id.* at 983 n.133 (citing Independent Commission on the Los Angeles Police Department, Report of the Independent Commission on the Los Angeles Police Department 83–84 (1991) ("'[F]emale LAPD officers are involved in excessive use of force at rates substantially below those of male officers . . . . The statistics indicate that female officers are not reluctant to use force, but they are not nearly as likely to be involved in use of excessive force,' due to female officers' perceived ability to be 'more communicative, more skillful at de-escalating potentially violent situations and less confrontational.'")).

CLASS 15

Asian Americans

CHAPTER 24
Understanding Asian Americans:
Background for Curriculum Development
Shin Kim

Shin Kim's work provides insight into the backgrounds of Asian Americans, one of the nation's fastest growing populations. As a result of the dynamic changes in Asian immigration to the U.S.A., this population is increasing at a faster rate than any other ethnic group in this society. This requires educators to know something about the backgrounds of these new students who will be in our nation's classrooms. Shin Kim's article provides a brief historical summary of key events leading up to the present.

CHAPTER 25
Educating Asian-American Students:
Past, Present, and Future
Ming-Gon John Lian

Ming-Gon John Lian provides insight on Asian culture that can help educators understand the differences as well as the similarities that Asian children bring to the classroom. The chapter also gives some insight into working with the parents of Asian students.

CHAPTER 24

Understanding Asian Americans: Background for Curriculum Development

Shin Kim

A doctoral candidate and adjunct professor in the School of Social Service Administration at the University of Chicago, Shin Kim taught economics at Chicago State University prior to beginning her Ph.D. program. She has published articles in the *Journal of Developing Areas* and the *International Journal of Aging and Human Development* and has edited *The Emerging Generation of Korean Americans.* Her areas of specialization are immigration policies, economics, and social work implications.

Introduction

Asian Americans, including immigrants from Asian countries and their descendants, have experienced an explosive growth since the 1965 revision in U.S. immigration laws. Early in the history of Asian immigration to the United States, severe and explicit restrictions had been placed on their immigration. As a consequence, the number of Asian Americans did not even reach one million by 1965 despite more than one hundred years of history here (Barringer, Gardner, & Levin. 1993). According to the 1980 U.S. census, there were 3.3 million Asian Americans in 1979, 1.5% of the total U.S. population. In a decade since then, the number jumped to 7 million or 2.8% of the population (U.S. Commission on Civil Rights, 1988, 1992). By the middle of the 21st century, projections indicate that one in ten Americans will claim their ancestry in Asian countries (Smith & Edmonston, 1997).

The second notable change in the post-1965 Asian American population is its ethnic diversity. Prior to 1965, Asian Americans generally were identified with only three ethnic groups: Chinese. Japanese, and Filipino. Presently, Asian Americans include Bengalis, Cambodians, Chinese, Filipinos, Hmongs, (Asian) Indians, Indonesians, Japanese, Koreans, Laotians, Pakistanis, Thais, Vietnamese, and several others with different languages and cultures. Some of these ethnic groups, such as the Indian and Chinese, encompass several languages and subcultures. In spite of their remarkable growth in numbers and diversity, the life experiences of Asian Americans have received insufficient attention among serious researchers of race/ethnic relations in the United States. This lack of understanding of Asian Americans' reality greatly hinders the curriculum development appropriate to Asian Americans. The task of developing curriculum relevant to Asian Americans, then, must begin with the effort to understand the Asian American reality.

Another noteworthy yet less apparent change in the 1990s is a growing presence of the children of immigrants in every ethnic community. The first generation of adult immigrants continues to be strong, except for Koreans. Nevertheless, as the history of mass Asian immigration lengthens, more and more children reach adulthood, and their presence in ethnic communities becomes more visible. On the whole, they are well educated and participate actively in various aspects of U.S. society. Whether they will be able to continue their active involvement as they grow older is difficult to predict and is not the task of this article. As their children grow in number and influence, the task of developing curriculum gains heightened urgency.

As mentioned, developing a curriculum appropriate to Asian Americans must begin with the proper understanding of their reality—their life experiences and structural positions—in the United States. I will discuss the similarities and differences among Asian Americans in terms of these experiences as well as their structural position in the U.S.; I begin with a brief discussion on the historical pattern of Asian American immigration.

Historical Pattern of Asian Immigration

Asian immigration historical patterns differ from those of nonAsian groups. Asian immigration to the United States occurred in two distinct stages. In the first stage—from the mid-19th century to the early decades of the 20th century—all Asian immigrations were labor immigrations. Moreover, several groups immigrated in a sequential order, one group at a time. Chinese immigrants were the first; they came from the mid-19th century until the passage of the Chinese Exclusion Act in 1882. As Chinese immigration ended, Japanese laborers immigrated until they too were stopped by legislation, the 1907 Gentlemen's Agreement between the Japanese and the United States governments. For a short three years between 1902 and 1905 during this Japanese immigration, approximately 7,000 Koreans arrived at Hawaiian shores. Japanese immigration was followed by Filipino workers until the Great Depression slowed down the whole immigration flow (U.S. Commission on Civil Rights, 1988).

A pull factor in this sequential immigration was the conflict of interests among members of the dominant group. That is, European American business owners' desire to obtain a cheap and reliable work force and the economic interests of European American labor unions led to a sequential immigration by different ethnic groups (Chan, 1991). This sequential immigration played out in a society with intense prejudice against Asians. Asian ethnic communities were looked down upon or outright despised. Native-born children could not find jobs even with advanced degrees.

From the 1930s to 1965, very little immigration from Asian countries was observed except for a limited number of Filipino workers. It is interesting to note that even though China was a U.S. ally in the second World War, severe restrictions on Chinese immigration were not lessened in any measurable degrees. Descendants of Asian immigrants of this first stage are outnumbered by children of the second stage immigrants in their respective ethnic communities. A notable exception is the Japanese.

As noted previously, the revision of the U.S. immigration laws in 1965 transformed the whole outlook on immigration. Since that revision, which abolished the highly discriminatory 1924 National Origin Act, immigration to the United States has been dominated by people from Asian and Latin American countries. Unlike the first stage, opportunities to immigrate are open to all ethnic groups simultaneously which results in the diversity among Asian immigrants. The society these immigrants migrate to is a society without *de jure* discrimination. Therefore, the push factor of immigration becomes more significant than the pull factor. Almost nonexistent immigration from Japan (in this stage) is a good example of this fact. Additionally, most immigrants in this second stage, especially ones in the early years, are professionals and/or skilled workers. It is a historical irony that the family reunification emphasis of the 1965 revision produced an immigration of highly skilled workers from Asian and Latin American counties. In recent years, the skill level of Asian immigrants has declined like nonAsian groups, as the population base of foreign-born Asian Americans has grown. Still, Asian immigration in this stage (the so-called 'recent' or 'new' immigrants) remains mostly a middle class and high skilled immigration (Smith & Edmonston, 1997). As the number of immigrants increases in most ethnic groups, each group develops its own vibrant ethnic community. Children of the immigrants of this second stage are growing up in different environments from first stage immigrants.

Characteristics of Asian Americans' Reality

STEREOTYPIC IMAGES

The public's stereotypic perception of Asian Americans includes both positive and negative images. Stereotypes are reflected in academic research and in mass media as well. Interestingly, this stereotypic image appears to have swung dramatically in recent years from an overt and summarily negative image to a positive one with subtle disparaging undertones. For example, for a long time—until the mid-20th century—Asian Americans were depicted as "inassimilable." "inscrutable," "cunning." and "filthy." (Chan, 1991; Fugita & O'Brien, 1991; Hurh & Kim. 1990). By the late 1960s. however, a new stereotype of Asian Americans as "successful groups" began to emerge in mass media as the United States was besieged by racial riots. Soon, this success image of Asian Americans became a *fait accompli.* Undoubtedly, stereotypes and changes of stereotypes affect the ethnic identity formation of children and their relationships with others, and, thus, merit further discussion (Min & Kim. 1999).

When Asian Americans were viewed negatively (in summary fashion) as in the past, children were deprived of developing healthy relations with parents and peers. They were prohibited from participating fully in U.S. society. Enduring life with such hardship took a great toll on individuals, and in some cases, created a vicious cycle. The U.S. response to Asian Americans in the past—"there would be discriminatory legislation prohibiting further immigration and for those already here, barriers to equal participation" (Kitano & Daniels, 1988, p. 5)—can be understood in this context as well. Two cases in point: 1) the 1882 Chinese Exclusion Act, the first federal law ever enacted to exclude a specific group, and several anti-Asian state and local laws in western states, and 2) a massive internment of Japanese Americans at the beginning of World War II in sharp contrast to U.S. treatment of German and Italian Americans (Fugita & O'Brien, 1991). In fact, Asian Americans were not allowed to obtain U.S. citizenship until 1952, and were commonly segregated in public facilities including schools (Chan, 1991: Kitano & Daniels, 1988).

The new stereotype of Asian Americans as "successful model minorities" who work hard but quietly, aspire to achieve the American (middle class) Dream, and abide by the law was (and still is) only part reality and part misperception. The post-1965 Asian Americans at the beginning were mostly professional and possessed a relatively high level of human capital. To be sure, this middle-class immigration was not solely an Asian American phenomenon. Immigrations from certain Latin American countries followed a similar pattern. Still, it was much more pervasive among Asian Americans than Latino Americans. In spite of their high level of education, skill, and ability, a majority of Asian immigrants could not find occupations corresponding to their human capital, and many ventured into self-employment in small businesses. Granted, they were quite different from traditional immigrants in terms of earnings and occupations, but perceiving them as a "successful group" is misleading and overlooks the harshness of their lives.

Moreover, since it is only partially based on reality, the success image brings detrimental effects to Asian Americans. For example, suicide rates among Asian American kids are found to be higher than the national average (Rue, 1993). With this image as a successful group. Asian Americans "do not have equal access to a number of public services, including police protection, health care, and the court system" (U.S. Commission on Civil Rights, 1992, p. 1). This public perception of Asian Americans includes a false idea that Asian Americans receive special favors from the government as well (U.S. Commission on Civil Rights, 1992; Kim, Kim & Gunn, 1997). The tragic killing of Vincent Chin and the 1992 Los Angeles racial disturbance, and their portrayals in mass media vividly illustrate the danger this success image poses to Asian Americans.

Surely, the positive image may boost the psychic ego of some Asian Americans and works as a positive reinforcer on some children. On the other hand, it disguises or ignores Asian Americans' experiences of discrimination in the United States and simplifies the Asian American life experiences. It thereby turns attention away from various social problems such as poverty and school dropouts that currently afflict many Asian Americans (U.S. Commission on Civil Rights, 1992, p. 24). The positive image also carries, erroneously, the message that this country is a land of opportunity open equally to any racial/ethnic group. It is used as a divisive wedge among minority racial/ethnic groups. For example, the attitude expressed in "if Asian Americans can make it, why can't African Americans make it?" (Hurh & Kim, 1990) blames African Americans for their current deprived life condition. At the same time, it arouses envy or jealousy that further aggravates the hostility of African Americans and others toward Asian Americans and results in "Asian bashing" (Kitano & Daniels, 1988).

Whether positive or negative, the stereotypic image conveys a simplistic and distorted picture of Asian American reality without a realistic understanding of their life experiences. All ethnic groups, Asian or nonAsian, suffer from stereotypes. What is unique to Asian Americans is the fact that their stereotypes had been changed somewhat superficially and applied in wholesale fashion. As a result, many children of Asian immigrants must deal with the clear as well as subtle duplicities of positive stereotypes while others suffer from invisibility.

The implications of this for curriculum development are several and revolve around the following considerations. First and foremost, great variance in life conditions among "Asian American" students exists. The success image is only partially correct: some Asian American students are from economically struggling and socially deficient households. Second, this positive image imposes a high expectation on Asian American students' academic accomplishment in general. Some could benefit from it at the same time others could be hurt by it. High expectation originates not only from teachers but also parents. Thus, Asian American students may face an overload of pressures. Third, Asian American students are viewed as "excellent" in mathematics but "not quite good" in humanities and social sciences. Once again, this too simplistic perception could hinder a proper cultivation of talents. Fourth, Asian Americans' peer relationships are much more complicated because of the flip side of the success image—the envy and jealousy it creates. Fifth, this success image may bring an over or false confidence that renders Asian Americans oblivious to possible obstacles they will face later in life.

COMMON EXPERIENCE OF MISTREATMENT

Coupled with stereotypes, the public's ignorance of Asian Americans often leads to mistreatment and victimization that grossly violates Asian Americans' civil rights. Recent studies stress that "Asian Americans are frequently victims of racially motivated bigotry and violence" (U.S. Commission on Civil Rights, 1992, p. 1). Due to their general ignorance and insensitivity, to most nonAsian Americans, Asian Americans look alike. Such an unfortunate perception creates numerous serious mishaps. For example, Vietnamese students are placed in Filipino, even in Spanish, bilingual programs. Or Asian students from various language backgrounds, such as Chinese, Vietnamese and Laotian, are placed together in a class so that the language of instruction has to be English (Chung, 1988). The killing of Vincent Chin (see endnote 11) is another good example of this. The trial verdicts—"not guilty" in the first trial and "guilty" with very light sentences in the second trial—are read by Asian Americans as expressions of pervasive ignorance and deep-down institutional racism in the United States.

Even though a significant proportion of current Asian Americans, with the exception of Japanese Americans, are foreign-born, many Asian Americans in the United States are native-born. Furthermore, the number of the native born is rapidly increasing as children of immigrants grow up. But most Americans tend to treat all Asian Americans as foreigners. When Asian Americans mention their home states in response to a question about where they are from, people are usually not satisfied with their answer and keep asking until the countries of the Asian Americans' ancestors are revealed. This kind of conversation, though perhaps unwittingly, carries a subtle message that Asian Americans are less than full citizens of the United States no matter how many generations they have lived here.

FAMILY LIFE OF ASIAN AMERICANS: SOLIDARITY AND CONFLICTS

Contrary to public expectation, the most prevalent family type among Asian immigrants is the residential and functional nuclear family (Min, 1998; Hurh & Kim, 1988). Without too much generalization, it can be argued that Asian Americans are high in family solidarity. Divorce rates and youth delinquency are still lower among Asian Americans (Smith & Edmonston, 1997), albeit rising, than in other groups. Some scholars trace this solidarity to Confucianism and Buddhism. Regardless of its cause, this strong family solidarity facilitates Asian Americans' economic advancement by easing the pressure to become independent too early, and/or by providing emotional supports. On the other hand, it also can complicate the family life of many Asian Americans.

To be sure, there are the usual generation gaps in Asian American families. Furthermore, there are language and Americanization gaps. Asian American parents (even the native-born) are known for their devotion to children. Children are expected to reciprocate the favor (?) by excelling in life and taking care of their parents in their old age. It is not difficult to imagine how this dimension of family solidarity complicates Asian Americans' family and kinship lives. Moreover, family conflicts are not solely between the native-born children and the immigrant parents. Frictions are observed between the adult children (immigrants) and their elderly parents (Kim, Kim, & Hurh, 1991). To the best of my knowledge, no paper has yet studied how this conflict (between parents and grandparents) affects children. As a matter of fact, the relationship between grandparents and grandchildren is one of the most understudied aspects of Asian American family life.

Another layer of Asian American family life to be mentioned revolves around its male-centeredness and its subsequent traditional gender role expectation. Without question, this male focus affects the self-concept of female children negatively (Min & Kim, 1999). This traditional gender role expectation is evident among the second generation Asian American churches (Chai, 1999) as well as within individual families. Unfortunately, possible adverse effects of this male domination on family life, such as domestic violence, are hushed subjects and receive little study. A great proportion of native-born Asian Americans marry out, that is, marry outside of their own ethnic group. Their marriage partners are as likely to be non-Hispanic whites as other Asian Americans (Kitano & Daniels, 1988).

Religious Activities: Highly Religious in Diverse Religions

Until recently, religious life among Asian Americans, especially among the native-born Asian Americans, had received very little attention. Like immigrants in the past, recent (i.e. post-1965) Asian immigrants brought their religion with them to the United States. Since immigration involves a psychologically upsetting experience of uprooting and re-rooting, immigrants are usually found to be more religious post-immigration than pre-emigration. Thus, it is not surprising to find many Asian immigrant communities religiously active. The unexpected, though, is the intense religious activities of the native-born chil-

dren of Asian American immigrants, and the significant role a religion plays in their ethnic identity formation (Warner & Wittner. 1998; Kim, Song, & Moon, 1998).

The heterogeneity of specific religions involved in Asian American communities must be stressed. Gone is the overwhelming dominance of western religions such as Christianity among native-born Asian Americans. Protestant religions are predominant among Koreans and Vietnamese, and Filipinos are mostly Catholic. At the same time, however, Hinduism is strong among Indians, and Pakistanis and Bengalis are often Muslims. Among Thais and Chinese, Buddhism is the dominant force (Chan, 1991; Warner & Wittner, 1998).

Socioeconomic Status: Education and Occupation

As expected, current Asian Americans include a high proportion of those who are well educated. Proportionally more native-born Japanese and Chinese Americans have completed a college education than their European American counterparts (Hurh & Kim, 1990; Kitano & Daniels. 1988: U.S. Commission on Civil Rights, 1988). Also, an unusually high proportion of Asian immigrants have completed their college education prior to emigration (Kim, Hurh, & Fernandez, 1989). Asian immigrant parents' emphasis on children's education is well known (Pai, 1993) and helps equip Asian American children to assimilate into the middle-class white United States regardless of their residential location (Zhou & Bankston, 1998). In short, Asian Americans are rich in human capital, especially in formal education on the whole. Even in this respect, though, there are some inter- and intra-group differences. Refugee groups except the Vietnamese are lower in educational attainment, on the average, than non-refugee immigrant groups. Likewise, members of the same ethnic group differ in education, ranging from those who have completed college or post-college education to those without high school diplomas. Due to the aforesaid stereotyping, the latter (the intra-group difference) is hardly acknowledged even among Asian scholars.

Such intra-group differences in education and post-industrial opportunities in the United States result in a high degree of intra-group occupational differentiations. Consequently, members of each Asian ethnic group are distributed among various occupational categories including professional/technical occupations, self-employed small businesses, and low-skill service or manual occupations (Kim, Hurh, & Fernandez, 1989). This occupational difference is exhibited among different ethnic groups, i.e. inter-group difference. One example: The inter-group difference in self-employed small businesses among immigrants is well documented. For instance, Koreans, South Asians, Chinese, and Vietnamese are active whereas Filipinos are hardly involved in such businesses. Japanese immigrants were once entrepreneurially very active, but their descendants shunned this sector (Fugita & O'Brien, 1991; Kim, Hurh, & Fernandez, 1989). In very recent years, cautious observations are voiced that children, primarily the foreign-born children, of entrepreneurially active Asian immigrants are entering self-employed small businesses in good numbers.

On the whole, Asian Americans are well represented in professional/technical occupations. Once in the professional labor market, though, Asian Americans encounter various kinds of subtle discrimination or difficulty such as peripheralization, underutilization of resources, and the glass ceiling, in spite of their high education levels (Kim, 1993; Hurh & Kim, 1990; U.S. Commission on Civil Rights, 1992). A report of the U.S. Commission on Civil Rights summarizes the problems highly educated native-born Asian males experience in the U.S. labor market as follows:

> For all groups that were studied, American-born Asian men are less likely to be in management positions than their non-Hispanic counterparts. Furthermore, adjusting for occupation and industry, highly educated American-born Asian men in all groups were found to earn less than similarly qualified non-Hispanic white men. These findings raised the possibility that men in all Asian groups face labor market discrimination at the top. (1988, p. 7).

Such diverse experiences of Asian Americans present dilemmas to researchers. As Kitano and Daniels observe, "no one model can encompass the experience of all Asian groups (1988, p. 7) or all members of any one group. Therefore, we need a creative application of the existing theories and development of new labor market models.

RESIDENTIAL PATTERNS AND LOCATIONS

Asian Americans are a highly urbanized group. Asian immigrants tend to settle in metropolitan areas rather than rural areas due to economic and ethnic sociocultural opportunities. A very small proportion of Asian Americans is engaged in agricultural production either an owner-farmers or hired farm workers. Most of the post-1965 Asian immigrants also formed ethnic communities of their own in urban areas. Such ethnic communities serve not only are a safe haven for immigrants but also as a vehicle to transmit sociocultural heritage. In other words, the native-born children of Asian immigrants are imbued in both U.S. and ethnic cultures by living in metropolitan areas around the country.

On the whole, Asian Americans are suburbanites more likely than not. Even here, there exists an inter-group difference. Thus, refugee groups are more likely to reside in inner cities than other immigrant groups. With an exception of Chinatown, other ethnic enclaves such as Little Saigon, Koreatown, and Japantown are commercial, not residential enclaves. Ethnic communities, then, are associational gatherings rather than territorially (or geographically defined ones. Even when they are residing inside cities, Asian Americans tend to assimilate to the suburban middle-class culture (Zhou & Bankston, 1998). One upshot of this pattern is that city and suburban educators must exert concerted efforts to develop an Asian American-appropriate curriculum. In addition, Asian Americans are concentrated heavily in the western states, particularly in California. Estimates of Asian Americans residing in the West (mainly California) range from 40 to 60 percent. One interesting observation: In Asian American circles, the term 'east of California' is uttered frequently to distinguish Asian Americans residing in California and those living outside of California. It succinctly depicts the eminence of California as the choice of residential location among Asian Americans.

Conclusion

Asian Americans can no longer be ignored in the United States. Their number is increasing rapidly and their activities are becoming more visible. So far. the general public's perception of Asian Americans is far from reality and often is based on erroneous stereotypes. Private and public treatment of Asian Americans has its origin in these incorrect perceptions. Developing curriculum that is in tune with Asian American experiences cannot and must not be based on these misperceptions. The very first step toward appropriate curriculum development, then, begins with efforts to understand and to appraise the Asian American reality.

As discussed throughout this article, the monolithic "Asian American" experience is nowhere to be found. Asian American groups differ significantly in their immigration history, culture, language, ethnic homogeneity, and other life experiences. Certain groups such as Koreans and Japanese are homogeneous while some, such as Indians and Chinese, are quite heterogeneous. Heterogeneous or homogeneous, each group also exhibits a high degree of intra-group variance in terms of education, occupation, and other socioeconomic factors.

Such inter- and intra-group differences notwithstanding, a common theme runs through various aspects of Asian American reality: the structural position of Asian Americans in U.S. society is that of a minority rather than of the majority. In economic terminology, the difference is micro and the similarity, more macro. To put it differently, Asian Americans are minorities with numerous attributes of the majority. A good proportion of Asian Americans succeed or 'make it' in the U.S. in terms of various observable indicators of success. At the same time. they are mistreated and downright discriminated against in some cases by the nonAsian public because of their racial minority status. This duality creates psychologically turbulent waters for Asian Americans to navigate. Curriculum developers must comprehend this extraordinary environment ordinary Asian Americans face and understand the efforts Asian Americans have to put into their everyday living.

Developing a new inclusive curriculum also requires a refinement of theoretical and conceptual frameworks for racial/ethnic study which goes beyond the traditional bi-racial bias of racial/ethnic studies in the United States. For a long period of time, the study of racial/ethnic relations has been dominated by the black (= the minority) vs white (= majority) polarity. Asian Americans, being neither white nor black, and being minority in some aspects and majority in some others, pose a special challenge. All in all, the case of Asian Americans as historically unique. Thus, developing a curriculum which adequately reflects Asian American experiences is a complicated task. Yes, it is a difficult undertaking. Yet it is an exciting challenge whose time has finally arrived.

References

Barringer, H., Gardner, R.W., & Levin, M. J. (1993). *Asian and Pacific Islanders in the United States.* New York: Russell Sage Foundation.

Bouvier, L.F., & Davis, G. B. (1982). *Future racial composition of the United States.* Washington, DC: Demographic Information Service Center of the Population Reference Bureau.

Chai, K. J. (2000). Beyond 'strictness' to distinctiveness: Generational transition in Korean Protestant churches. In H. Kwon, K. C. Kim, & R. S. Warner (Eds.). *Korean Americans: Religion and society.* University Park: Pennsylvania State University Press.

Chan, S. (1991). *Asian Americans: An interpretive history.* Boston: Twayne Publishers.

Chung, C. H. (1988). The language situation of Vietnamese Americans. In S. L. McKay & S. C. Wong (Eds.). *Language diversity: Problem or resource?* (pp. 276–292). New York: Newberry House.

Fugita. S., & O'Brien. D. J. (1991). *Japanese American ethnicity: The persistence of community*, Seattle: University of Washington Press.

Hurh, W. M., & Kim, K.C. (1990, October). The success image of Asian Americans: Its validity, practical and theoretical implications. *Ethnic and Racial Studies, 12,* 512–538.

Kim, K. C., Hurh. W. M., & Fernandez, M. (1989, Spring). Intra-group differences in business participation: A comparative analysis of three Asian immigrant groups. *International Migration Reviews. 12,* 73–95.

Kim, K. C., & Kim. S. (1999). The multirace/ethnic nature of Los Angeles unrest in 1992. In K. C. Kim (Ed.). *Koreans in the 'Hood* (chap. 2). Baltimore: Johns Hopkins University Press.

Kim, K. C., Kim, S., & Gunn, K. (1997, August 9–13). Self-reliance ideology and the African American view of Korean entrepreneurs: A case study on the South Side of Chicago. Paper presented at 92nd annual meeting of American Sociological Association, Toronto, Canada.

Kim, K. C., Kim, S., & Hurh, W. M. (1991). Filial piety and intergenerational relationships in Korean immigrant families. *International Journal of Aging and Human Development, 33,* 232–245.

Kim, K. C., Song, Y. I., & Moon, A. (1998, August 19–23). Pluralistic accommodation and young Korean Americans' ethnic identity. Paper presented at 93rd annual meeting of American Sociological Association, San Francisco.

Kim, S. (1993). Career prospect for Korean immigrants' children. In H. Kwon & S. Kim (Eds.), *The emerging generation of Korean Americans* (chap. 5). Seoul, Korea: Kyung Hee University Press.

Kitano, H. L., & Daniels. R. (1988). *Asian Americans: Emerging minorities.* Englewood Cliffs. N J: Prentice Hall.

Min, P. G. (1998). Korean American families. In R. L. Taylor (Ed.), *Minority families in the United States* (chap. 10). Upper Saddle River, NJ: Prentice Hall.

Min, P. G., & Kim, R. (Eds.). (1999). *Struggle for ethnic identity: Narratives by Asian American professionals.* Walnut Creek, CA: Alta Mira Press.

Pai, Y. (1993). Academic and occupational preferences of Korean American youth. In H. Y. Kwon & S. Kim (Eds.), *The Emerging generation of Korean Americans* (chap. 3). Seoul, Korea: Kyung Hee University Press.

Reimers. D. M. (1985). *Still the golden door: The Third World comes to America.* New York: Columbia University Press.

Rue, D. (1993). Depression and suicidal behavior among Asian whiz kids. In H. Y. Kwon & S. Kim (Eds.), *The emerging generation of Korean Americans* (chap. 4). Seoul. Korea: Kyung Hee University Press.

Smith. J. P., & Edmonston, B. (Eds.). (1997). *The New Americans: Economic demographic, and fiscal effects of immigration.* Washington, DC: National Academy Press.

CHAPTER 25

Educating Asian American Students: Past, Present, and future

Ming-Gon John Lian

He taught in Taiwan and Texas before joining the faculty at Illinois State University in 1983. Ming-Gon John Lian has served as the president of the Illinois Division for Culturally and Linguistically Diverse Exceptional Children and chair of the Multicultural Committee of the National Association for Persons with Severe Handicaps. He received the Outstanding Faculty Award from the Office of Multicultural Affairs in 1998 and the Strand Diversity Achievement Award in 1999.

Asian American children are one of the fastest-growing populations in U.S. schools. Between 1991 and 1996, Asian Americans in the United States increased by 28.9 percent, compared to 25.3 percent Hispanics/Latinos, 9.5 percent African Americans, and 2.9 percent Caucasians (see Table 1). It is predicted that, by the year 2050, the number of Asian Americans will increase from the current 3.7 percent to 10 percent, or 40 million, of the nation's total population (Chan, 1998).

Ong and Hee (1993) reported that there were three million Asian/Pacific American students in U.S. schools. They predicted that the number of these students may be increased to twenty million by the year 2020. Though Asian/Pacific Americans are frequently identified as a unified group, Asian ethnic groups vary greatly in culture, language and experience (Lian & Poon-McBrayer, 1997). Actually, members in the Asian American population may represent diverse familial and cultural backgrounds, including those from Bangladesh, Cambodia, China, Hong Kong, Cambodia, India, Indonesia, Japan, Korea, Laos, Malaysia Pakistan, Sri Lanka, Taiwan, Thailand, the Philippines, Vietnam, and many other Asian countries and areas. A broader classification of the Asian American population also includes the Pacific Islanders from Guam, Hawaii, Micronesia, Okinawa, Polynesia, Saipan, Samoa, Tonga, and other islands in the Pacific Ocean (Lian, 1995; U.S. Census Bureau, 1997a).

Asian Americans were previously referred to as "Orientals," a term that may critically disadvantage Asian American children. Through the years, a stereotype of the "Orientals" has existed. Some people, for example, may still relate Chinese Americans to illegal aliens, slanted eyes, chopsuey or chowmein-style ethnic foods, and funny speaking mannerism, thinking of them as different from persons of "the Western World." As a result, Asian American children in the school may suffer from cultural and social discrimination and racism (Luke, 1987).

"Asian American" is a preferred term, originating during the last ten to twenty years Just like African Americans, European Americans, Latin Americans, and Native Americans many persons with Asian descent are also Americans. Chinese Americans, Filipino Americans, Indian Americans, Indonesian Americans, Japanese Americans, Korean Americans, Malaysian Americans, Thai Americans, Urdu Americans, and Vietnamese Americans represent subpopulations of Asian Americans.

Characteristics of Asian American Students

Asian American students may include children and youth who have recently immigrated to

Table 1. Increase in Racial/Ethnic Populations (1991–1996)

	1991	July, 1996	Increase 1991–1996
African Americans	30,600,000	33,500,000	9.5%
Asian Americans	7,550,000	9,700,000	28.9%
Caucasians	188,500,000	194,000,000	2.9%
Hispanics/Latinos	22,500,000	28,200,000	25.3%
Total	231,900,000	265,284,000	14.4%

Source: U.S. Census Bureau (1997a).

the United States as well as those who were born or raised in this country and are second, third, fourth, or fifth generation. Some Asian American students may have limited-English-proficiency (LEP) or speak English as a second language (ESL), while others may speak only English. Some children may speak only one of numerous Asian languages, while others may be bilingual, trilingual, or multilingual (e.g., English, Vietnamese, and French). Even students who speak the same Asian language may use different dialects (e.g., Mandarin Chinese, Cantonese, Shanghainese and Taiwanese). Any of these linguistic factors could add to the complicated multicultural experience of school-age Asian American children.

Hu-DeHart (1999) points out that, in the next decade, more students will come from biracial (e.g., Asian American and Latino) or multiracial (e.g., African American, Pacific American, and Native American) families and cultural backgrounds. Another group of Asian American students are children who were adopted from Asian countries, such as China and Korea, by their African American, Asian American, Caucasian, or Hispanic/Latino parents. in 1993, 89 Chinese infants were brought to the U.S. by their adopting families. The number of adoptions went up to 4,000 in 1998.

For many years, Asian Americans were ignored in U.S. literature on ethnic relations, resulting in the general public knowing very little about this population. Wakabayashi (1977) describes Asian Americans as the "least acknowledged of the national minorities" (p. 430). Many

Americans developed their awareness and knowledge of Asian Americans based on false or stereotypic information eventually leading to prejudice, negative attitudes and discriminatory responses. Kim (1993) points out that, in the mid-19th to the mid-20th century, Asian Americans were often perceived to be "unassimilable," "inscrutable," "cunning," or "filthy." Because of the *exclusion legislation* enacted in 1882, most Asian Americans were not allowed to become U.S. citizens until 1952. Even today, Asian American children may be perceived by their teachers or peers in schools as foreigners or refugees (Cheng, Ima, & Labovitz, 1994) and many Asian Americans who are U.S. citizens are asked about their nationality or when they plan to "go back."

Since the 1960s, a new stereotypic image of Asian Americans has developed. Asian Americans are now often classified as diligent, hard-working, and high educational and economic achievers. Such overgeneralizations cause the public to overlook hidden issues and concerns among this population including poverty, limited health care, family violence, child abuse and neglect, and increased school failure and dropouts among Asian American children. As Sadker and Sadker (1994) indicate,

> Despite outstanding accomplishments, the statistics hide problems that many of the new immigrants from Southeast Asia and Pacific Islands face. Cultural conflict, patterns of discrimination, lower educational achievement, and the diversity of the Asian/Pacific Americans are all hidden by the title "model minority." (p. 411)

Similar situations occur in the classroom setting, as Pang (1997) suggests:

> . . . [Asian/Pacific American] students are often overlooked or misunderstood in schools. Many teachers do not feel pressured to attend to the needs of APA children since they are not discipline problems and do not seem to need special attention; however, many students may feel invisible and forgotten. Many APA students are seen and never heard. It happens in the classrooms of the best teachers and in classrooms where teachers have little interest in their students. (p. 149)

Chen (1989) expresses a concern about the lower self-concept which may exist among general Asian American students. He lists a number of positive characteristics of Asian American students, including bilingual and bicultural experiences, a long cultural history, respect within the culture for each other, strong family bonding, assertiveness, trustworthiness, high expectations, industriousness, a strong work ethic and moral values, flexibility, and adaptability. For example, Asian American students tend to be described as having "inner strength"—being flexible and able to bend but hard to break, especially during hardships. However, he worries that low self-concepts among Asian American students still exist.

Lian (1992) contends that the "melting pot" concept tends to force culturally and linguistically diverse students to assume Caucasian culture and language are priorities for learning and living. If the student does not learn well, he or she may be labeled a slow learner or even removed from the mainstream classroom. Such students may thus have lower self-esteem and expectations for educational achievement.

Leung (1990) indicates six major concerns related to educating Asian American students: physical differences, linguistic differences, culture-based differences, acculturation dilemmas (adjustment problems), identity crises, and uninformed and insensitive significant others. According to Leung, an example is provided when Asian American students speak their native language at school and other children laugh. It is not unusual for a child in this situation to say, "Mom, don't speak Chinese! It's embarrassing."

Like adults, students in the schools may face cultural differences and conflicts between the Asian American community and other ethnic populations. Lian and Poon-McBrayer (1998) suggest "Asian American youth may struggle with a number of issues such as racism and conflicts with traditional values" (p. 18). In a study by Poon-McBrayer (1996), teachers overwhelmingly reported that students from Asian American families tend to concentrate more on academic subject matter in school than do their nonAsian peers. However, Feldman and Rosenthal (1990) note that Asian American youth may often be torn by pressures associated with demands to conform to diametrical values: the Western notion of individualism and the traditional Asian value of collectivism. According to Rick and Forward (1992), Asian youth perceive themselves to be less connected to parental value systems as they become more acclimated to U.S. norms. This phenomenon is logically more apparent between the first-generation immigrant parents and the U.S.-born, second-generation youth. Cultural conflicts and linguistic differences between these parents and youth are more frequently found and severe than if the parents themselves were also U.S.-born. Other variables that may affect the severity of conflicts and differences between Asian parents and youth include the education of parents, where they received their education, parents' length of stay in the U.S., and their level of acculturation.

In U.S. schools, maintaining eye contact with the teacher during instructional activities is emphasized whereas Asian American students are told at home that it is rude to stare at or to look into the eyes of an adult whom they respect (Lian, 1995). Direct eye contact may give Asian American parents or teachers the impression that the child disagrees or wants to argue with them, or is showing disrespect toward them. Such a response, from an adult perspective, represents a serious behavioral problem. At the same time, teachers may find that Asian American students show politeness by standing while parents, teachers, or elderly persons sit and by remaining quiet or silent when adults are talking.

Asian American children may exhibit learning and response patterns that appear to be unusual in U.S. schools. In the classroom, Asian American children may feel more comfortable answering a yes-no question instead of an open-ended question. Also, in addition to "yes" and "no" answers, children may select the third choice—silence, which may mean yes, no, agree, disagree, no answer, no comment, didn't understand the question, or waiting for the answer to come up by itself (e.g., the teacher or other children eventually will answer the question). Heward and Orlansky (1992) state that "the toughest thing a teacher of Asian students must deal with is the silence; its reasons are complex" (p. 510).

Instead of showing and telling, an Asian American child in the classroom may define "sharing" as listening quietly. In addition, teachers may observe that Asian American children find it difficult to talk about their own achievement, to ask for or offer help, to ask questions in class, to answer a teacher's questions, or to express their own opinion (Brower, 1983). Teachers should avoid the conclusion that Asian American children are less active in classroom learning activities. This is especially true for a new, non- or limited-English-speaking child who may exhibit a great deal of silence in class.

Asian American children may show another type of passive resistance. When an Asian American child is selected to represent his or her class in an activity, the child may feel that his or her friends are more deserving of the honor and decline. This passive resistance should not be interpreted as a lack of willingness to volunteer.

A general autonomy issue also exists among Asian American children. Research indicates that Asian American children may take a few more years than European American children to become independent. Asian American parents may provide their children with extensive care, which often means doing as many nonacademic chores for them as possible. Asian American children may also rely heavily on adults for decision making. Asian American parents may expect their child's major responsibility in school to be to concentrate on academics, to study and to get good grades.

Uniqueness in Educating Asian American Children

Asian American students have unique cultural and linguistic backgrounds. Families of these students have special traditions and values affecting their daily life, including education. Members of Asian American families generally have a strong respect for parents, the elderly, teachers,

scholars, tradition, and the educational system, thinking of them as authorities. Asian American children are usually taught to be obedient and cooperative, to be dependent at home and in school, and to express unconditional loyalty to their ethnic community. As Barrett-Schuler (1997) notes,

> In sharp contrast to the Western emphasis on the individual, collectivist societies predominate in Asia. Individualism is viewed rather negatively in countries such as China and Japan. They have hierarchy-sensitive traditions with collectivist mentalities. (p. 165)

Education, in the eyes of Asian American parents, is of extremely high value and is perceived to be the vehicle for upward mobility. Heward and Olansky (1992) describe the influence of such a perception of education:

> For many years, teachers and scholars have been revered in China and other Asian countries. For parents influenced by their traditional cultural heritage, no sacrifice is too great to obtain a good education for their children. From the child's view point, scholastic achievement is the highest tribute one could bring to his or her parents and family. . . . This philosophy and work ethic has helped many Asian American students excel in schools. (p. 507)

Most Asian American parents and families value and support the education of their children. In fact, Chen (1989) identifies Chinese parental support and commitment as two of the major strengths and assets in the education of Chinese American children. However, educators need to be aware of the incongruencies between nonAsian teachers' expectations and Asian American parents' expectations (Cheng, 1987). In U.S. schools, students are encouraged by teachers to participate actively in classroom discussion and activities, while Asian American students may be told by their parents to "behave," i.e., to be quiet and obedient at school. Students may be encouraged by nonAsian teachers to be creative, while Asian American parents may think that students should be told what to do. In U.S. schools, students learn through inquiry and debate, while Asian American students may prefer to study and place their trust in what the teacher says and what is written in the textbooks, i.e., to learn through memorization. NonAsian teachers may believe Asian American students generally do well on their own, while Asian American parents may think the teacher's role is to teach and the student's job is to "study." In a U.S. school, critical thinking and analytical thinking are perceived to be important, while Asian American parents may believe that it is more important to learn the existing facts. Students' creativity and fantasies are encouraged by nonAsian teachers, while Asian American parents may perceive factual information to be much more important than imagination. Problem-solving skills are emphasized in U.S. schools, while Asian American parents may want their children to be taught the exact steps required to solve problems. In U.S. classrooms, students need to ask questions, while Asian American parents and their children may try not to ask questions, thinking that teachers should not be challenged. The teacher may think of reading as a way of discovering, while Asian American parents may think of reading as the decoding of information and facts.

Many Asian Americans believe and follow the thoughts of Confucianism, Buddhism, and/or Christianity, in which moral behaviors and a sense of forgiveness are strictly emphasized. Asian Americans also tend to rely on the **Yin-Yang philosophy.** Yin-Yang means a contrast between two extremes such as darkness and brightness, femininity and masculinity, interior and exterior, fast pace and slow pace, and happiness and sadness. Asian Americans tend to seek harmony and equilibrium between two distinct phenomena, feelings, or theories (Chan, 1998). In other words, Asians Americans may avoid either extreme or criticism of the opposite point of view. They may try to stay at the neutral-point in a controversial issue and attempt to make both sides in an argument happy—to avoid competition, conflict, and the related debate, and to work out a compromise. Asian Americans try to avoid conflict with nature. Many tend to accept their fate and do nothing to change it or create a "new" fate. This contrasts with the fighting-for-rights effort prevalent in the United States.

While differences between the Asian American culture and the majority culture may create educational obstacles, Asian American traditions and values significantly contribute to diversity in U.S. schools and society. Heward and Orlansky (1992) state that a great strength of the United States is cultural diversity. Our society is made up of immigrants from many lands, and we have all benefited from the contributions of the many ethnic groups. It is the educators' responsibility to attend to the Asian American heritage and the unique educational needs of children from the Asian American population.

Parents of Asian American Children

Asian American parents play a significant role in the education of their children. Most parents of Asian American children tend to treasure education and respect teachers and scholars highly, expecting high standards and academic achievement from educators. A Thai American parent, for example, may want his or her child to be educated to become an "ideal student" with the following traits (Sriratana, 1995):

1. values
   - to be well-rounded and honest,
   - to have confidence,
   - to be trustworthy and have integrity,
   - to have courage and dare to attempt difficult tasks and challenges,
   - to be peaceful, calm, and serene when dealing with conflict, and to be self-reliant and well-disciplined;

2. giving
   - to be dependable and loyal to family,
   - to respect life, property, and nature,
   - to love friends and neighbors,
   - to be sensitive to others' needs and feelings and to be unselfish,
   - to be kind and friendly, and
   - to act with justice and mercy.

However, Asian American families are generally reluctant to convey their expectations to teachers. Dao (1994), for example, reports that

Hmong, Cambodian and Lap parents tend not to speak up . . . because of a cultural politeness and respect toward the professional, who is seen as the expert. They don't want to insult him or her by asking too much—even though they have a right and even though the question or observation might help the professional. (p. 15)

This may lead to a reluctance to indicate when they need help. For instance, advocacy may be difficult for Asian American families to understand and engage in for a person with disabilities.

Asian American parents may also be unaware of how to participate actively in PTO or other school activities. Instead of concluding these parents are less willing to volunteer for school activities, it may be more appropriate to assume that they need more time to get acquainted or become comfortable with the U.S. school system, or that they might need to be informed or provided with information and opportunities before they become active volunteers to support school programs.

In the Asian American community, there is also general concern for "face." To challenge the educational system may not be acceptable because it causes trouble and, even worse, causes school administrators and teachers to lose "face." Parents and other family members may apologize repeatedly, worrying that they have bothered the school too much if they make requests for services.

Dao (1994) lists potential barriers that may prevent Southeast Asian American parents from accessing services:

- fear of persecution as a result of the experience in the war against the communists in Vietnam, Laos, and Cambodia;

- self-reliance which may cause Asian American families to be the main caregivers of children with special education needs, to solve educational problems, and to fulfill needs within the families;

- limited English proficiency which may slow the assessment process and cause a delay of service;

- a tendency to trust the psychoeducational system and authority and not to question;

- a perception and expectation based on a disabling condition, e.g., feeling of guilt;

- lack of training and experience in evaluating their child's progress and achievement;

- cultural and custom differences, e.g., trying not to be demanding, not to advocate, or to avoid court actions; and

- general misunderstanding on the part of the Asian American families.

Asian American parents may have different perceptions of a child's failure in school. Lynch (1994) identifies three educational failure paradigms perceived by Asian American parents:

1. *child deficit orientation* (the medical model)—the cause of failure resides within the child's physical body.

2. *environmental deficit orientation* (the behavioral model)—since behavior is learned, children fail as a result of inappropriate or inadequate environmental circumstances in which to learn;

3. *contextual or sociological paradigm*—learning and behavioral problems are not a result of within-child deficits or environmental inadequacies, but the product of inappropriate child-environment interactions.

Asian American parents may also misunderstand English-as-a-second-language (ESL) programs, or other educational support systems for limited-English-proficient (LEP) students, thinking that the ESL program is a type of special education program for slow learners and, thus, shameful for their children to be involved in. In addition, parents may be concerned their children are missing classes in other subject areas because of the pull-out for ESL instruction. Actually, ESL programs provide significant benefits for LEP students through individualized assistance to enhance their English language skills (San, 1992).

Professionals must be sensitive to each family's values and not judge the family based upon social status—poor or rich, educated or not. Nor should they assume the family knows the law or the educational system. Lian and Aloia (1994) recommend teachers utilize internal and external resources to support parents with specific needs related to the education of their children. Significant **internal resources** of parents include the degree of perceived control of the parenting situation, the extended family, parental relationships, health, energy, morale, and spiritual perspectives, problem-solving skills, and available financial and related resources. School personnel may also utilize **external resources** of parents, such as friends, neighbors, professionals, and community agencies and organizations, to meet parental concerns and fulfill their need to see their children successfully involved in the school program.

Suggestions for Teachers

When teaching and learning in a culturally and linguistically diverse environment, teachers and students should try not only to prevent stereotypes and prejudice, but they should also utilize more appropriate and less restrictive approaches in their teaching and learning activities (Lian 1990). Three different approaches may be implemented when teachers and culturally and linguistically diverse children interact with each other—aggressive, assertive, and passive.

The *aggressive approach* tends to be used by teachers and students who consider certain things only to be for themselves. For example, an aggressive teacher may view a culturally and linguistically diverse student as a burden on the class or a mismatch with other students. The teacher may determine that this student should "go back to where he or she belongs" or that the student deserves a lower grade in classroom evaluations. An aggressive nonAsian student may perceive Asian American students to be followers instead of leaders. Other aggressive stances to be made by some members of the nonAsian populations are expressed in statements such as: "Orientals are not good at sanitation," "They are always late for their appointments," and "They speak broken English or 'Chinglish'." Asian American students and their parents may also be aggressive. For example, parents might tell their children who are attacked by nonAsian peers that, "The only way for you to survive in this country is to fight back."

The *passive approach* is the opposite of the aggressive approach. A passive teacher or student may decide there is no need to deal with the issue because "everything is going to be all right." Persons using a passive approach may think totally for others, blame themselves, and "swallow" the complaint or the unfair situation.

The *assertive approach* represents an effort to consider both sides—one's own and that of one's counterpart. Persons utilizing the assertive approach may conduct rational thinking and find the balance point to understand and handle issues. They engage in a thoughtful evaluation of the situation, find each individual's needs and concerns, and fulfill as many personal and group goals as possible.

The following are general suggestions for teaching Asian American students.

Accept Asian American students as they are. A teacher needs to understand, accept, and appreciate students who are from Asian American cultural and linguistic backgrounds. Efforts must be made to develop an awareness of these students' specific needs, learning styles, and response patterns. Teachers must let the students work at their own pace and assure that major learning objectives are mastered. The major concepts children are to learn may be presented in different ways and then followed by the teacher giving repeated review. Teachers should avoid frustration, while encouraging students to think things out instead of supplying answers too quickly. Overall, teachers need to create learning environments which fit the students and not simply to ask the students to fit the school.

Strive to achieve unbiased assessment. Asian American students may be at-risk for socially, culturally, and linguistically biased assessment, educational placement, and instructional activities that may lead to misunderstandings, fewer opportunities, and lower expectations. School administrators and teachers need to help these students by providing opportunities to learn and achieve their maximum potential. Cheng (1991) suggests Asian American students be observed over time by the teacher in multiple contexts with various interactants to obtain a better understanding of their response patterns to different individuals and situations. Maker, Nielson, and Rogers (1994) suggest the use of the approaches of *multiple intelligence assessment* to prevent underestimating culturally and linguistically diverse children's giftedness and problem-solving abilities. A *portfolio assessment* system is highly recommended for limited-English-proficient students. Examples of various types of student work, such as art work, creative writing, math exercises, and book reports completed at different times, are collected to provide a more reliable evaluation of their ability, performance, and learning progress.

Promote meaningful communication. Teachers of new Asian American students should enunciate clearly, avoid speaking too quickly or too slowly, and use gestures to reinforce oral language, but not to replace it. Teachers should not introduce too much new information in one sentence; they should write on the chalk board or paper frequently to reinforce key terms and concepts. Also, the experiences they incorporate into lessons should be familiar to the students. Teachers should start out by asking yes-no questions and work up to "wh" questions (i.e., what, when, where, why, and how). Teachers should not assume a "yes" necessarily means the student has understood. They should praise the student's efforts and model the correct forms in both written and oral language.

In addition, meaningful communication should be facilitated between Asian American students and their parents, so they can reach consensus on appropriate value systems and mutual expectations (Lian, 1995; *The World Journal*, 1997). As indicated by Lian and Poon-McBrayer (1997), "The fact that more than half of the youth expressed a wish for parents to listen to them and trust them more while 90% of parents expressed that they trusted their children may confirm the need for better communication" (p. 20).

Develop new curricula. Kim (1993) suggests teachers should develop new curricula that will focus on life experiences of Asian Americans and their structural position in the United States. Major issues, such as immigration patterns, ethnic diversity among Asian American groups, socioeconomic diversity within groups, high and low educational achievement, experiences of discrimination and civil rights violations, and the complexity of family life, should be addressed.

Many local schools are still at the stage of emphasizing Asian foods and festivals as the major elements of Asian culture to which students are exposed. The multicultural education curriculum should include in-depth discussion of Asian families' traditions and values. It should help all students to develop more positive attitudes toward diverse cultural, racial, ethnic, and religious groups and to consider the perspectives of other groups (Banks, 1989).

Promote cooperative learning. Children learn quickly and effectively from each other. Teachers need to facilitate opportunities and encourage learning through cooperation. Cooperative learning assignments start with concrete and simple game-oriented projects. In such projects, an Asian American student will have the chance to take a role in which he or she feels competent and comfortable. Gradually, the teacher can move onto more complicated and abstract projects through which an Asian American student can increase his or her participation, contribution, and leadership.

Adopt collaborative teaching. Sadker and Sadker (1994) suggest that teaching be done in collaboration with other educators. Contemporary schools are more complicated than ever before, dealing with such issues as bilingual and multilingual special education services, limited English proficiency, low self-esteem, family crises, and poverty. A teacher cannot stand alone. He or she needs to be assisted and supported by experienced educators and professionals from various disciplines, for example, social work, counseling, nursing, and teacher education (Farra, Klitzkie, & Bretania-Schafer, 1994).

Summary

Asian American children are a special group of learners who bring unique cultural and linguistic backgrounds to U.S. schools. They have special traditions and values as well as learning styles which may significantly enrich school programs and society in general. These students may also have unique educational needs. Teachers of Asian American students will need to understand each individual student's attributes and learn to implement instructional strategies and contents which provide the optimal benefits and educational outcomes for these special learners.

References

Banks, J. A. (1989). Multicultural education: Characteristics and goals. In J. A. Banks & C, A. M. Banks (Eds.), *Multicultural Education: Issues and Perspectives* (pp. 2–26). Boston: Allyn & Bacon.

Barrett-Schuler, B. (1997). Module for Asian studies: The impact of culture on business behavior. In J. Q. Adams & J. R. Welsch (Eds.), *Multicultural prism: Voices from the field* (vol. 3) (pp. 159–177). Macomb, IL: Illinois Staff and Curriculum Developers Association.

Brower, I. C. (1983). Counseling Vietnamese. In D. R. Atkinson, G. Morten & D. W. Sue (Eds.), *Counseling American Minorities* (2nd ed.) (pp. 107–121): Dubuque, IA: William C. Brown.

Chan, S. (1998). Families with Asian roots. In E. W. Lynch & M. J. Hanson (Eds.), *Developing cross-cultural competence* (2nd ed.) (pp. 252–343). Baltimore, MD: Paul H. Brookes.

Chen, V. L. (1989). Know thyself: Self-concept of Chinese American youths. *Asian Week*, 8–9.

Cheng, L. L. (1987). *Assessing Asian language performance: Guidelines for evaluating limited English-proficient students*. Rockville, MD: Aspen Publishers.

Cheng, L. L. (1991). *Assessing Asian language performance: Guidelines for evaluating LEP students* (2nd ed.). Oceanside, CA: Academic Communication Associates.

Cheng, L. L., Ima, K., & Labovitz, G. (1994). Assessment of Asian and Pacific Islander students for gifted programs. In S. B. Garcia (Ed.). *Addressing cultural and linguistic diversity in special education* (pp. 30–45). Reston, VA: Council for Exceptional Children.

Dao, X. (1994, Winter/Spring). More Southeast Asian parents overcoming barriers to service. *Pacesetter*, 15.

Farra, H. E., Klitzkie, L. P., & Bretania-Schafer, N. (1994). Limited English proficient, bilingual, and multicultural special education students: Implications for teacher education and service delivery. *International Journal of Special Education*, 9(2), 128–134.

Feldman, S.S., & Rosenthal, D.A. (1990). The acculturation of autonomy expectations in Chinese high schoolers residing in two western nations. *International Journal of Psychology, 25*, 259–281.

Heward, W. L., & Orlansky, M. D. (1992). *Exceptional children: An introductory survey of special education* (3rd ed.). Columbus, OH: Merrill.

Hu-DeHart, E. (1999, April 20). *How to recruit and retain Asian American students at American colleges and universities*. Keynote speech at the MECCPAC Workshop, Illinois State University, Normal, IL.

Kim, S. (1993). Understanding Asian Americans: A new perspective. In J. Q. Adams & J. R. Welsch (Eds.), *Multicultural Education: Strategies for Implementation in Colleges and Universities* (pp. 83–91). Macomb, IL: Illinois Staff and Curriculum Developers Association. [See this volume, pp. 145–156 for a revision of this essay.]

Leung, E. K. (1990). Early risk: Transition from culturally/linguistically diverse homes to formal schooling. *The Journal of Educational Issues of Language Minority Students, 7*, 35–49.

Lisa, M-G. J. (1990). Enhancing ethnic/cultural minority involvement *TASH Newsletter, 16*(5), 1–2.

Lian, M-G. J. (1992). *Project TCLDSD: Teaching culturally and linguistically diverse students with disabilities*. Unpublished software program, Illinois State University, Normal, IL.

Lian, M-G. J. (1995, September). Education of Chinese-American students: Trends, issues, and recommendations. In A.M. Hue, C. Hwang, J. Huang & S. Peng (Eds.). *The 3rd annual national conference program proceedings of the Chinese-American educational research and development association* (pp. 155–169). Chicago: Chinese-American Educational Research and Development Association.

Lian, M-G.J., & Aloia, G. (1994). Parental responses, roles, and responsibilities. In S. Alper. P. J, Schloss, & C. N. Schloss (Eds.), *Families of persons with disabilities: Consultation and advocacy* (pp. 51–93). Boston: Allyn & Bacon.

Lian, M-G. J., & Poon-McBrayer, K. F. (1998, June). General perceptions of school and home among Asian American students and their parents. *New Wave—Educational Research and Development, 3*(3), 18–20.

Luke, B. S. (1987). *An Asian American perspective*. Seattle, WA: REACH Center for Multicultural and Global Education.

Lynch, J. (1994). *Provision for children with special educational needs in the Asia region* Washington, DC: World Bank.

Maker, C. J., Nielson, A. B., & Rogers, J. A. (1994). Giftedness, diversity, and problem solving. *Teaching Exceptional Children, 27*(1), 4–17.

Ong, N. T., & Hee, S. (1993). The growth of the Asian Pacific American population: Twenty million in 2020. In *The state of Asian Pacific America: A public policy report: Policy issues to the year 2020*. Los Angeles: LEAP Asian Pacific American Public Policy Institute and UCLA Asian American Studies Center.

Pang, V. O. (1997). Caring for the whole child: Asian Pacific American students. In J. J, Irvine (Ed.), *Critical knowledge for diverse teachers and learners* (pp. 149–189) Washington, DC: American Association of Colleges for Teacher Education.

Poon-McBrayer, K. F. (1996). Profiles of Asian American students with learning disabilities. *Dissertation Abstracts International, 58*(01), 65. (University Microfilms No. 9719430)

Rick, K., & Forward, J. (1992). Acculturation and perceived intergenerational differences among youth. *Journal of Cross-Cultural Psychology, 23*(1), 85–94.

Sadker, M. P., & Sadker, D. M. (1994). *Teachers, schools, and society* (3rd ed.). New York: McGraw-Hill.

San. (1992, June 14). Don't misunderstand ESL. *The World Journal*, 25.

Sriratana, P. (1995). *Education in Thailand: Past, present and future.* Paper presented at the Thailand Culture and Heritage Night, Illinois State University, Normal, IL.

The World Journal. (1997, July 23). How much do parents understand their children? Author, B1.

U.S. Census Bureau. (1997a). *Statistical abstract of the United States* (117th ed.). Washington, DC: U.S. Government Printing Office.

U.S. Census Bureau. (1997b, March). *The Asian and Pacific Islander population in the United States* (Document #P20–512). Washington, DC: U.S. Government Printing Office.

Wakabayashi, R. (1997). Unique problems of handicapped Asian Americans. In *The White House conference on handicapped individuals* (vol. 1) (pp. 429–432). Washington, DC: U.S. Government Printing Office.

CLASS 16

Arab Americans

CHAPTER 26
Image and Identity: Screen Arabs and Muslims
Jack Shaheen

Jack Shaheen, in this article, urges readers to consider the manner in which Arab Americans are depicted in the media. From modern media's past to the present the images of Arabs have been negative, regardless of the medium from cartoons to feature films. The question Shaheen asks is what are the long term effects of this negativity on the American consumers' consciousness?

Image and Identity: Screen Arabs and Muslims

Jack G. Shaheen

Professor Emeritus of Mass Communication at Southern Illinois University, Edwardsville, Jack Shaheen has written and lectured often on portraits of Arabs and Muslims in U.S. popular culture. He is author of three books, *Nuclear War Films, The TV Arabs, Arab and Muslim Stereotypes,* and Reel Bad Arabs: How Hollywood Villifies a People as well as numerous monographs and essays. A consultant on Arab issues with CBS News and a Department of State Scholar Diplomat, his work reflects his conviction that stereotypes of any grow narrow vision and blur reality.

"Arabs [and Muslims] have been the victims of ugly racial stereotypes in recent years . . . [and] the widespread casual violation of such standards threatens all potential victims of racial slurs. It ought to stop." (Editorial, *The New Republic*, March 1, 1980)

Regrettably, some Americans are still *"imprisoned because of their prejudices. I know that Arab Americans still feel the sting of being stereotyped in false ways. The saddest encounter of course [was] the heartbreaking experience of Oklahoma City."* (President Bill Clinton, Arab American Institute, Washington D.C., May 7, 1998)

"We are all diminished when a person is subject to discrimination." (Janet Reno, Attorney General, American-Arab Anti-Discrimination Conference, June 11, 1998)

Introduction

This essay presents an overview and analysis of selected media portraits, giving specific attention to television programs and motion pictures, and the impact the screen images have on America's Arabs and Muslims. For more than two decades I have been studying the manner in which purveyors of popular culture project Arabs and Muslims, and the effect their images have on individuals. Examples here are drawn from more than 800 feature films, and hundreds of television newscasts, documentaries, and entertainment shows, ranging from animated cartoons to soap operas to movies-of-the-week. Not included, although in themselves an extremely interesting study, are print and broadcast news stories, editorial and op-ed pages, editorial cartoons, children's books, comic books, textbooks, print advertisements, toys, and games. Explanations as to why these disenchanting images exist, and some possible ways of curtailing the stereotyping, will be considered. The underlying thesis is that stereotypes can lower self esteem, injure innocents, impact policies, and encourage divisiveness by accentuating our differences at the expense of those things that tie us together.

In 1982, I began soliciting information about stereotyping from a number of producers, writers, and network executives. I still recall the rationale for stereotyping offered by James Baerg, Director of Program Practices for CBS-TV in New York City: "I think," he remarked, "the Arab stereotype is attractive to a number of people. It is an easy thing to do. It is the thing that is going to be most readily accepted by a large number of the audience. It is the same thing as throwing in sex and violence when an episode is slow" (Shaheen, 1984, p. 122; Shaheen, 1980). Not much has changed since then. Research verifies that lurid and insidious depictions of Arab Muslims as alien, violent strangers, intent upon battling nonbelievers throughout the world, are staple fare. Such erroneous characterizations more accurately reflect the bias of Western reporters and image makers than they do the realities of the Arab and Muslim people in the modern world. Although the majority of Muslims are not Arabs, most Americans wrongly perceive Arabs and Muslims as one and the same people; the same attributes are almost always invariably linked to both peoples. Thus, in this essay, the terms "Muslim" and "Arab" are used interchangeably or substituted by the terms. "Arab Muslim" or "Muslim Arab."

On the silver screen, the Arab Muslim continues to surface as the threatening cultural "Other." Fear of this "strange" faith, Islam, keeps us huddled in emotional isolation. As Professor John Esposito (1992) says, "Fear of the Green Menace [green being the color of Islam] may well replace that of the Red Menace of world communism . . . Islam is often equated with holy war and hatred, fanaticism and violence, intolerance and the oppression of women" (p. 5). Esposito asserts that narratives about the Muslim world all too often assume that there is a monolithic Islam out there somewhere, as if all Muslims believe, think and feel alike. The stereotypical Muslim presented to Americans resembles Iran's Ayatollah Khomeini, Libya's Moammar Gadhafi, or Iraq's Saddam Hussein. Muslims and Arabs in this country, who overwhelmingly do not identify with these political leaders, feel that other Americans assume they do. As 30-year-old Shahed Abdullah, a native Californian, says, "You think Muslim, you think Saddam Hussein, you think Ayatollah" (Power, 1998. p. 35).

Through immigration, conversion, and birth Muslims are this nation's fastest growing religious group. Regrettably, the approximately five to eight million Muslims who live in the United States are confronted with a barrage of stereotypes which unfairly show them as a global menace, producers of biological weapons, zealots who issue *fatwas* or burn Uncle Sam in effigy. In reality, Muslims are an integral part of the American mainstream, individuals who respect traditions, who are committed to education, faith, family and free enterprise. Indeed, the community is generally a peace loving

blend of cultures: 25% are of South Asian descent, Arabs represent another 12%, and nearly half are converts, mainly African Americans. They contribute to their respective communities as teachers, doctors, lawyers and artists.

This mix of ethnic, racial, and cultural backgrounds offers a broad range of Muslim viewpoints. As Professor Sulayman Nyang (1996) of Howard University explains, "Muslims can be compared to Catholics. They are as different from each other as Mexican American Catholics in Southern California are from Polish and Italian Catholics in Chicago or Philadelphia" (p. B10). Muslims are a diverse group: the "seen one, seen 'em all" cliche does not apply. According to Steven Barboza (1993) in *American Jihad,* "There are more than 200,000 Muslim businesses [in the U.S.], 165 Islamic schools, 425 Muslim associations, 85 Islamic publications, and 1,500 mosques" spread from Georgia to Alaska (p. 9). Many Muslims hold prominent positions in business and public service. They appreciate the religious freedom in America, freedom not always available in the lands they left. Nevertheless, although Muslim Americans are an integral part of the American landscape, enriching the communities in which they live, the United States is seldom referred to as a Judeo-Christian-Muslim nation.

In a recent national survey, cited by John Dart (1996) of the *Los Angeles Times,* the Americans polled viewed Christians in general, Jews, and on balance, Mormons, as good influences on U.S. society, but more than 30% regarded Muslims as having a "negative influence" (p. 19). Muslims maintain they are perceived as a "negative influence" because producers of entertainment are ignorant of Islam and as a result tend to focus on a violent and extreme minority. On television and in feature films, they argue, you only see Arabs as bearded fanatics out to seduce blond, western heroines. Chanting "Death to the great Satan," they appear as the enemy, as anti-Jewish, anti-Christian terrorists out to destroy the U.S. and Israel.

Motion Pictures

It seems that most people have difficulty distinguishing between a tiny minority of persons who may be objectionable and the ethnic strain from which they spring. "The popular caricature of the average Arab is as mythical as the old portrait of the Jew," writes columnist Sydney Harris (1986). "He is robed and turbaned, sinister and dangerous, engaged mainly in hijacking airlines and blowing up public buildings." "If the Italians have their Mafia, all Italians are suspect; if the Jews have financiers, all Jews are part of an international conspiracy: if the Arabs have fanatics, all Arabs are violent," says Harris. "In the world today, more than ever, barriers of this kind must be broken, for we are all more alike than we are different."

Virtually since its inception the Hollywood film industry has promoted prejudicial attitudes toward numerous groups: viewers have seen the Asian as "sneaky"; the black as "Sambo"; the Italian as the "Mafioso"; the Irishman as the "drunk"; the Jew as "greedy"; the Indian as the "savage"; and the Latino as "greasy." In the "enlightened 90s," however, such offensive labeling is no longer tolerated. Now, "it appears that we're down to one group, the Arabs," writes columnist Jay Stone (1996). "When was the last time you saw an Arab character in a movie who was anything but one of three Bs (billionaire, bomber, belly dancer)" (p. 1C)? "One group should not be singled out as enemies of all that is good and decent and American," adds Stone. "Where are the movies about Arabs and Muslims who are just ordinary people? It is time for Hollywood to end this undeclared war?" Sam Keen (1986), author of *Faces of the Enemy*, shows how Arabs are still vilified: "You can hit an Arab free; they're free enemies, free villains—where you couldn't do it to a Jew or you can't do it to a black anymore (pp. 29–30)."

As President John Kennedy (1962) said, "The great enemy of truth is very often not the lie, deliberate, contrived and dishonest, but the myth, persistent, persuasive and realistic." For more than a century movies have created myths. Ever since the camera began to crank, the unkempt Arab has appeared as an uncivilized character, the outsider in need of a shower and a shave, starkly contrasting in behavior and appearance with the white Western protagonist. Beginning with Universal's *The Rage of Paris* (1921), in which the heroine's husband "is killed in a sandstorm by an Arab." Hollywood's studios have needlessly maligned Arabs. Motion pictures such as *The Sheik* (1921) and *Son of the Sheik* (1926), which starred the popular Rudolph Valentino as Sheikh Ahmed, displayed Arab Muslims as brutal slavers and promiscuous desert sheikhs. Of course, Valentino, as the hero, cannot really be an Arab:

> Purrs Diana, the heroine: "His [Ahmed's] hand is so large for an Arab."
>
> Ahmed's French friend: "He is not an Arab. His father was an Englishman, his mother, a Spaniard."

Hollywood's romantic sheikh of the 1920s became the oily sheikh of the 1970s and 1980s: concurrently, the industry's bedouin bandit of the 1920s became the "fundamentalist" bomber who prays before killing innocents. The cinema's sheikhs are uncultured and ruthless, attempting to procure media conglomerates (*Network*, 1977), destroy the world's economy (*Rollover*, 1981), kidnap Western women (*Jewel of the Nile*, 1985), direct nuclear weapons at Israel and the United States (*Frantic*, 1988), and influence foreign policies (*American Ninja 4: The Annihilation*, 1991) (Shaheen, 1990b, p. C1–C2).

Then and now Arab characters are carefully crafted to alarm viewers. Films project the diverse Islamic world as populated with bearded mullahs, billionaire sheikhs, terrorist bombers, backward bedouin, and noisy bargainers. Women surface either as gun toters or as bumbling subservients, or as belly dancers bouncing voluptuously in palaces and erotically oscillating in slave markets. More recently image makers are offering other caricatures of Muslim women: covered in black from head to toe, they appear as uneducated, unattractive, and enslaved beings. Solely attending men, they follow several paces behind abusive sheikhs, their heads lowered.

Mindlessly adopted and casually adapted, these rigid and repetitive portraits narrow our vision and blur reality. The screen Arab Muslim lacks a humane face. He/She lives in a mythical kingdom of endless desert dotted with oil wells, tents, run-down mosques, palaces, goats, and camels. These caricatures and settings serve to belittle the hospitality of Arabs and Muslims, their rich culture, and their history. Functioning as visual lesson plans, movies, like books, last forever. No sooner do Hollywood's features leave the movie theaters than they are available in video stores and broadcast on TV. From 1986 to 1995, I tracked feature films telecast on cable and network channels in St. Louis, Missouri. Each week, 15 to 20 movies mocking or denigrating Arab

Muslims were telecast. In numerous films such as *Navy Seals* (1990), *Killing Streets* (1991), *The Human Shield* (1992), *The Son of the Pink Panther* (1993), *Bloodfist V: Human Target* (1994) and *True Lies* (1994), viewers could see American adolescents, intelligence agents, military personnel, even Inspector Clouseau's son, massacring obnoxious Arab Muslims.

Since 1970, more than 300 major films have vilified Arabs. They have featured Arab curs drawing sabers (*Paradise*, 1982), abducting blondes (*Sahara*, 1983), buying America (*Network*, 1996), siding with the Nazis against Israel (*Exodus*, 1960), and tossing bombs—even nuclear ones—at the West (*True Lies*, 1994). Unsightly Arab Muslims and prejudicial dialogue about them also appear in more than 200 movies that otherwise have nothing at all to do with Arabs or the Middle East. In films such as *Reds* (1981), *Cloak and Dagger* (1984), *Power* (1986), *Puppet Master II* (1990), *The Bonfire of the Vanities* (1990), *American Samurai* (1992), and *Point of No Return* (1993), Muslim caricatures appear like phantoms. Libyans, especially, are a favorite target. In films like *Back to the Future* (1985), *Broadcast News* (1987), and *Patriot Games* (1992), Libyan "bastards" shelter Irish villains, bomb U.S. military installations in Italy, and shoot a heroic American scientist in a mall parking lot. *The American President* (1995), an otherwise agreeable romantic comedy about a widowed president falling for a lovely environmental lobbyist, mentions Libyans who bomb a U.S. weapons system. In this case, at least, writer Aaron Sorkin softens the anti-Libyan dialogue by expressing sympathy for the Arab janitor and other innocents about to be annihilated.

Egyptians are displayed as dirty, hostile, and sneaky in Universal's 1999 version of *The Mummy*, an $80 million remake of the 1932 Boris Karloff classic. In his review, critic Anthony Lane of *The New Yorker* (1999) writes: "Finally there is the Arab question. The Arab people have always had the roughest and most uncomprehending deal from Hollywood, but with the death of the Cold War the stereotype has been granted even more wretched prominence." Adds Lane, "So, here's a party game for any producers with a Middle Eastern setting in mind; try replacing one Semitic group with another—Jews instead of Arabs—and **then** listen for the laugh" (pp. 104–105).

Motion pictures such as *Not Without My Daughter* (1990) show the Muslim male as a religious hypocrite, a liar abusing Islam and kidnapping his American wife and daughter. Not only does he imprison and abuse his wife in Iran, he seems to do so in the name of Islam as when he slaps her face, boasting, "I'm a Muslim!" After breaking an oath sworn on the Qur'an he brags: "Islam is the greatest gift I can give my daughter." When he departs the mosque followed by his relatives, the camera cuts to a poster of a grim Ayatollah Khomeini. The editing implies that the offensive actions of Muslims towards American women and the behavior of Iran's late Ayatollah are clearly connected.

Palestinians are characterized by Hollywood as religious fanatics, threatening our freedom, economy, and culture. Producers portray the Palestinian as a demonic creature without compassion for men, women, or children. Palestinian Muslim images reflect a combination of past stereotypes, notably American Indians and Blacks as dark and primitive sexual predators. The "Palestinian equals terrorist" narrative initially surfaced in 1960, in Otto Preminger's *Exodus*. In the 1980s ten features, including *The Ambassador* (1984), *The Delta Force* (1986), *Wanted Dead or Alive* (1987), and *Ministry of Vengeance* (1989), put into effect images showing the Palestinian Muslim as Enemy Number One. Feature films tag him as "scumbag," "son of a bitch," "the Gucci Terrorist," "a fly in a piece of shit," "animals," "bastards," "f—in' pigs," and "stateless savages" who "massacre children." The slurs are not rebuked by other characters (Shaheen, 1990a, p. 50). Several made-for-television movies also paint the Palestinians as despicable beings, including TV movies such as *Hostage Flight* (1985), *Terrorist on Trial* (1988), *Voyage of Terror* (1990), Cinemax's April 1998 documentary, *Suicide Bombers Secrets of the Shaheed*, and HBO's January 1999 documentary, *Diary of a Terrorist: Mikdad*.

Two 1990s box-office hits, *True Lies* (1994) and *Executive Decision* (1996), also portray Palestinian Muslims as screaming, murderous "terrorists" killing American innocents, including a priest. In *True Lies* Muslims ignite an atom bomb off the Florida coast. Avi Nesher, a former Israeli commando working in the Hollywood film industry, was "incensed by the sick humor of a *Lies* scene in which an Uzi tossed down a flight of stairs inadvertently mows down a roomful of Arabs." Nesher told *Jerusalem Report* correspondent Sheli Teitelbaum (1996): "You were supposed to laugh?

I fought Arabs and I had Arab friends, but this was completely dehumanizing a group" (p. 49).

In *Executive Decision,* Muslims hijack a passenger jet, terrorize the passengers, kill a flight attendant, and prepare to unload enough lethal nerve gas to kill millions in Washington, D.C. and along the East coast. Throughout, Islam is equated with violence. Holding the Holy Qur'an in one hand and a bomb in the other, a Palestinian Muslim enters the swank dining room of London's Marriott Hotel and blows up innocent couples. Four days after the film was released, employees of a Denver radio station burst into a mosque and began heckling worshipers while the station broadcast their antics. Twentieth-Century Fox's recent feature *The Siege* (1998) displays stars such as Denzel Washington and Annette Bening as F.B.I. and C.I.A. agents. Their mission? To locate and destroy Palestinian Muslims who terrorize New York City. *The Siege* presents Arab immigrants, assisted by Arab American auto mechanics, university students, and even a Brooklyn college professor, killing more than 700 innocent New Yorkers.

Even the Walt Disney Company, a self-professed family-friendly mega-company, is guilty of the vilification of Arabs and Muslims. Since 1992, Disney has released seven features with harmful caricatures. In December 1995, Touchstone Pictures, a subsidiary of Disney, released a remake of Edward Streeter's 1948 book, *Father of the Bride.* In Disney's *Father of the Bride, Part II,* a sequel to the 1991 Steve Martin remake, disagreeable Mideast Americans are introduced for the first time. (In the original 1950 Spencer Tracy - Elizabeth Taylor film and all the earlier *Father of the Bride* movies Muslims and Mideast Americans do not appear at all.) Steve Martin and Diane Keaton appear as the happily married George and Nina Banks; they have everything, including a wonderful "Brady Bunch" home. When George convinces Nina to sell the house, the crass Arab family of Habibs is introduced. The rich and unkempt Mr. Habib (Eugene Levy) smokes, needs a shave, and talks with a heavy accent. When Mrs. Habib attempts to speak, her husband barks mumbo-jumbo, a mix of Farsi and Arabic, at her. Cowering like a scolded puppy, Mrs. Habib becomes mute, perpetuating Hollywood's image of the Arab woman as a submissive nonentity. Mr. Habib is portrayed as sloppy, mean, and tight-fisted. After he purchases the house he demands that

the Banks be out in ten days, crushing his cigarette on the immaculate walkway. The message is clear: there goes the neighborhood. Interestingly, no one working on *Bride II* denounced the stereotyping, nor did protests emanate from members of the Screen Writers', Actors', or Directors' Guilds of America.

Disney continued to demean Arabs in *Aladdin* (1992), the second most successful animated picture ever made, earning $217 million at domestic box offices. After sensitivity meetings were held between some Arab Americans and Disney executives in July 1993, Disney deleted two offensive lines from *Aladdin's* opening song before releasing the video. That was all. The line, "It's barbaric, but hey, it's home," remains. The storyteller is portrayed as a shifty, disreputable Arab, dastardly saber-wielding villains still try to cut off the hands of maidens, and a wicked vizier still slices a few throats. For generations, these scenes will teach children that Aladdin's home is indeed "barbaric" (Shaheen 1996, p. 7). A *New York Times* ("It's Racist," 1993) editorial complained that "To characterize an entire region with this sort of tongue-in-cheek bigotry, especially in a movie aimed at children, [itself] borders on the barbaric." Professor Joanne Brown (1992) of Drake University agrees that *Aladdin* is racist. The villains display "dark-hooded eyes and large hooked noses," writes Brown. "Perhaps I am sensitive to this business of noses because I am Jewish." Brown explains how she would feel if Disney studios created a cartoon based on a Jewish folk tale that portrayed all Jews as Shylocks (p. 12).

Following the *Aladdin* discussions, Disney executives promised not to demean Arabs in the future, but then went ahead and featured hook-nosed, buck-toothed Arab "desert skunks" in their home-video release of *Aladdin's* sequel, *The Return of Jafar* (1994). *Jafar* sold 10 million copies to rank among the 20 top-selling videos. That same year Disney also produced *In the Army Now,* in which "Glendale reservists" deride Arab cuisine, clobber desert Arabs, and encourage the U.S. Air Force to "blow the hell out of them." Americans of Middle Eastern heritage are again targeted in a Disney children's film called *Kazaam* (1996), starring Shaquille O'Neal, in which Malik, Hassan, and El-Baz, three dark-complexioned Muslim villains needing shaves and speaking with heavy accents, covet "all the money in the world."

Sloppy Malik gobbles "goat's eyes" like a pig swallowing corn. He punches good-guy Americans and tosses Max, a twelve-year-old boy, down a shaft presumably to his death.

In 1997, Disney subsidiaries Miramax and Hollywood Pictures released *Operation Condor* and *G.I. Jane.* Set in the Arabian desert, *Condor* displays Jackie Chan battling scores of evil Arabs such as a money-grubbing innkeeper and bedouin white-slavers. Chan also contests two hook-nosed Arabs, "Soldiers of the Faith," who speak fractured English and wear checkered headdresses that look like tablecloths pinched from a pizza parlor. The duo mock Islam by spouting such lines as, "We will never give up the struggle for the holy battle," and, "Praise Allah for delivering you (Chan) to us again." Watching the film, wondered why the talented Chan, whose 30 films are box-office hits here and abroad, would vilify anyone, especially since Asian performers are still trying to erase the Fu Manchu images. In *G.I. Jane,* viewers cheer as Demi Moore, a macho Navy SEAL officer, "guts is out" and kills Arabs. The Arabs surface only at the end, when the SEALs move to retrieve a U.S. nuclear-powered satellite containing weapons-grade plutonium off the Libyan coast. The camera reveals courageous Moore rescuing her drill sergeant's life, then blasting pursuing Arabs. Since 1986, Hollywood studios have released 22 films showing our military units and agents killing Arabs. As *New York Times* columnist Russell Baker (1997) wrote Arabs are the "last people except Episcopalians whom Hollywood feels free to offend "

Television

From 1950 until today, one Arab American and one Arab Christian immigrant have appeared as characters in a television series. The first was Uncle Tanoose, the Lebanese patriarch portrayed by Hans Conreid in "The Danny Thomas Show" (1953–71). Tanoose occasionally appeared in episodes, visiting his relatives in the United States. The second was Corporal Maxwell Klinger, an Arab American soldier in "M*A*S*H" (1972–1983) played by Jamie Farr, who tries to get himself discharged by wearing women's clothing People modeled on such public figures as heart surgeon Dr. Michael DeBakey, UPI's White House correspondent Helen Thomas, or radio's Top-40

celebrity Casey Kasem never appear. This absence is wounding. Since "M*A*S*H" debuted in 1972, there has not been a single series featuring an Arab American character. Surely image makers know what happens to young people when someone in authority portrays their society as one in which they have no public presence. Such an experience, writes Adrienne Rich (1995), can generate "a moment of psychic disequilibrium, as if you looked in a mirror and saw nothing."

Since 1974, when I began to document images on entertainment shows, the rogues have often been Arab Muslims. A selective overview of more than 200 programs, including network newscasts, documentaries, comedies, soap operas, children's cartoons, dramas, and movies-of-the-week yielded the following results. Fanatical Muslims surface in several mid-1980s television movies such as *Hostage Flight* (NBC, 1985), *Sword of Gideon* (HBO 1986), *Under Siege* (NBC, 1986), *The Taking of Flight 847* (NBC, 1988), *Terrorist on Trial The United States vs. Salim Ajami* (CBS, 1988), *Hostages* (HBO, 1993), *Freedom Strike* (SHO, 1997), *Path to Paradise* (HBO, 1997), and *Shadow Warriors II: Hunt for the Death Merchant* (TNT, 1999). These TV movies are now constantly rebroadcast on both cable and network systems.

In *Hostage Flight,* the protagonist says, "These [Arab Muslim] bastards shot those people in cold blood. They think it's open season on Americans." In *Under Siege,* the U.S. Secretary of State tells the Ambassador of a Muslim nation: "People in your country are barbarians. The FBI director in this film also scrutinizes Dearborn's large Arab American community for terrorists who have blown up shopping malls and threatened the White House, telling his African American colleague: "Those people are different from us. It's a whole different ball game. I mean the East and the Middle East. Those people have their own mentality. They have their own notion of what's right and what's wrong, what's worth living for and dying for. But we insist on dealing with them as if they're the same as us. We'd better wake up." In *Terrorist on Trial,* a Palestinian Muslim boasts that he ordered the deaths of American women and children and advocates the use of nuclear weapons, saying. "We will strike at them in their home country as well as overseas. Long live Palestine!"

Constantly rebroadcast on 40-plus cable and network systems, these disturbing TV movies show all Arabs, Muslims, and Arab Americans as abhorrent militants at war with the United States. Accomplished Arab American actors are obliged to play terrorists and to demean their heritage. Nicholas Kadi, for example, a competent character actor, makes his living playing Arab Muslim kuffiyeh-clad terrorists. In 1991, Kadi lamented on the news show "48 Hours" that he seldom speaks in films. Instead of talking, directors tell him to impart "a lot of threatening looks, threatening gestures, threatening actions. Every time we [he and others playing heavies] said 'America,' we'd [be directed to] spit." Says Kadi, "There are other kinds of Arabs in the world besides terrorists. I'd like to think that some day there will be an Arab role out there (Kadi, 1991)." Kadi has played stereotypical roles in films such as *Navy SEALS* (1990) and, in TV shows such as "Scimitar," a 1995 NBC *JAG* episode. In "Scimitar" the Iraqi-born Kadi impersonates a Saddam-like colonel holding Meg, an innocent U.S. army officer, hostage. The lusting Kadi tries to force himself on the attractive blond. One screen myth maintains that Arabs consider "date rape" to be "an acceptable social practice." The camera dwells on the drooling Kadi slowly wielding a Damascus scimitar to remove Meg's uniform. The rape is thwarted and Kadi is apprehended just in time. Interestingly, from 1995 to 1999 nine *Jag* episodes produced by Donald P. Bellisario vilified Muslims of the Middle East; with reruns that comes to 25 programs in five years. Programs such as "Embassy," "Act of Terror," and "Code Blue," like "Scimitar," revealed Arab Muslims lusting after American women and blowing up innocents overseas and in a Washington, DC hospital.

The demonization of Arab Muslims is reminiscent of the demonization of American Indians. As commentator Pat Buchanan pointed out at the annual Arab American Anti-Discrimination conference in Washington, DC on June 13, 1998: "The Arabs I see in Hollywood movies are like the movies I used to see with the cavalry and Indians." Clad in strange garb, Arabs are obliged to speak garbled English and to crave blond heroines. Just as screen protagonists call Indians "savages," they call Arabs "terrorists." The closing frames of "Scimitar" show an Iraqi helicopter pursuing Americans. When the chopper goes down in flames, the Marines cheer: "Yahoo. It's just like *Stagecoach* with John Wayne." Puzzled by the reference to Wayne, a motion picture idol, Meg asks

the Marine: "John Wayne was killed by Iraqis?" He replies. "No, Indians!" In the Gulf war movie, *Hot Shots Part Deux!* (1994). U.S. soldiers prepare for an Iraqi attack. Warns one G.I., "Indians on the warpath."

A November 1996 segment of *FX: The Series* depicts Rashid Hamadi as a stereotypical Arab drug addict who deliberately runs over and kills a New York City police officer in cold blood. But when policemen move to apprehend him, Hamadi boasts, "I have diplomatic immunity. You can't arrest me." In the end, Hamadi is caught smuggling counterfeit plates into New York City: his "Lebanese" and "Iranian" friends in Beirut fabricated the bills. Final scenes show policemen seizing Hamadi, that "piece of garbage" and "slimeball bastard." In 1998, two *Soldier of Fortune* segments, "Surgical Strike" and "Top Event," surfaced on UPN's television network. Produced by Rhysher Entertainment, the "Strike" episode depicts Arab Muslim "bastards" blowing up a passenger plane, killing all 230 passengers. And in Rhysher's "Event," Arab terrorists move to release three truck loads of poison gas "in the name of Allah," killing thousands of Los Angeles residents. When asked who she works for, the female militant barks, "I work only for Allah."

On the "Jon Stewart Show," U.S. soldier puppets kill white-robed Arab puppets. Waving the American flag, one soldier boasts: "I killed many of them!" Says another: "I decapitated quite a few of them myself." Stewart's audience applauds ("Jon Stewart," 1995). in "Twisted Puppet Theater." Ali, the Muslim puppet sporting a black beard and turban, shouts: "There is only one God and Mohammed is his prophet!" Then he turns and shoots Kukla, the good clown puppet, dead (Showtime, 1995). From December 1991 through early 1992, MTV featured "Just Say Julie" segments, sandwiched between music videos, showing Julie addressing unsavory Moroccan buffoons as "scum" and the "creep with the fez." In one segment the two "fiendish" Arabs armed with explosives move to blow up the television channel.

Cartoons

Over the years I have viewed and studied scores of American cartoons denigrating the Arab, starting with the 1926 animated short. "Felix the Cat Shatters the Sheik." In "Porky in Egypt"

(1938), for example, Arab Muslims in prayer suddenly become Amos 'n' Andy shooting craps and a sexy harem maiden removes her veil, revealing an ugly face. Favorite cartoon characters such as Popeye, Bugs Bunny, Woody Woodpecker, Daffy Duck, Superman, and Batman ridicule and trounce Arabs (Shaheen, 1993). Since 1975, more than 60 comparable cartoons have surfaced on television, depicting Arabs as swine, rats, dogs, magpies, vultures and monkeys.

Writers give cartoon Arabs names like "Sheikh Ha-Mean-ie," "Ali Boo-Boo," "The Phoney Pharaoh," "Ali Baba, the Mad Dog of the Desert, and his Dirty Sleeves," "Hassan the Assassin." "The Desert Rat," "Desert Rat Hordes," "Ali Oop," "Ali Mode," and "Arab Duck." While monitoring cartoons on November 23, 1996, I saw "Well-Worn Daffy" on the Nickelodeon channel. Wearing a white kuffiyeh and armed with a shotgun, Daffy shoots at three winsome Mexican mice. The mice call Daffy, among other things, "Arab Duck!" Adult viewers may be able to separate fact from animal, but for many children the animated world of cartoons consists of good people versus bad people, the latter often Arabs. What is particularly relevant about the TV shows/movies, cartoons, and feature films is that they are repackaged and exported back to the Arab world where the youth pick them up and begin to form a negative self-image through antagonistic Western eyes. This has a telling effect on the future of Arab society.

Effects on Children

Viewing these cartoons brings back memories of earlier portrayals of "stupid" African Americans, "savage" American Indians, "dirty" Latinos, "buck-toothed Japs" and "hook-nosed" Shylocks in burnooses. Jewish mothers in Europe of the 1930s and the 1940s, as well as African, Indian, Hispanic and Japanese mothers in the United States during this period, tried to shield their children from such imagery, but such hateful portraits cannot help but promote bigotry toward them. America's Muslim parents are increasingly aware of these dangers and work to counteract or eliminate them. Citing scores of old motion pictures being telecast on cable systems, along with cartoons, re-runs of television dramas and sitcoms, plus newly created TV programs and TV movies-of-the-week, they fear that stereotyping has become more pervasive than ever. Conversely, image makers are now giving children of other ethnic origins positive role models to identify with. Characters appear on the screen that make American children feel good about themselves: American Indians, African Americans, Hispanics, Asians, Jews, Italians, Polynesians, Irish, English, Poles, East Indians, Scots—just about every racial and ethnic group on the planet, except the Arabs. According to the American-Arab Anti-Discrimination Committee (ADC), many parents have complained that as a result of the pervasive stereotype, their children have become ashamed of their religion and heritage. Some have asked their parents to change their Arab names to something more American sounding. A Texas teen told his sister, "I lied about where our parents had come from." Especially alarming are the number of incidents targeting youngsters. After the Trade Center bombing several children of Arab descent in New York were told to "go back where you came from." They went home from school in tears, writes *New York Times'* Melinda Henneberger. "Classmates told them they were responsible for the attack." Muslim girls were taunted: schoolmates pulled off their head scarves (Moghrabi, 1995, p. 3C)." At a suburban Muslim day care center in Texas the driver of a passing car shouted, "Here's a bomb for you, lady!" and threw a soda can at a teacher and her students.

The *Anti-Arab-American Discrimination Hate Crimes* document, published by the American-Arab Anti-Discrimination Committee in November 1994, and the Council on American Islamic Relations' (CAIR) 1996 manual. *A Rush to Judgement: A Special Report on Anti-Muslim Stereotyping*, report many similar incidents. During the heartbreaking experience of Oklahoma City, Suhair al-Mosawia, a Muslim woman seven months pregnant, lost her son after teens pursued her, hammering her home with rocks. Following Muslim custom she gave the stillborn a name, Salam, Arabic for "peace." One Oklahoma City resident suggested putting Arab Americans in internment camps. In a *Cleveland Plain Dealer* op-ed essay. Palestinian activist Hamzi Moghrabi reported that "in Detroit, home of the largest Arab American population outside the Middle East, business owners, including the editor, Osama A. Siblani, of *The Arab American News*, were subjected to bomb threats" and trash was thrown at mosques (ADC, 1994, pp. 12, 14).

Media Images and Prejudicial Responses

Media images, points out media critic Jerry Mander (1978), "can cause people to do what they might otherwise never have thought to do (p. 13)." Following the April 1995 Oklahoma City tragedy, speculative reporting combined with decades of stereotyping encouraged more than 300 hate crimes against America's Arabs and Muslims. Abuses took place even as Muslims mourned, along with other Oklahomans, the disaster (CAIR, 1996). Mohammed Nimer of the Council on American-Islamic Relations told reporter Laurie Goodstein, "Most of these incidents have been completely unprovoked . . . just mere encounters with a person who looks like a Muslim, or a person praying, have prompted bias and violence. That is alarming" (Goodstein, 1996).

In Brooklyn, the police department reported that after the Oklahoma City bombing numerous Arab American businesses received hostile calls and death threats. One caller said, "We're going to put a bomb in your business and kill your family." A San Francisco mosque received 35 bomb threats. In Toledo, Ohio, the St. Francis de Sales High School yearbook, the 1995 ACCOLADE, printed in bold-letter capitals "**KILL ALL THE CAMEL JOCKEYS!**" The remark was part of a 500-word essay by a student. Officials immediately issued apologies, however, and the High School President, Rev. Ronald Olezewski, wrote to parents and friends saying that the "insensitive reference" should never have been either written or published. "We apologize," he said. "Please presume ignorance rather than malice and be assured that all at this institution of learning will learn from the wrong" (Briendel, 1996, p. 3).

The day of the Oklahoma City explosion, Abraham Ahmed, a U.S. citizen of Jordanian origin, boarded a plane in Oklahoma City en route to visit his family in Jordan. Two hours after the bombing, it was reported that Ahmed was a suspect. Immediately, some people in Oklahoma City began dumping trash on his lawn; others spit on his wife. While Ahmed was in Chicago waiting to make connections, FBI authorities escorted him into a room and interrogated him for six hours. Missing his flight, Ahmed arrived late in London. There he suffered a humiliating strip-search. After five more hours of interrogation, the handcuffed Ahmed was sent back to Washington, DC for another day of questioning. More than a year after he was cleared, Ahmed, who has lived in Oklahoma City for 14 years, still receives suspicious stares from neighbors.

Persisting in defiance of all evidence, hateful images have their impact on public opinion and policies. There is a dangerous and cumulative effect when repulsive screen images remain unchallenged. The negative images are sometimes perceived as **real** portrayals of Muslim culture, which come back to afflict Americans of Arab heritage as well as non-Arab Muslims in their dealings with law enforcement or judicial officials. For example, in January 1997, a judge in Dearborn, Michigan, was asked to rule whether an attorney could show *Not Without My Daughter* to a jury deciding on a child custody case between an Arab American father and a European American mother. Incredibly, the judge allowed this defamatory film portraying an Iranian man as a child abuser and child-kidnapper to be introduced in court, influencing the judicial proceeding (*ADC*, 1996–7, p. 33).

The Arab Muslim image parallels the image of the Jew in Nazi-inspired German movies such as *Robert and Bertram* (1939), *Die Rothschild Aktien von Waterloo (The Rothschilds' Shares in Waterloo,* 1940), *Der ewige Jew (The Eternal Jew,* 1940), and *Jud Suss* (1940). Resembling the hook-nosed screen Arab wearing burnooses, screen Jews also dressed differently than the films' protagonists, wearing yarmulkes and black robes. They, too, appeared as unkempt money-grubbing caricatures who sought world domination, worshiped a different God, killed innocents, and lusted after blond virgins (Hull, 1969, pp. 157–177). The simultaneous barrage of stereotypical films, editorial cartoons, radio programs, and newspaper essays helped make Jews scapegoats for many of Germany's problems (Hull, 1969, pp. 157–177).

Concerned that misperceptions might hinder genuine peace in the Middle East, *Newsweek* columnist Meg Greenfield ((1986) wrote, "Actually what I see coming is more like a reversion, a flight back to the generalized, hostile attitudes towards Arabs and/or Muslims as a collectivity that prevailed both as government policy and as public prejudice for so many years" (p. 84). Although progress has been real, Greenfield remains concerned about the kind of blanket, indiscriminate anti-Arab sentiment so often expressed in public, "If anything," she writes, "we should be seeking to sharpen and refine our involvement with those Arabs who are themselves enemies and targets of the violent, hate-filled elements in the region. We should be making more distinctions and discriminating judgments among them, not fewer" (p. 84). Greenfield's telling observations reveal the dangers of stereotyping. The Arab world accommodates peace-loving folk. Most Arabs live not in desert tents, rather in apartments and homes. The majority are poor, not rich; most have never mounted a camel, nor seen an oil well. They do not dally in palace harems, nor do they take vacations on magic carpets. Their dress is traditional or western; the variety of their garb and lifestyle defies stereotyping.

Why Vilify People?

No single factor leads to stereotyping. Undeniably, the Arab-Israeli conflict and ignorance, the handmaiden of bigotry, continue to be contributing factors. Most image makers do not have the religious, cultural or language background to understand Islam. To my knowledge, not one university, including those with Middle East and Near East centers, offers courses focusing on Arab and Muslim images in popular culture, and no university actively seeks to recruit faculty members to address this issue, even though comparable subjects are offered for other ethnic groups. In classroom discussions and research works, too few scholars document and discuss media images of Arabs and Muslims. It may take decades of education before misinformation is depleted.

One of the reasons why America's Arabs are not yet able to define themselves may be because none belong to America's "media elite." There are no Muslim communications giants comparable to Disney's Michael Eisner, Fox's Rupert Murdoch, or Time-Warner's Ted Turner. Few work as broadcasters, reporters, or filmmakers. Until Arabs and Muslims achieve some influence, their voices will not be heard. As producer Gilbert Cates (1993) says: "It's axiomatic. The more power you have, the louder your voice is heard (p. 3D)."

Inflexibility and indifference impact the stereotyping. Many Muslim and Arab leaders are reluctant to become involved. Although scores of films and television shows denigrating the Arab are purchased, rented, and screened throughout the Western as well as the Muslim world. Muslim information officials and media syndicators appear to be apathetic. Until very recently they have made little or no attempt to meet with image makers to discuss those images ridiculing them and their neighbors. Politics and fear are other reasons. In spite of many noteworthy accomplishments, American Arabs and Muslims do not yet have sufficient political clout to effect fundamental change. Efforts initiated by various groups, such as the American Muslim Public Affairs Council, the Council on American-Islamic Relations, and the American-Arab Anti-Discrimination Committee (an organization with 25,000 members and 75 campus and city chapters), however, have had some influence. Their efforts have resulted in limited apologies, minor edits, and some altered scenarios.

On June 11, 1998, Attorney General Janet Reno told Americans of Arab heritage attending an ADC conference that stereotypes should never influence policy or public opinion. Yet, when this writer asked CNN's Peter Arnett whether stereotyping had any impact on United States Middle East policies, he said: "The media elite follow U.S. policy," adding that those responsible for shaping policies are influenced in part by the stereotypical pictures in their heads.

Conclusion

Openness to change is an American tradition. There are numerous ways for image makers to humanize the Arab Muslim. They could reveal in television shows, documentaries, and motion pictures the telling effects of hate crimes brought about by stereotyping. They could show the impact of such prejudices on children, especially how some are taunted during the Muslim holy month of Ramadan, the time of purification and abstention. Although Ramadan has "a special meaning for Muslim children, their fasting makes them stand out in school," writes AP's Katherine Roth. Some children are distressed, saying "they often have to contend with anti-Muslim slurs" (1996, p. 4B).

Although harmful caricatures may not disappear soon, those professionals engaged in addressing harmful portraits merit recognition. In early March of 1998, this writer and Dr. Hala Maksoud, President of the American-Arab Anti-Discrimination Committee, informed Dr. Rosalyn Weinman, NBC-TV's Executive Vice President of Broadcast Standards and Current Policy, that the network's soap series, *Days of Our Lives, was impugning Arab Muslims. Dr. Weinman followed up immediately on our concerns. For weeks prior to our conversation the soap had displayed a kidnapped blond U.S. heroine held hostage in the "harem" of the Sultan's desert palace. Her kidnapper, a bearded clad-in-black Arab, warned that unless she pleased the Sultan, her head would be "chopped off by an Arabian axe, one of those long, curvy sharp swords." Not only did Dr. Weinman issue an apology, NBC promptly dropped all images and references to Arabs from the soap's plot, and as of March 27, the heroine's captors began appearing as generic villains.

During Jay Leno's January, 1996 appearance on CNN's *"Larry King Live"* he was asked whether he ever apologized to anyone he had made fun of. Leno replied that he had, "I said something about Iran or something. And I said instead of chopping the arm off, they were doing it surgically, or something [like that] now, to criminals. I made some jokes about it and I heard from some Arab Americans. And I called them up and I apologized, admitting that Arab Americans sometimes get a bad rap. When you are wrong, you do apologize. And in that case I was wrong. And I have no problem with that." Though Leno mistakenly assumes Iran to be an Arab country, his insights and candor are refreshing.

In ABC-TV's May 4, 1995, *Nightline* segment, "Muslims in America," host Ted Koppel remarked that "Muslims are the stereotyped religion in the United States" and that Muslims are "often the first we think of when there's a terrorist incident." Koppel displayed news clips from the Oklahoma City bombing containing the speculative statements made by several network correspondents about the connection to Middle East terrorism. His interviews and footage humanized Muslims: like other American Arabs, he reported, those living in Cedar Rapids, Iowa, "home of the oldest mosque in America," were "made to feel like aliens when the bomb went off in Oklahoma City." And on April 18, 1997 Koppel hosted a telling religious segment entitled *The Hajj,* focus-ing on producer-writer Michael Wolfe's pilgrimage to Mecca. This landmark production, narrated by Wolfe, a Muslim, illustrates the peaceful nature of Islam. Commenting on the success of *The Hajj,* one of the most watched segments in *Nightline's* history, Wolfe says, "I wanted to put front and center a very different view from the distortion that generally attends images of the Muslim world."

Some welcome exceptions to stale Arab caricatures in Hollywood features are beginning to appear. Party Picture's 1995 *Party Girl* represents a first: Mustafa, a Muslim Lebanese school teacher, is the romantic lead. Selling falafel to earn his way through college, Mustafa wins the American heroine's heart and helps her become a responsible person. Independent producer Michael Goldman's 1996 documentary film on singer Umm Kulthum, one of the most important figures in Arab popular culture (*Umm Kulthum: The Voice of Egypt*) was enthusiastically received during New York City's Film Festival at Lincoln Center on October 9, 1996. Fox's 1996 *Independence Day,* a movie depicting earthlings about to be exterminated by space aliens, shows the world's armies, including both Israeli and Arab combat units, preparing to repel an alien attack. Following a quick shot of scrambling Israeli soldiers, and the Israeli flag, actor Sayed Bayedra appears as an Arab pilot. Speaking Arabic, Bayedra rushes to his plane to stop the invaders. Coincidentally, during the summer of 1980, when I was interviewing executives and producers for my book, *The TV Arab,* writer Jack Guss told me that perhaps the best way to contest the stereotype would be to show outer-space aliens attacking earth. This way, said Guss, even Arabs and Israelis could be together, fighting off the invaders (Shaheen, 1980).

Two other 1996 features, Paramount's *Escape from Los Angeles* and New Line's *The Long Kiss Goodnight,* briefly display Muslim Arabs as victims of prejudice. The films may solicit mild sympathy for Arabs and Muslims, and though not yet an established trend, the images mark the beginning of a much needed change. In the 1998 feature, *A Perfect Murder,* a remake of the 1954 thriller, *Dial M for Murder,* actor David Suchet appears as a bright soft-spoken Arab American New York City detective, Mohamed "Mo" Karaman. Concluding frames show Mo, sympathetic to the heroine's ordeals, saying in Arabic,

"Allah ma'a kum" (May God be with you). In English, the heroine replies, "And you, as well."

Daily Variety has reported that actor Patrick Swayze has the lead role in a new film called *The White Sheik*. The story concerns an American boy adopted by an Arab couple who rose to become a prominent sheikh. Also, Disney Studios has produced *The Thirteenth Warrior* (1999), a motion picture based on Michael Crichton's book, *Eaters of the Dead*. The story is set ten centuries ago and stars Anthony Banderas as Ahmed Ibn Fahdlan, a heroic Arab Muslim scholar. "This Arab guy I play," said Banderas, "gets caught by cruel Vikings and their cultures clash completely. But they have a mission to carry out, and that starts pulling them together (*Movie Line*, 1998, p. 50)."

Former Disney Chairman Jeffrey Katzenburg has said, "Each of us in Hollywood has the opportunity to assume individual responsibility for creating films that elevate rather than denigrate, that shed light rather than dwell in darkness, that aim for the common highest denominator rather than the lowest." On December 6, 1996, Katzenburg, who is now one of the three executives in charge of DreamWorks Entertainment, solicited opinions from Arab and Muslim American specialists about DreamWorks' animated feature, the *Prince of Egypt*. The four-hour session included a presentation of the film in progress, followed by a candid question and answer session.

Regional and national Muslim organizations and agencies are beginning to pay increasing attention to the ways in which Arabs, Muslims, and Islam are portrayed in the public media. They point out instances of prejudicial depiction, and are working with non-Muslims in schools and other public arenas to help provide a more balanced, and accurate, picture of persons who have for so long been misrepresented and maligned in the news and in various forms of entertainment media. It seems reasonable to hope that as they become more vigilant, and as image makers and the American public gradually become more aware of the hurt that is caused by such misrepresentations as have been visible through much of this century, Arabs and Muslims may enjoy at least relative immunity from prejudicial portrayal and see themselves depicted at least as fairly as are members of other minority groups in America.

References

American-Arab Anti-Discrimination Committee (ADC). (1994, November). *Anti-Arab-American Discrimination Hate Crimes.*

American-Arab Anti-Discrimination Committee (ADC). (1996–97). *Report on hate crimes & discrimination against Arab Americans.*

Baker, R. (1997, September 1). More killing, Hollywood style. *Jacksonville [WI] Gazette.*

Barboza, S. (1993). *American Jihad.* New York: Doubleday.

Briendel, M. (1996, June 13). School yearbook scandal prompts surprise, anger. *Hills Publications*, p. 3.

Brown J. (1992, December 22). Stereotypes ruin fun of *Aladdin. Des Moines Register*, p. 12.

Cates, G. (1993, January 26). TV women portraying new image. *St. Louis Post-Dispatch*, p. 3D.

Council on American-Islamic Relations. (1996). *A rush to judgment: A special report on anti-Muslim stereotyping.* Washington, DC: Author.

Dart, J. (1996). *Deities and deadlines.* Nashville: Vanderbilt University Freedom Forum.

Downing, S. (Executive Producer). (1996). *FX: The Series.* New York City: UNP-TV.

Esposito, J. (1992). *The Islamic threat.* New York: Oxford University Press.

Goodstein, L. (1996, April 20). Report cites harassment of bombing. *Washington Post*, p. A3.

Greenfield, M. (1986, May 29). A Mideast mistake in the making. *Newsweek*, 84.

Harris, S. (1986, April 11). The world shrinks and stereotypes fall. *Detroit Free Press.*

Hull, D. S. (1969). *Film in the Third Reich.* Berkeley: University of California Press.

It's racist, but hey, it's Disney. (1993, July 14). Editorial, *New York Times.*

Jon Stewart show. (1995, February 25). St. Louis, MO: KMOV-TV.

Kadi, N. (1991, January 30). *48 Hours.* CBS-TV.

Keen, S. (1986, May 15). Speech to the Association of American Editorial Cartoonists, San Diego, CA. See Keen's book, *Faces of the Enemy.* Cambridge: Harper & Row.

Kennedy, J .F. (1962). Yale commencement address, New Haven, CT.

Lane, A. (1999, May 10). [Review of the film, *The Mummy* (1999)]. *The New Yorker,* 104–105.

Leno, J. (1996, January 24). *Larry King Live.* CNN Transcript #1652.

Mander, J. (1978). *Four arguments for the elimination of television.* New York: William Morrow.

Moghrabi, H. (1995, April 23). A rush to judgment,—again. *Cleveland Plain Dealer,* p. 3C.

Movie Line Magazine.(1998, June). p. 50.

Nyang, S. (1996, August 10). Campaign highlights Muslims' quandary. *Los Angeles Times,* p. B10.

Power, C. (1998, March 16). The new Islam, *Newsweek,* 35.

Rich, A. (1995, 1978). *Lies, secrets and silence: Selected prose, 1966–1978.* New York: Norton.

Roth, K. (1996, January 27). Muslims observe holy month of fasting and prayer. *Island Packet,* p. 4B.

Shaheen, J. G. (1980). American television: Arabs in dehumanizing roles. In M. C. Hudson & R. G. Wolfe (Eds.), *The American media and the Arabs* (pp. 39–40). Washington, DC: Center for Contemporary Arab Studies, Georgetown University.

Shaheen, J. G. (1980, July 15). Author's interview with Mr. Jack Guss. Los Angeles.

Shaheen, J. G. (1984). *The TV Arab.* Bowling Green, OH: The Popular Press.

Shaheen, J. G. (1990a). Screen images of Palestinians in the 1980s. In P. Loukides & L. K. Fullers (Eds.), *Beyond the stars: Stock characters in American popular film* (p. 50). Bowling Green, OH: Bowling Green State University Popular Press.

Shaheen, J. G. (1990b, August 19). Our cultural demon: The "Ugly" Arab. *Washington Post,* pp. C1–C2.

Shaheen, J. G. (1993, November 13). Cartoons as commentary. Paper presented at the Chicago Historical Society during the Illinois Humanities Council Festival.

Shaheen, J. G. (1996, February 3). There goes the neighborhood. *Atlanta Journal/Constitution.*

Stone, J. (1996, March 17). Billionaires, bombers and belly dancers. *Ottowa Citizen,* p. 1C.

Teitelbaum, S. (1996, October 17). *The Jerusalem Report,* p. 49.

Twisted puppet theater. (1995, July 23). Showtime.

CLASS 17

Emergence of New European Americans

CHAPTER 27
Beyond Vasco Da Gama:
Unlearning Eurocentric Phallacies in the Classroom
Nada Elia

Nada Elia discusses the difficulty of teaching from a non-Eurocentric
perspective without alienating some students in her classes. She
discusses a variety of strategies that have proven successful.

Beyond Vasco Da Gama: Unlearning Eurocentric Phallacies in the Classroom

Nada Elia

A Scholar-in-Residence in Afro-American Studies at Brown University, Nada Elia's areas of interest and research are counter-hegemonic, especially post-colonial and feminist, narratives. She contributed to *Food for Our Grandmothers: Writings for Arab-American and Arab-Canadian Feminist* and has just completed *Trances, Dances, and Vociferations: Agency and Resistance in Africana Women's Narratives.*

I was attempting to solve a crossword puzzle once when I came across a clue that struck me as unfathomable: "the first man who circled the southern tip of Africa." I left its space blank and moved on to the next line, hoping the empty squares would fill up as I completed the puzzle. But my roommate, who was looking over my shoulder, eagerly volunteered "Vasco da Gama." As an Arab in the United States, I have come to expect a lot of Eurocentric tunnel vision. But this was extreme in its presumption that not one of the millions of Africans, who for thousands of years had lived by the shores of southern Africa, could accomplish such an achievement until a Portuguese sailor showed them how.

As I wondered at how even highly intelligent Americans can accept such blatant falsehoods as facts, I was reminded of yet another incident that had puzzled me upon my arrival in the U.S. It was fall, the beginning of an academic year, and the end of the baseball season. During a class break, some students were discussing the World Series with the professor. I asked the professor, who seemed quite a sports fan, what countries were competing. "Canada and the U.S.," he said. Eager to learn new things—baseball not being a popular sport in the Middle East—I went on with more questions, about which countries had participated in the series and which had made the semi-finals. "Only Canada and the U.S. play in the World

Series," the professor responded matter-of-factly. Oddly enough, in a doctoral program in comparative literature at a respectable American university, I was alone in finding it absurd that any competition involving only two countries should claim to be universal. But more so, I was acutely aware of the arrogance behind this claim.

Today, as a teacher fully committed to offering my students a multicultural education and primarily concerned with providing alternatives to Eurocentric views, I begin each of my courses with my crossword anecdote, or the World Series one. For the last four years, I have taught courses in world literature and postcolonial literature in Indiana and Illinois. My students have been primarily European Americans, who took my class because it is required of education majors. In a few years, they will likely be teachers themselves. This article does not address a teacher's need to recognize the diversity of students ever present in all classrooms, even the most seemingly homogeneous—for diversity is not only ethnic, but manifests itself in numerous ways, in, for example, different sexual orientations, religious upbringing or the lack of it, having experienced child neglect and/or abuse, growing up in a traditional family or the much more common "contemporary" one. Rather, I want to provide the teacher with some suggestions as to how to approach students required to take multi-cultural classes they have little initial interest in or much prejudiced resistance to.

Over the last few years, I have developed a few strategies that counter the resistance of students hostile to diversity, as well as encourage them to view a multicultural education as a plus, as a wealth of information that, far from seeking to replace the traditional canon, attempts instead to revive it, to infuse it with a vitality that spares it the fate of Greek tragedy: classic, epic, but falling short of addressing contemporary issues.

On the first day of class, I ask my students for the name of the first person to have circled the southern tip of Africa. Occasionally, a student will volunteer the infamous piece of information. If nobody does, I write it on the board: Vasco da Gama. Then I tell my students that he was Portuguese and give them the dates of his birth and death: 1469–1524 A.D. Hungry for information (or eager to secure their A) they write it all down. I go on to ask them if they can suggest any reasons as to why no African had been able to circle Africa's southern tip, though they had navigated those shores for thousands of years before the first Europeans arrived there. Of course, no one can provide a satisfactory answer. There isn't one; that Vasco da Gama should be the first simply doesn't make sense.

My approach may be deemed a little harsh for a first day of class, but it has been my experience that this reality check is extremely effective. If it were a student who provided the name Vasco da Gama—and more often than not that student is a crossword puzzle fan—I make sure that they do not feel foolish by pointing out that, according to numerous reference books, they are correct. Moreover, haven't all the rest of the students copied the data down without any questions? Then I ask my students to please cross out whatever notes they have taken, since my class requires critical thinking, not dictionary knowledge, and, as we have just seen, the two are frequently at odds. Critical thinking, I explain, does not always provide the answers, but it avoids incorrect answers. Thus we will never know who made the first lap around the Cape of Good Hope, but we do know it does not make sense that it should be a Portuguese sailor.

Moreover, I find it important to lay the ground rules in that first session: we are here to unlearn certain misinformation we have received, as much

if not more than we hope to learn new material. And during the semester, when students are understandably frustrated at the lack of answers to some of the questions we raise, I can refer to this session and ask them "Do you want convenience? I can give you the 'Da Gama equivalent'. . . ." When I present lack of closure in these terms, they stop pressing for *the* correct answer. Indeed, da Gama has become one of my favorite historical examples, for he also allows me on that first day of class to introduce my students to the evils of racism (the denial of the humanity of Africans), sexism (Were there no women on Da Gama's ship? Why not?), and classism (Surely he had a whole crew to help him; why aren't they mentioned?). Da Gama also makes a good starting point for a discussion of European cultural hegemony and the numerous factors that contributed to the successful imposition of one paradigm over others.

Again, the importance of our first class must be emphasized, for it clearly establishes that the class allows, indeed favors, alternative modes of thinking. In a recent article, Linda Dittmar (1993) argues against leaving sensitive themes such as homosexual love till the end of a course. I agree with her, for the hegemonic discourse that has silenced these topics fully surrounds us, and the fourteen to sixteen weeks that make up a semester are barely sufficient for their discussion in a mature way. We should treat our students as adults. They are adults: they can drive a car, juggle credit cards, and, with very few exceptions, are of voting age. As I realize that the transition from sheltered home life to college campus is not easy, I help them recognize, or question, prejudices in a friendly environment.

One way I have found very effective in promoting individual thought is requiring students to formulate an opinion about the material they have just read. I require students to turn in, on the day we start discussing a new text, an index card with the following:

- three to five questions raised by the text;

- a page reference to a passage they would like discussed in class; and

- an opinion about the reading. Did they like it? Why or why not?

I emphasize to my students they will receive full credit for the index card, regardless of contents, the quality of their questions, or the positiveness of their response. Moreover, I stress that it is fully up to them to identify themselves, if they want to, when I answer their questions in class or read out their opinion. I identify them only in the case of the passage they would like to have us discuss together, since I then ask them to lead the discussion themselves. Whether it is because they indeed feel distance from the dominant discourse they would publicly express or because they are merely testing out alternatives or challenging assumptions, the students offer a rich array of responses that allow for lively debate.

The index cards are useful in many ways. They allow me to evaluate students' needs from the questions they ask and to prepare the next lesson accordingly. They give insight into the students' readings of texts. Through student-led discussion of the passage they have chosen—and quite frequently, two to three will choose the same passage, spontaneously creating group discussion—the learning experience becomes collaborative. Finally, students whose opinions would otherwise be underrepresented feel empowered when I read out their opinions. Here I do use my prerogative as a teacher in that I privilege original thoughts by sharing these with the rest of the class. In doing so, the traditionalists are not silenced, for they are, of course, entitled to respond, and most speakers of the hegemonic discourse feel safe speaking up.

A teacher communicates knowledge best when s/he successfully avoids alienating even the most resistant students, and humor plays an important role, helping in many instances to release tension. A few weeks into a course, as I feel my students weary of our politicized class, I tell them about the press conference I am calling next week, for I have a major announcement to make: I have discovered penicillin! Well, why not? Columbus discovered America, didn't he? Why can't I discover penicillin? Thus humor is not used to distract students from the seriousness of the matter at hand, but rather to present it to them in more acceptable ways, especially when their long-held beliefs are being shattered.

Despite my efforts to break classroom hierarchy, my students are ever aware that I am the authority, that I have special power in the classroom. When I am willing to show them that I, too, am quite fallible, they feel safer about acknowledging mistakes they have made. I tell them how readily I misjudged someone when I assumed that a man I had just met at a bar was drunk, simply because of his accent. He was an African American from a small town in Arkansas. Had I made a racist assumption? I meant no harm, but did I hurt him? Are we ever blameless?

It is easy to denounce racism. It is more challenging to do so without alienating European American students whose belief in a glorious heritage is shattered as they discover their ancestors, just like everybody else's, have at times murdered, pillaged, raped, stolen, and engaged in racial wars. When a student writes that s/he is ashamed of being white, it is essential to explain that shame and guilt can be paralyzing feelings or incitement to action, to change. Most are happy to know there is a positive way out. Yet I would in no way suggest my method is infallible. Very recently, I had a student who grew more angry at me, or the material I was presenting, with each class period and finally exploded during our discussion of the mistreatment of Native Americans by the Europeans. This student claimed that denouncing racism and sexism only aggravates these issues, and he argued that tolerance of others cannot be promoted through a discussion of past wrongdoings. Clearly, as a white male, he felt he had come under attack one time too many. Rather than turn this episode into a one-on-one confrontation between him and me, I asked the rest of the students if they in any way agreed with him. If that were the case, I would change my approach. Fortunately, the students came to my aid, as they explained to him the necessity of knowing how and why certain acts were wrong. Reassured, I was able to add that, just as with addictions or sexual abuse, one has to acknowledge the problem in order to treat it.

Because students learn in different ways, a combination of strategies is necessary when introducing them to concepts they have been trained to regard with suspicion, whether these concepts be feminism, anti-imperialism, or homosexuality. One simple yet effective way is to punctuate class handouts with empowering proverbs. Among my favorites are:

"Until the lions have their historians, tales of hunting will always glorify the hunter."

"The mind of a bigot is like the pupil of the eye: the more light you shine on it, the more it contracts."

"Freedom is merely privilege extended, unless enjoyed by one and all."

"Columbus didn't discover America, he invaded it."

I have included these on my syllabi or exams. You can ask students to contribute their own. One semester, our class started a racist/sexist/homophobic jokes bulletin board. This project was enlightening to those students for whom the prejudice was not evident, and who by the middle of the semester felt comfortable enough to inquire about how a joke was offensive. A bonus I had not anticipated was the broader audience this display reached, as other classes met in the same classroom and frequently commented on our clippings. Photocopies of the collage of some very prominent U.S. figures accompanied by the line "History has set the record a little too straight" never fails to affect students, as they realize that some of their heroes or role models were homosexual.

Students are also less likely to reject new concepts when they are presented to them not solely as the teacher's opinion, but as material of interest and validity to many of their classmates. Again, the index cards are helpful, since reading a positive student response to an alternative text makes the promoters and/or duplicators of the dominant discourse realize the diversity of opinions among their peers; the teacher's perspective is not singled out as that of a hostile authority to be resisted. This is especially helpful when the instructor is visibly other or when s/he openly acknowledges holding alternative views that are feminist, Marxist, or Afrocentric.

Some texts I have used in my classes have elicited very strong responses in my students. Two stand out at the top of a list of works that have sparked some of our best debates: Nawal el-Saadawi's *Woman at Point Zero* and Mehdi Charef's *Tea in the Harem*. The first is the narrative, defiant and unrepentant, of a prostitute on death row for killing her pimp. It is disturbing, as it confronts us with ugly aspects of life we would rather ignore. *Woman at Point Zero* also allows for a discussion of homosexuality, through hints that the prostitute may be lesbian, as well as for a critique of religion's role in the subjugation of women. The book does not contain a single passage that could be termed obscene even by the prudish. I generally also assign chapters from *Sex Works: Writings from Women in the Sex Industry*, which represents the views of COYOTE (Cast Off Your Old Tired

Ethics) and WHISPER (Women Hurt in Systems of Prostitution Engaging in Resistance).

Tea in the Harem is the autobiography of a young immigrant in the Parisian housing projects. He writes of doing drugs, torching neighborhood cars, pimping, harassing a teacher, all before being jailed for taking a joyride in a stolen car. Written in street language, the text is explosive. I am ever surprised at how readily my students say they relate to this criminal. Like the prostitute in *Woman at Point Zero*, he is also a victim, pulling us into the gray zone where absolutes are questioned. One of my students, a senior in law enforcement, wrote me that he feels he will be a different, more understanding police officer now that he has taken my class.

To counter the resistance of students who believe sexism is a thing of the past or only present today in nonWestern cultures, no book has proven more helpful than Gerd Brantenberg's *Egalia's Daughters*. Through a humorous role reversal, this novel by a contemporary Norwegian novelist successfully denounces the continuing pervasive male dominance in modern European society. After reading it, my students no longer find it perfectly natural, and fair, that they should be called freshmen their first year at college, or that they should earn a bachelor's degree, or a master's or that, even if they choose to retain their names after marriage, they will still be carrying a man's name, their father's. Men who say they would readily change their baby's diaper at a restaurant have to reconsider when they realize most baby-changing facilities are in women's restrooms. Interestingly, it has been my experience and that of my friend and colleague, Loretta Kensinger (who first suggested the novel to me), that most women thoroughly enjoy the novel, while men find it extremely disturbing.

Another text that produces a divided reaction allowing for valuable classroom discussion is the play, *Trial of Dedan Kimathi*, by Ngugi wa Thiong'o and Micere Githae Mugo. In this case, the divide falls along racial lines, since African American students find it empowering, while European Americans criticize it for any number of reasons, including that it is a racist text, a charge that is definitely incorrect. The polarized responses to both of these selections allow for an enriching exchange of ideas. Another text, Buchi Emecheta's

Second Class Citizen, tells of a Nigerian woman's successful struggle to overcome sexism at home as well as both sexism and racism in England. The response to this novel is generally unanimous, overwhelmingly positive, facilitating discussion of some of its underlying themes: domestic violence, marital rape, a woman's right to reproductive choice, mental emancipation.

These texts are but a few of a multitude of readily available, easily accessible titles that make the move away from a canon loaded with Eurocentric phallacies not only possible, but fun. Whether in women's studies classes or in general survey of literature courses, sociology courses or multicultural studies, we can and should assign them. We make a difference. We impact our students, who will impact others. Let us realize this potential for positive change by exposing our students to alternative texts, world views, and instructional methods.

References

Brantenberg, G. (1985). *Egalia's daughters*. (L. Mackay, Trans. In cooperation with Brantenberg). Seattle: Seal.

Charef, M. (1989). *Tea in the harem*. (E. Emery, Trans.). London: Serpent's Tail.

Dittmar, L. (1994). Conflict and resistance in the multicultural classroom. In J. Q. Adams & J. R. Welsch (Eds.), *Multicultural education: Strategies for implementation in colleges and universities*, Vol. 3. Macomb, IL: Illinois Staff and Curriculum Developers Association. (See this volume, pp. 235–244)

Emecheta, B. (1983). *Second class citizen*. New York: Braziller

Saadawi (1983). *Woman at point zero*. (S. Hetata, Trans.). London: Zed.

Ngugi wa Thiong'o N., & Mugo, M. G. (1976). *The trial of Dedan Kimathi*. London: Heineman.

CLASS 18

Creole and Mixed Ethnic Americans

CHAPTER 28
The Americanization of Black New Orleans, 1850–1900
Arnold Hirsch and Joseph Logsdon
Joseph Logsdon's article provides insight into the unique cultural
history of the city of New Orleans. The "Big Easy" is one of the most
intriguing areas in the U.S.A. It is a mixture of many distinct cultures
fused together in a way that has given birth to some of the most
distinctive colors, flavors and more concretely art forms.

The Americanization of Black New Orleans, 1850–1900

Joseph Logsdon and Arnold R. Hirsch

Professor of history and urban affairs at the University of New Orleans, Joseph Logsdon co-edited Solomon Northup's *Twelve Years a Slave* and is the author of *Horace White, Nineteenth-Century Liberal and Audubon Park: An Urban Eden.*

Chairman of the history department and professor of history and urban affairs at the University of New Orleans, Arnold R. Hirsch is also the author of *Making the Second Ghetto: Race and Housing in Chicago, 1940-1960.*

Several years after the collapse of Reconstruction, about fifty black and white Republican leaders of New Orleans met for dinner at Antoine's Restaurant in the French Quarter in an effort to heal some old wounds within their ranks. After their party's crushing defeats in 1876 and 1878, they were trying to recapture what one speaker at the dinner called "the fraternal feeling which characterized the early days of the party."

Dr. Louis Charles Roudanez, the founder of the state's first official Republican newspaper, had not for more than a decade spoken with two of the most prominent guests at the dinner—P. B. S. Pinchback and Henry Clay Warmoth, both former Republican governors of Louisiana. Racial differences could not explain the black doctor's deep disdain for these two men; Warmoth was white and Pinchback black. Nor was the shade of skin color the crux of their confrontation, for both Roudanez and Pinchback had complexions about as light as Warmoth's.

Pinchback understood the import of this rare meeting and tried to join in its spirit. He singled out Roudanez and declared that the doctor's decision to attend the party confab "demonstrated the possibility of Republican unity." His generous toast brought the normally taciturn physician to his feet. Roudanez politely acknowledged the flattery but did not reciprocate with any comparable praise for Pinchback. Instead, he took advantage of the moment to recall at some length "his own aims and purposes in the early days of reconstruction . . . to educate and advance the interests of his down-trodden race." When Roudanez finished, he reached across the table and shook hands with Governor Warmoth.

In an account of the meeting in his newspaper, Pinchback reported that these symbolic gestures showed Roudanez' "desire to let the past be forgotten." He was wrong. The old bitterness remained between these two black leaders. True, Roudanez never reentered politics to confront Pinchback, but other black friends of the doctor, such as Judge A. J. Dumont, took up the old cudgels against his nemesis. Indeed, Pinchback pointed to the new rivalry by observing that the party harmonizers had placed him and Dumont at one end of the banquet table, just as they had placed the two earlier protagonists, Roudanez and Warmoth, at the other end—"facing each other." The two new party leaders had already reopened the old Republican feud within Louisiana, and by

1882 newspaper columns emblazoned the clash of their forces as a contest of "Creoles vs Americans."

This lingering fifteen-year conflict among black leaders in New Orleans involved more than ordinary political factionalism and petty personal rivalry over patronage. It reflected a fundamental cultural duality in the city's black community that stemmed from different backgrounds and leadership and was similar to the division between white creoles and Americans. But the rift in black New Orleans may have even been more fundamental and lasting because no third group of later immigrants blurred the cultural distinctions and because black creoles seemed much more determined than their white counterparts to maintain their peculiar identity in the face of the relentless process of Americanization that worked on all segments of the city's population. As a result, the cultural duality continued well into the twentieth century and, although diminished and subdued, is still evident in New Orleans.

In 1907, almost three decades after the dinner at Antoine's, Rodolphe L. Desdunes reviewed the post-Civil War era in New Orleans for a younger historian, W. E. B. Du Bois. Desdunes felt that the duality within the New Orleans black community still endured. He did not seek simplistically to define the two groups by their skin color or antebellum status. Desdunes was born in 1849, and his firsthand experiences in New Orleans undoubtedly taught him that neither group could be incorporated into the racial categories of "black" and "mulatto" that have appeared so important to American census takers and later academic observers. He also knew that neither group had emerged from the Civil War either all slave or all free. Instead, he chose to describe them in ethnic categories—the "Latin Negro" and the "Anglo-Saxon or American Negro."

Desdunes felt that these two groups had evolved "two different schools of politics" and differed "radically . . . in aspiration and method." Keeping the "Latin Negro" as the former and the "American Negro" as the latter in his comparison, he tried to explain this unusual concept in American historiography: "One hopes, and the other doubts. Thus we often perceive that one makes every effort to acquire merits, the other to gain advantages. One aspires to equality, the other to identity. One will forget that he is a Negro in order to think that he is a man; the other will forget that he is a man to think that he is a Negro.

These radical differences act on the feelings of both in direct harmony with these characteristics. One is a philosophical Negro, the other practical." Desdunes refused to indulge in any of the fashionable racialism or biological determinism of his day to explain the makeup of the two groups. He insisted that their contrasting outlooks as well as their political disagreements "arise, partly from temperament, and partly from surroundings, just as a difference in the manner and thinking will soon crystallize between the Northern Negroes and the Southern Negroes."

Desdunes considered himself, as well as Roudanez and Dumont, to be Latin Negroes or creoles. They were an anomaly in the United States for both white and black Americans such as Warmoth and Pinchback. In turn, the creole Negroes regarded Americans, particularly those born outside of New Orleans, as members of a separate and sometimes hostile society. Creole blacks, particularly those like Roudanez and Desdunes, who formally learned French intellectual traditions and also carefully observed revolutionary movements in the nineteenth-century French world, staked their claim to equal status on unique political principles. English-speaking Protestants, by contrast, acculturated to Anglo-American traditions, approached events with strategies derived from their own historical experience in the Anglo-American world.

In Louisiana Reconstruction politics, white Democrats as well as white Republicans often exploited the ethnic differences among black New Orleanians and made it more difficult for them to achieve political unity. Nevertheless, in crucial struggles during Reconstruction, black leaders transcended their ethnic differences and helped to forge a new identity as free men and citizens not just for themselves but for all persons of African descent in the United States. What follows is a study of their difficult but important struggle.

Black Creoles and Americans

From the beginning of the nineteenth century, race relations in New Orleans had puzzled American newcomers, particularly those who were sent to govern the city in 1803. The new rulers encountered a black majority that grew larger with the addition of French-speaking West Indian immigrants. More perhaps than its size, the nature of the city's black population—particularly those who were free—confused and frightened American officials.

The free black creoles of New Orleans had emerged from French and Spanish rule not only with unusual rights and powers but also with a peculiar assertiveness and self-confidence. Many were armed and had gained military training and experience in the official militias of Louisiana. They had also secured wealth and a firm foothold in skilled occupations normally closed to free persons of African ancestry in Anglo-America. Most may have been fair-skinned but not all; they ran the spectrum of skin color. In the urban setting of New Orleans, moreover, free black men and women intermingled with slaves, often living in the same quarters and intermarrying or cohabiting with those still in bondage. In such a racial order, "the consummate linkage of negritude and servility, the dominant feature of race relations in the American Old South, never fully emerged in colonial Louisiana."

New American officials soon faced the self-confidence of free black creole leaders of the city, who felt that the Louisiana Purchase treaty had assured them of equal citizenship in the United States. Even before the transfer to the American authority, the explosive events of the revolutions in France and Haiti had raised the aspirations of black New Orleanians for equality and freedom. When they petitioned for civil rights, American leaders showed no desire to perpetuate, much less extend, the rights of black Louisianans. Instead, the new rulers tried to impose their own American racial order on New Orleans and the rest of Louisiana.

In the rural Louisiana countryside, little may have distinguished the severity of the Anglo-American slave order from that of the French or the Spanish. But in New Orleans American authorities faced a severe challenge to the racial policies that they wished to establish. The new American governor, William C. C. Claiborne, made no overt move against the armed free black population. Faced with the possibilities of insurrection by either slaves or some of the non-American white inhabitants, he and his associates tried to avoid creating any additional enemies. Time and events only compounded their ambivalence. The reverberations of the slave revolts in Saint Domingue brought more French-speaking black settlers into the territory. By 1810, the free

Negro population of the city rose to 4,950 from 1,566 in 1805, and the slave population rose to 5,961 from 3,105 (see Table 1). Among the West Indian newcomers were even more skilled, better-educated, and probably more assertive leaders—both free and slave—than those who had already disturbed the Americans in 1803.

Pressed by fearful white creoles and Americans, the territorial government thinned the ranks of the free black militia, imposed white officers, and finally allowed the legislature to disband it. Having already denied the creoles' petition for equal citizenship, Governor Claiborne forced their leaders to renounce any further public declarations. Slowly but surely the existing rights of the free black population were eroded. The territorial assembly's purpose was clear when it declared: "Free people of color ought never insult or strike white people, nor presume to conceive themselves equal to whites." To guard the color line, the assembly ordered that racial designation be applied to all persons of African ancestry in every public document.

In a generation or two, a resolute policy along these lines might have Americanized the racial order in New Orleans, but a slave revolt in 1811 and a British invasion in 1814 persuaded the American authorities to relent in their repressive policies toward the state's free black inhabitants. For their own survival, they recommissioned white-officered black militia units and almost created a legalized, triparte racial order similar to those of the Caribbean. From 1815 to 1830, state officials did not further reduce free black rights, and the economic boom in the city enabled skilled black workers and merchants to improve their already impressive occupational status.

When a repressive mood returned in the 1830s following the revived abolitionist movement and the Nat Turner insurrection, creole white lawmakers still had enough power in the state legislature to exempt many of the free black creoles from increased restrictions by giving special status to those who were in Louisiana at some earlier date. More significant, most of the black creoles of New Orleans—both free and slave—escaped much of the renewed severity by living within the virtually autonomous creole municipal districts of New Orleans that were created in 1836, where enforcement of almost all laws was notoriously lax. As a result, free and slave black creoles continued to gather for festivities, frequent bars and dance

Table 1. Whites, Free People of Color, and Slaves in New Orleans, 1769–1860

Population Figures

Year	Whites	Free People of Color	Slaves	Total
1769	1,803	99	1,227	3,129
1788	2,370	823	2,126	5,319
1805	3,551	1,566	3,105	8,222
1810	6,331	4,950	5,961	17,242
1820	13,584	6,237	7,355	27,176
1830	20,047	11,562	14,476	46,085
1840	50,697	15,072	18,208	83,977
1850	89,452	9,905	17,011	116,368
1860	144,601	10,939	14,484	170,024

Percentages

Year	Whites (%)	Free People of Color (%)	Slaves (%)
1769	57.6	3.2	39.2
1788	44.6	15.5	39.9
1805	43.2	19.0	37.8
1810	36.7	28.7	34.6
1820	49.9	23.0	27.1
1830	43.5	25.1	31.4
1840	60.4	18.0	21.6
1850	76.9	8.5	14.6
1860	85.0	6.4	8.5

SOURCES: Population figures and percentages for 1769 to 1820 are drawn from Paul F. Lachance, "New Orleans in the Era of Revolution: A Demographic Profile" (Paper presented at the American Society for Eighteenth-Century Studies, New Orleans, 1989). Respective figures for 1830 to 1850 are from Leonard P. Curry, *The Free Negro in Urban America, 1800–1850: The Shadow of the Dream* (Chicago, 1981). Figures for 1860 are taken from John W. Blassingame, *Black New Orleans, 1860–1880* (Chicago, 1973).

halls, and cohabit despite the state laws designed to constrain such activity.

In 1850, almost all free black creoles, and quite likely those enslaved as well, lived downriver from Canal Street in the First and Third municipalities. Their voluntary relationships across the color line were, it seems, not so much with the long-resident white creoles as with immigrants, especially those from France, who concentrated in the same areas during the 1830s and 1840s. Because European immigrants, who flowed constantly into the booming city before the Civil War, took a while to learn the mores of the United States, the racial order remained fluid during most of the antebellum period. The large number of immigrants from France and the French-speaking West Indies also nurtured the French culture, language, and institutional loyalty that pervaded black creole society. Music teachers, Catholic priests and nuns, shopkeepers, live-in lovers, radical émigrés, and saloonkeepers helped to maintain relationships between black and white New Orleanians that were more elaborate than those in any other city in the United States.

It was not accidental that the 1852 consolidation of the three separate municipalities coincided with a new serge of racial repression. For many years after the Civil War, creole black leaders recalled 1852 as the year of the breakdown of their sheltered and privileged order in New Orleans. At that point, the state legislature began an assault on their rights of manumission and began transferring enforcement of existing restrictions from local to state authorities.

Almost every major black creole leader of the Civil War and Reconstruction era was chastened by the repression of the 1850s. The large number who sought refuge outside of Louisiana fled not to the American North but to France and Latin America, especially Haiti and Mexico. Dr. Roudanez was just one of many who found greater freedom in France. There he not only gained a prestigious medical degree but also took to the revolutionary barricades. Both experiences helped him gain a radical vision of an alternative racial order for his native city and nation.

During the decade or so before the Civil War, the divergent racial policies of France and the United States helped shape the thinking and outlook of many black creole leaders. Edicts issued by officials of the Second Republic in 1848 not only ended slavery in the French West Indies but also gave full political rights to all black inhabitants of these islands. These radical actions outside the Anglo-American experience opened new possibilities in the minds of black creoles in New Orleans. Before the Civil War, even the Garrisonian abolitionists in the United States seldom reached the vanguard racial policies of the Second Republic in France. As a result, the black creoles of New Orleans looked less to the North Star than to La Belle France.

The Anglo-American assault on the anomalous world of the black creoles had some long-term results, producing among some a measure of acceptance and accommodation and among others nostalgia for the world that was lost. But far more important, the repression helped to develop a young leadership class that resisted American-

ization and stood poised to create a new order based not merely on French ideas but also on recent applications of those ideas in other areas of the New World.

The French-oriented creoles were not the only black New Orleanians. The role of black migrants from the United States during the first half of the nineteenth century has too often been forgotten in the story of social and cultural change in the city. Slaves and free men and women brought a highly developed way of life that had been fashioned over many decades in other areas of the United States. Their institutions and values often differed from those of the black creoles of New Orleans, and the resulting interchange between the two communities helped shape the peculiar way of life in the city for years to come. White American officials long tried to discourage the migration of free black men and women from the American seaboard or the upper South to the Mississippi Valley. Like other white Americans who moved out to the western frontier, the migrants to Louisiana passed laws to keep free black Americans from entering their new settlements. Despite the remarkable success of white leaders in other states, however, Louisianians failed in their efforts to keep out or effectively expel free black Americans.

The increase in the number of free black Americans was in part a result of American slaves gaining their freedom after arriving in New Orleans under the lenient manumission laws that survived from the colonial days of the city. Surprisingly large numbers of free black Americans also came to New Orleans voluntarily. For the most part, they came to work on coasting vessels or river steamers. Ship owners, in need of compliant, cheap labor, recruited them and even helped them evade the state laws and city ordinances passed to exclude them. The lure of jobs and the city's relatively open racial order made it an island of freedom and opportunity in the Deep South.

Most of the migrant workers probably returned to their home states, but some stayed in New Orleans. Few, if any, ever gained legal residency. Most had to subvert the law in order to remain, but in the labyrinth of a large seaport, evasion was often easy. In the 1850s the police, under employers' pleas for leniency, arrested fewer than ten free black residents per month for violating the exclusion laws. Only when a new city administration began enforcing a harsher law in 1859 did the monthly arrest total of almost one hundred free black aliens reveal the true level of their migration into the city.

So many fugitive slaves fled into the city that their presence began to undermine distinctions between free and slave in New Orleans, but their status proved very precarious and probably led to harassment of many blacks who were legally free. Because the underpaid and undermanned police force won private bounties for recovering runaways, the fugitives had a much more difficult time avoiding apprehension than did free black aliens. During the 1850s, more than eighty-five hundred fugitives fell into the hands of the police. Most had escaped from neighboring plantations, but slaves resident in the city also made at least two thousand attempts to escape bondage during that decade. Some of the latter may have managed to flee from the state, but most probably tried to disappear into the ranks of the free black community inside the city.

As slaves or as free men and women, black Americans brought with them a North American culture that was much older than that of the black creoles of New Orleans. It was not only rooted in different blends of African traditions but had been subsequently entwined with the lifestyles of the different European and Indian peoples whom African-Americans had encountered in North America. Central to the culture of most black men and women in Anglo-America was the Protestant church and the role of the black preacher. During the antebellum era, most religious leaders had realistically urged their followers not to revolt against the numbers and power arrayed against them in the Old South but rather to find shelter and solace in the church.

The Baptists laid the earliest foundations for the black Protestant church in Louisiana. In 1799, a black Baptist preacher landed in a Spanish jail for violating the colony's ban on all religious creeds except Catholicism. As soon as American control removed that restraint, another black American minister, Joseph Willis, became the first Baptist missionary west of the Mississippi River.

The first Baptist church in New Orleans, which lasted from 1818 to 1820, began like those on the rural frontier—with both black and white members and a tolerance for black preachers. The First African Baptist Church, with an all-black congregation, tried to set roots in New Orleans on October 31, 1826, but survived only until 1830, when its first pastor, Asa C. Goldsberry, died and harassment forced it to disband. In the early 1830s some Virginia slaves, led by a slave minister, Nelson D. Sanders, resuscitated it in a small house in Gentilly on the eastern outskirts of the city and sustained it there for the next decade. In 1843, under Sanders' leadership, the congregation built a church on Howard Street, in the uptown American sector of the city. Although frequently troubled by arrests, they eventually gained permission to meet "two hours on Sundays from 3 to 5 p.m. under the watch of a police officer who was paid $2 per hour." Three other African Baptist churches were established before the Civil War, all in the uptown American sector. In 1859, under increasing pressure, all four placed themselves under the supervision of the white Coliseum Baptist Church and the Mississippi River Association, and the slave pastors were required to work under the direction of a white minister.

It took longer for the Methodist church to gain a firm foothold in the city. The first white Methodist missionary, Elisha Bowman, met so much indifference to his efforts in 1806 that he gave up on the "ungodly city of New Orleans." Several other hardened circuit riders tried their hand during the next two decades but also gave up in despair. Benjamin Drake, who finally organized a congregation in 1824, reported that "New Orleans presents a more unyielding resistance to the evangelical gospel . . . than any other city in the South."

As in the case of the Baptists, black American newcomers anchored the Methodists in New Orleans. Of the first eighty-three members of Drake's church in 1826, at least sixty were black. During the first two decades, black and white Methodists worshiped together in New Orleans, but the black members had to sit in a segregated gallery. After Southern Methodists separated from the national Methodist Episcopal church and formed their own denomination in 1845—the Methodist Episcopal Church, South—they set up separate, subsidized congregations for black Methodists in New Orleans. In this arrangement, white presiding elders supervised the black congregations, and black preachers acted as subordinates.

The black preachers were not recent converts. Each, it appears, had chosen his religious persuasion well before he came to Louisiana. The

Reverend Scott Chinn, for example, had secretly learned to read by the age of thirteen and had been raised by Methodist parents. He began preaching at the age of fifteen and continued to do so after he was brought to New Orleans by his owner in 1849. There he joined two other slave preachers, Henry Green and Anthony Ross, in caring for the members of the three black congregations of the Methodist Episcopal Church, South. Ordained by a Methodist Episcopal bishop "without laying of hands," he was permitted to administer sacraments only "to the negroes and such white persons as may accept them."

Few free blacks, either Americans or creoles, appear to have joined the Baptist and Methodist Episcopal congregations. Some slaves who had gained their freedom while members of those churches remained as members, but most free black Americans turned to the African Methodist Episcopal (AME) church, a truly independent black institution that had its origins in eighteenth-century Pennsylvania. Although this denomination had been banned from the Deep South during the 1820s after the exposure of Denmark Vesey's 1822 slave revolt conspiracy in South Carolina, it managed to gain a foothold in New Orleans about two decades later.

In 1842, a small group of Methodists, tied together by Masonic loyalties, made contact with an AME minister, the Reverend Jordan Winston Early, who worked on a steamboat traveling between St. Louis and New Orleans. When Early advised them not to attempt to start an AME congregation unless they could get an act of incorporation from the state, one of the group, James Hunter, persuaded white friends to obtain the necessary charter from the Louisiana legislature in 1847, on the condition that the church meet only in daylight hours. Until then the group had met furtively in private houses, posting lookouts to warn them of approaching police.

In 1848, the group sent a member, Charles Doughty, to Indianapolis to ask the Indiana AME conference to send a minister to set up an AME church in New Orleans. The conference agreed to seek out a likely prospect but in the meantime ordained Doughty as a deacon to take pastoral charge of its "Louisiana Mission," subsequently called St. James Church. In the fall of 1852, Bishop Paul Quinn sent the Reverend John Mifflin Brown to guide the affairs of the congregation, which

existed near Canal Street, just inside the First Municipality. Brown had the misfortune to arrive just as the city was being consolidated and more severe restrictions were being imposed on the black community. During his five years in the city, Brown was arrested five times for not excluding slaves from the services of the church. Still he bravely continued to expand the AME operations by opening two other churches in the city, Morris Brown and Quinn chapels.

As the repressive mood grew worse in the late 1850s, city officials harassed the AME members with arrests. By 1857 the church's activities had been severely curtailed, but the authorities were not satisfied and, in 1858, finally closed the church by passing an ordinance that banned any black organization or church not under the control of whites. The AME members fought back by successfully suing the city on the basis of their state charter in the District Court, but the state Supreme Court overturned the decision, noting that the "African race are strangers to our Constitution, and are subject of special and exceptional legislation."

After this defeat, some of the AME members found shelter within the white Congregational church, while others went back to the secret meetings of the Prince Hall Masons, whose order had drawn heavily upon an Anglo-American heritage. From the beginning, the leadership of the AME churches was almost identical to that of the Prince Hall Masons in New Orleans. Many of the key figures had been in the state as free men before 1835. Without any state approval or charter, they had formed a secret Masonic group in the 1840s and in March, 1849, managed to obtain a charter from northern black leaders to open a Prince Hall (York Rite) unit in New Orleans. The newly sanctioned Richmond Lodge spawned two offspring before the Civil War, Stringer Lodge in 1854 and Parsons Lodge in 1857.

Almost all of the Prince Hall members before the Civil War were black Americans. In the repressive climate of the late 1850s, the lodge was one of the few organizations that allowed leaders from the free black American community to consider options to remaining in the United States. Even the moderate and long-settled black American Jordan B. Noble joined the group and represented Louisiana in the Negro Emigration Convention of 1854 in Cleveland, which commissioned agents to seek a place of refuge in Africa.

Like the black creoles, black Americans tried to protect their rights and dignity in face of the rising tide of racial discrimination during the 1850s. In establishing a black clergy and racially separate institutions, they expressed a desire to create a separate identity within the confines of the American racial order, and for a while they had some success. They repeatedly challenged laws prohibiting the assembly of free black men and women with those who were enslaved. Indeed, their assertiveness thoroughly alarmed white officials, who finally concluded that "such assemblages are dangerous to the institution of slavery. They create discontent among the slaves."

Neither the creole nor the American black leaders could resist the relentless pressure placed on all black residents. By 1860, fear and discouragement ran deeply through the entire black community of New Orleans, as the fragile rights and freedoms of those who were free or slave, creole or American vanished in the decade before the Civil War. Many fled the city. Of those who remained, most tried to make the best of a worsening situation by either enduring the conditions or finding whatever protection they could in paternalistic relationships with white New Orleanians. Some, however, secretly organized themselves and stood poised for action. In the late 1850s, few black New Orleanians could have predicted that the deteriorating racial climate in their city and other places in the Deep South would have led to emancipation and black suffrage, but they soon learned that liberation often comes to the oppressed when they least expect it.

Union Occupation and Black Troops

In the spring of 1862, the sight of the Union military forces was an occasion for rejoicing by almost all black New Orleanians. Union sailors recalled them thronging on the levees as their ships approached the city. The Lincoln administration had not yet dedicated itself to a policy of emancipation, but the slaves did not wait. Thousands poured into the city from the surrounding plantations, and many bade farewell to their former masters in the city.

How the new white American rulers from the North would react to the aspirations of black New Orleanians remained to be tested. The story of that relationship is the most complex in the Reconstruction saga. Nowhere did Reconstruction begin so early or advance so far in its legal changes as in New Orleans. And probably nowhere were black leaders so demanding or, on occasion, so divided in their response to the new American leadership.

In most areas of the South, particularly in the cities, the reaction to emancipation and Reconstruction may have differed among those who were already free and those who were slaves. Antebellum status and skin color may have led to differing outlooks and ideology, an inevitable result in a color-conscious society. But in most localities these differences did not produce anything like the lasting legal and political distinctions that arose in the postemancipation societies of the West Indies.

Still, some leaders tried to make color distinctions a basis for their programs. Such racialist appeals, for example, continued to sputter forth well into the late nineteenth century from the black and white leaders of the American Colonization Society, which tried to revive its antebellum program of sending black Americans to Africa. When one of the society's white officials blamed the organization's meager accomplishment in seventy-five years on the contempt in which light-skinned black leaders held Africa, a black New Orleans newspaper editor, A. E. P. Albert, responded with some interesting insights about the nature of the black community in his city. As a bilingual former slave of creole ancestry and a convert to Methodism, Albert understood the peculiar situation in New Orleans.

Albert did not deny the reality of color prejudice among Negroes in the United States, but he ridiculed the official's comparison of this antipathy to the once deadly clash of blacks and mulattoes in Haiti. He insisted that the occasional antagonisms that the official noticed in the American South were the "outgrowth of conditions and not of blood." Albert also observed that, because white southerners had indiscriminately classed "free people of color" with the freedmen, black southerners had "almost everywhere fused into one homogeneous people." He thought that Louisiana provided a "notable exception" but explained that the divisiveness there resulted "not so much from the perpetuation of antebellum lines of division as from difference in language and religion" because most of the free people had largely been "French and Roman Catholics" and most freedmen held to "English and Protestant religion."

Despite his own fervent anti-Catholicism, Albert admired the creole radicals of New Orleans and worked so closely with them that their shared assertiveness eventually jeopardized his career as a Methodist church official. His knowledge of French and his militant racial views enabled him to bridge the two ethnic communities and to discern their cultural and occasional political differences.

From the fall of the Confederates in New Orleans in 1862 until well into the twentieth century, black creole leaders remained in the forefront of thinking and planning about the destiny of black people in the city. But these leaders never gained the full adherence of their own ethnic group because some creoles were ambivalent about the dramatic changes the Civil War brought to the city's social and racial order. A sizable number had joined the Confederate army during the first months of the war. Some felt pressured to do so, but their motivations differed. A few were probably enthusiastic Confederates, but such sentiment was rare, even among those who did not at first enthusiastically welcome the Union army.

When the Union army first occupied the city, for instance, Armand Lanusse, director of the Catholic Institute for Indigent Orphans, ignored General Benjamin F. Butler's order to hoist the American flag over the school. But his hesitance did not proceed from pro-Confederate feeling. The Civil War had tormented him. He served as an officer in the Native Guards, as he later explained in a letter to a black newspaper, to contribute to the defense of "his native land." His devotion to his native soil transcended his contempt for racial injustice in Louisiana. Despite his own reluctance to take up arms and possibly kill antebellum friends who had joined the Confederacy, he supported those black New Orleanians who joined the Union army. But the skeptical Lanusse refused to throw his loyalties quickly to any group of white Americans. In another letter, he elaborated on his reluctance to embrace the Union cause in the spring of 1861: "Many men thought that the prejudice of caste was going to disappear with the arrival of federal troops in this city. They wanted to forget that in every free state of the Union, this prejudice is

twice as strong as it was here before and during the rebellion.

Other attitudes heightened the complexity of reactions within the black creole community to the changes wrought by the war. Some black creoles had been slaveholders for the same reasons that whites were slaveholders and may have wished to perpetuate the peculiar institution. Others wished to protect their antebellum privileges that had set them apart from the degraded lives of most slaves. Some added a racial justification for their distinctiveness and tried to perpetuate their light skin color among their descendants. Still others wished to pass to a white identity. But such individual reactions cannot define the general attitudes of the overwhelming bulk of the black creole community and its leaders during the last half of the nineteenth century.

During the Civil War, a new generation of black creole leaders emerged, who condemned such castelike attitudes and quickly came to guide and dominate the political views expressed by their community. Indeed, for the rest of the century, the most radical and consistent position on almost every subject came from creole leaders and the small number of American black spokesmen who regularly allied with them. Whatever may have been the case in other areas of the South, no one has found any correlation of political conservatism, wealth, and light skin color among the black political leaders of New Orleans during the Civil War and Reconstruction.

If there was any hesitancy about the Union cause among the black creole leaders, it resulted, as with Lanusse, from the apparent conservatism of the Yankee leadership. Benjamin Butler, Lincoln's choice to govern occupied New Orleans, did not come to liberate or to enfranchise black Louisianians. His goals were not much different from those of Governor William C. C. Claiborne, whom Jefferson had sent to govern the area in 1803. Butler came to pacify the city and adapt its future to the purposes and outlook of federal authorities. He, too, feared slave insurrection and found it difficult to understand the free black creole leaders. Little in his American experience had prepared him for their status or requests.

When Butler sought to disarm the civilian population of the city, a group of free creole black leaders who had joined the Confederate Native Guards sent a four-man delegation to check on his intentions. To protect their interests and safety, they had hidden their meager store of weapons in three different locations. At least one circle of the free black militia had become organized into a vigilance committee (Comité de Vigilance) as early as the spring of 1861 and met in the hall of the oldest black organization in the city, the Economy Society (Société d'Economie et d'Assistance Mutuelle). A sizable number of the inner circle of this group also appeared to be tied together in the late antebellum period in a radical spiritualist society.

Butler evidently admired the educated and dignified demeanor of the delegation. Like most northern observers, he was also fascinated by the near-white complexion of many of the free black creoles. But in these first meetings, he showed no willingness to accept their offers to transfer their armed support to his occupation army. He was not ready to transform the war into a campaign of racial liberation.

Meanwhile, some other creole black leaders had already gathered around the bolder initiatives of General John W. Phelps, a Vermont abolitionist, whose forces guarded the river road above New Orleans from Confederate army counterattacks. Because his outpost, Camp Parapet, became a haven for fugitive slaves, Phelps decided to drill the young black men in military fashion and eventually requested standard equipment for them. His actions shocked and frightened Butler, but they pleased and attracted free creole black leaders, who met with him to encourage his efforts to arm black troops.

Such activities by the creole leaders forced the issue of black troops upon Butler and the national administration. At first, Butler tried to stop black recruitment by forcing Phelps to retire; but when President Abraham Lincoln shortly thereafter supported the idea of black soldiers, the ambitious Butler quickly got the message. He called back the leaders of the Native Guards and urged them to raise the first black regiment for the Union. Within a few weeks, the black activists filled the ranks of one regiment with free black volunteers and began to raise two more with recruits who were both free and enslaved, creoles and Americans. Their call for bilingual black officers demonstrated their desire to cross old ethnic and status lines for the purposes of defeating the Confederates and ending slavery.

Few, if any, incidents of antagonism based on ethnicity or color emerged within the black mili-

tary units, demonstrating how a common agenda of liberation could bind their ranks. Captain Henry L. Rey celebrated the triumph in a letter to a compatriot: "Come visit our camp. . . . In parade, you will see a thousand white bayonets gleaming in the sun, held by black, yellow or white hands. Be informed that we have no prejudice; that we receive everyone into the camp; but that the sight of salesmen of human flesh makes us sick; but, since we know how to behave, though Negroes, we receive them, completely concealing from them the violent internal struggle that their prejudice forces us to wage within ourselves."

Military service allowed antebellum free black men such as Rey to become active agents of liberation. Perhaps the most famous example was the dramatic service of Francis E. Dumas, a young, wealthy free black creole. Although Dumas may have inherited slaves from his family, he had grown up in France, where he "imbibed his Republicanism and principles of the equality of men." After the Union capture of the city, he returned to the state just in time to hear Butler's call for black troops. He served as a captain in the first black regiment but then obtained the rank of major to begin enrolling the second regiment. Disregarding the restriction against slave recruits, he not only enlisted slaves but also equipped them with his own funds after white officers refused to accept his authority as a major. What is more, he led them successfully in battle.

Demands for Equal Citizenship and Suffrage

The struggle to become voting citizens of Louisiana paralleled the difficult effort to become fighting soldiers and officers in the Union army. Once again the radical creole leaders set the pace and helped to fashion a coalition with black Americans and white radicals to assert claims for black suffrage that soon set the entire national agenda. They may well have discussed their concerns with Butler in the fall of 1862 and received some encouragement from him to form Union clubs and to begin a newspaper that would establish their claims to equal citizenship. Whatever the precise genesis of the campaign, on September 27, 1862—just a few weeks after Butler's call for black troops—Paul Trévigne, a highly respected figure in the antebellum creole black community, began editing *L'Union,* a biweekly French-language newspaper.

With amazing bravado, Trévigne set forth the objectives of the creole radicals: "We inaugurate today a new era in the South. We proclaim the Declaration of Independence as the basis of our platform.... You who aspire to establish true republicanism, democracy without shackles, gather around us." Trévigne had taught French history and literature and could draw upon more resources than the unfulfilled promises of the American Revolution. A few weeks later, he wrote of "a new sun, similar to that of 1789 . . . on our horizon."

French-speaking radicals like Trévigne had carefully noted that when France emancipated all remaining slaves in her possessions in 1848, authorities had also granted universal male suffrage, which enabled black Antillians to take political control of Guadeloupe and Martinique. Almost immediately after *L'Union* appeared in New Orleans, Trévigne used the experience in the French Antilles as a model for the United States. Writers in the paper could spin off the names of "Pory-Papy, Mazaline, Charles Dain, Louisy Mathieu, Périnon, and other celebrated blacks and mulattoes," who represented their native land in the French Chamber of Deputies after 1848. One exclaimed: "Ah, la France, in proclaiming liberty for blacks, did not try to expatriate them or colonize them in Chiriqui: she wanted to make them men and honored citizens.... Nations of America! ... model your fundamental principles on those of France, and like her, reach the heights of civilization."

L'Union, in the vanguard of almost all radical opinion in the United States, moved quickly during the revolutionary events of the war. Trévigne's self-assurance stemmed not only from the recent experience of blacks in French-controlled areas but also from the rich history of the black creoles of New Orleans. He reached back to those traditions to find legal support for his claims for black suffrage, recalling the demands of his ancestors for equal citizenship that they felt was promised to all free men in the Louisiana Purchase Treaty. This claim became particularly pertinent after Lincoln's attorney general, Edward Bates, challenged the *Dred Scott* decision and declared in November, 1862, that native free black people were to be regarded as citizens of the United States.

Trévigne's objective of achieving the full rights of citizenship for African-Americans in the United States seemed almost as visionary in 1862 as it had been for the free black creoles in 1803. It became even more unlikely when Butler left his command in December, 1862, and was replaced by the more racially conservative General Nathaniel P. Banks. The new military ruler and former governor of Massachusetts tried to assuage the conservative white Unionists of the city as well as racist elements within his army who had become disturbed by the "arrogance and intolerable self-assertion of black officers." By insult, humiliation, and dogged persistence, Banks began to drum almost every black commissioned officer out of the occupation army and refused to consider suffrage rights for anyone in the city's black community.

In reaction to Banks's reversal of gains won under Butler, free black leaders—both creole and American—began to coalesce as never before behind the political struggle launched by *L'Union.* Central to this coalition were the Prince Hall Masonic lodges that had been forced underground during the late 1850s. Even before the Civil War, creole and American leaders had begun to transcend barriers of language and culture. Oscar J. Dunn, a free black New Orleanian of American parentage, recruited free black creoles into his unit, the Richmond lodge, and by 1864, when Dunn became grand master of all the Prince Hall units in the city, this Masonic group provided an important nucleus for political activism. Together with other creole activists, they joined with a small group of white radicals led by Thomas J. Durant, whose Union Association made *L'Union* its official French organ on June 5, 1863. Within a month, the French newspaper became a triweekly and extended its reach in both the white and black English-speaking communities by publishing a bilingual edition.

For these free black activists, cooperation with white allies never meant subordination. When they met for the first time in an interracial rally in November, 1863, to consider equal suffrage, a conservative white Unionist urged them "not to ask for political rights" because racial prejudice among whites would not permit anything beyond emancipation. Led by P. B. S. Pinchback, an American newcomer, and François Boisdoré, a creole resident, black leaders protested sharply and pushed their reluctant white associates into support of voting rights for all black men who had been free before the war.

This initial demand did not exclude the possibility of extending suffrage to slaves. At this point, the radicals tried to shape their short-term strategy to fit the Bates decision that declared as citizens only those African-Americans who were legally free. Because Louisiana slaves had not yet been freed either by Lincoln's decrees or by any state action, they tried to convince Banks to include at least the black men who had been free before the war in the voting scheduled for February, 1864, to select a new Louisiana constitutional convention. When Banks ignored their requests for voting rights, they vowed to "go to President Lincoln." But before they could organize their efforts, Lincoln also disappointed them when, on December 8, 1863, he announced general guidelines for Reconstruction that excluded all black voters.

Despite these severe setbacks, the black leaders pressed forward. They bolstered their case for free black suffrage by drafting a petition on January 5 that was signed by a thousand free black property owners in the city, as well as twenty-seven black veterans of the War of 1812 and twenty-two white radicals. Simultaneously, they raised funds to send two delegates to bring the petition not only to Lincoln but also to Republican leaders in Congress. In mid-February, the two delegates—E. Arnold Bertonneau, a wine merchant, and Jean Baptiste Roudanez, a mechanical engineer—set off on their revolutionary mission.

The assertive position of these Franco-Africans on black suffrage placed them in the political vanguard of the entire nation because even the most radical Republicans feared the political risks among their northern constituents of turning black Americans into voters. Indeed, almost all northern states still limited suffrage to white males, and virtually no one in the country had yet taken up the question of black suffrage in the South. Congress had already buried one bill introduced by James Ashley, the ultra-radical Republican congressman from Ohio, and Lincoln as well as the radical members of his cabinet were treating the issue in the most cautious manner, afraid to speak out publicly. Even the radical wing of the abolitionists, including William Lloyd Garrison, continued to view suffrage as impractical as long as emancipation still required their attention. True, a few stalwarts, like Wendell Phillips and Frederick Douglass, had begun to call for black suffrage about the same time as the free black radicals of New Orleans; but when this small band of northerners pressed the issue during the winter of 1863–1864, they caused a major

rift in the abolitionist movement that led to a bitter feud between Phillips and Garrison.

When Bertonneau and Roudanez arrived in New York during this clash, they knew none of the Garrisonians or free black leaders in the North such as Frederick Douglass, Henry Garnet, and John Mercer Langston. Indeed, black northerners apparently first learned of the political demands of the New Orleanians only after their petition was noted in the New York *Evening Post.* After they arrived in Washington, however, Bertonneau and Roudanez quickly discovered that Lincoln and Banks did not represent the most advanced thinking in the Republican party.

A conference with the Massachusetts senator Charles Sumner and Representative William D. Kelly of Pennsylvania showed these creoles a new brand of American opinion. Together, on March 10, they produced an addendum to the petition of the New Orleanians in the form of a memorial signed by Bertonneau and Roudanez, which clarified that the principles behind their petition for free black voting "require also the extension of this privilege to those born slaves, with such qualifications as shall affect equally the white and colored citizen; and that this is required not only by justice, but also by expediency, which demands that full effect should be given to all the Union feeling in the rebel States, in order to secure the permanence of the free institutions and loyal governments now organized therein."

When Lincoln met the black New Orleanians on March 12, he was obviously impressed by their demands and demeanor. For the first time, the president received a firsthand account of Louisiana events from black leaders. Reportedly, Lincoln listened to them attentively and "sympathized" with their objectives but concluded that he would not act on moral grounds but only on grounds of military necessity. On the very next day, unbeknownst to the visitors, Lincoln wrote to the newly elected governor of Louisiana, Michael Hahn, urging him to make voters of "some of the colored people . . . as, for instance, the very intelligent, and especially those who have fought gallantly in our ranks." But these cautious, confidential suggestions had little effect because the Banks-dominated convention of 1864 made no provision for black suffrage except to allow the legislature to grant limited voting rights if it so wished.

Bertonneau and Roudanez did not return to New Orleans discouraged. Before they set off for home, the instant celebrities accepted various invitations to meet with white and black northerners. At first, northern black leaders reacted negatively to the two strangers from New Orleans. Indeed, Robert Hamilton, the influential New York editor of the weekly *Anglo-African*, denounced them at public meetings because their petition, as reported in the daily press, seemed intended to limit suffrage to free black men and to create legal castes among African-Americans. For that reason, the black editor praised Lincoln for rejecting their petition. Until this time, most northern black leaders, like Hamilton, had paid little attention to suffrage questions and postwar reconstruction of the South. Many of younger leaders, moreover, had also rejected the integrationist leadership of Frederick Douglass and directed their energies to emigration schemes in West Africa and Haiti. The dramatic actions of the New Orleans delegation now compelled them to reconsider their own objectives.

When Hamilton finally met the New Orleanians in New York following their meeting with Lincoln, he publicly confessed that he had totally misjudged them. The editor learned that they had originally insisted "that the right to vote must be asked for all, and not for those only who have all their lives been free." They also explained to him in detail the strategy of their white allies that was embodied in the petition and noted that they had accepted it only "after much persuasion and long deliberation." After this meeting, Hamilton pulled all stops in praise of their revolutionary campaign: "We say all hail, faithful Louisiana! This act shall decorate the brow of her dusky children with a crown of glory that shall be coequal with civilization itself." Within weeks, the editor came out in solid support of the New Orleanians and made their civil rights drive the basis of a call for a national convention of black Americans.

Bertonneau and Roudanez drew similar reactions from white abolitionists and Radical Republicans. Accepting an invitation to go to Boston, they attended a dinner meeting in their honor that included William Lloyd Garrison, Wendell Phillips, Frederick Douglass, and the incumbent Republican governor of Massachusetts, John A. Andrew. Seated on either side of the governor at the head of the table, the two creoles elaborated upon their unusual outlook and vision of a new society in the Americas.

Roudanez reported on the meeting with Lincoln and noted that their petition and memorial had also been laid before both houses of Congress. Bertonneau, a former captain of black Union troops, got more readily to the point. He described how his compatriots had given "imagination full scope and play" after Butler encouraged them to think of themselves as "men and citizens." He explained that their immediate objectives were that "the right to vote shall not depend upon the color of the citizen, that the colored citizens shall have and enjoy every civil, political and religious right that white citizens enjoy; in a word, that every man shall stand equal before the law." Their ultimate goal, he said, was to change "the character of the whole people" by sending their children to schools "to learn the great truth that God 'created of one blood all nations of men to dwell on the face of the earth'—so will caste, founded on prejudice against color, disappear." Bertonneau then turned to Garrison, president of the Massachusetts Anti-Slavery Society, and to prolonged applause vowed that he would urge his compatriots in New Orleans to fight for the same integration of public accommodations and schools that the Garrisonians had helped to inaugurate in Massachusetts. Clearly moved by the cheers, Garrison stood up and praised the visitors for "their self-respect, their dignity, and the noble regard which they feel for their oppressed brothers." Although he noticeably failed to applaud their suffrage cause, his comments still managed to bring the gathering to a loud rendition of the "John Brown Song." Before the gathering ended, however, the seasoned activist Frederick Douglass warned the New Orleanians that "the prospect was not so sanguine."

Black Creoles and White Yankees

Douglass was right. Bertonneau and Roudanez returned to a state where white conservative Unionists, with General Banks's sanction, were still meeting in a convention that steadfastly refused to grant suffrage to any black Louisianians, free or slave. Even before their return, *L'Union* had already shown its true colors by coming out for extending the suffrage to all freedmen and calling for "harmony among all the descendants of the African race." The editor, Trévigne, urged that voting qualifications be based on "the rightful capacity of all native and free born Americans, by virtue of their nativity in the country, irrespective of national descent, wealth or intelligence—and that all not free, within the state, be immediately enfranchised by the abolition of slavery in the state forever, and by a statute or constitutional provision declaring the absolute equality of all free men as to their governmental rights." The newspaper also praised the emissaries and heralded the new support and publicity that they had gained in the North for the enlarged cause of universal male suffrage. At the same time, Trévigne warned his readers how Napoleon had divided black Haitians and undermined the freedom and citizenship granted by the French Revolution of 1789. He therefore urged "all those of our race" to remember that "United, we stand! Divided, we fall!"

Banks resented the creole black leaders' successful recruitment of support from important northern Republicans. He had wanted to succeed Lincoln based on his accomplishments in Louisiana both as a military leader and as the political maestro of Reconstruction. When the widened campaign of the black creole leaders complicated his efforts, Banks and his cohorts went on a counterattack. At first, they made a frontal assault against the oracle of the criticism, L'Union. Thomas A. Conway, a Baptist chaplain, who had been assigned by Banks to clean up the general's scandal-ridden labor program, cut off the subsidy the black newspaper had received from the army for printing public notices.

The tactics almost worked. The collapse of the economy in New Orleans had placed terrible burdens on every inhabitant, including those in the free black community. Without the army's support, sustaining the triweekly paper—indeed, even subscribing to it—required not only financial sacrifice but also great courage. Nonetheless, the free black creole community stuck to its guns when Paul Trévigne announced that his desperate financial situation was forcing him to fold the only organ "which the oppressed class of the State ever had." Within a few days, Dr. Louis Charles Roudanez, the brother of J. B. Roudanez and a participant in the Paris revolution of 1848, came forward to finance another paper, the New Orleans *Tribune*, and gave its editor, Paul Trévigne, a more secure forum.

To herald the new paper's first issue and to bolster racial solidarity, a key group of American black leaders founded a new organization, the National Union Brotherhood Association, which publicly endorsed the *Tribune*'s political program. Each rebuff by Banks only seemed to increase the radicalism and confidence of the assertive black leaders. By fall, the new surge of community support enabled the *Tribune* to become the first daily black newspaper in the history of the United States. Its new, regular correspondents in Boston, Washington, and Paris also kept black New Orleanians in touch with those major centers of political and ideological influence.

To meet the new, enlarged challenge of the *Tribune*, another Banks associate struck from a different front. Major B. Rush Plumly, an abolitionist soldier from Pennsylvania, who had switched sides in Louisiana from the radical camp to the Banks group in early 1864, took up Banks's defense among his fellow abolitionists in the North by questioning the motives and attitudes of the free black creoles. Aware that Garrison had broken with Wendell Phillips and the majority of the New England abolitionists over their demand for universal suffrage in Louisiana, Plumly shrewdly nurtured the deeply hurt editor of the *Liberator.* Plumly's task was made easier when the *Tribune* fiercely attacked Garrison for not endorsing their demands for suffrage. Plumly bolstered the Bostonian's resentment by noting that many of "the free colored men have not yet forgotten that they were slaveholders" and had "not attained to all the grace and wisdom of freedom." In an open letter to the *Liberator,* Plumly pleaded with the abolitionists to realize that the *Tribune* was the mouthpiece of an "aristocratic" and "exclusive" caste that still remained loyal to the Confederacy and was "bitterly hostile to the black, except as a slave."

Plumly blatantly lied. From the beginning the *Tribune* had endorsed suffrage for the freedmen. Indeed, at the very moment that Plumly was making his wild charges, the *Tribune* was leading a campaign against the Smith bill then pending in the new state legislature. Designed by Banks, the bill proposed to enfranchise those free black men who were quadroons or lighter in complexion by legally defining them as white men. The *Tribune* condemned such a racist approach and ridiculed Plumly's general knowledge of all but a handful of free black creoles. Deeply angered, the *Tribune* editors renewed their fierce attack on those Yankees who denied their demands for universal male suffrage and equal citizenship: "The Garrisonians do not often forget that they belong to the white race, and seem to say to the Negro: 'now that you are free, you will go no further.' . . . It is in rising up against an arrogant and vindictive race that we sometimes run afoul of the feelings of those who play the part of defenders of the principles of the Declaration of Independence, and who dare not throw off their irrational and absurd prejudices.

Once Plumly and Conway realized that their attacks on the creole leaders had backfired, they tried to make amends by calling a meeting with the creole leaders to plead for their support for the Banks program. But this time, the Banks surrogates had fatally injured themselves. Like so many American power brokers, Conway and Plumly had a difficult time fathoming the radical politics of the Franco-Africans in New Orleans who sought no mere political favor from their agitation but rather an entirely new social and racial order.

The *Tribune* editors tried to explain their rejection of the overtures to negotiate their differences: "We do not fight for a material advantage that we can peddle between the two parties: we defend a principle. We can compromise with interests, but we cannot compromise with principles. Assured of the sound basis of our rights, we proclaim them, we uphold them fully and completely, and we will hear nothing of sacrificing them. . . . This is why we do not accept the proposition of the Major [Plumly] of supporting the new Constitution of Louisiana. . . . The revolution moves forward; we await our hour; it will come, and we will enter into the temple not dressed in the garb of the catechumen, led to the altar by a godfather and a godmother, but in the dress of Uncle Sam's men in arms."

The *Tribune* leaders would not retreat; they had gone too far in their struggle to win universal male suffrage. They had cemented a political coalition among black New Orleanians by drawing upon key allies within the American black community, particularly Oscar J. Dunn and James Ingraham. The former was the grand master of the Prince Hall Masons and the latter a Freemason and an AME church member as well as a hero for leading the first black combat troops of the war at Port Hudson.

As an officer of the city's National Union Brotherhood Association, Ingraham did more than draw together black Americans and creoles in New Orleans. He also linked the political efforts of the New Orleans radicals to a national organization of black Americans, the National Equal Rights League. In early October, 1864, at Syracuse, New York, that new group had come into existence during a reassembling of the prewar Negro Convention called by Henry Garnet and the editors of the *Anglo-African*. At this meeting, black delegates from all parts of the country met under the direction of Frederick Douglass to consider their role in a postwar society. They demanded unequivocal abolition of slavery and universal male suffrage. To help establish those demands, they formed the National Equal Rights League as a permanent civil rights federation.

After Ingraham captured the limelight at the Syracuse convention by waving his regiment's battle standard and pledging the largest amount of money to the new federation, he rushed back home to create a state chapter of the newly christened league at a state convention of black leaders in January, 1865. The gathering endorsed the resolutions of the Syracuse convention, formed the first state chapter of the league, and voted for Ingraham as its president and the *Tribune* as its official organ. These steps only reinforced the determination of the black radical leaders to defeat Lincoln's Reconstruction plans for Louisiana just then before Congress and to urge Republicans to impose black citizenship and universal male suffrage over the entire South.

Creole-American Division

The strategy of the radical faction in New Orleans pushed the Banks "oligarchy" into taking desperate measures that exploited lingering divisions within the black community of New Orleans. Having failed to isolate the New Orleans leaders from Northern abolitionists, Plumly and Conway now tried to open a wedge within the city's black community by recruiting black American Protestants to help them in their struggle against the creole-dominated opposition. As northern Protestants, Plumly (a Quaker) and Conway (a Baptist minister) appealed to religious and cultural prejudice to divide the black political opposition and seek support for their more moderate plans.

By 1865, the demography of the black population in New Orleans had changed dramatically. The percentage of black creoles in the city declined when almost fifteen thousand slaves fled into the city from the countryside, badly in need of housing, employment, medical care, education, and spiritual support. Most of the freedmen and women were English-speaking Protestants of American heritage. The freedom to build community organizations took up most of the energies of both black creoles and Americans. Unlike the political movements for emancipation and suffrage, this activity, however, often bolstered ethnic autonomy among both the creoles and the Americans.

With greater resources and freedom in the antebellum period, black creoles had already fashioned a considerable number of organizations, but emancipation brought several important changes. First, without the prewar legal restrictions, they could more easily cross the old barriers between those who had been free and those who had been slaves. Many slave residents in the antebellum city as well as postwar refugees from southern Louisiana who were French-speaking Catholic creoles became part of a working black creole community in New Orleans.

Black Catholic benevolent organizations rapidly expanded after Union occupation, particularly under the forceful leadership of a radical French-born Catholic priest, Father Claude Pascal Maistre, who in early 1863 began a radical congregation that prayed for Union victory, celebrated emancipation, and memorialized John Brown. After he was suspended by the city's archbishop, he continued to hold the allegiance of many black Catholics within his schismatic church. In July, 1863, his role first became notable in the city newspapers when he organized over thirty-seven black societies, primarily creole groups, to follow in the funeral procession of Captain André Callioux, the black hero of Port Hudson.

The presence of this famous priest symbolized the troubled relationship that had developed between the Catholic church and the city's black community. Since its founding in the city, the Catholic church had remained in the hands of foreign-born, French-speaking prelates and clergy. Indeed, as late as 1869, only one priest in New Orleans was American-born, and all of the bishops and archbishops of the church since its formal organization in 1793 had been ordained in Europe by French-speaking orders. The non-American origins of the clergy and the nuns probably help to explain why the Catholic church in southern

Louisiana offered various services for its black members and long resisted the complete racial segregation of its congregations.

Integrated churches, however, had not brought much semblance of racial equality in Catholic circles. Well before the Civil War, the diocese had forbidden racial intermarriage, denied the entrance of black men into the priesthood, and implemented segregation in its schools, cemeteries, and lay societies. In some churches, particularly uptown churches that catered to pugnacious Irish immigrants, black members had to use segregated pews and special entrances. In addition, the church prelates sanctioned slavery and gave enthusiastic support to the Confederacy.

The attitudes of Catholic church leaders led many black creoles to seek other forms of organization to meet their spiritual and communal needs. Some left the Catholic church for Protestant churches, but the most defiant leaders turned to traditional French, anticlerical outlets— spiritualist societies and Masonic lodges. In the North, American spiritualism had spread rapidly during the 1850s, deriving strength from the conversion of leading politicians, activists, and journalists. A similar surge of spiritualism occurred in New Orleans about the same time, but it proceeded from distinctly French origins and remained confined during the antebellum period to a limited group within the French-speaking population. It was to this tradition that key black creole leaders, such as Joanni Questy, Nelson Desbrosses, Henry and Octave Rey, Charles Vêque, Aristide Mary, Antoine Dubuclet, and Rodolphe Desdunes, turned for inspiration and direction.

An even larger and perhaps more important organization in the black creole community was the Scottish Rite Masonic order, under the jurisdiction of the grand master of France. Unlike the leaders of the Catholic church, the well-established French-speaking Masons made a bold and radical departure from the city's antebellum racial order. Shortly after the Civil War, they responded favorably to orders from French superiors to open their lodges to black members. When the local leader, Eugène Chassaignac, invited black New Orleanians to join his group, they responded enthusiastically. Within newly formed lodges, many prominent black creole men found not only spiritual but also political support from the colony of radical white French émigrés in New Orleans.

By 1867, the organizational structure of black creole society was largely intact. Antebellum groups such as the Economy Society, the Veterans of 1812, and the Society of Artisans openly flourished, and their members overlapped into anticlerical organizations such as the Masons and spiritualists. At one time or another, all of these groups endorsed the New Orleans *Tribune* or made it their official organ.

Community building was much more difficult for black New Orleanians of American heritage, particularly the freedmen who fled into the city during the war. From the beginning, the Federal army had tried to disperse these rural refugees back into agricultural labor on Union-controlled plantations, but the forced evacuations had created a national uproar. By early 1864, Banks—in response to his critics—permitted greater freedom of movement and began to provide for some of the educational and health needs of the freedmen. Various northern Protestant church groups had also sent missionary teachers and ministers to help in this monumental effort. After considerable political infighting among Federal officials and the religious missionaries, Plumly had emerged in charge of the freedmen schools and Conway had gained control of the labor program.

These positions gave Plumly and Conway a perfect opportunity to try to use the freedmen against the army's political adversaries, the creole-dominated radicals. Because most of the refugee freedmen and women in New Orleans were Americans with ties to the Baptists and Methodists, the Banks group worked closely with those churches. Since most of the black Baptists as well as the black members of the Methodist Episcopal Church, South, had already been dependent on white southern churchmen and benefactors, their new relationship with the white army personnel represented only a slight departure from their earlier dependency.

Even if there had been no political disagreements, black Protestant ministers and their white northern co-workers would probably have run into conflicts with the black creoles of New Orleans. Both black and white Protestants abhorred the Catholic faith that predominated among black creoles. Evangelistic fervor also led some of the preachers into believing that the black creole communities offered a major potential for conversions. One black Methodist minister exhibited this outlook when he boasted that many black Catholics had already thrown away "the rosaries or beads and come to Jesus. . . . In their religious delight they declared that they like our American God."

Protestant ministers disliked more than just the creoles' Catholicism. They also scorned the city's deeply rooted Afro-Latin way of life that offended their Anglo-Protestant sensibilities. The ministers condemned dancing, desecration of the Sabbath, gambling, drinking, lavish entertainment, and the open sensual pleasures that infused Mardi Gras and other public festivals in New Orleans. When, for example, black creoles tried to raise funds for orphanages or schools by holding raffles, the clerics denounced them as gamblers and urged their fellow Protestants not to cooperate. In one case, they even removed Protestant children from a nondenominational creole orphanage to keep them free of such Catholic influence.

A fundamental difference about race relations also caused friction between the two groups. Creole leaders resented racial separation even in private institutions and constantly nagged black as well as white recalcitrants about any adherence to the color line. Most of the Protestant leaders, however, had responded to racial discrimination in Anglo-America by forming their own all-black institutions where they could find solace and support. The reluctance of most black creoles to adopt Victorian behavior or to accept the norms of the American color line struck some black Americans as a denial of racial solidarity.

The leaders of the *Tribune* tried to surmount the rivalries. In addition to printing their newspapers in English as well as French, they opened special columns for news of Protestant churches and fraternal organizations. They also hired a black American assistant editor, Moses Avery, who was the secretary of the National Union Brotherhood Association in New Orleans. In the midst of the intrablack power struggle, Dr. Roudanez made another important change by recruiting an outsider, Jean-Charles Houzeau, to edit the paper's English columns.

Houzeau, a radical Belgian émigré who had fled from Texas because of his abolitionist views, concentrated on healing the divisiveness stimulated by the Banks cohorts. He quickly recognized that the primary obstacle to greater unity stemmed from the "spirit of independence" among the "Franco-Africans." Their stubborn pride and assertiveness led them to resent the white Yankees who dominated Unionist politics in Louisiana. Houzeau never seemed to understand the depth of the antagonism that the racially conservative white Unionists had created among the black creoles before he arrived in November, 1864, but he realized that most black Louisianians of Anglo-American heritage rejected the creole leaders' hostility to the white northerners who were doing so much to help the Protestant freedmen.

When Houzeau reached New Orleans, the two-year-long battle between the *Tribune* leaders and the Banks forces was well under way; by early 1865, it had reached a critical stage. At that point, the creoles and their black American allies in the National Equal Rights League of Louisiana joined forces with Radical Republicans in Congress to defeat a bill backed by Lincoln's administration to restore Louisiana to the Union. Because the Radicals had insisted upon universal black male suffrage throughout the South, they felt that Louisiana's restoration without any black suffrage would jeopardize their larger goals.

The editors of the *Tribune* continued to direct their Gallic rage against all of their critics inside and outside of Louisiana. When, for example, William Lloyd Garrison justified his public endorsement of Lincoln's Reconstruction bill for Louisiana by noting that the British had not enfranchised the slaves they emancipated in the West Indies, the editors lashed out against him. They urged the abolitionists to broaden their vision to areas beyond the English-speaking world, where universal male suffrage had never been tried. They proclaimed that their own demands for equality came from the experiment in French territories, where "at the moment that liberty was proclaimed, legal equality was immediately a fact." They wanted America to follow that example and put into its Constitution what the French had done in theirs by declaring "all Frenchmen without distinction of class or color . . . equal before the law." The *Tribune* wondered why the "proud Anglo-Saxon" hesitated "to fulfill an act of justice."

To counter this resolute opposition in New Orleans, Conway and Plumly reached out to black American leaders, particularly the Baptist and Methodist Episcopal preachers. The two officials tried to placate some of the black opposition by circulating a petition to the Louisiana legislature in support of limited black suffrage. In part, their strategy worked. Conway and Plumly also gained enough support among black Protestant leaders to force a reconvening of the National Equal Rights League chapter in the city, but after several votes failed to reverse the group's earlier stand against the petition for limited suffrage, the Banks forces devised another strategem to offset the *Tribune*'s effective attack on their halfway measures.

In April, 1865, they launched the *Black Republican* under the apparent leadership of two Baptist ministers and several other leaders in the black American community. To Banks, who was directing the administration's efforts in Washington, Conway exaggerated his little conspiracy, claiming that "the American negroes are indignant" about the attacks of "the rich colored men" and were starting the paper "to more fully represent the cause of the black man." Plumly joined in the distortion by writing to Lincoln that "the American colored people here, disgusted with the 'N. O. Tribune'—the French Jesuit (color'd) paper, that under Durant and a few colored Creoles, has always been against us—are just starting another paper. . . . It will be out in a few days. I have been requested, by the Association to send the first copy to you, with the renewed expression of the undying gratitude and confidence of the People of Color."

The columns of the *Black Republican* nurtured the potential ethnic antagonisms within the black community of New Orleans. The paper repeated Plumly's old innuendos about wealthy, free black creoles and their non-American sentiments. It praised Banks and his labor program and found excuses for his failure to implement black suffrage in Louisiana. On the key issue of suffrage, the *Black Republican* meekly noted: "It would be an anomaly in the history of politics to change in a short season the usages of a State like this to such as to confer upon the colored race rights and privileges heretofore not enjoyed by them in any other state of the Union save one."

The Banks cohorts also turned to black American leaders who had come to New Orleans after the Union occupation. Some, like the Baptist minister S. W. Rogers, had come to establish new Protestant churches; some, like Edmonia Highgate, to teach in the freedmen schools; and still others, like P. B. Randolph, to take advantage of the new promising field for their political ambitions.

Randolph was an extraordinary man who had already traveled to Europe, Asia, and Africa. He was well-known in black communities of Boston and New York and had played a key role in the Syracuse convention of October, 1864. He came to New Orleans with the intention of "bringing my Southern brethren up to the highest standard of [the] men of Boston." Such presumptuousness, however, did not sit well with the proud creoles. They needed no one to lecture them about the world or their aspirations. When Randolph arrived, he met an "icy" reception and quickly learned that he had no understanding of New Orleans. He could compare the vast mixture of races, nationalities, and cultures only to "Beyrout, Syria." Because he was curious and fluent in French and English, he eventually discerned the "two totally distinct and widely divergent classes" of people within black New Orleans, which he perceptively labeled "Creole and American." Creoles, he also discerned, were "not as many suppose . . . the miscegens or mixed bloods, but . . . natives of the city." He noticed, too, that "the lines between the separate sections of colored Society here, are distinctly marked. Very few French live above Canal St., very few Americans below it, and save politically, they seldom affiliate."

Randolph, who arrived in the midst of the contest between the creoled *Tribune* faction and the Banks forces, picked his sides. After he and his cousin from Boston, Frank Potter, gained jobs in the army schools under Plumly, the newcomers joined the fray against the creoles. In the New York *Anglo-African*, Randolph insisted that the National Equal Rights League of Louisiana had been packed by black creoles and did not represent the view of most black Louisianians. "My entire sympathy," he declared, "is with the freedmen and the American people, for the reason that they do the fighting; but I see no French soldiers— not one. . . . There may be . . . but we outnumber them ten hundred to a single one, and therefore if any interest predominates, it ought to be ours, not theirs. Vive l'Amerique touts les jours!" Randolph ended his letter by complimenting General Banks, praising Conway as "the noble heart," and insisting that Plumly's "glorious acts in our favor deserve to be written in the same constellation."

The black creole leaders in New Orleans did not flinch. When they learned of Randolph's letter, they reprinted it openly in New Orleans and dared Randolph to prove his charges. They also declared him no "true representative of the North" and "unworthy of a place in our commu-nity." Thoroughly ostracized, he lost his job as a regular columnist of the *Anglo-African* and quietly disappeared from the political scene. He had more than met his match in New Orleans.

Despite their unscrupulous and damaging plots to divide the New Orleans black community, Banks and his cohorts failed to undermine the radical program for racial change in Louisiana. For the next three years the *Tribune* evoked the political demands of the New Orleans black community without any significant dissent. And no black leader appeared to take a more radical position than the *Tribune*.

The only notable division came during the terrible riots of 1866, when the last antebellum mayor of the city, John T. Monroe, returned to power and unleashed full police power against a pro-black suffrage convention in July, 1866. The repression caused Methodist Episcopal leaders to urge their black members to pull back from the political arena. Another black emigrationist leader, John Willis Menard, who came to the city from Illinois, via British Honduras and Jamaica, where he had seen a similar backlash in 1865, also recommended a retreat in a pamphlet entitled *Black and White*. He thought that the "African race" should turn inward and "help itself." The *Tribune* editors could sympathize with his racial pride, but they refused to accept Menard's view that universal suffrage had been demanded "too soon or too harshly" and should be abandoned in favor of "suffrage on the basis of intelligence" to encourage "the friendship of the dominant class" and to gain "security of life, liberty, and property." Instead, the *Tribune* editors bemoaned that the enactment of universal suffrage had not come before the end of the war and that its delay had only encouraged violent opposition. The right to vote, they insisted, had to remain "an attribute of citizenship."

The *Tribune* agenda held the day, despite some of the worst racial violence in the South. Black Louisianians not only gained universal male suffrage but also went beyond almost all other southern states in their attempts to end racial segregation. Indeed, the paper's Belgian editor played a major role in 1866 in winning support for universal male suffrage by continuing the paper during the height of the violence and broadcasting news about it, which helped turn the political tide against Andrew Johnson and pass the Fourteenth Amendment and the Reconstruction acts. In their constitution of 1868 and in subsequent legislation, the Louisiana radicals mandated the integration of all government facilities, including public schools, and also all private businesses licensed by the state to serve the public. In quest of these ends, black leaders remained united behind the agenda set by the *Tribune* leaders—at least for a time.

Cultural Transfers in Black New Orleans

More than a common political agenda in the early years of Reconstruction helped to diminish ethnic differences and unify the black community of New Orleans. Educational needs, particularly in the creole sectors, led many of the Catholic French-speakers into closer association with Protestant English-speakers. True, free black Catholics had reached relatively high levels of literacy before the Civil War, but only the wealthiest families could send their children outside the city for schooling beyond the elementary grades. A few orders of Catholic nuns offered elementary education in their antebellum parochial schools, but none opened their doors to black boys. And until after World War II, the Jesuits, Christian Brothers, and diocesan clergy limited the use of their schools and academies in New Orleans to white males.

Although the number of Catholic schools expanded rapidly after the Civil War from about ten elementary schools and three high schools to about sixty schools and academies by 1885, only five of them accepted a total of about three hundred black students out of the approximately ten thousand children in the entire Catholic system in the city. Most black creoles had to turn to public and Protestant schools for an education. Because Benjamin Butler ended the use of French as a teaching language when he consolidated the city's three separate public school districts in 1862, those institutions became a powerful instrument of Americanization for many French-speaking white and black creoles in the postwar era. To be sure, a few private tutors tried to keep alive the French language, history, and literature, but not many black creole families could afford to pay their fees.

For secondary or higher education, most black creoles also had to turn to Protestant colleges that opened during Reconstruction: Leland College (Baptist), New Orleans University (Methodist), and Straight University (Congregational). Straight University proved the most popular for black Catholics during the nineteenth century both because it was closer to their downtown neighborhoods and because it apparently made less effort to proselytize its student body. Some creole leaders tried to avoid this dilemma by founding a nondenominational, public land-grant college, the Agricultural and Mechanical College, but its duration as a desegregated college was too short to have much effect. During Reconstruction, all of the public high schools in the city enrolled black students, but between 1879 and 1917 no city-run high school was available for black students in New Orleans. For secondary education they had only the preparatory schools of the Protestant-dominated colleges or the meager facilities of the segregated, state-sponsored Southern University.

American black leaders also set the pace in establishing organizations that linked black New Orleanians to other black people in the United States. Drawing on national associations elsewhere, they duplicated local units in New Orleans after the Civil War. These included the Odd Fellows in 1866, the Knights Templar in the 1870s, the Knights of Pythias in 1881, and the Eastern Star, a women's auxiliary of the Prince Hall Masons. Because many of these benevolent organizations were nonsectarian, both Catholic and Protestant blacks in New Orleans could join in association. The Odd Fellows made a special point of downplaying religious views and concentrating on the sheer joy of camaraderie. The penchant for forming branches of national groups became such a craze by the 1880s that one newspaper found them "so numerous . . . that they can scarcely be enumerated." So it must have seemed, for by the early twentieth century, more than 280 clubs and organizations were meeting regularly in New Orleans.

In addition to their commingling in schools and benevolent societies, black Americans and creoles also transcended ethnic boundaries in their social life and entertainment. Black newspapers during the 1870s and 1880s regularly noted this interaction. The well-established creole lifestyle of good food, dance, music, gambling halls, ritualized festivals, and marching bands quickly caught the attention of the Protestant newcomers. One Protestant reporter who covered a sumptuous creole ball for the *Louisianian* confessed that he did not dance but still admired creole frolicking: "We love music and dancing, and chatting with the Belles." Although some creole societies showed religious exclusivity by beginning their parades and outdoor dances with a mass at the cathedral, uptown Protestants quickly copied the creole customs of "music, dancing, feasting, and romps" in their own neighborhoods. By the 1880s their own marching bands were stopping at Protestant churches to have their banners "blessed."

The pace of this creolization frightened some of the Protestant leaders. The *Louisianian* warned: "Whilst patronizing liberally balls and parades, our young men should not forget the revivals at St. James [AME] and Central [Congregational] churches. Remember the hereafter." The ministers were less restrained. The Methodist newspaper was particularly scornful of the regular frivolity in the city and noted that the lures of "the dance, the card table, and the theater" were leading the young people away from the church. The editor called for a revival of religion to "shut up theaters, dancing houses, and rum holes."

When one of the white Methodist Episcopal bishops, John F. Hurst, came from the North, he could hardly believe the city's scandalous behavior. He noted that "there is certainly no place in the country where it is more difficult . . . for a Christian to preserve his religious fervor, than in New Orleans." But at the same time he had to recognize that "there is a cheerful air throughout the city. In the French or English part, it makes no difference—all is bright, cheery, hopeful. . . . There is less anxiety in the face and speech than one generally finds among Americans." By 1894, even the more disciplined black Methodist preachers of this bishop's church were "sprinkling" banners, regalia, dolls, and other paraphernalia and holding festivals on Saturday night that extended "far into the Sabbath." Drawing from this peculiar creole-American cultural interchange, black New Orleanians added many new features to the city's vibrant folk culture—none more famous than the new musical forms of jazz.

Despite all these examples of erosion in the ethnic boundaries of their communities, black creoles and Americans continued to concentrate in different neighborhoods and often formed separate social and cultural institutions. And if they worked together in the early years of Reconstruction to win impressive political and civil rights, their leaders never fully surmounted the rivalries that reflected their different values, goals, and aspirations. Throughout the late nineteenth century, the major division among black politicians still ran along the creole-American rift that had been exacerbated by the Banks leaders in 1865. New black and white leaders may have entered the political scene, but, like earlier leaders, some still continued to stir the ethnic divisions.

Henry C. Warmoth and the Creoles

After 1867, the radical creole leaders who had so brilliantly maintained their agenda of revolutionary demands found it more difficult to exert the same dominance in the more normal electoral politics initiated by the Reconstruction acts of 1867. They did not shrink away from the new political arena, but they found it difficult to win elective office, proving to be better agitators than pragmatic politicians. By 1868, they lost control of the Republican party to a coalition of white carpetbaggers and American black leaders.

The nature of the electoral districts in New Orleans helps to explain the meager number of black creoles in the Reconstruction legislatures. Since less than 30 percent of the city's population was black from 1860 to 1900, no creole electoral district had a black majority to provide a secure voting base for their candidates. In their racially mixed neighborhoods, only Algiers on the west bank of the river contained even a substantial black voting plurality, and it was from this ward that a key black creole politician, A. J. Dumont, found the base for his leadership position in the local Republican party during the 1870s and early 1880s.

The large mass of black voters in Louisiana lived outside of New Orleans. After the war, several black creoles left the city to seek office in black rural districts, such as Jacques Gla in Carroll Parish and Louis Martinet and Emile Detiège in St. Martin Parish. Particularly in the south Louisiana sugar parishes, where French-speaking Catholic slaves had been concentrated, a few New Orleans creoles managed to find an electoral base, but not many, it seems, wished to uproot themselves from their urban homes and life-styles to seek office in the isolated countryside. Besides, resident black leaders in those areas had their own ambitions.

Some black creole leaders from New Orleans managed to win major statewide positions. In addition, they vied to retain control of the Louisiana Republican party and sought the governorship for a black candidate more energetically than any comparable group of black leaders elsewhere in the South. But they lost those two power struggles in Louisiana, largely because of the ethnic division within the black population both in the city and the state.

By 1867, Henry C. Warmoth, a brilliant young politician, fell heir to the Banks forces after Andrew Johnson dismissed the Massachusetts general and restored Confederate leaders to power in Louisiana. During the summer of 1865, in the face of Johnson's obdurate and reactionary policies, Warmoth brought about a fusion of the Banks moderate forces and the *Tribune* radicals to create the Republican party of Louisiana and then shrewdly used it to push his own candidacy for governor. Anticipating opposition, he not only stacked the nominating convention of 1867, but he also carefully nurtured the rivals of the black creoles in the black American community.

As a member of the Ames Methodist Episcopal Church pastored by the Reverend John P. Newman, Warmoth formed an important alliance with that key white leader among the black Methodists. Only several months before the nominating convention, Newman had reopened the old ethnic feud among black New Orleanians when he condemned the *Tribune*'s call for a black mayor in New Orleans. In his weekly newspaper, the New Orleans *Advocate,* Newman rhetorically asked, "Shall white men or black men rule this city?" He answered by warning his largely black Methodist readership against "certain men of color in New Orleans who now claim the exclusive right to rule this city." When Newman threatened to encourage Protestant freedmen to revolt against the black creole radicals, the *Tribune* editors flew into a rage against the northern "philanthropists" who wished to divide black New Orleanians "in politics, in religion, in social relations." They countered the Methodist editor with charges of their own: "We understand fully, Mr. Advocate, why you do not like us. It is because

when you came here, you expected to find a servile population, and you have found MEN."

The *Tribune* insisted that "the idea of having the freedmen cut away from the creoles will not work." The paper admitted that the two groups differed "somewhat in religious matters" but confidently declared that "the interests and the blood of both classes will keep them as a unit." In making this prediction, the *Tribune* editors drew confidence, no doubt, from their earlier victories over the Banks forces, but this time they clearly underestimated the political abilities of Warmoth as well as the new divisions that had been developing between themselves and some key black American leaders.

The conflict with Newman involved much more than a black or white mayor. The *Tribune* had been pressing for a new state constitution that would bring not just universal male suffrage but also desegregated schools and public accommodations. The paper's vision of a new society threatened many conservative and moderate white Louisianians: "We want to inaugurate a state of things in which the law and authorities will know but citizens, and in no case discriminate, be it at the school door, between any class of these citizens. . . . Our society should be one—formed of one people instead of two—keeping only as immaterial varieties, unknown to the law and its officers, the differences of origin, color, fortune, education, language, religion and physical strength. . . . None is a true Republican who says 'it is too soon.'"

To counter this concept of a color-blind civil order, many white Republicans excoriated "Africanization" and "social equality" with almost as much ease as their Democratic opponents. Few white Republicans endorsed the black radicals' vision of civic fraternity. Indeed, Henry C. Warmoth mobilized his conservative faction of white Republicans around opposition to the *Tribune*'s call for the integration of public schools.

Just when the *Tribune* leaders were quarreling with Warmoth and Newman, several of the paper's staff engaged in another, more damaging conflict with their most important black American ally, Oscar J. Dunn. When the white French Masons opened their Scottish Rite lodges to black New Orleanians, many of those who accepted the invitation were French-speaking creoles who had earlier joined the Prince Hall (York Rite) lodges headed by Dunn. As leading creoles, including *Tribune* editor Paul Trévigne, formed rival lodges, both sides engaged in rancorous accusations that produced lasting bitterness between the competitive Masonic organizations. The wrangling also exposed a serious difference over racial values among black New Orleanians.

Dunn had long supported the radical demands of the black creole leaders to remove all color bars from public life, but he did not feel that the logic of integration extended to the voluntary societies that blacks had fostered within their communities. He also accused the white French-speaking Masons of avoiding the challenge of true integration by forming all-black units within their grand lodge. He was wrong in this charge, but such accusations demonstrated how severely the creole desertions had antagonized some of their key American allies. The mutiny in Prince Hall ranks coincided, moreover, with Dunn's personal defeat as a delegate to the constitutional convention from a ward with numerous black creole voters. Both losses made Dunn ready to seek political revenge.

Carefully nurturing these divisions, Warmoth gained critical support from black delegates when he sought the Republican nomination for governor of Louisiana. When the creole radicals could not get their trusted white ally, Thomas J. Durant, to accept the nomination and instead turned to a black candidate, Major Francis Dumas, Warmoth's friends raised the fear of black rule among whites and, at the same time, portrayed Dumas among black Americans as a conservative former slaveholder. Relying primarily on a rising black American leader, P. B. S. Pinchback, to convince black delegates that it was not time to elect a black governor, Warmoth won the nomination by just one vote and then named Oscar J. Dunn as his nominee for lieutenant governor.

In their most serious mistake of the entire Reconstruction era, the owners of the *Tribune*—forcefully led by Dr. Louis Charles Roudanez—refused to support the Warmoth-Dunn ticket. They rejected the advice of their Belgian associate, Jean-Charles Houzeau, to wait for another chance to win control of the party. Instead, they discouraged Dumas from accepting the lieutenant governorship proffered by the Warmoth wing and set up an alternative ticket headed by a white Republican, James G. Taliaferro, with Dumas running for lieutenant governor. It was a terrible

blunder born of anger and stubbornness. True, Taliaffero had been a remarkably defiant Unionist, but he also had been a slaveholding planter. Even some of the *Tribune*'s most loyal creole supporters, such as the Rey brothers and Emile Detiège, refused to join the bolt by Roudanez from the regular Republican ticket, and the mass of Louisiana's black voters, particularly the freedmen outside of the city, remained loyal to the party of Abraham Lincoln.

After Warmoth's victory, black creole leaders never recovered their dominant leadership role in black political circles. When the national Republican party cut off its subsidies to the *Tribune*, the discouraged Belgian managing editor decided to quit, and a more conservative, white newspaper, the New Orleans *Republican*, replaced it as the official organ of the party in Louisiana. Although the *Tribune* continued sporadically as an independent Republican weekly until 1870, it never regained its former stature as the daily oracle of the black community in New Orleans. The sudden turn of political events made many of those who had sacrificed so much to keep it going for three years as a daily newspaper reconsider their careers. Both the primary owner, Dr. Roudanez, and the managing editor, Jean-Charles Houzeau, felt that their political work had reached a fitting conclusion with the passage of the national Reconstruction acts and the new Louisiana constitution. The Belgian radical returned to Europe, and the black doctor virtually abandoned politics.

It was inevitable, moreover, that black American leaders such as Dunn and Pinchback would assume greater influence and visibility among the overwhelming numbers of black voters in the city and especially the state who shared their Anglo-American cultural background rather than the Franco-African traditions of the New Orleans creoles. The alliance between Pinchback and Warmoth also appeared to lay a more practical base for the new era of electoral politics. Pragmatic and gifted, Pinchback extracted major rewards and benefits from the Warmoth administration for himself and a growing circle of his political associates, who like their boss had honed their skills elsewhere in the United States and only recently migrated to New Orleans.

The dominance of American leadership did not, however, mean that the creoles abandoned politics in a fit of disillusionment and despair.

Quite the contrary: in 1869, they staged a comeback of sorts after Warmoth vetoed various measures to enforce the integration of public schools and public accommodations that had been mandated in the constitution of 1868. By mending their quarrels with Oscar J. Dunn, black creole leaders also temporarily restored their old radical, biethnic coalition, first to pass measures in the legislature to enforce desegregation and then, in the face of continued opposition from Warmoth, to help make Dunn the state's governor by impeaching Warmoth. And they almost succeeded despite Pinchback's backing of Warmoth. But Dunn's sudden death in 1871, under mysterious circumstances, ended the campaign and allowed Warmoth to use his influence in the state senate to elevate Pinchback to Dunn's old position as lieutenant governor.

The creole leaders continued the struggle after Dunn's death. Joining with an anti-Warmoth faction of white Republicans led by William P. Kellogg, they helped remove Warmoth from office in 1872. Scornful of the temporary governor, Pinchback, they tried to nominate another black creole, Aristide Mary, as the Republican candidate for governor in 1872. When that effort failed, the creole leaders helped elect Kellogg as governor and C. C. Antoine, a bilingual black Methodist from northern Louisiana, as lieutenant governor. For the next decade, the black creoles warily backed Kellogg's customshouse faction, which controlled the Republican party in Louisiana. But this loose alliance was powerless either to advance the radical cause of the creoles or to stop the violence that, after 1874, engulfed the northern part of the state and kept black voters there from participating freely in local and state elections. When the Grant administration refused to intervene any longer in the South to ward off such violence, the white Democrats gained control of Louisiana in the disputed election of 1876 and proceeded to undermine almost every gain that black Louisianians had made during Reconstruction.

The ethnic division within the New Orleans black community may help to explain some of the factionalism among black New Orleans leaders, but it cannot explain the collapse of Reconstruction in Louisiana. If anything, black Louisianians, despite their divisions, held off the relentless force of white violence longer than black southerners did in other states. Warmoth rightly recalled the black creoles in his history of Louisiana Reconstruction as the ultra-radicals, even if he distorted their objectives as an attempt to "Africanize" the state.

Creoles, Americans, and the Redeemers

For black New Orleanians, the collapse of Reconstruction ended neither political involvement nor their old ethnic and personal antagonisms. The latter survived the restoration of white conservative control, not only because the black creoles never forgave Warmoth and Pinchback for undermining their plans during Reconstruction, but also because their political rivalry continued after the Democrats returned to power under Governor Francis T. Nicholls. When Pinchback's conciliatory gestures about the Compromise of 1877 won political patronage from both President Rutherford B. Hayes and Nicholls, creole leaders accused him of party and racial treason. The conflict reached a zenith, however, when Pinchback extended his cozy relationship by supporting the Redeemers' new constitution of 1879 in exchange for the black college, Southern University.

Pinchback defended his actions as realistic in face of the abandonment of southern blacks by the national Republican party. He declared: "I have learned to look at things as they are and not as I would have them . . . this country, at least so far as the South is concerned, is a white man's country. . . . What I wish to impress upon my people, is that no change is likely to take place in our day and generation that will reverse this order of things."

The creole leaders rejected such talk and never forgave his apostasy. Their chief political spokesman after 1876, Judge A. J. Dumont, maintained a running battle with Pinchback for control of the Republican party. Despite the apparent futility, Dumont and other creoles in New Orleans also opposed the Constitution of 1879 because it sanctioned segregated public schools and public accommodations. Many years later, in 1893, at the funeral of Aristide Mary, Rodolphe Desdunes expressed the bitterness that still lingered among his fellow creoles for Pinchback's betrayal.

In his memorial, Desdunes contrasted Pinchback with Aristide Mary in much the same way that he later, in remarks addressed to W. E. B. Du Bois, tried to contrast the political viewpoints of

"Latin Negroes" and "Anglo-Saxon Negroes." Desdunes made Pinchback's outlook a symbol of "American reasoning" in which "the first principle was to succeed." Mary, he felt, operated on "entirely French ideas" in insisting on principles and self-respect. He extended the parallel by portraying Mary as the principal architect of the state's radical constitution of 1868 and Pinchback as the apologist of the reactionary Redeemers' constitution of 1879.

To explain Mary, a dark mulatto, Desdunes made no reference to skin color but instead referred to an episode in which Mary refused to give up his candidacy for governor in 1872 in exchange for the lieutenant governorship. Desdunes explained: "Mary understood that equality could not take up its residence within the domain of subordination, and that compromises which resulted in this political anomaly, only postponed the solution which we envisioned with the abolition of slavery." The real test of contrasting political outlooks, however, came over the constitution of 1879, when Pinchback publicly acceded to the segregation of the public schools in return for the creation of the all-black Southern University. Desdunes recalled how Mary "thundered with indignation against the scheming of men of color who took part in the Convention of 1879." Because Mary saw Pinchback as the leader of the group who accepted a segregated black college, the creole radical "never spoke a word to Pinchback from that time until his death" because of his "contempt for the man who had said that 'this government is a government of whites,' in order to justify his conduct on this occasion." Mary's stance, Desdunes claimed, had "the support and sympathy of the population called creole.

Although something of a hyperbole, Desdunes' polarization of political outlooks rings true. Creole leaders such as Mary and Desdunes refused to accommodate to the new color line in Louisiana or the rest of America. Despite their obvious abandonment by the national Republican party, they undertook various forms of resistance to Jim Crow laws and other denials of civil rights. When Democrats resegregated the city schools and public accommodations in 1877, they sued under the state constitution of 1868. When the Bourbons passed the state constitution of 1879, which sanctioned such segregation, they turned to the federal courts for relief.

Although many prominent black Americans joined with the creole leadership in these battles, increasing numbers of black American leaders in the South followed the path of Pinchback in seeking some form of racial accommodation with the more moderate southern white Democrats. After 1876, black and white Methodist Episcopal leaders in the region, for example, began to articulate such ideas. When the more assertive black Methodists in Louisiana under the leadership of the white radical presiding elder, Joseph C. Hartzell, resisted the general Methodist tendency, national church leaders tried to halt the carping dissent in Louisiana by removing Hartzell from the editorship of the *Southwestern Christian Advocate*. His replacement, Marshall Taylor, was a black minister from Kentucky, who proved more acceptable to the national leaders.

Within a few months, the newspaper took a new line. It defended the development of racially exclusive Methodist districts in the South, condemned interracial marriages, and urged its black readers to turn inward and away from politics and the white community. Taylor, who had been free in antebellum Kentucky and Ohio, acknowledged that "deeds of violence here and there now occur" but insisted that the post-Reconstruction South offered black residents opportunities to find "a life of wealth and power." He therefore urged "less of politics and more acres for awhile." Still later he suggested that his readers "let politics alone and attend strictly to getting money, land, education, sound morals and religion."

To be sure, many creole families also turned inward toward their own communities and kinship networks to escape the wave of racial oppression and humiliation that was overtaking the South, but their organized leadership in New Orleans seldom, if ever, took the conservative and racialist stand of Marshall Taylor and other leaders who were assuming greater authority in the black American communities of the city and the state. Instead, the creole leaders used what few weapons they had to resist the reactionary movement of the southern Bourbons.

Rodolphe Desdunes and the *Crusader*

The primary strategist of creole resistance was the remarkable young intellectual and activist

Rodolphe Desdunes. He not only saw himself as a leader following in the traditions of the Civil War radicals but was their protégé, since he had not only studied French literature and history as their student but also modeled his life after their examples. He wrote in both French and English, but most elegantly in French. And throughout his life he turned to the radical ideals of France in 1848 "because all Frenchmen were equal before the law."

Although too young to play a major role in the events of the 1860s in New Orleans, Desdunes emerged in the public eye during the mid-1870s because of his refusal to surrender to the violent counterrevolution in Louisiana. He felt certain that the virtual lack of organized protest and resistance among blacks only encouraged the growing number of lynchings of rural blacks in the northern part of the state. He also came forward to challenge the corruption and conservatism that had infiltrated the Republican party in Louisiana. In 1878, to instill renewed militancy and idealism among younger black leaders, he helped organize a key group of creoles and Americans into the Young Men's Progressive Association. "If we are citizens of this great and free country," they declared, "we demand our rights as such." Desdunes openly labeled himself a "radical" and allied with the creole-dominated faction of the party against the cautious approach of Pinchback's largely American faction.

While attending the integrated law school of Straight University, from which he gained a law degree in 1882, Desdunes became convinced that the federal courts offered black southerners the best opportunity to reverse their declining status. By 1881, he began to agitate for an "Association of Equal Rights" to support a counterattack in the courts to protect black voting rights. "It is time," he wrote, "that some of these 'unregenerates' should know that we mean to test their legal right to humiliate us. . . . It is the duty of colored men to fight for an equal chance in the race of life and not depend upon the generosity of others to do so for them."

Desdunes increasingly reached back into his French and creole heritage for a radical ideology and militant tradition. Not only did he draw on his knowledge of French history and literature, but he also nurtured his outlook inside several organized groups of like-minded French-speaking radicals in the city, particularly a black spiritualist society and an integrated Masonic lodge. Discouraged by the methods of other black leaders in the South, Desdunes urged his fellow black creoles to return to the methods that had worked during Reconstruction. Without the centrality of a black Protestant church or the leadership of black clergymen in the creole communities, he knew that they needed an ideological organization and a newspaper—their own bold, militant newspaper—to unify and lead them. In 1887, he helped form the organization L'Union Louisianaise and circulated its prospectus for a revolutionary paper with French columns: "Our efforts to create here a republican organ in the language that is still spoken with pride by a class of men who have drawn their republicanism from reading the great philosophes of the 18th century. . . . Those to whom it [L'Union Louisianaise] has entrusted the editing will put all their efforts . . . into continuing its progressive work. They will endeavor to graft, so to speak, the truth onto the side of error, in order to produce a result, which . . . assures to each the plenitude of his civil and political rights."

The call eventually resulted in a community corporation to support the New Orleans *Crusader*. Printed in both French and English, it was an aggressive vehicle for racial protest in New Orleans. The managing editor, Louis A. Martinet, had once been an ally of Pinchback and had even joined him in support of the constitution of 1879, which overturned many of the key features of the 1868 Reconstruction constitution, but Martinet later abandoned the narrow patronage politics of his former mentor and closed ranks with his fellow creoles. The newspaper obviously struck a chord in the black community and helped encourage a new assertive spirit in the city as its founders had hoped. By 1894, the editors received enough support from black New Orleanians that the *Crusader* became the only black daily newspaper in the United States during the 1890s.

That the *Crusader* resounded with the same spirit of the earlier *Union* and *Tribune* from the Reconstruction era was not accidental, because one of its regular contributors, Paul Trévigne, then an old man, helped in its founding and reminded its readers how he and an earlier generation had originally won the rights that the *Crusader* now proposed to regain three decades later. The new paper rallied the community to protest an upsurge of political violence in the sugar parishes of southern Louisiana and condemned police brutality in New Orleans. Calling itself a "Labor and Republican" paper, it also supported labor unions, including the Knights of Labor, and any other movement in the South such as the early Populist party that seemed to offer protection for the rights of black citizens.

But above all, the *Crusader* served as the organ of an assertive civil rights effort in the courts that Desdunes had envisioned at the beginning of the 1880s. The editor, Louis Martinet, who had also graduated from the Straight University Law School, agreed with Desdunes that well-chosen legal suits offered more hope than the fraudulent politics of the state to recapture basic constitutional rights under the Fourteenth and Fifteenth amendments. In early 1890, the editors helped to gather other leaders throughout the South at Washington, D.C., to form a new national civil rights group, the American Citizens Equal Rights Association (ACERA). The *Crusader* purposely insisted upon a name that would open the group to all sympathizers irrespective of race, setting it at odds with all those—black or white—who sought racial isolation. Within a few weeks of the group's formation, a cause emerged for the Louisiana branch of the association: the state legislature passed laws forbidding interracial marriage and mandating segregation of blacks on all railroads operating within Louisiana.

Initially both American and creole leaders participated in the campaign to protest these new laws. Some American leaders joined the board of the *Crusader*, and even Pinchback helped at the beginning. But before too long, black creoles had to maintain the burden of the struggle as other leaders, particularly the black Protestant ministers, backed away from the dangerous challenge to the white supremacists. A few were forced out. At the outset, the Reverend A. E. P. Albert, the first president of the state branch of the American Citizens Equal Rights Association, aligned his Methodist newspaper with the *Crusader*; but when he gathered support for the campaign and called upon Methodist churches to pledge opposition to the state laws, national church officials removed him from the editorship of the *Southwestern Christian Advocate* and left him without any comparable base of leadership in Louisiana.

Before long, black creoles stood virtually alone. They provided almost all of the financial support as well as the plaintiffs for the test cases. Daniel F. Desdunes, the son of Rodolphe Desdunes, served as the plaintiff in their first case, and Homer Plessy, another creole activist, served in the second and more famous suit. After the national organization of the ACERA also collapsed, the black creole leaders, under Desdunes' leadership, formed a Citizens Committee with financial help from the old Reconstruction radical Aristide Mary to support the expensive court suits. The New Orleanians also cooperated with another civil rights group, headed by the white activist Albion Tourgée, for national assistance and publicity.

Jubilation greeted their impressive victory in the first case, which dismissed Louisiana's efforts to segregate trains that crossed state borders. Desdunes and his compatriots confidently pronounced Jim Crow "dead as a door nail." Desdunes, a regular columnist for the *Crusader*, hammered away at the white supremacists while the lawyers continued the long process of legal maneuvers and appeals that brought their second, more significant suit based on the Thirteenth and Fourteenth amendments to the Supreme Court of the United States. "No theory of white supremacy," Desdunes reminded the fainthearted, "no method of lynching, no class legislation, no undue disqualification of citizenship, no system of enforced ignorance, no privileged classes at the expense of others can be tolerated, and, much less, openly encouraged by any citizen who loves justice, law and right."

The group did not organize simply to attack segregated railroads. They pursued several other legal cases, especially one against the denial of the right of black citizens to sit on criminal juries. Between 1892 and 1896, Desdunes also tried to rally opposition against the efforts of southern legislatures to disfranchise black voters by literacy and property requirements. In 1895, after the *Crusader* became the only daily black newspaper in the nation, he assumed the role of associate editor and brought a greater class appeal to the paper: "This question of qualified suffrage," he warned, "is one in which all the common people, whether colored or white, are vitally interested." He rued the day "when once the wealthy classes get the laws as they want them. The elect of creation, as they believe themselves to be, aim to kill the right [of universal suffrage] as a short cut to assured and permanent ascendancy."

In 1896, however, the paper's bravado ended when the Supreme Court of the United States ruled against Plessy and explicitly sanctioned segregation. It must have seemed that the total weight of American power suddenly arrayed itself against the long struggle of the black New Orleans leaders. Even most of the stalwarts who helped pursue the case were too discouraged or fearful to continue any further protests. With the numbing efficiency of undertakers, they dismantled the Citizens Committee and distributed a published accounting of their fund-raising before they called a large public meeting to announce their formal disbandment. Desdunes later recalled that pessimism and fear had finally taken their toll. Most of the leaders, he said, "believed that the continuation of the *Crusader* would not only be fruitless but decidedly dangerous." They believed that "it was better to suffer in silence than to attract attention to their misfortune and weakness."

The end to organized resistance did not lessen the violent determination of the white supremacists to subordinate black Louisianians. Within the next few years, black New Orleanians lost the right to vote and were slowly deprived of almost all access to public education. Even the leaders of the Catholic church in the New Orleans diocese finally imposed the color line. For a while the storm of black creole protest in 1895 led by Desdunes and Martinet in the *Crusader* had confined the creation of exclusively black "national" parishes to two small churches. In that battle, Desdunes had urged the church to maintain its universal principles and to uphold "justice, equality and fraternity" within its ranks. He repeated his constant refrain: "Whether we be citizens or Christians, we never cease to be the children of God and the brothers of other men." But here, too, he could only delay the inevitable. By the end of World War 1, the prelates of the city segregated all of the city's Catholic churches.

Church leaders praised these and other developments as part of the Americanization of their church. As in other private organizations in the city, almost all of the foreign white leaders, particularly the foreign French, had died off by the early twentieth century, and few new French immi-

grants took their place. Other integrated institutions, like the Scottish Rite Masonic lodges, either became all black as older white members died or, like the French Opera House, disappeared from the city. Even from afar, colonialist France itself must have lost much of its glow as a beacon of liberation for black New Orleanians. Most of the younger creoles also lost the ability to speak French or to read French literature and history. Increasingly, New Orleans became, in its race relations, very similar to other American cities in the South.

From the perspective of the early twentieth century, the promise that Radical Republicans and abolitionists once held out for black New Orleanians of freedom, opportunity, and equal citizenship had turned into a nightmare of peonage, segregation, and disfranchisement. In the face of such reality, even the black creoles of the city turned inward. By 1915, a new generation of their leaders greeted Booker T. Washington with almost the same enthusiasm as did other black southerners. If creoles and Americans still maintained their own distinctive churches and benevolent societies in different neighborhoods, both groups apparently had conformed to the American color line.

The unusual nineteenth-century resistance led by the black creoles to the Americanization of the city's race relations had not been a prolonged fool's errand. The complex traditions that had produced their peculiar militant resistance had left a proud legacy not only for themselves but for the whole nation because they played a major role in embedding a policy of racial justice into the Reconstruction amendments to the U.S. Constitution. Indeed, even the *Plessy* case had not been a total failure, for it generated a powerful dissent that would be used to rescue those amendments in later Supreme Court decisions.

And, finally, the peculiar traditions of black New Orleanians survived within their own communities, for they have preserved their own memories and written history. Even after the defeat of the *Plessy* suit, not all the leaders accommodated to the new racial order. Many maintained a militant interracial labor organization in the city; hundreds boycotted segregated streetcars; and before the end of the 1920s, black leaders returned to the federal courts to reopen their old battles. None of these recalcitrants was more defiant than Rodolphe Desdunes. He decried any accommodation to the prevailing American racial order. From the beginning of the struggle against the state laws that segregated railroad cars, Desdunes recognized that he was fighting against all odds in resisting racial oppression in the American South.

Early in that battle, when a subscriber complained to the *Crusader* that Desdunes was calling the black community to a "battle which is forlorn," Desdunes refused to be shaken from his faith that "liberty is won by continued resistance to tyranny." What is more, he would not succumb to the obvious burden of the federal judiciary's opinion that "colored men ought to be satisfied with the enjoyment of the three first natural rights" of the Declaration of Independence. He insisted that there must be more than life, liberty, and the pursuit of happiness. He argued that equal rights could not be divided among groups of humanity living within the same society. Fraternity and equal rights were inseparable. His reading of history told him that "forlorn hopes like utopias have been the cause or beginnings of all the great principles which now bless ... the free and progressive nations of the earth." In his mind a "forlorn hope" should not be "a disconcerting element to a true lover of the good and the just, and ... his devotion to principle must be above perturbation from the most threatening prospects of temporary disappointment." In this response, Desdunes frankly warned his compatriots that they should be prepared to "show a noble despair" and be ready to "face any disappointment that might await them at the bar of American justice." He seemed to know that he was fighting not just for them but for a generation yet unborn. He proudly admitted on a later occasion that he fought in the tradition of Victor Hugo, Alphonse de Lamartine, and John Brown as a "champion of impossible doctrines, or as a debater of dreams, just fallen from the skies." It was in this spirit that he responded to W. E. B. Du Bois' remarks when that younger leader seemed to be at wit's end after the terrible Atlanta race riot of 1906.

Before an accident blinded him about 1910, Desdunes completed a history in French of his people so that their achievements and struggles would be remembered and used by its readers to continue the fight against racial prejudice in America. He wanted the accomplishments of the creoles to be absorbed by all blacks, whether American or creole. But above all, Desdunes wanted any reader to learn from the story of the creole radicals that "it is more noble and dignified to fight, no matter what, than to show a passive attitude of resignation. Absolute submission augments the oppressor's power and creates doubt about the feelings of the oppressed."

Endnotes

1. *Louisianian*, January 4, 1879.

2. *Ibid.*

3. *Ibid.*, January 4, 1879, April 15, 29, 1882.

4. Rodolphe Lucien Desdunes, *A Few Words to Dr. DuBois: "With Malice Toward None"* (New Orleans, 1907), 13. For a sketch of Desdunes, see the foreword by Charles E. O'Neill in the new edition and translation of Desdunes' original history, *Nos hommes et notre histoire* (Montreal, 1911): *Our People and Our History*, ed. and trans. Dorothea Olga McCants (Baton Rouge, 1973), ix–xix.

5. Desdunes, *Few Words to DuBois*, 13. For an elaboration of Desdunes' definition of the creoles as "one community, alike in origin, language, and customs," see Desdunes, *Our People*, 3.

6. Thomas Marc Fiehrer, "The African Presence in Colored Louisiana: An Essay on the Continuity of Caribbean Culture," in *Louisiana's Black Heritage*, ed. Robert R. Macdonald *et al.* (New Orleans, 1979), 30. See also Ira Berlin's comparative treatment of the free people of color in the former French and Spanish colonies of the Gulf Coast, *Slaves Without Masters: The Free Negro in the Antebellum South* (New York, 1974). For two comprehensive studies of free blacks in Louisiana, see H. E. Sterkx, *The Free Negro in Ante-Bellum Louisiana* (Rutherford, N.J., 1972), and Donald E. Everett, "Free Persons of Color in New Orleans, 1803–1865" (Ph.D. dissertation, Tulane University, 1952). On the question of phenotype among slaves and free blacks, see John W. Blassingame, *Black New Orleans, 1860–1880* (Chicago, 1973), 21.

7. Marcus B. Christian, "Demand by Men of Color for Rights in Orleans Territory," *Negro History Bulletin*, XXXVI (March, 1973), 54–57. For Jefferson's approval of the repressive policies, see his notes on the cabinet meeting, October 4, 1803, in Thomas Jefferson Papers, Library of Congress.

8. David C. Rankin, "The Tannenbaum Thesis Reconsidered: Slavery and Race Relations in Antebellum Louisiana," *Southern Studies*, XVIII

(Spring, 1979), 5–31; Paul F. Lachance, "The Politics of Fear: French Louisianians and the Slave Trade, 1786–1809," *Plantation Society,* 1 (June, 1979), 162–96; Laura Foner, "The Free People of Color in Louisiana and St. Domingue: A Comparative Portrait of Two Three-Caste Slave Societies," *Journal of Social History,* III (1970), 421–22. For population data, see *New Orleans in 1805: A Directory and a Census* (New Orleans, 1936), 11; and *Third Census, 1810: Population,* 295.

9. Berlin, *Slaves Without Masters,* 114–23; Everett, "Free Persons of Color," 55–74.

10. Berlin, *Slaves Without Masters,* 130; Foner, "Free People of Color," 424–27; Everett, "Free Persons of Color," 101–104, 123–25.

11. A sample study (by the authors) of the 1850 census shows that creoles constituted 76 percent of the adult free male black population in the First Municipality of the city (82 percent below St. Louis Street) and 88 percent in the Third Municipality. By contrast, Americans constituted 78 percent of the comparable population in the uptown Second Municipality. The methodology for this study was based on the work of D. L. A. Hackett, "The Social Structure of Jacksonian Louisiana," *Southern Studies,* XII (Spring, 1973), 324–53. For a similar preponderance of the 10,564 white French immigrants in the downtown wards, see Victor Hugo Treat, "Migration into Louisiana, 1834–1880" (Ph.D. dissertation, University of Texas, 1967), 328–32.

12. On the crisis of the 1850s, see Desdunes, *Our People,* 111, 134–35, and a speech by Robert B. Elliot (*Louisianian,* September 17, 1881), who learned from creole leaders that their struggle to challenge racial subordination began in 1852.

13. Jean-Charles Houzeau, *My Passage at the New Orleans "Tribune,"* ed. David C. Rankin (Baton Rouge, 1984), 25–29; Paul Trévigne, "Dr. Louis Charles Roudanez," New Orleans *Daily Crusader,* March 22, 1890.

14. Shelby T. McCloy, *The Negro in France* (Lexington, Ky., 1961), 145–59; McCloy, *The Negro in the French West Indies* (Lexington, Ky., 1966), 141–59; Lawrence C. Jennings, *French Reaction to British Emancipation* (Baton Rouge, 1988), 194–98.

15. In the 1860 census, Texas had only 355 free blacks, Mississippi had 753, and Arkansas had 114, whereas Louisiana had 18,647.

16. Biographies of some manumitted black Americans appear in *Southwestern Christian Advocate,* March 27, 1879, March 22, 1888,

September 10, 1896. Loren Schweninger provides a revealing autobiography of James P. Thomas, a black migratory worker, in "A Negro Sojourner in Antebellum New Orleans," *Louisiana History,* XX (1979), 306–308. For Thomas' comparative views of northern cities and their racial mores, see John Hope Franklin, *A Southern Odyssey: Travelers in the Antebellum North* (Baton Rouge, 1976), 141–44. For a similar appraisal of antebellum New Orleans by other black informants, see John Freeman Clarke, *Condition of the Free Colored People* (1859; rpr. New York, 1969), 253–54.

17. Richard R. Tansey, "Out of State Blacks in Late Antebellum New Orleans," *Louisiana History,* XXII (1981), 375–84.

18. Richard R. Tansey, "Economic Expansion and Urban Disorder in Antebellum New Orleans" (Ph.D. dissertation, University of Texas at Austin, 1981), 124–30; Richard B. Wade, *Slavery in the Cities: The South, 1820–1860* (New York, 1964), 219.

19. John W. Blassingame, *The Slave Community: Plantation Life in the Ante-bellum South* (New York, 1972); Lawrence W. Levine, *Black Culture and Black Consciousness: Afro-American Folk Thought from Slavery to Freedom* (New York, 1977); Eugene D. Genovese, "Black Plantation Preachers in the Slave South," *Louisiana Studies,* XI (1972), 196–214.

20. William B. Posey, "The Early Baptist Church in the Lower Southwest," *Journal of Southern History,* X (1944), 161–73; William Paxton, *A History of the Baptists in Louisiana* (St. Louis, 1888), 140–48; John T. Christian, *A History of the Baptists in Louisiana* (Shreveport, 1923), 42–43, 50–51.

21. Marcus Christian, "The First African Baptist Church of New Orleans, 1817–1842" (Typescript in Marcus Christian Papers, University of New Orleans), 6–8. The quotation is from R.W. Coleman, "Church Anniversary of the First African Baptist Church," quoted in Marcus Christian, "The Negro Church in Louisiana" (Chapter in MS WPA history of the Negro in Louisiana, in Christian Papers).

22. Walter N. Vernon, *Becoming One People: A History of Louisiana Methodism* (Bossier City, La., 1987), 8, 13.

23. *Southwestern Christian Advocate,* July 20, 1882. For information on smaller black Protestant groups, see Robert C. Reinders, "The Church and the Negro in New Orleans, 1850–1860," *Phylon,* XXII (Fall, 1961), 244–46; John F. Nau, *The Lutheran Church in Louisiana* (New Orleans, n.d. [ca. 1952]), 45–50; and Hodding Carter and Betty Werlein

Carter, *So Great a Good: A History of the Episcopal Church in Louisiana* (Sewanee, Tenn., 1955), 169.

24. Charles Spencer Smith, *A History of the African Methodist Episcopal Church* (Philadelphia, 1922), 20, 33–36.

25. *Ibid.*, 33–36.

26. City ordinance No. 3847, April 7, 1858, cited in *African Methodist Episcopal Church v. City of New Orleans*, 15 La. Ann. 441 #6291 (1858). The original records and testimony of this case are filed in the Louisiana Supreme Court Records, Case 6342, in the Department of Archives of the University of New Orleans. The quotation is taken from page 4 of the Supreme Court ruling.

27. *Proceedings of Eureka Grand Lodge, 1863–69* (New Orleans, 1869); and *100 Years of Legitimate and Progressive Free Masonry, Centennial Souvenir* (New Orleans, *ca.* 1963), both in George Longe Collection, Amistad Research Center, Tulane University, New Orleans.

28. Howard H. Bell, ed., *Search for a Place: Black Separatism and Africa* (Ann Arbor, 1969), 38; *Louisianian*, February 11, 1882. Noble's interest in immigration to Liberia is documented in "Letters to the American Colonization Society," *Journal of Negro History*, X (April, 1925), 271–72, 275.

29. *African Methodist Episcopal Church v. City of New Orleans*, 15 La. Ann. 441 #6291 (1858).

30. *Southwestern Christian Advocate*, January 28, 1886, August 22, 1889, February 13, 1890, August 13, 1891, March 17, 1892.

31. *Ibid.*, August 2, 1888. On color consciousness among black Americans, see Joel Williamson, *New People: Miscegenation and Mulattoes in the United States* (New York, 1984).

32. The discussion of the Native Guards by Rodolphe Desdunes may be the most balanced appraisal. Errors in the recent translation of his history of the black creoles unfortunately reversed his original meaning and led some scholars to use his work to prove widespread pro-Confederate views among the Native Guards. Compare Desdunes, *Our People and Our History*, 120, with Desdunes, *Nos hommes et notre histoire*, 161. See also the judicious work by Mary F. Berry, "Negro Troops in Blue and Gray: The Louisiana Native Guards, 1861–1863," *Louisiana History*, XIV (Winter, 1973), 21–39.

33. Desdunes, *Our People and Our History*, 22–23; *L'Union*, October 18, 1862, July 12, 1864.

34. For a different view, see the work of David Rankin, "The Impact of the Civil War on the Free Colored Community of New Orleans," *Perspectives in American History*, XI (1977–78), 379–416; and Rankin, "The Politics of Caste: Free Colored Leadership in New Orleans During the Civil War," in *Louisiana's Black Heritage*, ed. Macdonald *et al.*, 107–46. Rankin's sample of Reconstruction leaders, in Howard N. Rabinowitz, *Southern Black Leaders of the Reconstruction Era* (Urbana, 1982), 181–88, shows both the youthfulness and the small number of slaveholders among the younger black creole leaders. Of the two hundred identified leaders, only twenty-three were identified as slaveholders. Of that number, about eighteen were clearly creoles, but none except Francis Dumas and V. E. Macarty were closely identified with the radical *Tribune* faction. The circumstances that had led Dumas and probably others to owning slaves undercuts the idea that a large number of the Reconstruction leaders had either bought slaves or held them for profit or social prestige.

35. Howard Westwood, "Benjamin Butler's Enlistment of Black Troops in New Orleans in 1862," *Louisiana History*, XXVI (1985), 14–15. See minutes of Economy Hall Native Guards for June 11, 15, 1861, in the back of the 1864 seance register, in René Grandjean Collection, Department of Archives, University of New Orleans.

36. Desdunes, *Our People and Our History*, 118–20.

37. J. W. Phelps to Benjamin Butler, August 2, 1862, in *Freedom: A Documentary History of Emancipation, 1861–1867*, ed. Ira Berlin (Cambridge, Eng., 1982), 11, 63–64. For memoirs of two black leaders who offered help to Phelps—Emile Detiège and Robert Isabelle—see the *Louisianian*, February 20, 1875, and the *Anglo-African*, June 13, 1862.

38. *L'Union*, October 18, 1862.

39. Manoj K. Joshi and Joseph P. Reidy, " 'To Come Forward and Aid in Putting Down This UnHoly Rebellion': The Officers of Louisiana's Free Black Native Guard During the Civil War Era," *Southern Studies*, XXI (1982), 330, 336. For conflicting versions of Dumas' slaveholding, see George Washington Williams, *A History of the Negro Troops in the Rebellion, 1861–1865* (1888; rpr. New York, 1969), 214–23; Joseph T. Wilson, *Black Phalanx* (1888; rpr. New York, 1968), 207–11; New Orleans *Tribune*, July 2, 1867; and *Crusader*, July 19, 1890.

40. *L'Union*, September 27, October 18, 1862, as translated in James McPherson, *The Negro's Civil War* (New York, 1969), 276, 61. The paper expanded to

a triweekly on December 23, 1862, and to a bilingual edition on July 6, 1863 (Desdunes, *Our People and Our History*, 66–68; *Pelican*, September 10, 1887; *Picayune*, September 1, 1907).

41. *L'Union*, October 18, 1862. A recent comparative study of emancipation by Eric Foner failed to note the French action of 1848, claiming that emancipation in the United States was "distinctive" because "uniquely in postemancipation societies, the former slaves during Reconstruction enjoyed universal manhood suffrage and a real measure of political power" (*Nothing but Freedom: Emancipation and Its Legacy* [Baton Rouge, 1983], 3). The French emancipation of 1848 shocked white creoles in New Orleans but equally impressed the black creoles, who eventually began an annual celebration of the radical French decrees. See Guillaume de Berthier de Sauvigny, *La Révolution parisienne de 1848 vue par les américains* (Paris, 1984), 112, 139–41.

42. Recognizing the importance of the policy decision, the publishers of the paper reprinted Bates's opinion, first in the newspaper and then in a separate pamphlet, *Opinion de l'Avocat-Général Bates sur le droit de citoyenneté* (New Orleans, 1863). Trévigne felt, as he stated in the pamphlet's preface, that the "truly remarkable" opinion should get into the hands of "those most directly affected by it."

43. The quotation on black officers comes from Richard B. Irwin, adjutant to Banks, as cited in Joshi and Reidy, " 'To Come Forward,' " 331.

44. *Louisianian*, November 26, 1871. See also *100 Years of Legitimate and Progressive Freemasonry: Centennial Souvenir* (New Orleans, ca. 1963) in the George Longe Papers at the Amistad Research Center, Tulane University. The membership rolls of the Prince Hall Masons of New Orleans can also be found in the Longe Papers.

45. Peyton McCrary, *Abraham Lincoln and Reconstruction: The Louisiana Experiment* (Princeton, 1978), 183–84; *L'Union*, December 1, 1863. Pinchback's migration to New Orleans as a steamboat worker followed the pattern of many American free blacks who settled in New Orleans. See James Haskins, *Pinckney Benton Stewart Pinchback* (New York, 1973), 11–27.

46. New Orleans *Times*, November 6, 1863; Charles Vincent, *Black Legislators in Louisiana During Reconstruction* (Baton Rouge, 1976), 19.

47. For the petition see *Liberator*, April 17, February 5, 1864; Herman Belz, "Origins of Negro Suffrage," *Southern Studies*, XVII (1978), 115; James M.

McPherson, *The Struggle for Equality* (Princeton, 1964), 238–46.

48. *Liberator*, April 17, 1864.

49. *Ibid.*, April 15, 1864. For some additional speculation about this meeting with Lincoln, see LaWanda Cox, *Lincoln and Black Freedom* (Columbia, S.C., 1981), 94–95. Although Lincoln and Hahn showed the letter to several people, the black leaders in New Orleans did not learn its contents until after Lincoln's death (New Orleans *Tribune*, July 7, 1865).

50. *Anglo-African*, April 2, 16, 23, July 23, 1864.

51. Boston *Daily Advertiser*, April 13, 1864, as quoted in the *Liberator*, April 15, 1864.

52. *L'Union*, April 9, 14, May 26, 1864.

53. *Liberator*, March 11, April 8, 1864.

54. *L'Union*, July 19, 1864.

55. *Anglo-African*, August 27, September 24, October 1, 1864.

56. New Orleans *Tribune*, August 4, October 12, 1864.

57. Donald E. Everett, "Demands of the Free Colored Population for Political Equality, 1862–1865," *Louisiana Historical Quarterly*, XXXVIII (1955), 56; New Orleans *Tribune*, December 7, 1864.

58. New Orleans *Tribune*, October 11, 1864.

59. *Ibid.*

60. *Ibid.*, November 16, 1864.

61. *Proceedings of the National Convention of Colored Men Held in the City of Syracuse New York, October 4, 5, 6, and 7, 1864* (Boston, 1864), 13, 36–43, as found in *Proceedings of the National Negro Conventions, 1830–1864*, ed. Howard Bell (New York, 1969).

62. *Anglo-African*, October 8, 15, 1864.

63. For the complicated relationships of free and slave status within a single black creole family, see Document 295 in *Freedom*, ed. Berlin, II, 684–85. Two very prominent black creole leaders in postwar Louisiana had been slaves until the war began: Basile Barrès, the musician, and Theophile T. Allain, a state senator.

64. Ted Tunnell, *Crucible of Reconstruction: War, Radicalism, and Race in Louisiana, 1862–1877* (Baton Rouge, 1984), 71–73; New Orleans *Bee*, January 13, 1859. For a list of some of these organizations, see Roger Baudier, *Centennial: St. Rose of Lima Parish* (New Orleans, 1957), 21. For a good analysis of Maistre, see Geraldine M. McTigue, "Forms of

Racial Interaction in Louisiana, 1860–1880" (Ph.D. dissertation, Yale University, 1975), 37–41. *L'Union,* January 26, 1864; New Orleans *Tribune,* June 13, July 31, November 30, December 27, 1867, January 9, 1869; Baudier, *Centennial,* 20–24; Roger Baudier, *The Catholic Church in Louisiana* (New Orleans, 1939), 393–413.

6 5. John T. Gillard, *The Catholic Church and the American Negro* (Baltimore, 1929), 38–42, 72–73. Also see a later, expanded work by the same author, *Colored Catholics in the United States* (Baltimore, 1941), 122–23. For a critical appraisal of segregation in the Catholic churches in New Orleans, see Charles B. Rousséve, *The Negro in Louisiana: Aspects of His History and His Literature* (New Orleans, 1937), 139–41.

66. *L'Union* and the *Tribune* often criticized the Catholic church for its conservatism. See *L'Union,* November 15, December 6, 1862, May 31, 1864; New Orleans *Tribune,* November 6, 1864, May 11, 1865, December 1, 1867. Paul Trévigne, however, also noted the strong attachment of black Catholics to the Catholic church, despite the political conservatism of its clergy. See *L'Union,* May 31, 1864.

67. New Orleans *Tribune,* October 7, 1865. The French Masonic leader, Felix Vogeli of Lyons, appealed to French Masons in the United States: "Let us be the first to combat on this land of Liberty . . . prejudices of all kinds; let us furnish the example of their irrationality."

68. *Ibid.,* June 18, 23, July 25, 26, November 6, 8, 1867. In late 1868, the integrated Scottish Rite lodges gave Chassaignac a gold medal "as a Token of esteem for his courageous action in the cause of humanity in opening the Masonic temples to all men without distinction of color" (*ibid.,* January 5, 1869).

69. William F. Messner, *Freedmen and the Ideology of Free Labor: Louisiana, 1862–1865* (Lafayette, La., 1978), 99–105, 171–72. For a discussion of the rivalry among Protestant leaders, see Jacquelyn S. Haywood, "The American Missionary Association in Louisiana During Reconstruction" (Ph.D. dissertation, University of California at Los Angeles, 1974), 67–75, 129–37.

70. Methodist Episcopal Church, *Proceedings of the Second Session of the Mississippi Mission Conference* [1866], 8.

71. *Louisianian,* May 18, 1871; Methodist Episcopal Church, *Journal of Louisiana Conference* [1876], 20–22; *Southwestern Christian Advocate,* November

6, 1873, February 26, 1874, May 9, 1876, June 22, September 14, 1882, March 15, 1883, April 3, 1884. For a discussion of the orphanage quarrel, see New Orleans *Tribune,* October 25, November 23, December 5, 1865, June 14, November 24, 1866, May 21, 1867.

72. New Orleans *Tribune,* June 18, 1867, January 21, February 5, May 7, 1865. See also Houzeau, *My Passage at the New Orleans "Tribune,"* 48–49, 82–84.

73. See the letters of Houzeau to his parents, March 2, April 2, 1868, in the Houzeau Collection at the Bibliothèque Royale in Brussels, Belgium.

74. New Orleans *Tribune,* January 28, 1865.

75. *Ibid.,* January 14, February 4, 5. 1865.

76. Cox, *Lincoln and Black Freedom,* 128. Before he set up the black rival paper, Conway apparently tried to get the army to shut down the *Tribune.* See Henry A. White, *The Freedmen's Bureau in Louisiana* (Baton Rouge, 1970), 18–19.

77. *Black Republican,* April 15, 22, 29, 1865.

78. *Anglo-African,* October 1, 1864, January 21, 28, 1865.

79. *Ibid.,* February 25, 1865; New Orleans *Tribune,* March 10, 11, June 30, July 17, 1865.

80. Although initially an outspoken proponent of black racialism, Randolph (1825–1874) ended his career as a bizarre apostle of spiritualism and free love and even denied his African ancestry. See Pascal Beverly Randolph, *P. B. Randolph: His Curious Life, Works, and Career* (Boston, 1872).

81. Methodist Episcopal Church, *Proceedings of the Second Session of the Mississippi Mission Conference,* 20–21. At this conference, Methodist officials urged their Louisiana flock to "command better relations with conservatives"; "to banish all erroneous and strange notions, instilled in them by impractical men, concerning their own destiny"; and "to counsel obedience to law and patient endurance for righteousness sake." See also New Orleans *Tribune,* October 31, November 6, 1866; J. Willis Menard, *Black and White* (New Orleans, 1866), 4.

82. *Catholic Directory,* 1858–1900; Gillard, *Colored Catholics,* 203; Carolo E. Nolan, *Bayou Carmel: The Sisters of Mount Carmel of Louisiana* (Kenner, La., 1977), 17–23. Among the ten elementary schools and three secondary academies in 1860, there was only one elementary school for black girls and none for boys (Edward D. Reynolds, *Jesuits for the Negro* [New York, 1949], see the foreword and pp. 162–66, 174–75).

83. *Catholic Directory*, 1885. See also Mary Di Martino, "Education in New Orleans During Reconstruction" (M.A. thesis, Tulane University, 1935), 172–81.

84. Blassingame, *Black New Orleans*, 107–30.

85. *Louisianian*, February 1, August 9, 1879, September 24, 1881; *Southwestern Christian Advocate*, December 6, 1883. See also Dorothy Rose Eagleson, "Some Aspects of the Social Life of the New Orleans Negro in the 1880s" (M.A. thesis, Tulane University, 1961), 77–80. For a list of the many black groups in New Orleans, see *Woods Directory: A Classified Colored Business, Professional and Trade Directory of New Orleans* (New Orleans, 1912).

86. *Louisianian*, February 26, 1871, February 12, 1881. For examples of social activities at which newspaper reporters noted creole and American commingling, see *ibid.*, February 16, May 14, 21, September 28, October 1, November 30, 1871. A decade later the interchange still drew notice: *ibid.*, December 25, 1880, June 25, July 30, August 27, 1881, February 18, 25, 1882. In a careful review of the social columns and editorials of New Orleans black newspapers, we found no mention of any society formed on the basis of light or dark skin color as happened in Charleston, South Carolina. Another historian recently came to the same conclusion: Virginia R. Dominguez, *White by Definition: Social Classification in Creole Louisiana* (New Brunswick, N.J., 1986), 164.

87. *Louisianian*, January 8, 1881; *Southwestern Christian Advocate*, June 22, September 14, 1882, March 15, 1883.

88. *Southwestern Christian Advocate*, March 15, 1883, May 17, 31, 1894; Alan Lomax, *Mister Jelly Roll: The Fortunes of Jelly Roll Morton, New Orleans Creole and "Inventor of Jazz"* (1950; rpr. Berkeley, 1973), ix–xvii.

89. In 1912, all of the black Baptist churches were on the upriver side of Canal Street, as were the overwhelming number of black Methodist churches. Of thirty-seven black Protestant churches in 1912, thirty were uptown. When the Catholic church, by 1945, established ten so-called "national" churches for black Catholics, all but two small churches were downriver from Canal Street. See *Woods Directory* (unpaginated). See also *Catholic Directory*, 1925, and *Claverite*, XXV (October, 1945), 5.

90. For information on the racial composition of electoral districts in New Orleans see Londa L. Davis, "After Reconstruction: Black Politics in New Orleans, 1876–1900" (M.A. thesis, University of New Orleans, 1981), 222–25.

91. *Louisianian*, February 20, 1875; Vincent, *Black Legislators in Louisiana*, 226–38.

92. Tunnell, *Crucible of Reconstruction*, 135, 145.

93. New Orleans *Tribune*, May 19, 1867.

94. *Ibid.*, May 21, 1867. The quarrel between Newman and the editors of the *Tribune* continued through 1867. Indeed, it went on for years and finally resulted in his removal from New Orleans by Methodist Episcopal bishops because of the antagonism he had engendered within the black community of New Orleans. See *ibid.*, May 26, June 12, July 2, 1867, January 6, 1869.

95. *Ibid.*, October 23, 1867.

96. Roger Fischer, *The Segregation Struggle in Louisiana, 1862–77* (Urbana, 1974), 47–48.

97. New Orleans *Tribune*, June 18, 23, July 25, 26, 1867.

98. In his report, as grand master, to the Eureka Grand Lodge in December, 1867, Dunn excoriated the defection and admitted that "our Temple has been shaken to its foundation" when many of the members "became demoralized and unruly, and were consequently lopped off from our jurisdiction." See the "Proceedings of the Most Worshipful Grand Lodge of Louisiana, 1863–1869," 48, in the George Longe Collection at the Amistad Research Center.

99. Tunnell, *Crucible of Reconstruction*, 135, 145.

100. Well after this election, black leaders recalled Roudanez' decision a serious political error but honored him as a man of independence and integrity. See *Southwestern Christian Advocate*, March 19, 1885.

101. Houzeau, *My Passage at the New Orleans "Tribune,"* 47–57, 149–53.

102. Tunnell, *Crucible of Reconstruction*, 77. Pinchback kept up his contacts in the North, particularly in Ohio, by leaving New Orleans almost every summer. On the staff of his newspaper, the *Louisianian*, he gathered a coterie of political lieutenants who had come from northern states: J. Henri Burch (New York), William G. Brown (New Jersey), James Kennedy (Washington, D.C.), and several others.

103. Fischer, *Segregation Struggle in Louisiana*, 66–69; Marcus B. Christian, "The Theory of the

Poisoning of Oscar J. Dunn," *Phylon,* VI (Fall, 1945), 4–10.

104. Henry C. Warmoth, *War, Politics and Reconstruction: Stormy Days in Louisiana* (New York, 1930), 51–54; Tunnell, *Crucible of Reconstruction,* 164–72.

105. *Louisianian,* June 14, 1879.

106. Rodolphe Lucien Desdunes, *Hommage rendu à la mémoire de Alexandre Aristide Mary* . . . (New Orleans, 1893), 5–9.

107. Fischer, *Segregation Struggle in Louisiana,* 143–46; *Louisianian,* February 22, March 8, 1879.

108. *Southwestern Christian Advocate,* June 5, 1884.

109. *Ibid.,* March 25, 1886, January 27, 1887.

110. *Daily Crusader,* undated clipping from 1892 signed by Desdunes, in *Crusader* Scrapbook, 7, Xavier University of Louisiana, New Orleans.

111. *Louisianian,* October 30, December 4, 1875, December 28, 1878.

112. *Ibid.,* July 2, 9, 16, 23, 30, August 6, 13, 1881, May 6, 1882.

113. Editorial Committee, *Prospectus,* (September 15, 1887), in Charles Roussève Papers, Amistad Research Center, Tulane University.

114. *Crusader,* March 29, 1890, in Roussève Papers.

115. *Southwestern Christian Advocate,* March 3, 1892.

116. Desdunes, *Hommage rendu à la mémoire de Alexandre Aristide Mary,* 3.

117. Martinet to Tourgée, October 5, 1891, as quoted in Otto H. Olsen, *The Thin Disguise: Turning Point in Negro History, "Plessy v. Ferguson": A Documentary Presentation, 1864–1896* (New York, 1967), 55–61.

118. R.L. Desdunes, "Judge Ferguson and Allies," *Crusader,* n.d. [1893], in *Crusader* Scrapbook, 19.

119. *Crusader,* June 12, 1895, in *Crusader* Scrapbook, 53.

120. Desdunes, *Our People and Our History,* 147; Citizens Committee, *Report of the Proceedings for the Annulment of Act 111 of 1890* (New Orleans, [*ca.* 1897]). This publication and an earlier one, L.A. Martinet, ed., *The Violation of a Constitutional Right* (New Orleans, 1893), demonstrate the large following that the committee gathered at various meetings to protest discrimination and to support various legal cases.

121. See Dolores Egger Labbé, *Jim Crow Comes to Church: The Establishment of Segregated Parishes in South Louisiana* (Lafayette, La., 1971).

122. New Orleans *States,* February 29, 1915; New Orleans *Times-Picayune,* April 13, 14, 1915.

123. ΩCharles A. Lofgren, *The Plessy Case: A Legal-Historical Interpretation* (New York, 1987), 204–207.

124. *Crusader,* August 15, 1891, in Roussève Papers, and May 14, 1895, in *Crusader* Scrapbook, 45.

125. Desdunes, *Our People and Our History,* 147.

CLASS 19

Ethnocentric Groups In America

CHAPTER 29
The Evolution of Race
David Duke

David Duke's perspective on African Americans represents a skewed interpretation based on stereotypical notions and myths about black ability, intellect, brawn and black male sexuality. His racialist viewpoints come through in rather startling ethnocentric terms. While his message may not be mainstream, his logic finds coherence for a significant number of Americans seeking to maintain Eurocentric notions of superiority in a country reflective of white supremacy in its views and policies towards minorities.

The Evolution of Race

David Duke

A political activist and white racialist, David Duke has held public office in the Louisiana State Legislature and unsuccessfully ran for the U.S. Congress in 1998. He publishes the *David Duke Report* and continues to speak out in defense of white supremacy, traveling far and near espousing his views.

In looking into the issue of race, much of my attention had dealt with the impact of heredity on intelligence, but evidence accumulated showing the powerful role of genetics in human behavior in many areas beyond IQ.

The popular version of psychology packaged by the liberal media continued to insist that upbringing or conditioning shaped all human personality traits. It is an article of faith that criminal behavior comes from a bad environment or dysfunctional family. It seemed that every societal problem blamed poverty, poor education, or bad parenting. Some even blamed high robbery and murder rates on the availability of guns.

Few Americans know that numerous studies show that a person's disposition toward criminality can be inherited. One extensive study analyzed the data compiled from 14,427 adoptions in Denmark from 1924-1947. Over two decades of data revealed that the biological children of criminals, even when adopted by non-criminal parents, had much higher rates of criminality than that the adopted children whose genetic parents were law-abiding.

Every major adoption study of criminality in the 20th century shows similar results. Studies of identical and fraternal twins raised together show that identical twins are more than twice as much alike in their criminal behavior as are fraternal twins. In a number of scientific research studies done in the 1990s, it has been shown through MRIs and electrical scans that there are differences in the functioning of the average brains of criminals as compared to the law abiding. The follow-ing is from the *Journal of Biological Psychiatry* in 1997 about a study of the brains of 41 murderers who pled not guilty by reason of insanity and 41 age and sex matched non-criminals. It shows that their brains revealed differences in structure between them and the non-criminal group.

> These preliminary findings provide initial indications of a network of abnormal cortical and sub cortical brain processes that may predispose to violence in murderers found NGRI [not guilty by reason of insanity].

Numerous studies show that extraversion, introversion, altruism, selfishness, self-esteem, dishonesty, truthfulness, and many other character traits have a strong hereditary influence. I had always believed that those kinds of personality traits were a product of environment rather than genes, but once I read the scientific journals, I found the evidence persuasive. While I learned these things as a teenager, William Hamilton and others launched a whole new scientific discipline called sociobiology. It advanced the idea that much social behavior both of individuals and groups is dramatically affected by heredity. In the three decades since I first looked into the issue in the mid 1960s, what's called *behavioral genetics*, *sociobiology* and recently, *evolutionary psychology*, have become respected academic disciplines.

From the period of the beginning of the Second World War to the 1960s, the media associated genetic and racial understanding with the image of German Nazism. While the media dubi-

---

ously attempted to shape public opinion pertaining to these matters, the scientific world learned the truth of the gene and its powerful social role. Important research findings were ignored by the mass media. However, as increasing evidence of the power of human genetics became known, the breakthroughs could no longer be kept from public knowledge.

Genes were directly linked with certain kinds of diseases such as cancers, mental conditions such as schizophrenia, and depression; and of course, intelligence and behavior. Social problems such as alcoholism and homosexuality were shown to be influenced by genes, and there was a reaffirmation, at least in scientific circles, of a genetic influence on criminality. Discoveries were made as to dramatic differences in the architecture of the male and female brain. So many possibilities opened up for the understanding and improvement of the human condition through genetics that a number of governments joined together in eventually launching perhaps the most ambitious scientific investigation of all time: the Human Genome Project, an attempt to identify all the genes affecting mankind.

Studies on identical twins, which had begun in the 1920s, suddenly began to be pursued again by psychologists and geneticists. In the 1960s and 1970s, the public was astounded to learn what many psychologists had known almost the entire century, that many identical twins separated from birth and living in entirely different environments cultures—had remarkably similar personality traits and habits. Amazing stories filled the press of identical twins, who although growing up thousands of miles from each other, smoked the same brand of cigarettes, pursued identical occupations and had almost identical personal habits. Also, a wealth of evidence was amassed comparing personality differences between identical and fraternal twins. Below is a chart showing results of just a few of the more recent studies of behavioral genetics showing the heritibility of personality traits.

Personality Traits Shown to Have a Significant Genetic Component

The following chart shows a number of character traits are strongly influenced by heredity. If there is no hereditary correlation to a factor it would show up as around plus or minus 0. If a trait is 100 percent caused by heredity, it would show up as 1.00. Theoretically a perfect balance of heredity and environment would be represented by .5

Aggression	Plomin 1990	.46
	Rushton, Fulker, et al 1986	.5
	Tellegen, Lykken, et at 1988	.44
Alienation	Plomin 1990	.48
	Tellegen, Lykken, et al 1988	.45
Emotional reactivity	Floderus-Myrhed 1980	.56
Altruism	Rushton, Fulker, et al. 1986	.5
	Keller et al 1992	.37
Cautiousness	Plomin 1990	.5
Extraversion	Plomin 1990	.3-.5
	Bouchard 1984	.54
obey rules/ authority	Tellegen, Lykken et al 1988	.53
Constraint	Tellegen, Lykken et al 1988	.58
Work values	Keller et at 1992	.4
Stress reaction	Tellegen, Lykken et al 1988 Rushton 1992	.53

RACIAL DIFFERENCES IN PERSONALITY

Just as all IQ studies show a marked difference in IQ between the White and Black races, psychologists report dramatic personality differences as well. In high school I had subscribed to a few racially conscious publications. They often referred to scientific studies on the race question. I had the habit of looking up the articles for myself in the journals and books that could be found in university libraries close to my home. Every month, I would go to Tulane or LSU and make Xerox copies of the articles that interested me. I have kept it the habit of reading them over the years and have found much more corroborating evidence since those early days, but there was a wealth of material available, even then.

One interesting publication I read was the *Psychological Bulletin*. I found a couple of articles from the early '60s that discussed how Blacks tend to be more impulsive and unrestrained than Whites. Dreger and Miller called some of the Black personality traits "estrangement and impulse ridden fantasies."

In later years, numerous articles detailed other Black personality differences. An extreme liberal, Thomas Kochman, noted clear racial distinctions in personality between Blacks and Whites, and he expressed his preference for black characteristics. He argued that Black males perceive being ignored as the highest insult and recommends that White women should react to Black sexual aggression with sassy rejoinders just as Black women do. He even went so far as to suggest the typical non-black behavior style of White women caused violent Black male attacks.

Kochman also noted that blacks have "intense and spontaneous emotional behavior" and that the Black "rhythmic way of walking" is "a response to impulses coming from within." He criticized White debating techniques as 'low-keyed, dispassionate, impersonal and nonchallenging . . . cool, quiet, and without affect," while he describes Black approach to argument as "animated, confrontational, . . . heated [and] loud . . ." and that Blacks argue not simply the idea but the "person debating the idea."

After personally experiencing the Black style of argument on many occasions, I had to agree with Kochman's evaluation. However, I disput his notion that such primitive and emotional behavior enriches our culture. After I read Kochman, I noticed the frequent news reports of Black males who argue in precisely the way he descibed, "heated, confrontational, and loud," leading them to impulsively use their Saturday Night Specials. Our public hospitals are full of the victims of such heated and unrestrained Black styles of argument.

Many studies showed the greater levels of impulsiveness, aggression and emotionalism in Blacks as compared to Whites. A study that took place in Trinidad compared Blacks and Caucasian immigrants from India. Walter Mischel conducted a study of children in Trinidad in which he gave White and Black children the choice between a candy bar immediately or a larger one a week later. Blacks almost always chose the immediate gratification while Whites usually chose to wait for the bigger reward. The inability of the blacks to delay gratification was so great in comparison with Whites, that Mischel stated that measuring it seemed "superfluous." Mischel also fried to compare the familial patterns of the blacks who almost always had female-headed households to the East Indian households, but he could not find enough East-Indian households with absent fathers to constitute a statistically meaningful study.

Other books such as *The Unheavenly City Revisited* by Edward Banfield noted that inner cities' inhabitants, that include many Blacks, have less tendency to defer gratification, and an extreme orientation to the present. Most of the men who noted these psychological differences between the races took for granted their cultural origins, but many new studies reveal that such tendencies had hereditary implications.

One of the more interesting aspects of the study of criminal behavior I learned about was its links with testosterone. Researchers have long noted that males are about ten times more often found guilty of violent crimes than are women, and high crime rates coincide with high levels of testosterone in adolescence. Criminal youths are also found to have higher average levels of testosterone than non-criminals of the same age. Interestingly enough, young Negroes are found to have significantly higher levels of testosterone than do young Whites. The Black crime rate is about 300 percent higher than that of Whites on a world-wide basis.

Higher levels of testosterone could contribute to greater sexual aggression as well, contributing both to rape and assault of women as well as instability in relationships. It is also easy to see how it could damage the family. In my reading, I learned that in Africa as well as in every New World Black society, illegitimacy and promiscuity is far more common than in European societies. In the United States, for instance, the African-American illegitimacy rate is fast approaching 75 percent of all newborns.

The chronic social problem of absent Black fathers in America is found repeated on a world-wide scale. In a research paper on African marriage systems, Patricia Draper describes the parenting role of Negro fathers in Africa and the Americas:

> The psychological, social, and spatial distance of husbands/fathers, together with their freedom from direct economic responsibility relieves them of most aspects of the parental role as Westerners understand the term.

I wanted to understand the reasons why the Black differences existed. That meant a look into the evolutionary aspects of the formations of the major races. But, before I did that, I had to answer a more pertinent question. Ashley Montagu maintained in his books and articles that Race is simply a cultural myth. In recent times this view has been parroted frequently in the media. Is race *real*, or is it a socially-contrived *invention*?

THE REALITY OF RACE

Ashley Montagu's, *Man's Most Dangerous Myth: the Fallacy of Race* had impressed me before I began my look into the other side of the scientific studies on race. The "myth of race" position is essentially that skin color, hair type and other traits that influence racial classification are completely arbitrary traits of mankind and are as unimportant as are different types of fingerprint designs.

After almost thirty years of the media proclaiming the "myth of race," race-critic Jared Diamond refined the argument in the 1994 issue of the very popular *Discover* magazine. Diamond chose a few traits such as lactose intolerance and fingerprint patterns that varied geographically among human populations and suggested by those traits alone, Swedes could be put in the same "racial category as the Ainu of Japan or the Xhosa of Africa. He asserted, therefore, that racial classification was nonsensical. Another media-popular disclaimer of race is Cavalli-Sforza, who in the preface of his major work, *The History and Geography of Human Genes*, gave lip-service to the arguments of Diamond and Montagu. Interestingly enough, when one looks at Cavalli-Sforza's world gene-distribution maps in his book, they show the same geographic boundaries that reflect the traditional racial groupings.

I had realized back in the 1960s that the "myth of race" argument is perfectly analogous to saying that the dozens of different breeds of dogs is a myth because one can find some specific traits that exist in varying breeds. I thought about the question long and hard, and I asked myself, "Because some similar traits are found in different breeds of dogs, does that mean that there are no St. Bernards or Chihuahuas?"

If Ashley Montagu were attacked by a dog, I think it might matter to him if the dog were a Doberman Pinscher or a Toy Poodle. As the Doberman began to chow down on him, would he still insist that the differences among the breeds of the canines don't exist? Even Montagu could predict that a Doberman offers a great deal more potential danger than a toy Poodle. If Diamond wants to be technical about it, many human traits and sets of traits, can be found that exist in other mammals. In fact, humans share 98.5 percent of their genes with Chimpanzees. If one follows Diamond's rationale, there is no difference between humans and Chimpanzees because we can find sets of arbitrarily selected genetic traits we share.

A number of scientists in recent times have brought up the fact that the DNA in Blacks and Whites differs by less than a percent, and therefore such a small difference could not mean much distinction in races. Yet, with only a 1.5 percent difference in DNA between humans and chimpanzees, humans have brains that are about twice as large. Small differences in DNA can make big differences in biological structure. Only a small number of genes set the structure of an organism. It is similar to the fact that only a small set of paper architectural plans make a big difference in the way wood, steel, concrete and glass construct a house.

Saying that the races are the same because similar genes make up the bulk of the physical structures of both Blacks and Whites is analogous to saying that because a shack is built of wood, steel and glass—it is the same as a skyscraper made of the same materials. The vast majority of the basic genes that make up the races are not only shared by them, but also by all mammals and even other orders of life. What makes the important distinctions are the small percentages of genes that effect the structure and composition of those life forms.

A race is a more or less distinct combination of inherited physiological, morphological and behavioral traits. J. Phillippe Rushton describes it this way:

> A race is what zoologists term a variety or subdivision of a species. Each race (or variety) is characterized by a more or less distinct combination of inherited morphological, behavioral, physiological traits. In flowers, insects, and non-human mammals, zoologists consistently and routinely study the process of racial differentiation. Formation of a new race takes place when, over several generations, individuals in one group reproduce more frequently among themselves than they do with individuals in other groups. This process is most apparent when the individuals live in diverse geographic areas and therefore evolve unique, recognizable adaptations (such as skin color) that are advantageous in their specific environments. But differentiation also occurs under less extreme circumstances. Zoologists and evolutionists refer to such differentiated populations as races. (Within the formal taxonomic nomenclature of biology, races are termed subspecies). Zoologists have identified two or more races (subspecies) in most mammalian species.

Differences between the major races of mankind include over 50 physiological and social variables. Other than the obvious differences in skin color and hair texture, they include brain size, cranial structure, dentition, intelligence, musculature, hormonal levels, sexual norms, temperament, longevity and a wide range of personality trait. As Rushton says eloquently, "If race were an arbitrary, socially-constructed concept, devoid of all biological meaning, such consistent relationships would not exist."

Science has long established different species and subspecies as a recognizable group having a common heredity. Take a look at what the Random House Webster's Dictionary has to say about the subject.

species
> *Biol.* the major subdivision of a genus or subgenus, regarded as the basic category of biological classification, composed of related individuals that **resemble one another,** are able to breed among themselves, but are not able to breed with members of another species.

race
> **1.** a group of persons **related by common descent or heredity.** a population so related.

breed
> *Genetics.* **a relatively homogenous group of animals within a species, developed and maintained by humans.**
> *lineage; stock; strain:* **She comes from a fine breed of people.**
> *offensive:* **half-breed** (emphasis mine)

Even though many scientists argue for the existence of many races of mankind, most accept the existence of at least three major divisions: Mongoloid, Caucasoid and Negroid. Obvious differences in facial features, skeletal and cranial characteristics, skin color and hair types make the three major races easily distinguishable. Blood, semen and molecular information can determine the race or even an estimate of the racial mixture in an individual. Scientific investigators can readily identify the race from just the skeletal parts of badly decomposed human remains, and the race of criminal perpetrators can readily be identified by traces of hair, semen, skin, or blood. The O.J. Simpson case gave the world a lesson in genetic racial identification.

Denying the reality of race is a good example of how egalitarians are grasping for straws. A mass of scientific evidence proves the existence of traits and features that identify the genetically differentiated breeds of mankind, just as there are genetically differentiated breeds of dogs or cats, or as I had found out years earlier in my garage — domestic and wild breeds of rat. One does not need molecular studies to know that race exists, all one must do is use his eyes and some common sense.

Imagine, for example, that a hypothetical extra-terrestrial that had no prior knowledge of humanity and no prejudices about race suddenly landed on the Earth to study its higher orders of life. He would immediately classify mankind into its different groups by the general observable differences that exist among them, just as he would the rest of the mammals and all other life forms. He would do it in the same way that we have genealogically classified the orders, species and subspecies (races or breeds) of the animal kingdom by their physical characteristics, appearance and genetic imprint. When the *Times-Picayune* ran its article, "White/Black: The Myth of Race", my campaign lawyer, James McPherson, quipped that it might as well have been called, "Light/Heavy, The Myth of Gravity."

In school, I discovered that anti-race bias had become almost like a religion with some people. They parroted back the silliest and most illogical concepts about race. For instance, someone would tell me that there are no such things as races because there are some individuals who may be racially mixed or who are not clearly of one race or another. That argument is much like saying that there is no day or night because for a few minutes every day at dusk it is hard to tell whether it is night or day.

Even a high-school teacher of mine maintained that there were no racial differences because some Whites are darker than some Blacks and that some Blacks are smarter than some Whites. Trying to negate group differences by citing individual exceptions is the poorest logic I could imagine. It is much like saying that because some grade school children are more knowledgeable than some college students, that there is no difference between the knowledge of college students and grade school students.

I have heard people say that individual variation within a race is greater than the average difference between races, so therefore race is irrelevant. One could easily take that fallacious argument to its logical conclusion and point out that since some humans unfortunately have less intelligence than some dogs, therefore there is no difference between humans and canines in intelligence. The racial egalitarians are just that silly, but like the fable of the emperor's new clothes; nobody dares to stand up and tell the truth!

Arguments erupted frequently at school, often with teachers. One teacher told me that there is no point to race because it is impossible to really know who is Black and who is White. I simply pointed out to her that the government seems to have no trouble in distinguishing between Blacks and Whites for affirmative action programs and for forced racial integration of education, and that she obviously believes that Blacks and Whites can be identified and therefore "integrated."

By far, the most popular saying among egalitarians is that Blacks and Whites differ only in color of skin. If that were true, one would be quite stupid to believe in racial differences in intelligence, and that is the direct implication. But, the idea that skin color is the only difference is patently absurd. Yet, the media consistently repeats it like a holy incantation, "We are all the same other than color of skin", How is it then, that every one of the top 16 semi-finalists in the 1996 Olympics 100 meter sprint were black, when one hundred times more Whites participate in organized track and field in the world? If the Black difference is just a darker skin color, how could skin color make one run faster? There are genetic qualities in Black people that make them, on average, more efficient sprinters and that talent has an *association* with skin color. If there are differences that can make one group have faster runners, it stands to reason that there can be differences that make other groups have faster thinkers.

I have already argued in this volume that IQ is primarily inherited and that Blacks and Whites differ dramatically in IQ—even when Blacks and Whites come from similar socioeconomic backgrounds. I have shown that there is abundant evidence of difference in the size of the brains of Africans as opposed to Europeans or Asians. Does the fact that there are at least 40 times more Whites per capita who have a genius level of intelligence have to do with the fact that they have lighter skin color than Negroes? Lighter skin has no direct effect on the brain. Intelligence is obviously created by genetic differences other than color of skin, although there may be an association of skin color with brain size and structure as representative of racial heritage. So although lighter skin does not make one smart, it can be associated with other racial genetic features that can.

Until very recent times, American society completely segregated people with any visible degree of black blood, even those only one-eighth or one-16th Negro. Is it an odd coincidence that lighter-skinned, and Caucasian-featured Blacks have a tremendous over-representation among Negroes who have achieved prominence in academic and scientific disciplines? Or could it simply be that their lighter skin color and Caucasian facial features are somewhat indicative of their predominant White genetic component, making their intelligence closer to the White norm. As I have noted previously, in repeated intelligence testing of mulattos and full-blooded Blacks, even when environmental factors are controlled, mulattos average somewhere between Whites and Blacks.

Yes. Whites, Blacks and Yellows have obvious differences in skin color and hair texture, but also in skeletal and cranial structure, blood groups and DNA fingerprinting. The latest DNA studies in fact indicate that ancestors of Blacks and Whites split at least as long as 110,000 ago (many say 200,000) and Whites and Asians about 40,000 years ago. Subspecies, which is the scientific term for race, has always denoted a geographic genetic differentiation of a species. Europeans, Asians and Africans obviously developed on different continents under different environments. I came to the conclusion that race is certainly *real* and that racial differences are *inherent* and profound. I then wanted to better understand how racial differences originated and their possible impact on modern society. To do that I had to look into evolutionary theory.

THE EVOLUTION OF RACES

To understand the evolution of the races, I found it instructive to understand the genetic development of dogs. All dog breeds are members of the same species, *Canis familiaris*, just as all humans are members of the same species *Homo sapiens*. We call the different varieties of dogs breeds, and we call the different varieties of humans, races, although breed can also describe human varieties. The only difference in the two terms is that breed usually denotes genetic selection by humans, while races denote genetic selection by the forces of the geographic environment.

Selective breeding from a single species created the spectacular variety of dog breeds over a relatively short period of time, perhaps only five or six thousand years. Humans selected dogs for certain physical and personality traits, segregated them from other dogs and created the vast differences in dog breeds we see today. Before the Black and White race as we know it, mankind's remote ancestors fanned out around the globe. The populations encountered vastly differing environments that selected for many characteristics, the most readily recognizable being the physical traits of skin color, hair texture and color, and eye color.

Once I understood the realities of racial difference, I realized that by learning about the evolutionary forces that created the different races, we can understand the character and conduct of the various races, our own included.

Numerous anthropological theories speculate about the origin and age of modern mankind and its varied races. The two dominant theories are called the Single Origin Hypothesis and the Multi-Regional Hypothesis. The Multi-Regionalists argue that a parallel evolution of the races has been going on since the *Homo erectus* stage of our evolution. According to this theory, Homo erectus emerged in Africa and migrated all over the Old World. In the different regions, shaped by different environmental conditions, they separately crossed the threshold of *Homo sapiens*. Homo erectus independently evolved to form the Mongoloid race in Asia, the Caucasian Race in Europe and the Negroid race in Africa. Anthropological artifacts seem to support this theory in that specimens of Homo erectus have been found in east Asia with tooth characteristics similar to those of the modern race that inhabits those regions. But, the DNA and other genetic evidence suggests a contradictory hypothesis.

Geneticists maintain that after mankind's ancestors reached an archaic *Homo sapiens* stage in Africa, they then evolved separately into two distinct genetic groups, the African and the non-African about 120,000 years ago. Later, a split between Europeans and Asians occurred around 40,000 years ago.

The latest DNA research seems to support the theory that the separate races evolved after crossing the *Homo sapiens* level, but the issue is far from decided. Whether or not the different races crossed the Homo sapiens threshold separately, the White and Black races have been divided for at least 110,000 years, even by the single origin theory. Asians and Whites, being separated for only 40,000 years have far more similarities than exist between Blacks and Whites. While scientists argue a bit about the timing, there is little doubt that the major races have been in existence for quite a long time, many tens of thousands of years, more than enough time for geography and climate to have created the profound differences that exist.

When I considered that the great differences in dogs had been created by selective breeding over only 5,000 years, it made sense to suppose that varying environments could have easily created the differences we see in mankind. For example, 100,000 years is time enough for over 5,000 human generations. To cause a 15 point higher increase in the average IQ of a population, it would only have to be increased on average by a tiny fraction of one percent (.003) each generation. That is an average of less than one-one-hundredth of an IQ point per generation. Five thousand generations is at least twice the number of generations needed to make the vast differences we see in dog breeds.

The geographically separated populations of mankind facing dramatically different climatic challenges, created what we recognize as the major races of mankind.

THE EFFECT OF CLIMATE ON THE RACIAL EVOLUTION

The Black race developed in the relatively warm, more tropical regions of Sub-Saharan Africa, while the European and Asian races had their origins in the colder, harsh regions of Europe and Asia. Obviously, the environment of the two regions was dramatically different. It explains the lighter skin of Whites, as a colder, wetter climate and the less available sunlight of Europe made lighter skin more advantageous for the absorption of needed Vitamin D. In the tropics, dark skin is important to protect the body from the damaging rays of the sun. Another example of climatic adaptation can be seen in the development of the protective eye fold of the Asians. The epicanthic fold is likely an evolutionary response to the extremely cold and windy weather of North East Asia

Lighter skin color is just one of the many genetic adaptations for survival by both

Europeans and northern Asians The very harsh, cold climate also selected for certain psychological and behavioral traits that facilitated survival. A cold climate selects for mental fitness and behavior in the same way it favors lighter skin.

My interest in the effects of evolution on the races was stirred by Professor Carleton Coon, who at the time of my inquiry, was the president of the American Association of Physical Anthropologists and the premier physical anthropologist in the world. I read all of his books I could find, including *The Living Races of Man, Story of Man, Origin of the Races,* and *The Races of Europe.*

Later, I read his classics *The Hunting Peoples* and in 1982 *Racial Adaptations.* Coon wrote extensively in his books of the impact of the extremely cold climates on prehistoric mankind. Two other books that made a great impact on me were *Man the Hunter* and *Hunters of the Northern Ice.*

From my reading, I began to sketch a broad outline of life that existed in the Northern Hemisphere during prehistoric times. Much of the last two hundred thousand years the northern world has been in periods of advancing and retreating glacial ice ages. The Northern Hemisphere is currently in a lull between ice ages. Survival for prehistoric man in Europe was far more difficult, even in the lulls between the ice ages, than for man in the milder African climate. During most of the last 80,000 years, Europe endured temperatures much colder than today. Modern Europeans emerged about 35,000 years ago and met the crucible of the Würm glaciations (24,000–10,000 B.C.). Temperatures in Europe and Asia probably averaged about 18 degrees (F) colder than the present.

I traveled on a short trip with my father to Kansas City and while there experienced a snow storm on the road to Lawrence, Kansas. As I read about the trials of prehistoric Europeans, I thought about the sub-zero temperatures, and the miles upon miles of nothing but snow. and ice I had seen. With that picture in my mind, I thought about how difficult it must have been for prehistoric Europeans to survive such rigors. Yet, the temperatures of the Würm glaciations would have been far colder than that of Kansas.

As the ancestors of modern man migrated further to the North, they needed a number of vital skills and behavioral qualities to survive. Unlike tropical Africa, the technology to create warm, well-made clothing and sturdy shelter became necessary for survival. The ability to make and control fire became an essential survival skill. Dealing with the deadly forces of winter demanded skills not required in the tropics. Scarcity of edible plants and small game, and even the fact that birds migrated south for the winter, posed unique problems, as early man relied a great deal on eggs and young animals, for food. These were scarce in the cold months.

In Africa, numerous kinds of edible vegetation existed, as well as small rodents and insects and other varied and abundant food sources. By contrast, the ground in Europe was a frozen sea of snow and ice for many months each year and even many trees had no leaves. In the mildest of months, the inhabitants had to prepare for the harsh periods by deferring gratification and putting aside stores of food and supplies. In such cold climates, hunting large game rather than gathering edibles became the chief source of food and supplies.

Prehistoric European-Asian Conditions	Prehistoric Sub-Saharan Africa
complex—sturdy shelter—critical	minimal shelter needed for survival
winter—extremely harsh climate	no winter—comfortable climate
Warm, well-made clothing—critical	no clothing required for survival
ability to make/control fire critical	fire not required for survival
Long periods of resource deprivation	resources more abundant
periods of little vegetation, few small animals or birds—hunting necessary	food gathering less problematic in tropical climes—gathering favored
foresight, planning and delayed gratification necessary for survival	little seasonal change, immediate gratification favored
In resource scarce male-provisioned hunting-society, monogamy favored	in female provisioned gathering society, polygamy favored
male provisioned society, less sexual and physical aggression favored	female provisioned society favors male aggression and sexual drive
promiscuous behavior resulting in fights often leads to death of mate and children	death in fights from sexual competition not critical for survival of mates and children

Because hunting provided most resources, females and children became dependent on male provisioning, leading to a strong bond between men and their immediate family. In both Europe and Asia men had to provide for their mates and children if they were to survive.

FAMILY PATTERNS OF EUROPEANS AND AFRICANS

In the more tropical climate of Africa, survival depended mostly on gathering rather than hunting. The lush vegetation and abundant small animal life provided far greater food resources than in the northern climes. The African mother could feed herself and her children with little help from the father. On a pretty fall day, there was no necessity for the inhabitants of the tropics to control an impulse to lie upon a bed of leaves with a mate and satisfy sexual desires, but in the cold north; such an indulgence could affect survival in the winter months ahead.

In the North, those who survived were more likely the ones who had the self-control to defer sexual and other forms of immediate gratification. On those pretty warm days they had to use that precious time and good weather to prepare for the extremely difficult winter days ahead. When the inevitable months of bad weather came, often they had to ration their food rather than completely satisfy their hunger.

In Europe, the prehistoric economy found dependence on several primary animals. Probably the most important were the mastodon and the various breeds of deer and reindeer. Now extinct, the mastodon was the largest animal ever to walk the Earth contemporaneous to man. A great hairy beast adapted to the cold temperatures of Europe and Northern Asia, it stood about twice the size of the great African Elephant, had huge tusks and was easily strong enough to lift weight equivalent to a small automobile. To hunt such creatures demanded technologically-effective weapons, as well as effective teamwork and planning. Much of the prehistoric economy of Europe found its base in products harvested from the Mastodon. Meat and fat, thick skins for clothing, shoes and shelter, bone and sinew for weapons and tools, oil for their lamps, organs used for thread and containers—the Mastodon provided all these products and more. Obviously, it was hunted exclusively by males. The same was true for deer and other game.

With food supplies coming mostly from hunting rather than gathering, females and children were very dependent on male provisioning. At the same time, males depended on females for much of the work involved in preparing and processing the products of the kill, as well as the gathering needs of the clan, work which could be done while caring for the children.

If the male would randomly have sexual relations with females and then abandon them and his children, they had a greatly lessened chance of survival. Dr. Edward Miller of the University of New Orleans has done much work on these concepts in his groundbreaking paper: *"Paternal Provisioning versus Mate Seeking in Human Populations."* Even when surviving relatives shared some of the hunt with fatherless families, in times of scarce food resources they were likely to be the last fed. If the male had multiple mates and many children, even if he fried to take care of all of them he could have difficulty providing for them. In Africa, because women generally supported themselves and their children, male bonding and support was not nearly as important to survival. In fact, male bonding, empathy and time spent with the wife and children only lessened the male's opportunities to mate with more females. It was an environment and social system that greatly rewarded male sexual aggressiveness and infidelity. Evolutionary success for the African male found reward in his immediately gratifying his own sexual desires with as many females as possible. It favored male genes leading to strong sexual drive, aggression, and genetic advantages in fighting that comes from intense male competition for women.

Biologists call the strategy of having few children combined with high parental investment a "K" strategy, and that of having more children which is naturally accompanied by less paternal investment per child an "r" strategy. The tropical climate of Africa tended to support an *r* strategy among males and selected for males who employed it. Because of female provisioning, an effective reproductive strategy for males was to father as many children as possible since such conduct would give the most assurance that their genes would survive.

In the harsh and resource scarce environment of the cold climes, if a male were to father many children by many women, he would not likely be able to provision them. The result could well be the loss of them all. However, males having a single family and fewer children could provide greater paternal sustenance and care, enabling survival of a much higher percentage. The European environment thus encouraged a K reproductive strategy.

AGGRESSION AS REPRODUCTIVE STRATEGY

In any society where males attempt to mate aggressively with as many females as possible there is great potential for violence. Efforts to mate with other male's mates would encounter risk of retaliation. Any biological group in which males frequently fight for females favors genes in males that lead to combative success. Hand-to-hand fighting is very anaerobic and usually only takes a few moments to determine a winner. It favors those who have muscles favored for quick bursts of speed rather than raw strength. A fighter with longer arms than his foe has a distinct advantage, making it easier to strike his enemy while avoiding his enemy's blows. A thicker cranium allows him to withstand blows to the head which could otherwise render him insensible and vulnerable. 196 A flat nose with wider nostrils allows greater airflow needed for quick exertion, and it is harder to break than the longer nose Europeans need to warm the cold air as well as filter out viruses and bacteria.

In prehistoric Europe, fighting could occur for many reasons, including pursuit of females and territorial conflicts, but the pattern of male provisioning of their mates and children certainly encouraged restraint. Although the European or Asian might sexually desire a female belonging to someone else, he had more reason to control his emotions and sexual urges, for if he was killed or seriously injured in a fight, his children could likely die as well. Until very recent times, most marriages were arranged by the parents, so reason would suggest that they would attempt to select males for their daughters who were more inclined to fidelity.

Many studies show that even in the modern world, woman are far more selective and reticent than men in regard to mating. Among European and Asian women this is especially true. Just as there is a striking difference between males and females, there is also a difference between European and African women. In prehistoric Europe, choosing the right mate was critical to the female's survival. For if her mate did not provision her, she and her children would face much greater hardship and possible death.

In Africa, although there could be advantages for a woman if the male helped provide for her, it was not nearly as important to her survival. Surveys of Blacks worldwide show that Black males and females begin sexual relations earlier, have more sexual partners, more frequent sexual relations, more absent fathers, more polygamy, higher testosterone levels in males, more prominent secondary sexual characteristics, and much higher rates of sexually transmitted diseases. For instance, even in the United States, African-Americans are 50 times more likely to have syphilis, and in some areas, an incredible 100 times greater likelihood of gonorrhea. Blacks are 14 times more likely to have AIDS than are non-Hispanic Whites. "I don't think there is any question that the epidemic in this country is becoming increasingly an epidemic of color," said Surgeon General David Satcher.

PHYSICAL MANIFESTATIONS

In colder climates, strength and endurance became the deciding physical factors for survival rather than speed. Men had to be strong enough to build complex and heavy structures of wood or stone, or sometimes even of ice. It made more evolutionary sense for the European to have a bit more insulating body fat and a larger body cavity than Africans, as such helps protect the body from times of intense cold. Africans having a lower percentage of body fat, arms and legs proportionately larger to body size, smaller body cavities, and smaller heads—helps make them more efficient in running, jumping and fighting.

In the modern world, Black domination of boxing illustrates the physical differences created by the differing evolution of the races. Soon after Blacks were permitted to participate freely in the organized sport, they quickly asserted their superiority in it. Black athletes have muscle types that can provide quick bursts of speed, while Whites tend to dominate sports that require maximum strength and endurance. Weightlifting, for example, is overwhelmingly dominated by Europeans and Asians.

When I was looking into the evolutionary questions, one of the most heavily-promoted sporting events in history was the Mohamed Ali,

Chuck Wepner fight. I remember the statistical differences to this day. Wepner stood six foot six inches in height, but interestingly, Ali who stood three inches shorter, had a reach that was six inches longer. Wepner however, was much stronger and could lift dramatically heavier weights than Ali. It became obvious in the fight that although Wepner had a tremendously powerful blow, Ali's speed allowed him to simply strike, bob, weave and dance around his slower European-American opponent. Despite Ali's evolutionary advantage, in a courageous effort, Wepner lasted 15 rounds with Ali, and inspired the Rocky movie series based on his character. I was probably the only one in the neighborhood who thought about the evolutionary racial differences between Ali and Wepner as the replay of the fight came on TV.

The Roots of Higher Intelligence

In an extremely cold and inhospitable natural environment higher human intelligence is dramatically favored. Europe demanded a higher technology for survival. If a society depends almost wholly on hunting, development of advanced weapons, traps and sophisticated strategies can be critically important when there is scarce game. Effective hunting, fishing and trapping in such an environment can demand well-developed cognitive skills. The invention and rigging of ingenious traps can demand high intelligence. The skills and the tools necessary to make a fire, no easy task in a cold wet environment, can mean the difference between life and death. If a heavy shelter constructed to keep out winter collapses on its occupants because of poor design, they could well die. In equatorial Africa, if the leaves or straw huts blow away in a rainstorm, the occupants can just build another one tomorrow. If a native gets lost in the rain forests of Africa, he can live on the fauna and flora while he finds his way back, while if the European gets lost in winter he could freeze to death.

A number of writers on European prehistory believe that navigating on long winter hunts with nondescript landscapes, favored survival of Europeans and Asians with high levels of spatial reasoning. Tracking the movements of reindeer and other arctic herds from great distances demanded the intelligence to weigh past information and develop strategies to anticipate the herd movement.

Parents and prospective brides naturally tried to choose potential mates who they thought would be faithful to the wife and children. Even the female intelligence needed to detect male deception became an important genetic advantage. It was important for a female and her parents to determine if a prospective male had other families on the side. If a male had other mates and children he could well have to choose whom to provide with the dwindling stores when the shortages of winter came. On the male side, it was evolutionarily important for him to figure out if his mate was cheating and thus avoid provisioning a wife and children who were not carrying on his genes.

An important aspect of intelligence is the ability to think abstractly. To conceive of winter on a warm spring or summer day is an abstract thought, as is the very concept of the future. In harsh climates one must be able to conceive of tomorrow, and even more importantly, the more distant future such as next winter. In tropical zones, life is much more immediate. Without the prospect of a harsh winter, there was little need to plan for the future. If one lives only in the immediate, one is less likely to control or restrain impulsive behavior and to delay gratification.

In the long, cold hunts of the north, the hunter often had to be quiet and restrained for long periods of time, and other than occasional hunts for herds or Mastodons, he often was likely to be alone for long periods of time. Such would tend to favor restraint and introversion rather than talkativeness and extraversion. We can see this evolutionary model as represented in the strong, silent prototype of the classic European. On a popular level we find it in our attraction to the stoic heroes of our Western movies. Such is represented by men such as Gary Cooper or John Wayne, or even the classic Clint Eastwood films. That behavioral characteristic can be readily contrasted to the jive talk or the trash talk of the stereotypical Black athlete, or the sexual rap by Black males ever on the prowl in the African village or the American high school hallway.

Although a wide range of personality types are present in Europeans, on the whole, our people are quieter, more restrained, more under control. The difference between races can be seen in everything from the intricate musical melodies of Mozart as compared to the elemental beat of rap, from quiet fashion to flashy dress, from thoughtful and considerate speech, to the loud and boisterous nature that Kochman admired in his study of the Black personality.

In the cold north, as the European was more restrained and less aggressive, so the European had to develop an intense sense of community and social justice. In an African tribe of gatherers everyone can provision themselves. They can eat and indulge themselves while they gather and no one will be the wiser. They have no vital need to share or develop higher systems of social justice or common welfare. In the small hunting bands of Europe, sometimes game was so scarce that an individual hunter may not have luck bringing home any game for weeks, but one hunter's reindeer kill might fend off starvation for the whole group. Pressures for community needs and a group altruism must have been intense, creating the social conscience and ethics of Europe.

Successfully hunting the great mastodons of Europe took a tremendous group effort. Bringing one down took planning, coordination, and effective and precise communication. There was a high risk of death. Under such circumstances, the gene pool would favor genes of altruism and self-sacrifice, for each one had to take great individual risks so that the clan could survive. After the kill there had to be a well-organized effort and division of labor to process and preserve its valuable resources.

Fire became vital for survival. In inclement conditions it is much easier to keep a fire going than to light one. Some ancient bands likely lit a fire when it was warm and dry in the fall and then endeavored to keep it going all winter. To do that took teamwork, responsibility, accountability, emotional restraint and self-discipline. If just one member of the group who had responsibility for keeping the fire going fails for reasons of stupidity or irresponsibility, the whole group could die. If the exhausted hunter does not rise when it is his watch; delay his immediate need for the gratification of sleep and willfully stay awake to tend the fire, many could die.

I believe that these were some of the evolutionary forces that forged the European's intelligence, self-control, altruism and sense of social justice. From the crucible of Europe's environment came our legal systems, our government forms, our principles of self-government and freedom, as well as our social conscience.

In a hunting society where birthrates are low and death rates are high, both the female and the male must protect, provision and treasure each child. In Africa where men were driven more by sexual coupling than the love of family, and where the most honored are those with the greatest number of sexual conquests, an individual child or its mother meant little to those males who had many. When human life is too abundant it tends to lose value. On the other hand, in a struggling small band that faces the severest challenges of survival, each life becomes precious. In its rarity comes the appreciation of life's beauty. Our ancestors had that appreciation. A man who has many sexual partners is not as selective about his mate as one who must choose for a lifetime. And, in the hard climes, women and their families had to select men for their loyalty and responsibility. So evolved our race and so arose the nuclear family.

CLASS 20

Sexual Orientation Issues

CHAPTER 30
Opening Classroom Closets: Teaching About Lesbians, Gay Men, and Bisexuals in a Multicultural Context

Jovita Baber and Brett Beemyn

Brett Beemyn and Jovita Baber's article discusses the changing views of family and sexuality in American society. The authors also discuss the need to include issues about gender and sexual orientation in our educational curriculums.

Opening Classroom Closets:
Teaching About Lesbians, Gay Men,
and Bisexuals in a Multicultural Context

R. Jovita Baber and Brett Beemyn

Currently pursuing a doctorate in Latin American history at the University of Chicago, Jovita Baber's experience includes five years in education and educational reform as a bilingual social studies teacher in the Chicago public schools. She served as a history teacher in Oak Park and River Forest schools, and a bilingual literacy coordinator at the University of Chicago Center for School Improvement.

The co-editor with Mickey Eliason of *Queer Studies: A Lesbian, Gay, Bisexual, and Transgender Anthology* and the editor of *Creating A Place for Ourselves: Lesbian, Gay, and Bisexual Community Histories*, Brett Beemyn is currently writing a history of LGBT life in Washington, DC and finishing an anthology about male bisexuality.

The following article was originally written by R. Jovita Baber in 1993 and updated by Brett Beemyn in 1999 to incorporate more recent studies and examples. Sadly, many of the arguments about the failure of schools to foster acceptance of lesbian, gay men, and bisexuals remain as valid today as they were six years ago.

Family, the mass media, and formal education are probably the most powerful institutions influencing and maintaining our present culture. The family in the United States has undergone dramatic changes in the last century. The media reflects these changes, while education is caught in a political battle over its role in teaching about them. Among the most contested changes are those related to the place of lesbians, gay men, and bisexuals within our society. Educational institution need to teach acceptance of lesbians, gay men, and bisexuals, since they are members of our pluralistic society but are subject to discrimination and harassment based on their sexual and gender identities.

In the early sixties and seventies, the traditional nuclear, heterosexual family came under critical examination with the rise of the women's liberation movement. The release of Betty Friedan's book *The Feminine Mystique* (1963)—in which she wrote about "the problem that has no name"—helped spark a change in attitudes. Instead of asking, "What's wrong with women who can't adjust to marriage?" people started to ask "What's wrong with marriage that so many women can't adjust to it?" Thereafter, many studies of marriage placed the traditional nuclear family under closer scrutiny (Tavris & Wade, 1984).

Our society's ideas about what defines a family and the roles of men and women in families have been revolutionized since the early sixties. For example, the rate of divorce has doubled since 1960, and the Census Bureau now projects that 40% of new marriages will fail (National Center for Health Statistics, 1995; Vobejda, 1998). As of 1998, there were nearly 12.5 million single mothers in the U.S., and 72% of all mothers were in the paid work force(Bureau of Labor Statistics, 1999a; 1999b). The number of children born out of wedlock increased from under 4% in 1950, to 11% in

1970, to more than 32% in 1997 (Magnet, 1992; National Center for Health Statistics, 1998). At the same time, the number of lesbian, gay, and bisexual parents has grown tremendously in the 1980s and '90s; studies estimate that from four to 14 million children are currently being raised by two to eight million lesbian/gay/bisexual parents (Patterson, 1995). As a result of these changes, the "traditional" family, with the father going off to work and the mother remaining at home to take care of the children, represents just 10% of U.S. families today (Bates, 1992). Educational institutions need to acknowledge these new realities in their policies and curricula.

Many of these changes are related to changing ideas about sexuality. We have inherited many of our sexual mores from the Victorian era, when sex was considered "dirty, dangerous and disgusting." A Victorian female was expected to "save herself" for her husband. But since the 1960s, several studies on sexual behavior have shown that the number of women having pre-marital sex is increasing and that people's attitudes and behaviors about sex in general have become more liberal. As a result, sex is no longer seen as something dirty, but rather, as a natural part of intimate relationships.

At the beginning of the century, the idea of contraceptives was a radical notion. Today, though, most people do not question an adult's right to use birth control. Contraceptives and their acceptance have allowed people to separate sex as a pleasurable, intimate activity from its reproductive function. When this occurred, lesbian, gay, and bisexual relationships were increasingly able to assume a more logical place as part of a new understanding of sexuality.

Within the context of society's changing attitudes around family and sexuality, the lesbian, gay, bisexual, and transgender (LGBT) rights movement has grown and developed. Those who oppose equal protection for lesbians, gay men, and bisexuals generally want to maintain traditional sexual mores and the nuclear family. The Reverend Pat Robertson has charged that laws that limit discrimination against lesbians, gay men, and bisexuals would legitimize their lifestyle and "would destroy the American family." This argument is often part of a larger philosophy that equates the erosion of the traditional family with the demise of our society: "this revolution [the result of an epidemic of divorce, remarriage, ille-

gitimacy, and new strains within intact families] ... has deeply troubling implications for the American social order" (Magnet, 1992).

People who are more accepting of the changes in the family are often more receptive to lesbians, gay men, and bisexuals. They typically argue that the family is a flexible institution that has always changed with the times and will continue to do so. Doherty (1992) describes today's family arrangements as the "pluralistic family":

> no single family arrangement ... [but] a plethora of family types ... including dual career families, never-married families, post-divorce families, step families, and gay and lesbian families. Legislative bodies and courts are beginning to codify the Pluralistic Family by redefining the terms to include arrangements considered deviant, nonfamily forms in the past. Tolerance and diversity, rather than a single family ideal, characterizes the Pluralistic Family. (p. 35)

Although some of these new arrangements have become embedded in society's perceptions of family. Doherty acknowledges that the plethora of family types has left many people feeling very ambivalent. "Surveys indicate that most Americans still believe in the traditional family values ... that the stable two-parent family is the best environment for raising children." However, she cites family sociologist Dennis Orthner, who points out a difference between family "values" and family "norms." While our values and ideals have remained traditional, our norms and expectations have changed remarkably, as indicated by the earlier statistics on families in the U.S.

Similar ambivalence is felt toward acknowledging lesbian, gay, and bisexual relationships. Polls in the last few years have consistently shown that large majorities support equal rights for gays in job opportunities (84%) and housing (80%), but oppose same-sex sexuality itself. For example, 56% of the respondents to a 1996 survey said they believed sexual relations between two consenting adults were "always wrong," while 46% of those polled in another survey thought such relationships should be illegal (Yang, 1997; Yang, 1998). Even higher numbers believe that same-sex marriage should not be legalized—about two-thirds of respondents to recent polls. Although the level of disapproval for same-sex relationships is down from highs of 70–75% in the 1980s and early '90s

(Yang, 1997), these findings demonstrate that while people may ideally believe in equality for all, they are not ready to give up their conviction that nuclear families are better than other family arrangements. They will not "endorse homosexuality as equal to heterosexuality" (Shapiro, 1993). The conflict that arises when schools want to teach about lesbians, gay men, and bisexuals is embedded in the differences between family "values" and family "norms," and sexual "values" and sexual "norms."

Social trends indicate that our society will probably not return to the traditional nuclear family as the dominant family arrangement (Wallis, 1992). Doherty (1992) writes: "The forces of gender equality, diversity, and personal freedom may never again permit a single ideal family structure. . . ." Doherty further states that the "Pluralistic Family has redefined our notions about relationships, parenthood, and homelife. Increased tolerance for multiracial and single-sex couples who are raising children will be necessary as this type of family is here to stay for an indefinite future." Thus schools need to play an active role in encouraging acceptance of multiracial and same-sex relationships.

The mass media is already giving greater and often more positive attention to lesbians, gay men, and bisexuals. For example, searches of *The New York Times* and *The Washington Post* for stories that mention "lesbian and gay" resulted in 267 and 214 articles, respectively, for the past twelve months alone. Whether it is features on brain studies that seek to unravel the mysteries of sexual orientation, news reports about the Senate's refusal to confirm an openly gay man to an ambassadorship, or the critical treatment of the assertion by Jerry Falwell's group that one of the Teletubbies is gay, stories involving gay people have become a regular feature of the national print media. In popular magazines, lesbians, gay men, and/or bisexuals were the cover stories of the June 21, 1993 and July 17, 1995 editions of *Newsweek*, the July 5, 1993 edition of *U.S. News and World Report*, and the July 19, 1993 edition of *Christianity Today*. In 1998, the press gave unprecedented coverage to the hate-motivated murder of Matthew Shepherd, and many newspapers and magazines responded to his death by calling for passage of a national hate crimes law that would increase penalties for attacks motivated by someone's actual or perceived sexuality. Undoubtedly, part of the reason the story received so much attention was because Shepherd was a white, middle-class gay college student. (In the six months following Shepherd's death, six transgendered people, most of whom were people of color and poor, were killed because of their gender identity, but their murders were entirely ignored by the mainstream media, even in some of the places where the attacks occurred (Meyer, 1999].) Nevertheless, the story of Shepherd's death would not have been considered as newsworthy if lesbians, gay men, and bisexuals were not becoming more accepted.

Human sexuality, in its many forms, is also increasingly being represented on television and in movies. In 1997, there were a record 30 lesbian, gay, and bisexual television characters, led by the show *Ellen*, which became the first prime-time series to have its lead character come out (Gay and Lesbian Alliance Against Defamation, 1997). Although it was canceled after the 1998 season, the widespread coverage given to *Ellen* demonstrated the growing visibility of gay people on television. Likewise, Hollywood movies are including more—though not necessarily more realistic—depictions of lesbians, gay men, and bisexuals, with recent popular films ranging from *The Silence of the Lambs* (1991) and *Basic Instinct* (1992) to *The Birdcage* (1996). *In and Out* (1997), and *As Good As It Gets* (1998).

Historically, the few lesbian, gay, and bisexual personalities in the entertainment media were often characterized negatively. More recently, they are included because their sexuality is key to the story line: "The story focuses on their sexuality rather than their day-to-day nonsexual lives" (Herek & Berrill, 1992). While the images of lesbians, gay men, and bisexuals are increasing and becoming less hostile, they are still seldom portrayed as compassionate, whole (sexual and nonsexual) people. This is no small matter, for the mass media affect how people perceive lesbians, gay men, and bisexuals. In a *U.S. News and World Report* poll, 56% of voters worried that media portrayals of gays had had a negative influence on society (Shapiro, 1993). Schools need to balance the continuing stereotypical depictions of lesbians, gay men, and bisexuals in the media with more realistic representations.

Teaching about lesbians, gay men, and bisexuals is riddled with the political controversies surrounding the changing family and sexual morality. Schools throughout the nation are cautiously beginning to question when and where to teach children about lesbians, gay men, and bisexuals (Lacayo, 1992). One of the most heated debates erupted in New York City in 1992 when the "Children of the Rainbow" curriculum suggested that first graders read the gay/lesbian-positive books *Daddy's Roommate*, *Heather Has Two Mommies*, and *Gloria Goes to Gay Pride*. Half of the 32 local school boards balked. The borough of Queens had an outright revolt, as sexual morality and "traditional family values" became the focus of debate (Tucker, 1993).

Other places have avoided this kind of political battle by introducing lesbians, gay men, and bisexuals into the curriculum at a later grade level and by including community leaders in the process of policy development (Celis, 1993; Ribadeneira, 1992; Tucker, 1993). Massachusetts created the nation's first Governor's Commission on Gay and Lesbian Youth in 1992 to work towards the creation of a safe, supportive environment for lesbian, gay, and bisexual students in the state's public schools, which led the following year to Massachusetts banning sexual orientation discrimination in its educational institutions (Massachusetts Governor's Commission on Gay and Lesbian Youth, 1997). Most changes, though, are occurring on the city or county level: Fairfax County in Virginia, Broward County in Florida, Houston, San Francisco, and Seattle have begun to include lesbians, gay men, and bisexuals in various areas of their curricula (Celis, 1993; Tucker, 1993).

At the same time, a growing number of colleges and universities are establishing sexuality or lesbian and gay studies programs and offering courses in the field. At least fourteen schools currently have a minor, concentration, or certificate in sexuality/lesbian and gay studies, San Francisco City College provides a bachelor's degree, and Brandeis University and Barnard College are currently planning degree programs (Younger, 1999). More than a hundred colleges and universities now offer regular classes on lesbians, gay men, and bisexuals, and numerous others are incorporating such material into more general courses. Why are so many schools integrating lesbians, gay men, and bisexuals into their curricula when their inclusion often sparks controversies over the family and sexual morality?

The Importance of Integrating Lesbians, Gay Men, and Bisexuals into the Curriculum

The primary reason for including lesbians, gay men, and bisexuals in the curriculum is because they are members of our pluralistic society. Some people argue that 10% of the population is lesbian and gay, citing the Kinsey studies (Kinsey, Pomeroy, & Martin, 1948; Kinsey, Pomeroy, Martin, & Gebhard, 1953). More recently, surveys conducted by the Alan Gultmacher Institute and the National Opinion Research Center found that only 1% and 2.8% of men, respectively, were **exclusively** gay. These figures are in line with the 1–3% findings of surveys in Britain, France, and Denmark (Barringer, 1993a; Schmalz, 1993). But a distinction has to be made here between behavior and identity: many people who are involved in same-sex relationships don't consider themselves lesbian, gay, or bisexual. Another recent study reported that 22% of men and 17% of women had had same-sex sexual experiences, but just 9% of the men and 5% of the women self-identified as homosexual or bisexual (Keen, 1993). The fact that people tend to underreport behavior that might be considered anti-social and overreport behavior that is socially sanctioned makes it even more difficult to assess the exact number of lesbians, gay men, and bisexuals in our society (Barringer, 1993b). But whether lesbians, gay men, and bisexuals make up 1%, 10%, or 20% of the population, they are members of our society and should receive the same benefits, rights, and respect as other people.

In a pluralistic society such as the United States, we must teach the acceptance of difference. One can see the results of social intolerance in the 1990s by observing the ethnic cleansing in Bosnia, Rwanda, and Kosovo, the neo-Nazi attacks on Turkish people in Germany, the Iraqi treatment of the Kurds, and other international crises (Breslau, 1992; Lief, 1992; Lane & Breslau, 1992). Similar violence created by social intolerance is seen within the U.S. in 1997, 8,049 hate-crime incidents were reported to the FBI by local law-enforcement agencies. The actual number of incidents was undoubtedly even higher, as jurisdictions representing 17% of the U.S. population did not provide any information and many others submitted inadequate reports. For example, not a single hate crime was recorded for the year in the entire states of Alabama, Mississippi, and Arkansas. Crimes motivated by race made up the largest category of the incidents that were reported (58%), followed by religion (17%), sexual preference (14%), and ethnicity (11%) (Freiberg, 1998).

Groups whose mission is to monitor hate crimes against lesbians, gay men, bisexuals, and transgendered people receive many more reports of violence. The National Coalition of Anti-Violence Programs documented 2,445 hate crimes against individuals who were known or perceived to be lesbian, gay, bisexual, or transgendered in 1997, more than twice as many incidents as were submitted to the FBI. But even these statistics are incomplete, as they are based on reports from only 14 violence tracking programs, and many areas of the country lack any means to document such crimes (Freiberg, 1998). A 1998 study of nearly 500 college students in the San Francisco Bay area conducted by psychologist Karen Franklin found that the majority had participated in or witnessed anti-gay incidents. Half of the male respondents admitted to some form of anti-gay attack: 18% said that they had engaged in physical violence or threats against people whom they believed were lesbian, gay, or bisexual, and another 32% had taken part in anti-gay name calling. And far from being guilty over their involvement in hate crimes, nearly half of the assailants said they would likely assault again in similar circumstances. "Indeed, assaults on gay men and lesbians were so socially acceptable that respondents often advocated or defended such behaviors out loud in the classrooms, while I was administering my survey," Franklin states. Many of the students who had never assaulted or harassed someone perceived as gay were not more tolerant so much as they were concerned about getting into trouble or experiencing retaliation. Franklin argues that "[a]s long as the schools are breeding grounds for intolerance and abuse, hate crimes will continue" (American Psychological Association, 1998; Ness, 1998).

Because of their power to influence society, educational institutions can help limit the number of hate crimes committed by teaching acceptance of diversity. The majority of these crimes are committed by youth and young adults. The general profile of the "gay basher" is a young male acting alone or with other young men. One study indicated that 54% of the assailants were under 21 years of age, and 92% were male. Another report, by the Governor's Task Force on Bias-Related Violence, revealed that high school students were more prejudiced against gays than any other group (Herek & Berrill, 1992). Franklin concludes from her research that "the majority of young people who harass, bully, and assault sexual minorities do not fit the stereotype of the hate-filled extremist. Rather, they are average young people who often do not see anything wrong with their behavior. And the reason they do not see anything wrong is simple—no one is telling them that it is wrong" (American Psychological Association, 1998; Ness, 1998). Educators must attempt to reduce the fears, intolerance, and ignorance behind violent attitudes such as these by teaching about difference. In U.S. society, opposing opinions—even hatred—are and should be admissible by the First Amendment, but violent acts that stem from intolerance cannot be permitted.

Either lack of policies or the lax enforcement of policies has permitted much of the harassment and hate crimes against lesbians, gay men, and bisexuals to happen in our educational institutions. A study conducted by psychologist Anthony D' Augelli found that 17% of lesbian, gay, and bisexual youth had been assaulted, 44% had been threatened with physical attack, and 80% had been subjected to direct verbal abuse (Gay, Lesbian and Straight Education Network, 1999b). Another survey found that they were seven times more likely than their nongay classmates to be threatened with a weapon while at school. In one Des Moines high school, students found that their classmates experience anti-gay epithets 25 times a day on average, and teachers who overhear such slurs fail to respond to them 97% of the time. Given such an atmosphere, it is not surprising that the most recent Youth Risk Behavior Survey of the Massachusetts Department of Education revealed that the state's lesbian, gay, and bisexual students are more than five times as likely as other students to skip classes because they feel unsafe at or en route to school (Gay, Lesbian and Straight Education Network, 1999a).

The same intolerance is found at colleges and universities. In 1989 alone, a total of 1,329 anti-gay episodes were reported to the National Gay and Lesbian Task Force by lesbian, gay, and bisexual student groups on just 40 campuses (Herek & Berrill, 1992). Such acts of violence and harassment have led a number of institutions to investigate their campus climate for LGBT students, staff, and faculty in recent years. Examining the results of investigations at 30 colleges and universities, diversity specialist Sue Rankin found that anti-gay incidents were prevalent at all of them:

> For example, in studies where surveys were used as the primary tool, the data indicated that LGBT students are the victims of anti-lgbt prejudice ranging from verbal abuse (2%–86%)to physical violence (6%–59%) to sexual harassment (1%–21%).
>
> In those investigations that utilized qualitative data, analogous findings were reported indicating the invisibility, isolation, and fear of LGBT members of the academic community. Their lives are filled with secret fears. For the professor, counselor, staff assistant or student who is gay, lesbian, bisexual or transgendered, there is the constant fear that, should they be found out, they would be ostracized, their careers would be destroyed, or they would lose their positions (Rankin, 1999).

To cite just one campus study, a survey at the University of Oregon found that 61% of lesbian, gay, and bisexual students feared for their personal safety (Herek & Berrill, 1992). An environment in which nearly two-thirds of a group of people feel threatened does not nurture tolerance, pluralism, or democratic ideals. Educational institutions need to encourage the exploration of new and opposing ideas, while penalizing violent and bigoted behavior. Policies that clearly state a punishment for harassing or victimizing a person because of their minority status should be implemented and enforced.

A second reason for schools to integrate lesbians, gay men, and bisexuals into the curriculum is because they are likely to have students, including lesbians, gay men, and bisexuals, who are struggling with their sexuality. Lesbian, gay, and bisexual youth often take to heart the hatred that is directed at them through harassment. They internalize the rejection they received from peers and family and find few available role models to assist them in developing positive self-images. These factors put lesbian, gay, and bisexual youth in a high-risk group for dropping out of school, committing suicide, and abusing drugs and alcohol (U.S. Department of Health and Human Services, 1989; Uribe & Harbeck, 1992).

The U.S. Department of Health and Human Services' "Report of the Secretary's Task Force on Youth Suicide" (1989) states that "gay youth are 2 to 3 times more likely to attempt suicide than other young people. They may comprise up to 30 percent of completed youth suicides annually." Subsequent studies have confirmed these results. A 1995 survey of public high school students in Massachusetts found that lesbian, gay, bisexual, and questioning youth were 3.41 times more likely to report a suicide attempt than their peers, and one-third had attempted suicide in the previous year. Among adolescent males, being gay or bisexual was the strongest independent indicator of suicide risk (Sun, 1998; Garofalo et al., 1999). In a similar study of Minnesota middle and high school students, 28.1% of self-identified gay and bisexual males reported making at least one suicide attempt, compared to 20.5% of self-identified lesbians and bisexual females, 14.5% of heterosexual females, and 4.2% of heterosexual males (Boodman, 1998).

Self-destructive behavior and unhealthy coping skills are also seen in the high level of alcohol and drug addiction among lesbians and gay men, with estimates suggesting that "about 25% of such persons suffer from definitive drug and alcohol abuse problems, while an additional percentage experiences 'suggestive or problematic' abuse patterns" (Bickelhaupt, 1995). The messages of our society have distorted some of the self-perceptions of lesbians, gay men, and bisexuals. Educators at all levels of academia are in a position to provide information and support that can help end these abuses. "We have a moral obligation to combat a devastating trend," says Gerald Newberry, coordinator of the Fairfax County's family-life education programs. "We need to communicate to our kids [and young adults] that people are different, and that we don't choose our sexual feelings—they choose us" (qtd in Lacayo, 1992).

Lastly, schools need to integrate lesbians, gay men, and bisexuals into the curriculum because an increasing number of children are being raised by lesbian, gay, and bisexual parents. Research has shown there are no disadvantages to being raised by a same-sex couple: no impact on gender identity, self-esteem, self-concept, or sexual orientation (Goleman, 1992; Bliss & Harris, 1999; Freiberg, 1999). Developmental psychologist Virginia Casper says that school is probably the most difficult arena for children raised by same-sex parents, as peers and staff retain traditional ideas about family arrangements and sex-role models. Casper and her colleagues argue that teachers and administrators should acknowledge that some children and young adults have lesbian, gay, or bisexual parents (Goleman, 1992). To do this effectively, not only should the curriculum be integrated to teach students acceptance, but staff development needs to include acceptance education for teachers.

There are many humanitarian reasons for teaching about lesbians, gay men, and bisexuals in academia, yet the process of integrating them into the curriculum will be neither easy nor quick. A *U.S. News and World Report* poll indicates that 52% of respondents oppose teaching about lesbians and gay men in public schools, while 44% favor it (Shapiro, 1993). Attitudes toward lesbian, gay, and bisexual teachers are also very ambivalent. A 1996 survey found that respondents were almost equally divided over whether gays should be hired as elementary school teachers (although this was much improved over the nearly two-to-one opposition of a decade ago), and just 60% felt that they should be allowed to instruct high school (Yang, 1998). Lesbians, gay men, and bisexuals maybe more visible, but ignorance about their lives still exists among the general public. Frances Kunreuther, executive director of the Hetrick Martin Institute, says, "This is not the first issue this country has faced that has been emotional. I expect it to be painful. But fortunately in this country, we just don't protect the majority" (qtd in Ribadeneira, 1992).

Including Lesbians, Gay Men, and Bisexuals in the Classroom

Lesbians, gay men, and bisexuals should be included in multicultural education. While lesbian, gay, and bisexual communities are extremely diverse, and critics say that the only commonality is attraction to the same sex, lesbians, gay men, and bisexuals share a history of being oppressed as members of a sexual minority. This common experience pulls lesbians, gay men, and bisexuals together throughout the world, as seen by the emergence of international lesbian, gay, and bisexual organizations. While internal rifts exist, lesbians, gay men, and bisexuals have learned to celebrate their commonality by creating communities and cultures that include their own

newspapers and magazines, literature, music, radio and cable television programs, web pages, and internet chat rooms. These communities and cultures need to be integrated into multicultural studies.

Lesbians, gay men, and bisexuals together constitute a cultural group that can be identified and studied, but their experiences vary widely according to such factors as nationality, gender, race. religion, class, and age. For example, while some in the U.S. see same-sex couples as threatening to the nuclear family, they enjoy many of the same rights as heterosexual couples in Denmark and Sweden and have won major victories in Canada (Wright, 1999). In a study of 77 cultures, C. S. Ford and F. A. Beach found that 28 of them condemned same-sex sexuality with punishments ranging from mild sanctions to death, while in the remaining 49, "homosexual activities . . . are considered normal and socially acceptable for certain members of the society" (qtd in Blumenfeld & Raymond, 1992). Since one's perceptions of homosexuality and bisexuality are highly culturally bound and often linked to how family and sexuality are defined within the culture, a full discussion of lesbians, gay men, and bisexuals is appropriate in the context of studying cultural groups.

James Banks (1989) defines four distinct levels at which teachers can integrate multicultural perspectives and information into the curriculum: contributions, additive, transformation, and decision making and social action. When applying Banks's theory to lesbians, gay men, and bisexuals, one should not necessarily assume that one level of curriculum integration is inherently better than another. The approach educators use should be carefully selected after considering the political environment in which the curriculum will be taught, the educators' level of comfort with discussions of sexual and gender identities, and the educators' security in their own sexuality. These factors will play a role in the level of success attained.

The contributions level does not alter the traditional curriculum a great deal, but rather, systematically inserts underrepresented cultures into the course. Since, as is commonly stated, lesbians, gay men, and bisexuals are everywhere, every field of study has famous lesbian, gay, and bisexual people already within it. If an English professor traditionally gives background information about the authors being read, the teacher should include the fact that numerous famous writers, such as Gertrude Stein, Walt Whitman, Herman Melville, Virginia Woolf, James Baldwin, and Alice Walker, had or have relationships with people of the same sex. If biography is an important aspect of an art history course, one might mention that Michelangelo and Leonardo da Vinci, as well as more contemporary artists like Andy Warhol and Robert Mapplethorpe, had same-sex relationships. Or political science and history courses could discuss the same-sex sexuality of monarchs such as King Richard II, Pope Julius III, Queen Christina, and King James I, or of more recent leaders such as Susan B. Anthony, Eleanor Roosevelt, and Bayard Rustin (Blumenfeld & Raymond, 1992; Folliard, 1999).

Including lesbians, gay men, and bisexuals in the curriculum through a contributions approach allows for the identification of some famous gay people. This approach does little to break down stereotypes and myths about lesbians, gay men, and bisexuals as a group, however, since an educator is simply acknowledging the same-sex relationships of individuals, most of whom are already part of the curriculum. To take a more proactive stance, a teacher could adopt Banks's additive approach. This method would modify the traditional curriculum slightly by including material that describes the wider experiences of lesbians, gay men, and bisexuals and the concepts and themes unique to gay communities. In a discussion of the literary and historical figures mentioned above, for example, a teacher could address how same-sex sexuality was viewed during their lives and the impact it might have had on their work. If the class was considering the ongoing struggle for women's reproductive freedom, an educator could bring in information on the legal battles that lesbians have fought in order to conceive and to keep their children. In a unit on civil rights movements in the United States, one could present material on the LGBT movement for equal rights.

The additive approach allows teachers to introduce their students to lesbian, gay, and bisexual issues without making tremendous waves in a school system. But the approach is limited in that it reinforces the idea that lesbian, gay, and bisexual history is not an integral part of U.S. history, as people are viewing lesbians, gay men, and bisexuals from a heterosexual point of view. Further, it does little to explain the tensions, relationships,

and connections among lesbians, gay men, bisexuals, and heterosexuals.

In contrast, a transformative approach would critique stereotypes and myths by asking students to question why we take for granted what we do. They begin to see how concepts of sexuality, family, and gender have shaped our society and to explore their heterosexual assumptions through being presented with material from lesbian, gay, and bisexual world views. A direct application of Banks's transformation approach could, however, be unsuccessful, for a mainstream community might rebel if an educator offered only lesbian/gay/bisexual perspectives. Exposing students to all sides of any argument would be important. Heterosexual students would be faced with the dilemma of resolving the internal conflict that arises when world views collide. If students truly take on the challenge of resolving this conflict, they can recognize their own world views and the subjectivity of their positions. At the same time, lesbian, gay, and bisexual students would be empowered by having their perspectives validated.

In adapting Banks's transformation approach, the educator could pose difficult questions, such as how the United States should react to lesbians, gay men, and bisexuals. When the question is posed, the teacher must be very careful to provide the students with sufficient information from all sides to enable critical thinking about the issue. For background material, the teacher should present the students with information arguing that homosexuality is an immoral **decision** that will destroy the nuclear family and information arguing that homosexuality is an **orientation,** not a choice, and a legitimate alternate family arrangement. Then students could be shown the contradictions within our own legal system that reflect the various attitudes toward homosexuality. The 14th Amendment says that no state can deny any person equal protection under the law. However, 18 states currently have enforceable sodomy laws against people who pursue same-sex relationships, with penalties of up to ten or more years in prison in six states, including a possible sentence of five years to life in Idaho (American Civil Liberties Union, 1999). On the other hand, nine states and the District of Columbia prohibit discrimination against lesbians, gay men, and bisexuals in employment, housing, and public accommodations, and two others ban anti-gay bias just in employment (Roundy, 1999). How is it that in one country, different states can have such opposite interpretations of how the Constitution should or should not be applied?

In order for the transformation approach to work, an environment must be established in which students are able to honestly explore their beliefs, feelings, and reactions to the material. Finding and creating materials that provide lesbian/gay/bisexual perspectives and making sure points of view are equally represented is more time consuming than adopting a contributions or additive approach, especially if one considers the need for ongoing staff development to make the approach truly effective. Banks suggests this kind of training be institutionalized, even though this can be costly as well as time consuming.

The last level Banks mentions is the decision making and social action model of curriculum integration. This approach is organized around the students' identifying an important social problem, learning about the issue, and taking action. There are many advantages to this method. The students interact directly with the material presented in the process of developing their thinking, research, decision making, and social action skills. Students would also be called upon to analyze their own values and to improve their cooperative skills as they work together on a final project. One of the drawbacks to this approach when applied to lesbians, gay men, and bisexuals is the extent of controversy that could erupt. The students may find that they do not have political efficacy, for example, if the status quo is too threatened by the action they decide to take.

The students in a class organized around a decision making and social action agenda could study homophobia and biphobia and then resolve to start a project to raise awareness and limit the number of homophobic and biphobic incidents on campus. The students could also research the extent of discrimination and anti-gay related incidents at the institution and work to have sexual orientation included in the school's non-discrimination clause or sexual harassment policy.

Teachers need to consider their situation carefully to create a curriculum that can be effectively and successfully implemented within their own classrooms and institutions. As educators and administrators, we need to examine our own attitudes for ways we are maintaining the ignorance and hatred that have oppressed lesbians, gay men, bisexuals, and other persons in underrepresented groups. We need to work toward a time when we stop simply talking about integrating underrepresented groups into the curriculum and actually begin to teach students, as a matter of course, about the increasingly complex and pluralistic society in which we live. As key persons in institutions that have the power to influence society, we have a responsibility to educate our students about our shared humanity.

References

American Civil Liberties Union. (1999, January). Status of U.S. sodomy laws. http://www.aclu.org/issues/gay/sodomy.html.

American Psychological Association. (1998, August 6). Anti-gay aggression: Expressions of hatred or of perceived cultural norms? News release. http://www.apa.org/releases/react.html.

Anderson, J. (1993, January 10). Portraits of gay men, with no apologies. *New York Times*, p. M5.

Banks, J. A., & Banks, C. A. M. (Eds.). (1989). *Multicultural education: Issues and perspectives.* Boston: Allyn & Bacon.

Barringer, F. (1993a, April 15). Sex survey of American men finds 1% are gay. *New York Times*, p. A1.

Barringer, F. (1993b, April 25). Polling on sexual issues has its drawbacks. *New York Times*, p. L23.

Bates, T. D. (1992, October 9). Paying for values: The real needs of real families. *Commonweal*, 6–7.

Bickelhaupt, E. E. (1995). Alcoholism and drug abuse in gay and lesbian persons: A review of incidence studies. *Journal of Gay and Lesbian Social Services, 2,* 5–14.

Bliss, G. K., & Harris, M. B. (1999). Teachers' views of students with gay or lesbian parents. *Journal of Gay, Lesbian, and Bisexual Identity, 4,* 149–71.

Blumenfeld, W., & Raymond, D. (1992). *Looking at gay and lesbian life.* Boston: Beacon Press.

Boodman, S. G. (1998, March 3). Gay teen boys likelier to commit suicide. *Washington*, p. Z5.

Breslau, K. (1992, August 3). The push for national purity. *Newsweek*, 36–7.

Bureau of Labor Statistics. (1999a). Employment characteristics of families in 1998. http://stats.bls.gov/news.release/famee.nws.htm.

Bureau of Labor Statistics. (1999b). Families by presence and relationship of employed members and family type, 1997–98 annual averages. *Labor force statistics from the current population survey.* http://stats.bls.gov/news.release/famee.t02.htm.

Celis, W. (1993, January 6). Schools across U.S. cautiously adding lessons on gay life. *New York Times,* p. A 18.

Doherty, W. J. (1992, May/June). Private lives, public values: The future of the family. *Psychology Today, 25,* 32–37.

Folliard, P. (1999, April 16). Love letters: Historian looks at a first lady and the most important person in her life. *Washington Blade,* pp. 39–40.

Freiberg, P. (1998, December 4). Gay hate crimes rise 8 percent: Annual FBI statistics document 1,102 incidents nationwide. *Washington Blade.*

Freiberg, P. (1999, February 26). Study finds lesbian parents as good as straights: Researchers say sharing partnering duties allows more time to spend with children. *Washington Blade.*

Friedan, B. (1963). *The feminist mystique.* New York: Norton.

Garofalo, R., et al. (1999). Sexual orientation and risk of suicide attempts among a representative sample of youth. *Archives of Pediatric and Adolescent Medicine, 153,* 487–93.

Gay and Lesbian Alliance Against Defamation. (1997). '97 Television lineup includes record number of "out" characters: 23% increase in gay characters over last season. http://www.glaad.org/glaad/press/970813.html.

Gay, Lesbian and Straight Education Network. (1999a, June 6). GLSEN expresses disappointment over loss of California's AB 222. News release. http://www.glsen.org/pages/sections/library/news/9906-1.article.

Gay, Lesbian and Straight Education Network. (1999b). What's it like to be young and gay in American schools today? http://www.glsen.org/pages/sections/library/reference/014.article.

Goleman, D. (1992, December 2). Gay parents called no disadvantage. *New York Times,* p. C3.

Herek, G., & Berrill, K. (1992). *Hate crimes: Confronting violence against lesbians and gay men.* Newbury Park, CA: Sage Publications.

Keen, L. (1993, March 5). Study finds 20% report same-sex experiences. *Washington Blade,* pp. 1, 23.

Kinsey, A., Pomeroy, W. B., & Martin, C. E. (1948). *Sexual behavior in the human male.* Philadelphia: W. B. Saunders.

Kinsey, A., Pomeroy, W. B., Martin, C. E., & Gebhard, R. H. (1953). *Sexual behavior in the human female.* Philadelphia: W. B. Saunders.

Lacayo, R. (1992, December 14). Jack and Jack and Jill and Jill. *Time,* 52–53.

Lane, C., & Breslau, K. (1992, December 7). Germany's furies. *Newsweek,* 30–32.

Lief, L. (1992, July 27). Europe's trail of tears: 'Ethnic cleansing' threatens to unleash another holocaust. *U. S. News & World Report,* 41–43.

Magnet, M. (1992, August 10). The American family, 1992. *Fortune,* 42–47.

Massachusetts Governor's Commission on Gay and Lesbian Youth. (1997). Mission and history. http://www.magnet.state.ma.us/gcgly/mssn.htm.

Meyer, L. (1999, May 25). The hidden hate epidemic: Violence against the transgendered is widespread, brutal—and often unnoticed. *Advocate,* pp. 61–63.

National Center for Health Statistics. (1995, March 22). Divorces and annulments and rates: United States, 1940–90, *Monthly Vital Statistics Report,* p. 9. http://www.cdc.gov/nchswww/fastats/divorce.htm.

National Center for Health Statistics. (1998, October 7). *National Vital Statistics Report,* p. 15. http://www.cdc.gov/nchswww/fastats/pdf/47_4t6.pdf.

Ness, C. (1998, August 15). Survey: Alarming rate of anti-gay violence. *San Francisco Examiner.* http://www.examiner.com/980816/0816antigay.shtml#top.

Patterson, C. J. (1995). Lesbian mothers, gay fathers, and their children. In A. R. D'Augelli & C. J. Patterson (Eds.), *Lesbian, gay, and bisexual identities over the lifespan: Psychological perspectives* (pp. 262–90). New York: Oxford.

Rankin, S. (1999). Queering campus: Understanding and transforming climate. *Metropolitan Universities: An International Forum, 9,* 29–38.

Ribadeneira, D. (1992, December 13). Gay, lesbian students live with harassment. *Boston Globe,* p. 49.

Roundy, B. (1999, May 28). Nevada passes civil rights law: State poised to be 11th to ban sexual orientation bias. *Washington Blade,* pp. 1, 29.

Schmalz, J. (1993, April 16). Survey stirs debate on number of gay men in U.S. *New York Times,* p. A20.

Shapiro, J. P. (1993, July 5). Straight talk about gays. *U. S. News & World Report,* 42–48.

Sun, L. H. (1998, July 20). As gay students come out, abuse comes in: Changing attitudes, new laws push ambivalent schools to confront harassment. *Washington Post,* p. A8.

Tavris, C., & Wade, C. (1984). *The longest war: Sex differences in perspective.* Chicago: Harcourt Brace Jovanovich.

Tucker, W. (1993, February). Revolt in Queens. *The American Spectator,* 26–31.

Uribe, V., & Harbeck, K. M. (1992, October). Project 10 addresses needs of gay and lesbian youth. *The Education Digest,* 50–54.

U.S. Department of Health & Human Services (1989). Report of the Secretary's Task Force on Youth Suicide. Washington, DC: Public Health Service, Alcohol, Drug Abuse, and Mental Health Administration.

Vohejda, B. (1998, May 28). Traditional families hold on: Statistics show a slackening of 1970s, '80s social trends. *Washington Post,* p. A2.

Wallis, C. (1992, Fall). The nuclear family goes boom. *Time,* 42–44.

White, B. (1992, October 16). Advisory panel urges Ga. schools to broaden definition of a family. *Atlanta Constitution,* p. D2.

Wright, K. (1999, May 28). Couples win in Canada: Ruling expected to change laws that exclude gays. *Washington Blade,* pp. 1, 12.

Yang, A. S. (1997). The polls—trends: Attitudes toward homosexuality. *Public Opinion Quarterly 61,* 477–507.

Yang, A. S. (1998). *From wrongs to rights: Public opinion on gay and lesbian Americans moves toward equality.* Washington, DC: National Gay and Lesbian Task Force Policy Institute.

Younger, J. (1999). Academic programs and opportunities for LGB study in the U.S. and Canada. http://www.duke.edu/web/jyounger/lgbprogs.html.

CLASS 21

Physical/Mental Ability Issues

CHAPTER 31
The Microculture of Disability
Jacqueline Rickman
Jacqueline Rickman's chapter provides an historical perspective on our nation's
attitude and behavior toward people with disabilities. She then discusses the
responsibilities schools should take in providing equitable opportunities
for people with disabilities.

CHAPTER 31

The Microculture of Disability

Jacqueline C. Rickman

Is currently a Supervisor for the Northwestern Illinois Association (NIA). She provides technical assistance for special education teachers in the areas of visual and multiple disability. Before coming to NIA Rickman was an Associate Professor in the Education and Interdisciplinary Studies Department at Western Illinois University. Her research interest focus on ableism, prodigiousness, and equity.

Freak shows are not about isolated individuals, either on platforms or in an audience. They are about organizations and patterned relationships between them and us. "Freak" is not a quality that belongs to the person on display. It is something that we created: a perspective, a set of practices—a social construction.

(Bogdan, 1988, p. x)

Higher education has a unique opportunity to assume a leadership position in the preparation of a generation of citizens with disabilities who have positive images of themselves and who are socially engaged, rather than socially estranged. To accomplish this task, postsecondary institutions must recognize the characteristics of students with disabilities as well as the level of disability stereotypes and misconceptions operating on campus. They must assume responsibility for meeting the needs of students with disabilities and for countering the stereotypes and misconceptions. Increasingly, postsecondary educators and administrators are assuming that responsibility; they are learning to respond resourcefully to a growing demand that the needs of students with disabilities be met and that they be helped in their efforts to develop positive self images and become socially engaged citizens.

Characteristics of Postsecondary Students with Disabilities

At present, approximately 10% of students enrolled in U.S. institutions of higher education report that they have a disability. The microculture of disability is comprised of subcultures consisting of specific disabilities such as hearing impairment. Within each subculture are further subsets such as the totally deaf and the partially deaf. Individuals within these subsets reflect a great variety of medical diagnoses and are representative of the population at large in their heterogeneity.

Four major disability subcultures and five onset categories exist in postsecondary institutions. The most common disability subcultures and their subsets include: 1) learning disabilities (perceptual, perceptual-motor, and general coordination problems, disorders of attention and hyperactivity, disorders of memory and thinking, language disorders), 2) physical disabilities and other health impairments (neurological impairments, musculoskeletal and chronic medical conditions), 3) visual disabilities (totally blind, partially sighted), and 4) hearing impairments (totally deaf, partially deaf). Onset categories include: a) special education early onset, b) special education adventitious onset, c) recently diagnosed, d) self referral, and e) other referral. These categories can be differentiated further depending on whether the conditions are permanent or uncertain and degenerative.

Although it would be illogical to assume that all students with disabilities have the same levels of independence and productivity or that they have identical needs for adaptations and services, all share the experience of interacting on a regular basis with social stigmas based on inaccurate assumptions and ambivalence. At present, many

Reprinted by permission of the author.

drop out of college, and those who stay perceive themselves in a distinct marginal status with inequitable access to programs and services.

Reported stigmatic reactions from nondisabled faculty and peers have included: discomfort, admiration, patronizing or pitying attitudes, avoidance, fear, an assumption of low intelligence, an assumption of talent, treatment like that of a child, an assumption that all members of a disability subculture are alike, a public disclosure of special accommodations needed, and simply ignoring the situation. Most students practice self-advocacy and do not expect preferential treatment; most want faculty to ask about their disability and to collaborate with them for appropriate environmental and academic accommodations. Their expectations parallel those of their collegiate peers. They expect their postsecondary experience to provide them with the tools to achieve rewarding, productive, and integrated adult lives. They expect the institution to respect them and to be sensitive to their beliefs and experiences. I would like to examine the sources of disability stereotypes before discussing current stereotypes and misconceptions about postsecondary students with disabilities and then suggesting ways educators can help meet their needs.

A Chronology of Evolving Disability Stereotypes

In his book, *Freak Show: Presenting Human Oddities for Amusement and Profit.* Robert Bogdan (1988) suggests that "whenever we study deviance, we must look at who are in charge—whether self-appointed or officially—of telling us who the deviant people are and what they are like" (p. 279). Through the years, those who have been in charge of people with disabilities as well as the media have misunderstood, incorrectly categorized, and stigmatized individuals within the microculture of disability. Bogdan's pioneering text explores and evaluates the gradual evolution of those who were in charge of people we would identify today as having disabilities—from the managers, promoters, and audiences of "freak shows," through the administrators of professional organizations and charities, to medical practitioners, to present-day professionals and human service providers.

FREAK SHOWS (CIRCA 1840–1940)

Barbara Baskin sought to ban freak shows from the New York State Fair in 1939 contending that they were to disabled people as *Amos 'n Andy* was to African Americans and as the striptease show was to women (Bogdan, 1988). In the carnival culture, people with differences were seen as valuable presentations; indeed, their abnormalities and human variations translated into meal tickets and security. An exhibits, these individuals were part of the public domain. They were presented in two unique modes to their audiences; the exotic mode that exploited the public's curiosity about the unusual or sensational and the aggrandized mode that capitalized on the public's need for superior status and power.

The exotic mode was rooted in racism, imperialism, and handicapism. It presented people with disabilities as human curiosities—specimens to be feared and held in contempt. As exhibits, they were the devalued victims of institutionalized discrimination, hopelessly stigmatized and devoid of human dignity. Paradoxically, Bogdan's research revealed that these marginal citizens thought of themselves as having high status and as very elite carnival insiders who arrogantly viewed their audiences with disdain and contempt.

The aggrandized mode exploited the exhibits, that is the persons on display, as mere objects in a tainted amusement world. In doing so, it capitalized on the audience's need to maintain a sense of superior status and power. It contended that people with disabilities were not competent enough to be part of society. They were to be excluded and kept with their own kind. The most insidious features of this mode were the underlying contentions that exhibits were not capable of achieving, and that normal accomplishments by people with disabilities were to be flaunted as extraordinary. The aggrandized mode thereby served as the foundation for the perceptions of not only **Jerry Lewis's pitiful poster child,** the indigent **idiot,** and the blind **beggar,** but also the disabled **wonder-kid,** the **amazing crippled prodigy,** and the blind **genius.** All of these images were manufactured when audiences determined that people with disabilities were exhibits who were amusing, but tainted, incompetent, disgusting, and ultimately unworthy of inclusion in the larger world.

THE MEDICAL ESTABLISHMENT AND CHARITIES (CIRCA 1940s–1960s)

A later conception of disability was basically **pathological** in that people with disabilities were seen as **patients.** Several premises were operant within this philosophy. They were: (1) people with disabilities could be treated and possibly cured; (2) people with disabilities were to be secluded from the public; and (3) people with disabilities were to be feared, and in many cases locked away to protect the **normal** citizenry from danger. The trend was followed by the emergence of organized charities, professional fund raisers, and poster children. It is likely that freak shows are perceived as repulsive today because members of society, including many with disabilities themselves, have embraced the pathological disabled imagery of pity as an artifact of the medical establishment's monopoly over the presentation of people with disabilities.

FREEDOM MOVEMENTS: REHABILITATION REFORM (CIRCA 1960s–1970s)

Beatrice Wright (1960) was a pioneer in the provision of counseling and rehabilitation services for people with disabilities. Her mentor was Carl Rogers, who emphasized the importance of investigating the perspective of individuals with disabilities, of valuing what they were saying about their experiences. Her sensitization developed into an awareness of and objection to the presence of gross societal distortions and misconceptions about this population. Wright observed the medical establishment's presentation of people with disabilities as pathological cases and formulated the "fundamental negative bias" as a powerful source of prejudice that steers perception, thought, and feeling along negative lines to such a degree positives remain hidden. She reports that one's perception, thinking, and feeling regarding deviance will be negative if three conditions for the functioning of the fundamental negative bias are met. These conditions are saliency (what is observed stands out sufficiently), value (it is regarded as negative), and context (it is vague or sparse). Her view appears to be based on an integration of Heider's (1958) balance theory of sentiments and Sherif, Sherif, and Nebergall's (1965) social judgment theory. This theoretic combination suggests that when similarity with the self is perceived, the similarity will be exaggerated and liking and belonging will be induced; when differences are perceived, however, the dissimilarity will be exaggerated, resulting in a host of complex rejection reactions Dembo, Wright, and Leviton (1975) identify as negative spread effects.

Perhaps an indication of these negative spread effects can be found in Zimbardo and Ebberson's (1970) observation that "the United States has spent millions of dollars on unsuccessful information campaigns to correct stereotypes about minority groups, to present the facts, and to help people get to know one another" (p. 101). Though U.S. universities were becoming beacons of protest against structural exclusion during the 1960s and 1970s, the fundamental negative bias against people who differed from the norm was too strong to overthrow, as evidenced in the spread effects of bigoted and prejudicial attitudes held by many postsecondary personnel and students. Many with disabilities were denied admission; those who were admitted were perceived as dependent, unattractive, and not eligible for special services or adaptations.

UNAWARENESS AND AMBIVALENCE AS SOURCES OF NEGATIVE ATTITUDES TOWARD PERSONS WITH DISABILITIES (CIRCA 1980s)

During the 1980s, researchers began to report that the origins of conscious and unconscious negative attitudes toward disability range from full awareness to total unawareness. They emphasized that unawareness, or mindlessness, was the overwhelming determinant of negative societal attitude formation (Livneh, 1988; Langer & Chanowitz, 1988). At postsecondary institutions, an increase in mindfulness about the situations of students with disabilities was noted in females, younger personnel, faculty at institutions with disability service programs, faculty within education and the social sciences, and in faculty with previous extended contact with students with disabilities (Fonosch & Schwab, 1981; Yuker, 1987; Amsel & Fichten, 1990). Less supportive attitudes were held toward students with learning disabilities and socioemotional problems than for those with hearing, visual, or physical disabilities (Leyser, 1989).

In contrast, other findings during the 1980s discounted the notion of discriminatory practices based on a fundamental negative bias in favor of ambivalence. Ambivalence is best described as confusion about enduring cultural myths derived from freak show, medical, and rehabilitation images. Among those myths is the idea that disability and mainstream cultures exist without conflict within a harmonious world family, its Woodstock imagery reinforcing the false belief that interactions between members of mainstream and marginal cultural groups are easy. Ambivalence results when normal interpersonal discomfort and miscommunication occur, as they most certainly will, and mainstream individuals revive other myths that suggest persons with disabilities are eccentric (according to Bogdan's exotic mode) or inferior (as in Bogdan's aggrandized mode).

SOURCES OF STIGMA IDENTIFIED BY CONSUMERS WITH DISABILITIES (1980s–PRESENT)

In the late 1980s and early 1990s, the seeds of Wright's client-centered emphasis began to blossom. Consumers with disabilities themselves began to speak on their own behalf. They presented intriguing arguments such as the idea that even a focus on disabled superstars, which implies more respect for disabled persons' accomplishments, can be a prejudicial reaction rather than a recognition of the person as an individual (Yuker, 1987). In contrast, protests against current counseling practices were illustrated in Kalter's (1991) caution against the treatment of disability exclusively as a drama of personal adjustment with no social context since the consequence would be the reduction of the issue to one of individual character and courage rather than of societal stigma and discrimination.

Legislation such as the 1990 Americans with Disabilities Act (ADA) has increased environmental and academic accessibility in both public and private postsecondary institutions and has enhanced employment opportunities for people with disabilities. However, negative attitudes towards students with disabilities on the part of faculty, administrators, and peers remains a challenging enigma. Unfortunately, current investigations have revealed that nondisabled students attributed fewer socially desirable and more undesirable traits to students with disabilities than to their nondisabled peers (Fichten & Bourdan, 1986). In fact, circumplex scales that tested for sameness and difference disclosed that the perception of traits of students with disabilities and their nondisabled peers were clearly opposite. Persons with disabilities were characterized as aloof-introverted, lazy-submissive, and unassuming-ingenuous, while nondisabled persons were seen to be more gregarious-extroverted, ambitious-dominant, and arrogant-calculating (Fichten & Amsel, 1986).

The microculture of persons with disabilities perceives social isolation and underparticipation in campus life as common and all-encompassing problems (Hanna & Rogovsky, 1991; Oakes, 1990; Jenkins, Amos, & Graham, 1988). A hypothesized cause for this exclusion can likely be found within the intersection of self-concept and a sociocultural system that encompasses the attitudinal barriers of apathy, paternalism, fear, curiosity, stereotyping, need for stability, and focus on disabled superstars (Pati & Atkins, 1981; Levi, 1975; Lenhart, 1976/1977). Low self-esteem resulting in social isolation as well as gross societal misconceptions and deep-seated discrimination must be addressed.

Assuming Responsibility for Meeting the Needs of Students with Disabilities

Higher education administrators, faculty, and staff must take responsibility to insure awareness and communication between nondisabled and disabled students and between university personnel and students with disabilities. Programming to counteract negative stereotypes and misconceptions can help. Fragmented and destructive interactions will continue, however, without vigorous and consistent upper administrative support. At the grass-roots level, formal in-services and workshops will be exercises in futility unless every participant believes he or she can be a change agent with the individual and collective power to make a difference. Fortunately, the higher education community has a history of solving problems, and student interest in social values is growing (Astin,

1991; Fichten & Bourdon, 1986; McLoughlin, 1982).

HIGHER EDUCATION ADMINISTRATORS, FACULTY, AND STAFF

Disability awareness is now the responsibility of professionals in postsecondary settings who enjoy easy access to "a broad and rich literature on the lived experience of persons with disabilities, attitudes toward disability, stigma and discrimination, the disability rights movement, and laws and public policies affecting citizens with disabilities" (Hahn, 1991, p. 18). They are privy to action research from sociological, historical, philosophical, psychological, legal, educational, and scientific perspectives. But are universities willing to develop solutions to the marginal status of their students with disabilities? The facilitation of such opportunities means the surrender of the comforts of tradition and prejudice to close analysis, systematic evaluation, collaborative research efforts, and creative innovations (Feldman & Newcomb, 1969).

Campuswide assessment of needs and problems is the first priority. Recommended mechanisms are town meetings, surveys, interviews, and other interpersonal strategies designed to gather information from as many stakeholders as possible. Yuker's Attitudes Toward Disabled Persons Scale (ATDP) (see Yuker & Block, 1986) is one example of a survey that has been used effectively to reveal the level of disability stereotypes held in specific institutional contexts. Demographics should be investigated for retention rates and resiliency factors related to successful completion of studies on the part of students with disabilities. Former students should be surveyed for information on what worked for them. Myers' (1994) investigation, designed to reveal communication patterns and preferences of college students with visual disabilities, offers an excellent research base for a parallel inquiry.

The next priority is the generation of strategies to counteract the campus community's identified miscommunication patterns and misconceptions. Implicit in such counteraction is the need to adjust and refocus attitudes at every level: student workers, receptionists, custodial staff, faculty, and administrators, as the following case study illustrates.

Donna was a first-year student with learning disabilities (LDs) enrolled at an eastern university with a well known disability support service program. The legal documentation of her condition with an explanation of prescribed adaptations had been sent to her professors. She had forgotten to attend the orientation meeting for new students with disabilities, so she did not know the procedures for accessing accommodations. Her specific learning deficit, like that of the majority of adults with LDs, was in written language and necessitated a word processor with a spell check for written assignments and exams. She affirmed this need with each of her professors, including the one she had for U.S. history. He verbally agreed to allow her to take his essay exams using a word processor at the disability service center. On the day of the first exam, a graduate student was filling in for the professor. Nervously, Donna explained her circumstances to him and he reluctantly gave her a copy of the exam and excused her.

When she arrived at the disability service center, she asked the receptionist for directions to the word processors explaining she had to take an exam. The receptionist scolded her for not having faculty authorization to take the test under special circumstances. The student attempted to protest but the receptionist threw a faculty authorization form at her, frowned, and went back to his typing. The student meekly trekked back to get the required signature. The graduate student, however, was confused and unsure of what to do and ended up refusing to sign, stating he hadn't been given the authority. He suggested she return to the disability service center. When she arrived at that office, the clerk was on the phone and chose not to acknowledge her presence. She broke into tears, dropped the exam, and fled. When she returned to class the next week, the professor refused to give her a makeup exam. She dropped out shortly thereafter.

The smugness of one clerk, the lack of concern of a faculty member, the ignorance and confusion of a graduate student, forgetfulness, and inadequate procedural communication between a student and disability service personnel were combined factors culminating in one student's failure to make it through the maze of higher education. Could these causative variables have been avoided? Are proactive strategies possible for counteracting negative stereotypes and discriminatory interactions? I believe so.

Receptionists and Other Front-Desk Personnel

Anti-discriminatory procedural safeguards need to be built into job descriptions and monitored and evaluated on a regular basis. Because of their highly visible interactive positions, receptionists and other front-desk personnel merit extensive training in how to guide and direct students who may not do things the way they do. To practice creative resourcefulness and sensitive responsiveness, they would ideally possess flexibility, interest in problem solving and networking, and openness to new strategies for meeting students' needs. It is absolutely critical their success be acknowledged and rewarded by superiors to generate respect for themselves and those they were hired to serve. If the first priority of the receptionist Donna met was the student, an alternative scenario would have included his timely and undivided attention to her specific problem. While Donna did not fulfill her own responsibilities to learn and follow through on test-taking procedures, her unawareness did not warrant the treatment she encountered.

Faculty and Graduate Assistants

While large scale institutional reform is underway, specific changes can be made by faculty that will make a major impact on students. Attention needs to be given to the way language, environment, and course methodology perpetuate myths. Language in course descriptions and lectures must not isolate people who are not in the mainstream. Consider, for example, the following course description for an introductory U.S. history course:

> . . . investigate the great heterogeneity of the population in the U.S. in the 1960s, from powerful citizens like those in positions of medicine, politics, and business to the disabled and infirm who struggled in less fortunate situations.

Discussing those in successful positions and those who were struggling without considering the impact each had on the other is aggrandizing behavior. Those who struggled did not suffer oppression in isolation: those who succeeded did not acquire power through natural giftedness and physical inheritance. We need to talk about the balance sheet—to note that social disadvantage not only limited some individuals, it also enhanced the self-esteem and opportunities of others.

Like language, environment can help or hinder the interaction among students with disabilities and those without. According to Sherif, Sherif, and Nebergall (1965), students are likely to sit and socialize with those who most resemble them. By changing the seating arrangement purposefully and often, faculty can build in opportunities for a variety of interactions that provide extended contact among nondisabled students and students with disabilities and opportunities for them to learn from each other. Carefully facilitated classroom interactions may have afforded Donna a more focused and proactive test-taking action path.

Recommended course adaptations to access individual abilities (versus deficits) fall into two categories: methods utilized to disseminate course content and methods used to measure subject mastery. The case of an educator at a large Midwestern university illustrates both.

The faculty member observed nonverbal reactions to the peer-tutoring method she routinely used in her political science course. Students who achieved mastery over specific content were paired up to drill those who were struggling. She saw an attitude of superiority developing in the tutors and a concurrent lack of confidence and helplessness in those being tutored, many of whom were students with learning disabilities. It became apparent the tutors perceived themselves as solutions to the "problem" of inept students.

Because grouping for the learning of rote facts and principles was the only type of peer tutoring within her course, the industry of the tutors, who were very capable in the sequential organization of information, was operationalized at the expense of the academic identity of the tutorees whose ordering tendencies were less linear. She did not consider the tutorees incapable of the work, having observed their streaks of brilliance in class discussions and their creativity in problem solving and relating real-life case studies. She also noted untapped abilities in role playing, technological aptitude, critiquing films and readings, debate, research, interviewing, mediation, and oral presentations. Once aware of this, she began using a variety of creative pairings and team work to recognize and exercise the strengths of all the students.

Similarly, to level the playing field of evaluation, faculty who always use timed, computer-scored, multiple-choice tests may want to add alternate evaluative formats. The heterogeneity of students' learning styles are responsive to taped, project, portfolio, self-paced, developmental, collaborative, computer assisted, oral, short answer, and untimed assessments. These types of course adjustments do not necessitate additional cost or extreme revisions in planning or teaching style for most faculty, yet they benefit all students, not just those with disabilities.

Disability Support Service Personnel

The directive to disability support administrators is clear. While one might expect them to be directly responsible for programs counteracting identified miscommunication among students, faculty, administration, and staff, it must be stated it is no easy task to combat rampant negative bias, arrogance, mindlessness, ambivalence, and delivery system breakdowns. In order to implement effective interventions, collaboration with students with disabilities and representatives from all campus departments and services is imperative.

The content of disability awareness interventions should be innovative and include: a) the college's legal responsibilities, b) characteristics of disabilities, c) methods of providing reasonable architectural and academic adaptations, and d) ways to gain and maintain productive communication and collaboration. They should contain clearly defined short- and long-term anticipated outcomes to be used for formative evaluation. Additionally, a chorus of researchers recommends campus interventions that attend to the credibility of the presenter. Successful attitude modifying inservices have included talk show, panel discussion, and interview formats featuring qualified students with disabilities, expert speakers from off-campus sites, and university personnel who have effectively collaborated with students to achieve productive academic and physical accommodations (Gerber, 1990; Wright, 1988; Yuker & Block, 1986; Cortez, 1983; Pomerantz, 1983; Donaldson & Martinson, 1977; Dembo, 1970).

Summary

Assessing campuswide needs and problems, building in procedural safeguards, and recommending changes are the first steps toward the successful inclusion of students with disabilities within the campus community. Subsequently, campuswide programming must be designed as a direct response to identified institutional exclusion since every communication, environmental, and attitudinal barrier has a critical effect on students with disabilities. It is only when we gain a comprehension of the inherent challenges in our interactions with students with disabilities that we can engage in the construction of images of disability that dismantle the shameful and destructive freak show and pathological patterns. Bogdan (1988) has identified and contributed to the growth and success of all our students in his imperative to move beyond appearances, first impressions, stereotypes, and misconceptions to get to know our students, not as they have been presented but as they are.

References

Amsel, R., & Fichten, C. S., (1990). Interaction between disabled and nondisabled college students and their professors: A comparison. *Journal of Postsecondary Education and Disability, 8,* 125–140.

Astin, A. (1991). The changing American college student: Implications for educational policy and practice. *Higher Education, 22*(2), 129–144).

Bogdan, R. (1988). *Freak show: Presenting human oddities for amusement and profit.* Chicago: University of Chicago Press.

Cortez, D. M. (1983). A study of the effects of an in-service program for postsecondary faculty on mainstreaming handicapped students (Doctoral dissertation. New Mexico State University, 1983). *Dissertation Abstracts International, 39,* 2865 A.

Dembo, T. (1970). The utilization of psychological knowledge in rehabilitation. *Welfare Review, 8,* 1–7.

Dembo, T., Leviton, G. L., & Wright, B. (1975). Adjustment to misfortune: A problem of social and psychological rehabilitation. *Artificial Limbs, 3,* 4–62. (Original work published 1956)

Donaldson, J., & Martinson, M. C. (1977). Modifying attitudes toward physically disabled persons. *Exceptional Children, 43*, 337–341.

Feldman, K. A. (1972), & Newcomb, T. M. (1969). *The impact of college on students.* San Francisco: Jossey-Bass.

Fichten, C. S., & Amsel, R. (1986). Trait attributions about college students with a physical disability: Circumplex analyses and methodological issues. *Journal of Applied Social Psychology, 16*(5), 410–427.

Fichten, C. S., & Bourdon, C. V. (1986). Social skill deficit or response inhibition: Interaction between disabled and nondisabled college students. *Journal of College Student Personnel, 27*, 326–333.

Fonosch, G. G., & Schwab, L. O. (1981). Attitudes of selected university faculty members toward disabled students. *Journal of College Student Personnel, 22*, 229–235.

Gerber, D. A. (1990). Listening to disabled people: The problem of voice and authority in Robert Edgerton's *The cloak of competence. Disability, Handicap, and Society, 5*(1), 3–23.

Hahn, H. (1991). Alternative views of empowerment: Social services and civil rights. *Journal of Rehabilitation, 57*(4), 18–20.

Hanna, W. J., & Rogovsky, B. (1991). Women with disabilities: Two handicaps plus. *Disability, Handicap, and Society, 6*(1), 49–63.

Heider, R. (1958). *The psychology of interpersonal relations.* New York: Wiley.

Jenkins, C., Amos, O., & Graham, G. (1988). Do black and white college students with disabilities see their worlds differently? *Journal of Rehabilitation, 54*(4), 71–76.

Kalter, J. (1991). Good news: The disabled get more play on T. V. Bad news: There is still too much stereotyping. In E. Lessen (Ed.), *Exceptional persons in society* (pp. 55–6). Needham, MA: Ginn.

Langer, A. L., & Chanowitz, B. (1988). Mindfulness/mindlessness: A new perspective for the study of disability. In A. Yuker (Ed.), *Attitudes toward persons with disabilities* (pp. 69–81). New York: Springer.

Lenhart, L. C. (1977). The stigma of disability (Doctoral dissertation. The University of Oklahoma Health Services Center, 1976). *Dissertation Abstracts International, 37*, 5439B.

Levi, V. (1975). *Disabled persons: attitudes formation and the effect of the environment: An experimental research.* Unpublished manuscript. York University, Toronto.

Leyser, Y. (1989). A survey of faculty attitudes and accommodations for students with disabilities. *Journal of Postsecondary Education and Disability, 7,* 97–108.

Livneh, H. (1988). A dimensional perspective on the origin of negative attitudes toward persons with disabilities. In A. Yuker, (Ed.), *Attitudes toward persons with disabilities* (pp. 35–47). New York: Springer.

McLoughlin, W. P. (1982). Helping the physically disabled in higher education. *Journal of College Student Personnel, 23*, 240–246.

Myers, K. (1994). *Preferences of communication styles and techniques of persons with visible visual disabilities: Implications for higher education.* (Doctoral dissertation submitted for publication, Illinois State University, 1994).

Oakes, J. (1990). *Lost talent: The underparticipation of women, minorities, and disabled persons in science.* Santa Monica, CA: Rand.

Pati, G., & Atkins, J. (1981). *Managing and employing the handicapped: An untapped potential.* Chicago: Brace & Jovanovich, Human Resource Press.

Pomerantz, R. M. (1983). *The effectiveness of training modules designed to improve the attitudes of college faculty toward students with disabilities: An evaluation study* (Doctoral dissertation. Temple University, 1983), *Dissertation Abstracts International, 44*, 1604B.

Sheriff, C. W., Sherif, M., & Nebergall, R. E. (1965). *Attitude and attitude change: The social judgment-involvement approach.* Philadelphia: Saunders.

Wright, B. A. (1960). *Physical disability—A psychological approach.* New York: Harper & Row.

Wright, B. A. (1988). Attitudes and the fundamental negative bias. In A. Yuker (Ed.), *Attitudes toward persons with disabilities* (pp. 3–21). New York: Springer.

Yuker, H. (1987). Labels can hurt people with disabilities. *Et Cetera, 44*(1), 16–22.

Yuker, H., & Block, J. R. (1986). *Research with the attitudes toward disabled persons scales (1960–1965).* Hempstead, NY: Hofstra University. Center for the Study of Attitudes Toward Persons with Disabilities.

Yuker, H. E. (1988). *Attitudes toward persons with disabilities.* New York: Springer.

Zimbardo, P. G., & Ebberson, E. (1970). *Influencing attitudes and changing behavior,* Reading, MA: Addison-Wesley.

CLASS 22

Age Issues: From Young to Old

CHAPTER 32
Breaking Down the Myths of Aging
John Rowe and Robert Kahn

John Rowe and Robert Kahn's chapter seeks to shatter six long held myths about the aged in our society. Their positions are supported by some of the most extensive research data on aging that has ever been available.

Breaking Down the Myths of Aging

John Rowe and Robert Kahn

President of the Mount Sinai School of Medicine and Mount Sinai Hospital in New York City, John Rowe has chaired the MacArthur Foundation Research Network on Successful Aging since its inception and is a member of the Institute of Medicine of the National Academy of Sciences.

Professor emeritus of psychology and public health at the University of Michigan, Robert L. Kahn is also research scientist emeritus at the Institute for Social Research. He is a member of the Mac Arthur Foundation of Research Network on Successful Aging and a member of the American Academy of Arts and Sciences.

The Topic of aging is durably encapsulated in a layer of myths in our society. And, like most myths, the ones about aging include a confusing blend of truth and fancy. We have compressed six of the most familiar of the aging myths into single-sentence assertions—frequently heard, usually with some link to reality, but always (thankfully) in significant conflict with recent scientific data.

MYTH #1: To be old is to be sick.
MYTH #2: You can't teach an old dog new tricks.
MYTH #3: The horse is out of the barn.
MYTH #4: The secret to successful aging is to choose your parents wisely.
MYTH #5: The lights may be on, but the voltage is low.
MYTH #6: The elderly don't pull their own weight.

Contrasting these myths with scientific fact leads to the conclusion that our society is in persistent denial of some important truths about aging. Our perceptions about the elderly fail to keep pace with the dramatic changes in their actual status. We view the aged as sick, demented, frail, weak, disabled, powerless, sexless, passive, alone, unhappy, and unable to learn—in short, a rapidly growing mass of irreversibly ill, irretrievable older Americans. To sum up, the elderly are depicted as a figurative ball and chain holding back an otherwise spry collective society. While this image is far from true, evidence that the bias persists is everywhere around us. Media attention to the elderly continues to be focused on their frailty, occasionally interspersed, in recent years, by equally unrealistic presentations of improbably youthful elders. Gerontologists, an important group of scholars which has become prominent during the last few decades, have been as much a part of the problem as the solution. Their literature has been preoccupied with concerns about frailty, nursing home admissions, and the social and health care needs of multiply impaired elders.

That we as a society are obsessed with the negative rather than the positive aspect of aging is not a new observation. Robert Butler, a pioneering gerontologist and geriatrician who was founding director of the National Institute on Aging and established the United States's first formal Department of Geriatric Medicine at Mount Sinai Medical Center in New York, coined the term "ageism" in his Pulitzer Prize-winning book *Growing Old in America—Why Survive?* in 1975. Butler saw ageism as similar to racism and sexism—a negative view of a group, and a view divorced from reality. More recently Betty Friedan, a leading architect of the women's movement, wrote about the mystique that surrounds aging in America, and our obsession with "the problem of aging." The persistence of the negative, mythic view of older persons as an unproductive burden has been underlined in recent congressional debates as to whether America can "afford the elderly." Ken Dychtwald, founder and CEO of Age Wave, Inc., has consistently sounded the call for a realistic view of aging and of older persons, exhorting American corporations to become more responsive to elders' needs.

. . .

Most of us resist replacing myth-based beliefs with science-based conclusions. It involves letting go of something previously ingrained in order to make way for the newly demonstrated facts. Learning something new requires "unlearning" something old and perhaps deeply rooted. Acknowledging the truth about aging in America is critical, however, if we are to move ahead toward successful aging as individuals and as a society. In order to make use of the new scientific knowledge and experience its benefits in our daily lives, we must first "unlearn" the myths of aging. Here we present each myth with a glimpse of the scientific evidence that corrects or contradicts it. In the following chapters of this book, we will explore that evidence in greater detail and discover its implications for how long, and how well, we live.

MYTH #1
"To Be Old is To Be Sick"

Ironically, myth #1 could be the title of many a gerontological text. Happily, though, the MacArthur Study and other important research has proved the statement false. Still, a central question regarding the status of the elderly is, "Just who is this new breed of seniors?" Are we facing an increased number of very sick old people, or is the new elder population healthier and more robust?

The first clue comes in the prevalence of diseases. Throughout the century there has been a shift in the patterns of sickness in the aging population. In the past, acute, infectious illness dominated. Today, chronic illnesses are far more prevalent. The most common ailments in today's elderly include the following: arthritis (which affects nearly half of all old people), hypertension and heart disease (which affect nearly a third), diabetes (11 percent), and disorders which influence communication such as hearing impairment (32 percent), cataracts (17 percent), and other forms of visual impairments including macular degeneration (9 percent). When you compare sixty-five- to seventy-four-year-old individuals in 1960 with those similarly aged in 1990, you find a dramatic reduction in the prevalence of three important precursors to chronic disease: high blood pressure, high cholesterol levels, and smoking. We also know that between 1982 and 1989, there were significant reductions in the prevalence of arthritis, arteriosclerosis (hardening of the arteries), dementia, hypertension, stroke and emphysema (chronic lung disease), as well as a dramatic decrease in the average number of diseases an older person has. And dental health has improved as well. The proportion of older individuals with dental disease so severe as to result in their having no teeth has dropped from 55 percent in 1957 to 34 percent in 1980, and is currently approaching 20 percent.

But what really matters is not the number or type of diseases one has, but how those problems impact on one's ability to function. For instance, if you are told that a white male is age seventy-five, your ability to predict his functional status is limited. Even if you are given details of his medical history, and learn he has a history of hypertension, diabetes, and has had a heart attack in the past, you still couldn't say whether he is sitting on the Supreme Court of the United States or in a nursing home!

There are two key ways to determine people's ability to remain independent. One is to assess their ability to manage their personal care. The personal care activities include basic functions, such as dressing, bathing, toileting, feeding oneself, transferring from bed to chair, and walking. The second category of activities is known as nonpersonal care. These are tasks such as preparing meals, shopping, paying bills, using the telephone, cleaning the house, writing, and reading. A person is disabled or dependent when he or she cannot perform some of these usual activities without assistance. When you look at sixty-five-year-old American men, who have a total life expectancy of fifteen more years, the picture is a surprisingly positive one: twelve years are likely to be spent fully independent. By age eighty-five, the picture is more bleak: nearly half of the future years are spent inactive or dependent.

Life expectancy for women is substantially greater than that for men. At age sixty-five, women have almost nineteen years to live—four more than men of the same age. And for women, almost fourteen of those will be active, and five years dependent.

It is important to recognize that this dependency is not purely a function of physical impairments but represents, particularly in advanced age, a mixture of physical and cognitive impairment. Even at age eighty-five, women have a life expectancy advantage of nearly one and a half years over men and are likely to spend about half of the rest of their lives independent.

There are two general schools of thought regarding the implications of increased life expectancy on the overall health status of the aging population. One holds that the same advances in medical technology will produce not only longer life, but also less disease and disability in old age. This optimistic theory predicts a reduction in the incidence of nonfatal disorders such as arthritis, dementia, hearing impairment, diabetes, hypertension, and the like. It is known as the "compression of morbidity" theory—in a nutshell, it envisions prolonged active life and delayed disability for older people. A contrasting theory maintains just the opposite: that our population will become both older and sicker.

The optimistic theory may be likened to the tale of the "one-horse shay" by Oliver Wendell Holmes. Some sixty-five to seventy years ago, when one of us (RLK) was reluctantly attending the Fairbanks Elementary School in Detroit, students were required to memorize poetry. One of Robert's favorites was a long set of verses by Oliver Wendell Holmes entitled "The Deacon's Masterpiece or The Wonderful One-Horse Shay." (A shay was a two-wheeled buggy, usually fitted with a folding top. The word itself, shay, is a New England adaptation from the French *chaise*.)

The relevance of all this to gerontology becomes clear early in the poem. The deacon was exasperated with the tendency of horse-drawn carriages to wear out irregularly; one part or another would fail when the rest of the vehicle was still in prime condition. He promised to build a shay in which every part was equally strong and durable, so that it would not be subject to the usual breakdowns of one or another part. And he was marvelously successful. The shay showed no sign of aging whatsoever until the first day of its toist year, when it suddenly, instantly, and mysteriously turned to dust. The poem concludes with a line that stays in memory after all the intervening years. It is the poet's challenge to those who find the story difficult to believe. Since every part of the shay was equally durable, collapse of all had to come at the same moment: "End of the wonderful one-hoss shay; logic is logic; that's all I say."

The second, more negative theory—in which older people become sicker and more dependent with increasing age—is losing favor. MacArthur Studies and other research show us that older people are much more likely to age well than to become decrepit and dependent. The fact is, relatively few elderly people live in nursing homes. Only 5.2 percent of older people reside in such institutions, a figure which declined significantly from the 6.3 percent found in a 1982 survey. Furthermore, most older Americans are free of disabilities. Of those aged sixty-five to seventy-four in 1994, a full 89 percent report no disability whatsoever. While the proportion of elderly who are fully functioning and robust declines with advancing age, between the age of seventy-five to eighty-four, 73 percent still report no disability, and even after age eighty-five, 40 percent of the population is fully functional.

Between 1982 and 1994, the proportion of the population over age sixty-five that reported any disability fell from 24.9 percent to 21.3 percent, a meaningful reduction. And another statistic really sends the message home: in the United States today there are 1.4 million fewer disabled older people than there would be had the status of the elderly not improved since 1982. Furthermore, many studies show that the reduction in disability among older people appears to be accelerating. This is true at all ages, even among those over age ninety-five.

And so, the optimistic vision of aging seems to hold true—and the fact that the elderly population is relatively healthy and independent bears on the future of social policies for older people. It has important implications for issues as broad as establishing the proper eligibility age for Social Security benefits, and projecting the likely future expenses of federal health care programs including Medicare and Medicaid. Furthermore, beyond social policy implications, the greater our understanding of disability trends, the greater, in turn, will be our insights into the degree of biological change in our aging population. Disability in older people results from three key factors: 1) the impact of disease, or more commonly, many diseases at once; 2) lifestyle factors, such as exercise and diet, which directly influence physical fitness and risk of disease; and 3) the biological changes that occur with advancing age—formally known as senescence. It is not clear whether the reduction in the incidence of many chronic diseases—and the reduction in many risk factors for those diseases—is connected to a more general slowdown in the rate of physical aging. There is increasing evidence that the rate of physical aging is not, as we once believed, determined by genes alone. Lifestyle factors— which can be changed—have powerful influence as well. We will discuss this in much greater detail later in the book, but it's a very empowering notion to keep in mind. We can, and should, take some responsibility for the way in which we grow older.

So far, we have been focusing on objective information about older people's ability to function. But another important issue is how older people *perceive* their own health status. Again, we are optimistic. Research finds that older people have a quite positive view of their own health. In one major study, older people were asked to rate their health as excellent, very good, good, fair, or poor. In 1994, 39 percent of individuals over the age of sixty-five viewed their health as very good or excellent, while only 29 percent considered their health to be fair or poor. Even among those over age eighty-five, 31 percent considered themselves to be in very good or excellent health, while 36 percent viewed themselves as in poor health. Men and women were equally positive, but there were some racial differences—for instance, older African Americans were more likely than Caucasians to rate their health as poor. In general, however, a growing body of evidence shows that older people perceive themselves as healthy, even in the face of real physical problems. Why the occasional dissonance between objective measures of health and people's perceptions of it? It may reflect a remarkably successful adaptation to disability. Despite society's view of older persons as frail and in poor health, older people simply

don't share that view, even when they have objective evidence of disability.

In sum, decades of research clearly debunk the myth that to be old in America is to be sick and frail. Older Americans are generally healthy. Even in advanced old age, an overwhelming majority of the elderly population have little functional disability, and the proportion that is disabled is being whittled away over time. We are delighted to observe increasing momentum toward the emergence of a physically and cognitively fit, nondisabled, active elderly population. The combination of longer life and less illness is adding life to years as well as years to life.

At the same time, as a result of the MacArthur Foundation Studies of Aging in America and other research, we now can identify the lifestyle and personality factors that boost the chance of aging successfully. This book discusses strategies to reduce one's risk of disease and disability, and to maintain physical and mental function. Our main message is that we can have a dramatic impact on our own success or failure in aging. Far more than is usually assumed, successful aging is in our own hands. What we can do for ourselves, however, depends partly on the opportunities and constraints that are presented to us as we age—in short, on the attitudes and expectations of others toward older people, and on policies of the larger society of which we are a part.

MYTH #2
"You Can't Teach an Old Dog New Tricks"

The pervasive belief among young and old that the elderly cannot sharpen or broaden their minds creates a disturbing cycle of mental inactivity and decay. Certainly, the less people are challenged, the less they can perform. But research shows that older people can, and do, learn new things—and they learn them well. True, the limits of learning, and especially the pace of learning, are more restricted in age than in youth. And the conditions for successful learning are different for older people than for the young. The trouble is, our institutions of learning—schools and work organizations—have not yet adapted to these age differences. One result is that the myth about older people's capacity to grow and learn becomes further entrenched.

MacArthur research on mental function in old age is also encouraging. First of all, the fears of age-related loss are often exaggerated. Older people have become so sensitized to the threat of Alzheimer's disease that every forgotten name or misplaced key ring strikes fear. Alzheimer's is indeed a terrible disease, both for those afflicted and their caregivers. But current estimates are that no more than 10 percent of all elderly people, aged sixty-five to one hundred or more, are Alzheimer's patients. In fact, even among those aged seventy-four to eighty-one, a full half show no mental decline whatsoever over the following seven years. Ninety-five percent of older people live in the community at large; only 5 percent are in nursing homes. And that small percentage has been decreasing since 1982! The MacArthur Studies have added to our understanding of the factors that maintain high mental function. As we discuss in chapter 8, three key features predict strong mental function in old age: 1) regular physical activity; 2) a strong social support system; and 3) belief in one's ability to handle what life has to offer. Happily, all three can be initiated or increased, even in later life.

OLDER MEN AND WOMEN CAN AND DO LEARN NEW THINGS

Research has demonstrated the remarkable and enduring capacity of the aged brain to make new connections, absorb new data, and thus acquire new skills. In one experiment, older people who showed a decline in two important cognitive functions, inductive reasoning and spatial orientation, participated in five training sessions designed to improve these functions. The improvements were significant, and permanent. The same can be said of short-term memory among older men and women. Before training sessions, older people were able to recall fewer than five words from a randomly presented long list. After training, they were able to recall almost fifteen words. (In chapter 8, we go into this in more detail.) As consumers, older people learn to use household appliances that were unknown in their youth—food processors, microwave ovens, automated bank teller machines, and even "user-friendly" VCRs (video cassette recorders).

Secretaries who learned their craft on manual typewriters make the transition to electric machines and then to word processors and computers.

The stereotype in organizations is that older people oppose innovation while younger ones urge it—the stereotypical old fogies versus the young Turks. But in fact, corporate battles often involve young fogies and old Turks! Intimate knowledge of a given organization, the security that often comes with long tenure and, ultimately, the freedom that accompanies impending retirement combine to yield significant advantages to older people in the workplace. Specifically, elders may have an innovative advantage that compensates for (or even exceeds) the flexibility of youth.

SOME ASPECTS OF LEARNING ARE MORE LIMITED IN AGE

Science confirms what all of us have observed; young people tend to have sharper vision and better hearing than older people, their reaction time is quicker, and they outperform elders in terms of short-term memory. As a result, some kinds of learning, especially those that require perceptual speed, physical coordination, and muscular strength, become more difficult and ultimately impossible in old age. One of us (RLK) was, in his late teens, an aspiring gymnast. Robert mastered some modest feats, but the giant swing, in which the performer does a handstand on the high bar, was beyond his reach. Back then, he probably could have prevailed with a little extra training (and perhaps courage). At age eighty, the giant swing is beyond the realm of possibility. As we write this, however, we have before us a picture of the man who, as a senior Olympic competitor, holds the national record for pole vault. He is sixty-seven years old! So while there are certainly limits, there are limit-breakers as well.

WHAT IT TAKES TO LEARN CHANGES WITH AGE

While it is true that older people have, in general, weaker short-term memories than younger people, these deficits can be overcome with proper training. For instance, older people can significantly improve their short-term memory by making lists and training their memory with practice games. Admittedly, similarly trained young people do still better, but trained elders often do better than untrained young people.

There are many examples of ways in which older people can boost their performance when given the right opportunity for improvement. The key is for older people to develop at their own pace, and with respect for both their practical and emotional needs. One good example is the case of a large company that was converting to computer-controlled operation of a decentralized staff. They soon found that older workers were relatively slow, and reluctant to adapt to the new procedures. Young people, already computer proficient, were assigned as coaches, but the difficulties continued. In time, older clerks were seen staying at their desks beyond the usual working hours, in order to practice in relative privacy and at their own pace. And indeed, their performance improved significantly. This episode illustrates several of the key requirements for learning new skills in old age. It is critical that older people be able to 1) work at their own pace; 2) practice new skills; and 3) avoid the embarrassment so common among older people when they cannot keep up to speed with their younger counterparts. From childhood, we become accustomed to older people teaching those who are younger. It is often difficult for older people to accept the reversal of roles in which the young become the mentors.

TEACHING INSTITUTIONS HAVEN'T ADAPTED TO LEARNING NEEDS

When it comes to learning, our society is still age-graded. Times have changed, the need for lifelong learning and relearning has increased, but our institutions have not caught up with the new realities. They operate as if life consisted of three compartmentalized periods—education, work, and retirement, in that order.

There was a time when that was adequate. The traditional skills of reading, writing, and arithmetic were sufficient for many jobs. More specific skills, once learned, were practiced for the rest of one's working life. That time is long gone. Technological change means that most people will need to learn several new jobs in the course of their working lives. We now know that the capacity to learn is lifelong. The next step will be to create the conditions under which lifelong learning can be nurtured and achieved.

MYTH #3
"The Horse Is Out of the Barn"

We've all heard the claims of lifelong smokers that there's "no point stopping now"—the damage is already done and the habit permanently ingrained. This is an easy way out, but far from the truth. It's time to dispel the false and discouraging claim that old age is too late for efforts to reduce risk and promote health. Many older persons believe that after decades of risky behavior—overindulgence in alcohol and fat-laden food, lack of exercise, and so on—there is no point changing. They feel that what they have lost is gone forever and cannot be recovered, or they deny that their habits are dangerous in the first place. Many consider age-related changes irreversible, and hold no hope for either recovering lost function or lessening their risks of developing diseases. Fortunately, they are mistaken. Not only can we recover much lost function and decrease risk, but in some cases we can actually increase function beyond our prior level.

Mark Twain amused his audiences by reversing the relationship between health and bad habits. He told a story about an elderly woman whose doctor, after careful examination, informed her that she would have to quit smoking, drinking, and gorging herself on rich food.

"But doctor," she protested, "I have never done any of those things in my life!"

At this point, Twain looked out at the audience. There was a moment of silence, he shook his white head sadly, and pronounced the grim verdict: "There you are. There was nothing to be done. She had neglected her habits!"

Certainly, it's better to start healthy habits early and sustain them for a lifetime. But for those who have strayed—that is, most people!—nature is remarkably forgiving. Research shows that it is almost never too late to begin healthy habits such as smoking cessation, sensible diet, exercise, and the like. And even more important, it is never too late to benefit from those changes. Making these changes can mark the transition from the risky state we call "usual aging" to the goal we all share: "successful aging"—growing old with good health, strength, and vitality.

We're not, however, promoting a fantastical fountain of youth. Attempts at rejuvenation are probably as old as aging itself. Early in this century one of the more interesting (though ineffective) attempts involved injections of extracts of tiger testes. Though many anti-aging remedies and nostrums continue to be commercially available, most have little to offer or are, at best, of unproven value. We discuss these in greater detail in chapter 9. Despite the lack of proven "rejuvenators," however, there are many ways in which older people can recover function and decrease the risk of disease or disability. Perhaps the greatest anti-aging "potion" is good old-fashioned clean living.

CIGARETTE SMOKING

Everyone knows that smoking is bad for the health. But we've heard it so often, and for so long, it often falls on deaf ears. Cigarette smoking and other tobacco use increases the risk of lung cancer and other lung diseases, coronary heart disease, stroke, and other life-threatening illnesses. A person who smokes a pack of cigarettes a day is four times more likely than a nonsmoker to have coronary heart disease. Even a person who smokes less than half a pack a day is twice as likely to have coronary heart disease as a nonsmoker. That's the bad news.

The good news is that the risk of heart disease begins to fall almost as soon as you quit smoking—no matter how long you've smoked. Within a few months, smokers who have managed to quit begin to reap the benefits. In five years, an ex-smoker is not much more likely to have heart disease than a person who has never smoked! That's only part of the good news about smoking and heart disease. The rest of it is that the good effects of quitting smoking hold regardless of age, the number of years one smokes, or how heavy the smoking habit.

Like heart disease, the risk of stroke drops quickly when cigarette smoking stops. We know that among people aged third-four to fifty-five, those who stopped smoking within the past two to four years were no more at risk for stroke than those who had never smoked at all.

Lung disease, especially lung cancer and emphysema, is perhaps the main fear of cigarette smokers. In this case, too, the research is encouraging to former smokers and should spur those who are planning to stop. As with heart disease, the risk of lung cancer begins to fall when smoking stops, although much more slowly. It takes at least fifteen years after quitting for a smoker's risk of lung cancer to become as low as that of a lifetime nonsmoker. But the good news remains; when you quit, your lungs begin to heal and the risk of lung disease begins to drop. That holds for people of all ages.

Being overweight and eating too much of the wrong things is like smoking in some ways. Psychologists call these activities oral gratification—and like smoking, eating habits are hard to change. Unfortunately, overeating is like smoking in another way: it increases the risk of many diseases. Several factors fit together like a puzzle and conspire to raise the risk of disease: eating too many calories, eating too much fat, and becoming obese. All of these—independently and as a group—may raise the risk of heart disease as well as certain cancers.

SYNDROME X

Researchers have identified a new condition known as Syndrome X, in which a cluster of risk factors together raise the risk of heart attack and premature death. These factors include high blood sugar and insulin levels (the so-called pseudodiabetes of aging); high blood pressure; and increases in blood fats like cholesterol and triglycerides, which accompany the pot-bellied obesity so common in middle-aged and elderly people (especially men). But the good news for people with Syndrome X is that the increased risk of heart disease is related to their weight, not their age. When their weight drops and stays down, so do the risk factors for heart disease. These results hold in old age. When obese middle-aged and older men lose 10 percent of their body weight, they reduce their risk factors significantly. In one study, older men lost less weight than younger ones, but interestingly, they did almost as well in reducing their risk of disease.

HIGH BLOOD PRESSURE

High blood pressure, especially the systolic blood pressure (the higher of the two numbers in your blood pressure reading), is an important risk factor for heart disease and stroke. In the United States and other similarly prosperous countries, systolic blood pressure generally rises with age. In fact, the increase in blood pressure is so common that it is often taken for granted, and considered the inevitable result of "normal" aging. But in developed countries, not *all* older people show increases in blood pressure; and on the flip side of the coin, in less-advantaged countries, where people eat less meat, more grains and vegetables, and keep physically active, blood pressure tends *not* to rise with age.

Diet and exercise tend to reduce blood pressure, but they are not failproof. Some people do neither, and have low blood pressure. And others do both, but are unable to lower their blood pressure to an acceptable level. In a reversal from previous practice, such older individuals are now commonly advised to take medication to get their blood pressure under control. But many older people resist drug treatment, arguing that they have tolerated their hypertension well for many years, and that certainly the damage is already done. But we now know that treatment of systolic hypertension is safe, inexpensive, and lowers risk. One large study, in which all the participants were over the age of sixty and some were over eighty, showed that drug treatments for high blood pressure reduced the risk of stroke by more than a third and the risk of heart attacks by more than a quarter. The horse may have been headed out of the barn, but some good rope tricks lured it back in.

PHYSICAL FITNESS

"Doc, I've been a couch potato for so many years, I can't possibly get back in shape" is a common refrain in my (JWR) office. Physical function does indeed decrease with age, especially in the realm of the upper limits of physical performance. The best race times of elderly marathon runners and master swimmers do not equal those of similarly trained young athletes (nor of their own performance in the days of their youth). Nerve function, heart capacity, kidney function, breathing capacity, and maximum work rate all show age-related reductions. Vision and hearing, muscle mass, and strength show similar age-related patterns. That's the bad news. But set against this tale of diminishing capacities are three reassuring facts.

First, the aged body is more than able to meet the demands of everyday life. Losses in elite athletic ability do not create handicaps for most activities.

Second, most age-related reductions in physical performance are avoidable and many are reversible. They are often the cumulative result of lifestyle—what we do with our bodies and what we take into them—rather than the result of aging itself. Years of cigarette smoking, excessive use of alcohol, too little exercise and too much food, especially fats and sugars, do physical damage that is often wrongly attributed to age.

The facts are that exercise dramatically increases physical fitness, muscle size, and strength in older individuals. Besides rejuvenating muscles, resistance exercises (pumping iron) also enhance bone strength, limiting the risk of osteoporosis and fractures of the hip, spine, and wrist. Exercise also improves balance, thereby decreasing the risk of falling, a common and life-threatening problem in older persons. And as we discuss in detail in chapter 7, the MacArthur Studies now show that physical exercise is just the first of several ways to maintain one's physical abilities. It turns out that active mental stimulation, and keeping up relationships with friends and relatives, also helps promote physical ability. For instance, many people are surprised to learn that frequent emotional support (listening, encouragement, cheering up, understanding, and so on) is associated with improved physical function in old age. This is just one of countless connections between mind and body—mental vigor and physical well-being—that are seen in the aging process. A healthy physical and emotional lifestyle seems to be of even greater value to older people than younger ones. It's never too late to start.

MYTH #4
"The Secret to Successful Aging Is to Choose Your Parents Wisely"

People commonly assume that genes (or heredity) account for the rate at which one's body functions decline with advancing age. And it's not hard to find examples to support that assumption—families in which everyone seems to live past ninety or not make it to age sixty-five. True, there is a meaningful connection between genetics and aging. For instance, it has long been recognized that the length of life of nonidentical twins varies much more than that of identical twins. But while the role of genetics in aging is important, it has been tremendously overstated. A common error is to assume that one's genetic predisposition is equivalent to genetic "control" of life expectancy, and that we are all preprogrammed for a given duration of life. Our MacArthur twin studies leave very substantial room for factors *other* than genetics in determining life expectancy.

When considering what factors promote long life, it is essential to distinguish familial habits and experiences from genes. Members of a family may share many characteristics as they grow old, but this should not be misinterpreted as evidence for a pure genetic role in aging. It is possible that these similarities are related more to common environmental conditions, such as diet, which are shared by family members. Not everything that runs in families is genetic. For example, apple pie recipes, though passed from generation to generation, are clearly not genetically determined. But the contents of those apple pies, and all other foods shared by families, have a meaningful impact on the health of all family members—their weight, blood sugar levels, you name it.

Regardless of our genes, we as individuals can play an important role in how successfully we age. Just how big a role can we play? That depends on the balance between the influence of genes and environment. Let's take a look at the ways in which heredity does—and does not— play an important role in the three key components of successful aging: 1) avoiding disease and disability; 2) maintaining high mental and physical function; and 3) continuing to engage actively in life, through productivity and strong interpersonal relationships.

The strongest influence of heredity on aging relates to genetic diseases that can shorten life, such as numerous forms of cancer and familial high cholesterol syndromes (which lead to heart disease). Certainly, it would behoove us to choose parents who don't carry genes for these diseases. Would that it were so easy. Still, however, heredity is not as powerful a player as many assume. For all but the most strongly determined genetic diseases, such as Huntington's disease, MacArthur Studies show that the environment and lifestyle have a powerful impact on the likelihood of actually developing the disorder. This is wonderful news for individuals with strong family histories of some cancers, heart disease, hypertension, rheumatoid arthritis, and many other conditions. We now know that diet, exercise, and even medi-

cations may delay, or completely eliminate, the emergence of the disease. Genes play a key role in promoting disease, but they are certainly less than half the story.

What about the role of genetics on mental and physical function, the second important component of successful aging? In this arena, MacArthur research has shown that heredity is *less* important than environment and lifestyle. A major study of Swedish twins that was part of the MacArthur Research Program on Successful Aging shed light on the factors that influence the physiological changes that occur with advancing age. By studying both identical and nonidentical twins who were raised apart, researchers were able to tease apart the relative importance of heredity and environment on mental and physical changes with age. The bottom line is very clear: with rare exceptions, only about 30 percent of physical aging can be blamed on the genes. Additional studies of Swedish twins over the age of 80 show that only about half of the changes in mental function with aging are genetic. This leaves substantial room for a healthy lifestyle to protect the mind and body. And better yet, as we grow older, genetics becomes *less* important, and environment becomes *more* important. The likelihood of being fat, having hypertension, high cholesterol and triglyceride levels, and the rate at which one's lung function declines with advancing age are, by and large, largely *not* inherited. These risks are due to environmental or lifestyle factors. How we live, and where we live, has the most profound impact on age-related changes in the function of many organs throughout the body, including the heart, immune system, lung, bones, brain, and kidneys. We will discuss these important findings in greater detail in chapters 5–8.

The third component of successful aging, continuing active engagement with life, is for the most part not inherited. While certain personality traits may be, in part, heritable—the maintenance of good health certainly enhances the likelihood of remaining active and engaged in life—one's degree of vitality and interpersonal connection late in life is largely determined by *nongenetic* factors.

These findings are exceptionally optimistic and shatter the myth that our course in old age is predetermined. MacArthur research provides very strong scientific evidence that we are, in large part, responsible for our own old age. We have the powerful capacity to enhance our chance of maintaining high mental and physical ability as we grow older. Throughout this book, we will show you just how that can be accomplished.

MYTH #5
"The Lights May Be On, But The Voltage is Low"

This metaphorical assertion has at least three implications about aging—all negative and none accurate. The myth suggests that older people suffer from inadequate physical and mental abilities. And the electrical metaphor hints that older men and women are sexless, or at least uninterested in sex (and, in the case of men, unable to perform adequately regardless of interest). MacArthur research shows that while there is some modicum of truth to these beliefs, they're far more fiction than fact. Let's sift out the facts.

SEXUALITY IN OLD AGE

At the time of this writing, a popular TV beverage commercial pokes fun at a silver-haired couple engaged in passionate foreplay on the living room couch. The image is presented as absurd, and a humorous reference is made to the parents (supposedly 100-plus years old) being home. Apparently, the age-old assumption that sexual interest and activity in later life are rare and inappropriate is still in full force. These stereotypical images are examples of what psychologists call "pluralistic ignorance"—that is, most people as private individuals know the image is false, but remain silent on the subject because they think that others see it as true.

We remind ourselves that myths do contain some truth. Sexual activity *does* tend to decrease in old age. However, there are tremendous individual differences in this intimate aspect of life. We know also that these differences are determined in part by cultural norms, by health or illness, and by the availability of sexual or romantic partners. When it comes to sexual activity, as in so many other aspects of aging, chronological age itself is not the critical factor. In men, the decline in testosterone with age is highly variable and linked only loosely with sexual performance.

Certainly there are older people who have lost interest in sex and are glad to be done with it. When Sophocles, the great tragic poet of ancient Greece, was in his eighties, he was asked rather delicately whether, at his advanced age, he "had yet any acquaintance with Venus." "Heavens forbid!" the sage is said to have replied, "I thank the gods that I am finally rid of that tyranny."

Had surveys been conducted in the Greece of 400 B.C., it is unlikely that all of his elderly countrymen (and women) would have agreed with him. Certainly it is not the dominant view of older men and women in the United States today. There is a gradual decline in sexual interest and ability beginning around the age of fifty. However, this decline has many causes besides age itself, including certain chronic diseases and the medications with which they are treated. Diabetes, heart disease, and hypertension are perhaps the most frequent impediments to sexual function, especially for men.

At least since the famous Kinsey report in 1953, there have been occasional attempts to put numbers to the question of sexual activity in old age. One important early study found that at age sixty-eight, about 70 percent of men were sexually active on a regular basis. At age seventy-eight, however, the percentage dropped to about 25 percent of men. In addition to age itself, health status was the major factor in determining the frequency of sexual activity among men. For older women, however, regularity of sexual activity depends primarily on the availability of an appropriate partner. If this study were repeated today, the substantial improvements in health among older people and the changes in social norms that have occurred during the past two decades would likely yield evidence of even greater interest and participation in sex in later life.

Finally, our wish list for research on this important subject includes a distinction between the sex act itself and the many other forms of physical intimacy. The basic human need for affectionate physical contact, which is apparent even in newborn infants, persists throughout life. The voltage is never too low for that—in fact, it may help keep the lights on.

MYTH #6
"The Elderly Don't Pull Their Own Weight"

The widespread belief that older people are relatively unproductive in society is wrong and unjust in three ways: I) the measures of performance are wrong; our society doesn't count a great deal of productive activity; 2) the playing field is not level; older men and women aren't given an equal chance for paying jobs; and 3) millions of older people are ready, willing, and able to increase their productivity; paid and voluntary. Let's look at the facts that bear on each of these claims.

THE MEASURES ARE WRONG

The accusation that older people are burdens rather than contributors to society is heard in many places, from the halls of Congress to the living rooms of overworked young men and women. The unstated assumptions are that everybody who works for pay is pulling his or her weight, and that everyone who does not work for pay is a burden.

Both assumptions are wrong. Some people who are paid do little or nothing useful, and some are paid to do things that are damaging—writing advertisements for cigarettes, for example. It is ironic and misleading, as well as unfair, that such things are counted as productive, while raising children, maintaining a household, taking care of an ill or disabled family member, or working as a volunteer in a hospital or church are considered unproductive (or at least not "counted" as productive). While it is important to distinguish between paid and unpaid work, it is wrong to omit unpaid productive work from our national accounting. As people age, and especially as they retire from paid work, their continuing productive activities are increasingly unpaid. Our national statistics thus ignore a great deal of productive activity, a great deal of what keeps our society functioning.

Almost all older men and women are productive in this larger sense. One-third work for pay and one-third work as volunteers in churches, hospitals, and other organizations. Others provide informal, much-needed assistance to family members, friends, and neighbors. It would take more than three million paid caregivers, working full time, to provide that assistance to sick and disabled people!

In 1997, a national campaign was mounted to increase volunteerism in America. The president and several ex-presidents spoke of the country's need for voluntary activity and urged people to contribute as volunteers. We propose one way of making it more attractive to volunteer: start counting voluntary work as productive. The ways we measure productive activity are broken; fix them!

THE PLAYING FIELD IS NOT LEVEL

Older men and women aren't given an equal chance for paid employment. Retirement used to be compulsory. When you reached the ages of fifty-five or sixty or sixty-five, you had to retire. While it is now illegal to force people to retire solely because of their age, downsizing, corporate mergers, and other organizational changes affect older people disproportionately. For many people retirement, while not legally compelled, is nevertheless involuntary.

In addition to the stick of involuntary retirement, there is the carrot of pension entitlements, both private and through Social Security. These make retirement attractive or, for some, downright irresistible. We should remember, however, that the reasons for creating Social Security in the first place were not only to prevent poverty in old age but also to make way for youth. In an economy plagued by unemployment, getting older workers out of the labor force was an attractive idea. It exchanged unwanted joblessness among younger people for a more acceptable kind of joblessness (retirement) at the other end of the age range. In combination, both public and private policies urge older people to retire and we then blame them for doing so.

Older people who want to continue working beyond the usual retirement age see the inflexibility of employers as the main obstacle. Many of those who are still working and would like to continue with the same employer want fewer hours, a change in work content, or greater flexibility in scheduling. Ninety percent of those who want such changes, however, say that their employers will not accommodate them. Older people who are seeking new jobs report that companies are reluctant to hire older workers. Many employers seem to believe, mistakenly, that older workers are less productive, more often absent, or are liabilities in some other respect. When it comes to job-hunting by older people, the playing field has yet to be leveled.

THEY ARE READY, WILLING, AND ABLE

When Old Age and Survivors Insurance (OASI) was first enacted, most people did not live to the legal retirement age of sixty-five years. Most of those who did, it was assumed, would be neither willing nor able to work. Since the early twentieth century, life expectancy has greatly increased and the health of older people has greatly improved. Although some are not able to work and some do not wish to work, there are millions of older men and women who are ready, willing, and able to work. Among nonworkers aged fifty to fifty-nine, almost half would prefer to work, and among those sixty to sixty-four, more than one-third agree. Companies that have emphasized the recruitment and retention of older workers confirm that older employees meet or surpass expectations, often bringing the added value of increased insight and experience to the work environment.

CLASS 23

A New South Africa?: Lessons for the USA

CHAPTER 33
Now That The TRC Is Over:
Looking Back, Reaching Forward
Charles Villa-Vicencio
Charles Villa-Vicencio recounts some of his experiences in South Africa during and after the Truth and Reconciliation Commission wherein he served as the director of research.

CHAPTER 34
African Mysteries
Patti Waldmeir
Anatomy of A Miracle: The End of Apartheid and the Birth of the New South Africa. (1997). Patti Waldmeir provides an account of her personal observance of racial social change in two countries on two different continents.

CHAPTER 33

Now That The TRC Is Over
Looking Back, Reaching Forward

Charles Villa-Vicencio[1]

Currently residing in Cape Town, South Africa, Charles Villa-Vicencio is former director of research for the Truth and Reconciliation Commission.

The South African Truth and Reconciliation Commission (TRC) is over. It must be over. It must close. It is time to move on. It is useful, however, to look back at the drama of the TRC experience in order to reach forward to something new—a milieu within which the atrocities of the past are not repeated. Given the response by some within the political spectrum to the Report of the Commission, it is expedient and it is right that the quest for what is indeed new be vigorously promoted. The habits of the past are not yet behind us.

In looking for the new it is fashionable to ask: Did the TRC work? Did it attain its objectives? How much truth did it uncover? How much reconciliation did it accomplish? Has it discerned a new way forward? There captivity, in pursuit of something new. While not forgetting—we need to free ourselves from debilitating into a paralyzing form of memory.

Behind the Mask

Melodrama is to be avoided. I also do not wish to be seen to be too pessimistic about human nature—portraying some kind of Protestant propensity to what theologians call original sin. On the contrary, I believe that it is in facing the capacity of humanity for evil that we can unleash within ourselves an energy to do good.

When hope seems least likely, it can only emerge from the cauldron of that which seems to deny its very existence. The TRC has reached into the cauldron of suffering and despair—creating a space within which those who have borne this suffering could tell their stories. Those directly responsible for this suffering as well as those who simply stood by and allowed it to happen (sometimes out of fear or a sense of helplessness, sometimes because they benefited from a system that generated this suffering) were invited to listen to these stories. In the context of this drama the nation has been compelled to *acknowledge* the suffering of the past. If earlier most whites refused to acknowledge the extent of black suffering, today few deny that it happened—although few whites chose to attend TRC hearings or are ready to take responsibility for the restitution of those who suffered most. Some victims and survivors who have testified before the Commission have spoken of a sense of cathartic relief which the experience afforded them. Others still feel that the Commission has not done enough to dress their wounds.

I tell the story of but one such person, Joe Seremane—whose brother Timothy Tebogo Seremane was executed in 1981 in the Quatro detention camp in Angola by cadres of the African National Congress who judged him to be a spy, working for the South African apartheid regime.

Is a sense in which the Commission was doomed to failure before it began, if it was ever

---

thought that it could resolve all the entrenched problems associated with centuries of colonial and racial oppression. This is a past that included the Dutch occupation of the Cape in 1652, a century of British imperialism and almost fifty years of statutory apartheid. The long and tired saga came to the beginning of an acknowledged end in 1990— as the first stages of a negotiated political settlement to a civil war began to unfold.

Such settlements do not occur with textbook clarity. The expectations of those who demanded Nuremberg trials, as well as those who thought 'now that it is all over' we could forget the past and live happily ever after, were simply not realistic. South Africans were required instead to embrace a process the Chileans called *reconvivencia*. This is a period involving the need to learn to live together, after years of separation and conflict. For the ship of state in this context to veer either too far towards retribution or too close to amnesia would be fatal. Accountability is necessary, while unbridled retributive justice undermines the possibility of peace.

I propose not to address the South African TRC in any detail in what follows—while using it as a model to explore related but broader concerns - concerns from which no gender, tribe, nation or ethnic group is immune. Universal in nature, they are vividly illustrated in the deep-seated human passions, concerns and afflictions which have emerged from the stories of perpetrators and victims during the life of the Commission. It is only acknowledging the brooding presence of these emotions in humanity itself that makes it is possible for them to be dealt with in a constructive manner.

I seek to do two things: One, to provide an insight into humanity as gleaned from the South African experience—both its evil nature and the quest for something new that resides within it. Two, I appeal to proponents, essentially, of the arts—poets, story-tellers, musicians, creators of fine art, artists of the stage (for reasons to which I return later) to assist this generation to break out of what Max Weber has called the 'iron cage' of.

In brief, Seremane's concern is that the matter was not probed sufficiently by the Commission. "Memories are not so short that it can be forgotten that many have been killed under trumped-up charges of being a spy or a sell-out by fanatic elements in our struggle for liberation," he notes.[3] In his appearance at the Commission he made several requests: The return of his brother's bones.

"Where," he asked, "was my brother buried?" He demanded access to the records of his brother's trial. He asked for the names of his interrogators, prosecutors and executioners, so that he and his family could make peace with them. He asked that both sides of the allegations concerning his brother's alleged spying activities be disclosed in public so that society could judge whether or not he was a South African agent. "You owe us a lot; not monetary compensation, but our bones buried in shallow graves in Angola and heaven knows where else." He quotes words from Langston Hughes's M*instrel Man*:[4]

> Because my mouth
> Is wide with laughter
> And my throat deep with song,
> Do you not think
> I suffer, after I have held
> My pain so long.

Whatever the truth of the various allegations (by Seremane and the counter charges by the ANC) the pathos of Seremane's story should not be missed. His *perception* is that his brother was unjustly sentenced—and alienation is driven by perception. A fierce critic of the apartheid regime, he was imprisoned and tortured by the apartheid police. He was a dedicated member of the liberation struggle. Appointed by the African National Congress (ANC) led government to be chief commissioner of the newly formed Land Claims Court (and later dismissed), he now discovers that his comrades in struggle had executed his brother. "I have been on [Robben] Island, I have gone through hell. I have been tortured, nearly lost my life . . . I have seen what it means to be tortured. But when I think of Chief Timothy and compare the way he died . . . my suffering is nothing . . .," he told the Commission's special hearing on prisons in July 1997.

A dramatic story. Whatever the truth concerning detail, it illustrates the extent to which healing needs to take place. His story is the stuff of which drama and poetry is written. And yet, tragically, Seremane's story is but one of many that have shaped the story-telling experience of the Commission. It identifies the agony of alienation among brothers—and there are many such stories. Yasir Henry, a young and vulnerable *Umkhonto we Sizwe* (the armed wing of the African National Congress) soldier reflects on the experience of having been dreadfully tortured and forced to lead the security police to the hiding-place of a comrade-in-arms, Ashley Fransch. Unbeknown to Yasir Henry, they were intent to kill not capture. "I heard a very big explosion, it sounded like a rocket had been launched and then . . . (whispers) there was silence . . . And they shouted that it was over. In my head all the time, and even now— although now I am asking the same question: Who sold me to the police? . . . (cries) Anton died! . . . With that question on his mouth . . . And I wake up at night with the same question! . . . (cries)."[5] Yasir Henry struggles, inter alia, to be reconciled with himself.

Alienation between those who fought on the same side is, of course, as (perhaps more) vividly portrayed within the structures of the State. The resentment experienced by apartheid's operatives who see their political masters as cowards and sellouts for refusing to stand by them in their hour of need has resulted in a cleavage within Afrikanderdom, equal to anything the *volk* has known in its divisive history. Former State President, FW de Klerk's, dismissal of those who carried out the orders of the State Security Council as a 'few bad apples,' will fester for decades to come in the minds of those whose task it was to do the evil deeds of the past.

The anger and hostility of war between enemies is equally devastating. The atrocities afflicted by one side on the other leave deep and gaping wounds. The reaction to the exhumation of bodies buried in shallow graves across the country is but a single window into the wounded memories that haunt this nation. The stories of the more than fifty bodies exhumed are the stories, sometimes of *askaris* (former cadres of the liberation movements who were 'turned' and became spies) who had served their purpose, sometimes of brave soldiers of the liberation movements who refused to capitulate to their captors and often of operatives who were captured, tortured and when no further information could be extracted from them, killed. The Commission has identified a further 200 graves that it was simply not able to open. I offer you the comment of Richard Lyster, a Commissioner in the TRC who witnessed the exhumation of the body of Portia Ndwandwe, acting commander of *Umkhonto we Sizwe* in Natal at the time of her death:

> To me this was the most poignant and saddest of all exhumations, for a number of reasons . . .

She was a woman, then the extreme remoteness of the terrain, and the conditions of her detention and death. She was held in a small concrete chamber on the edge of the small forest in which she was buried. According to information from those that killed her, she was held naked and interrogated in this chamber, for some time prior to her death. When we exhumed her body, she was on her back in a foetal position, because the grave had not been dug long enough, and she had a single bullet wound to the top of her head, indicating that she had been kneeling or squatting when she was killed. Her pelvis was clothed in a plastic bag, fashioned into a pair of panties indicating an attempt to protect her modesty. She must have heard them digging her grave . . .

It is not easy for the wounds of memory which Portia Ndwandwe's young son and others bear to be healed. Less dramatic but equally painful suffering festers behind the mask of normality and respectability for all who have suffered in the South African conflict. We laugh and we drink our wine. It is not polite to over-burden society with the suffering of our age. A new nation has been born.

> Poor chap, he always loved larking
> And now he's dead
> It must have been too cold for him his heart gave way,
> They said
>
> Oh, no no no, it was too cold always
> (Still the dead one lay moaning)
> I was much too far out all my life
> And not waving but drowning[6]

A new nation *must* be born. There *must* be wine. There *must* be laughter in life. We must, however, also take time out to face the tragic dimensions of the reality of the past that continues to gnaw at the heart of this new land. Only in facing the memories of the past can we travel with them, not only weeping, but (dare I say it) also laughing.

South Africa is a tragic place for so many of its unhealed citizens. There is unfinished healing waiting to be happen. Yes, it is absurd to suggest a Commission of two and half year's duration can heal the wounds of he past, make reparation and reconcile a nation. The Commission's attempt to enable the nation to acknowledge the truth about itself has, however, hopefully created a space for the nation to begin the difficult process of healing itself. It is a process that must necessarily include many facets—including material restitution and psychological counseling, political confrontation, residual criminal trials and the refusal of some to ever forgive. Life is a bag of mixed virtues. Perhaps it is only this mix, which will sadly but inevitably leave some in perpetual pain, that can contribute to meaningful nation-building.

If *reconvivencia* (learning to live together) is to be a reality, it necessarily involves getting to know one another—getting to know what has shaped one another's character, driven one another to war and motivated one another to commit the most heinous gross violations of human rights. This involves sharing life's stories one with the other. A new genre of South Africa's stories which peer into the past and expose the present—not in order to fuel ideological divisions nor to preach moralisms, but to sensitise and to heal, is only beginning to be born. Poets, dramatists, musicians, song-writers, painters, sculptors and story-tellers can help heal the nation. The irony is, however, that the arts are starved of funding in South Africa at the very time when they are needed most.

- Timothy Garton Ash speaks of "the more adventurous current fiction" and the theatre as providing "a partial substitute for the lack of a free press" in the East Germany of the 1980s. He describes, for example, the Deutsches Theater and the Volksbuhne as a "kind of sly cultural resistance so familiar from my studies of Berlin in the 1930s" comparing it to the "anti-Nazi resistance writings of Brecht and others".[7] The *Story of Anne Frank* has produced an empathetic understanding of anti-Semitism in the Netherlands that no political analysis can rival. Ariel Dorfman's play, *Death and the Maiden*,[8] has probably done more to quicken the minds of readers around the world about the Latin American dictatorships than all the analytical texts on the subject put together. The anti-war ballads of the Vietnam war era stirred the minds of the American populace—contributing to the creation of a climate that persuaded Nixon to end the war. The impact of poet and artist in anti-apartheid resistance at home and abroad is beyond calculation. Similar artistic resources need now to be mobilised in the creation of a reconciled

nation. Artists and the arts generally, need to facilitate the process of mutual understanding and sensitivity, to promote nation-building and reconciliation in South Africa but also in situations of more guarded and subtle forms of personal, economic and political alienation elsewhere in the world. There is healing waiting to be done. The mask of normality hides the cries of the heart. South African writer and poet, Antjie Krog, sees truth, the quest for which stands at the center of the South African experiment in transition, "as the widest possible compilation of people's perceptions, stories, myths and experiences." In pursuit of this many-sided truth, the artist, story-teller and poet can "restore to memory and foster a new humanity." This wide truth, she suggests, is "perhaps justice in its deepest sense."[9] The genre of memory must be allowed to flow where it will, giving expression to bitterness and anger as well as life and hope. It is at the same time important to recognise that the "politics of memory" can be abused by politicians to fuel the fires of hatred—as seen in the case of the Anglo-Boer war, in Northern Ireland and the situation in the former Yugoslavia. This makes it important to include stories that look forward (rather than backwards) towards restoration in the nation's repertoire of story telling. Memory as *justice* and not least as *healing* is at the same time often about victims working *through* their anger and hatred, as a means of rising above their suffering—of getting on with life with dignity.

The Non-Fascist Life

The flip-side of the challenge to heal the victims of past suffering, is the challenge to heal those responsible for this suffering. Some in South Africa were directly responsible for past suffering, others simply allowed the gross violations of human rights to occur. I want to focus on a general rather than a specific aspect of the challenge associated with perpetration. It involves the creation of an open, inclusive society—a society in which, to quote Michel Foucault, "all forms of fascism, whether already present or impending" are excluded.[10] There seems little remarkable in what he says—until we expose ourselves to his understanding of the notion of 'impending' or, if you like, subterranean forms of fascism that so easily find a place in human nature.

I suggest there is perhaps a little perpetrator in all of us. Leon Jaworski, chief prosecutor in the earliest European war crimes trials after World War II, asks himself how it is that decent people murdered others so systematically? The question haunted him all his life and in 1960 he published a book entitled *After Fifteen Years*, in which he effectively said: "Watch out." "It can happen to you."[11] Josef Garlinski, a member of the Polish resistance army and Auschwitz survivor reflects on the brutality he was required to endure from his Nazi captors and reminds us, in his book, *Fighting Auschwitz*. Having told his story with devastating human impact, he goes on to remind us that the young SS officers responsible for such deeds "could have been your sons or mine."[12] A black South African artisan, proud of his son's educational achievements and advancement in the South African Police, asked in disbelief how his son, a sensitive and deeply religious young man, could possibly have become a culpable member of the police riot squad sent into Mlungisi, the African township outside of Queenstown, to quell an anti-apartheid uprising.[13] The moving testimony of Ginn Fourie, mother of Lyndi Fourie who was killed in the Heidelberg Tavern massacre, carried out by three young APLA (Azanian People's Liberation Army) operatives in December 1993, captures the importance of discovering the humanity, compassion and courtesy of her daughter's assassins. At the close of the amnesty hearing for the young men responsible for the deed, Mrs Fourie met with them as they were about to be returned their prison cells. She had on a previous occasion offered them her forgiveness. They had suggested that perhaps there was a need for joint counseling, involving perpetrator and victim or survivor. I quote her account of the meeting:

> The warders insisted that the meeting adjourn, a hug for each indicated the depth of community we had entered into in this short while. The amnesty applicants then shackled themselves, which at that moment symbolised to me the enormous responsibility which accompanies freedom of choice and the sad outcome of making poor choices. Tears came to my eyes. Humphrey Gqomfa (one of the killers) turned to

the interpreter and said: "Please take Mrs Fourie home." Once more I was amazed by the sensitivity and leadership potential of this man, the same man who was also a perpetrator of gross violations of human rights against my own daughter.[14]

The focus of the TRC has been on what could be regarded as the exceptional. The nation was, in the process, horrified by the killers of Vlakplaas. It is outraged by the poisoning exploits and drug industry which emerged from South Africa's experiments in chemical and biological warfare. The media has understandably focused on these events—labeling Eugene de Kock, the Vlakplaas commander, "prime evil". Jeffrey Benzien, a Western Cape Security Branch policeman, who demonstrated his notorious "wet bag" method of torture before the amnesty committee, was seen on television screens and captured on the front page of most newspapers in the country. Such killers and torturers have been represented as psychopaths, aberrations and misfits. The stories of 'the ordinary' within apartheid have not made it to television screens with the same impact as these more horrific events. Steven Robins, perhaps a little too zealously, suggests that all too often the public representation of the perpetrator before the TRC conformed to the Hollywood notion of a white South African policeman, portrayed as "evil-looking Nazis with thick Afrikaans accents"[15]. The outcome has been the undermining of the ability of ordinary South Africans to see themselves as 'represented' by those who the TRC defines as perpetrators. It was too easy for too many to walk away, saying "Well, at least I did not kill anyone." In crypto-biblical style, many have silently observed, "thank you God that I am not a murderer, a torturer or an assassin—like those evil people paraded on our television screens. I thank you, God, that I am not like Eugene de Kock or Jeffrey Benzien." The focus on the outrageous has drawn the nation's attention away from what Hannah Arendt has called the "banality of evil". Foucault suggests that "fascism is in us all, in our heads and in our everyday behavior, the fascism that causes us to love power; to desire the very thing that dominates and exploits us."[16]

We too often fail to recognise the little perpetrator—the impending or latent fascist, within. Indeed, the size of the perpetrator, and its capacity to do harm, is perhaps determined by the circumstances in which we find ourselves. To recognise the possibility of evil in each of us is to take responsibility to ensure that past evil does not, in one form or another, reoccur in the future. The attempt by some within the African National Congress to stop the publication of the TRC report, because it was unhappy with the Commission having found this organisation to be responsible for certain gross violations of human rights, is suggestive in this regard. The Archbishop in his prophetic way (and prophets at times speak without nuance) was quick to warn that the seeds of tyranny were present in this initiative. Suffice it to say, however, South Africa's new constitutional democracy allowed for the challenge to happen and for the court to rule against the ruling party. This is the good news. Constitutional democracy is working. The saga suggests the reality of political gain as well as the need for vigilance in the promotion of human rights—more specifically, the freedom of information, as the basis of democracy.

Itzhak Fried suggests that individuals in most societies know that a constellation of high fever and coughing may indicate pneumonia, our society needs to be aware of symptoms that suggest the possibility of human rights violations being committed.[17] I suggest the following are, inter alia, among them:[18]

- The curtailing of free speech in favour of a paranoiac promotion of 'the truth'.

- Threats to the freedom the press and political exchange.

- The marginalisation, let alone the demonisation, of 'the other'—those who challenge 'our truth'. In South Africa they used to be labeled communists, anarchists and unSouth African. It is a process that begins, however, not with demonisation *per se*, but with an inability to empathise and an unwillingness to understand the other. It is this "incapacity for identification," suggests Adorno, that is the root of fascism.[19]

- Interference in the process of the rule of law.

- The suspension of basic human rights in the interest of the state (what is usually called national) priorities.

- The restriction of the activities of civil society.

The role of the satirist, comic, cartoonist, storyteller, artist and court jester—as well as the harshest political critic, is required for democracy to flourish. This is a process which must go beyond cerebral response—it must include those emotions that can only be captured in story-telling, poetry and song. Joseph Jaworski, in reflecting on his father, Leon Jaworski's, book *After Fifteen Years*, takes the scenario further in suggesting that it is decidedly not only governments that exploit power. It happens in business, academic institutions and similar organisations where power is frequently wielded without the restraints of public criticism and open debate. Needless to say, it can raise its ugly head in every human relationship—wherever "two or three are gathered." It occurs, he suggests, wherever the 'undiscussibles' that impede a healthy exchange of ideas remain undiscussed[20]

Reconciliation

I have referred to two deep-seated human passions: The *legacy of past suffering* which resides in all but the most remarkable of people, and the reality of the *little perpetrator*, the *potential fascist*, within in each of us. These passions are counterbalanced, I suggest, by an equally deep-seated desire among most (but not all) people to move beyond past legacies and above petty fascist tendencies toward an existence that allows for the possibility of peace, justice and ultimately reconciliation. It involves the human impulse to move both beyond being a *victim* and ceasing to be a *perpetrator*.

The South African political settlement, described by some as a 'miracle', is but one example of this impulse. It is the story of two warring groups—divided by all the *isms* of the modern world, entrenched in generations of prejudice and oppression, coming together around a table to talk peace. The historic compromise (for all its strengths and weaknesses) is today celebrated around the world—a compromise, the details of which still need to be worked out. With the initial euphoria over and the demands of the challenge that awaits the nation needing to be faced, there are fewer and fewer people who are still prepared to talk of the South African 'miracle'. The compromise has huge economic and other implications that reach beyond the scope of this paper.

The legislation governing the TRC presupposes the need for national reconciliation. It, at the same time, gives expression to two related but distinct conceptions of reconciliation. The one is captured in what the Act calls "peaceful coexistence". The other is a higher notion of "reconciliation".

Coexistence involves working together as a basis for putting in place those things that make for mutual survival—an appropriate legislative structure, a civil service, legitimate policing and the like. It involves arguing with one's political adversaries late into the night, accepting that the next day it will be necessary to live and work together at a number of different levels. As such it requires the first step (often reluctantly) towards honoring one's political commitments—if only out of self-interest. It involves ways of identifying and responding to the fears and aspirations of those on the extremes of the political spectrum, with a view to incorporating as many as possible within these groups into the bigger national agenda. It involves refusing to allow past wrongdoing and resentment towards others to undermine the political process.

Reconciliation involves more. It implies the restoration and sometimes the establishment of a hitherto non-existent relationship of trust. This takes time. It involves hard work and persistence. It is likely to include compromises. It requires an understanding of the other person's fears and aspirations. It necessitates the building of trust and respect for the rights and legitimacy of political opposition groupings. It does not necessarily imply forgiveness.

Forgiveness involves more than reconciliation. It usually comes, if at all, at the end of a process of cooperation and reconciliation. It is deeply personal. Jeffrie Murphy, in a helpful essay on forgiveness, argues that "we do all need and desire forgiveness and would not want to live in a world where forgiveness was not regarded as a healing and restoring value."[21] It is more than a Christian imposition as some have suggested.

These different levels of *connecting-up* tend to nest inside each other—a bit like Chinese boxes or Russian dolls. Different groups within society find themselves at different levels of interaction and no one group or individual within society is perhaps ever fully at home in either one or other category of engagement.

A powerful dialogue between the Polish dissident, Adam Michnik, and the then Czechoslovakian President, Vaclav Havel, in November 1993, captures the tension inherent to a nation seeking to redeem itself. Michnik tells that when he was in prison he resolved never to seek revenge. Yet he kept repeating to himself a fragment of Zbigniew Herbert's poem: "And do not forgive, as it is not within your power to forgive on behalf of those betrayed at dawn." We can forgive harm done to *us*. It is not in our power to forgive harm done *to others*. "We can try to convince people to forgive, but if they want justice, they are entitled to demand it."[22] Think, however, of the impact that forgiveness could have on the nation.

It is essential that South Africans agree to coexist. National reconciliation is necessary for South Africans to become dedicated citizens of one nation. Forgiveness involves more. It is a coveted ideal to be gently pursued. It cannot be imposed.

The dialectic between coexistence and reconciliation should not be easily surrendered as South Africans learn to live together. If it is surrendered, we surrender too much. We loose what Horkheimer calls the "theological moment"—let's call it the "artistic moment," which allows for a space for critique, openness and renewal in society."[23] No nation can afford the loss of this moment. The political quest must be to cut the Gordian knot of the past. It is to reach towards what Karl Jaspers in his celebrated essay, written shortly after the institution of the Nuremberg Trials, called the "new world waiting to be built." "Unless," he warned, "a break is made in the evil chain, the fate which overtook us will overtake the victors—and all mankind with them."[24]

Question: Can the resources of the arts be harnessed, as they were harnessed in opposing apartheid, to reconcile those who carry within them the burden of past memory and guilt of perpetration? Resistance art was, of course, experiential art—it emerged out of resistance. It is this that suggests the burden of *art that heals,* lies on the shoulders of those directly affected by the past, or at least sufficiently moved by it to be committed to the healing of the future. The responsibility of those so committed is to facilitate the emergence of a genre of art that speaks even to those who would prefer not to engage themselves in healing process. It is likely to involve not merely the weight of the past, but also the joy and celebration of what can emerge as the future.

Why the Arts?

Why an appeal to the arts? I return to Max Weber's 'iron cage'. He feared nothing more than, what he called, the "inescapable universal bureau-cratization" which hangs over society like the sword of Damocles. Agreeing with Karl Marx that revolution was the "expropriation of the expropri-ator," he was at the same time not convinced that the new would be fundamentally different from the old.[25] He feared most the power of the all-encompassing structural forces of society—which are capable of surviving the most radical revolu-tions. For him they are epitomized in the domi-nant culture, in habit, social convention, political structures, the economic order and the love of power—all of which militate against the possibili-ty of what is new. Trapped in the past, we perpet-uate the norms, behaviour and (all too frequently) the gross violations of human rights of the past. Camus' warning of the danger of the revolution-aries of the past becoming the hangmen of tomor-row can from Weber's perspective, never be dis-missed as mere bourgeois pessimism. In the words of Foucault, "How does one keep from being a fascist, even (especially) when one believes oneself to be a revolutionary militant?"[26]

The question is how to break out of the captiv-ity of the past? Rubem Alves, the Brazilian poet and social analyst suggests it has something to do with *imagination*. It has to do, he suggests, with the need for humanity to break out of what he calls the "arrogance of power"—which perpetuates past thoughts, answers and structures.[27] Look, he argues, not to those who epitomize what contem-porary society regards as 'success'—a brand of success which succeeds only within the limita-tions of the very structures that need to be breached. Look rather to those who dream new thoughts and see new visions: poets, artists, visionaries, musicians—those who dare to dream new dreams, those who celebrate the possibility of a different kind of future. It is only as alternatives visions confront the long held presuppositions that the possibility emerges of the iron cage being sprung. Creativity, new ideas and imagination is, however, rarely acceptable to the status quo.

"Creativity," suggests Alves, is for those who ben-efit most from the existing order, a "forbidden act."[28] It is dismissed as absurd, as ridiculous, as heresy. Yesteryear, society burned heretics at the stake. At least they were taken seriously. Today they are simply ignored.

But every now and again an alternative option grasps public attention—perhaps only because it emerged from a situation within which there *was* no other real alternative. The TRC was, in a sense, that kind of necessity. Seeking neither revenge nor amnesia (because neither were politically possi-ble), an alternative to dealing with the past had to be found. It is still too early to say whether it has worked. The nation is not yet healed. There is no broad-based reconciliation. But there is a chance for this to happen and South Africa needs all the help is can get to ensure that the best use is made of this time of grace. We need material and eco-nomic assistance, as well as links with other cul-tural and human rights institutions international-ly. We also, however, need the *will* to overcome the past—to deal with the *memory of wrongs* and the *guilt of perpetration.* It constitutes an inward need—driven by spiritual and psychological forces, which enables people to embrace one another, even when material restitution, that is so vitally necessary, is not fully available. The forces that challenge and provoke the human soul need to be tapped to enable this to happen. It is here that artists have a role to play. Values cannot be imposed. Hope cannot be demanded. The soul of a nation cannot be bought. It can all be gently nur-tured and artistically nudged and massaged into reality.

WS Merwin's prose poem entitled, "Unchopping a Tree," provides a powerful metaphor, reminding us of the limitations of any human attempt to heal. The author describes the incredibly difficult process of how one could go about reconstructing a tree—placing each fallen branch, withered twig and dried leaf in its appro-priate place, as well as relocating birds' nests. Herewith the final lines of the poem:

> The first breeze that touches its dead leaves . . .
> You are afraid the motion of the clouds will be
> enough to push it over. What more can you do?
> What more can you do?

> But there is nothing more you can do
> Others are waiting
> Everything is going to have to be put back.

Have the leaves been placed in the correct place? How many twigs are missing? Will the birds recognise their nests? Will the tree take root and grow? Perhaps endurance, not restitution, never full recovery, not even full healing, is all that survivors can strive for. Some dare to hope.

Endnotes

1. Charles Villa-Vicencio is the former national research director of the South African Truth and Reconciliation Commission.

2. Dag Hammarskjold, *Markings* (London: Faber and Faber, 1964), 31.

3. In *Mail and Guardian*, July 24–30, 1998.

4. Ibid.

5. Antjie Krog, *Counrty of My Skull* (Cape Town: Random House, 1998), 54.

6. Stevie Smith, *Not Waving but Drowning*.

7. Timothy Garton Ash, *The File: A Personal History* (London: Flamingo, 1997), 62; 65.

8. Ariel Dorfman, *Death and the Maiden* (London: Nick Hern Books, 1991).

9. Krog, 16.

10. Gilles Deleuze and Felix Guattari, *Anti-Oedipus: Capitalism and Schizophrenia* (London: Athlone Press, 1984).

11. Leon Jaworski, *After Fifteen Years* (Houston, TX: Gulf Publishing Company), 1961.

12. Jozef Garlinski, *Fighting Auschwitz* (London: Orbis Books, 1994), 139.

13. A conversation with the author of this paper.

14. In a paper "The Psychology of Perpetrators of Political Violence in South Africa: A Personal Experience," delivered at a Medical Research Unit on Anxiety and Stress Disorders conference, Mental Health Beyond the TRC, 8 October 1998.

15. Cape Times, 6 August, 1997.

16. Foucault, iii.

17. Itzhak Fried in *The Lancet*, December 1997.

18. See Foucault.

19. In H Schreir and M Heyl (eds), *Never Again: The Holocaust Challenge for Educators* (Hamburg: Kramer, 1997), 18.

20. In a draft article unpublished article, "When Good People Do Terrible Things".

21. Jeffrie G. Murphy and Jean Hampton, *Forgiveness and Mercy* (Cambridge: Cambridge University Press, 1988), 30–31.

22. In *Journal of Democracy*, Volume 4, No. 1, January 1993.

23. M Horkheimer, *Die Sehnsucht nach dem ganz Andern*, (Hamburg: Furche, 1975), p.60.

24. Karl Jaspers, *The Question of German Guilt* (New York: The Dial Press, 1947).

25. Arthur Mitzman, *The Iron Cage* (New York: Knopf Books, 1970), 5.

26. Foucault, in *Anti-Oedipus*, iii.

27. Rubem Alves, *Tomorrow's Child: Imagination, Creativity and the Rebirth of Culture* (London: SCM, 1972), 15f.

28. Ibid., 67.

CHAPTER 34

African Mysteries

Patti Waldmeir

A native of Detroit, Michigan whose early life was shaped by the Detroit riots and the civil rights movement, Patti Waldmeir spent most of her adult life living and working in Sub-Saharan Africa. Between 1985-95 she lived in South Africa where she witnessed the transition of power from extreme apartheid to a struggling democracy.

WE COULD NOT HEAR THE RIOTING, but we could see the fires burning all around, as we stood on the roof of the stadium. Black smoke spewed forth from looted shops and houses, blocking the streets and filling us with the vicarious thrill of violence. Snipers, aiming down into the urban gully of the freeway, had cut off our escape route. Already, they had killed one white woman.

We chose instead a circuitous route that took us past the heavily barricaded police headquarters. This was before the troops arrived and police said the situation was "completely out of control." In the days that followed, we could hear the drone of troop transports overhead, as five thousand soldiers were flown in to restore order. Gatherings of more than five people were banned. There was a nighttime curfew. Troops patrolled in tanks.

The year was 1967, the city was Detroit, and I was three days shy of my twelfth birthday. That was my introduction to the politics of race: the Sunday afternoon when I was caught with my father and brother watching baseball in the middle of Detroit's race riots. The issue of race defined my childhood, as I grew up in a pure white suburb of this overwhelmingly black city. It would dominate most of the next thirty years of my life.

This time we could hear the sounds of violence, as we stood on the highway overpass looking down into the squatter camp. The noises were surreal: the gentle pop of gunfire, the crackle of the fires; none of it sounded lethal. But there were victims, black men hacked to death by other black men, or killed by white police. It was nearly twenty years since my initiation on the Tiger Stadium roof, and I was once again playing voyeur to violence, this time in South Africa.

For the better part often years—from 1985 to 1995—I was a spectator to the political drama that was the death of apartheid. I came to the theater bearing the baggage of my childhood in Detroit, marked by vicious battles over the forced integration of Detroit area schools through busing. I came armed with a child's outrage at discrimination, and with adolescent dreams of revolution nurtured by voracious reading of the words of Malcolm X. The question of race had always held a romantic fascination for me. But the romance really bloomed when I went to live in Africa.

I went first to black Africa, that part of the continent north of South Africa, most of which had been independent of white rule by then for two decades. My first African home was Ghana, on the western slave coast of Africa, where I went to live in 1980. I arrived to teach English literature at the University of Ghana, and quickly succumbed to the charms of a continent that became my home off and on for fifteen years. Like other whites before me, I was overcome by the warmth and hospitality of black people, who welcome white visitors as honored guests in their country. Human intercourse is so much more direct in

Africa, where there is no First World cloak of sophistication and mistrust to shroud it. Africa is a seductive continent; for a girl from Detroit, raised in a world of racial hatred, its warmth proved addictive.

I soon learned that Africa is also a continent of extremes. If Ghanaians took their virtues to extremes, they did the same with vices. About a year after I arrived, I started to do freelance journalism, and went to visit the scene of a tribal massacre in the north of the country. There, in the dusty main street of a nameless village, the local authorities showed me the partly decomposed body of a man half buried in a shallow grave. There were other bodies in surrounding huts, but this was my first one. It was the first dead body I had ever seen, except in a funeral home.

This struck me at the time as barbaric—the death was the result of fighting between two tribes that had been enemies for decades—but it was to prove only a mild prelude to South African atrocities. Ghanaians are a mostly peaceful people. The real tragedy of Ghana was not physical brutality but an entirely more subtle form of abuse: the incompetence and corruption of Ghana's leaders.

By the time I arrived, Ghana had lived under a series of military and civilian black governments for nearly a quarter of a century. They had reduced the country to utter penury. Even as a privileged lecturer living in a university apartment, I had running water only sporadically. To flush the toilet, I had to collect water by bucket from a tap several hundred yards away. The electricity supply was erratic, so I could seldom use the ceiling fan to dispel the oppressive heat of the tropics. Meat was exceptionally hard to come by: every year, the university issued its staff with one chicken for the Christmas meal. (These were live chickens. I took mine home, locked it up in the kitchen, and went off to seek the wisdom of Africa to deal with the situation.)

Medical care was virtually nonexistent. When my Ghanaian boyfriend fell ill and was admitted to the University Hospital, the authorities told me to bring bed linens and food, and to buy medicine for him on the black market. That was by then the only source of many basic necessities—canned fish, toilet paper, condensed milk, beer. The prices were far out of reach of most Ghanaians.

Yet Ghana had been one of the richest countries in colonial Africa, before independence in 1957. It used to be called the Gold Coast, because of its rich reserves of the metal, and of diamonds. Older Ghanaians had a great nostalgia for the days of white rule, and said so. They blamed black rule—and the confused socialism of Ghana's early rulers—for ruining their wonderful country. Thousands of miles away in South Africa, it was exactly that African nightmare which disturbed the white man's sleep.

None of what I had seen in Ghana was any excuse for apartheid. I had no doubt about that. So when I arrived in South Africa for the first time in 1985, I came bearing the certain knowledge of good and evil that was the baggage of every foreigner. The Afrikaner was demon and the African saint; there were no mixed tones in the black and white morality of the times. I relished the idea of having a front-row seat at the twentieth century's best morality play.

I soon realized that the characters in my drama were not drawn exactly according to script. The main story line was fairly accurate: the white government kept blacks in oppression, denying them the vote, and detaining, harassing, sometimes even killing those who resisted. Blacks responded, by and large, with nobility, patience, and a breathtaking generosity of spirit. Black South Africans refused to indulge the racial hatred which would have been so much more rational than tolerance. They welcomed me to their townships and their homes, as the Ghanaians had done. The old African potion began to work on me, again.

Still, there were unaccountable departures from text. On my first visit to a township, to attend the funeral of four guerrillas of the African National Congress, a black bystander was nearly burned to death by the mob. The crowd thought he was a police informer and sentenced him to death on the spot. He was spared after the intervention of a clergyman. But I wondered whether I had got my casting quite right. I found it hard to grasp the hatred that could spur such a deed, hard to condone the glee that filled the eyes of those preparing to carry it out. These were not the saints of Central Casting.

The sinners, too, proved disturbingly sympathetic. For many of the same reasons that Africans had won my heart, I found myself drawn to the white tribe of Africa, the Afrikaners, a tiny nation of 3 million people whose language, Afrikaans, was spoken almost nowhere else on earth. They were people of the South African soil, often descendants of the original handful of Dutch, French Huguenot, and German settlers who colonized this harsh and distant land in the seventeenth and eighteenth centuries. Afrikaners had no automatic right of refuge in Europe: South Africa was their homeland. They feared for their language, their culture, and their prosperity under black rule. Afrikaners were fighting for ethnic survival, and they were battling the Ghana syndrome. I felt a kind of guilty sympathy for their plight.

One knew immediately that Afrikaners were not modern people, any more than their black compatriots. Both dressed like fashion refugees from the 1960s American South, with their absurdly bouffant hairdos (in the case of whites) and their veiled churchgoing headgear (in the case of blacks). This was part of their appeal: they lacked the sophistication to hide their flaws. Both were as simple and straightforward in good as in evil. Chillingly brutal and heartwarmingly kind by turns, they taught me confusing lessons in the nature of the human spirit.

They also taught me that in Africa, politics is about power, and it was a lesson I would not forget in the years to come. The attitude of African and Afrikaner to power was like their approach to everything else—straightforward. Power in Africa is naked, like the hard stone and harsh scrub of the African bush. It is elemental, and it can be frightening. Democracy will not easily tame it.

The Afrikaner was not so much evil in fighting to maintain that power as blind to the consequences of the battle. By then, I had begun to worry about my eyesight as well. I had thought my moral vision perfect when I arrived in South Africa in 1985. By the time I left at the end of my first short visit, I could no longer see things in quite such stark relief.

The main purpose of my 1985 visit was not journalistic but commercial. I had been posted by the *Financial Times* to Lusaka, in neighboring Zambia, from which base I spent two years covering the whole of black Africa. But Zambia was another African economic cripple, and I could not buy a car there. So I flew to Johannesburg, bought a slightly used Volkswagen, and drove 1,200 kilometers across the African bush back home to Zambia.

Lusaka was also home to the African National Congress (ANC), the main liberation movement fighting white rule. By then, many of its leaders had been in exile for twenty-five years. My home was a simple cottage at 14B Twin Palm Road, in the verdant Lusaka suburb of Kabulonga. It was to prove a choice location: my landlords, Harry and Marjorie Chimowitz, were South African exiles who were not only immensely kind but politically well connected. One of their closest friends was Joe Slovo, the white Communist who commanded the ANC's guerrilla army, *Umkhonto we Sizwe,* or "Spear of the Nation." A few houses away lived Mac Maharaj, a brilliant, ebullient Indian South African who had been Mandela's confidant in prison, and was now a senior leader of the ANC. In another part of Kabulonga was the house of Thabo Mbeki, who is now deputy president of South Africa.

These men exploded most of my remaining South African stereotypes. Slovo was the first real revolutionary I had ever known. Yet he was not grim, obsessive, and charmless, a textbook terrorist; he was a rotund, grandfatherly Communist, with an impish sense of humor and a disarming openness of manner. No doubt, he was also a killer—for that was his job. But I knew him as the portly gentleman who did laps in the Chimowitz swimming pool. I often silently cursed Slovo for waking me—he swam before 7:00 A.M.—and worried that his regular visits might attract the murderous attentions of South African intelligence. But I never found him frightening.

The ANC were careful to court the international press, which was not widely represented in Lusaka. So I had time to get to know the men who would one day rule South Africa. They gave me courses in their philosophy of non-racialism, which decreed that the ANC's enemy was not whites themselves, but the system whites had built—apartheid. And I thought, if the ANC can look beyond black and white, how dare I refuse to do so?

I returned to South Africa in July 1989, at what seemed to me the country's darkest hour. After an absence of nearly three years, I was posted to Johannesburg as bureau chief by the *Financial Times.* I found the township revolt of the mid-1980s crushed by a brutal state of emergency. Nelson Mandela was finishing his twenty-sixth year in prison and some fifty thousand ANC activists had been detained. I felt certain South Africa would never escape its twisted past.

The years that followed were the most exhilarating of my life. Almost from the moment I returned, the political landscape began to shift beneath my feet. Soon there were grand figures to people the new landscape—Nelson Mandela, freed from prison, and F. W. de Klerk, the new white president. There were vignettes of remarkable African warmth and scenes of unspeakable horror. There were brains in a basin on the floor, amid the blood-soaked detritus of a township massacre; but there was also the inspiring refusal of the relatives to attack my white skin, though they blamed whites for the carnage. This was drama writ large, with characters to match. Apartheid brought out the best in people, or it brought out the worst; it left scant room for mediocrity.

You will read, in the pages that follow, a strange and wonderful tale of collective liberation, the story of how the African was freed from apartheid and the Afrikaner released from the bondage of his fear. I would ask you to remember throughout that though both sides will say this was a struggle for democracy, it was also a battle for power.

More than anything, it was a compelling mystery story, one of the great political thrillers of the late twentieth century. Why did the Afrikaners do what so few ruling groups had ever done in history, voluntarily relinquish power? How is it that they, too, felt liberated when Nelson Mandela ascended the throne built by them? Why did the Boers give it all away?

I spent much of my seven years in South Africa looking for the answers to those questions, seeking to explain the miracle of a peaceful transition to majority rule. It was a study in the psychology of capitulation; a journey into the mind of South Africa. This book is my record of that journey, which took me to the listless "platteland," the white rural areas of South Africa where the prejudice of centuries dies hardest. It took me to the hills of Natal and the townships around Johannesburg, to witness scenes of barbarity and small epiphanies of joy. I spoke to the great and the humble in my quest to understand; I went to the heart of South Africa's humanity and its inhumanity; and the trip left me changed forever.

Perhaps I will never be the same again, but neither will South Africa. Just after the first all-race elections in April 1994, South Africans cherished a sense of infinite possibility. They thrilled to the notion of creating a new country, complete with symbols and systems and languages, entirely from scratch. It was like a new marriage, or the beginning of a new life. Inevitably, that exhilaration has faded.

No one knows how the ANC will react to having power. The demographics of South Africa—Africans represent a vast and growing majority of the population—are likely to keep the ANC in a position of dominance for a decade, perhaps much more. Until Africans decide to vote against blood and tribe, for some future party whose appeal is based on economic and social policies, the ANC will face no effective opposition. Parties which hold power unchallenged inevitably abuse it.

But the future is another country that I cannot hope to visit. The present is quite extraordinary enough. For a girl who learned her race politics on the top of Tiger Stadium, South Africa was a dream impossibly come true. It was a powerful rebuke to the memories of my girlhood, a chance to do what South Africans had taught me: To liberate myself from my past.

Chronology

1652	Jan van Riebeeck lands at the Cape of Good Hope, to establish the first European settlement
1899–1902	Anglo-Boer War
1910	Union of South Africa formed from the former Boer republics of Transvaa and Orange Free State and the British colonies of the Cape and Natal
1912	South African Native National Congress formed, later renamed the African National Congress
1914	National Party formed
1918	Nelson Mandela born
1936	F. W. de Klerk born
1948	National Party comes to power
1950	South African Communist Party banned
1955	Congress of the People adopts the Freedom Charter
1958	Hendrik Verwoerd becomes prime minister
1960	Sharpeville massacre; ANC banned

1961   South Africa declares itself a republic

1962   Mandela arrested, given five-year sentence

1963   Police raid headquarters of *Umkhonto we Sizwe* at Rivonia farm, arrest many ANC leaders

1964   Mandela sentenced to life imprisonment

1966   Verwoerd assassinated; John Vorster replaces him

1976   Soweto revolt

1977   Death of black consciousness leader Steve Biko

1978   P. W. Botha becomes prime minister, later president

1979   Black trade unions legalized

1982   Right-wing whites break away to form Conservative Party

1983   New tricameral Constitution denies power to blacks; United Democratic Front formed to fight it

1984–86   Township uprising; states of emergency declared (1985 and 1986)

1985   *August:* the Rubicon debacle and the unilateral debt moratorium
November: Nelson Mandela and Kobie Coetsee begin secret meetings

1986   Thabo Mbeki and Pieter de Lange meet secretly in New York; National Party holds crucial Federal Congress

1987   Mells Park House talks begin

1988   Niël Barnard team begins meeting Mandela in prison

1989   *February:* F. W. de Klerk elected National Party leader after P. W. Botha suffers stroke
July: Botha and Mandela meet at Tuynhuys
September: de Klerk elected president, legalizes ANC Cape Town march
October: Walter Sisulu and ANC leaders released from prison
December: de Klerk meets Mandela

1990   *February:* de Klerk legalizes ANC and SACP and releases Mandela
May: talks begin at Groote Schuur estate in Cape Town
August: ANC suspends armed struggle; violence escalates

1991   *January:* Nelson Mandela and Chief Mangosuthu Buthelezi meet
July: ANC holds key policy conference in Durban
December: start of formal multi-party talks, the Convention for a Democratic South Africa (Codesa I)

1992   *March:* whites-only referendum endorses reform
May: Codesa II collapses
June: ANC supporters killed at Boipatong
September: Bisho massacre, followed by conclusion of the Record of Understanding between the ANC and government
October: Joe Slovo publishes article offering "sunset clauses"

1993   *April:* Chris Hard assassinated
July: agreement on election date, Inkatha walks out
August: Mandela secretly meets Constand Viljoen
November: agreement on interim constitution
December: Transitional Executive Council, the multi-party interim government, begins to operate

1994   *March:* overthrow of Bophuthatswana, rout of the white right
April: Inkatha enters elections
April 26–28: ANC wins South Africa's first democratic elections
May: Mandela inaugurated, government of national unity formed

1995   *June:* South Africa wins Rugby World Cup on home turf

1996   *May:* New Constitution adopted, to take force in 1999
June: National Party withdraws from government of national unity

Prologue

ON A BRILLIANT WINTER'S DAY in 1994, the vanguard of apartheid's air force swooped over a hilltop in Pretoria and tipped its wings to the force's new commander in chief, Nelson Mandela. The same Impala and Mirage jet fighters that bombed black guerrillas during South Africa's liberation war pledged their allegiance to apartheid's most hated enemy on the day he became their president. It was an event of great national catharsis, the moment when white hands finally let go their 350-year grip on power. Africa and the Afrikaner were reconciled at last.

Until the first planes appeared on the horizon, trailing smoke in the garish colors of the new South African flag, this sight would have been unimaginable. Every spectator knew, rationally, that white rule had ended; but reason alone could not grasp the enormity of this truth. This simple signal of white loyalty to black rule made South Africa's unlikely revolution seem finally real. It was a transcendent moment, and I was not alone in hiding tears once it had passed.

Emotion was a constant companion in those days when the South African morality tale reached its storybook climax—especially for someone who had spent a decade following each twist in the tortured plot. Hastily, I donned sunglasses to mask unprofessional tears when Nelson Mandela placed hand over heart in sign of reverent respect for the singing of *die Stem,* the anthem of his oppression; when white army sharpshooters, deployed to guard a black president, proved as fervent in their protective duty as ever they were in persecution; when white lips struggled to form the unfamiliar syllables of South Africa's new anthem, *Nkosi sikelel'iAfrika,* paying homage to Africa at last.

Theirs is an implausible tale of collective liberation, one that might have ended so tragically otherwise: Afrikaners might have fought to keep Africa at bay until well into the new millennium, and left the new black rulers to inherit a wasteland. Africans might have merely changed the complexion of South African oppression, replacing white hegemony with black domination.

Those who believe in a God or gods—which includes most South Africans—rely on the rhetoric of divine intervention to explain their narrow escape from such a fate. But they do scant justice to the very human personalities and the very real historical forces that drove the apartheid drama to its end. For those who observed the protracted demise of white rule, it was like living a political thriller. The combined forces of history, economics, demography, and morality hastened apartheid on its way; but the outcome remained uncertain until the last plane disappeared over the horizon on the crisp bright day of Nelson Mandela's inauguration.

Disaster may yet descent on the "rainbow nation." Zhou Enlai said, when asked what he thought of the French Revolution, "It's too soon to tell." It is too soon to pronounce on South Africa, either way. But the plot thus far is gripping by any standard. History provides few enough examples of the triumph of common sense over ethnicity, or religion, or the myriad other forces which divide human populations; how rare the opportunities to savor what Nelson Mandela calls the "poetry of the triumph of the oppressed."

So how is it that white South Africans—scarcely renowned for their good sense in the decades of apartheid—managed finally to accept the dictates of reason? How could black South Africans subdue hatred and reject revenge to defy the logic of a tortured past that might have doomed them to ceaseless conflict? Why did the Afrikaner hand over power? What was it that catapulted this dour, Calvinistic, Old Testament people so abruptly into the modern world?

That story begins nearly thirty years ago, when doubt first began to enter the Afrikaner mind; in the decades that followed, Afrikaner thinking was transformed, by reformist leaders, timorous churchmen, troublesome academics, vocal editors, and ultimately, by the nagging sense of being out of step with history. Eventually, Afrikaners knew that they were wrong; but even before that, they knew they could not carry on. This is the story of their revolution, a study in the psychology of capitulation. Why, after all, did the Boers give it all away?

No single human being, no single historical force, provoked this reversal. But standing on the inaugural podium that day, May 10, 1994, and later appearing in a giant, bulletproof glass cage to greet tens of thousands of well-wishers, were the two men who did more than any others to drive South Africa's transformation: Nelson Mandela and F. W. de Klerk, black victor, white subordinate, their roles reversed by fate, and by their own courageous vision.

History will surely claim these two men as its heroes. They have guided South Africa as it grappled with the grandest question of the political life of nations: how to order the relations between man and the state: how to balance rights and responsibilities, the demand for equality with the quest for freedom; in short, how to invent a new democratic nation from the ruins of a state built on institutionalized injustice. To South Africans, democracy is not the old and devalued friend familiar to citizens of mature nations; it is the promised land. And whatever their flaws, the two men who led South Africa to that haven will dominate its history for years to come.

They have never been friends—indeed, they are so different as to be almost incompatible—but at last they are compatriots, jointly devoted to the land of huge and empty beauty which is their common fatherland. It is that shared patriotism which carried the two men through the years of negotiated struggle; it is that reality which Nelson Mandela recognized at the pinnacle of his triumph, when he declared that F. W. de Klerk, taking the oath of office beside him as deputy president, was "one of the greatest sons of Africa."

A capricious history brought the forefathers of these two very different "sons of Africa" to live on this disputed tip of a troubled continent, in separate worlds of race, language, ethnicity, and ideology. But eventually they learned to recognize, if not a common destiny, at least a common danger: the risk of mutually assured destruction. None could live without the other. Now they would no longer try.

The fact of racial interdependence had been self-evident for many decades. White capital drove South Africa's mines, but black hands hewed the rock which held the precious metal; white farmers brought skills and machinery to till the African soil, but blacks did the hardest labor; whites managed the banks, but the tellers were mostly people of color; white matrons built a society of comforts for their men, but black domestics made comfort a reality.

Yet for just as many decades both Afrikaners and Africans denied those obvious facts. The story of how they came to accept the central reality of mutual need, how Afrikaners set out on their last Great Trek to a new multi-racial fatherland, begins with another flyover, and yet another burst of patriotic color from the exhaust trail of more jet fighters. But if the planes were the same, the colors were radically different—as was the complexion of the man they served. For this was the apartheid state at the height of its self-delusion, the nadir of its cruelty. This was the land of Hendrik Verwoerd, the man who dreamed the dream that became South Africa's nightmare.

Class 24

Diversity Issues and Answers

CHAPTER 35
Surprisingly Singing and Women's Day Song
Barry Feinberg
Barry Feinberg's poetry expresses the pain, the commitment, and the hope
that comes from years of struggle against the monolithic power
of South Africa's Apartheid system.

CHAPTER 35

Songs and Commemorations

Feinberg, Barry

Born in South Africa in 1938, Barry Feinberg attended Benoni High School and the Johannesburg School of Art. Because of his activism against apartheid he was in exile in London from 1961-1991. He is an award winning film director and his publications include *Bertrand Russell's America* a biography and *Poets to the People,* an anthology of liberation poems.

Surprisingly Singing

While whites
on sabbath greens
slowly bowling
on weekdays
growing gold
back home
black men
break backs
surprisingly
singing

Women's Day Song

Celebrate our women in campaigns
Celebrate our women in the jails
Celebrate our women over many fighting years
Celebrate our women for their triumphs
and for their tears

There is no day
from which women are exempt
no day in which women
do not play their part;
every day in fact
is women's day;
freedom day tomorrow
is women's day today

From *Gardens of Struggle* by Barry Feinberg. Mayibuye Center, University of Western Cape, South Africa. Used with permission.

Remember all our women in campaigns
remember all our women in the jails
Remember all our women over many fighting years
Remember all our women for their triumphs
and for their tears

There is no struggle
from which women are exempt
no struggle in which women
do not play their part;
our struggle is in fact
for women's day;
to struggle for tomorrow
is a woman's fight today

Celebrate our women in campaigns
Celebrate our women in the jails
Celebrate our women over many fighting years
Celebrate our women for their triumphs
and for their tears

There is no freedom
while women are not free
no freedom when women
do not have their say;
freedom day in fact
is women's day
freedom day tomorrow
is women's day today

Remember all our women in campaigns
Remember all our women in the jails
Remember all our women over many fighting years
Remember all our women for their triumphs
and for their tears

Fight for an Africa
where women are not slaves
fight for an Africa where women
do not waste their lives;
South Africa in fact
is on its way
to celebrate its freedom
and to honour women's day.

INDEX

A

Absolute deprivation, 128
Acculturation of ethnic minorities, 16–17. *See also* Immigration
Adaptation, 46
Adarand Constructors Inc. v. Peña, 139–140
Affirmative action
  African Americans and, 6
  discussion of, 137–141
  key decisions on, 139
Affirmative admissions to colleges
  changes to, 63–66
  Regents of the University of California v. Bakke, 63–64, 66, 69–70, 138–139
  standard admission tests and, 66–70
  University of Texas Law School (UTLS) and, 294–297
African Americans. *See also* Afrocentricity; Slavery
  access to college prior to 1978, 63
  affirmative admissions in colleges and, 69, 294–297
  black creoles of New Orleans, 354–360
  Civil War and, 10
  Directive No. 15 of racial classification and, 92
  doctorates awarded (1989-1990) to, 113
  educational techniques towards Chinese Americans for, 298
  Federal Naturalization Act of 1870 and, 83
  integration as goal and, 239–245
  Kwanzaa and, 259–263
  media representation of, 247–255
  origins in America of, 6
  Pell Grant educational funding and, 293–294
  perceptions of aging according to, 432
  personality stereotypes of, 401–402
  potential fascist in all people and, 444–447
  racial differences in personality and, 392–393
  results of South African TRC, 444–447
  style of communication and, 44
  "Top 25" institutions and doctorates awarded to, 115–123
  as underclass, 131
African National Congress (ANC), 444–445, 448, 455–457. See also Ghana perspectives
Afrocentricity
  conceptual contributions of, 268–276
  definition of, 265–268
After Fifteen Years, 447–448
Age of Jackson, The, 6
Aging population
  disabilities in the, 431
  heredity myths and, 436–438
  intelligence myths and, 432–434, 438
  lifestyle myths and, 434–436
  productivity myths and, 438–440
  sexuality and, 438
  sickness myths and, 430–432
Agriculture. *See also* Immigration
  Asian Americans and, 314
  Kwanzaa and, 259
  moral codes in agrarian societies, 198
  Native American "Civilization Acts" (1802,1819) and, 169
American-Arab Anti-Discrimination Committee (ADC), 336, 338
American Citizens Equal Rights Association (ACERA), 379
American Indians. *See* Native Americans
Americans with Disabilities Act (ADA), 422

Apartheid in Africa, 454–459, 463–464
Arab Americans and communication styles, 44
Ash, Timothy Garton, 446
Asian Americans
  Asian Indian and racial classification, 97
  changes to affirmative admissions and, 66
  characteristics of students, 317–320
  Directive No. 15 of racial classification and, 93
  diverse backgrounds of, 317
  doctorates awarded (1989-1990) to, 113
  educational failure paradigms by, 322
  Federal Naturalization Act of 1870 and, 83
  funereal traditions and, 129–130
  immigration since 1965, 309–310
  importance of religion for, 312–313
  origins in America of, 6–7
  as political label, 94–95
  socioeconomic status and, 313–314
  style of communication and, 44
  "Top 25" institutions and doctorates awarded to, 115–123
Assimilation, 46
Azanian People's Liberation Army (APLA), 447

B

Bakke, Regents of the University of California v., 63–64, 66, 69–70, 138–139
Baline, Israel (Irving Berlin), 9
Banfield, Edward, 393
Behaviorism, 106–107
Bell Curve, The, 104

Berlin, Irving, 9
Bilingualism, 15. *See also* Language
    acculturation and, 17
    affirmative admissions in
        colleges and, 70
    Asian American students and,
        319
    Hispanic/Latin American
        education and, 223–224
    teachers and, 15
*Black Culture and Black
    Consciousness*, 6
Black English, 289–290
Black Republican (newspaper), 370
Bloom, Allan, 4
Board of Education, Brown v., 135
Bogdan, Robert, 420
Bok, Derek, 19
Brantenberg, Gerd, 348
Brown, Dee, 6
Brown v. Board of Education, 135
B.S. Thind, United States v., 97
Buried Mirror, The, 11
*Bury My Heart at Wounded Knee:
    An Indian History of the
    American West*, 6
Business initiatives. *See* Workplace
    initiatives
Butler, Benjamin, 361–363
Butler, Robert, 429

C

Camarillo, Albert, 6
Campus activism, 59–60
Carver, George Washington,
    103–105
Cavalli-Sforza, 394
Census Bureau's racial
    classification, 93
Charef, Mehdi, 348

Cherokee Nation v. Georgia, 167–168
Cherokee people, 167–169. *See also*
    Native Americans
Chicanos in a Changing Society, 6
Chinese Americans. *See also* Asian
    Americans
    "Asian American" as political
        label for, 94–95
    educational techniques
        towards, 298
    immigration of, 82–84
Chinese Expulsion Act of 1882,
    6–7, 84, 310, 318

*City of Cleveland, International
    Association of Firefighters v.*,
    139
*City of New York, New York State
    Clubs Association v.*, 136
Civil rights. *See also*
    Discrimination
    African Americans and, 6
    Asian Americans and, 312
    higher education as, 64
    Indian treaty rights and,
        164–166
    Jews and African Americans
        and, 8
Civil Rights Act of 1964
    affirmative admissions in
        colleges and, 66
    elimination of discrimination
        and, 135–136
Civil War, 10
Closing of the American Mind, The, 4
College admission policies. *See*
    Affirmative admissions to
    colleges
Columbia Teachers College (CTC),
    123–124
Commission on Interracial
    Cooperation, 105
Communication (intercultural)
    analysis of perspective of, 37–38
    cultural adaptation and, 46–49
    definitions of, 34
    differences in peoples and,
        33–34
    humanism and, 38–39
    language and, 39–41
    levels of culture and, 35
    nonverbal behavior and, 41–43
    perceptual relativity and, 41
    style of, 43–45
    values and, 45–46
Conway, Thomas A., 366–367,
    370–371
Corporal punishment, 197–198
Council on American Islamic
    Relations (CAIR), 336
Creoles. *See also* African
    Americans
    demands for equality by,
        362–365
    Desdunes, Rodolphe and
        Crusader and, 377–381
    history in New Orleans of,
        354–360
    racial solidarity in 1860s of,
        365–372

reconstruction after Civil War
    and, 372–376
Criminal behavior
    aggression as reproductive
        strategy, 400
    behavior genetics and, 392
    hate crimes as, 409–410
    media representation of,
        247–255
    racial differences in personality
        and, 392–393
Croson Company, Richmond v., 139
Crusader (newspaper), 377–381
"Cultural awareness" workshops,
    58
*"Cultural Literacy" What Every
    American Needs to Know*, 4
Culture
    adaptation to, 46–49
    ambivalence towards
        disabilities and, 422
    Asian American students and,
        319–322, 324
    campus research project on
        multiculturalism and, 55–61
    communication (intercultural)
        and, 35
    as distributive model, 16
    evolution of man and, 397–402
    group-oriented concept of,
        14–15
    Hispanic/Latin Americans
        literacy model and, 204–206
    Hispanic/Latin Americans
        values/morals and, 195–200
    image of the aging and, 429
    immigration study between
        Mexican and American,
        225–233
    individual-oriented concept of,
        15–17
    Kwanzaa and, 259
    language modifications and, 34
    lifestyle myths of the aging and,
        434–436
    productivity myths of the aging
        and, 438–440
    second generation immigration
        concerns and, 221–224
    social interaction model (SIM)
        and, 25–29
    sociological structure of Native
        Americans, 178–179
    South African TRC and,
        450–451

stereotypes/generalizations and, 35–36
understanding/appreciation and Native American, 177–178
values and, 45–46
women's liberation movement and, 405–406
Cynical Americans, The, 19

D

Daddy's Roommate, 408
Dangerous Memories, Invasion and Resistance since 1492, 180
Dawes Act, 168
Denmark. *See* Scandinavians
Deprivation, 128
Desbrosses, Nelson, 368
Desdunes, Rodolphe, 368, 376–381
Development Model of Intercultural Sensitivity (DMIS), 47
"Did Women Have a Renaissance?", 157
Directive 15, 92, 96
Disabilities
    in the aging, 431
    characteristics of postsecondary students with, 419–422
    discrimination and, 423–425
    self-advocacy and, 422
Discrimination. *See also* Racism
    affirmative action and, 137–141
    affirmative admissions in colleges and, 65–67
    of the aging, 429–430
    curricular revision of women's studies and, 150
    demands for equality by creoles and, 360, 362–365
    earning power and, 132–133
    educational apathy from, 227–228
    elimination of, 133–136
    eugenics and, 105–106
    Ghana perspectives and, 453–459
    glass ceiling, 141–142
    importance of media content analysis to fight, 255
    informal economy and, 130–131
    institutional, 129–130
    integration as goal and, 239–245
    of Irish Catholics, 79–80

measuring contemporary, 132–133
media representation and, 337–338
nativism, 80–81
organization of anti-Indian groups and, 171
physical requirements in police departments and, 298
reverse, 140–141, 294
South African Truth and Reconciliation Commission (TRC), 444–448
in sports, 136
total, 128–129
toward disabled postsecondary students, 423–425
voting rights of creoles of New Orleans (mid-1800s) and, 364–366
Distant Mirror, A, 11
Dorsey, J. O., 15
Double jeopardy, 132
Dred Scott decision, 135, 363
Du Bois, W. E. B., 269
Dual labor market model, 130
Dubuclet, Antoine, 368
Duke Power Co., Griggs v., 139
Dumas, Francis E., 362
Dunn, Oscar J., 374–376

E

Earning power. *See* Labor/unions
Easter Star, 372
Economic conditions. *See also* Immigration
    affirmative action and, 138
    Asian Americans and, 313–314
    immigration study between Mexican and American and, 225–233
    Pell Grant educational funding and, 293–294
Education. *See also* Women's studies
    affirmative admissions in colleges and, 294–297
    African Americans in science, 104–106
    African Americans' language and, 285–291
    Afrocentricity and, 266–270, 266–270, 272–275
    Asian Americans and, 313–314

campus research project on multiculturalism, 55–61
changes to affirmative admissions, 63–66
characteristics of Asian American students, 317–321
corporal punishment and, 197–198
cultural models for Hispanic/Latin Americans, 189–196
culture of school, 17–18
curricular revision of women's studies, 148–159
curricular revision of women's studies and, 148–159
doctorates awarded (1989-1990) in, 113
early discrimination in higher, 9
ethnicity and, 279–282
group culture concept and, 14–15
Hispanic/Latin American achievement and, 222–223
Hispanic/Latin American literacy studies, 188–189
Hispanic/Latin American values towards, 186–188
Hispanic/Latin Americans continuities/discontinuities of, 207–210
Hispanic/Latin Americans literacy model and, 204–206
Hispanic/Latin Americans parental involvement in, 207
Hispanic/Latin Americans values/morals and, 200–203
immigration study between Mexican and American and, 225–233
importance of multicultural, 4–6, 10–11
individual culture concept and, 16–17
IQ testing as institutional discrimination, 129
law school enrollment, 63–64
lesbians/gays/bisexuals in curriculum, 408–411
meeting needs of postsecondary students with disabilities, 422–425
Native American "Civilization Acts" (1802,1819) and, 169
Native American curriculum material and, 171, 177–180

Native Americans in textbooks and, 165, 170–171
nonverbal behavior of communication and, 41–43
Pell Grant funding for, 293–294
perceptual relativity of communication and, 41
postsecondary students with disabilities, 419
pursuit of truth and, 61
reconstruction after Civil War and, 372
segregation of Japanese (1907) and, 84
social interaction model (SIM) and, 25–29
standard admission tests and, 66–70, 138
of stereotypes/generalizations, 36–37
strategies for teaching of diversity, 346–349
style of communication and, 43–45
teachers of Asian American students and, 323–324
teaching in cultural contexts, 18–21
teaching of lesbian/gays/bisexuals and, 407–413
texts for teaching diversity in, 348–349
Thematic Apperception Test (TAT) and, 227–233
"Top 25" institutions and doctorates awarded (1984-1985) to students of color, 115–123
total discrimination and, 128–129
universities most successful in advanced degrees, 113, 115–123
Egalia's Daughters, 348
El-Saadawi, Nawal, 348
Elderly. *See* Aging population
Emecheta, Buchi, 348–349
Emigrants and Exiles: Ireland and the Irish Exodus to North America, 6
Employers and discrimination, 138–142. *See also* Labor/unions

Environmental justice, 136–137
Equal Employment Opportunity Commission (EEOC), 135–136
Essay on the Principle of Population, An, 105
Ethnic diversity origins in America, 6–11
Ethnicity in education, 279–282
IPEDS research project of postsecondary education and, 115–123
Ethnocentricity definition of, 47
style of communication and, 44–45
Ethnorelativity definition of, 47
ethics of, 49–50
Eugenics, 105–106
European Americans, 345–349. *See also* White Americans
Evolution, 397–401

F

Faces of the Enemy, 331
Fair Employment Practices Commission (FEPC), 134
FCC, Metro Broadcasting v., 139
Federal Naturalization Act of 1870, 83
Feinberg, Barry, 463–464
"Female World of Love and Ritual, The: Relations Between Women in Nineteenth Century America", 157
Feminine Mystique, The, 405
"Field and Function of the Negro College, The", 269
Fighting Auschwitz, 447
Filipino Americans, 94-95. *See also* Asian Americans
Firefighters Local Union No. 1784 (Memphis, TN) v. Stotts, 139
"Forty-Eighters", 78
Freak Show: Presenting Human Oddities for Amusement and Profit, 420
Friedan, Betty, 405
Fuentes, Carlos, 11

G

Galton, Francis, 105
Gangs, 223–224
Garlinski, Josef, 447
Gender cultural models for Hispanic/Latin Americans and, 193
discrimination in the sciences and, 143
double jeopardy of discrimination and, 132–133
effect of women's liberation movement, 405–406
employment criteria and, 135
glass ceiling and, 141–142
racial classification and, 94
General Allotment Act of 1887, 166
Generalizations. *See* Stereotypes/generalizations
Genetic basis of intelligence, 106–107
Georgia, Cherokee Nation v., 167–168
Georgia, Worcester v., 167–169
German Americans immigration (1820-1920) and, 77–79
style of communication and, 44–45
World War II and, 7
German Sterilization Act of 1933, 105–106
Ghana perspectives, 453–459
Gilligan, Carol, 157
Glass ceiling, 141–142
Gloria Goes to Gay Pride, 408
Goddard, Lewis, 106
Graham, Lawrence Otis, 127–128
Grant's Peace Policy, 168
Griggs v. Duke Power Co., 139
Growing Old in American—Why Survive?, 429

H

Handlin, Oscar, 6
Harvard Civil Rights Project, 69
Harvard University, 115–123
Hate crimes. *See* Criminal behavior
"Have Only Men Evolved?", 157
Heather Has Two Mommies, 408

Hereditary Genius, 106
Heritability, 107
Hirsch, E. D., 4
Hispanic Americans
    Chicanos in a Changing Society, 6
    corporal punishment and,
      197–198
    cultural models for, 189–196
    Directive No. 15 of racial
      classification and, 92–93
    doctorates awarded (1989-1990)
      to, 113
    immigration (1980-1990) of, 185
    literacy models and, 204–206
    literacy studies and, 188–189
    origins in America of, 7
    style of communication and, 44
    "Top 25" institutions and
      doctorates awarded to,
      115–123
    as underclass, 131
    values/morals and, 195–200
    values/morals and education,
      200–203
    values toward education of,
      186–188
    years completed of education
      of, 186
Historically Black Colleges
    (HBCs), 104–105
History
    Afrocentricity and, 268, 271,
      273–275
    of black creoles of New
      Orleans, 354–360
    curricular revision of women's
      studies and, 148–159
    of freak shows (1840-1940), 420
    of Ghana, 454–457
    incorporating Indian
      perspective into, 176–177
    South African Truth and
      Reconciliation Commission
      (TRC) and, 444
    strategies for teaching of
      diversity in, 346–349
*History and Geography of Human
    Genes, The*, 394
Hopwood v. Texas, 69, 139
Horsman, Reginald, 164
Houzeau, Jean-Charles, 369–370
"How Psychology Constructs the
    Female", 157
Howe, Irving, 6
Hubbard, Ruth, 157
Hypodescent, principle of, 91

I

Ichioka, Yuji, 6
Immigration. *See also specific
    peoples, i.e.* Hispanic
    Americans
    of Chinese (1850-1882), 82–84
    Chinese Expulsion Act of 1882
      and, 6–7, 310
    eugenics and, 105
    of Germans (1820-1920), 77–79
    increase in racial/ethnic
      populations (1991-1996), 318
    of Irish (1820-1924), 79–80
    of Japanese (1880-1924), 84
    of Latin Americans, 219–220
    Naturalization Law of 1790
      and, 7
    paradox of gains and losses due
      to, 220–221
    post-Civil War, 81
    reasons (1820-1860) for, 75–78,
      82–83
    of Scandinavians (1800-1910),
      81–82
    second generation concerns
      and, 221–224
    since 1965 of Asian Americans,
      309–310
    study between Mexican and
      American, 225–233
    transportation's effect on, 76, 82
In a Different Voice, 157
Indian Nations at Risk Task Force
    (INAR), 178
"Indian New Deal", 168
Indian Reorganization Act of 1934,
    166, 168
Informal economy, 130–131
Ingraham, James, 367
Institutional racism, 129
Integrated Postsecondary
    Education Data System
    (IPEDS), 115
Integration as goal, 239–245
Intelligence and race, 106–107
*International Association of
    Firefighters v. City of
    Cleveland*, 139
Internment camps of World War
    II, 7
IQ (intelligence quotient) testing,
    129
Irish Americans
    immigration (1820-1924) and,
      79–80

Market Revolution and, 8
    origins in America of, 7
Iroquoian Confederacy of Nations,
    176
*Issei, The: The World of the First
    Generation Japanese
    Immigrants*, 6
Italian Americans, 7
Iverson, Sherrice, 251–252, 254

J

Janeway, Elizabeth, 148
Japanese Americans. *See also* Asian
    Americans
    "Asian American" as political
      label for, 94–95
    immigration of, 84, 310
    internment camps of World War
      II and, 7
Jaworski, Leon, 447–448
Jewish Americans
    eugenics and, 106
    immigration from Germany
      and, 78–79
    origins in America of, 7–8
*Johnson v. Transportation Agency,
    Santa Clara, CA*, 139
Just, Ernest Everett, 103–105

K

Kanter, Donald L., 19
Karenga, Maulana. *See* Kwanzaa
Kawaida philosophy, 259
Kelly-Gadol, Joan, 157
Kerner Commission, 247, 255
King, Martin Luther, Jr., 6
King, Rodney, 5
Knights of Pythias, 372
Knights Templar, 372
Know-Nothing Party, 81
Korean Americans, 94–95. *See also*
    Asian Americans
Krog, Antjie, 446
Kwanzaa, 259–263

L

Labor/unions
    acceptance of
      lesbians/gays/bisexuals and,
      406
    affirmative action and, 137–141
    the aging and, 439–440

California farm laborers strike of 1903, 8–9
creoles of New Orleans (mid-1800s) and, 379
doctoral recipients and, 122
dual labor market model and, 130
earning power and discrimination and, 132–133
Equal Employment Opportunity Commission (EEOC) and, 135–136
Informal economy, 130–131
Irish immigrant strike of 1870, 8
Jewish garment workers' strike of 1909, 9
music and, 9–10
National Union Brotherhood Association, 366, 369
physical requirements in police departments and, 298
total discrimination and, 128–129
underclass and, 131
workplace diversity initiatives, 85–88
Language
African Americans and, 285–291
Afrocentricity and, 273–274
Asian American students and, 318, 322
bilingual, 15, 17, 223–224
civil rights of Asian Americans and, 312
as ethnic symbolic tool, 224
intercultural communication and, 39–41
of Kwanzaa, 261–263
Latin Americans. *See also* Hispanic Americans
affirmative admissions in colleges and, 69
"Asian American" as political label for, 95
cultural models for, 189–196
immigration (1980-1990) of, 185
literacy models and, 204–206
literacy studies and, 188–189
racial classification and, 93
schools in Texas and, 67–70
style of communication and, 44
as underclass, 131
values/morals and, 195–200
values/morals and education, 200–203

values toward education of, 186–188
years completed of education of, 186
Legal issues/laws
Adarand Constructors Inc. v. Peña, 139–140
Americans with Disabilities Act (ADA), 422
Cherokee Nation v. Georgia, 167–168
Chinese Expulsion Act of 1882, 6–7, 6–7, 84, 310, 318
Dawes Act, 168
Dred Scott decision, 135
environmental justice and, 136–137
Federal Naturalization Act of 1870, 83
Firefighters Local Union No. 1784 (Memphis, TN) v. Stotts, 139
General Allotment Act of 1887, 166
Grant's Peace Policy, 168
Griggs v. Duke Power Co., 139
"Indian New Deal", 168
Indian Reorganization Act of 1934, 166, 168
International Association of Firefighters v. City of Cleveland, 139
Johnson v. Transportation Agency, Santa Clara, CA, 139
Martin v. Wilks, 139
Metro Broadcasting v. FCC, 139
National Origin Act of 1924, 310
Native American "Civilization Acts" (1802,1819) and, 169
Naturalization Law of 1790, 7
New York City v. Sheet Metal, 139
Phipps case of racial classification, 91–92
Plessy suit, 380–381
Regents of the University of California v. Bakke and, 63–64
Richmond v. Croson Company, 139
San Antonio Independent School District v. Rodriguez, 133
Texas v. Hopwood, 139
treaty rights of Native Americans, 164–166
United States v. B.S. Thind, 97
United States v. Paradise, 139

United Steelworkers of America v. Weber, 139
Worcester v. Georgia, 167–169
Levine, Lawrence, 6
Linton, Ralph, 14
Los Angeles race riot of 1992, 5
L'Union (French creole newspaper), 362–363, 365–366

M

Malcom X, 241
Man Made Language, 156
Manifest Destiny, 168, 176
Man's Most Dangerous Myth: the Fallacy of Race, 394
Manzie, Sam, 250–251, 254
Market Revolution, 8
Martin v. Wilks, 139
Mary, Aristide, 368, 376
Masons, 368, 374
McCaffrey, Lawrence J., 7
Measurement of Intelligence, The, 106
Media representation
acceptance of lesbians/gays/bisexuals and, 407
"accepted" societal order and, 254–255
Arabs and Muslims and responses to, 336–338
of Arabs and Muslims in motion pictures, 330–334, 339–340
of Arabs and Muslims in television, 334–335, 338–339
of Asian Americans, 310–312
of creoles of New Orleans (mid-1800s), 362–363, 365–366, 377–381
of race, 394
research overviews and, 250–252
Metro Broadcasting v. FCC, 139
Mexican Americans
immigration study between Mexican and American, 225–233
restricted college enrollment of, 67
Miller, Jean Baker, 157
Miller, Kerby, 6

Minorities. *See also specific peoples, i.e.* Hispanic Americans
affirmative admissions in colleges and, 294–297
Asian Americans treated as, 315
doctorates awarded (1989-1990) to, 113
media representation of, 247–255
as underclass, 131
universities most successful in advanced degrees and, 115–123
Mirvis, Philip H., 19
Model Eugenical Sterilization Law, 106
"Model Minority", 7
Models
Development Model of Intrcultural Sensitivity (DMIS), 47
Social interaction model (SIM), 25–29
Montagu, Ashley, 394
Morals. *See* Values/morals
Motion pictures featuring Arabs and Muslims, 330–334, 339–340
Mugo, Micere Githae, 348–349
Multiculturalism. *See also* Education
acceptance of lesbians/gays/bisexuals and, 411–413
Afrocentricity and, 265–266
campus research project on, 55–61
educational curriculum material and, 177–180
importance of, 6
multiracial identification, 95
social interaction model (SIM) and, 25–29
Music
Berlin, Irving (Israel Baline) and, 9
labor/unions and, 9–10
slave songs and Irish ballads, 8

N

National Advisory Commission on Civil Disorder, 247

National Association for the Advancement of Colored People (NAACP), 241
National Equal Rights League, 367
National Origin Act of 1924, 310
National Union Brotherhood Association, 366, 369
Native Americans. *See also* American Indians
affirmative admissions in colleges and, 69
cultural understanding/appreciation for, 177–178
Directive No. 15 of racial classification and, 92
discrimination of, 164
doctorates awarded (1989-1990) to, 113
educational curriculum material and, 165, 171, 177–180
environmental justice and, 137
Indian Nations at Risk Task Force (INAR) and, 178
"Indian New Deal" and, 168
mock "Indian Shoot" of 1980s and, 164
origins in America of, 8
racial classification and, 92–93
stereotypes in education of, 17
Termination Policy (1950s), 176
"Top 25" institutions and doctorates awarded to, 115–123
treaty rights of, 164–169
Nativism, 80–81
Naturalization Law of 1790, 7
Nazi Eugenics Court, 105–106
Negro Emigration Convention of 1854, 359
Nepotism, 138
New Orleans *Crusader*, 376–377
New Orleans, Louisiana. *See* Creoles
New York City v. Sheet Metal, 139
New York State Clubs Association v. City of New York, 136
New York University, 115–123
Noble, Jordan B., 359
Norway. *See* Scandinavians

O

Odd Fellows, 372
Ojibwe people. *See also* Native Americans
educational curriculum material and, 171
Indian treaty rights and, 164–169
Old Age and Survivors Insurance (OASI), 439–440

P

Panethnicity, 94–95
Paradise, United States v., 139
Pell Grant, 293–294
Peña, Adarand Constructors Inc. v., 139–140
People of the Three Fires, 177
Phelps, John W., 362
Phipps, Susie Guillory, 91–92
Plessy suit, 380–381
Plumly, B. Rush, 366–367, 370–371
Poland's early immigration, 75
Politics
acceptance of lesbians/gays/bisexuals and, 408
affirmative action programs and, 293–294
Afrocentricity and, 276
black creoles of New Orleans (1769-1860), 355–358, 363–365
campus research project on multiculturalism and, 58–61
elimination of discrimination and, 133–136
equality/suffrage and, 362–363
government Indian programs and, 167
integration as goal and, 242–244
nativism and, 80–81
perspectives from Ghana and, 453–459
potential fascist in all people and, 446–448
reconstruction after Civil War and, 373–376
results of South African TRC, 444–447
Potato famine, 77–80

Poverty. *See* Economic conditions
Powers of the Weak, The, 148
Preponderance of belief, 36
Project RACE (Reclassify All
    Children Equally), 95
"Push-pull" theory of
    immigration, 75–77

Q

Questy, Joanni, 368

R

RACE. *See* Project RACE
    (Reclassify All Children
    Equally)
Race and Manifest Destiny, 164
Racial classification. *See also*
    Racism
    IPEDS research project of
      postsecondary education
      and, 115–123
    problems in, 93–96
    proposed genetic differences
      among races and, 104
    social science and, 96–97
    state definitions of race, 92–93
Racism. *See also* Discrimination
    absence due to affirmative
      college admissions, 64–65
    apartheid in Ghana and,
      454–459
    behavior genetics and, 391–392
    campus research project on
      multiculturalism and, 57–58
    East St. Louis race riot of 1917,
      7–8
    environmental, 136–137
    eugenics and, 105–106
    genetic basis of intelligence
      and, 106–107
    importance of media content
      analysis to fight, 255
    institutional, 129
    integration and, 243–244
    King, Rodney and, 5
    mock "Indian Shoot" of 1980s
      and, 164
    nativism, 80–81
    personality stereotypes, 401–402
    racial differences in personality,
      392–393
    science and racial differences,
      394–395

songs/commemorations
    regarding, 463–464
Randolph, P. B., 370–371
Reconstruction after Civil War,
    372–376. *See also* Creoles;
    Slavery
Reconvivencia, 444
*Regents of the University of
    California v. Bakke,* 63–64, 66,
    69–70, 138–139
Relative deprivation, 128
Religion
    Asian American families and,
      312–313, 321
    black creoles of New Orleans
      and, 358–359, 369–370,
      379–380
    discrimination of Catholics,
      79–80
    Kwanzaa and, 260
    Muslims and, 330
    reconstruction after Civil War
      and, 372–373
Research
    into aging (MacArthur Study),
      430
    media representation and,
      250–252
    universities most successful in
      advanced degrees, 115–123
Reverse discrimination, 140–141,
    294
Rey, Henry, 368
Rey, Octave, 368
Richmond v. Croson Company, 139
*Rodrigues, San Antonio Independent
    School District v.,* 133
Rogers, Carl, 421
Roosevelt, Theodore, 105
Roudanez, Louis Charles, 353–354,
    364–365, 375. *See also* Creoles
*Rush to Judgement, A: A Special
    Report on Anti-Muslim
    Stereotyping,* 336

S

*San Antonio Independent School
    District v. Rodriguez,* 133
Sankofa, 273–274
Scaffolding, 18
Scandinavians, immigration of,
    81–82
Schlesinger, Arthur M., Jr., 6, 12
Schurz, Carl, 78

Science
    African Americans in, 103–105
    behavior genetics and, 392
    curricular revision of women's
      studies and, 148–159
    discrimination in field of, 143
    eugenics and, 105–106
    evolution, 397–399
    genetic basis of intelligence
      and, 106–108
    racial differences and, 394–397
*Science and Politics of Racial
    Research, The,* 107
Scottish Rite Masonic order, 368,
    374
Second Class Citizen, 348–349
Segregation, 6, 63–64. *See also*
    Discrimination
Seremane, Joe, 443
Seremane, Timothy Tebogo, 443
*Sex Works: Writings from Women in
    the Sex Industry,* 348
Sexuality. *See also* Gender
    acceptance of
      lesbians/gays/bisexuals,
      406–408
    the aging and, 438
    as part of multiculturalism,
      411–413
    teaching of
      lesbian/gays/bisexuals,
      407–413
Sheet Metal, New York City v., 139
Slavery
    Afrocentricity and, 271–272
    black creoles of New Orleans
      and, 355–356, 358, 360–362
    Civil War and, 10
    "coolie" labor systems, 83
    Douglass, Frederick and, 367
    effect on racial classification, 92
    immigration (1820-1860) and, 77
    Know-Nothing Party and, 81
    origins in America of, 6
    racial classification and, 91–92
Smith-Rosenberg, Caroll, 157
Smith, Susan, 248, 250–253
Social interaction model (SIM)
    cultural scene component of,
      26–28
    decision-making process
      component of, 28–29
    ego component of, 25–26
South African Truth and
    Reconciliation Commission
    (TRC), 444–448

Spender, Dale, 156
Sports (tribal fishing), 171
Stanford University, 115–123
Statistical analysis
  generalization distribution
    curve, 36
  hidden problems in, 318
  Hispanic/Latin Americans
    years of education, 186
  immigration (1980-1990) of
    Hispanics, 185
  lesbians/gays/bisexuals in
    society, 408–410
  postsecondary students with
    disabilities, 419
  shifting meaning of 1980
    Census, 95–96
  Statistical Directive No. 15, 92,
    96
  of values and life preferences,
    46
  women's liberation movement
    and, 405–406
Stereotypes/generalizations
  of Asian Americans, 310–312,
    317
  children and, 336
  intelligence and, 401–402
  intelligence myths of the aging
    as, 432–434, 438
  lesbians/gays/bisexuals and,
    412–413
  Native Americans in textbooks
    and, 165
  of postsecondary students with
    disabilities, 419–421
  rationale for media
    representation of, 329–330
  sickness myths of the aging as,
    430–432
  types of, 35–36
  Yuker's Attitudes Toward
    Disabled Persons Scale
    (ATDP) and, 423
Sterilization and eugenics, 105–106
Stotts, Firefighters Local Union No.
  1784 (Memphis, TN) v., 139
Stuart, Charles, 252–253
"Surprisingly Singing", 463
Sweden. See Scandinavians

T

Talented Tenth, 272
Tea in the Harem, 348

Teaching in cultural contexts. See
    also Education
  necessities of, 18–21
Technology and the aging, 433
Television. See Media
Terman, Lewis, 106
Texas A&M University, 67
Texas, Hopwood v., 69, 139
Thematic Apperception Test (TAT),
    227–233
Thiong'o Ngugi wa, 348–349
Toward a New Psychology of Women,
    157
Transportation Agency, Santa Clara,
    CA, Johnson v., 139
Transportation's effect on
    immigration, 76, 82
TRC. See South African Truth and
    Reconciliation Commission
    (TRC)
Treaty rights of Native Americans,
    164–169, 176
Trévigne, Paul, 362–363, 365–366,
    375. See also Creoles
Trial of Dedan Kimathi, 348–349
Truth and Reconciliation
    Commission (TRC). See
    South African Truth and
    Reconciliation Commission
    (TRC)
Tuchman, Barbara M., 11
Tucker, William, 107
Turner, Charlie, 103–105
Tylor, Edward, 14

U

Underclasses, 6, 131–132, 142
Unheavenly City Revisited, The, 393
United States v. B.S. Thind, 97
United States v. Paradise, 139
United Steelworkers of America v.
    Weber, 139
Universities and the Future of
    America, 19
University of California-Los
    Angeles, 115–123
University of Maryland-College
    Park, 123
University of North Carolina, 66
Uprooted, The, 6
Urban areas, immigration (1820-
    1860) to, 77. See also
    Immigration
U.S. Office of Management and
    Budget (OMB), 92

V

Values/morals
  Afrocentricity and, 268, 275–276
  American perception of, 45
  Asian American families and,
    321–322
  campus research project on
    multiculturalism and, 55–61
  Hispanic/Latin American
    educational, 186–188, 207–210
  Hispanic/Latin American
    family, 195–198
  Japanese perception of, 45
  Kwanzaa and, 260–261
  sexuality and, 406–407
Vêque, Charles, 368
Violence. See Criminal behavior

W

War
  Civil War and creoles, 357,
    360–362
  curricular revision of women's
    studies and, 150
  effect on immigration, 75–76
  German Americans and World
    War II, 78
  post-Civil War reconstruction,
    372–376
Warmoth, Henry C., 373–376
Weber, United Steelworkers of
    America v., 139
Weisstein, Naomi, 157
Wellesley College Center for
    Research on Women, 147–148
Werner, Edward P., 250–251, 254
White Americans. See also Creoles
  Directive No. 15 of racial
    classification and, 92
  Eurocentric perceptions and,
    345–349
  immigration study between
    Mexican and American,
    225–233
  integration as goal and, 239–245
  as minority, 4
  perceptions of aging according
    to, 432
  personality stereotypes of,
    401–402
  racial identification and, 95–96
  style of communication and,
    43–45
  as underclass, 131

White supremacy. *See* Racism
Whorf/Sapir hypothesis, 39–41
Wiggins, Cynthia, 127–128
Wilks, Martin v., 139
Women at Point Zero, 348
Women Look at Biology Looking at Women, 148
"Women's Day Song", 463–464
Women's studies, curricular revision of, 148–159

Wood, Tiger, 136
Worcester v. Georgia, 167–169
Workplace initiatives, 85–88, 247–248
World of Our Fathers: The Journey of the East European Jews to America, 6
Wright, Beatrice, 421

Y

Yerkes, Robert, 106
Yuker's Attitudes Toward Disabled Persons Scale (ATDP), 423